D0727695

An introduction to modern economics

Philip Hardwick

Bahadur Khan

John Langmead

WITHDRAWN FROM THE LIBRARY

UNIVERSITY OF WINCHESTER

Ac

KA 0010943 6

Longman
London and New York

Longman Group Limited
Longman House, Burnt Mill, Harlow
Essex CM20 2JE, England
Associated companies throughout the world

Published in the United States of America
by Longman Inc., New York

© Longman Group Limited 1982

All rights reserved. No part of this publication may be reproduced, stored in a retrieval system, or transmitted in any form or by any means, electronic, mechanical, photocopying, recording, or otherwise, without the prior permission of the Copyright owner.

First published 1982
Second impression 1982

British Library Cataloguing in Publication Data

Hardwick, Philip
An introduction to modern economics.
1. Economics
I. Title II. Khan, Bahadur
III. Langmead, John
330 HB171 80-41105

ISBN 0-582-44051-3

KING ALFRED'S COLLEGE
WINCHESTER.
330
HAR
95914

Set in 10/12 pt Compugraphic English Times
Printed in Singapore by
Selector Printing Co. (Pte) Ltd

Contents

Macroeconomic policy issues

Foreword

Yet another textbook on economics takes some justifying. When I first met the authors, however, I had no hesitation in suggesting to them that what was missing was a rigorous text which did something authors of first year texts seem reluctant to do, namely, discuss welfare economics. I am delighted that the authors took up the challenge and, in my view, succeeded in following through their aims.

The oddity of current ideological standpoints in respect of economics is that a naive philosophy – logical positivism – expounded in its most severe form in the 1920s and 1930s should have such a hold over modern economics teaching. In essence positivism asks us to define the economist's role in such a way that he or she is precluded from making 'value judgements'. The term 'value judgement' is itself a source of confusion but we do not stray too far from a useful definition if we say that a value judgement is almost always expressible in the sentential form 'x is good' or 'x is bad'. The positive economist thus refrains from prescription and recommendation, since such activities imply value judgements to the effect that some event, outcome or activity is good or bad. The most that can be done is to say 'If you (usually some entity called the "policymaker") wish to achieve such and such a result, then my recommendation as to policy is as follows.' In this way the economist is removed from direct association with the end result the policy maker seeks to achieve.

To isolate further the subject of welfare economics, that branch of economics concerned with normative statements to the effect that such and such a course of action *ought* to be pursued, the welfare economist is normally caricatured as someone who 'imposes' his or her own value judgements when normative analysis is undertaken. The end result is a whole generation of economists raised on a false distinction and based on an outmoded philosophy. Much of the harm can be undone in further courses at university or polytechnic level on ideology and on methodology in economics. What the current authors have done is to attempt to reverse the ideological bias that has arisen, and reverse it at an earlier stage than has hitherto been considered. In this respect alone their book is to be applauded as a hoped-for turning point in economics teaching. They may not have gone far enough. My own view is that students can accommodate far more welfare economics than is normally thought possible. Indeed, I would go further and argue that the positivist teaching of economics is one of the dominant factors explaining the widespread image of economics as an arid and dull subject.

The argument that economics is unavoidably normative, inextricably bound up with value judgements, can be rehearsed at a fairly simplistic level. To 'economise' actually means to make the *best* use of resources. But best has no meaning unless it is related to some desired outcome. The best use of resources might be to give them all to me if the underlying value judgement is that my wants and desires are supreme and should dominate. In reality the best use is some combination of an efficiency objective – making sure that we minimise the use of resources for any given amount of desired outcome – and some concept of 'fairness' which obviously will vary from person to person. Yet if the very meaning of economics involves a value judgement what becomes of the positivist view that economics ought not to engage in normative activity? Indeed, the irony is that the recommendation is itself a normative statement implying a value judgement about the status of a science.

For these reasons it is a distinct pleasure to see authors facing head-on the efficiency-equity distinction and not shying away from the fact that economics is ultimately about a value-loaded science. What matters is that the value judgements be made clear and that we are given guidance as to how the science would change if a different value basis was used. This helps us to understand, partly, how radical economists can come up with such different prescriptions to 'orthodox' economists, although the radicals, in so far as they build upon the works of Marx and others, also have differing positive explanations of relationships between the various actors in an economy. It also explains how economists steeped in ecology can produce different answers to the same questions, and so on. Quite rightly, the authors have not taken us down these paths. The logic of this omission is simple – it is better to build a framework in order to understand the jargon that economists use but to use that framework like a ladder and pull it away when the student is well versed enough to face 'alternative' views of society and the economy. What is certain is that repeated avoidance of welfare economics will have the opposite effect.

Finally, the authors have also introduced the student gently to words and issues that some years ago would have been held to be 'beyond the ken' of the average student. The constructions that have now been built upon the concept of disequilibrium as opposed to the traditional preoccupation with equilibrium cannot be carried very far in an introductory text. Again, however, the authors have justly used the terminology and explained the basic ideas. In the same way students using this book will come to recognise that the world does not consist of sets of stable equilibria with economies and markets simply hopping from one to the other without any apparent upset. This refreshing recognition of reality may cause some problems – the old economics was easier to hold on to and reassuring in its assessments. The truth now is that economics is undergoing a revolution probably far more fundamental than those that overtook it at the end of the 19th century or in the inter-war years. It would be pretentious of anyone to suggest that this textbook offers reassurance in an unassuring world. What it does do is give some basic insights into the modern way of thinking. It is to be welcomed and, I hope, widely used.

David Pearce
Professor of Political Economy
University of Aberdeen

Preface

This book has been written with the objective of introducing students to the interesting and important subject of economics. It is intended primarily to be of value as a textbook for students in first-year degree courses in economics, the social sciences, business studies and other areas of study which include economics among their foundation subjects. The material covered is also suitable for many Business Education Council and other professional courses. A careful selection of parts of the book should be helpful to 'A' level students in the United Kingdom and to students of similar courses overseas.

As teachers of economics at degree and higher national diploma level, we have felt for some time that the efficiency and equity aspects of resource allocation have been inadequately treated in introductory textbooks (where the analysis is often omitted completely) and in intermediate microeconomics books (where the topic is normally left until the last few chapters). In an attempt to correct this deficiency, we have included at an early stage two chapters entitled 'Resource allocation' (Ch. 7) and 'Introduction to welfare economics' (Ch. 8): these come *after* chapters on production and demand (which cover isoquant and indifference curve analysis), but *before* the chapters on the theory of the firm, the public sector and the theory of distribution. This lay-out enables us to compare more rigorously the efficiency and equity aspects of different market structures and different policy changes. None the less, much of the material in the chapters on the theory of the firm, the public sector and distribution can be used (with the omission of the welfare sections) by those teachers who prefer the more traditional introductory course. We think, however, that the early introduction of a simple treatment of welfare economics is of great value to beginning students.

An important development in modern economics has been the increasing recognition that disequilibrium, rather than equilibrium, may be the normal state of affairs. As a result, we have attempted to discuss some of the major aspects of microeconomic disequilibrium analysis in Chapters 6 and 15 and macroeconomic disequilibrium analysis in Chapter 23.

Although not intended to be primarily a book on applied economics, there is throughout an emphasis on economic policy. Chapters 11–14 are concerned entirely with the activities of the public sector. Chapter 18 outlines the major macroeconomic policy objectives and Chapters 26–30 are concerned with issues of macroeconomic policy. These sections on economic policy draw heavily on examples from the United Kingdom economy. This does not mean, however, that readers from other countries have been forgotten: in many chapters, there are references to the problems of less developed countries and, in many cases, statistics are quoted, not just for the United Kingdom, but for a selection of the developed and less developed countries.

Now a brief note on the structure of each chapter. Each one begins with an introduction designed to link the chapter with related ones and to summarise the material to be covered. Each one ends with a brief conclusion, a list of further reading and a set of exercises. As its name implies, the list of *further* reading provides some more advanced references which will take the interested reader to a higher level of analysis than that reached in the text. The exercises are designed to reinforce the reader's understanding of the chapters and, of course, to help in the preparation for examinations. Nearly all chapters have at least one numerical exercise or data-response question in addition to a number of essay questions.

We should like to thank Professor David Pearce for encouraging us to embark on the project. We are also considerably indebted to Stuart Wall whose many comments and suggestions have been extremely helpful to us in revising an earlier draft. For selflessly typing a large part of the manuscript, our thanks go to Jenny Gibbins and Pauline Lever. Finally, special thanks go to our wives for putting up with our over-long preoccupation with the book. We three, of course, bear full responsibility for all errors and omissions.

Philip Hardwick
Bahadur Khan
John Langmead

Introduction

1 The nature and scope of economics

Introduction

Economics is a social science which seeks to explain the economic basis of human societies. The purpose of this introductory chapter is to identify the basic *economic problem* encountered by all societies and to focus attention on the basic concepts which modern economists employ in their attempts to analyse this problem.

Human existence has been preoccupied with the production and consumption of wealth, the desire for which seems to arise from man's basic impulse to increase his welfare. The concepts of *wealth* and *welfare*, therefore, stand at the heart of economics. A nation's wealth consists of its stock of goods and services – that is to say, it includes tangible goods like cars and houses as well as intangibles like the services of teachers and musicians. Welfare, on the other hand, refers to the satisfaction that an individual or society derives from wealth and can be regarded as being synonymous with that individual's or society's standard of living. If the welfare of one person or group of persons is increasing without at the same time anyone being made worse off, we could say that this is a definite improvement in the welfare of society as a whole. As a criterion for judging welfare changes, though, this is rather too simple because the world we live in is exceedingly complex and most economic changes make some people better off and others worse off. For example, cheap imports of cloth make a lot of people better off as they can buy cloth at lower prices, but many domestic textile workers may lose their jobs and so be made worse off. It is because economic changes generally impose gains and losses on different groups in society that we need criteria of both *efficiency* and *equity* in order to judge policy measures designed to increase social welfare.

In this chapter, we first of all consider the economic problem itself; then we return to the important concepts of efficiency and equity; in the remainder of the chapter, we explain economic concepts like equilibrium and disequilibrium, microeconomics and macroeconomics and we outline the methodology of economic analysis.

The economic problem

The production of wealth is necessary because it enables individual and collective wants to be satisfied. Unfortunately, wants are virtually limitless whilst the resources to satisfy them are scarce. The most pressing wants are food, housing, clothing and warmth – these essentials are the first to make a call on a nation's resources. Advances in technology and the development of new means of transport and communications, however, have added new wants and brought about new ways of satisfying existing wants. For example, our wants for cars and television sets were unknown to previous generations and the wants for travel, regarded as difficult in the past, have become capable of being satisfied easily from several modes of transport.

The scarcity of resources in relation to the call made upon them imposes a choice on society as to the range of wants it wishes to satisfy. A decision to satisfy one set of wants necessarily means sacrificing some other set: this sacrifice is called by economists the *opportunity cost* of satisfying given wants. In a regime of scarcity and restricted choice, economic welfare is determined to a very large extent by the quantity and quality of goods and services which can be produced. This leads us to the next important point: the constraints on economic production.

The quantity of resources available and the state of technology are the major constraints on production. Many resources, like coal and oil, are non-recoverable – the faster the rate at which they are used up in production the sooner will be the limit to the growth in wealth. New and improved technology opens up new ways of doing old things more efficiently and may lead to the discovery of new resources. More modern techniques enable a larger output to be produced, whereas antiquated methods of production act as a barrier to increased wealth and prosperity. Unfortunately, technical changes usually take a long time to come about so that it is the existing technology which determines how efficiently resources can be used at any given time.

To sum up, we can say that the basic economic problem is that of *allocating scarce resources among the competing and virtually limitless wants of consumers in society*. All nations have to decide in some way *what* goods and services to produce, *how* to produce them and *for whom* to produce them. These three questions of what, how and for whom are central to the economic problem and we shall be considering them in greater detail in Chapter 7. For now, consider how the economic problem can be illustrated by means of a production possibility frontier and the concept of opportunity cost.

The production possibility frontier and opportunity cost

A production possibility frontier joins together the different combinations of goods and services which a country can produce using all available resources and the most efficient techniques of production. Assume for simplicity that a country produces only two goods, food and cloth. Figure 1 shows the different combinations of these two commodities which can be produced. The vertical axis measures the quantity of food in tonnes and the horizontal axis measures the quantity of cloth in metres. The straight line AB is the production possibility frontier. It shows that when all resources are efficiently employed in the production of food, OA tonnes can be produced and when all resources are employed in the production of cloth, OB metres can be produced. *All points on the production possibility frontier represent combinations of food and cloth which the country can just produce when all its resources are employed. All points inside the line, such as point* M, *represent combinations which can be produced using less than the available supply of resources or by using the available supply with less than maximum efficiency. Points outside the line, such as* N, *represent combinations which*

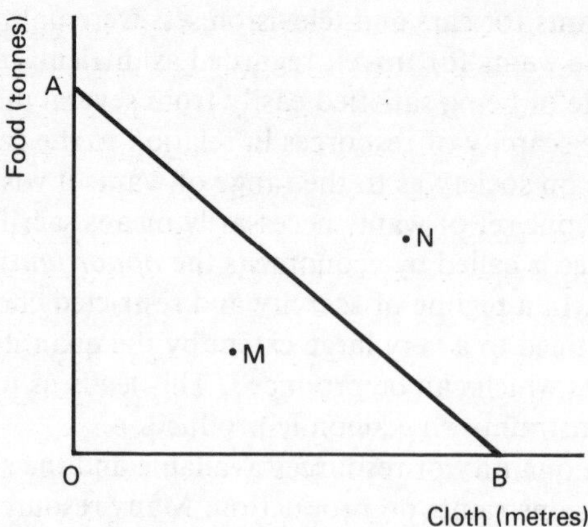

Fig. 1. A country's production possibility frontier.

are unattainable.

Suppose initially that the country is producing at point A. That is, all resources are being used in the production of food. If it now decides to produce cloth, it is obvious from the downward slope of the production possibility frontier that some food production must be given up. The quantity of food which has to be forgone is called the opportunity cost of producing cloth. In Fig. 1, where the production possibility frontier is drawn as a straight line, the slope of the line, equal to OA/OB, measures the opportunity cost in terms of food of producing 1 extra metre of cloth. Similarly, the reciprocal of the slope, equal to OB/OA, measures the opportunity cost in terms of cloth of producing 1 extra tonne of food. All this means is that every additional metre of cloth produced requires that OA/OB tonnes of food be forgone and that every additional tonne of food produced requires that OB/OA metres of cloth be forgone.

As well as measuring opportunity cost, the slope of the production possibility frontier can be interpreted as measuring the rate at which food can be 'transformed' into a metre of cloth by shifting resources from food production into cloth production. Thus, the slope of the production possibility frontier is sometimes called the *marginal rate of transformation* – in this case, of food into cloth. The marginal rate of transformation is a concept we use later in the book, particularly when we deal with welfare economics in Chapter 8. Notice that in Fig. 1, where the production possibility frontier is drawn as a straight line, the opportunity cost and the marginal rate of transformation remain unchanged no matter how much cloth is produced. This is said to be the case of *constant* opportunity costs.

The assumption of constant opportunity costs is very unrealistic. It implies that all factors of production can be used equally efficiently in either the production of food or the production of cloth. It is much more likely that some factors are more efficient in the production of cloth. To illustrate the effects of this on the production possibility frontier, suppose that the country is once again using all of its resources in the production of food; that is, production is taking place at point A′ in Fig. 2. If the country now decides to produce some cloth, we might expect the opportunity cost of the first few metres of cloth to be relatively small as those resources which are more efficient in the production of cloth move from food production into cloth production. As more and more metres of cloth are produced, however, it becomes necessary to move into cloth production those factors which are more efficient in the production of food. As this happens, the opportunity cost of the extra metres of cloth produced will get larger and larger. This is the case of *increasing* opportunity costs.

In Fig. 2, the production possibility frontier A′B′ is concave to the origin. Starting from point A′, the production of 1 metre of cloth requires that A′C tonnes of food be given up. The production of a second metre of cloth requires that an additional CD tonnes of food be given up. A third requires that DE be given up, and so on. From the concavity of the production possibility frontier, it must be true that EF > DE > CD > A′C. In other words, the opportunity cost of cloth in terms of food increases as more and more cloth is produced. It is also true, of course, that the opportunity cost of food in terms of cloth increases as more and more food is produced. Just as with the straight line production possibility frontier, the opportunity cost of cloth in terms of food and the marginal rate of transformation of food into cloth are measured by the slope of the production possibility frontier. This time, however, the slope is not constant, but increases as more and more cloth is produced. The actual slope of the production possibility frontier can be measured at any point by drawing a tangent to the curve at that point (like GH in Fig. 2) and measuring the slope of the tangent.

The production possibility frontier thus provides us with an illustration of the problem of scarcity and choice facing a country when deciding what goods and services to produce. The analysis of production is dealt with in greater detail in Chapter 2.

To ensure that resources are devoted to those uses which result in maximum welfare for a society, we need to be able to judge the production and consumption of wealth by some rules of efficiency and equity. So we turn now to a preliminary consideration of these two important concepts.

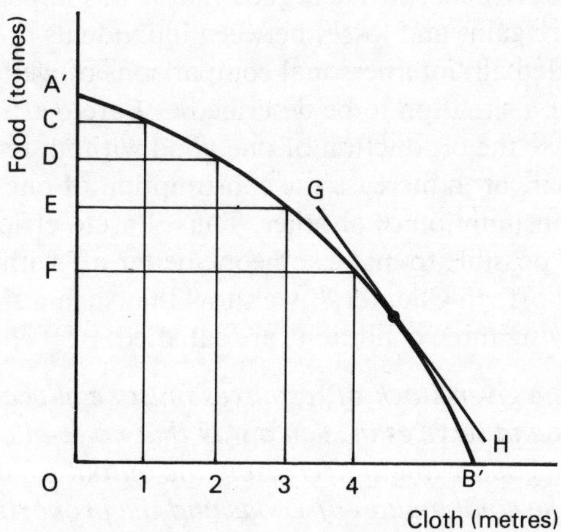

Fig. 2. A country's production possibility frontier with increasing opportunity costs.

Efficiency and equity

One of the major aims of this textbook is to introduce the reader, at an early stage, to the study of welfare economics at the heart of which are the concepts of efficiency and equity. It is with the aid of these concepts that economists are able to judge whether the existing arrangements about: (a) the methods of production; (b) the types and quantities of goods and services produced and consumed; and (c) the relative share of goods and services going to each household, are satisfactory. A 'satisfactory' situation may be said to exist when no rearrangement of the systems of production, consumption and distribution can increase the welfare of one person or group of persons without hurting someone else. Envy apart, many people would agree that a change which increases the welfare of one individual without harming others is desirable.

However, most welfare changes in real life are associated with gains and losses accruing to different people as a result of actions initiated by producers and consumers. In other words, economic changes cause alterations in the pattern of the distribution of income and wealth. If we had an economic theory which told us what the 'optimal' or 'ideal' distribution of income and wealth was, we should be able to judge whether a given change in the distribution pattern would be socially desirable or undesirable. There are no clear-cut rules, however, and so the problem of distribution has become very controversial.

Economists have managed to separate the problems of an efficient allocation of resources from the controversial question of the distribution of income and wealth. The latter is concerned with value judgements and is dealt with under the heading 'equity'. In order to facilitate understanding, in what follows the efficiency and equity aspects of welfare are treated separately. It should be emphasised, however, that questions of economic policy can scarcely be settled satisfactorily by relying on efficiency or equity considerations alone.

Efficiency

The famous Italian economist Vilfredo Pareto (1848–1923) concentrated on the efficiency aspects of welfare because he believed that welfare was a highly subjective concept. He argued that it was impossible to measure and compare welfare gains and losses between individuals or groups – that is to say, he excluded all 'interpersonal comparisons of welfare' from his analysis.

For a situation to be described as Pareto efficient, it must be impossible to increase the production of one good without reducing the production of another, or to increase the consumption of one household without reducing the consumption of another. Thus, Pareto efficiency is a situation in which it is not possible to make someone better off without making someone else worse off. In Chapter 8, we show that such a situation results when the following three conditions are satisfied.

(a) *The given stock of resources must be allocated in the production of goods and services in such a way that no re-allocation can increase the output of one good without decreasing the output of any other.*
(b) *The combination of goods and the proportions in which they are produced must be in response to the tastes and preferences of the community – i.e. the goods produced must be the ones that the community wants.*
(c) *The distribution of goods and services must be in conformity with*

consumers' preferences, given their tastes and incomes.

As we have already mentioned, however, a Pareto better situation (that is, one which is reached by moving from a Pareto inefficient point to a Pareto efficient one) necessarily involves both gains and losses in real life. This has led to the development of compensation tests in welfare economics. Consider a situation where a gain to group A is worth, say, £100 million while the loss to group B is valued at £80 million. If A compensates B, the latter is restored to the original position whereas A is left with a gain of £20 million. Some economists say that for a Pareto better situation to exist the compensation should actually be paid to the losers, while others contend that it is sufficient to show that compensation could be paid.

Equity

The word 'equity' means fairness or justice. Questions about what is equitable are moral and ethical ones which have their basis in the norms of society. Individual members of society are bound to have differing and often conflicting views about what is equitable. For instance, what is a fair distribution of wealth and income? How do we judge whether a monopolist is or is not acting in the public interest? Economists have shown increased interest in such questions of equity over the last fifty years. According to one argument, economists are able to give expert advice on issues related to economic efficiency, but equity considerations are outside the purview of economics and should be left to philosophers, politicians and social reformers.

A counter-argument is that the economist is as good a judge as anyone else in society and by the very nature of his role cannot neglect equity considerations. Balanced, expert advice involves appraising the system of production and consumption on the grounds of both efficiency and equity. According to this argument, equity considerations are important because every policy action, like building a road or raising a tariff, makes some people better off and others worse off.

Equilibrium and disequilibrium

Most economics textbooks stress the idea of an equilibrium. Unfortunately, in the real world, equilibria are hardly ever achieved and even when they are, they are not easy to identify.

An equilibrium is a state of rest. In economics, it comes to be established when there is a single price for identical products in a market and when no economic forces are being set up to change that price. In other words, in equilibrium, the price and quantity of a commodity match both consumers' and producers' *expectations* and thus there is no discrepancy between the *actual* and *desired* prices and quantities. Consequently, the market is cleared and there are no involuntary holdings of unsold stocks. The equilibrium behaviour of consumers and producers, whether in a single market or in the economy as a whole, is characterised by the fact that there exists no feeling of urgency on the part of buyers and sellers to change their behaviour.

In contrast, a disequilibrium position is one in which some buyers and sellers feel impelled to change their behaviour because forces are at work that change their circumstances. By changing their behaviour, however, they unwittingly change the circumstances of other producers and consumers who may initially have been in equilibrium. A disequilibrium, then, sets in motion a chain of *adjustment* and *readjustment* processes: for example, on the London commodity markets and on stock exchanges, buyers and sellers change their behaviour daily in response to changing circumstances.

An important point is that the adjustment of output and employment takes time and there are wide variations in time-lags in different lines of production and consumption activities. Disequilibrium economics is concerned with the investigation of the time-lags involved in the path to equilibrium as well as the *speed* and *direction* of the adjustment to equilibrium. Unfortunately, it is very difficult to identify time-lags in every conceivable circumstance: producers and consumers react differently to changed situations and the rate of response tends to vary between different classes of consumers and different groups of producers. One possible reaction to a changed situation may be to 'wait and see'. For instance, an unemployed worker may wait and *search* for work over a period of time before deciding to accept an offer of a job at a reduced money wage. Similarly, producers may, despite a slump in their sales, continue to maintain existing levels of output and employment before eventually deciding to cut back on their production plans.

Apart from the time-lag in diagnosing a disequilibrium, there is a time-lag in deciding to implement a particular policy action. It then takes time for the effects of the action to work through the system. By the time all these things have happened, the original situation may have changed in such a way that the selected policy action is no longer appropriate. It follows that, to formulate an effective policy measure, it is essential to have *sufficient information* about time-lags and the speed and direction of the adjustment process. In practice, buyers and sellers generally trade goods and services with insufficient information: that is to say, they transact business in disequilibrium. This point is well illustrated by the market for housing in the United Kingdom where actual house prices frequently diverge from desired (or expected) prices and consequently supply and demand conditions overshoot or undershoot the equilibrium position. The unsold 'mountains' of butter, meat and cereals in the European Economic Community further illustrate disequilibrium conditions in the real world.

In this book, particularly in Chapters 6 and 23, we shall be dealing with the analysis of both microeconomic and macroeconomic disequilibria.

The distinction between microeconomics and macroeconomics

Over the past twenty-five years or so, economists have divided their subject matter into two main branches, microeconomics and macroeconomics. This book maintains that tradition by dealing with microeconomics in Chapters 3–17 and macroeconomics in Chapters 18–30. It must be pointed out, however, that these two branches of economics can never be completely separated from each other – there are many linkages and overlaps between them.

Microeconomics, broadly speaking, is concerned with the behaviour of individual firms, industries and consumers (or households) and deals with the effects of individual taxes and specific public spending programmes. A study of the determination of the level of output and employment in the British textile industry, for example, would belong to microeconomics. An examination of the activities of a firm by the Monopolies Commission or the Office of Fair Trading would also come within the purview of microeconomics. This branch of economics deals with the problem of resource allocation, considers problems of income distribution, and is chiefly interested in the determination of the *relative* prices of goods and services.

Macroeconomics, on the other hand, concerns itself with large aggregates, particularly for the economy as a whole. It deals with the factors which determine national output and employment, the general price level, total spending and saving in the economy, total imports and exports, and the demand for and supply of money and other financial assets. It must be remembered that these large aggregates are the sums of individual variables – total national output, for example, is the sum of the outputs of all individual business units; total consumption is the sum of the consumption spending of all individual consumers. The problems associated with such aggregation are dealt with in Chapter 17.

Economic methodology

The term 'methodology' refers to the way in which economists go about the study of their subject matter. Broadly, they have followed two main lines of approach: *positive* economics and *normative* economics.

Positive economics is concerned with the investigation of the ways in which the different economic agents in society seek to achieve their goals. For example, positive economists may analyse how a firm behaves in trying to make as much profit as it can or how a household behaves in trying to reach the highest attainable level of satisfaction from consumption. Positive statements, therefore, are concerned with *what is, was or will be* and are statements whose validity can be tested against the available evidence. The statement 'an increased budget deficit *will* bring down the present high level of unemployment but *will* increase the rate of inflation' belongs to positive economics.

Normative economics is concerned with making suggestions about the ways in which society's goals might be more efficiently realised. From the standpoint of policy recommendations, this approach involves economists in ethical questions of what *should or ought to be*, so much so that they may take up strong moral positions on the propriety of goals themselves. For example, the statement 'the present high level of unemployment and inflation in Britain *ought to be* reduced' and 'the distribution of income in Britain *should be* made more equal' are normative statements.

The basic economic theories, problems and policies set out in this book include both the positive and normative approaches, though it must be pointed out that it is not always easy to draw a clear line of demarcation between the two. For instance, if the goal is to eliminate poverty, then the question of whether to give cash or help in kind (like free medical care or free school meals) to low-income families is an issue of both positive and normative economics.

Deduction and empirical testing

The process of deduction and empirical testing is the most important method of approach followed by modern economists. It is illustrated in Fig. 3. The starting point is an *a priori* proposition or theory. (Note that an *a priori* proposition is one which seems reasonable to the investigator and is based on innate ideas and not derived directly from statistical evidence.) This proposition or theory is then demonstrated logically in the context of a simple model which is set up by specifying a number of assumptions concerning the behaviour of the economic variables under investigation. This logical reasoning (called deduction) may yield in turn a number of predictions or testable hypotheses and it is these which can be subjected to empirical (or statistical) testing. If the evidence supports the theory, we cannot simply accept it: instead, we say that the theory is not rejected but that continued testing is required. This is essential because economic events are rarely sufficiently stable for us to be certain that a theory that is thought to be satisfactory in one period of history will continue to be satisfactory in later periods. If, on the other hand, the evidence fails to support the theory, it must be rejected and either replaced by a new theory or modified in some way which improves its predictive power.

It is through this process, carried out rigorously by economists and statisticians, that economics progresses – unsatisfactory theories are rejected, whilst more satisfactory ones are continually subjected to empirical testing.

Figure 3 also provides a specific example of the way in which the deductive method works. The reader should find the example more illuminating after reading Chapter 7, but for now it provides a good illustration of modern economic methodology. First, the reasonable proposition is stated that a good's market price is determined by the demand for and supply of it. A simple model is then set up in which it is assumed that the market is competitive and that demand and supply themselves both depend on the good's price. Logical reasoning demonstrates that the proposition is true in the context of the model and yields the testable hypothesis that changes in supply conditions will cause the market price to change. The final step is to test these predictions in the real world and the market for agricultural goods is seen to provide some evidence in support of the theory.

There has been much debate among economists about how realistic the assumptions upon which a theory is based should be. Let us just state here that a model with highly unrealistic assumptions is extremely unlikely to perform well in empirical tests. In a sense, then, in testing a theory, the assumptions upon which the theory is based are also being tested. There is a strong case for arguing (as Milton Friedman has done in his *Essays in Positive Economics*) that if a model is giving predictions which stand up to rigorous testing, it ought not to be rejected on the grounds that its assumptions can be shown to be unrealistic.

Induction

An alternative methodological approach in economics is known as induction. This involves, first, the collection, presentation and analysis of economic data and then the derivation of relationships among the observed variables. In other words, the available statistics are closely examined in the search for general economic principles. A major problem with this approach is that

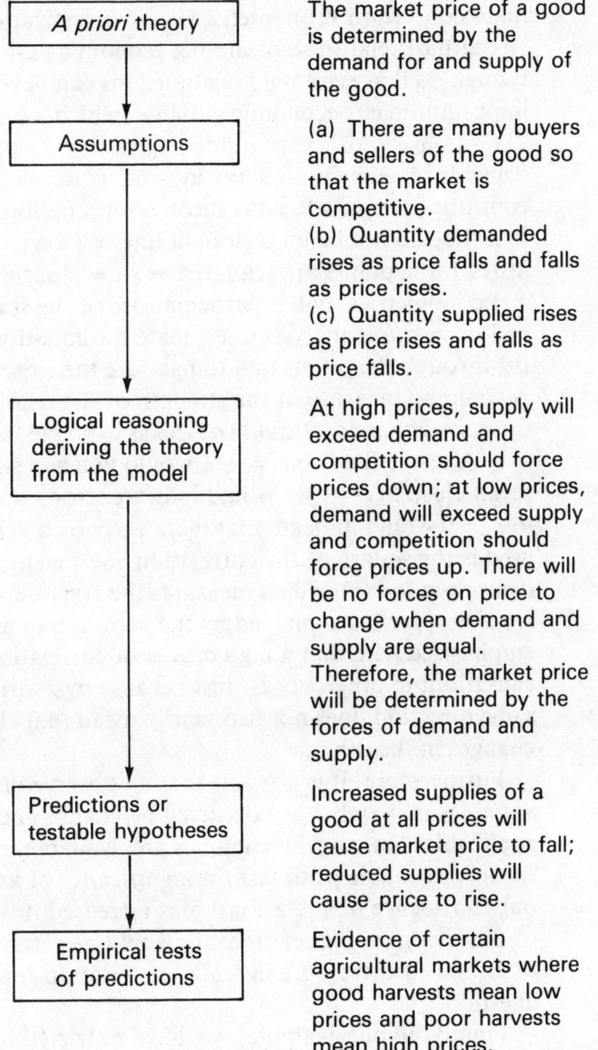

Fig. 3. Deduction and empirical testing.

economic statistics are so complex that it is often difficult to disentangle them and, of course, economists cannot perform laboratory experiments in the same way as the physical scientists can. Another difficulty is that some economic variables cannot be directly measured or are extremely difficult to measure accurately – for example, the 'satisfaction' that a household derives from consuming a good cannot be measured and a country's stock of plant and machinery cannot be measured in physical units with any accuracy. None the less, the collection and analysis of data is of crucial importance in economics, and, as mentioned above, plays a large role in the empirical testing of predictions derived from the deductive method.

Introducing econometrics

The use of statistical methods to test or derive economic theories has developed into a growing branch of economics, known as econometrics. The main concern of econometrics is the investigation of the direction and strength of relationships among economic variables. A serious problem, though, is that economic relationships can never be precisely quantified. One important macroeconomic variable (which we consider in detail in Chapter 21) is households' consumption spending: according to one theory, this depends on current after-tax income. If we plot combinations of total consumption and after-tax income for a period of years on a graph, we find that they do not lie on a straight line or along any well-defined curve: instead, the points are scattered as shown in the *scatter diagram* in Fig. 4.

Econometrics makes particular use of the statistical methods of *regression* and *correlation* analysis to estimate the equation of the line or curve of 'best fit' through the points and to measure the closeness of the points to the line. A common measure of the strength of the relationship between variables is the *correlation coefficient* (r): this is expressed as a figure between -1 and $+1$. A result close to $r = -1$ would indicate strong *inverse* correlation; a result close to $r = +1$ would indicate strong *direct* correlation; a result close to $r = 0$ would indicate that there was no correlation at all. More commonly used is the square of the correlation coefficient, known as the *coefficient of determination* (r^2) which measures the fraction of the variation in one variable which is explained by the variation in another. It has to be emphasised here that a high degree of correlation does not necessarily imply causation: in other words, just because two variables tend to move in the same direction does not necessarily mean that changes in one are causing changes in the other.

Furthermore, it is possible that an observed relationship between two variables may only have occurred by chance and so may not be generally applicable. Statistical techniques are available, making use of probability theory, to enable us to test the *significance* of any relationship. For example, our confidence in a relationship is increased if we can show that the chances of observing such a relationship would be extremely small (say, one in a thousand) if there were in reality no relationship between the variables in question.

Finally, in our examples, we have restricted ourselves to relationships between two variables only. It is possible, though, for a relationship to exist

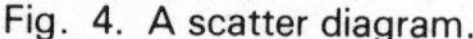
Fig. 4. A scatter diagram.

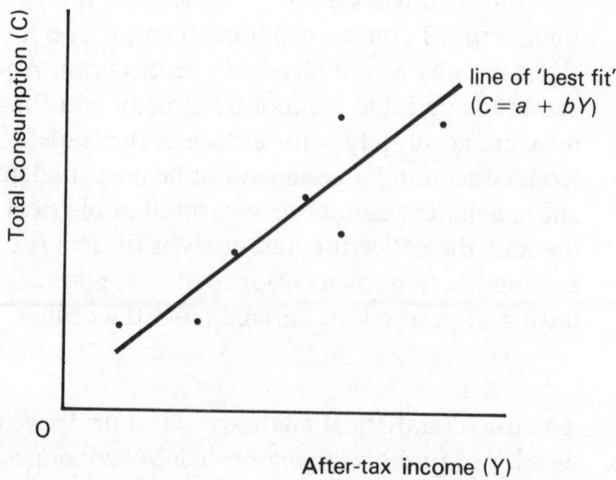

among more than two variables. The analysis of such relationships is called *multiple regression* analysis.

Although not essential for the study of this introductory textbook, serious students of economics are recommended to follow a course of statistics or introductory econometrics at an early stage.

Conclusion

In this chapter, we have attempted to explain the nature of economics, to outline some of the major concepts which modern economists employ and to discuss the methodology of economics as a 'science'.

It should be clear by now that the basic function in an economy is the production of goods and services. Without production, no economy as such could exist. For this reason, before delving into the main areas of micro- and macroeconomics, it is useful to set out the major concepts of production. This is our objective in Chapter 2.

Further reading

Friedman, M., 'The methodology of positive economics' in *Essays in Positive Economics,* University of Chicago Press, Chicago, 1953.
Robbins, L.C., *Nature and Significance of Economic Science*, Macmillan, London, 1935.
Koplin, H.T., *Microeconomic Analysis*, Harper and Row, New York, 1971 (Ch. 1).
Stewart, J., *Understanding Econometrics,* Hutchinson, London, 1976.

Exercises

1. Review your understanding of the following terms:

the basic economic problem	equilibrium
wealth	disequilibrium
welfare	microeconomics
opportunity cost	macroeconomics
production possibility frontier	positive economics
efficiency	normative economics
equity	deductive method
marginal rate of transformation	inductive method

2. Consider a country which, using all its resources efficiently in food production, can just produce 1,000 tonnes and, using all its resources efficiently in cloth production, can just produce 600 metres. Assuming constant opportunity costs:
(a) draw the production possibility frontier; and
(b) find the marginal rate of transformation.
Explain why the production possibility frontier is unlikely in reality to exhibit constant opportunity costs.

3. Discuss the opportunity cost of: (a) your attendance at college for the duration of the course; (b) the construction of an extra mile of motorway;

(c) the development of Concorde; (d) the development of nuclear energy in the United Kingdom.

4. Make *positive* and *normative* statements concerning: (a) the level of unemployment; (b) the rate of inflation; (c) the balance of payments; and (d) the distribution of income and wealth in your country.

5. Discuss which of the following can be classified under the heading *microeconomics* and which can be classified under the heading *macroeconomics*:
(a) the determination of the price of wheat in the European Economic Community;
(b) the influence of changes in the stock of money on the economy;
(c) the contribution of oil to the United Kingdom balance of payments;
(d) the effects on the distribution of income of a reduction in the basic rate of income tax.

6. Discuss the implications for the demand and supply analysis outlined in Fig. 3 of an observation that a bumper crop of apples did not lead to a fall in the price of apples. What evidence would be needed for the theory to be rejected in favour of an alternative theory?

2 Production

Introduction

Production can be defined as the creation of wealth which, in turn, adds to society's welfare. It is a vital link in the process of satisfying wants for, as we saw in Chapter 1, man's wants are almost unlimited relative to the resources available. It is important in production, then, that the limited resources be used efficiently in order to create the maximum possible welfare.

At a general level, all economies, irrespective of their organisation, face the same basic decisions of what, how and for whom to produce, subject to their production possibilities. In a mixed economy, such as the United Kingdom, some production decisions are left to private enterprise and the market mechanism whilst others are taken by the government: the production of shoes, for example, is the result of the decisions of private firms, whereas the quantity of hospital services or military tanks produced is the result of political decisions. In a command economy, such as the USSR or China, most production decisions are taken by a state planning agency. The allocation of resources by the price mechanism and by a central planning agency, and their respective merits, is taken up in detail in Chapter 7.

In this chapter, we concentrate on firms operating in a market economy or in the market sector of a mixed economy. We discuss the objectives of such firms and describe the types of business units that exist. We then turn to the growth of firms and consider the motives for growth and the ways in which firms grow. Finally, we discuss the characteristics of the factors of production and consider the relationship between the input of factors and the output of goods and services both in the short- and long-run.

The firm and its objectives

The total level of output in an economy is, of course, the sum of the outputs of all the individual firms. It is important at the outset, therefore, to explain what is meant by a firm and to consider some of the main factors which motivate firms to produce goods and services.

Definition: ***A firm is a decision-making production unit which transforms resources into goods and services which are ultimately bought by consumers, the government and other firms.***

Traditional economic theory has assumed that the typical firm has a single objective – to maximise its profits. No distinction is drawn between the objective of a corner-store proprietor and that of the largest firm. The modern theories of the firm, however, do acknowledge that firms may have other objectives, such as sales-revenue maximisation or the maximisation of managerial utility.

The significance of the divorce between the ownership and the control of the modern firm has occupied many economists since it was observed by Berle and Means in their book *The Modern Corporation and Private Property* (1932). They pointed out that, typically, the owners of a large public company, the shareholders, delegate their authority to a board of directors who, in turn, place the effective control of the company in the hands of professional managers. The interests of the shareholders and the managers may diverge. The shareholders are presumably interested in obtaining the maximum dividends possible over a reasonable time period, which implies that the firm should aim to maximise its long-run profits. The managers, though, who do not necessarily share in the profits, may not have profit maximisation as their primary objective: instead, they may aim for an increased market share or greater sales revenue which they feel will bring them more prestige, greater security or a higher salary. The managers cannot forget about profits entirely, however, because they need to earn a satisfactory level of profits in order to declare reasonable dividends to keep the shareholders satisfied.

We consider managerial and other models of the firm in more detail in Chapter 10. In this chapter, we assume in the main that firms have the single objective of profit maximisation – that is to say, they attempt to make as large as possible the excess of revenue over costs.

A firm has to decide what level of output to produce. This decision will in turn determine the firm's purchases of factor inputs and may also influence the price at which its output can be sold. The firm's production decisions will be conditioned by the type of market in which it operates. Some firms operate in highly competitive markets, such as catering, foreign exchange dealing and agriculture. As we see in Chapter 9, a firm operating in a *perfectly competitive* market cannot charge a price higher than that of its competitors, or no one will buy its output.

Other markets are less competitive. In the United Kingdom, for example, commercial banking is dominated by a few large firms, namely the 'Big Four' banks, each of which reacts to each other's actions, thereby constituting an *oligopoly*. The motor-car market is similarly dominated by four large domestic car assemblers, although they also face competition from imports. The market for soap powders is dominated by two large firms, Unilever and Procter and Gamble: such a market is a special case of oligopoly called a *duopoly*. A market dominated by a single firm producing a good for which there are no close substitutes is called a *monopoly*. In the United Kingdom, the Post Office had a monopoly in the supply of telecommunication services.

There are a large number of degrees of competition in the thousands of markets of a modern economy; these can be viewed as a continuum stretching from pure monopoly at one extreme to perfect competition at the other. We consider models of market behaviour in Chapters 9 and 10.

Types of business units

Consider now the legal status of the different types of firms to be found in a western economy, such as the United Kingdom.

One-man business

In terms of numbers, the one-man business (or sole proprietorship) is the most common type of firm. Typically, it is a small-scale operation employing at most a handful of people. The proprietor himself is normally in charge of the operation of the business, with the effect that he is likely to be highly motivated as he benefits directly from any increase in profits. As the one-man business is small, it can provide a personal service to its customers and can respond flexibly to the requirements of the market. Decisions can be taken quickly as the owner does not have to consult with any other directors.

Disadvantages associated with a one-man business are that the owner cannot specialise in particular functions but must be a jack-of-all trades, and that the finance available for the expansion of the business is limited to that which the owner himself can raise. An even bigger disadvantage is perhaps that there is no legal distinction between the owner and his business. The owner has, therefore, unlimited liability for any debts incurred by the business, so that in the eventuality of bankruptcy all his assets (for example, his house and car) are liable to seizure.

One-man businesses are common in retailing, farming, building and personal services, such as hairdressing.

Partnership

The logical progression from a one-man business is to a partnership. An ordinary partnership contains from two to twenty partners. The main advantages over a one-man business are that more finance is likely to be available with the influx of partners, and that each partner may specialise to some extent (for example, in the marketing, production or personnel functions). The major disadvantage, once again, is that of unlimited liability. As each partner is able to commit the other partners to agreements entered into, all of the others may suffer from the errors of one unreliable or foolhardy partner.

Partnerships are often found in the professions – for example, among doctors, dentists, solicitors and architects. Ultimately, the upper limit on the number of partners is likely to restrict the amount of finance available to the partnership and so place a limit on its growth. This, together with the disadvantage of unlimited liability, means that many growing businesses eventually form joint-stock companies.

Joint-stock company

The joint-stock company with limited liability developed in the second half of the nineteenth century. It helped to promote the development of large companies by providing a relatively safe vehicle for investment in industry and commerce by a wide cross-section of the community. The liability of the shareholders is limited to the amount they have subscribed to the firm's capital and each shareholder knows the extent of his potential loss if the company goes bankrupt. To make information available to potential shareholders, all joint-stock companies are required to file annually with the

Registrar of Companies details of their profits, turnover, assets and other relevant financial information, such as the remuneration of the directors.

A joint-stock company can be either a *private limited company* or a *public limited company*. The shares of a *private* company cannot be offered for sale to the public and thus are not traded on the Stock Exchange. The shares cannot be transferred without the consent of the other shareholders. Private companies require a minimum of two and a maximum of fifty shareholders (or members), though the upper limit may be exceeded in the case of employees or former employees of the company.

The shares of a *public* company can be offered for sale to the public. A public company requires a minimum of two shareholders, but there is no upper limit. Shares are freely transferable and the company is required to hold an annual general meeting where shareholders are able to question the directors, to change the company's articles of association, to elect or dismiss the board of directors, to sanction the payment of dividends, to approve the choice of auditors and to fix their remuneration. In practice, attendance at annual general meetings is low, and normally the approval of the director's recommendations is a formality.

Although only about 3 per cent of companies are public companies, most large companies are public companies. Indeed, they account for about two-thirds of the capital employed by all companies.

Co-operatives

In the United Kingdom, consumer co-operatives have been relatively successful since the first co-operative was formed at Rochdale in 1844. The movement, which comprises a familiar section of the retail trade, is based on consumer ownership and control, although there is a professional management. There are about thirteen million members of co-operative societies in the United Kingdom. Producer co-operatives, on the other hand, have not generally been successful and are not particularly significant in the United Kingdom.

Public corporation

The public corporation is the form of enterprise that has developed in the United Kingdom for those areas where the government has decided to place production in the hands of the state. Whilst there are early examples of the formation of public corporations, such as the Port of London Authority (1909) and the British Broadcasting Corporation (1927), most were formed in the period of the postwar Labour government of 1945–51. The government appoints the chairman and the board of directors which is responsible to a minister of the Crown for fulfilling the statutory requirements for the public corporation laid down by Parliament. The minister is supposed not to concern himself with the day-to-day running of the company. Public corporations contribute about 10 per cent of the total output of the United Kingdom and in 1975 employed more than two million people. We consider public corporations and their operations in detail in Chapter 14.

The growth of firms

Motives for growth

A firm may have one or more motives for growth. Some firms may see expansion as a way of ensuring their survival in the long-run: they may fear that if they should stagnate at their present size they may become the target of a take-over bid. Diversification may similarly be seen as a key to survival and the best prospect for growth. It can be argued that a diversified firm will be better able to withstand depressed trading conditions because whilst the markets for some of its products may be stagnating or falling in size, other markets may be growing. In recent years, for example, cigarette and tobacco firms have been faced with relatively stagnant traditional markets, largely because of the publicity given to the health risks of smoking. As a result, they have diversified into new areas: the diversification of the Imperial Group (formally the Imperial Tobacco Group) into areas such as food production, packaging, educational supplies, woollen textiles and distribution is a case in point.

Another possible motive for growth is to achieve higher profits. These may result, first, from the likely fall in unit production costs as the firm expands and, secondly, through the firm increasing its market share and, therefore, its ability to control the price of its product. A firm with a dominant position in a market may be acknowledged by other firms as a price leader. Alternatively, if the expansion of firms leads to the market being dominated by a few firms, they may engage in some form of collusion whereby they all charge similar prices – it should be pointed out, though, that this practice of oligopolistic collusion is not legal in the United Kingdom.

The ways in which firms grow

A firm can grow as a result of internal or external growth. *Internal growth* occurs when a single firm expands its scale of operation within its original management structure. This process is easier if the markets for the firm's product are expanding rapidly and if the firm is efficient relative to its competitors. The raising of finance may be a constraint on the speed at which a firm can grow. It may be able to plough back some retained profits into the business or it may be able to borrow funds from one or more of the financial institutions. The large public company is able to raise finance by floating a new share issue, but this option is normally too expensive for the smaller firm.

External growth occurs when two or more firms join together to form a larger firm. This may be a result of a take-over where a dominant firm acquires a controlling interest in a smaller firm which then loses its separate identity. Alternatively, two or more firms may agree to a merger to form a new company. We can classify the integration of firms into three categories: vertical, horizontal and conglomerate. Consider these in turn.

Vertical integration This occurs when two or more firms in the same industry, but at different stages in the production process, join together. Most of the major oil companies, for example, do not confine their interests to oil refining: they are also involved in the exploration for and extraction of oil (vertical integration backward) and they own chains of filling stations (vertical integration forward).

Vertical integration backward occurs when a firm acquires another firm which produces at an earlier stage of the production process. Other examples include the acquisition of tea plantations by tea companies and the acquisition of a body-building firm by a motor-car assembler. The motives for this kind of integration might be the desire for greater security of vital supplies or better control over the quality of raw materials. In addition, the company might see the prospect of increased profits by capturing the previous supplier's profit margin. Finally, control over an important supplier might give the company a competitive advantage over other companies who may now be denied access to a source of supplies.

Vertical integration forward occurs when a firm acquires another firm which produces at a stage of the production process nearer the consumer. Examples include the purchase of a rolling mill by a steel producer, and the acquisition of public houses by a brewery. As before, the firm may see the prospect of extra profits which formerly accrued to the acquired firm. Also, it may wish to improve upon the marketing of the final product with a view to increasing its sales.

Vertical integration may lead to a reduction in production costs, as, for example, in the iron and steel industry where the location of iron and steel production on a single site enables the molten pig-iron to be transferred directly into the converter with a saving in energy costs. There may also be a saving in transport costs, as when a rolling mill is located adjacent to a steelworks.

Horizontal integration This refers to the combining of firms that produce at a similar stage of an industry's production. Examples include the mergers between British Motor Holdings and Leyland Motors to form British Leyland in 1968, and Tate and Lyle's take-over of Manbre and Garton in the sugar refining industry in 1976. Horizontal integration may be undertaken to achieve economies of scale – that is, a reduction in the average production costs (see Ch. 9). Alternatively, it may be undertaken to carry out the rationalisation of capacity, as in the Tate and Lyle–Manbre and Garton case. If two companies have excess capacity, they may be able to close one or more plants and still be able to meet the market demand.

In practice, horizontal integration does not always result in economies of scale being achieved. The integration of different units may prove difficult, especially in cases where the plants are physically separate, and the increased size of the business may give rise to managerial diseconomies of scale. Rationalisation, too, may prove difficult to achieve as it is painful to close plants and to declare redundancies, especially in the face of concerted trade union opposition.

Conglomerate mergers These take place between firms whose activities are not directly related. Thus, the possibility of achieving economies of scale is not so great as in the case of horizontal integration. However, even if two companies' operations are not directly related, they may depend indirectly on similar marketing or financial expertise. Thus, one justification for a conglomerate merger might be that it has the effect of replacing an inefficient management by a more efficient one. This might in turn lead to a more efficient use of the company's assets.

Because of the difficulty of achieving economies of scale, however, and because conglomerate mergers lead to increased concentration in the ownership of resources, the case for conglomerate mergers does not appear to be very strong. In some cases, the skills required for efficient management have been specific to the industry and the mergers have not been successful as, for example, in the case of Burton the tailor's take-over of Rymans the business stationers which finally led to the sale or closure of many of the Rymans stores.

Another type of conglomerate merger has occasionally occurred when an ailing company with a depressed stock market valuation has been taken over with a view to 'asset stripping'. This involves the running down of the company and the sale of the company's assets, such as factories, land and machinery, so that the work-force loses its livelihood.

The factors of production

There are many different inputs into most production processes. The production of pig-iron, for example, requires a blast furnace, iron ore, coking coal and limestone, in addition to the human effort necessary to control the production process. For the purposes of analysis, economists typically place each of the many different factor inputs into one of three categories - land, labour and capital.

Definition: ***Land includes all the natural resources which are used in production.***

Definition: ***Labour refers to all human attributes, physical and mental, that are used in production.***

Definition: ***Capital consists of goods which are not for current consumption, but which will assist consumer goods to be produced in the future.***

Sometimes a fourth factor of production, *enterprise*, is added to the list. Consider these four factors in turn.

Land

It is important to note that land as a factor of production includes minerals, forests, water and all other natural resources as well as the land itself used in agriculture and as a site upon which economic activities take place. Unfortunately, the classification of factor inputs is not always clear-cut. Take, for example, the 'land' on which the Southampton container port is built: this land has been reclaimed from the sea and so in fact represents both land and capital. (Perhaps a better known example is that of the Netherlands where large areas have been reclaimed from the sea.) Similar remarks apply to agricultural land which has been cleared of bushes and weeds and fertilised. Indeed, a few economists argue that land should be regarded as a form of capital, and they prefer to distinguish only between labour and capital as separate factors of production.

Labour

In many ways, labour is a special factor of production as it refers to human effort and as ultimately all production is carried out to satisfy *human* wants. Clearly, labour is not a homogeneous factor of production as some jobs require little, if any, training (for example, petrol pump attendants and ice-cream salesmen) whilst others require several years of training (for example, surgeons and civil engineers). The education that is invested, or embodied, in trained labour is sometimes referred to as 'human capital', yet another reminder that the distinction between factors of production is not water-tight. The compelling argument for retaining a distinction between labour and capital, however, is that whereas capital yields future services that can be bought and sold, trained labour cannot be bought and sold in a society without slavery.

The labour force in the United Kingdom consists mainly of males aged from sixteen to sixty-five and females aged from sixteen to sixty. Not everybody, of course, in these age groups is either working or actively looking for work. Many women (and a few men) are unable to work because of family commitments; many young people are still in full-time education; some people retire early; and there are many other reasons why some members of the potential work-force are not in a position to work. The characteristics of the labour market and the determination of wages are considered in detail in Chapters 15 and 16.

Capital

Capital goods (sometimes called investment or producer goods) are not wanted for their own sake, but because of the contribution they make to production. They are goods which produce a flow of services over a time period – it is estimated, for example, that each of the Concorde supersonic airliners will have a working life of at least twenty-five years. Capital, then, includes all plant, machines and industrial buildings that contribute to production. Most definitions of capital also include all intermediate goods (or semi-finished goods) and all unsold stocks of finished and intermediate goods. What all these have in common is that they are not to be consumed in the current period, but they enable a greater flow of consumer goods to be made available in the future.

Capital is a *stock* – that is to say, it exists at a point in time. In principle, the capital stock could be measured at a particular moment. With an army of investigators, a list could be made of all the lathes, cranes, lorries, power-tools – in fact, of every piece of plant and machinery in the economy – together with the stocks of finished and intermediate goods. This list would be extremely long and would make very little sense since all the items contained in it would be measured in different units. A more practical approach is to add up the monetary value of each piece of capital. Unfortunately, estimates of the current value of the different components of the capital stock are notoriously inaccurate. The value of a machine, for example, depends on the expected future demand for the final product. An additional problem in an inflationary world is that the price actually paid for a machine may bear little relationship to its current replacement cost.

The heterogeneity of capital and the problems of valuation have led some economists, like Joan Robinson, to argue that the capital stock cannot be measured in any meaningful way. In practice, estimates of the value of the capital stock are made in the United Kingdom using arbitrary rules for tax purposes in order to estimate the extent of *depreciation*. Depreciation (or capital consumption) is a measure of the extent to which the capital stock falls in value as a result of use (or 'wear and tear') during the relevant time period, normally a year.

Note that the purchase of new plant and machinery by firms is called *investment*. Investment is a *flow* - that is to say, it can only be measured as 'so much' per time period. Since part of total (or 'gross') investment is needed to make good the depreciation of the capital stock, it is only *net* investment (that is, gross investment minus depreciation) which represents an addition to the capital stock. Investment is considered in greater detail in Chapter 20.

Enterprise

To land, labour and capital, we could add a fourth factor of production - enterprise or entrepreneurship. It is the entrepreneur who organises the other factors of production; he decides what goods to produce and what quantities of the factors of production to use. The entrepreneur bears the risks of production because he incurs the costs of production before receiving any revenue from the sale of the finished product. The risk is whether or not there will be sufficient demand for the product. If he has chosen to produce a successful product, he will make a profit; if not, he is likely to make a loss.

It has been argued that this formulation of the role of the entrepreneur was perhaps more appropriate in the nineteenth century when one-man businesses were the typical production units. Since production is dominated now to a large extent by large firms, owned by perhaps thousands of shareholders, the concept of the entrepreneur is often not appropriate as the risks of failure fall mostly on the shareholders. The professional management which makes the day-to-day decisions does not bear all the risks, though it is of course possible that the managers and the other employees will lose their jobs if the firm is unsuccessful. In this book, we consider management as a specialised type of labour, thereby allowing the list of factors of production to be reduced to three - land, labour and capital.

The production function

As we saw earlier, production involves the transformation of resources into final goods and services. The relationship between inputs and output is a technological relationship which economists summarise in a production function. Suppose that the production of good X requires inputs of capital, labour and land. Using *functional notation*, we can write:

$$Q_X = f(K, L, L_D)$$

where Q_X is the output of X per time period; f is the functional relationship; and K, L and L_D represent the inputs of the services of capital, labour and land respectively into the production process. This production function states that the output of good X is a function of (or depends on) the inputs of the services of capital, labour and land – that is to say, Q_X depends on all the variables included in the brackets. Note that the precise form of the relationship between Q_X and the variables upon which it depends has not been specified.

In this book, we confine our analysis to the consideration of *technologically efficient* methods of production. A method of production is said to be technologically efficient if, for a given level of factor inputs, it is impossible to obtain a higher level of output, given the existing state of technology. As we saw in Chapter 1, the existing state of technology acts as a constraint on production possibilities. An improvement in technology, of course, would enable more output to be produced from a given level of inputs and this is a possible source of economic growth. For the purposes of analysis, however, we assume that the state of technology only improves in the *very* long-run.

The short- and long-run

Given the state of technology and assuming technological efficiency, a firm can only increase its level of production by employing more inputs. Very often, though, a firm that wishes to increase production quickly is unable to increase the input of all the factors of production that it employs. For example, a manufacturing firm wishing to increase its output is unable to have a bigger factory built overnight and so in the *short-run* can only produce more by employing more of its variable factors, such as labour, raw materials and fuel. Only in the *long-run* can factors such as capital and land be increased. We shall distinguish between the short-run and the long-run so far as a firm's production decisions are concerned as follows:

Definition: ***The short-run is that period of time over which the input of at least one factor of production cannot be varied. Those factors which can be varied in the short-run (typically labour, raw materials and fuel) are called variable factors; those which cannot be varied (typically capital and land) are called fixed factors.***

Definition: ***The long-run is that period of time over which the input of all factors of production can be varied. Consequently, all factors are variable factors in the long-run.***

Note that the actual length of the short-run does not correspond precisely to any particular time period. It varies from industry to industry and from firm to firm. In the North Sea oil industry, for example, it may take several years to install a new platform and to make it operational; meanwhile, output can only be increased by more intensive use of the existing capital stock. In the case of a shirt factory, on the other hand, the company can probably acquire extra equipment and have it installed within a few weeks.

Short-run changes in production

The 'law of diminishing returns'

As a firm increases its level of production in the short-run, it eventually comes up against the 'law of diminishing returns'. This 'law' can best be illustrated by means of a simple arithmetic example. Consider a wheat farmer with a given area of land (say, 1 hectare) and a given quantity of capital equipment, and assume that neither the land nor capital can be varied in the short-run - in other words, they are both fixed factors. Assume further that the state of technology is constant and that labour (the variable factor) is homogeneous - that is to say, each worker is exactly like any other worker.

Under these circumstances, the firm's production function for wheat can be written as:

$$Q_W = f(L, \overline{K}, \overline{L_D})$$

where Q_W is the output of wheat in tonnes per time period. The bars on the last two variables indicate that the inputs of the services of both capital and land are held constant.

Table 1 shows how wheat output varies as additional workers are employed on the fixed area of land. Column (2), labelled *total product* (TP), shows what happens to total wheat output as the number of workers is varied. Notice that maximum wheat output is achieved when nine workers are employed. When a tenth worker is added, output falls because there are then too many workers employed on the fixed area of land and they begin to get in each other's way.

Table 1. Wheat production illustrating the law of diminishing returns.

(1) Number of workers (*L*)	(2) Total product (TP)	(3) Average product (AP)	(4) Marginal product (MP)
1	4	4	4
2	14	7	10
3	25.5	8.5	11.5
4	40	10	14.5
5	60	12	20
6	72	12	12
7	77	11	5
8	80	10	3
9	81	9	1
10	75	7.5	−6

Column (3), headed *average product* (AP), tells us the output per worker. It is found by dividing total product by the number of workers employed, or in symbols,

$$AP = \frac{TP}{L}$$

where L is the number of workers employed by the farmer. Notice that average product is at its highest when six workers are employed. The addition of any more workers causes average product to decline.

Column (4) shows the *marginal product* of labour (MP). This can be defined as the change in total product resulting from the employment of an additional worker. When three workers are employed, for example, the total product is 25.5 tonnes and when four workers are employed, this increases to 40 tonnes; the marginal product of the fourth worker, then, is 14.5 tonnes. The marginal product of labour can be defined more generally (to take account of the fact that the labour input might be altered in terms of man-days or man-hours) as the change in total product divided by the change in the labour input. In symbols, we can write:

$$MP = \frac{\triangle TP}{\triangle L}$$

where $\triangle TP$ is the change in total product and $\triangle L$ is the change in the labour input. Strictly speaking, this formula is only valid for very small changes in the variables.

From Table 1 it is apparent that the marginal product of labour is at a maximum when five workers are employed; the fifth worker adds 20 tonnes to total wheat output. After this point, the marginal product of labour declines.

The result (derived arithmetically from our example) that both the average and marginal products of labour eventually decline as more and more units of labour are added to a fixed amount of other factors is an illustration of the 'law of diminishing returns'.

Definition: ***The 'law of diminishing returns' states that as additional units of a variable factor are added to a given quantity of fixed factors, with a given state of technology, the average and marginal products of the variable factor will eventually decline.***

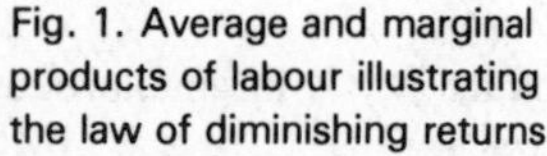
Fig. 1. Average and marginal products of labour illustrating the law of diminishing returns.

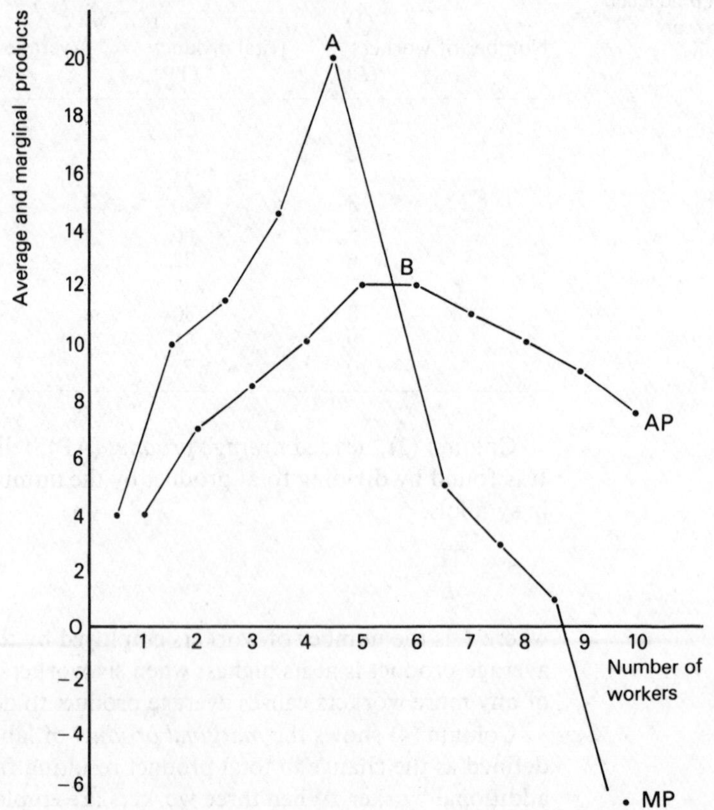

Plotting the average and marginal products from our example on a graph, we can see how the 'law' comes into operation. This is shown in Fig. 1. Notice that the data for the marginal product are plotted at the mid-points of the class intervals.

The AP and MP 'curves' in Fig. 1 are not smooth because of the discrete nature of the data used in our example where the labour input increases by 'whole workers'. If we had used continuous data, so that the labour input could be increased in very small quantities, we would have obtained smooth curves for AP and MP, as shown in Fig. 2.

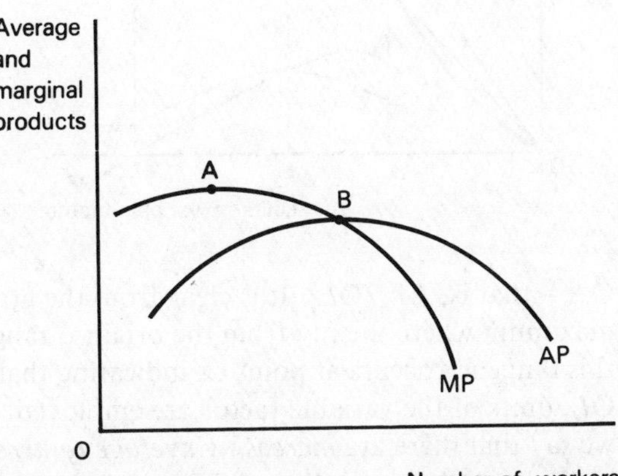

Fig. 2. Average and marginal products of labour for continuous data.

In both Fig. 1 and Fig. 2, the point at which MP reaches its maximum is point A. This is known as the point of *diminishing marginal returns.* Similarly, the point at which AP reaches its maximum (point B in both diagrams) is known as the point of *diminishing average returns.*

Notice from the graphs that MP begins to fall before AP does. In fact, MP cuts AP at the maximum point on the AP curve. This is an arithmetic relationship: when AP is increasing (up to point B), MP is above AP, pulling it up; when AP is at its maximum and constant (at point B), AP is equal to MP; when AP is falling (after point B), MP is below AP, pulling it down. To clarify this, the analogy with a cricketer's batting average may be helpful: if a batsman's average score is to increase from its present level, his next (or marginal) score must be greater than his present average; if his next score is exactly equal to his present average, the average remains unchanged; finally, for the average to fall, the batsman's next score must be below his present average.

The relationship between total, average and marginal products

The relationship between total, average and marginal products can be illustrated diagrammatically. Consider Fig. 3 which presents the TP, AP and MP curves for continuous data.

Since AP is equal to TP divided by the number of units of the variable factor employed, it follows that AP is given by the slope of the ray from the origin to the relevant point on the TP curve. Thus, for example, when OL_1 units of the variable factor are used, the AP is equal to the slope of the ray

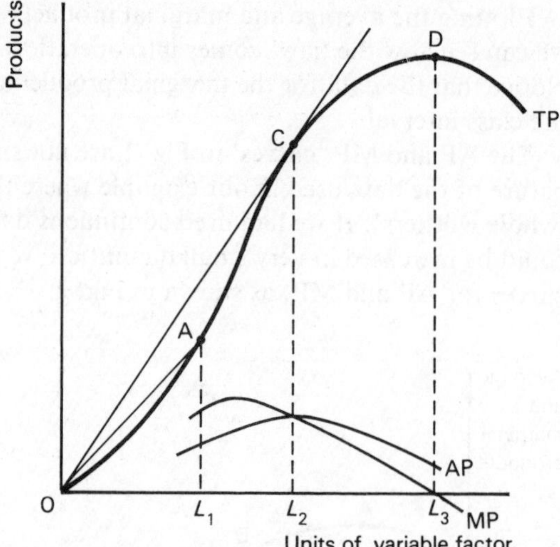

Fig. 3. The relationship between total, average and marginal products.

OA – that is, AL_1/OL_1. It is clear from the graph that AP reaches its maximum where the ray from the origin is tangent to the TP curve. In Fig. 3, this tangency occurs at point C, indicating that AP is at a maximum when OL_2 units of the variable factor are employed. Until OL_2 units are employed, we say that there are *increasing average returns to the variable factor*.

We have defined MP as $\triangle TP/\triangle L$, where the changes in the variables are very small. This also measures the slope of the TP curve. Thus, when OL_2 units of the variable factor are employed, the slope of the TP curve is given by CL_2/OL_2 which also represents AP at that point, confirming that AP = MP when AP is at its maximum. Total product reaches its maximum when OL_3 units of the variable factor are employed. At this point, MP is equal to zero, confirmed by the slope of the TP curve at point D. If additional units are hired, total product falls and marginal product is negative.

Finally, note that a firm operating with a fixed factor may not actually be encountering diminishing returns if it is producing at a level of output below the point where diminishing marginal returns set in. Any firm increasing its output with a fixed factor, though, must eventually come up against diminishing returns. Remember also that the model assumes that the state of technology is held constant. In practice, improvements in technology may offset the operation of the law. This has been the case in western agriculture where productivity has greatly increased over time despite a relatively fixed supply of agricultural land.

Long-run changes in production

In the long-run, all factors of production are variable. Firms wishing to maximise their profits, therefore, will attempt to produce their chosen output by employing combinations of capital, labour and land which minimise their production costs. We can illustrate this cost-minimisation graphically with the use of *isoquants* and *isocost lines*. These also enable us to trace out the path along which a firm can expand in the long-run.

Isoquants

Consider the production of a single good, say good X, and suppose (for purposes of graphical representation) that only two factors of production, labour and capital, are employed. Suppose further that it is always possible to substitute capital for labour and labour for capital continuously in the production process.

Given these assumptions, it follows that a given quantity of good X can be produced using many different combinations of capital and labour. This is shown in Fig. 4, where the vertical axis measures units of capital per time period (K) and the horizontal axis measures units of labour per time period (L). Point A, on the isoquant labelled Q_1, represents just one possible combination of capital and labour (OK_1 units of capital and OL_1 units of labour) which can be used to produce Q_1 units of output. There are in fact an infinite number of other points on the isoquant Q_1 all of which represent different combinations of capital and labour which can be used to produce Q_1 units.

Fig. 4. Isoquant map for good *X*.

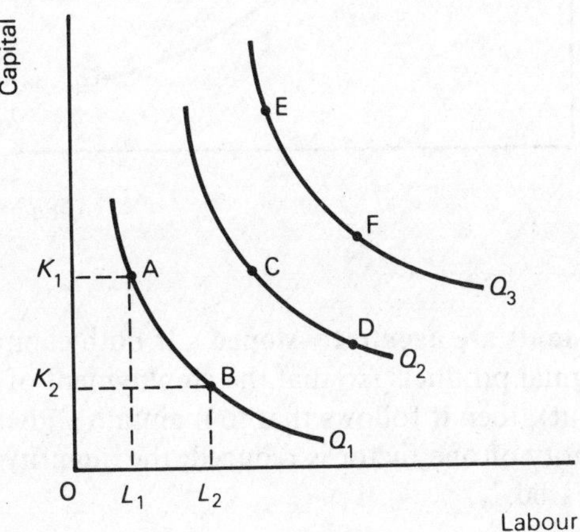

An output of Q_2 units (bigger than Q_1) can be produced using any of the combinations of capital and labour represented by points along the isoquant labelled Q_2, such as points C and D. Similarly, an output of Q_3 (bigger than Q_2) can be produced using any of the combinations of capital and labour represented by points along the isoquant labelled Q_3, such as E and F.

Definition: ***An isoquant, sometimes called an isoproduct curve, is a contour line which joins together the different combinations of two factors of production that are just physically able to produce a given quantity of a particular good.***

An *isoquant map,* then, is a family of isoquants which illustrates graphically the production function for a good. The isoquants themselves have three important properties: first, no two isoquants can intersect; secondly, isoquants normally slope downwards from left to right (that is to say, they have a negative slope); thirdly, they are convex to the origin. Consider these properties in turn.

Isoquants cannot intersect Figure 5 shows two intersecting isoquants, Q_1 and Q_2. As drawn, point H represents a combination of capital and labour which, when used efficiently, can apparently produce two different quantities of good *X*, Q_1 units and Q_2 units. This absurd result confirms the statement that isoquants cannot intersect.

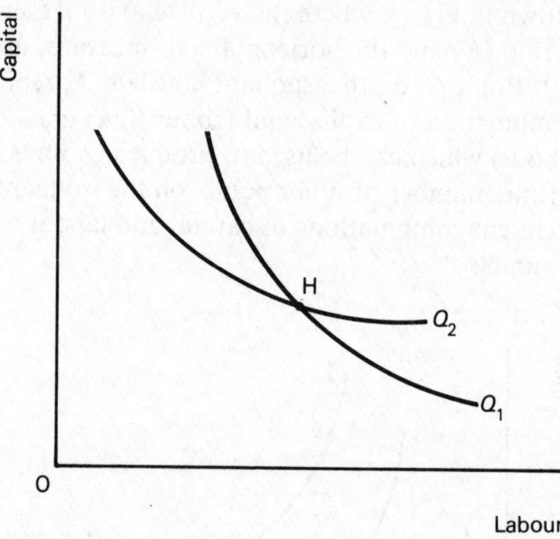

Fig. 5. Two intersecting isoquants for good *X*.

Isoquants are negatively sloped If both capital and labour have positive marginal products (so that the employment of extra units increases total output), then it follows that to maintain a given level of output when the quantity of one factor is reduced, the quantity of the other must be increased.

Isoquants are convex to the origin If labour and capital are substitutes for each other, though not *perfect* substitutes, then isoquants will be curves which are convex to the origin. As bigger quantities of labour and smaller quantities of capital are employed to produce a given level of output, labour becomes less and less capable of substituting for capital. Similarly, as bigger quantities of capital and smaller quantities of labour are employed to produce the same level of output, capital becomes less and less capable of substituting for labour. This is illustrated in Fig. 6. Notice from the graph that as the quantity of capital employed is reduced by one unit from OA to OB units, the quantity of labour employed must increase from OD to OE for output to remain unchanged at Q_1 units. If the quantity of capital is now reduced again by one unit to OC units (where AB = BC = 1), the quantity of labour employed must increase to OF units to maintain output at Q_1. Clearly, EF is bigger than DE. Thus, as more and more units of capital are given up, successively larger quantities of labour must be hired in order to keep the output level unchanged.

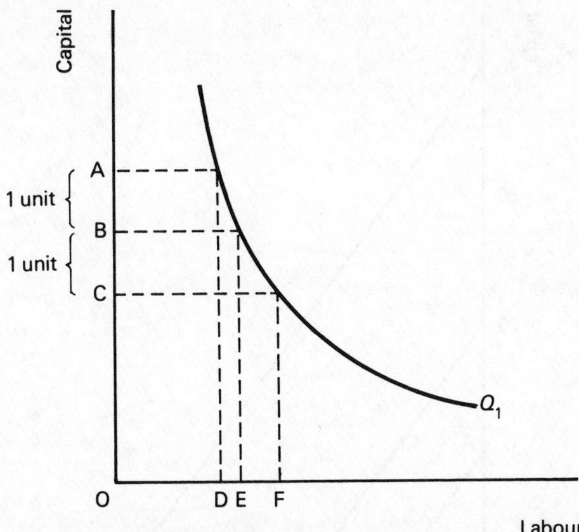

Fig. 6. An isoquant convex to the origin.

Note that the *slope* of an isoquant measures the rate at which capital can substitute for labour, keeping output constant. This slope is called the *marginal rate of technical substitution of capital for labour.*

Isocost lines

On the same labour and capital axes, we can plot an isocost line which joins together all those factor combinations which have the *same cost*. This, together with the isoquant map, enables us to identify the cost-minimising combination of factors that a profit-maximising firm will employ to produce its chosen output level.

Definition: ***An isocost line illustrates all the combinations of capital and labour that can be bought for a given monetary outlay.***

As an example, suppose that the price of capital is £1 per unit and the price of labour £2 per unit. Table 2 shows the combinations of the two factors that can be bought for an outlay (or cost) of £20. These combinations are plotted as the isocost line AB in Fig. 7: notice that the slope of the line (OA/OB = 2) represents the relative factor price ratio – in fact, it is the price of labour in terms of capital. The isocost line for an outlay of £40 is plotted as A′B′ on the graph: as might be expected, it is parallel to AB and

Table 2. The combinations of labour and capital for a £20 outlay.

Labour (price = £2)	Capital (price = £1)
10	0
8	4
6	8
4	12
2	16
0	20

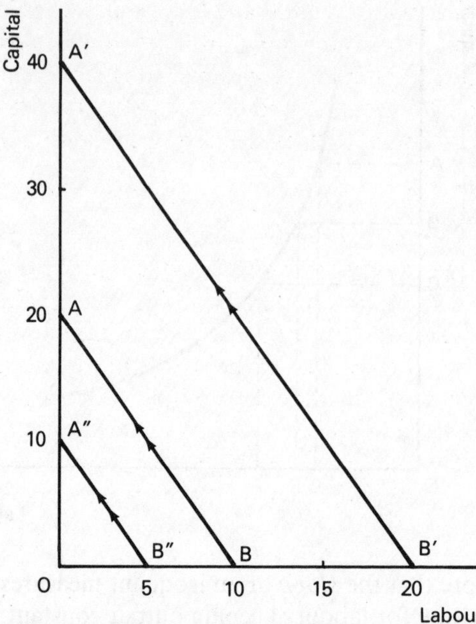

Fig. 7. Isocost lines.

lies to its right. Similarly, the isocost line for a £10 outlay, A″B″, is also parallel to AB but lies to its left. Isocost lines further to the left represent lower cost factor combinations; those further to the right represent higher cost factor combinations.

A change in the relative factor price ratio will change the slope of the isocost lines. If the price of capital should rise in terms of labour, the isocost lines in Fig. 7 would become less steep; if the price of labour should rise in terms of capital, the lines would become steeper.

Cost-minimisation

To produce a given output of good X, say Q_1, at minimum cost, a firm will produce at the point where isoquant Q_1 is just touching, or is tangent to, an isocost line. This is the isocost line nearest to the origin that can be achieved. Point C in Fig. 8 represents this point of cost-minimisation: all other

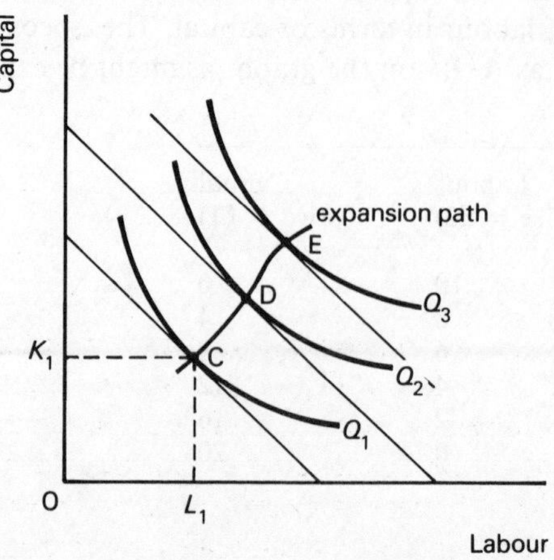

Fig. 8. Cost-minimisation and a firm's expansion path.

combinations of capital and labour along the isoquant Q_1 would involve the firm in a larger monetary outlay. As the firm expands in the long-run, it will continue to attempt to minimise its costs. Thus, production of output Q_2 would be at point D and production of output Q_3 would be at point E. The locus of points CDE is referred to as the firm's long-run *expansion path*.

Returns to scale

In economic theory, it is often found convenient to assume that there are *constant returns to scale* in production. What this means is that when a producer employs more labour and more capital, his output increases proportionally. For example, if a producer doubles the quantities of labour and capital employed in the production of good *X*, output will also double; if he triples the quantities of capital and labour, output will triple; and so on. If the increase in output is more than proportional to the increase in the quantities of capital and labour employed, we say that there are *increasing returns to scale*. Similarly, if the increase in output is less than proportional, we say that there are *decreasing returns* to scale.

Figure 9 illustrates a production function which exhibits constant returns to scale; such a production function is said to be *linearly homogeneous*. In the graph, $OL_1 = L_1L_2 = L_2L_3$ and $OK_1 = K_1K_2 = K_2K_3$, so that when labour and capital are doubled from OL_1 and OK_1 to OL_2 and OK_2 respectively, output doubles from 500 to 1,000 units. Similarly, when labour and capital are tripled from OL_1 and OK_1 to OL_3 and OK_3 respectively, output triples from 500 to 1,500 units. Notice that the isoquants representing 500, 1,000 and 1,500 units of output must be equally spaced when there are constant returns, so that OP = PQ = QR along the ray OR. The same is true for any other ray from the origin, so that, for example, OS = ST = TU along the ray OU.

Fig. 9. A production function with constant returns to scale.

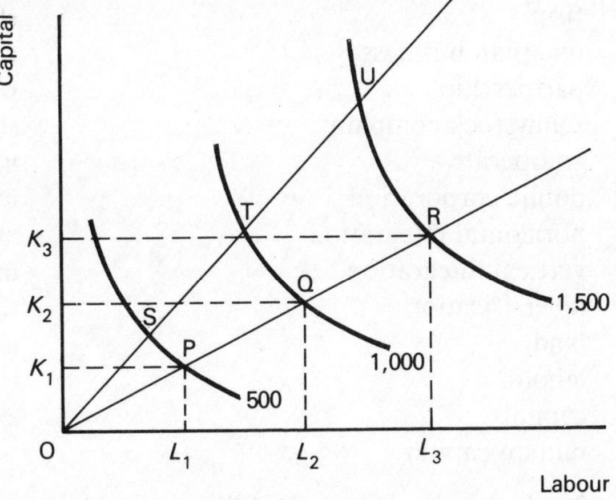

Although we sometimes find it convenient to assume that there are constant returns to scale, we shall see in Chapter 9 that this is not realistic for most producers. It is more likely that, in expanding his scale of operations, a producer will first experience increasing returns to scale, as he is able to take advantage of increased specialisation and division of labour. However, when all the inefficiencies of small scale have disappeared, the firm may experience a period of constant returns to scale. Finally, decreasing returns may set in as the scale of production becomes very large.

Conclusion

In this chapter, we have seen that production is an activity carried out by the many different types of firms in an economy. We have considered the main objectives of these firms and their motives for growth.

In the final sections of the chapter, we have analysed changes in production in the short- and long-run. In doing this, some very important concepts have been introduced which will be applied in later chapters. In particular, the section on isoquant/isocost analysis should be re-read before Chapter 8 on 'welfare economics' and the entire chapter should be re-read before tackling Chapters 9 and 10 on the 'theory of the firm'.

Further reading

Koplin, H.T., *Microeconomic Analysis*, Harper and Row, New York, 1971 (Ch. 7 and 8).

Lancaster, K., *An Introduction to Modern Microeconomics*, Rand McNally, Chicago, 1974 (Ch. 4).

Ryan, W.J.L. and **Pearce, D.W.**, *Price Theory*, Macmillan, London, 1977 (Ch. 3–5).

Exercises

1. Review your understanding of the following terms:

production
firm
one-man business
partnership
joint-stock company
co-operative
public corporation
horizontal integration
vertical integration
diversification
land
labour
capital
human capital
enterprise
stock variable
flow variable
production function
short-run
long-run
law of diminishing returns
average product
marginal product
returns to scale
isoquants
isocost line
expansion path

2. Using the data in the following table, which shows the variations in the output of good X as the labour force is increased, calculate the average and marginal products of labour. Plot these on a graph and indicate the points of diminishing average returns and diminishing marginal returns.

Labour	1	2	3	4	5	6
Total product	100	300	480	560	600	600

3. Suggest reasons why there are many more sole traders in retailing, farming and personal services than in manufacturing industries.

4. Discuss the reasons for the growth in the size of firms and outline the ways in which firms can grow.

5. Indicate the factors which influence the production functions of the textile industries in: (a) rural India; and (b) Japan.

6. Sketch the isoquant maps for a good: (a) where labour and capital are perfect substitutes for each other; (b) where labour and capital have to be used in fixed proportions; (c) where the average and marginal products of one of the factors of production is zero.

Demand and supply

3 Demand

Introduction

We have seen in Chapters 1 and 2 that the basic economic problem faced by all societies is that of allocating the scarce resources of land, labour and capital among competing uses in an attempt to satisfy the limitless wants of consumers. Later in this book, in Chapter 7, we examine in some detail the different methods of resource allocation: from the free market economy, where government intervention is kept to a minimum and the forces of demand and supply are left free to determine relative prices, to the command economy, where all economic decisions are planned by the central administration. In doing this, we highlight the role played by the *price mechanism* in allocating resources in a market economy.

Before looking in detail at the working of the price mechanism, however, we must examine how the economic forces of demand and supply can interact with each other to determine the market prices of goods and services: this is the objective of the present and the next three chapters. In this chapter, we concentrate on the determinants and measurement of demand, one of the most important concepts in economics. First, we consider an individual's demand and the market demand for a commodity; secondly, we explain the concept of the 'elasticity of demand'; finally, we consider some of the problems which arise in attempting to identify a demand curve statistically and in attempting to measure elasticities.

An individual's demand for a commodity

As a first step, consider the main factors which influence an individual consumer's demand for a particular commodity, say good X.

Definition: ***An individual's demand for a commodity may be defined as the quantity of that commodity that the individual is willing and able to buy during a given time period.***

Suppose we list some of the factors which may be expected to influence this consumer's demand for good X over a given time period (d_X):

- the price of good X (P_X)
- the prices of other goods which are related to good X (P_R)
- the consumer's income (y)
- the consumer's taste for good X (T)
- the consumer's expectations about future prices (E)
- other relevant factors (Z)

Using functional notation, we can write the following *demand function:*

$$d_X = f(P_X, P_R, y, T, E, Z)$$

This states simply that the individual's demand for X is a function of all the factors listed in the brackets.

Although all the factors are undoubtedly important, the price of a commodity is in many cases the most important factor influencing an individual's demand for it. Economists analyse the relationship between a consumer's demand for X and the price of X by assuming that all the other influencing factors remain unchanged: this is the important *ceteris paribus* assumption which is used so widely in all branches of economics. (*Ceteris paribus* is a Latin phrase meaning 'other things being equal'.) We can now write:

$d_X = f(P_X)$, *ceteris paribus*

This states simply that the individual's demand for X is determined by the price of X, assuming that all the other influencing factors are held constant.

Now look at Table 1 where different prices of X are listed together with our consumer's weekly demand for X, *ceteris paribus*. As price rises from 10p per unit to 20p per unit, weekly demand falls from 3 units to 2 units. As price rises from 20p to 30p, demand falls to 1 unit. If the price should rise to 40p, our consumer would choose to buy no units at all.

Table 1. Individual consumer's demand schedule for good *X*.

Price of *X* (pence per unit)	Consumer's demand (units per week)
10	3
20	2
30	1
40	0

Demand schedules can be represented most conveniently by using graphs. It has become conventional to represent the price of a commodity on the vertical axis and the quantity demanded per time period on the horizontal axis. Thus, in Fig. 1, the vertical axis measures the price of X in pence per unit and the horizontal axis measures the quantity demanded per week. The line AB reproduces the information contained in Table 1 and is called the individual's *demand curve* for X. Notice that the quantity axis is labelled the 'quantity of *X per week*'. Demand is a *flow* concept, so in measuring the quantity of a good demanded, it is imperative to refer to some time period. A demand for 3 units has no meaning whatever unless it is expressed over some specified period of time.

The demand curve for X represented in Fig. 1 is a straight line and slopes downwards from left to right (that is to say, it is negatively sloped). It certainly need not be a straight line – it is only a straight line in Fig. 1 because of the simple numbers used in our example. The negative slope of the demand curve reflects the reasonable expectation that as the price of X falls, *ceteris paribus*, our consumer's demand for it will rise. This proposition is examined in greater detail in the following chapter where we deal with the theory of consumer behaviour and where we bring the important concept of utility into the analysis.

Fig. 1. An individual's demand curve for good *X*.

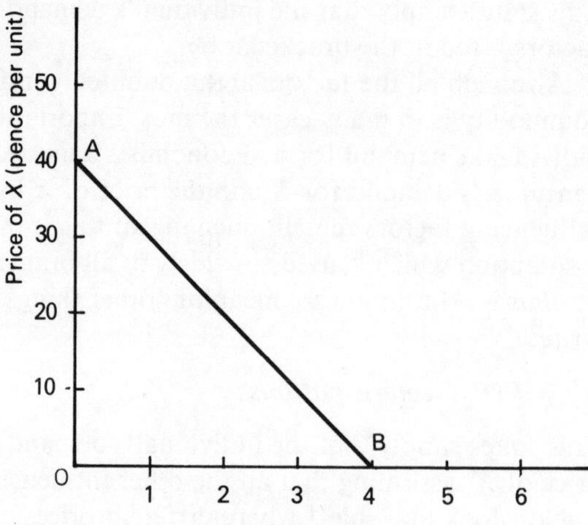

Market demand

The *market* for a good can be thought of as the area in which buyers and sellers of the good come into contact with each other to transact their business. It is important to remember that the limits of a market are not necessarily defined by national or geographical boundaries – the markets for certain goods, like black puddings, are very localised, but the advanced nature of communications these days has enabled the markets for many other commodities, like wheat and gold, to become world-wide.

In this chapter, we assume for simplicity that the market for good X is restricted to the home economy. We can say, therefore, that the *market demand* for good X is the sum of all the individuals' demands in the economy. As with our individual's demand, we may expect this market demand (D_X) also to be influenced by the price of X (P_X) and the prices of other related goods (P_R). It obviously will not, however, be much influenced by a single consumer's income; this time, instead of the income of an individual, we use the income of the economy as a whole – that is to say, national income (Y). If T represents society's taste for X and Z represents other relevant factors (including expectations about future price changes), we can write the following *market demand function* for X:

$$D_X = f(P_X, P_R, Y, T, Z)$$

Making the *ceteris paribus* assumption and holding all the influencing factors constant except the price of X, we can write:

$$D_X = f(P_X), \textit{ceteris paribus.}$$

Representing this on a graph, and assuming that a fall in the price of X will cause an increase in the total quantity demanded, we have the downward-sloping market demand curve, DD, shown in Fig. 2. As price falls from Op_1 to Op_2, the total quantity demanded in the market rises from Oq_1 to Oq_2; if price should rise back to Op_1, quantity demanded would fall back to Oq_1.

Fig. 2. Market demand for good *X*.

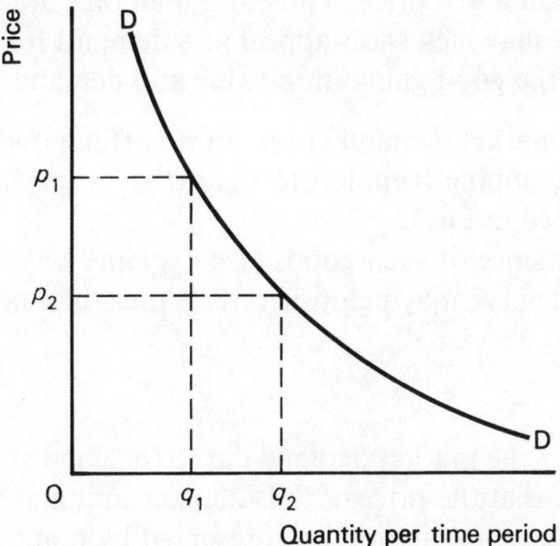

This inverse relationship between the price of a commodity and the quantity demanded in the market is summed up in the so-called 'law of demand'.

Law of Demand: ***A rise in the price of a good leads to a fall in the total quantity demanded. A fall in the price of a good leads to a rise in the total quantity demanded.***

It must be emphasised, however, that this 'law' is not an unassailable truth. There are two major exceptions to it.

(a) *Giffen goods.* A Giffen good (named after the economist Sir Robert Giffen) is a very inferior good for which demand increases as price rises, and demand decreases as price falls. This is possible when consumers in certain less developed countries, such as Bangladesh, are so poor that most of their income is spent on a commodity necessary for subsistence, like rice. If the price of rice should fall in such circumstances, consumers may reduce their demand for rice and use their extra real income to purchase meat or some other more nutritious food.

(b) *Veblen goods.* A Veblen good (named after the economist Thorstein Veblen) is a luxury good, like jewellery, which is in greater demand at a high

Fig. 3. The demand curve for a Giffen or Veblen good.

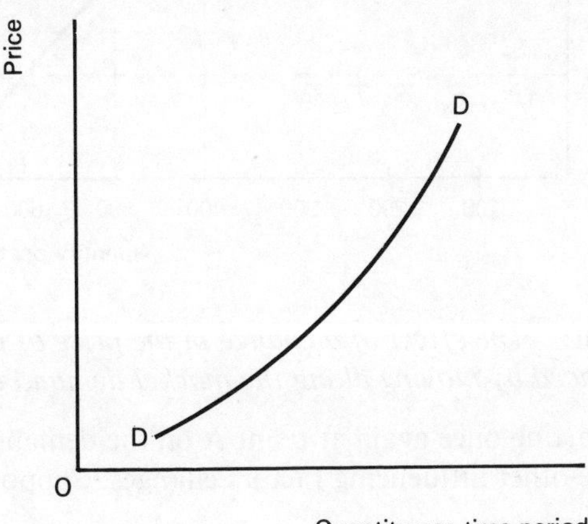

price than a low price. Thus, if a diamond bracelet is put up for sale at a low price, it may lack snob-appeal and demand for it may be low. As the price is raised, the good gains snob-value and demand for it increases.

The market demand curve for a Giffen good and for a Veblen good will be upward-sloping from left to right (that is, positively sloped). This is illustrated in Fig. 3.
The existence of such goods also explains why an individual consumer's demand curve may be positively, rather than negatively, sloped.

Movements along and shifts of the demand curve

Consider the market demand curve for good X in Fig. 4. To start with, suppose that the price of X is 20p per unit and the quantity demanded is 500 units: this combination is represented by point A on the curve. If price should fall to 10p per unit, *ceteris paribus,* quantity demanded will rise to 600 units. This fall in price means that we have simply *moved along* the demand curve from point A to point B. If price should rise to 30p per unit, quantity demanded will fall to 400 units. Again, we have simply moved along the demand curve - this time from point B to point C. Such movements along a demand curve are sometimes called *expansions* of demand (for an increase in quantity demanded following a price change) or *contractions* of demand (for a decrease in quantity demanded following a price change).

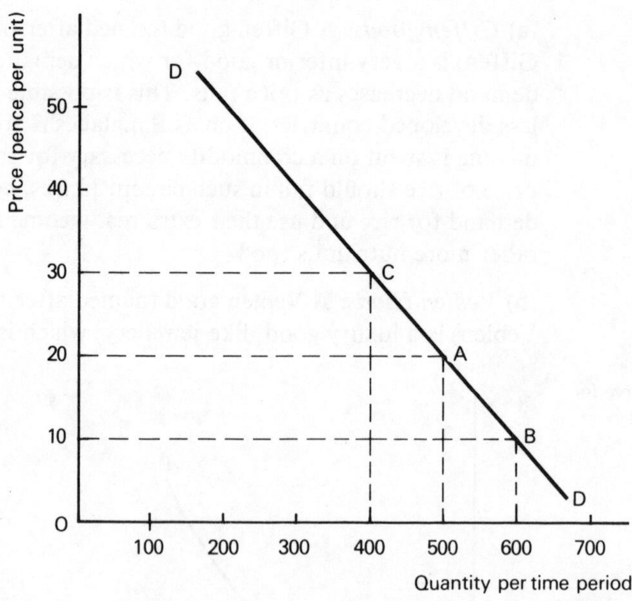

Fig. 4. Movements along a demand curve.

Result: *The effect of a change in the price of good X,* ceteris paribus, *can be traced by moving along the market demand curve for good X.*

Starting once again at point A on the demand curve, suppose now that one of the other influencing factors changes. Suppose in fact that real national income increases so that everyone has more to spend on all goods. The market demand for good X will now increase *at all prices.* In other words, we must draw a new demand curve to represent the new relationship between quantity demanded and price. Figure 5 shows the original demand curve, DD, together with the new one, D′D′, which lies above and to the right of the original one.

Fig. 5. A shift in a demand curve.

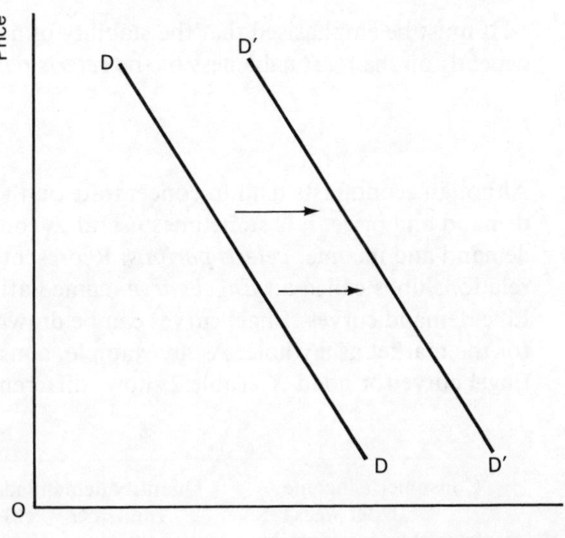

Result: *A change in any of the influencing factors except the price of X causes a shift in the demand curve for X.*

To illustrate this, consider the following likely causes of shifts in the demand curve for a particular good, say cod:

Cause	Effect
1. Increase in national income.	Increase in demand for cod at all prices. Demand curve shifts *right*.
2. Decrease in national income.	Decrease in demand for cod at all prices. Demand curve shifts *left*.
3. Rise in the price of substitute goods (such as haddock or plaice).	Demand curve for cod shifts *right*.
4. Fall in the price of substitute goods.	Demand curve for cod shifts *left*.
5. Rise in the price of complementary goods (such as chips).	Demand curve for cod shifts *left*.
6. Fall in the price of complementary goods.	Demand curve for cod shifts *right*.
7. Change in tastes in favour of cod.	Demand curve shifts *right*.
8. Change in tastes against cod.	Demand curve shifts *left*.

	Cause	Effect
9.	Expectation of a rise in the future price of cod.	Demand curve shifts *right*.
10.	Expectation of a fall in the future price of cod.	Demand curve shifts *left*.

It must be emphasised that the stability of any given market demand curve depends on the reasonableness of the *ceteris paribus* assumption.

Engel curves

Although economists tend to concentrate on the relationship between demand and price, it is sometimes useful to consider the relationship between demand and income, *ceteris paribus*. Represented graphically, such a relationship is called an *Engel curve*, named after the economist Ernst Engel. Like demand curves, Engel curves can be drawn either for an individual or for the market as a whole. As an example, consider an individual consumer's Engel curve for good *X*. Table 2 shows different levels of income for the

Table 2. Consumer's income and demand for good *X*.

Consumer's income (£ per week)	Quantity demanded (units per week)
50	1
60	2
70	4
80	7

consumer together with his demands for good *X* on the assumption that the price of *X* and all other influencing factors (except, of course, the consumer's income) remain constant. Plotting this information on a graph with income on the vertical axis and quantity demanded on the horizontal axis, we obtain the consumer's Engel curve for good *X*. This is shown in Fig. 6.

Note that Engel curves can also be drawn for the economy as a whole – in that case, though, the vertical axis must be labelled 'national income' and the horizontal axis the 'total quantity demanded in the market'.

Engel curves are useful for distinguishing between *normal* and *inferior* goods. When income rises, the quantity demanded of a normal good increases (as in our simple example) and this is indeed the result one would normally expect. But the quantity demanded of an inferior good falls. To explain this, consider the market demand for black and white television sets. As real national income rises, more and more people may find that they can afford to buy colour sets so that the demand for black and white sets falls. If this is the case, black and white television sets are said to be inferior goods and will have an Engel curve which slopes downwards from left to right.

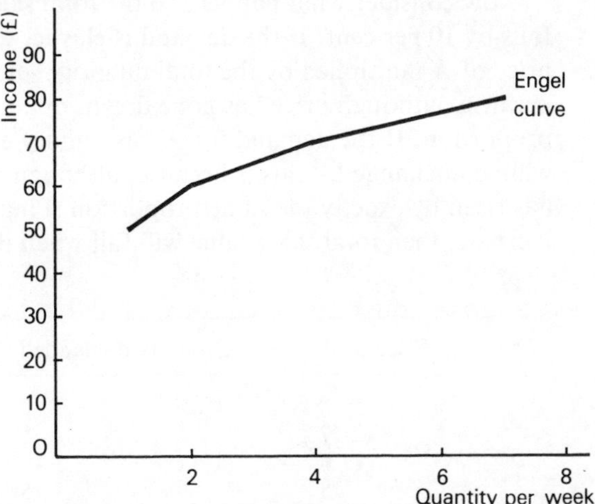

Fig. 6. Engel curve for good *X*.

Finally, it is important to note that inferior goods and Giffen goods are not exactly the same. The difference between them is explained in the next chapter.

Elasticity of demand

The 'elasticity of demand' is a measure of the extent to which the quantity demanded of a good responds to changes in one of the influencing factors. The main measures are the *price* elasticity of demand (which is a measure of the responsiveness of quantity demanded to a change in price); *income* elasticity of demand (which measures the responsiveness of quantity demanded to a change in income); and *cross* elasticity of demand (which measures the responsiveness of quantity demanded to a change in the price of some related good). Of these, the price elasticity is the most commonly used. It is calculated by using the following general formula:

$$\text{Price elasticity of demand, } e_D = \frac{\text{Proportionate change in quantity demanded}}{\text{Proportionate change in price}}$$

This means that if the price of good *X* should rise by 10 per cent (or 0.1) and the quantity demanded should fall in consequence by less than 10 per cent, say 5 per cent (or 0.05), then the price elasticity of demand would be 0.05/0.1 = 0.5. In this case, since the elasticity is less than one, we say that the demand for *X* is *inelastic: a given percentage change in price gives rise to a smaller percentage change in quantity demanded.* Now suppose that when the price of *X* increases by 10 per cent, the quantity demanded falls by more than 10 per cent, say 20 per cent (or 0.2). The price elasticity of demand will now be 0.2/0.1 = 2. This time, since the elasticity is greater than 1, we say that the demand for *X* is *elastic: a given percentage change in price gives rise to a bigger percentage change in quantity demanded.* If, when the price of *X* increases by 10 per cent, the quantity demanded should fall by exactly 10 per cent, the price elasticity of demand would be exactly equal to 1 – this is called *unitary elasticity.*

Now consider what happens to the total sales of good *X* when its price falls by 10 per cent. If the demand is elastic, total sales value (which is the price of *X* multiplied by the total quantity sold) will rise – this must be so because, although price has gone down, quantity has risen by a bigger proportion. If the demand for *X* has unitary elasticity, then total sales value will be unchanged – this is because, although price has fallen, quantity sold has risen by exactly the same proportion. Finally, if the demand for *X* is inelastic, then total sales value will fall when the price of *X* falls.

Table 3. The quantity demanded and total sales value of good *X* at different prices.

Price of *X*	Quantity demanded	Total sales value
8	0	0
7	5	35
6	10	60
5	15	75
4	20	80
3	25	75
2	30	60
1	35	35
0	40	0

To illustrate these points, consider the example shown in Table 3. As the price of *X* falls from 8p to 0p, quantity demanded increases steadily from 0 to 40. The third column of the table shows the total sales value of *X* at each price. All this information is reproduced in graphical form in Fig. 7. The market demand curve, which reproduces the information contained in the first two columns of Table 3, turns out to be a straight line. The total sales value curve starts at the origin, rises to a maximum of 80p when price is 4p and quantity sold is 20, then falls off to zero again when price is zero and quantity sold is 40. It should be clear that demand is elastic in the price range greater than 4p, inelastic for all prices less than 4p, and of unitary elasticity when price is exactly 4p.

It is only possible to calculate price elasticity with complete accuracy *at a point* on a demand curve. Such a calculation yields what is called the *point elasticity of demand*. An estimate of the elasticity along a range of a demand curve is called the *arc elasticity of demand*. Consider these in turn.

For a straight-line demand curve, *point elasticity* can be found using the following formula:

$$\text{Point } e_D = -\frac{\triangle q/q}{\triangle p/p} = -\frac{\triangle q}{\triangle p}\frac{p}{q}$$

In this formula, p/q is the price divided by the quantity at the point and $\triangle q/\triangle p$ is the reciprocal of the slope of the line. The minus sign is conventional: it ensures that the elasticity of demand for a normal good is positive.

Examples:

From Table 3, find the price elasticity of demand when price = 6p.
The slope of the line, $\triangle p/\triangle q = -8/40 = -1/5$

Fig. 7. Demand curve and total sales value curve.

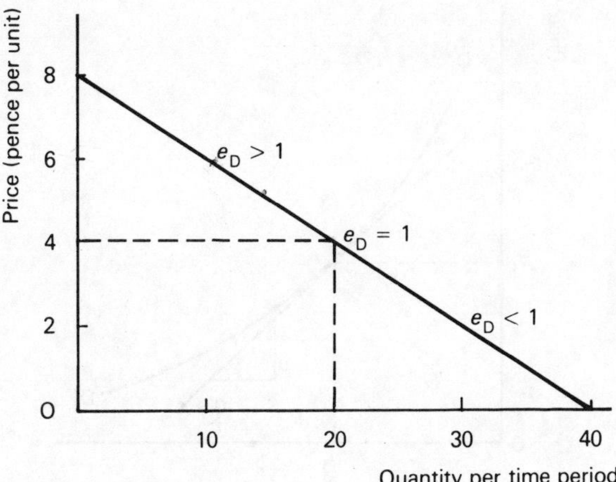

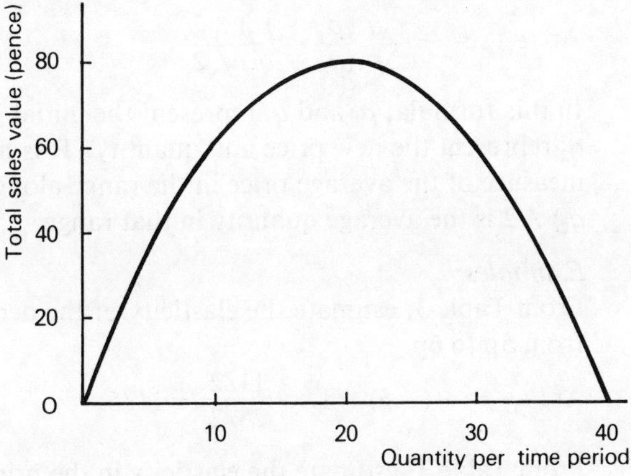

Reciprocal of the slope, $\triangle q/\triangle p = -5$
Point elasticity, $e_D = -(-5) \times 6/10 = 3$.

From Table 3, find the elasticity when price = 4p.
Point elasticity, $e_D = -(-5) \times 4/20 = 1$.

The same formula can be used to find the elasticity of demand at a point on a non-linear demand curve, but this time $\triangle q/\triangle p$ refers to the reciprocal of the slope of the tangent to the curve at the point. This is illustrated in Fig. 8, where the elasticity at point A is:

$$e_D = -\frac{\triangle q}{\triangle p}\frac{p_1}{q_1}$$

Note that the slope of the tangent is the same as the slope of the curve at point A. This slope (written as dp/dq) can only be determined exactly using differential calculus and is not pursued in this book.

Arc elasticity is an estimate of the elasticity along a range of a demand curve. It can be calculated for both linear and non-linear demand curves using the following formula:

Fig. 8. Point elasticity on a non-linear demand curve.

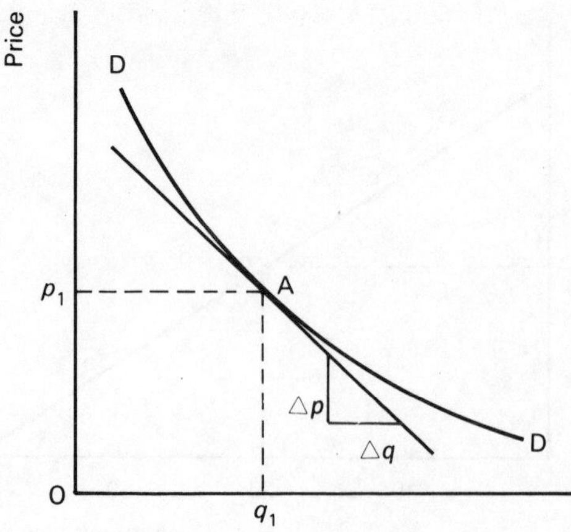

$$\text{Arc } e_D = -\frac{\Delta q \,(p_1 + p_2) / 2}{\Delta p \,(q_1 + q_2) / 2}$$

In this formula, p_1 and q_1 represent the initial price and quantity, and p_2 and q_2 represent the new price and quantity. This means that $(p_1 + p_2) / 2$ is a measure of the average price in the range along the demand curve and $(q_1 + q_2) / 2$ is the average quantity in that range.

Examples:
From Table 3, estimate the elasticity of the demand curve in the price range from 5p to 6p.

$$\text{Arc } e_D = -(-5) / 1 \times \frac{11/2}{25/2} = 11/5.$$

From Table 3, estimate the elasticity in the price range from 1p to 2p.

$$\text{Arc } e_D = -(-5) \times \frac{3/2}{65/2} = 3/13.$$

Since the price elasticity of demand changes as we move along a demand curve, it follows that the initial price of a good is one of the determinants of its price elasticity. Other factors which influence the price elasticity of demand are: (a) *The availability of substitutes*: the more substitutes a good has, the more elastic the demand for it is likely to be. (b) *The proportion of consumers' incomes spent on the good*: goods, like cars, which take up a large proportion of consumers' incomes tend to have a more elastic demand than goods, like salt, which take up only a very small proportion of consumers' incomes. (c) *Time*: since it may take time for buyers to react to changes in price, the demand for many goods may be inelastic in the short-run but more elastic in the longer-run.

A demand curve is said to be *perfectly inelastic* ($e_D = 0$) when changes in price cause no change in quantity demanded; the vertical straight line AB in Fig. 9 depicts such a perfectly inelastic demand curve. A demand curve is said to be *perfectly elastic* ($e_D = \infty$) when any quantity will be bought at the prevailing price, but any rise in price will cause quantity demanded to fall to zero; the horizontal straight line in Fig. 9 depicts a perfectly elastic demand curve.

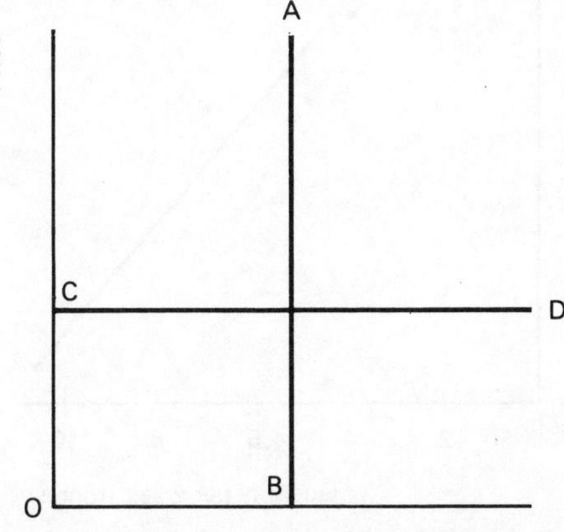

Fig. 9. Perfect elasticity and perfect inelasticity.

Other elasticity formulae

To calculate the *income* elasticity of demand, the following general formula can be used:

$$\text{Income } e_D = \frac{\text{Proportionate change in quantity demanded}}{\text{Proportionate change in income}}$$

An income elasticity of demand greater than 1 means that a given proportionate increase in national income will cause a bigger proportionate increase in quantity demanded. It follows that producers of such goods may need to plan extra capacity in times of rising incomes.

To calculate the *cross* elasticity of demand, the following general formula can be used:

$$\text{Cross } e_D = \frac{\text{Proportionate change in quantity demanded}}{\text{Proportionate change in the price of a related good}}$$

This will be positive if the related good is a substitute good and negative if the related good is a complement.

Problems of measurement

Suppose that we were to collect some actual sales figures for a particular good, say potatoes, and plot the quantities sold at different prices on a

Table 4. Hypothetical figures of the quantity of potatoes demanded at different prices.

Price of potatoes (pence per kg)	Quantity demanded (tonnes per week)
5	10
10	6
15	7
20	4
25	3

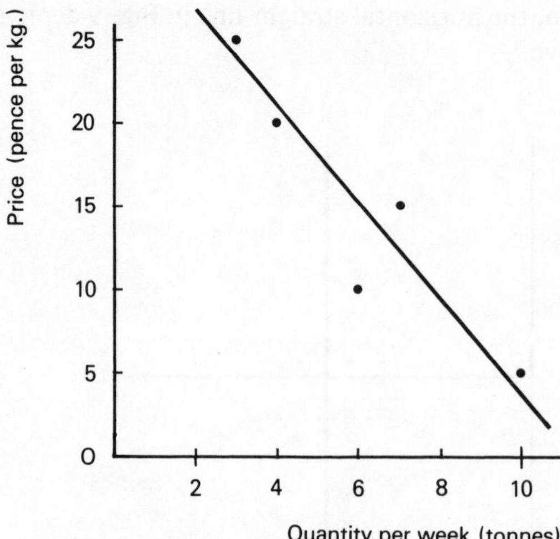

Fig. 10. Best-fitting line through a scatter diagram.

graph. Table 4 shows some hypothetical statistics of the quantity of potatoes sold at different prices and these are plotted as a scatter of points on the graph in Fig. 10. Can the best-fitting line through the scatter diagram be properly called the demand curve for potatoes and can we use it to calculate the price elasticity of demand for potatoes? The answer to both questions is likely to be no for three main reasons.

(a) The figures can only have been collected over time and we cannot be certain that the other influencing factors all remained unchanged during that time-period. If any single one of them did change, then the best-fitting line will not trace out a demand curve and any calculations we make of the price elasticity of demand will be unreliable. Since controlled experiments are usually impossible to perform in economics, we have to rely instead on the statistical techniques of multiple regression analysis to estimate the influences of individual variables on the quantity demanded of a good. As we pointed out in Chapter 1, such techniques are the subject matter of a branch of economics called econometrics and are beyond the scope of this book.

(b) As we shall see in Chapter 5, the supply of a good also depends on the price of the good. Thus, when we plot our observed combinations of prices and quantities sold of potatoes on a graph (even assuming *ceteris paribus*), we cannot be certain whether we are plotting the demand curve or the supply curve, or even some combination of the two. This problem of identifying the demand curve separately from the supply curve is called the *identification problem*. It is a problem which can also be overcome to some extent by using econometric techniques, but it does illustrate the danger of drawing inferences about demand curves from observed price-quantity changes.

(c) Supposing that all the other influencing factors remain constant and that the identification problem is satisfactorily solved, can we now describe our best-fitting line as the demand curve for potatoes? Assuming that a sufficiently large sample has been taken, then it certainly does provide an estimate of the demand curve *at the time the study was made*. But is it a good estimate of that relationship today, and will it still be a good estimate next year, and in ten years' time? This depends on how long the *ceteris paribus* assumption holds over time. The stability of the relationship can only be determined by continuous empirical testing.

Conclusion

Demand is a very important variable. It plays a crucial role in allocating resources via the price mechanism (see Ch. 7). Knowledge of demand and the elasticity of demand is of great importance to firms in planning how much to produce and in setting their prices (see Ch. 9 and 10). It is also of importance to governments in many areas: for example, in formulating their taxation policies (see Ch. 13) and in estimating the effectiveness of exchange rate changes in correcting a balance of trade deficit (see Ch. 28). We have seen, however, that the estimation of the demand for a good (or for a series of goods) poses a number of statistical problems. This is one of the areas in which statistical and econometric analysis plays an important role in economics.

Further reading

Lancaster, K., *An Introduction to Modern Microeconomics*, Rand McNally, Chicago, 1974 (Ch. 2 and 3).
Cole, C.L., *Microeconomics*, Harcourt Brace Jovanovich, New York, 1973 (Ch. 2).
Baumol, W.J., *Economic Theory and Operations Research*, Prentice Hall, New Jersey, 1977 (Ch. 9 and 10).

Exercises

1. Review your understanding of the following terms:

demand function	Engel curve
demand curve	price elasticity of demand
ceteris paribus	point elasticity
market	arc elasticity
normal good	income elasticity
inferior good	cross elasticity
Giffen good	substitutes
Veblen good	complements

2. Consider the following price and quantity demanded data for good *X*:

Price (£)	2	4	6	8	10	12
Quantity demanded	100	80	60	40	20	0

(a) Plot the demand curve and sales revenue curve on separate graphs.
(b) Calculate the point elasticity of demand at price = £4 and at price = £10.
(c) Estimate the elasticity between the prices of £6 and £8.
(d) Suppose now that a rise in real income causes quantity demanded to increase by 50 units at every price. Repeat exercises (a), (b) and (c).

(e) Given that the new demand curve is parallel to the original one, explain why the elasticities have changed.

3. Discuss the main determinants of the market demand for: (a) ice creams; (b) holidays in the United Kingdom; and (c) fashionable clothes.

4. Explain what is depicted by a demand curve and sketch demand curves which exhibit: (a) negative price elasticity; (b) perfect price elasticity; and (c) perfect price inelasticity.

5. What are the main determinants of the price elasticity of demand? How elastic would you expect the demand to be for: (a) salt; (b) petrol; (c) cigarettes; (d) sausages; and (e) black and white television sets?

6. In drawing the market demand curve for butter, what other things do we assume to remain unchanged?

4 Utility and demand

Introduction

In the last chapter, we considered a consumer's demand and the market demand for a single good only. In reality, of course, consumers have to choose from the many thousands of different goods available on the market. In other words, consumers are faced with the problem of choice. In examining the shape of a demand curve for a single good, therefore, we must look closely at the behaviour of consumers when faced with this problem of choice. The 'theory of consumer behaviour' or 'theory of consumer choice' has developed into one of the major branches of microeconomics.

In this chapter, we first explain the important concept of *utility* and discuss whether or not it can be measured. Secondly, we set out, rather briefly, the 'cardinalist' or 'marginal utility' approach to the theory of demand. Thirdly, and in much greater detail, we set out the 'ordinalist' or 'indifference curve' approach – this is a very important section since it introduces concepts and techniques which are now widely used in all branches of modern economics. Finally, we consider two of the more recent developments in the theory of consumer behaviour: Samuelson's 'revealed preference' approach and Lancaster's 'characteristics of goods' approach.

Cardinal and ordinal utility

When a good is consumed, the consumer presumably derives some benefit or satisfaction from the activity. Economists have called this benefit or satisfaction *utility*, and have assumed that, in choosing among goods, a consumer will attempt to gain the greatest possible utility, subject to the size of his income.

Some nineteenth-century economists thought that utility might be measurable as if it were a physical commodity. In other words, just as coal can be measured in tonnes, they believed that utility could similarly be measured in its own units (like utils). These economists (amongst whom Alfred Marshall figured prominently) have become known as *cardinalists* because they believed that cardinal numbers could be used to express utility measurements. For example, a consumer may obtain 20 utils of utility from a helping of carrots, but only 10 utils from a helping of beans. The cardinalists would conclude from this that he obtains twice as much utility from the carrots as from the beans and that the absolute difference between the utility derived from the carrots and that derived from the beans is 10 utils.

Utility, however, is an abstract, subjective concept and there are two major problems involved in trying to measure it for an individual.
(a) It is difficult to find an appropriate unit of measurement. If we call the unit a util, what is a util? How do we calculate the number of utils enjoyed

by an individual at a moment in time? Are 10 utils enjoyed by one individual equivalent to 10 utils enjoyed by another – in other words, can we make *interpersonal comparisons of utility*?

(b) To measure the utility derived by an individual in consuming a good requires that all the other factors which affect his level of satisfaction be held constant and it is clearly impossible to carry out such a controlled experiment. There are too many other factors (economic, social and psychological) which influence an individual's level of utility.

By the 1930s, many economists were coming to the view that utility could not be measured cardinally and that cardinal measurement was not essential for a theory of consumer behaviour. These economists (who included Hicks and Allen, who in turn were influenced by the earlier work of Pareto and Slutsky) have become known as *ordinalists*. This is because they claimed that an individual can rank bundles of goods in order of preference and say that he derives more utility from one bundle than from another, or that he derives equal utility from two or more bundles. It is impossible, though, to measure by how much one bundle is preferred to another. For example, a consumer may say that he prefers carrots to beans, but, according to the ordinalists, he will be completely unable to attach a numerical measure to the degree of preference. In this case, only ordinal numbers (first, second, third and so on) can be used to 'measure' utility and these say nothing about the absolute difference or any other relationship between utilities. Indifference curves and budget lines are the means of illustrating this ordinalist approach to demand theory and these are now widely used in all branches of modern economics.

The cardinalist approach

The objective of this section is to outline the cardinalists' explanation of why an individual's demand curve normally slopes downwards from left to right. Central to this approach are the concept of *marginal utility* and the *hypothesis of diminishing marginal utility*.

Definition: ***Marginal utility is the extra utility derived from the consumption of one more unit of a good, the consumption of all other goods remaining unchanged.***

Definition: ***Marginal utility per penny is the extra utility derived from consuming one extra penny's worth of a good.***

Consider an individual's consumption of good *X* over a particular time period, say a week. Table 1 shows what happens to the consumer's total utility and marginal utility (both measured in utils) as he consumes more and more units of the good in the week. When the individual consumes no units of *X* at all, he derives no utility from the activity. Consuming one unit, though, yields 20 utils. Apparently, this whets the consumer's appetite for the good because when he consumes two units in the week, his total utility rises to 50 utils so that the second unit adds more to his total utility than the first. Adding further units up to the fourth continues to increase total utility, but at a decreasing rate so that marginal utility is falling. Finally, consuming

Table 1. An example illustrating diminishing marginal utility.

Quantity of *X* consumed per week	Total utility (utils per week)	Marginal utility (utils)
0	0	
1	20	20
2	50	30
3	60	10
4	62	2
5	60	−2

a fifth unit actually causes total utility to fall so that marginal utility is negative.

This example illustrates the reasonable proposition that as more and more units of a good are consumed in a given time period, the extra utility derived from the consumption of additional units *eventually* falls. This is called the hypothesis of diminishing marginal utility.

Definition: ***The hypothesis of diminishing marginal utility states that as the quantity of a good consumed by an individual increases, the marginal utility of the good will eventually decrease.***

To illustrate this hypothesis further, consider the utility derived by a thirsty consumer from successive cups of tea. The first cup will yield a great deal of utility: in other words, the marginal utility of the first cup is very high. A second cup may also be very welcome, but is unlikely to yield as much utility as the first, and a third cup is likely to yield even less utility. Having quenched his thirst, the consumer may have no further desire for liquid refreshment: we say that any more tea would yield *disutility*. It seems reasonable to regard this hypothesis as a valid generalisation about consumer behaviour: the more a consumer has of a commodity, the less utility he is likely to derive from the consumption of an additional unit.

Now consider a consumer who has to choose between two goods, *X* and *Y*, which have prices P_X and P_Y respectively. Assume that the individual is rational and so wishes to maximise his total utility subject to the size of his income. He will be maximising his total utility when he has allocated his income in such a way that the utility to be derived from the consumption of one extra penny's worth of *X* is equal to the utility to be derived from the consumption of one extra penny's worth of *Y*. In other words, when the marginal utility per penny of *X* is equal to the marginal utility per penny of *Y*. Only when this is true will it not be possible to increase total utility by switching expenditure from one good to the other. The condition can be written as follows:

$$\frac{MU_X}{P_X} = \frac{MU_Y}{P_Y}$$

where MU_X and MU_Y are the marginal utilities of *X* and *Y* respectively and P_X and P_Y are the prices of *X* and *Y* respectively. In order to derive the individual's demand curve for good *X*, consider what happens to this condition when the price of *X* falls. It must be true (assuming that the price of *Y* remains unchanged) that:

$$\frac{MU_X}{P_X} > \frac{MU_Y}{P_Y}$$

The consumer can now increase his total utility by consuming more units of good X. This will have the effect of decreasing the marginal utility of X (because of the hypothesis of diminishing marginal utility) and he will continue increasing his expenditure on X until the equality is restored. We now have the result we have been seeking: that a fall in the price of a good will, *ceteris paribus*, give rise to an increase in a consumer's demand for it – that is to say, the demand curve slopes downwards from left to right.

As an illustration of this, suppose initially that $MU_X = 20$ utils, $MU_Y = 25$ utils, $P_X = 4$p and $P_Y = 5$p, so that the condition is satisfied:

$$\frac{MU_X}{P_X} = \frac{MU_Y}{P_Y} = 5 \text{ utils per penny.}$$

Now let the price of X fall to 2p. With consumption unchanged, the MU per penny of X rises to 10 utils and exceeds the MU per penny of Y. How will the consumer respond to this? By spending an extra penny on good X, he derives 10 utils of utility; by spending an extra penny on good Y, he derives only 5 utils. Clearly, he will buy more units of good X, thus reducing their MU until the MU's per penny for X and Y are once again equal.

Since economy of space allows us to present only a brief treatment of the cardinalist approach here, the interested reader is recommended to consult the references listed at the end of the chapter for a more detailed account.

The ordinalist approach

Indifference curves

To simplify the analysis of the ordinal utility approach so that it can be represented graphically in two dimensions, consider again a consumer's choice between two commodities only, say X and Y. The consumer's preferences for X and Y are represented by the indifference map in Fig. 1, where I_1, I_2 and I_3 are three of his indifference curves.

Definition: ***An indifference curve joins together all the different combinations of two goods which yield the same utility to the consumer.***

In Fig. 1, the vertical axis measures the quantity of good Y and the horizontal axis measures the quantity of good X. Thus, every point on the graph represents some combination of X and Y. Points very close to the origin, like point A, represent very small quantities of X and Y; points further away from the origin represent bigger quantities. Since combinations B (10 units of Y and 2 units of X) and C (5 units of Y and 4 units of X) are on the same indifference curve, the consumer is said to be indifferent between them – that is to say, both combinations yield the same utility to him. Combination D, however, is on a higher indifference curve than B or C. We say that he prefers D to either B or C. Similarly, he prefers combination E to A, B, C, or D.

We assume that the consumer is able to rank his preferences over the entire field of choice. This means that he must be able to consider any two possible combinations of X and Y and say either that he prefers one to the

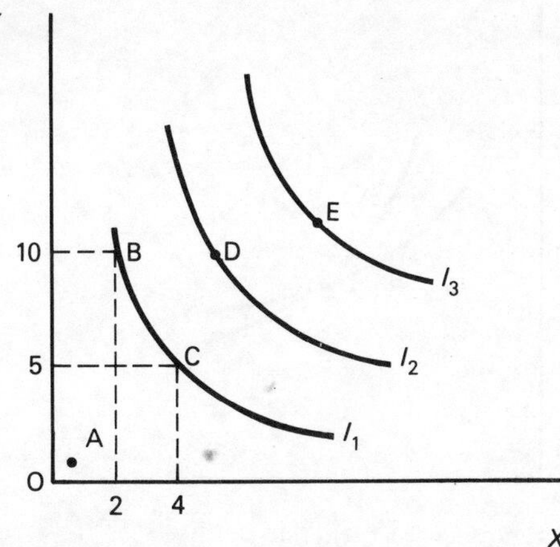

Fig. 1. An indifference map.

other, or that he is indifferent between them. It should be clear from this that there must exist an indifference curve passing through every possible combination of *X* and *Y* – that is, through every point on the graph. This means that, although we have only drawn three of them in Fig. 1, there are an infinite number of indifference curves making up the indifference map.

Note at this stage the similarity between indifference curves and isoquants (see Ch. 2). There is, though, an important difference between them: this is that whereas an isoquant represents a given level of output which is *cardinally* measurable, an indifference curve represents a given level of utility which is only *ordinally* measurable.

Before taking the analysis further, we need to make the assumption that our consumer is rational. To be rational, he must satisfy the following conditions:

(a) He must be able to rank his preferences over the entire field of choice facing him.

(b) His behaviour must be *transitive*: this means that if he prefers combination A to combination B, and combination B to combination C, then he must also prefer A to C.

(c) He must never have all he wants of all goods – he must always want some more of at least one good.

For a rational consumer, indifference curves have three important properties:

Indifference curves can never intersect To show this, consider Fig. 2 which shows two intersecting indifference curves. Since both combinations A and C are on the same indifference curve, the consumer must be indifferent between them. Combinations B and C, however, are also on the same indifference curve, so the consumer must be indifferent between them as well. If the consumer is indifferent between A and C, and between B and C, he must (by the rule of transitivity) be indifferent between A and B. This, however, is absurd because A contains more *Y* and the same amount of *X* as B and so must be preferred to it. This kind of absurd result occurs whenever indifference curves cross. We conclude, therefore, that indifference curves can never intersect each other.

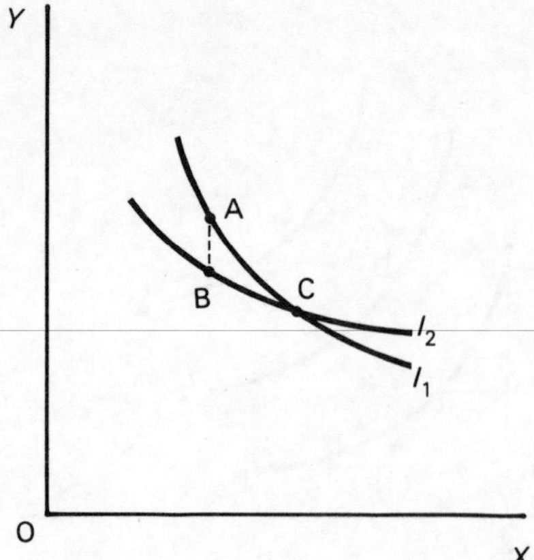

Fig. 2. Intersecting indifference curves.

Indifference curves slope downwards from left to right If both *X* and *Y* are goods (so that the consumer derives utility rather than disutility from them) and if the consumer is not satiated with either *X* or *Y*, then as some of one good is given up, more units of the other good must be obtained if the consumer is to remain at the same level of utility. Consider Fig. 3. In moving from point A to B, as units of *Y* are given up, more units of *X* are obtained and the utility derived is unchanged. For this to be true, the indifference curve must slope downwards from left to right.

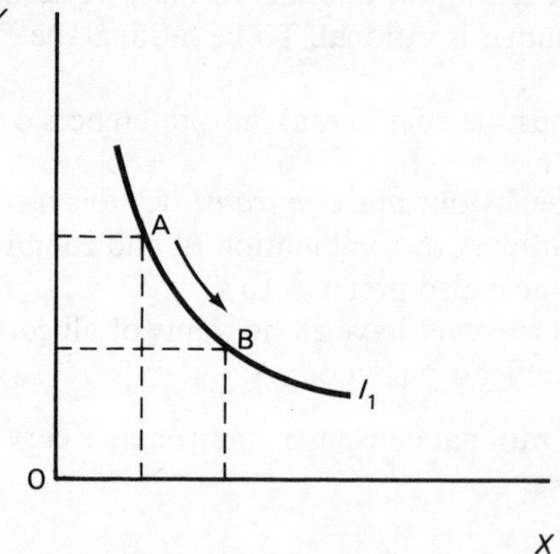

Fig. 3. The negative slope of an indifference curve.

Indifference curves are convex to the origin As more and more units of one good, say *Y*, are given up, it is reasonable to suppose that successively bigger quantities of *X* must be obtained to compensate the consumer for his loss and leave him at the same level of utility. Consider Fig. 4 where this proposition is illustrated. Since the slope of an indifference curve is called the *marginal rate of substitution* (that is, the rate at which good *Y* can be substituted for by good *X*, leaving the consumer at the same level of utility), the proposition is sometimes summed up as the *diminishing marginal rate of substitution*.

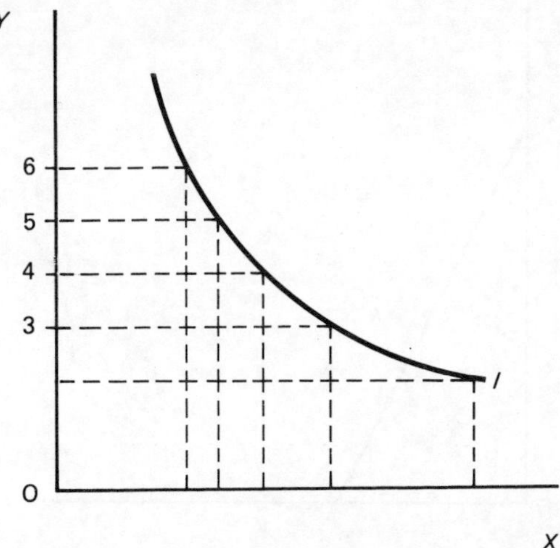

Fig. 4. The convexity of an indifference curve.

Budget lines and 'consumer equilibrium'

Indifference curves only tell us about the consumer's preferences for the two goods. By themselves, they cannot tell us which combinations will be chosen. In addition to the consumer's preferences, we need to know his *income* and the *prices of the two goods.* Given this information, and assuming that he will choose the combination of the two goods which will yield him greatest utility (that is, put him on the highest attainable indifference curve), we can determine the combination of *X* and *Y* that the consumer will choose.

As an example, suppose the price of *X* is £20, the price of *Y* is £10, and suppose the consumer's income is £100. Table 2 shows the combinations of *X* and *Y* that he can just afford to buy. Plotting these points on the same graph as the indifference map, we obtain what is called the *budget line.* This is illustrated in Fig. 5; it shows the combinations of the two goods that can just be afforded with an income of £100. The (absolute) slope of the budget line

Table 2. The combinations of *X* and *Y* that the consumer can just afford to buy with an income of £100.

Quantity of *X* (price = £20)	Quantity of *Y* (price = £10)
0	10
1	8
2	6
3	4
4	2
5	0

(10/5 = 2) measures the relative price of *X* in terms of *Y* – that is, two units of *Y* must be given up in order to buy one unit of *X*. If we let P_X denote the price of *X* and P_Y the price of *Y*, then we can write the slope of the budget line as equal to P_X/P_Y.

Figure 6 shows the indifference map and budget line on the same graph. Assuming that the consumer spends all his income on *X* and *Y*, he will choose the combination represented by point A. This is the point where the

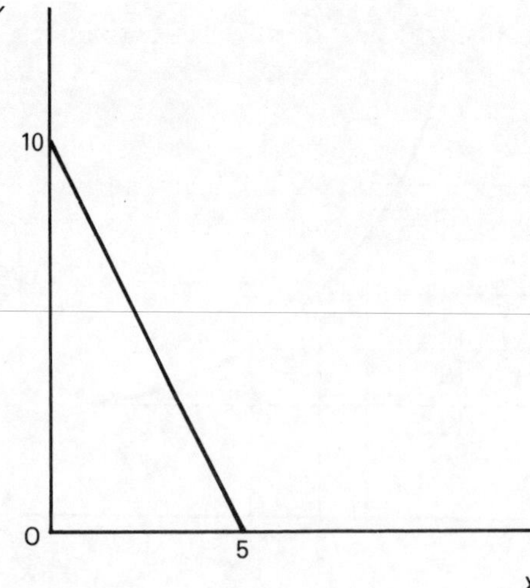

Fig. 5. A budget line.

budget line is just tangent to an indifference curve – the indifference curve I_2 is the highest one that can be reached. Point A is called the 'consumer equilibrium' point. The consumer is said to be *maximising his utility subject to his budget constraint.*

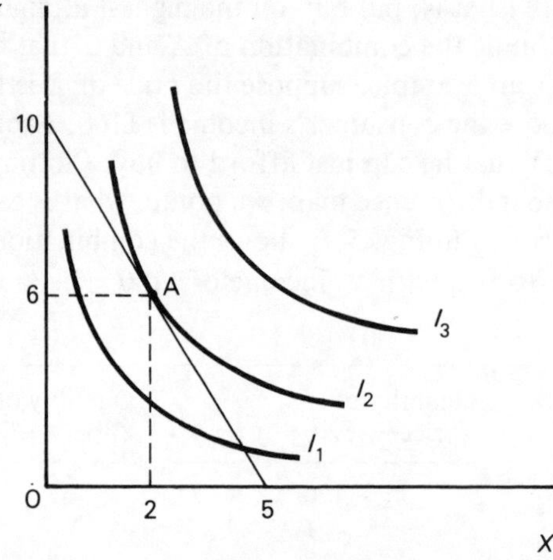

Fig. 6. Consumer equilibrium.

Since the budget line is tangent to the indifference curve at point A, it must be true that the slope of the indifference curve (the marginal rate of substitution) is equal to the slope of the budget line at that point. Thus, we can write that, at the 'consumer equilibrium' point,

$$\text{Slope of budget line} = \frac{P_X}{P_Y} = \text{Marginal rate of substitution.}$$

Effect of an income change

If the consumer's income increases, his budget line will shift upwards remaining parallel to the original one. Similarly, if his income falls, his budget line will shift downwards remaining parallel. To show this, suppose that his income rises from £100 to £200. Table 3 (a) shows the combinations of *X* and *Y* that he can afford after the income rise; the new budget line FG, together with the original one DE, is shown in Fig. 7. Now suppose that his income falls to £50: the combinations he can just afford are shown in Table 3 (b) and the new budget line HJ is shown with the others in Fig. 7.

Table 3. The combinations of *X* and *Y* that the consumer can afford to buy with different incomes.

(a) Income = £200		(b) Income = £50	
Quantity of *X* (price = £20)	Quantity of *Y* (price = £10)	Quantity of *X* (price = £20)	Quantity of *Y* (price = £10)
0	20	0	5
2	16	$\frac{1}{2}$	4
4	12	1	3
6	8	$1\frac{1}{2}$	2
8	4	2	1
10	0	$2\frac{1}{2}$	0

With an income of £200, the 'consumer equilibrium' point is shown as point B in Fig. 7. With an income of only £50, the 'consumer equilibrium' point is shown as point C. The important result to remember is that when income changes, the budget line shifts but remains parallel. Notice that the dotted line CAB in Fig. 7 is called the *income-consumption curve.* It shows what happens to the consumer's demand for the two goods as his income changes.

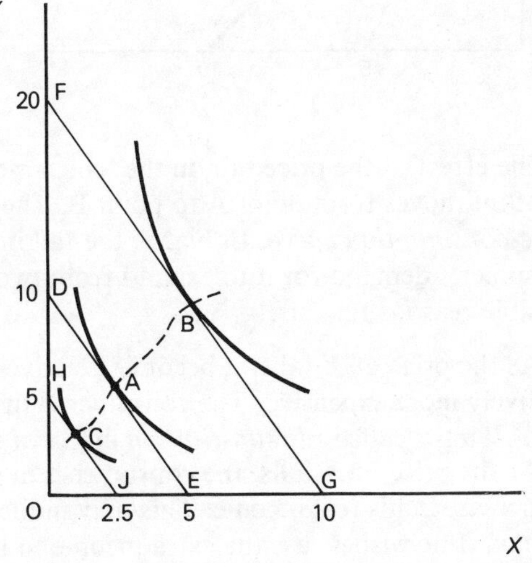

Fig. 7. Effects of an income change.

Effects of a price change

To examine the effect of a price change, suppose that the price of *X* falls, *ceteris paribus.* Table 4 shows the combinations that the consumer can just afford to buy when his income is £100, the price of *Y* is £10 and the price of *X* has fallen to £10. The new budget line DE′ is graphed, together with the original one DE, in Fig. 8. Notice that when the price of one of the goods falls, the budget line shifts, but this time it *pivots* and so does not remain parallel to the original one. It becomes less steep reflecting the fall in the relative price of *X*.

Table 4. The combinations of *X* and *Y* that the consumer can afford to buy after a price change.

Quantity of *X* (price = £10)	Quantity of *Y* (price = £10)
0	10
2	8
4	6
6	4
8	2
10	0

Fig. 8. Effect of a price change.

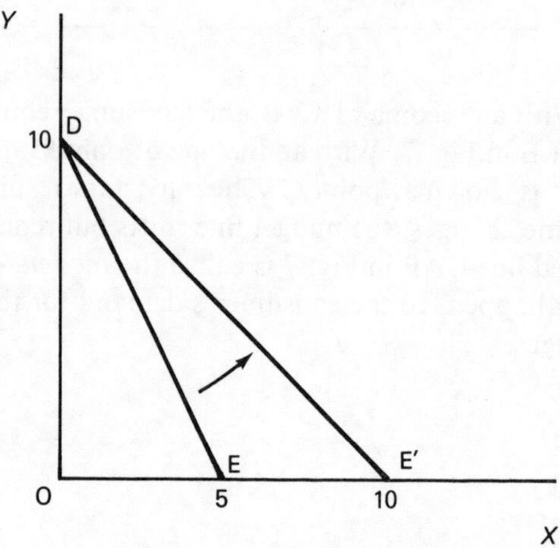

The effect of the price fall on the 'consumer equilibrium' point is shown in Fig. 9: it moves from point A to point B. The dotted line AB is called the *price-consumption curve*. In Fig. 9, the fall in the price of *X* causes the consumer's demand for it to expand from two to six units. There are two possible reasons for this:

(a) As the price of *X* falls, it becomes relatively cheaper and *Y* becomes relatively more expensive. The consumer is therefore induced to substitute *X* for *Y*. This is called the *substitution effect* of the price change.
(b) As the price of *X* falls, the consumer is made better off – he experiences an increase in his real income. This may induce him to buy more *X*, although he may, if he wishes, use the extra income to buy more *Y*. This is called the *income effect* of the price change.

It is possible to identify these two effects graphically and this is done in Fig. 10. The first step is to eliminate the income effect: to do this, we assume that, accompanying the fall in the price of *X*, there is a *compensating variation* in income which leaves the consumer at the same level of utility as before the price change. In Fig. 10, the original budget line is labelled DE

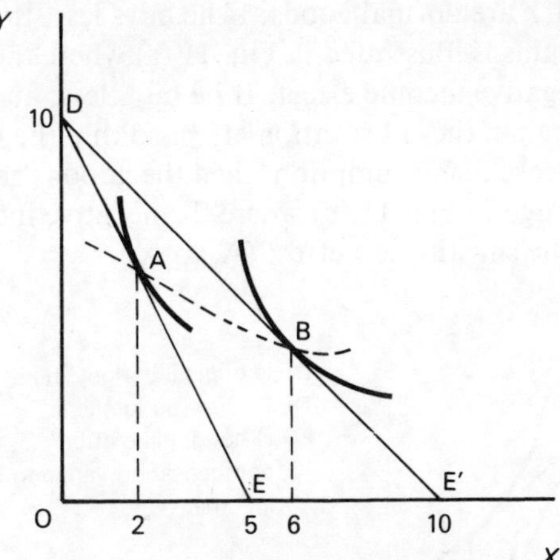

Fig. 9. The price-consumption line.

whilst the budget line after the price fall is labelled DE′. To make the compensating variation in income, we shift the budget line to the left, keeping it parallel to DE′ until it becomes tangential to the original indifference curve I_1. This is the budget line FG. The movement from point A_1 to A_3 is the *substitution effect* – the consumer is no better off, but has substituted X_1X_3 of X for Y_1Y_3 of Y because of the change in relative prices. The movement from point A_3 to A_2 is the *income effect* – the consumer buys X_3X_2 of X and Y_3Y_2 of Y because of his increase in real income.

Normal, inferior and Giffen goods again

The substitution effect always acts in such a way that when the relative price of a good falls (real income remaining constant), more of it is purchased. The income effect, however, can work either way – when the consumer's real income rises, he may buy more or less of good X. If he buys more, the good is said to be a *normal* good; this is the case illustrated in Fig. 10, where both

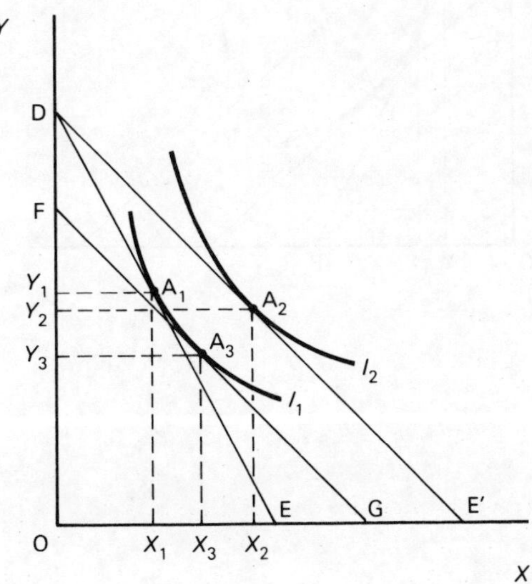

Fig. 10. Income and substitution effects.

X and Y are normal goods. If he buys less, the good is said to be an *inferior* good; this is illustrated in Fig. 11 (a) where the movement from A_3 to A_2 is the negative income effect. If he buys less, and the income effect is actually bigger than the substitution effect so that the overall effect of the price fall is a decrease in consumption, then the good is said to be a *Giffen* good; this is illustrated in Fig. 11 (b) where the negative income effect (A_3 to A_2) is bigger than the substitution effect (A_1 to A_3).

Fig. 11. The case of an inferior good and a Giffen good.

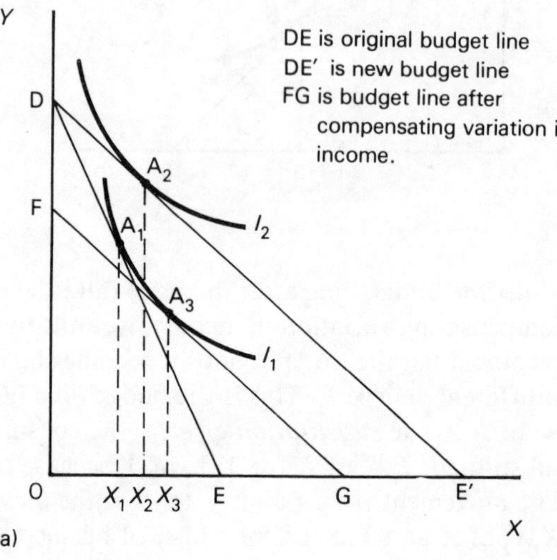

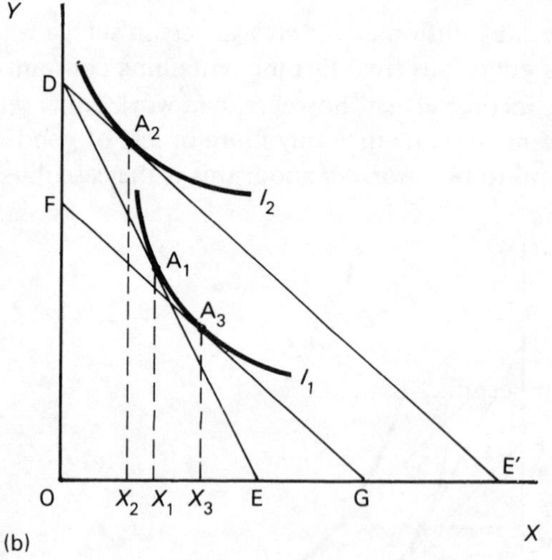

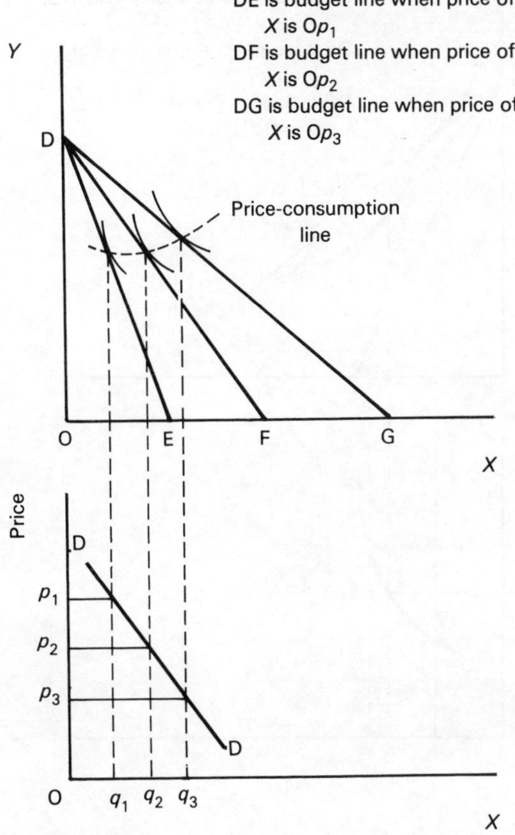

Fig. 12. Derivation of the demand curve for a normal good.

The demand curve again

The preceding analysis can be used to derive a consumer's demand curve. The price-consumption curve in Fig. 9 shows the different points of 'consumer equilibrium' as the price of X is varied, *ceteris paribus*. It gives us enough information, therefore, to draw the consumer's demand curve. This is done in Fig. 12 where X is a normal good: as the price of X is reduced from Op_1 to Op_2 to Op_3, the quantity of X demanded expands from Oq_1 to Oq_2 to Oq_3. The resulting demand curve is downward-sloping from left to right. The same analysis is carried out in Fig. 13 where X is a Giffen good and the resulting demand curve is upward-sloping from left to right.

We have now completed a full circle. Having started by considering an individual consumer's demand curve in isolation in Chapter 3, we have now looked at the concept of utility and the theory of consumer behaviour which underlies demand. Furthermore, we have seen that by making certain assumptions about the consumer's preferences and assuming *ceteris paribus*, we can derive a demand curve which slopes downwards from left to right. We have also seen that under certain exceptional circumstances, a demand curve which slopes upwards from left to right can be derived.

Consumer surplus

Consider now an individual's demand curve for good X as shown in Fig. 14

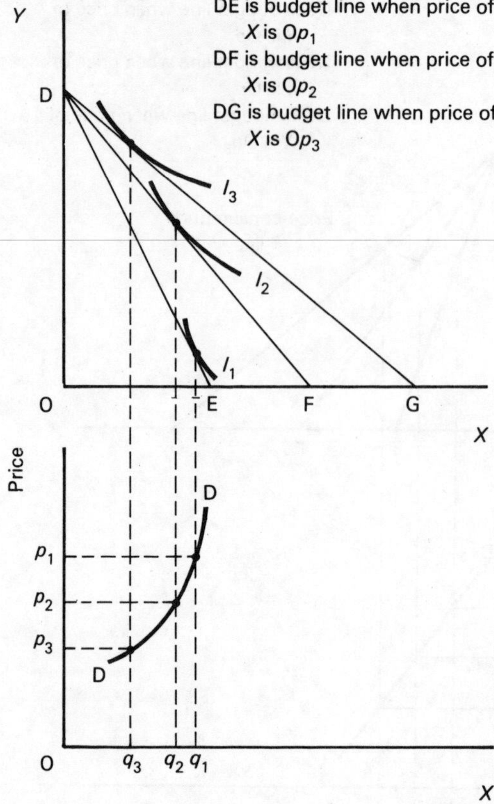

Fig. 13. Derivation of the demand curve for a Giffen good.

and suppose that the prevailing market price is £4. The graph indicates that the individual will buy 6 units of the good per week, paying out a total of £24. We have seen in the foregoing analysis that the individual will maximise

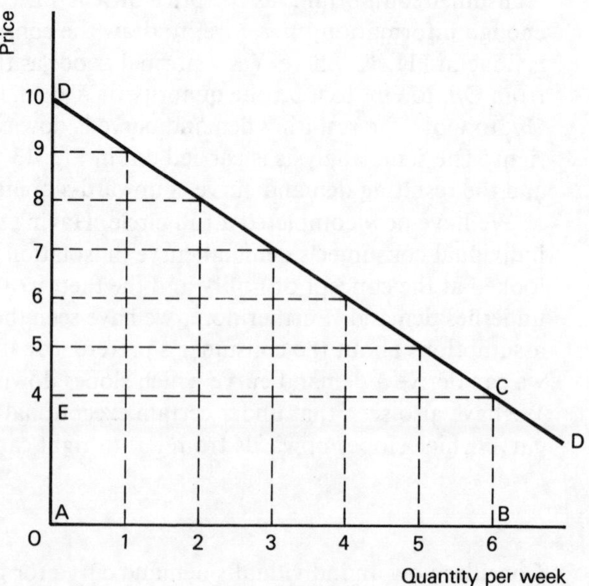

Fig. 14. Consumer's surplus.

his utility by these purchases. Consider, though, the first unit of good *X* that the individual buys – it yields him so much utility that he would have been prepared to pay as much as £9 for it. Similarly, he would have been prepared to pay as much as £8 for the second unit, £7 for the third unit, and so on. Since a single price of £4 prevails in the market, he has only had to pay £24 for the six units (area ABCE), instead of £(9 + 8 + 7 + 6 + 5 + 4) = £39 which he would have been prepared to pay – for continuous data, this is equal to the area under the demand curve, ABCD. The £15 difference can be thought of as the *consumer's surplus* and is represented by the area under the demand curve and above the price line (ECD in Fig. 14).

For a market demand curve, *consumer surplus* is a monetary indicator of the gap between the total utility that society derives from a good and the good's actual market value. We see in later chapters that it is a useful concept in illustrating the welfare effects on an economy of taxes, quotas and certain elements of imperfect competition.

Recent developments in demand theory

The revealed preference theory

The 'theory of revealed preference' is based on the reasonable proposition that a consumer will actually choose to consume that collection of goods that he prefers. Paul Samuelson used this proposition to derive a consumer's downward-sloping demand curve in such a way that required neither the subjectivity of the utility concept used in both the ordinal and cardinal utility approaches, nor the assumption of diminishing marginal utility of the cardinal utility approach. All that was required was that the consumer behaved consistently.

The 'revealed preference' theory can demonstrate that the consumer's demand curve for a good will be downward-sloping from left to right so long as the consumer is observed to increase his purchases of the good when his income increases. Consider Fig. 15. Suppose that the line AB is a consumer's

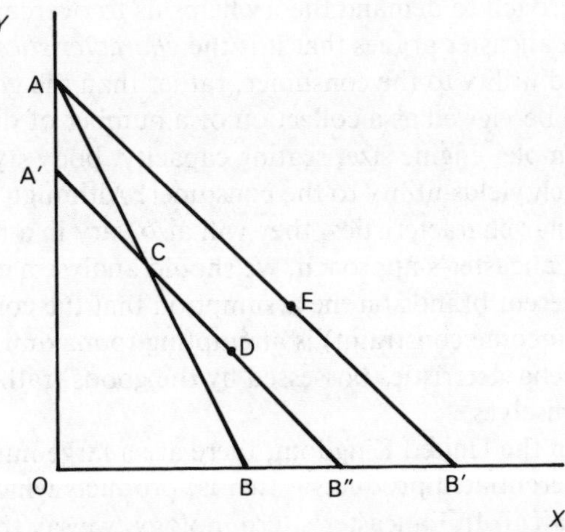

Fig. 15. The revealed preference approach.

budget line and that point C is the combination of X and Y that the consumer reveals preferred to all the other attainable combinations in the triangle AOB. If the price of X falls, the budget line will shift to AB′. We can eliminate the income effect of this price change, as before, by shifting the budget line back to AB″ (parallel to AB′). Having revealed point C preferred to all other points in the triangle AOB, the consumer will clearly not now choose any points along the section A′C. He must, therefore, choose a point on the line CB″, say point D. The movement from C to D is the substitution effect of the price fall; according to this effect, the consumer purchases more of X following the price fall. If, as we have assumed, the income effect also causes him to buy more of X, then he must end up at a point on the budget line AB′ somewhere to the right of point D, say at E. Since the fall in the price of X has caused the consumer to buy more, *ceteris paribus*, we can conclude that the consumer's demand curve slopes downwards from left to right.

It is important to notice that, in arriving at this conclusion, no mention was made of the abstract concept of utility. The 'revealed preference' approach can be described as a more objective approach to the theory of consumer behaviour. However, it cannot be denied that some subjective evaluation is implicit when consumers reveal their preferences for goods.

The 'characteristics of goods' approach

So far in this chapter, we have been concerned with consumers' choice between different goods on the assumption that a consumer will make a choice which will maximise his utility (whether cardinal or ordinal), subject to his income constraint. In this traditional approach, however, it is difficult to analyse a consumer's choice between different brands of the same product. One good must be treated either as the same as another or as a different good altogether. How then can we analyse a consumer's choice between two different brands of, say, a car? Is a Mini the same as a Jaguar or are they to be treated as completely different products? Lancaster's approach to demand theory helps us to overcome this problem.

Lancaster argues that it is the *characteristics* or attributes of goods which yield utility to the consumer, rather than the goods themselves. Thus, a car can be viewed as a collection of a number of different attributes – for example, engine size, seating capacity, body style, colour and so on, each of which yields utility to the consumer. Although different cars will clearly have similar characteristics, they will also vary in a number of respects. According to Lancaster's approach, we should analyse a consumer's choice between different brands on the assumption that the consumer (subject as always to his income constraint) is attempting to maximise the utility he derives from the characteristics possessed by the goods, rather than from the goods themselves.

In the United Kingdom, there are a large number of so-called differentiated products – that is, products which are very similar but not identical. In Lancaster's terminology, we say that such goods have similar characteristics. Clearly, traditional economics can be criticised for its inability to analyse a consumer's choice between these goods, and Lancaster's approach welcomed for throwing some light on this previously untrodden ground.

Conclusion

The main objective of this chapter has been to examine the various approaches to the analysis of consumer behaviour, and to look more closely into the proposition that a fall in the price of a normal good will cause an increase in the quantity of that good demanded by an individual consumer.

The next step is to consider the main determinants of the supply of a good. It is to this, therefore, that we now turn our attention in Chapter 5.

Further reading

Lancaster, K., *Introduction to Modern Microeconomics*, Rand McNally, Chicago, 1974 (Ch. 7).

Ryan, W.J.L. and **Pearce, D.W.**, *Price Theory*, Macmillan, London, 1977 (Ch. 1 and 2).

Baumol, W.J., *Economic Theory and Operations Analysis*, Prentice Hall, New Jersey, 1977 (Ch. 9).

Laidler, D., *Microeconomics*, Philip Allan, Deddington, 1974 (Ch. 2–6).

Exercises

1. Review your understanding of the following terms:

cardinal utility	income-consumption curve
ordinal utility	price-consumption curve
marginal utility	income effect
indifference map	substitution effect
budget line	compensating variation
marginal rate of substitution	consumer surplus
consumer equilibrium	revealed preference

2. Suppose an individual spends all his weekly income on two goods, *X* and *Y*. Draw the individual's budget line if his income is £150 per week, the price of *X* is £10 per unit and the price of *Y* is £15 per unit. Draw the new budget lines: (a) if the price of *X* doubles; (b) if the price of *Y* halves; (c) if the individual's income rises to £250 per week.

3. Draw an individual's indifference maps for two goods, *X* and *Y*:
(a) where the individual regards *X* and *Y* as perfect complements;
(b) where the individual regards *X* and *Y* as perfect substitutes;
(c) where the individual derives utility from good *X*, but disutility from good *Y*.

4. Suppose that *X* is a normal good, but that *Y* is an inferior good. Illustrate graphically the income and substitution effects following: (a) a fall in the price of *X*; (b) a fall in the price of *Y*.

5. Discuss the precise meaning of the term 'utility'. To what extent can it be measured cardinally?

6. 'The revealed preference approach eliminates the abstract concept of utility from the theory of demand.' Discuss.

5 Supply

Introduction

As we saw in Chapter 2, it is the primary function of firms to hire and organise factors of production in order to produce goods and services which are then offered for sale. Firms, then, whether sole traders, partnerships, limited companies or public corporations, are the economic agents responsible for the supply of goods and services.

To give a full treatment of supply, it is necessary to analyse in detail how firms under different market structures make their price and quantity decisions. Firms in highly competitive industries, for example, operate differently from those with some monopoly power. This detailed analysis, however, is left for Chapters 9 and 10. In this short chapter, a preliminary discussion of supply is presented. This includes an outline of some of the problems facing all suppliers, the main factors likely to influence the market supply of a good *under competitive conditions*, the supply curve and the elasticity of supply.

Definition: ***The market supply of a good is the sum of the quantities of that good that individual firms are willing and able to offer for sale over a given time period.***

Problems facing suppliers

Whatever its objectives, every firm needs to earn sufficient revenues to cover its costs if it is to remain in business in the long-run. In Chapter 2, we saw that a profit-maximising firm attempts to produce that quantity which will yield biggest possible profits and, of course, firms with other objectives must aim at least for some satisfactory level of profits (if only to keep their shareholders happy). In striving to achieve their objectives, then, firms would like to be able to estimate their current and future *sales revenues* and their current and future *production costs* with a reasonable degree of accuracy. It is this estimation of revenues and costs which represents a major problem to many firms.

Consider a firm which is thinking of expanding its output. To determine whether or not such a policy will be profitable, the firm has to *search* for a certain amount of information. In particular, the firm must be able to estimate the profitability of employing extra labour and capital, the cost of acquiring additional raw materials and the future demand for its product. In an uncertain world with imperfect knowledge, none of this information is easy to obtain.

The *profitability of employing extra labour*, for example, depends on the productivity of that labour and the new wage rates required to attract it to the firm, bearing in mind that the wage levels paid to newly-employed labour will in most cases also have to be paid to the existing work-force. The productivity of extra labour is not known with certainty by the firm. Similarly, the wage rates and any overtime rates which the firm may have to pay to expand its output are also initially unknown – they depend to some extent on the rates prevailing in the market and will in many cases be the result of negotiations with trade unions.

Similarly, the *profitability of employing more capital*, say a new machine, depends on the price of the machine and the rate of interest which has to be paid on money borrowed to finance its purchase. This cost (which presumably can be estimated with a reasonable degree of accuracy) must then be compared with the estimated future yield of the machine, and this is not so easy to determine – it depends on future demand conditions and future prices which are not known with any certainty by the firm.

Even the *cost of acquiring additional raw materials* may not be known with certainty as it depends on future raw material prices. In the 1970s, for example, the unanticipated and very rapid rise in oil prices, together with the difficulty of finding alternative sources of energy, posed many problems for firms throughout the world. If a firm is a very large one, its own increased demand for raw materials as it expands may push prices upwards unexpectedly. On the other hand, of course, a new discovery of raw materials may cause their prices to fall substantially.

Finally, the *future demand for a firm's product* depends (as we saw in Chapter 3) not only on the future price of the product, but also on many factors which are not under the firm's control, like the prices of related goods, family income, tastes and expectations. These can be very volatile and therefore difficult to predict. Firms receive information about the demand for their product through price changes, changes in their stocks and market research. They have to use this information to estimate future trends.

Imperfect knowledge and uncertainty in the modern business world mean that firms have to employ time and resources searching for current information. The more information that is collected, the greater are the potential future profits, but, of course, the more time-consuming and costly is the search.

In spite of the fact that firms face some quite severe problems in making their price and quantity decisions, it is still possible to isolate some of the factors which are likely to influence the total market supply of a good. In doing this, however, it is important to bear in mind that firms make their quantity decisions in the light of imperfect knowledge, and having determined their preferred output may even fail to produce it because of factors outside their control. In the following section, we list the likely determinants of the total supply of a *competitive* industry – that is, one in which there are many firms competing with each other and where there is relatively free entry into and exit from the industry.

Determinants of supply

The main determinants of the market supply of a good, say good X, are (a) the objectives of the firms in the industry; (b) the price of good X; (c) the prices of certain other goods; (d) the prices of factors of production; (e) the state of technology. Consider these in turn.

Objectives of the firms (B) We saw in Chapter 2 that firms can have different objectives. The nature of a firm's objectives will affect the decisions it takes. A firm which aims to maximise its sales revenue, for example, will generally supply a greater quantity than a firm aiming to maximise profits. This is illustrated in Fig. 1 where a single firm's total costs and total revenues are plotted against quantity supplied – the difference between the two curves representing the firm's profits. Sales revenue is maximised at output Oq_1 where the total revenue curve reaches its maximum. Profits are maximised at output Oq_2 where the difference between the total revenue and total cost curves is greatest: on the graph, this is also the point where the profits curve reaches its maximum. It follows from this that the total market supply of good *X* depends on the primary objectives of all the firms in the industry. Changes in these objectives will usually lead to changes in the quantity supplied.

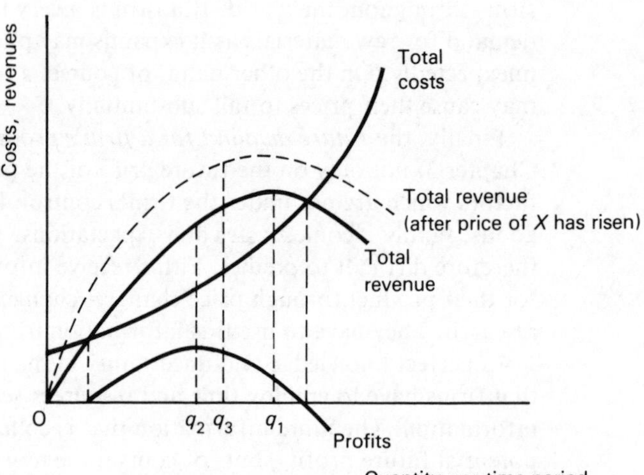

Fig. 1. Different objectives yielding different outputs.

Price of good *X* (P_x) As the price of good *X* rises, with all costs and the prices of all other goods unchanged, production of *X* becomes more profitable. Existing firms are likely, therefore, to expand their outputs and eventually new firms will be attracted into the industry. Hence total market supply will expand when price increases. This is also illustrated in Fig. 1 where the price rise causes the total revenue curve to shift upwards and the profit-maximising quantity to increase to Oq_3. It should also be pointed out here that it is not just current prices, but also expectations concerning future prices, which may motivate producers.

Prices of certain other goods (P_g) If the price of some other good, say *Y*, should rise, with the price of *X* unchanged, some of the firms now producing

X may be tempted to move into *Y* production, motivated by their search for profits. A producer of wheat, for example, who sees that the price of barley has risen may decide to use more of his land for barley production and so reduce his wheat output. Wheat and barley are said to be *substitutes in production* and in this case there is an inverse relationship between the supply of one good and the price of the other.

However, this is not the result we should expect for goods which are *complements* (like cars and petrol) or *jointly-supplied* (like petrol and paraffin). An increase in the demand for, and therefore the price of, cars will lead to an increased demand for petrol: this should raise the price of petrol and so lead to an expansion rather than a contraction of supply. With petrol and paraffin, increasing the supply of one necessarily increases the supply of the other. Thus, if the demand for and price of petrol should rise, the supply of petrol should expand leading at the same time to an increase in the supply of paraffin.

It is also true, of course, that the extent to which firms can move from one industry to another in search of higher profits depends on the ease with which resources can be shifted from one use to another.

Prices of factors of production (P_f) As the prices of those factors of production used intensively by *X* producers rises, so do the firms' costs. This will cause supply to fall as some firms reduce output and other, less efficient, firms make losses and eventually leave the industry. Similarly, if the price of one factor of production should rise (say, land), some firms may be tempted to move out of the production of land-intensive products, like wheat, into the production of a good which is intensive in some other factor of production.

The state of technology (*T*) This is another factor which influences the firms' costs. Technological improvements (such as the invention of a new machine or the development of a more efficient technique of production) will reduce costs and increase the profit margin on each unit sold. Total supply can, therefore, be expected to increase.

Using functional notation, we can write the following *supply function* for good *X* (just as we wrote the demand function in Chapter 3):

$$S_x = f(B, P_x, P_g, P_f, T, Z)$$

This states simply that the market supply of good *X* (S_x) is a function of, or is determined by, all the variables listed in the brackets, where *Z* represents all other relevant factors, such as natural events (like the weather or an invasion of pests which destroys an agricultural crop) and the levels of taxes and subsidies.

The supply curve

Definition: ***The supply curve for good X shows the relationship between the prices of X and the quantities that firms are willing and able to sell at those prices,*** ceteris paribus.

In order to isolate the relationship between the supply of good *X* and its price, we need to make the *ceteris paribus* assumption and hold all the other influencing factors unchanged. We can then write:

$S_x = f(P_x)$, *ceteris paribus.*

As stated above, in a competitive market where the profit motive is a major objective of firms, this relationship between supply and price is likely to be a direct one. When plotted on a graph, then, the supply curve will slope upwards from left to right so that as the price of the good increases, so does the quantity that firms are willing to supply. Table 1 shows some figures for the price and quantity supplied of good *X* which reflect this proposition. The corresponding supply curve is graphed in Fig. 2. Note that in plotting a supply curve, it is most important to specify the time period under consideration along the horizontal axis.

Table 1. Quantities supplied of good *X* at different prices.

Price of good *X* (pence per unit)	Quantity supplied (units)
10	0
20	100
30	200
40	400

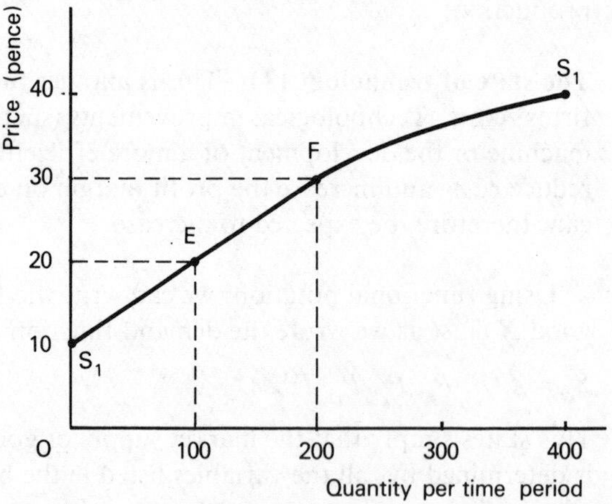

Fig. 2. Supply curve.

Movements along and shifts in the supply curve

Consider the market supply curve S_1S_1 in Fig. 2. Suppose that the price of *X* is 20p per unit so that the total quantity that firms are willing to supply is 100 units: that is, the combination represented by point E on the curve. If the price should rise to 30p per unit, *ceteris paribus*, quantity supplied will expand to 200 units. The change in price means that we have simply moved along the supply curve from point E to point F. (Note that this is similar to the movement along the demand curve described in Chapter 3.)

Result: *The effect of a change in the price of good X,* ceteris paribus, *can be traced by moving along good X's market supply curve.*

The whole supply curve will shift if any of the other influencing factors should change. For example, an improvement in technology which reduces the firms' costs of production will cause an increase in supply at every price and the supply curve will shift to the right. This is illustrated in Fig. 3 where the original supply curve for *X*, S_1S_1, is reproduced. After the improvement in technology, the curve shifts to S_2S_2, so that now at a price of 20p per unit, quantity supplied has risen to 150 units and at price 30p per unit, quantity supplied has risen to 260 units.

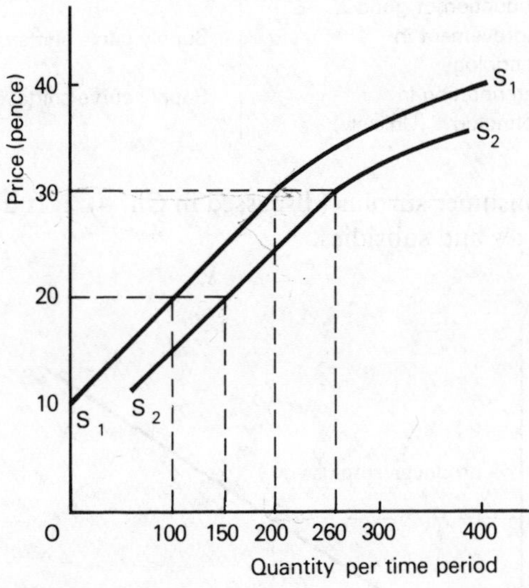

Fig. 3. A shift of a supply curve.

Result: *A change in any of the influencing factors, except the price of X, causes a shift in good X's market supply curve.*

The most likely causes of shifts in good *X*'s supply curve are summarised in Fig. 4.

Producer surplus

Consider the market supply curve SS in Fig. 5. Recall that it shows the quantity of good *X* that producers are willing and able to supply over a given time period at different prices. Suppose that the prevailing market price is actually Op_0, so that quantity Oq_0 is being supplied. The firms in the industry are receiving a total revenue of $Op_0 \times Oq_0$, represented by the total area Op_0Aq_0. It can be seen from the graph that the producers in the industry would have been prepared to supply the first unit at the much lower price of Op_1, the second unit at price Op_2, the third at Op_3 and so on. Since all the firms are receiving the same price (Op_0) for each unit sold, the area above the supply curve and below the price line, Sp_0A, can be interpreted as a gain to the producers over and above that required to keep them in business. This area is therefore sometimes called *producer surplus*. Like the related concept

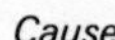

Fig. 4. The most likely causes of shifts in the supply curve of good *X*.

Cause	*Effect*
1. Change in firms' objectives from profit maximisation to sales maximisation.	Supply curve shifts *right*.
2. Rise in the price of good *Y* or expectation of such a rise, where *Y* is a substitute in production.	Supply curve shifts *left*.
3. Fall in the price of good *Y* or expectation of such a fall.	Supply curve shifts *right*.
4. Rise/fall in the prices of those factors of production used intensively in the production of good *X*.	Supply curve shifts *left/right*.
5. Improvement in technology.	Supply curve shifts *right*.
6. Deterioration in technology. (Unlikely)	Supply curve shifts *left*.

of consumer surplus (discussed in Ch. 4), it is useful in examining the effects of taxes and subsidies.

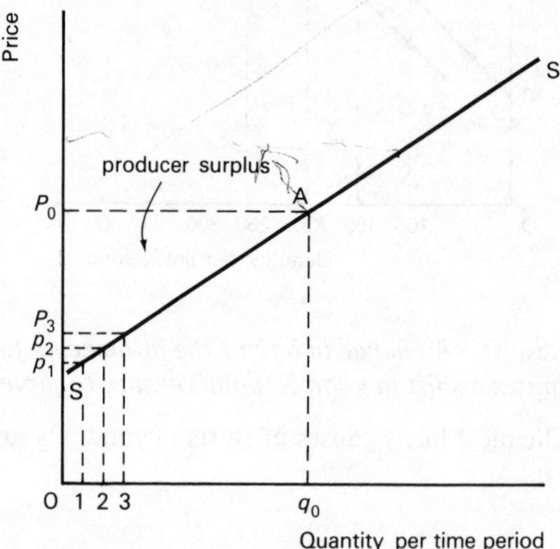

Fig. 5. Producer surplus.

Elasticity of supply

The *elasticity of supply* is a measure of the extent to which the quantity supplied of a good responds to changes in one of the influencing factors. In this chapter, we concentrate on the *price* elasticity of supply (which is a measure of the responsiveness of quantity supplied to a change in the good's own price, *ceteris paribus*). It can be calculated by using the following formula:

$$\text{Price elasticity of supply} = \frac{\text{Proportionate change in quantity supplied}}{\text{Proportionate change in price}}$$

Or in symbols, $$e_s = \frac{\Delta q/q}{\Delta p/p}$$

where $\Delta q/q$ represents the proportionate change in quantity supplied and $\Delta p/p$ represents the proportionate change in the good's price.

Supply is said to be *inelastic* ($e_s < 1$) when a given percentage change in price causes a smaller percentage change in quantity. It is said to be *elastic* ($e_s > 1$) when a given percentage change in price causes a bigger percentage change in quantity. Figure 6 (a) illustrates perfect supply inelasticity ($e_s = 0$). This means that the fixed quantity Oq_1 will be supplied at any price; it will be supplied even at a zero price. The total supply of land in the world may be regarded as being perfectly inelastic (unless, that is, we take into account the possibility of reclamation schemes). Now consider the other extreme illustrated in Fig. 6 (b): that of perfect supply elasticity ($e_s = \infty$). In this case, nothing at all will be supplied at prices below Op_1; any amount will be supplied at Op_1; presumably (unless the supply curve eventually turns upwards) an infinite quantity will be supplied at prices above Op_1. Although these extremes of elasticity are possible over a certain range of prices or quantities, they are extremely unlikely over the entire range of a supply curve.

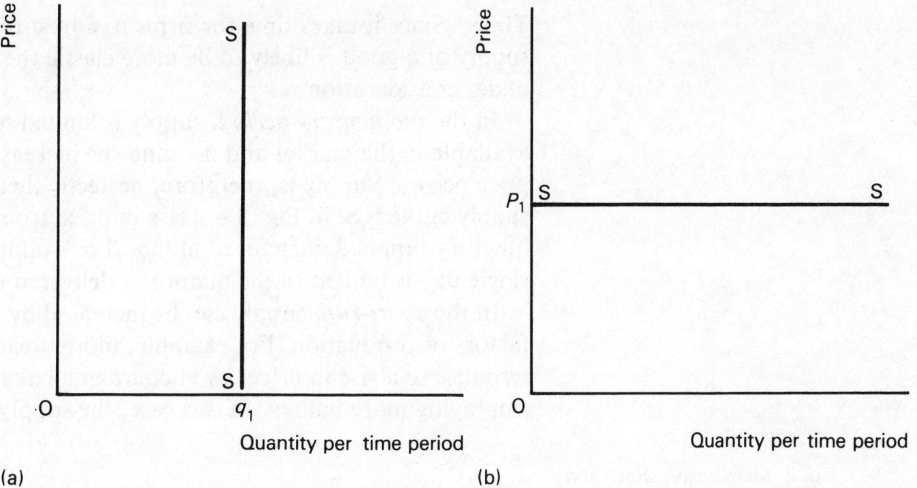

Fig. 6. Perfectly inelastic and elastic supply curves.

Figure 7 illustrates unitary elasticity of supply ($e_s = 1$). This is the case where the percentage change in quantity supplied is exactly equal to the percentage change in price. Thus, in moving from point A to point B along the supply curve in Fig. 7, a 100 per cent rise in price causes a 100 per cent rise in the quantity supplied. In fact, it can be demonstrated that any straight-line supply curve passing through the origin has an elasticity equal to 1.

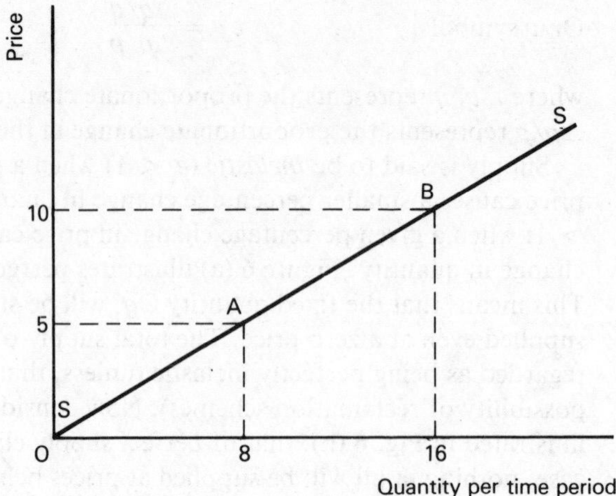

Fig. 7. Unitary supply elasticity.

Determinants of the elasticity of supply

Consider in turn the following three main factors which are likely to influence the elasticity of supply: (a) time; (b) excess capacity and unsold stocks; (c) the ease with which resources can shift from one industry to another.

Time Since it takes time for firms to adjust the quantities they produce, the supply of a good is likely to be more elastic the longer the period of time under consideration.

In the *momentary period*, supply is limited to the quantities already available in the market and it cannot be increased even if a substantial rise in price occurs. Supply is, therefore, perfectly inelastic and is represented by the supply curve S_1S_1 in Fig. 8 – a rise in price from Op_1 to Op_2 leaves the quantity supplied unchanged at Oq_1. For example, the supply of bread in a single day is limited to the quantities delivered to bread shops.

In the *short-run*, supply can be increased by employing more variable factors of production. For example, more bread can be produced (in response to a rise in price) by encouraging bakers to work overtime or by employing more bakers. In this case, the supply curve will slope upwards

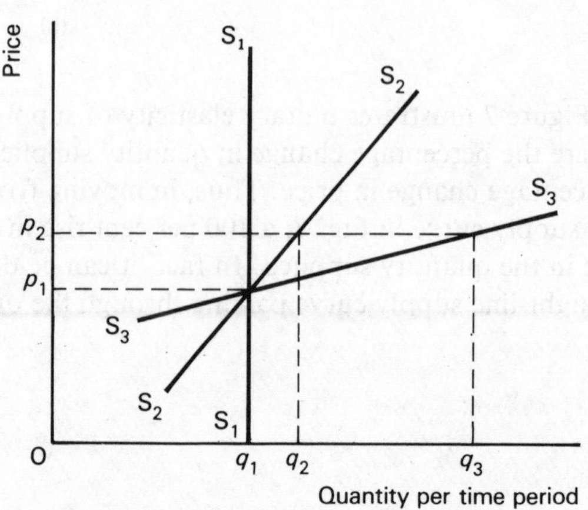

Fig. 8. Momentary, short- and long-run supply curves.

from left to right exhibiting some degree of elasticity, but there is a limit to the increase in supply that is possible without an expansion of the scale of operations. The short-run supply curve is illustrated by S_2S_2 in Fig. 8 and this time a rise in price from Op_1 to Op_2 brings forth an increase in supply from Oq_1 to Oq_2.

In the *long-run*, the quantities of all factors of production can be increased. Existing firms can be expanded and new firms may enter the industry. In our example of bread production, existing bakeries can be expanded and new ovens and other forms of capital equipment can be installed; new bakeries may also be set up. Supply in the long-run, then, is likely to be much more elastic than in the short-run and the long-run supply curve is illustrated by S_3S_3 in Fig. 8. A rise in price from Op_1 to Op_2 this time brings forth an increase in supply from Oq_1 to Oq_3

Excess capacity and unsold stocks In the short-run, it may be possible to increase supplies considerably if there is a pool of unemployed labour and unused machinery (known as *excess capacity*) in the industry. Similarly, if the industry has accumulated a large stock of unsold goods, supplies can quickly be increased. It follows that supply will be more elastic the greater the excess capacity in the industry and the higher the level of unsold stocks.

The ease with which resources can be shifted from one industry to another In both the short- and long-runs, in the absence of excess capacity and unsold stocks, an increase in supply requires the shifting of factors of production from one use to another. This may be costly because the prices of the factors may have to be raised to attract them to move.

There are, however, other problems which may limit the *mobility* of factors between industries. Labour may be reluctant to move away from family and friends and may need retraining before it is suitable for the new occupation. Similarly, capital equipment which is suitable for one use may be totally unsuitable for another. It is this heterogeneity of labour and capital which can severely restrict their mobility. In certain industries this is not such a serious problem and, given sufficient time, supply can be very elastic. In agriculture, for example, it is quite possible for both labour and capital to shift from barley production to wheat production in response to a rise in wheat prices, though in this particular example time must be allowed for reaping the old crop and sowing the new one. In many other industries, however, labour may have to be completely retrained and new capital equipment may have to be acquired. In such cases, supply will be inelastic, except over a very long time period.

Note that the mobility of labour is discussed in greater detail in Chapter 15.

Conclusion

The supply of a good is influenced by many factors and we have discussed the main ones in this chapter. We have also defined the supply curve as a graphical representation of the relationship between quantity supplied and a good's price, *ceteris paribus*. We have to wait until Chapter 9, though, to see how a firm's supply curve can be derived from the costs of production. In economics, price is highlighted as the major determinant of both the demand for a good and the supply of a good. In the next chapter, we move a step further forward and show how the good's price itself is determined in a competitive market.

Further reading

Lancaster, K., *An Introduction to Modern Microeconomics*, Rand McNally, Chicago, 1974 (Ch. 2).

Ryan, W.J.L. and **Pearce, D.W.**, *Price Theory*, Macmillan, London, 1977 (Ch. 4 and 5).

Ferguson, C.E. and **Maurice, S.C.**, *Economic Analysis*, Irwin, Homewood, Illinois, 1974 (Ch. 2).

Exercises

1. Review your understanding of the following terms:

market supply
supply function
supply curve
joint supply
producer surplus
elasticity of supply
momentary period
short-run
long-run

2. Consider the following price and quantity supplied data for good *X*.

Price	2	4	6	8	10	12
Quantity supplied	25	35	45	55	65	75

(a) Plot the supply curve on a graph;
(b) calculate the elasticity of supply at price = £4 and at price = £10;
(c) suppose that a rise in raw material costs causes the producer to reduce supply by 15 units at every price. Repeat exercises (a) and (b).

3. Discuss the main determinants in the United Kingdom of the market supply of: (a) beef; and (b) guest house accommodation in a holiday resort.

4. Discuss the main determinants of the elasticity of supply of: (a) oil; and (b) shoes.

5. Describe the likely effect on the market supply curve for wheat of:
(a) a prolonged drought;
(b) the introduction of a cost-reducing combine harvester;
(c) an increase in the demand for barley.

6 Equilibrium and disequilibrium

Introduction

In Chapters 3–5, we have analysed separately the important concepts of demand and supply. Our next task is to bring these two concepts together and see how interaction between them can determine the market price of a good. We start by explaining the meaning of an equilibrium in economics and by considering some applications of equilibrium analysis. By examining the effects of shifts in the demand and supply curves, we are able to make predictions about the effects of certain changes in the economy on the equilibrium price and equilibrium quantity of particular goods and services.

In the second half of the chapter, the more modern approach to demand and supply analysis is considered. This takes us into the area of disequilibrium economics and search theory where we study the dynamics of the movement from one equilibrium to another.

Equilibrium

Figure 1 shows the demand and supply curves of a 'normal' good X on the same graph. Remember that these curves are drawn on the assumption that all influencing factors except price remain unchanged (that is, *ceteris paribus*). When the price of X is Op_e, the demand for X and the supply of X are just equal: this is called an equilibrium position and Op_e is called the *equilibrium market price*. At this price, the amount that producers are willing and able to supply to the market is just equal to the amount that buyers are willing and able to buy: both producers and buyers can be satisfied and there will be no pressure on the price to change.

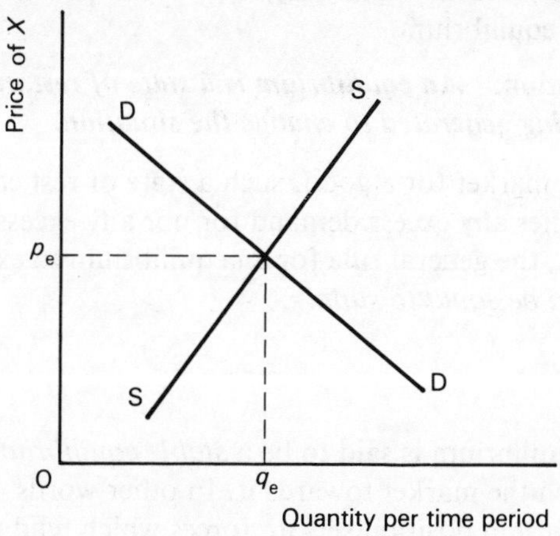

Fig. 1. Equilibrium in the market for good X.

Now consider Fig. 2. When the price of X is Op_1, quantity demanded is Oq_1, but producers are willing to supply Oq_2. There is an *excess supply* of X equal to q_1q_2. Note that an excess supply exists whenever quantity demanded is less than quantity supplied at the prevailing market price. Producers may react to this by reducing price in an attempt to sell off their unsold stocks – excess supply, then, represents an economic force which exerts downward pressure on price. When the price of X is Op_2, however, quantity demanded is Oq_4 but producers are only willing to supply Oq_3. Now there is *excess demand* for X equal to q_3q_4. Excess demand exists whenever quantity demanded is greater than quantity supplied at the prevailing market price. This time it is not unreasonable to suppose that competition amongst buyers will bid the price upwards. Producers are in a position where they can sell all they are producing and more at higher prices. Excess demand, then, is an economic force which exerts upward pressure on price. Prices Op_1 and Op_2 and all other prices except Op_e are called *disequilibrium* prices.

Fig. 2. Graph illustrating excess demand and excess supply.

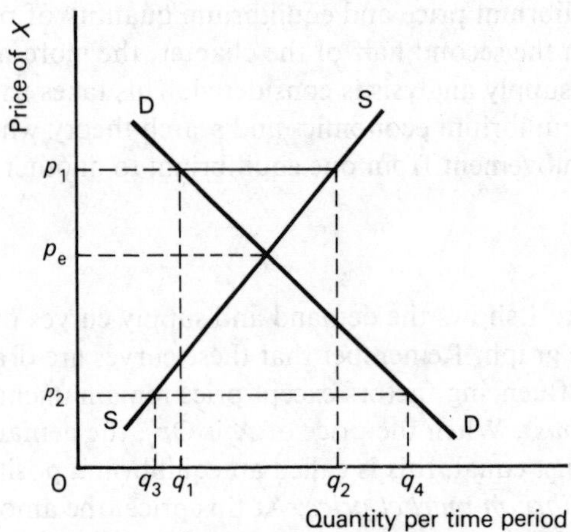

Since much work in economics has been concerned with comparing one equilibrium state with another at a moment in time (often called *comparative static equilibrium analysis*), it is very important to understand what is meant by an equilibrium.

Definition: ***An equilibrium is a state of rest in which no economic forces are being generated to change the situation.***

In the market for a good, such a state of rest can be said to exist when there is neither any excess demand for nor any excess supply of the good. In other words, the general rule for an equilibrium to exist in a market is that *demand should be equal to supply.*

Stable and unstable equilibria

An equilibrium is said to be a *stable equilibrium* when economic forces tend to push the market towards it. In other words, any divergence from the equilibrium position sets up forces which tend to restore the equilibrium.

This is the case in the market for good *X* illustrated in Fig. 1 and Fig. 2. The equilibrium at price Op_e is stable because the establishment of any disequilibrium price, like Op_1 or Op_2, sets up economic forces (excess supply in the case of Op_1 and excess demand in the case of Op_2) which, given competition among buyers and sellers, tend to push the price back towards Op_e.

Now consider Fig. 3 which illustrates the market for good *Y*, which has a demand curve sloping upwards from left to right. Good *Y* might be a Giffen or a Veblen good. Price Op_e is the equilibrium price and quantity Oq_e is the equilibrium quantity. This equilibrium, however, is an unstable one. To show this, suppose the disequilibrium price, Op_1, is established. This creates excess demand equal to q_1q_2 which pushes the price upwards, even further away from Op_e. Similarly, if the price were Op_2, the excess supply equal to q_3q_4 would tend to push the price even further downwards.

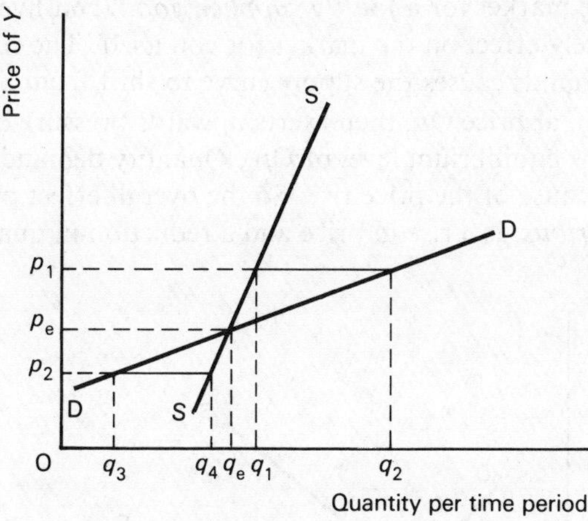

Fig. 3. An unstable equilibrium.

Thus, although equilibria are states of rest at which no economic forces exist to change the situation, it is important to remember that not all equilibria are stable. The equilibrium in Fig. 3 is sometimes called a *knife-edge* equilibrium, because a small change in price sends the system well away from equilibrium.

Some applications of equilibrium analysis

In this section, we consider two main applications of equilibrium analysis: the first enables us to analyse the interaction which can occur among the markets for related goods; the second illustrates a possible (though admittedly oversimplified) approach to the problem of environmental pollution.

Substitutes, complements and jointly-supplied goods

As a simple illustration of the interaction that can occur between markets, consider the market for *cod* in the United Kingdom. Cod is a fish which can be bought by consumers in a number of different forms: for example, it is available fresh from fishmongers, frozen from supermarkets and cooked in batter and served with chips from the famous English fish and chip shops! It has a number of close *substitutes,* like haddock, and a number of less close substitutes, like hamburgers. It also has a number of complementary goods like batter, bread-crumbs, chips and cooking-oil, the demands for which tend to increase as the demand for cod increases. These are all demanded jointly with cod. (Other examples of jointly-demanded or complementary goods include cars and petrol, and right and left shoes.)

A by-product of cod is cod-liver oil. Since an increase in the supply of cod also increases the supply of cod-liver oil, they are said to be *jointly-supplied* goods. (Other examples of jointly-supplied goods are petrol and paraffin, and coal gas and coke.)

Now suppose that the supply of cod to the United Kingdom is reduced following a political decision to restrict access to fishing grounds. Consider the likely effects of this on the market for cod, the market for a *substitute good* (say, haddock), the market for a *complementary good* (say, chips) and the market for a *jointly-supplied good* (cod-liver oil). Figure 4 illustrates the likely effect on the market for cod itself. The restriction of access to fishing grounds causes the supply curve to shift from SS to S′S′. Excess demand of q_3q_1 at price Op_1 then exerts upwards pressure on price until it rises to the new equilibrium level of Op_2. Quantity demanded will fall from Oq_1 to Oq_2 because of the price rise. So the overall effect on the market for cod, *ceteris paribus,* is a rise in price and a reduction in quantity consumed.

Fig. 4. The market for cod.

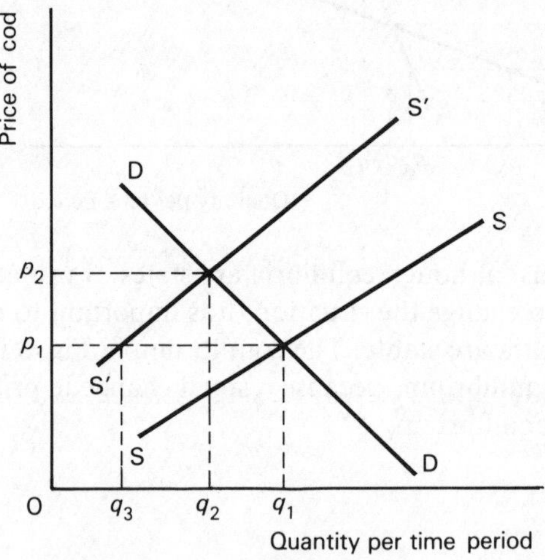

Figure 5 (a) shows the likely effect on the market for haddock. The rise in the price of cod causes consumers to shift their spending on to a variety of substitute goods, including haddock. Thus, there will be an increase in the demand for haddock, shown in the graph as a shift in the demand curve from DD to D′D′. This will push up the price of haddock from Op_1 to Op_2. The total quantity supplied will also expand (because of the price rise) from Oq_1 to Oq_2. So the overall effect on the market for haddock, *ceteris paribus,* is a rise in price and an increase in quantity consumed.

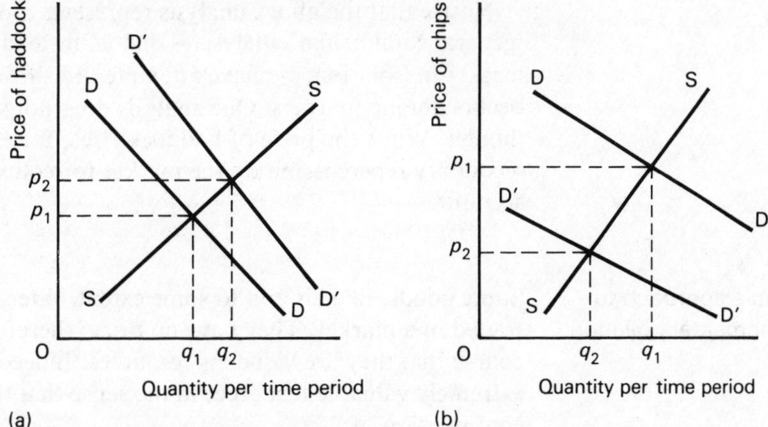

Fig. 5. (a) The market for haddock (a substitute for cod).
(b) The market for chips (a complement to cod).

Result: *A rise in a good's price will tend to put upward pressure on the price of substitutes.*

Figure 5 (b) shows the likely effect on the market for chips. The fall in the consumption of cod and the increase in the consumption of substitute goods (some of which are not normally accompanied by chips) should reduce the overall demand for chips. This is shown in the graph as a shift in the demand curve from DD to D′D′. The final effect, *ceteris paribus*, is seen to be a fall in both the price and quantity consumed.

Result: *A rise in the price of a good will tend to put downward pressure on the prices of complementary goods.*

Finally, Figure 6 shows the effect on the market for cod-liver oil, a jointly-supplied good. The fall in the supply of cod necessarily reduces the supply of cod-liver oil as well. This is shown in the graph as a shift of the supply curve from SS to S′S′. The price of cod-liver oil is likely to rise and the quantity consumed fall.

Result: *A fall in the supply of a good will reduce the supply of jointly-supplied goods, thereby raising their prices.*

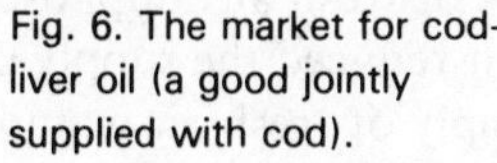
Fig. 6. The market for cod-liver oil (a good jointly supplied with cod).

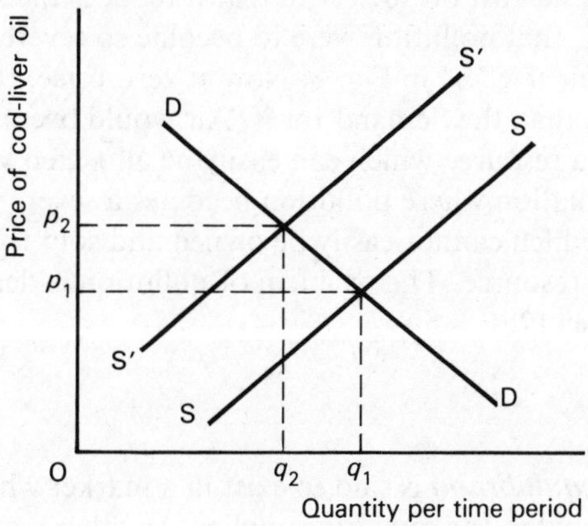

Notice that the above analysis represents a preliminary approach to 'general equilibrium' analysis – that is, instead of merely examining a single market in isolation, we have attempted to show some of the interaction that occurs among markets. Our analysis does not show all the interaction, though. When the price of haddock rises, for example, this will have a secondary repercussion on the market for cod which we have not taken into account.

A simple approach to environmental pollution

Some goods, like air and to some extent water, cannot easily be owned and traded in a market. They have no price, therefore, but this does not mean of course that they are valueless resources. Indeed, both air and water are extremely valuable resources in the sense that they are crucial to the continuation of life.

Suppose that Fig. 7 represents the market for fresh air. As drawn, fresh air is a *free good* because supply exceeds demand even at zero price. It is, therefore, of no real consequence that fresh air cannot be allocated via the price system.

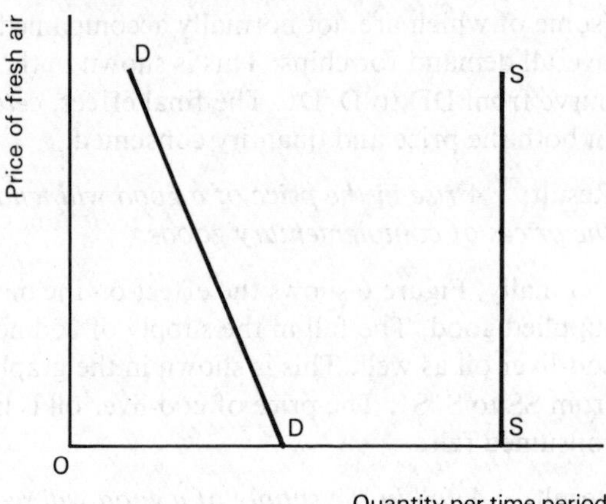

Fig. 7. Fresh air as a free good.

Environmental pollution, in the form of smoke emissions, for example, imposes a cost on society in that it reduces the supply of fresh air. Suppose, in fact, that pollution were to become so severe that it reduced the supply of fresh air to S′S′ in Fig. 8. Now at zero price, the supply of fresh air would be less than the demand for it. Air would become a scarce resource and yet it is not a resource which can easily be allocated via the price mechanism. This is a situation where pollution becomes a severe problem – when it converts a good which cannot easily be owned and sold from being a free good into a scarce resource. The problem of pollution is dealt with in greater detail in Chapter 12.

Disequilibrium analysis

A *disequilibrium* is said to exist in a market when the quantity demanded is not equal to the quantity supplied. In other words, it is a state in which either

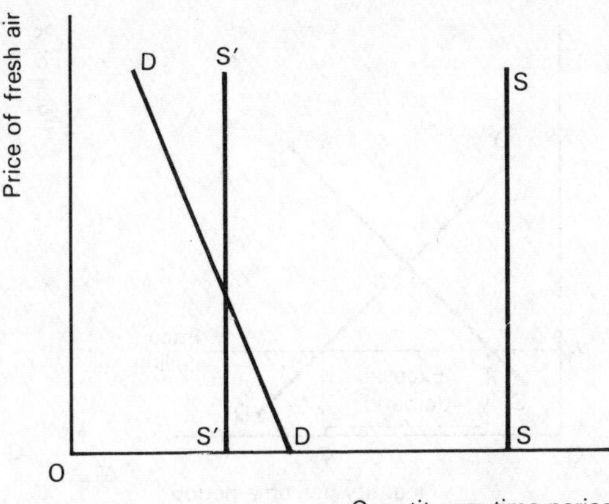

Fig. 8. The market for fresh air after environmental pollution.

excess demand or excess supply exists.

In our analysis so far, we have assumed that when either of these two economic forces exists, equilibrium will quickly be restored. For example, if we start from an equilibrium position and the supply of good *X* is reduced for any reason, excess demand in the market exerts upward pressure on price until a new equilibrium position is reached. If this return to equilibrium were instantaneous, or at least very speedy, there would be little point in studying disequilibrium economics. If the disequilibrium state should persist for any length of time, however, disequilibrium analysis would perhaps be more important and relevant than equilibrium analysis. Disequilibria can, and do, persist in markets in the following circumstances:

(a) where the government or other bodies impose artificial restrictions on either price or quantity;
(b) where the market equilibrium is an unstable one;
(c) where production plans are not realised;
(d) where there are lagged responses.
Consider these in turn.

Artificial restrictions on price or quantity Occasionally, in an attempt to stop the price of a particular good from rising to an 'unacceptable' level, governments have set by law a maximum price, sometimes called a *price ceiling*. Such price ceilings were common during the Second World War, particularly on items which played a big part in the cost of living. Rent controls, which are another form of maximum price, have been in operation in the United Kingdom since 1917.

Alternatively, in order to guarantee producers a certain return on their sales, governments can impose minimum prices or *price floors* below which the price cannot legally fall. The 'intervention price' on certain agricultural goods sold in the Common Market is a kind of price floor – it is that price at which the authorities will intervene to buy up excess supplies so as to prevent the price from falling any further.

The effects of these two forms of government intervention are illustrated for good *X* in Fig. 9 (a) and (b). Figure 9 (a) shows that an excess demand

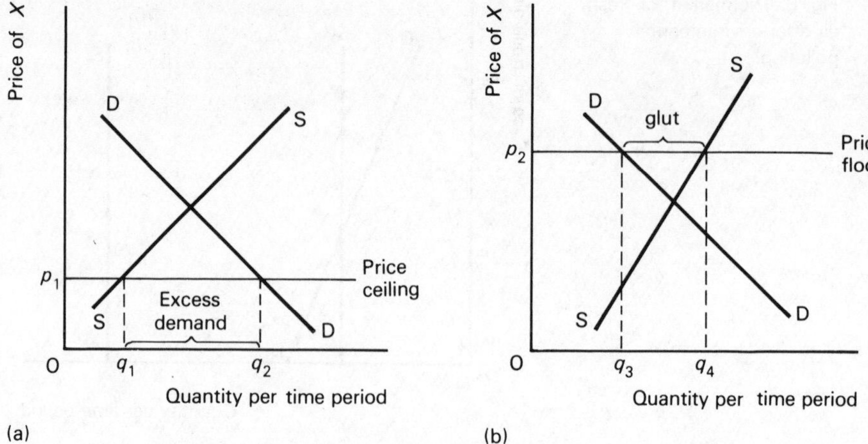

Fig. 9. (a) A price ceiling. (b) A price floor.

for good *X* occurs when a price ceiling is imposed at Op_1 which is below the equilibrium price. Since the price is not allowed to rise back towards the equilibrium, unsatisfied demand exists and this will show itself in queues forming.

At first, *X* may be allocated on a 'first come, first served' basis, but often sellers start to restrict sales to 'so many' per customer, or even to serve only their regular customers. Eventually a 'black market' may develop. In an attempt to allocate the limited supplies fairly, the government may adopt a system of *rationing* – with ration coupons being issued which enable the recipients to buy a limited quantity at the maximum price. Rationing (which involves restricting quantity as well as price) is never entirely satisfactory because many buyers are still unable to obtain the good in the quantities they desire, but it can be argued that it is fairer than simply controlling price.

Figure 9 (b) shows the effects of a price floor at Op_2 which is above the equilibrium price. This time, there is an excess supply of good *X*, sometimes called a *glut*. Where the price floor is established by the authorities intervening to purchase excess supplies, the glut will show itself mainly in an increase in the authorities' stocks of the good. This is the origin of the so-called 'butter mountains' and 'wine lakes' of the Common Market. In the event of a price ceiling or price floor being set on a good at a price which is not the equilibrium one, the economic forces of excess demand and excess supply will not be able to restore the equilibrium. The disequilibrium will persist, then, for as long as the restrictions are maintained.

Unstable equilibria Where an equilibrium is unstable so that any divergence from it generates an economic force which pushes the market even further away from it, disequilibrium positions may be expected to persist. As an example, consider Fig. 10 which shows the market for a Giffen good, like rice in a country where most people spend most of their income on rice. Suppose that at price Op_e (an equilibrium price) people are able to afford a small quantity of more expensive food products, like meat, in addition to rice. If a disturbance occurs so that the price of rice should rise above Op_e, consumers will find that they can no longer afford so much meat and have to spend a bigger and bigger proportion of their incomes on rice. The rising price, therefore, creates excess demand and so no pressure is being generated which will restore the original equilibrium. In other words, the equilibrium at point A in Fig. 10 is an unstable one.

Fig. 10. The market for rice, a Giffen good.

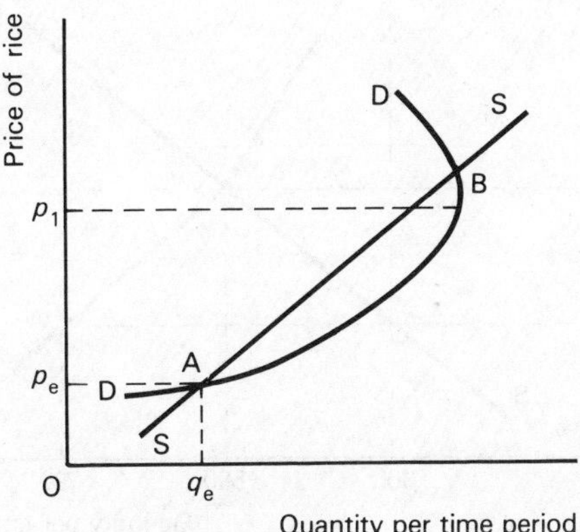

How long a disequilibrium position of this kind can persist will depend on how abnormal the demand curve for the good is. In the case of a Giffen good, there must be some point beyond which demand will fall if price continues to rise. Eventually, when rice is the only food being eaten, it will no longer be possible to substitute rice for meat and, at that price (Op_1 in the graph), total consumption of rice must be cut back. A new equilibrium will then be restored, as at point B in Fig. 10. Notice that point B represents a stable equilibrium.

Failure of production plans to be realised In some industries, because of the possibility of unforeseen events happening, the quantities that producers *plan* to supply may fail to be achieved for a variety of reasons. On the one hand, *actual* supply can fall short of *planned* supply if events not under the producers' control (for example, strikes) mean that production targets cannot be met. On the other hand, *actual* supply may exceed *planned* supply if producers underestimate the productive capacity of their resources. Unplanned fluctuations in supply will affect the market price and also, therefore, the producers' incomes.

This problem of fluctuating supply from one period of time to another has been particularly severe in the case of *agriculture,* and this explains why the prices of agricultural products tend to fluctuate more than the prices of manufactured goods. To show this, consider the graph in Fig. 11 which illustrates the market for the agricultural good *A*. Suppose that at the equilibrium price of £1 per unit, farmers plan to produce 500 units (point E on the supply curve). Assume, however, that because of unexpectedly unfavourable weather conditions or an unexpected attack by destructive insects, actual production is only 300 units. At price £1 per unit, excess demand will exist and this will exert upward pressure on price until it reaches £2 per unit (point V on the demand curve).

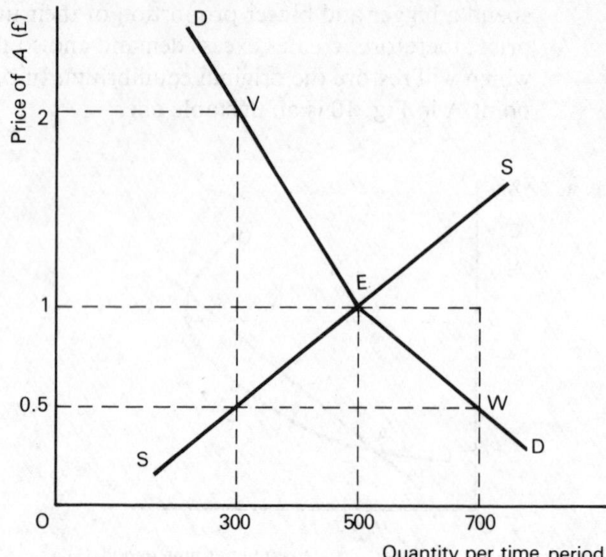

Fig. 11. The market for an agricultural product.

Another possibility is that there may be unexpectedly favourable weather conditions or an unusual absence of pests, so that actual production exceeds the planned 500 units – say, 700 units as shown in Fig. 11. This time, at a price of £1 per unit, excess supply will put downward pressure on price until it reaches 50 pence (point W on the demand curve).

In this example, points V and W cannot be regarded as equilibrium points even though quantity demanded is equal to the actual quantity supplied. The reason is that in the next period, producers would plan to produce 700 units if price remained at £2, and only 200 units if price remained at 50 pence. Quantity supplied would then not equal quantity demanded at those prices. It can be argued with some force that agricultural markets, even where they are very competitive, are extremely unlikely ever to be in equilibrium. Disequilibrium analysis, therefore, is very important in such markets.

Lagged responses For an equilibrium to be restored following a disturbance, we require that the buyers and sellers involved should behave in a particular way. For example, suppose that there is a change in tastes in favour of good *X* so that the demand for it increases. The demand curve for *X* shifts to the right as shown in Fig. 12 and the equilibrium point shifts from A to B. For the movement from A to B to be a swift one, the following behaviour is necessary: (a) the excess demand q_1q_3 must cause sellers to raise their prices from Op_1 to Op_2; (b) the higher prices must cause sellers to expand quantity supplied from Oq_1 to Oq_2; and (c) the higher prices must cause buyers to contract their purchases from Oq_3 to Oq_2. These responses are indeed the most likely ones, but they may not occur instantaneously – instead, there may be *lags* which will cause the market to remain in disequilibrium for some period of time. Lags may occur because of *imperfect information, expectations, inertia* or for *technological reasons.*

Lags on the supply side For firms to respond to the increased demand they

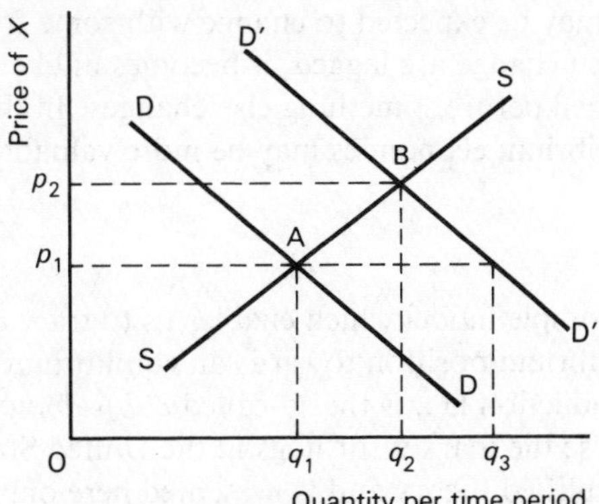

Fig. 12. An increase in demand for good *X*.

have to be aware that it has occurred. Since they only have *imperfect information*, it may take some time before increased sales figures or an increased number of enquiries concerning their product convinces them that an actual increase in demand has taken place. Even then, they will not necessarily increase price immediately – it depends upon whether they expect the increased demand to be permanent or temporary. Only if their *expectations* are optimistic will price finally be raised and, as we shall see later, the formation of expectations can be very time-consuming. Apart from the formation of expectations, some firms may respond very slowly because they suffer from *psychological inertia* – that is, they are set in their ways and insensitive to changing conditions. Assuming that firms do eventually recognise the increase in demand, do expect it to be permanent and are not suffering from inertia, the price of the product will be raised. Our model next predicts an expansion of quantity supplied, but in many industries this will only be possible after a time-lag for technological reasons. This kind of lag is sometimes called a *production lag*. It arises because it takes time for firms to organise the additional factors of production necessary to increase output and this will be particularly difficult if the economy as a whole is close to full employment – then additional labour and capital will be scarce and expensive to acquire. Agriculture provides a good example of a production lag – output can only be increased after one whole season because time has to be allowed for the growing of the new crop.

Lags on the demand side For the equilibrium in Fig. 12 to be restored quickly, we require that buyers should reduce their demand from Oq_3 to Oq_2 as price rises from Op_1 to Op_2. Assuming that the demand curve D′D′ is an accurate and stable relationship, this must eventually happen – but again the crucial question is: how long will it take? Recall from Chapter 3 that we listed 'time' as one of the determinants of the 'elasticity of demand,' arguing that demand is likely to be less elastic in the short-run than in the long-run. Any time-lag on the demand side, then, will depend on (a) the buyers' *expectations* (do they believe the price change to be permanent or temporary?); (b) the buyers' state of knowledge (are they aware of the prices of available substitutes?); (c) whether or not they too suffer from inertia.

Since an economy is a very dynamic place, the conditions of demand and supply may be expected to change with some frequency. If the responses to any given change are lagged, it becomes unlikely that a new equilibrium will be reached before something else changes. In the presence of lags, therefore, disequilibrium economics may be more valuable than equilibrium economics.

An application of disequilibrium analysis

A very simple model which enables us to trace out a time-path from a disequilibrium position towards an equilibrium position, given the presence of a production lag, is the so-called *cobweb model.* This was originally used to analyse the market for hogs in the United States, but it is a rather oversimplified theory and is presented here only as an illustration of dynamic, disequilibrium analysis. More complex versions of the cobweb model are unfortunately outside the scope of this book.

Suppose that the demand for hogs depends on this year's market price, but that this year's supply depends on *last* year's price. This is not unreasonable because if prices were high last year, farmers would have reared many hogs in the expectation of high prices this year; if prices were low last year, though, farmers would have reared fewer hogs in the expectation of low prices this year. Using functional notation, we can write:

$$D_h = f(p_t)$$
$$S_h = f(p_e), \text{ where } p_e = p_{t-1}$$

D_h and S_h represent the demand for and supply of hogs respectively, p_t is this year's price, p_e is the price which farmers last year expected would prevail this year, and p_{t-1} is last year's price. The important point to remember is that any change in price leads to an immediate change in quantity demanded, but only a lagged change in quantity supplied, the production lag being one year. Consider Fig. 13. Suppose we start in year 1 with a disequilibrium price of Op_1. The quantity supplied in year 2 (which depends on the price in year 1) will be Oq_2, but to sell this quantity of hogs the price in year 2 will have to be reduced to Op_2. This price will bring forth a supply of Oq_3 in year 3. This quantity can, however, be sold at the higher price Op_3 and this will bring forth a supply of Oq_4 in year 4. This process will continue year after year, tracing out a cobweb pattern on the graph, with the market slowly approaching the equilibrium position. As drawn in Fig. 13 and assuming *ceteris paribus,* the equilibrium will eventually be reached. This is an example of a *damped* cobweb. The *ceteris paribus* assumption is rather unrealistic in this case since the path to equilibrium takes several years. It is also possible for the cobweb pattern to be *explosive* so that instead of moving closer and closer to the equilibrium each year, the market moves further and further away from it. (See exercise.)

It must be emphasised that the above cobweb model represents a very simple approach to disequilibrium analysis. It only introduces a production lag – it does not take any account of inertia, expectations or imperfect knowledge on the demand side. Expectations are introduced on the supply side in a very simple form with no learning. It does, however, enable us to trace out a dynamic time-path and is therefore a useful starting-point for disequilibrium economics.

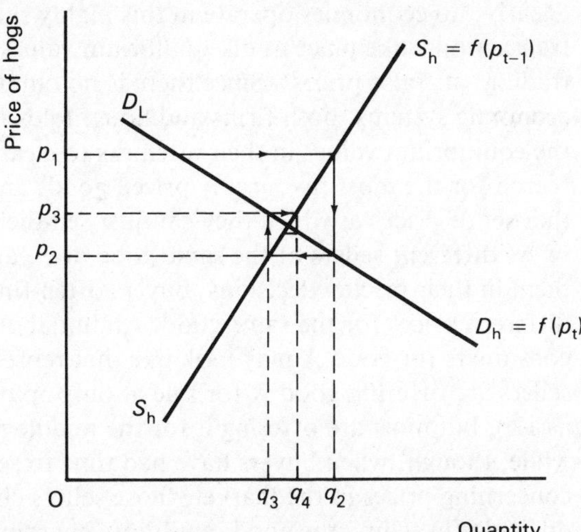

Fig. 13. The cobweb model.

Introduction to search theory

It can be seen from the foregoing discussion that one of the major reasons for the persistence of disequilibrium states is the existence of *imperfect knowledge*. This term can be used to explain the inability of producers to predict both their own output and the demand for their product, and is one of the main reasons for lagged responses.

Imperfect knowledge of equilibrium values means that the economic agents involved (that is firms and consumers) have to *search* for the relevant prices and quantities. The analysis of this search process has been called 'search theory' and is being incorporated into that branch of microeconomics which concerns itself with disequilibrium analysis (sometimes referred to as the 'new microeconomics'). For equilibrium analysis to be perfectly accurate, we require that all transactions should take place in equilibrium and that no transactions should be allowed to take place in disequilibrium. To this end, 'classical' economists (in particular, Leon Walras) constructed a fable, known as the *'tâtonnement' process* which is admittedly unrealistic but which at least provides us with an illustration of how an economy would have to work if equilibrium economics were to be completely acceptable. Here is a summary of that fable:

Consider an economy which consists of firms and households and which is ruled by an all-powerful *auctioneer*. Before any transactions can take place, the auctioneer has to call out a set of prices for all goods and services and command all willing buyers and sellers to indicate their demands and supplies. If the demand for any good is not equal to its supply, *no* transactions are allowed to take place. Instead, the auctioneer calls out a new, revised set of prices and again counts the demands and supplies. This process of 'groping towards' the general equilibrium position continues until the demand for each good and service is just equal to its supply. Then, and only then, transactions are allowed to take place. Should any change in demand or supply occur, all transactions must stop and the whole process of 'tâtonnement' be repeated.

Clearly, no economies operate in this highly simplified way. Indeed, many transactions take place at disequilibrium values – sometimes called 'false trading' at 'false prices'. Since there is no omnipotent auctioneer controlling economic systems, both firms and households themselves have to search for the equilibrium values in their attempts to clear markets. Buyers have to search for the most favourably priced goods and sellers have to search for that set of prices at which they can just sell their output.

As different sellers of the same good are searching for information to help them in their pricing decisions, buyers often find themselves faced with different prices for the same good. An initial distribution of prices facing consumers for good *X* may look like that represented in Fig. 14 (a). A few sellers are offering good *X* for sale at only 5p per unit and a few for as much as 12p, but most are offering it for the middle prices, like 9p or 10p. After a while, though, when buyers have had time to search for information concerning prices in the market, those sellers charging 12p will find some difficulty in selling the good, and those charging 5p will experience an excess demand for their product. Because of this, the distribution of prices will eventually tend to cluster around the middle prices as shown in Fig. 14 (b).

Fig. 14. Distribution of prices among different sellers.

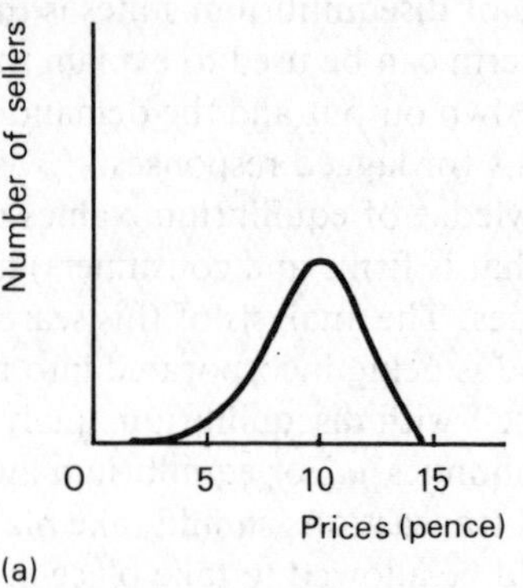

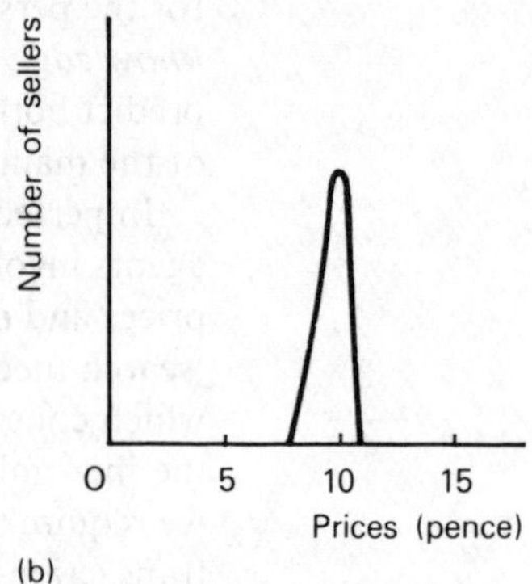

Only if perfect information is available will a single equilibrium price be determined and such an equilibrium can only be achieved immediately if perfect information is available costlessly and without the need for searching. Such single equilibrium prices are hardly ever achieved because search processes are costly and time-consuming and even after a long period of searching, only improved (not perfect) information is acquired.

Conclusion

In this chapter, we first outlined the traditional equilibrium analysis of demand and supply and showed how in competitive markets with perfect information on the part of buyers and sellers, equilibrium market prices and quantities would be determined. As a first approach to general equilibrium analysis, we then considered some of the interaction which occurs among the markets for substitutes, complements and jointly-supplied goods.

Modern economists, though, are becoming increasingly aware that there are many reasons why equilibrium states may not be achieved - for example, because of government restrictions, unstable equilibria, imperfect information and lags. We considered these in turn and then briefly examined the theory of search. In the remainder of this book, we make use of equilibrium analysis in our study of the firm, the theory of distribution, and in macroeconomics. We point out the limitations of this analysis and, where appropriate, show how modern economists have been attempting to incorporate disequilibrium analysis and search theory into the subject.

Further reading

Lancaster, K., *An Introduction to Modern Microeconomics*, Rand McNally, Chicago, 1974 (Ch. 3, 9).
Ferguson, C.E. and **Maurice, S.C.,** *Economic Analysis*, Irwin, Homewood, Illinois, 1974 (Ch. 2).
Stafford, L.W.T., *The Modern Economy*, Longman, London, 1976 (Ch. 2).
Van Doorn, J., *Disequilibrium Economics*, Macmillan, London, 1975.

Exercises

1. Review your understanding of the following terms:

equilibrium
disequilibrium
equilibrium market price
equilibrium market quantity
excess demand
excess supply
stable equilibrium
jointly-supplied goods
free good
price ceiling
price floor
rationing
lagged response
cobweb model
search theory
tâtonnement

2. Consider the following price, quantity demanded and quantity supplied data for good *X*:

Price (£)	2	4	6	8	10	12
Quantity demanded	100	80	60	40	20	0
Quantity supplied	25	35	45	55	65	75

(a) Plot the demand and supply curves on the same graph and identify the equilibrium price and quantity.
(b) Calculate the elasticities of demand and supply at the equilibrium.
(c) Suppose a sales tax of 2p per unit is imposed on good *X*. Show the effect of this on the graph and identify the new equilibrium price and quantity.

3. Suppose good *X* and good *Y* are substitutes. Show the effects in the market for good *X* of:
(a) a new discovery which increases the supply of good *Y*;
(b) an industrial dispute which reduces the supply of good *Y*.
Repeat (a) and (b) on the assumption that *X* and *Y* are complements.

4. Explain why the prices of agricultural goods usually fluctuate more than

the prices of manufactured goods. How has the EEC attempted to stabilise the prices of agricultural goods?

5. Consider a competitive agricultural market with the following demand and supply curves respectively

$$q_t^d = 1000 - 2p_t$$

$$q_t^s = 3p_{t-1}$$

where q_t^d and q_t^s represent the quantities demanded and supplied in the current period, p_t represents the current price and p_{t-1} is the price in the previous period.

(a) Draw the demand and supply curves on a graph and find the equilibrium price and quantity.
(b) From the graph, estimate the prices in the first four periods following a disturbance which moves the price 50 units below its equilibrium.
(c) Comment on the stability of the adjustment to a disturbance in the market.

6. Discuss the characteristics that would indicate that the market for a good or service was in disequilibrium.

General equilibrium and welfare

7 Resource allocation

Introduction

The aim of this chapter is to analyse society's decisions about resource allocation and to consider the different methods societies use to allocate resources. Chapter 1 introduced the fundamental economic problem of allocating scarce resources amongst the competing wants of society. Although resources like labour and capital have increased over time and technology has made steady advances, society's wants have continuously exceeded the means to satisfy them.

Positive economics does not pronounce judgement on the desirability of wants – society's wants and scales of preferences are assumed to be given. This means that efforts have to be directed towards making the most efficient use of scarce resources. With given scales of preferences, the problem of scarcity imposes choices on society. Decisions have to be taken as to which set of wants society must forgo in order to satisfy that set of wants which will maximise the welfare of its members. Such decisions essentially belong to the branch of economics known as *general equilibrium analysis* which is concerned with the allocation of resources in the production of commodities and with the distribution of those commodities among the members of society.

We propose in this chapter to focus attention on the following aspects of the allocation problem: (a) the meaning of general equilibrium and its relation to resource allocation; (b) the types of allocation decisions in a general equilibrium system; (c) the methods of resource allocation in a *closed* economy (that is, one with no international trade); (d) the advantages and disadvantages of the different methods of allocation; (e) resource allocation in an *open* economy (that is, one with international trade).

General equilibrium and welfare maximisation

The term *general equilibrium* refers to equilibrium in the markets for all commodities and resources simultaneously throughout the economic system. Such an equilibrium is reached when no forces exist to compel buyers and sellers in these markets to change their behaviour. The equilibrium behaviour of every individual is then compatible with the equilibrium behaviour of all the other members of society. It can be seen that a general equilibrium is in sharp contrast with a partial equilibrium in the analysis of which no attempt is made to relate the market under consideration to the rest of the economic system.

Economists are interested in general equilibrium because all markets are interdependent. Given full employment, a decision to shift resources to one industry to meet an increased demand for one commodity means a reduced quantity of resources in other industries and reduced supplies of other commodities. Consider, for example, the limited stock of energy resources in an economy: if it is decided to use more energy to produce goods for future consumption, there will be less energy available to produce goods for current consumption.

It follows that the level of output of one industry cannot be determined in isolation, but only in relation to the output levels of other industries which compete for society's limited stock of resources and available technology. These interrelationships are illustrated in Fig. 1 for a simple closed economy, producing only two goods (food and cloth) with two factors of production (labour and capital). The curve AB is the production possibility frontier with the output of food measured along the vertical axis in tonnes and that of cloth measured along the horizontal axis in metres.

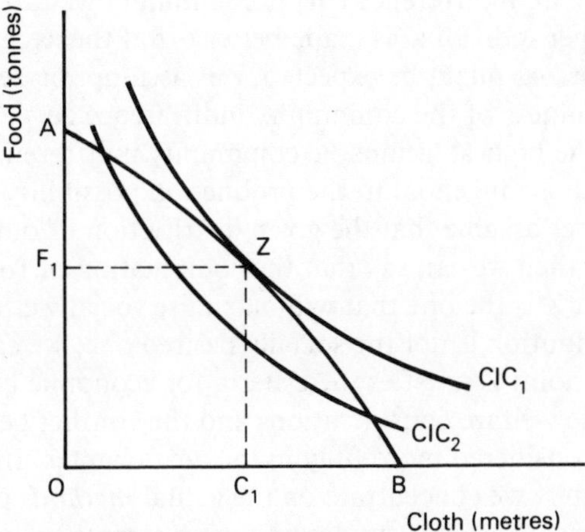

Fig. 1. Social welfare maximisation.

The slope of AB measures the amount by which the production of food must be reduced to increase the production of cloth by 1 metre. As we saw in Chapter 1, this is called the *marginal rate of transformation*. If all resources are transformed into food, the largest possible output is OA tonnes; if, on the other hand, all resources are transformed into cloth, the largest possible output is OB metres. Between these two extremes is a range of possible combinations of food and cloth along AB that can just be produced using all resources efficiently. Point Z is one such combination with OC_1 metres of cloth and OF_1 tonnes of food being produced. At this point and at all other points on the frontier, it is not possible to increase the output of one of the goods without reducing the output of the other. Recall from Chapter 1 that points inside the frontier imply either that there are unused resources or that resources are being used inefficiently – at such points, it is always possible to increase the output of one good without reducing the output of the other.

Assuming that the country can reach its production possibility frontier, the problem then is which combination of food and cloth actually to produce. The 'desired' combination is the one that maximises social welfare. To find this, though, we have to know something about consumers' preferences for the two goods. Just as we were able to express an individual's preferences for two goods by means of an indifference map in Chapter 4, so we can express a community's preferences for two goods by using what is called a *community* indifference map. In Fig. 1, CIC_1 and CIC_2 are two of the community indifference curves which make up such a map for our hypothetical economy.

Definition: ***A community indifference curve joins together all the different combinations of two goods which yield the same utility to a community.***

Note that a community indifference map can only be drawn on the important assumption that the distribution of output amongst the members of the community *remains unchanged.* This heroic assumption is essential because, as we have stressed, community welfare (or utility) depends not only on the quantities of the two goods available for consumption, but also on the distribution of those goods. Thus, as we move from one point to another along an indifference curve, community welfare will only be unchanged if neither individual is made better off at the expense of the other - an unlikely event. As might be expected, this assumption severely restricts the analytical usefulness of the community indifference curves.

The highest attainable community indifference curve in Fig. 1 is CIC_1 which is tangential to the production possibility frontier at point Z. If we further assume that the given distribution of output is the socially desired one, then we can say that the combination of food and cloth represented by point Z is the one that will maximise social welfare. However, if that given distribution is not the socially desired one, we can only go so far as to say that point Z satisfies the criteria for economic *efficiency* and not equity. These welfare considerations and the conflict between efficiency and equity are considered more fully in the next chapter. In the remainder of this chapter, we concentrate on the actual *methods* of resource allocation that different societies employ in their attempts to maximise social welfare.

Types of allocation decisions

All societies strive to achieve point Z in Fig. 1 by making the three types of interrelated decisions of *what, how* and *for whom* to produce. Consider these in turn.

The question of *what to produce* arises essentially from scarcity and choice and the existence of opportunity costs. A decision to produce more cloth, for instance, has the opportunity cost of fewer tonnes of food. This can be seen from Fig. 1: starting at point A, an extreme position, a rightward movement along the frontier to point Z means giving up AF_1 tonnes of food in order to gain OC_1 metres of cloth. Similarly, a leftward movement along the frontier means giving up cloth in order to gain more food. Note that the problem of what to produce is a general one - it applies to all human societies.

The second question of *how to produce* arises because every country, apart from the limited technological know-how at its disposal, possesses a mixture of relatively cheap and expensive resources. India, for example, has relatively abundant (and therefore cheap) labour but a shortage of capital. The United States has relatively cheap capital but expensive labour. Such differences in 'factor endowments' between countries influence the factor combinations used to produce the chosen output-mix at minimum cost. A technologically efficient combination of factors is one which makes greater use of the relatively cheap resources and more sparing use of the relatively expensive ones.

The third question of *for whom to produce* leads us into normative economics because it involves value judgements concerning the pattern of the distribution of income and wealth. This is undoubtedly the most difficult question of all as it reflects society's attitudes to fairness and economic equality. Unlike positive economics, normative economics does pronounce judgements on the desirability of different distributional patterns on the basis of interpersonal comparisons of welfare. This means that normative economics is concerned with public sector redistribution policy decisions whose aim it is to maximise social welfare. In terms of Fig. 1, we said that point Z was the social welfare maximising point *only so long as the given distribution underlying the community indifference map was the socially desired one.* This implies that all societies have to decide in some way what it is that they regard as an equitable distribution and then what method to use to achieve it. In practice, a decision to have more equity may mean forgoing some efficiency – in this case, societies have to decide how much efficiency they are prepared to give up in order to gain more equity.

It should be clear from the foregoing account that the problem of resource allocation is that of making decisions in a general equilibrium system about efficiency and equity. These decisions (*what, how* and *for whom*) all arise from the universal problem of scarcity and choice. Thus, all societies, irrespective of their political complexions and stages of development have to tackle the same basic economic problem. It is the *methods* of allocation that differ between countries and, in what follows, we outline and appraise these different methods of allocation.

Methods of resource allocation in a closed economy

In this section, we consider three methods of resource allocation, assuming for now that there is no international trade: (a) the hypothetical case of the price mechanism under *perfect conditions* – an economy characterised by this method is sometimes referred to as a *pure market economy*; (b) the price mechanism under imperfect conditions, as employed by the *mixed economies* of the western industrialised countries; (c) central planning, as used by the *command economies* of, for example, eastern European countries.

The price mechanism under perfect conditions

With a freely operating price mechanism, the economy's decisions of what, how and for whom to produce are not taken consciously by individual consumers and firms. There is no central authority for fixing prices or setting output targets, so that both prices and output levels are determined by the interaction of the free forces of demand and supply. Firms supply goods and services motivated by their desire for profits, and consumers demand those goods and services which will maximise their utilities.

By the phrase *perfect conditions*, we mean a situation in which there are so many buyers and sellers competing freely with each other in the markets for *homogeneous* goods and services that no individual buyer or seller is in a position to influence any market price by his own actions. Also, there is perfect information, so that a single price can be established for identical goods, and there are no restrictions on the movement of resources between industries or between firms in the same industry. Buyers and sellers are said to be *price takers* in the sense that all prices are market-determined.

Under these (admittedly unrealistic) conditions, *what* to produce is determined by consumers' preferences expressed freely in the market. This power of consumers to determine the allocation of resources in the production of different goods and services has been called *consumer sovereignty*. Consumers make their preferences known to producers through money 'votes'. In fact, there is a sort of general election every day where consumers cast their money 'votes' for the millions of different commodities on the market. Note that this general election, though, is unlike a political election of 'one man, one vote' because a rich man has more money 'votes' than a poor man and so has a bigger say in what is produced.

The decision *how* to produce is determined by competition among firms for the available factors of production whose prices are determined by demand and supply conditions. Profit-maximising firms can only achieve their objective by keeping their costs at a minimum and making use of the most efficient methods of production. This means, for example, that if a change in demand or supply conditions in the labour market should lead to a fall in the price of labour relative to other factors, firms who can do so will adopt more labour-intensive methods of production. It is the demand for and supply of the different factors of production which determine their relative prices and so influence the factor combinations which profit-maximising firms employ.

The decision *for whom* to produce in a market economy is also determined by demand and supply conditions in the factor markets. Households can be thought of as the owners of factors of production, the services of which they sell to firms to earn their incomes. The distribution of these incomes, therefore, depends on the distribution of the ownership of factor services and the prices of the factors. If we take the distribution of the ownership of factors as given, then the distribution of incomes depends on factor prices. The majority of households, of course, own little land and capital, so that the command they have over goods and services depends largely on the wage rate that they can earn by selling labour services. In a market economy under perfect conditions, this wage rate will depend on the demand for and supply of labour. The important topic of the distribution of incomes is taken up in Chapters 15 and 16.

To illustrate the working of the price mechanism under perfect conditions, consider the following simple example. Suppose that goods *X* and *Y* are substitutes for each other and are produced using two factors of production, labour and capital. Suppose further that *X* is a *labour-intensive* good and that *Y* is a *capital-intensive* good. Now let consumers in general suddenly develop an increased preference for good *X* so that the demand for *X* increases and the demand for *Y* correspondingly falls. The effects of these shifts in demand in the markets for the goods are illustrated in Fig. 2 (a) and (b), where the demand curve for *X* (DD_x) shifts to the right to $D'D'_x$ and the

Fig. 2. Interaction between the markets for goods *X* and *Y*.

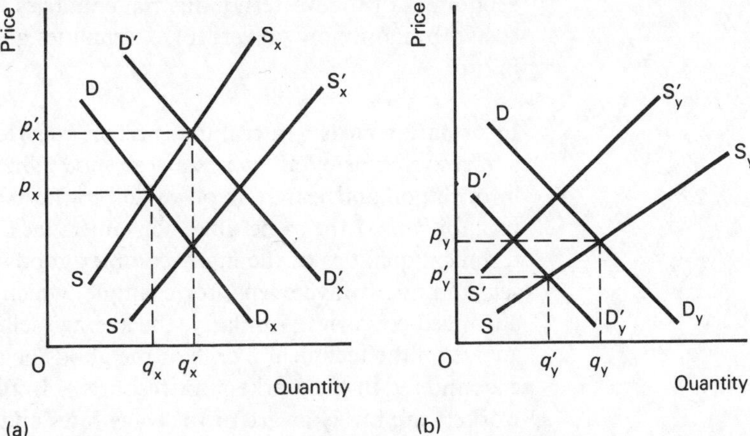

demand curve for *Y* (DD_y) shifts to the left to $D'D'_y$. The supply curves illustrated in Fig. 2 are short-run supply curves. The result in the short-run is that the price of *X* rises from Op_x to Op'_x and the price of *Y* falls from Op_y to Op'_y. These price changes now act as signals to producers. The production of good *X* is seen to be more profitable, so existing producers expand their supplies (from Oq_x to Oq'_x in Fig. 2) and in the long-run new firms are attracted into the industry, causing the supply curve to shift from SS_x to $S'S'_x$. The production of *Y*, though, is seen to be less profitable, so existing firms contract their supplies (from Oq_y to Oq'_y) and some are eventually forced to leave the industry, causing the supply curve to shift from SS_y to $S'S'_y$. It is in this way that the price mechanism automatically responds to changes in consumers' demand to ensure that what is demanded is produced.

In the factor markets, similar automatic forces are at work. The expanding labour-intensive *X*-industry is demanding more labour than is being released by the contracting capital-intensive *Y*-industry. This puts upward pressure on the price of labour. At the same time, more capital is being released by the contracting *Y*-industry than is being demanded by the expanding *X*-industry. This puts downward pressure on the price of capital. Thus, the distribution of income is affected as the owners of labour gain at the expense of the owners of capital. This change in the distribution of income in turn affects the pattern of consumer demand for good *X* and good *Y*. Adjustments continue to take place until all markets are back in equilibrium.

The important point to notice is that the price mechanism under perfect conditions operates automatically. Price changes, the profit motive and the self-interest of consumers all interact to channel resources away from unprofitable lines of production and into the more profitable ones.

The price mechanism under imperfect conditions

The term *imperfect conditions* refers to the frictions or impediments which prevent a free market economy from reaching an otherwise attainable point on its production possibility frontier. There are several types of impediments to perfect allocational efficiency and these are all features of the mixed economies of the western industrial countries. They include: (a) information costs; (b) monopoly power; (c) externalities and public goods. Consider these in turn.

Information costs In real life, perfect knowledge about the prices of goods and resources is by no means a *free good*. There are considerable costs of information and search involved and to the average consumer these may be prohibitive. At the same time, consumers lack information about the technical qualities of the many complex goods and services (cars, television sets and microwave ovens, for example) which are for sale in the industrially advanced countries. Similarly, the average seller is not competent to give advice on the technical merits of the goods he sells. The same problems are encountered in the markets for resources. In the labour market, for example, workers are rarely aware of the wage rates and career prospects in rival firms and industries in the same locality or in the same firms and industries in different localities.

Monopoly power Monopoly power is the ability of a firm to control its prices. It can be achieved through collusion or mergers which give a firm a substantial market share and can be maintained by making it difficult for new rival firms to enter the industry or by differentiating the product through branding, labelling and advertising. Some firms are *natural* monopolies - these occur where the nature of the industry requires a single supplier in order to avoid overlapping and duplication of activities. The supply of water is an example of a natural monopoly, for it would clearly be wasteful to have more than one company supplying water to the same town. Other examples include gas, electricity and telecommunications.

Given the motive to maximise profits, a firm with monopoly power is likely to set price above competitive levels and, as we see in Chapter 10, this will lead to a misallocation of resources. The control of monopoly profit is part of the explanation for government intervention in the price mechanism through legislation and nationalisation, as discussed in Chapter 14.

Externalities and public goods The economic organisation of every human society is characterised by certain social costs (such as pollution and noise) and certain social benefits (such as the panoramic view of a row of beautiful houses) which are not taken into account by firms in determining their price levels. Such social costs and benefits are called *externalities* and their existence means that the price mechanism fails to reflect the true opportunity cost of resources. Externalities are tackled in mixed economies by government measures such as taxes, subsidies and legislation. These are discussed in Chapter 12.

Also, the price mechanism by its very nature is not well-equipped to provide certain types of goods whose benefits cannot be attributed to individual users. These goods are called *public goods*: examples include defence, the police service and roads. Such goods are produced and consumed in great 'lumps' and the users cannot easily be charged through the pricing system. This explains why the state intervenes to provide these types of goods in mixed economies.

Resource allocation in a command economy

A command economy is one in which decisions about production and distribution are taken by a central planning authority (CPA). This CPA is generally made up of a large administrative machinery responsible for issuing directives to factory managers about: (a) what to produce; (b) where to get the supply of resources; (c) what techniques of production to use; (d) where to dispose of the finished product. Thus, the CPA is a centralised decision-making body concerned with allocating resources. This method of allocation is common in eastern European countries and in other socialist countries, such as China and Cuba. Although allocation by a CPA is the most common method in these countries, they cannot be described as *pure* command economies.

In a pure command economy, there would be no place for money and prices. People would most probably be issued with ration cards telling them to which commodities they were entitled and at what distribution centres they could obtain them. Moreover, a pure command economy would be likely to direct labour to occupations and industries decided upon by the CPA. Judging by these criteria, it is clear that the present-day command economies are far from being pure command economies. Like the economies of the western industrialised countries, command economies depend on the use of money for allocational decisions. Hungary, Poland, Yugoslavia and others, for instance, have developed highly sensitive markets designed to mirror consumers' choices more accurately. We can conclude that in practice the CPA allocates resources to a limited degree in response to consumers' choices expressed in these markets.

Advantages and disadvantages of the different methods of resource allocation

The mixed economies of western industrialised countries depend upon the price mechanism as the principal instrument of allocating resources. Several advantages can be claimed for this method of allocation. Consider the following.

Advantages of the price mechanism

Economic efficiency Given that consumers are the best judges of their interests, it can be shown that the price system working under perfect conditions ensures economic efficiency in the sense that no one can be made better off without making someone else worse off. *This important result is demonstrated fully in Chapter 9.* It is argued that the impersonal and sensitive price mechanism fulfils consumers' choices more accurately than central planning.

Freedom of choice Given that firms enjoy freedom of entry into industries, competition amongst firms gives rise to a large number of goods and services being offered for sale. This means that consumers, in seeking to maximise their utilities, have the freedom to choose from a much wider range of goods and services than would be made available in a centrally planned economy.

Automatic bias towards full employment Supporters of free market forces claim that there is an automatic bias towards long-term full employment of society's resources, including manpower. Cyclical unemployment is regarded as merely a short-term phenomenon. This means that a free market economy working under perfect conditions would be pushed to operate on its production possibility frontier.

Sensitivity in international markets In an open economy, free markets become sensitive to changes in the prices of labour, capital and raw materials (such as oil). Thus, before its abandonment in the 1930s, the Gold Standard generated such sensitivity in the export and import markets. In the postwar years, the International Monetary Fund and the newer institution of the European Monetary System have been designed to aid domestic markets to adjust to changes in the prices of internationally traded goods.

Greater incentives to bear risks It is possible that free markets with minimum state intervention will encourage competition and thus stimulate the incentive to take business risks. If this, in turn, leads to a faster rate of technological advance, it may result in a higher rate of economic growth.

Disadvantages of the price mechanism

Critics of the free forces of markets point to the following disadvantages.

Inequalities of income and wealth It is maintained that the pricing system operates in the face of extreme inequalities of income and wealth. As goods and services are produced in response to money 'votes' cast in their favour, scarce resources are diverted to the production of luxuries for the rich who have more money 'votes' before an adequate output of goods for the poor is produced. The pricing system, therefore, ignores the equity objective of resource allocation.

Cyclical unemployment of resources It is claimed that the free market mechanism subjects an economy to cyclical unemployment when production and consumption decisions get out of line. Experience has shown that the total demand for output (in the absence of government intervention) periodically falls short of the total supply of goods. As a result, unsold stocks of goods accumulate forcing producers to cut back on production plans and to lay off workers.

Inflation Experience of the 1970s and 1980s has led many economists to argue that, in spite of government intervention in market economies, the pricing system is prone to severe inflation. Most of the industrialised and less developed countries have experienced persistently rapid rises in prices in their economies. This has in turn led to social and political tensions in many of these countries.

Contrived demand Recall that a result of the operation of the price mechanism under perfect conditions is that the consumer is sovereign. It can be argued, though, that the advertising and sales promotion media which have evolved over the years in western capitalist societies have actually created new wants. Thus, consumers' demand is contrived by advertising and this has resulted in a substantial loss of consumer sovereignty.

Market imperfections As mentioned above, market imperfections (such as information costs, monopoly power, externalities and public goods) are inherent in a price mechanism. With such imperfections, price and output levels are unlikely to satisfy the conditions for economic efficiency.

Advantages of a command economy

Some of the disadvantages of allocation by the price mechanism disappear when allocation decisions are made by a CPA. A CPA is in a better position to match decisions of production with decisions of consumption so that: (a) full employment of resources can more easily be achieved; (b) because the prices of many goods and labour services are fixed, a much lower rate of inflation can be maintained than under the price mechanism; (c) the waste of resources arising from monopoly can be minimised; (d) some externalities can be taken into account when deciding upon the pattern of output; (e) inequalities of income and wealth can be minimised.

In a regime of fixed prices for commodities and resources, it becomes relatively easy to switch resources from one line of production to another in response to changes in consumers' demand, as reflected in shortages and gluts. This is particularly so because the CPA manipulates demand to match its production decisions. This enables the CPA to make adjustments only at the margin in the pattern of production, without resorting to the large-scale closures of production units with widespread redundancies sometimes experienced in market economies.

Disadvantages of a command economy

Several criticisms can be levelled against centralised decision-making as a means of achieving efficiency in resource allocation. Consider the following.

Information costs It is pointed out that the cost of gathering information about *what, how* and *for whom* to produce is likely to be very high as it requires an army of experts in several fields, such as statisticians, engineers, planners and administrators. The collection of sufficient information on the three inter-related decisions is, however, unavoidable given that the objective of a CPA is to achieve efficiency in resource allocation. In contrast, the device of casting money 'votes' under the free market mechanism is a costless source of information, provided that society is prepared to tolerate the existing distribution of income and wealth.

Difficulty of estimating demand Without price signals, it is immensely difficult to estimate the existing and future pattern of demand for goods and services. Consequently, shortages and gluts have been recurring features of command economies.

Lags in the implementation of plans Even if the required information about allocation decisions is collected, the pattern of consumers' preferences and society's composition of resources might well change before production and distribution plans are implemented. There is a time-lag between the collection of information and the formulation of production plans based upon that information. Then, there is a further time-lag between the implementation of production plans and the realisation of production targets.

Possible lack of incentives As we saw above, the price mechanism stimulates incentives to greater effort and to take business risks. In a command economy, with administered prices and wages, workers and managers may lack such motivation.

Restricted choice and dull conformity Because demand is manipulated to match the limited range of goods available on the market, consumers can be said to have restricted choice. Also, the goods produced tend to be standardised with practically no regard for individual tastes.

Resource allocation in less developed countries

In less developed countries, the method of allocation is normally a blend of the price mechanism and central planning. The governments of these countries are typically active interventionists in the markets for both commodities and resources with a view to promoting the objectives of economic growth and development.

The policy instruments employed by the governments of such countries typically include: (a) subsidies to capital and exports; (b) import controls; (c) taxes on labour and capital in selected industries and occupations; (d) rationing of foreign exchange to capital and food imports; (e) price controls on essential foods; (f) licensing of industrial and residential buildings, plant and equipment; (g) land reforms, redistributing the ownership of land and fixing the optimum size of holdings. These policy instruments are a reflection of these countries' dissatisfaction with the unfettered working of the price system. Indeed, certain features of a CPA can be observed from the fact that almost all the less developed countries have comprehensive economic plans where the public sector is assigned a key role in influencing decisions about production and distribution.

Such economic plans assess the availability of total domestic and overseas resources over the plan period (typically, five years). In the light of this information about resources, the plans then set *production targets* and the *strategy* – that is, the way in which the public and private sectors are expected to contribute to the realisation of the plan. A typical development plan of a less developed country reviews the performance, targets and availability of resources in its third year of implementation and, in the light of experience and new information, identifies bottlenecks and revises its expectations accordingly.

Unfortunately, a number of difficulties arise in implementing development plans. In particular, there are great problems of estimating and then acquiring the foreign exchange component of investment expenditures. In the agricultural sector, natural factors, such as droughts and floods, militate against the implementation of production plans. See Chapter 25 for additional comments on the difficulties of implementing economic plans.

Resource allocation in an open economy

Earlier in this chapter, we considered resource allocation within a simple general equilibrium model of a closed economy with only two goods (cloth and food). The preferences of the community were reflected in the community indifference map in Fig. 1 and we saw that the optimum output combination was at the point on the production possibility frontier where the economy was on its highest attainable indifference curve.

In such a closed economy, the community can of course only consume goods produced within the economy – that is to say, it can only consume at points on or inside the production possibility frontier. With an open economy, though, mutually advantageous trade between countries may enable the participating economies to consume combinations of goods to the north-east of their production possibility frontiers. In this section of the chapter, we consider how a freely operating price mechanism can give rise to international trade and thus influence the pattern of the allocation of resources within the countries. We also demonstrate that such trade may be beneficial to those who take part in it.

Clearly, much trade takes place because an economy is better able to produce particular products than its trading partners. A tropical country, for example, is better suited to growing fruits that require a lot of sunshine than a temperate country; similarly, some natural resources are only found in plentiful supplies in certain locations. Japan, for example, has to import oil from Indonesia, the Middle East and other oil-rich areas. A large amount of trade in the world, however, is in goods that could conceivably be produced in either the importing or the exporting country; many countries, in fact, choose to specialise in producing particular products. The case where country A is more efficient than country B at producing, say, cloth and country B is more efficient than country A at producing, say, food is known as *absolute advantage.* It is fairly obvious that if A specialises in cloth production and B in food production, the total production of both goods will increase, giving rise to the possibility of mutually beneficial trade.

But what if country A is more efficient than B at producing all products? David Ricardo in the early nineteenth century developed the theory of *comparative advantage* which showed that it was relative efficiency that was relevant when considering the possibility of gains from trade. So long as the relative costs of production in countries A and B differ, increased specialisation and exchange can potentially benefit both countries. Ricardo's original theory was based on the *labour theory of value,* but was refined in the 1930s by an approach based on opportunity costs developed by Haberler. Consider now an illustration of the theory based on opportunity costs.

The theory of comparative advantage

The theory of comparative advantage demonstrates that trade is potentially beneficial to the welfare of a country if it specialises in the production of those commodities in which it has a comparative advantage. To illustrate the theory by means of a numerical example, consider the two countries, A and B, both of which produce and consume the two goods, food and cloth. Suppose that when both countries use all their resources efficiently to produce food, the corresponding outputs are as follows:

Country A – 100 tonnes
Country B – 200 tonnes

Similarly, suppose that when they use all their resources efficiently to produce cloth, the corresponding outputs are:

Country A – 100 metres
Country B – 100 metres

Assume that both countries face constant opportunity costs of production and have full employment at all times. Assume further that factors of production are perfectly mobile between the cloth and food industries within each country, but immobile between the countries. The *perfect conditions* we had earlier in considering the operation of the price mechanism in a closed economy are assumed to prevail in both countries.

Given the assumption of constant opportunity costs, the two countries' production possibility frontiers will be straight lines. Country A's frontier is shown as line ab in Fig. 3 (a) and country B's frontier is line cd in Fig. 3 (b). To discover whether or not it would pay the countries to specialise in production and to trade with each other, we have to consider each country's opportunity costs of production. Country A can produce either 100 tonnes of food or 100 metres of cloth: the opportunity cost of producing one extra tonne of food is one metre of cloth. Country B can produce either 200 tonnes of food or 100 metres of cloth: in this case, the opportunity cost of producing one extra tonne of food is 0.5 metres of cloth.

We see then that country B can produce food at a lower real cost (that is, in terms of cloth) than country A. *Country B, therefore, is said to have a comparative advantage in food production. Country A, on the other hand, has a comparative advantage in cloth production*: this is so because the opportunity cost of an additional metre of cloth in country A is 1 tonne of food, whilst in country B the opportunity cost of a metre of cloth is 2 tonnes of food. Under *perfect conditions*, 1 metre of cloth will exchange for 1 tonne of food in country A and for 2 tonnes of food in country B. These exchange ratios represent the pre-trade relative prices of the two goods in the two

Fig. 3. The gains resulting from trade between two countries.

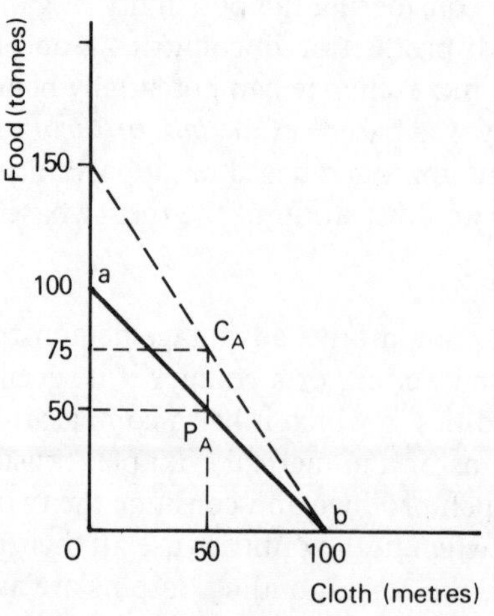

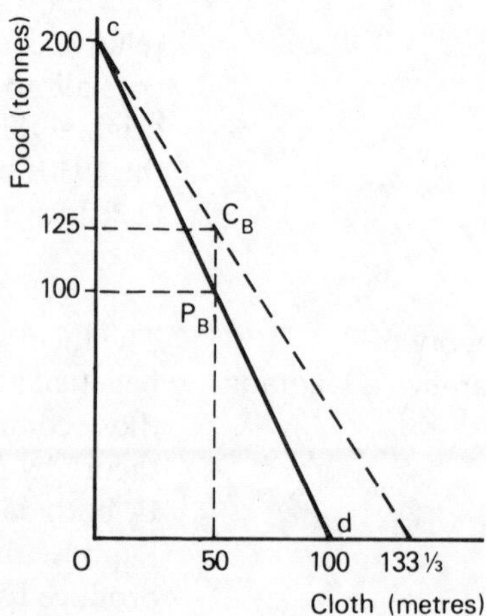

countries. Both countries can potentially gain if they specialise along the lines of their respective comparative advantages and then trade with each other.

To illustrate this, suppose that before any trade takes place, both countries divide their resources equally between food and cloth production. The resulting outputs are as follows:

	Pre-trade output and consumption	
	Food (tonnes)	Cloth (metres)
Country A	50	50
Country B	100	50
World total	150	100

In the pre-trade situation, of course, each country's consumption coincides with its production. If each country exists in isolation, the rate at which it can substitute one product for another is fixed by technology and is represented by the slope of its production possibility frontier.

Suppose now, though, that the possibility of trade is introduced. If a mutually acceptable exchange rate is agreed upon, each country will be able to substitute one commodity for another at a more favourable rate. The international terms of trade will, in fact, be determined through the interaction of international demand and supply. In the absence of knowledge about the scales of preferences in the two countries, we can only say that 1 tonne of food will exchange for something between 0.5 and 1 metre of cloth. This must be so because at an exchange rate of 1 tonne for 0.5 of a metre, country B would have no incentive to trade as it could obtain extra cloth at this rate domestically. Similarly, at an exchange rate of 1 tonne for 1 metre, country A would have no incentive to trade. It follows that country A would prefer the terms of trade to be close to 1 tonne for 0.5 of a metre, whilst country B would prefer them to be close to 1 tonne for 1 metre.

To show that both countries can benefit from specialisation and trade, suppose that competitive forces between the two countries establish the international terms of trade at 1 tonne of food for $\frac{2}{3}$ of a metre of cloth. If both countries specialise completely in the production of the good in which they have a comparative advantage, their outputs will be as follows:

	Production after specialisation	
	Food (tonnes)	Cloth (metres)
Country A	0	100
Country B	200	0
World total	200	100

Notice that the total world production of food has increased with cloth production remaining unchanged. One possible post-trade position might involve country A in exporting 50 metres of cloth in return for imports of 75 tonnes of food. The post-trade consumption pattern will be as follows:

	Post-trade consumption	
	Food (tonnes)	Cloth (metres)
Country A	75	50
Country B	125	50
World total	200	100

Compared with their pre-trade consumption, both countries are consuming 25 extra tonnes of food and no less cloth. *Specialisation and exchange have unambiguously benefited both countries.*

In terms of Fig. 3, before trade, country A is consuming at point P_A and country B is consuming at point P_B, both points being on the production possibility frontiers. After trade, country A is able to reach point C_A and country B is able to reach point C_B – notice that both of these points are outside the countries' respective production possibility frontiers. If we were, in addition, to draw the two countries' community indifference maps on the graphs, it would be clear that international trade can enable both countries to reach indifference curves which without trade would be unattainable. International trade can, therefore, increase social welfare.

The theory of comparative advantage developed by Ricardo took as its starting-point the assumption that different countries had different production costs for the same good. It is logical now to ask what lies behind these cost differences.

The *Heckscher-Ohlin theorem* (named after the Swedish economists, Eli Heckscher and Bertil Ohlin) attributes these cost differences to differences in factor endowments between countries. A country with an abundance of natural resources and agricultural land can be described as land-abundant and may be expected to have a comparative cost advantage in the production of commodities which are land-intensive. Conversely, a country with an abundant labour force may be expected to have a comparative cost advantage in goods whose production uses labour intensively. Thus, the theorem predicts that a country will tend to export those goods which are intensive in the country's relatively abundant factor and import those goods which are intensive in the country's relatively scarce factor.

Trade resulting from technological change

In recent years, increasing attention has been paid to the importance of technological progress in the generation of international trade. A country which makes a technological breakthrough and develops a new product will have a temporary monopoly in its production. If a demand for the new product exists (or is developed) in other countries, trade is likely to result. This trade is sometimes described as *technological gap* trade, referring to the time-lag or gap before other countries start to produce the new good with equal efficiency. Some empirical evidence does indicate that those American industries with a high level of 'research and development' effort (such as aerospace and electronics) do have an export performance significantly above average.

In addition, R. Vernon has developed a 'product-cycle' model which describes the development of, in particular, labour-saving products which meet demands in countries with high *per capita* incomes. He argues that initially production of the new product will take place in the country for whose market it is intended. When the product is being developed, producers require continuous feedback from consumers and need good communications with numerous suppliers. Later, though, when the product becomes standardised, other countries may offer comparative cost advantages so that gradually production shifts to these countries. It is possible that exports back to the country which originally developed the product will then occur.

Conclusion

In this chapter, we have considered the problem of resource allocation in the context of both domestic and international economies. As far as domestic economies are concerned, we outlined three methods of resource allocation: the price mechanism under perfect conditions, the price mechanism under imperfect conditions and central planning. We presented some of the advantages and disadvantages of planned and market economies, pointing out that all modern economies exhibit characteristics from both. As for the international economy, we concentrated on explaining how a freely operating price mechanism can give rise to trade which will be beneficial to the participating countries in the sense that it will potentially increase their social welfare.

Throughout the chapter, we have been concerned to emphasise that all methods of allocation have as their aim social welfare maximisation. It is time now, therefore, to consider the topic of 'welfare economics' in greater depth.

Further reading

George, K.D. and **Shorey, J.** *The Allocation of Resources,* Allen and Unwin, London, 1978 (Ch. 2).

Baumol, W.J., *Economic Theory and Operations Analysis,* Prentice Hall, New Jersey, 1977 (Ch. 21).

Wagner, L. and **Baltazzis, N.** (eds), *Readings in Applied Microeconomics,* Oxford University Press, 1973 (Ch. 1 and 4).

Haveman, R., *The Economics of the Public Sector,* John Wiley, Santa Barbara, 1976 (Ch. 2 and 3).

Exercises

1. Review your understanding of the following terms:

general equilibrium	money 'votes'
community indifference map	theory of comparative advantage
allocation decisions	terms of trade
price mechanism	factor endowments
market economy	factor intensity
central planning	Heckscher-Ohlin theorem

command economy
mixed economy
consumer sovereignty
product cycle
technological gap

2. 'The price mechanism operating under perfectly free conditions allocates resources to the production of those goods and services for which consumers have expressed their preferences through money votes in the market place.' Explain and criticise this statement.

3. Outline the circumstances under which you think government intervention in the working of the pricing system can be justified in: (a) an industrially advanced country; (b) a less developed country.

4. 'It is the method of allocation rather than the nature of allocation decisions that distinguishes command economies from the mixed economies of western industrialised countries.' Do you agree?

5. Assess the achievements and failures of the allocation methods of the USA and the USSR since the Second World War.

6. Superimpose community indifference curves on the graphs in Fig. 3 (a) and (b) to show that trade has increased social welfare in both countries.

7. Consider two countries, A and B, which produce and consume two goods, X and Y. Assume that both countries face constant opportunity costs and operate under the perfect conditions described in this chapter. Suppose that when both countries use all their resources efficiently to produce X, the resulting outputs are:

Country A: 1,000 units
Country B: 1,000 units.

When they use all their resources to produce Y, the resulting outputs are:

Country A: 600 units
Country B: 200 units.

(a) Draw the countries' production possibility frontiers.
(b) Explain which country has a comparative advantage in X and which has a comparative advantage in Y.
(c) Choose a plausible international terms of trade and use your diagrams to show how specialisation and trade between the two countries can be mutually beneficial.

8 Introduction to welfare economics

Introduction

Welfare economics has grown in recent years into a complex body of analysis. It is our intention in this chapter to introduce the reader to the subject in as simple a way as possible and, later in the book, to show how welfare economics may be applied in the theory of the firm, in the analysis of the public sector and in the theory of distribution.

We saw in the last chapter and to some extent in Chapter 1 that economic systems, in whatever way they are organised, all face the same problem of resource allocation, and we examined the different ways in which the free market economies and the planned economies tackle this problem. This chapter is concerned not with the actual methods of allocation, but with identifying those allocations which are *efficient* and *equitable* and determining that allocation which maximises social welfare.

First, then, we must decide what is meant by *social welfare*. It can be thought of as being synonymous with the level of satisfaction or utility enjoyed by the members of society. It includes, therefore, a variety of objective and subjective factors. In Chapter 1, we pointed out that it has two main aspects – economic efficiency and equity. A given allocation can be said to be *economically efficient* in the Pareto sense when no re-allocation is possible which makes anyone better off without making someone else worse off. In addition, an allocation can be said to be *equitable* when it is associated with a 'fair' distribution of income and wealth. Clearly, there is a good deal more subjectivity in equity than in efficiency considerations.

A *social welfare function* is a statement of the factors which determine social welfare (SW) and must at least include the total quantity of goods and services produced (Q) and some measure of the way in which these goods and services are distributed (D). Such a function might also include factors such as the health of the community (H), the amount of leisure time (L), the degree of environmental pollution (P), political stability (S) and even the quantity of rainfall (R). Thus, letting Z denote other relevant factors, we could write:

$$\text{SW} = f(Q, D, H, L, P, S, R, Z).$$

Alternatively, we could suppose that the welfare of society as a whole depends on the welfare or utilities of the individuals who make up society – in which case, we could write:

$$\text{SW} = f(U_1, U_2, \ldots, U_N)$$

where $U_1, U_2, \ldots, U_N$ are the utilities of the N individuals who make up a society.

Unfortunately, writing the social welfare function in either of these forms does not enable us to determine whether any specific change in the economy which makes some people better off and others worse off will increase or decrease social welfare. It is the purpose of this chapter to move us a step closer to being able to make such judgements. First, we consider economic efficiency in the Pareto sense and derive the conditions necessary for Pareto optimality in the context of a very simple model. Secondly, we consider some equity criteria for judging welfare. Thirdly, we examine the possible conflict which can arise between efficiency and equity and, finally, consider the use of 'compensation tests' and 'cost-benefit' analysis to reconcile this conflict.

Economic efficiency

It has been stated a number of times in this book that economic efficiency in the Pareto sense can be said to exist when it is not possible to change the allocation of resources in any way which makes someone better off without at the same time making someone else worse off. In Chapter 1, we explained the implications of this in greater detail, pointing out that in *production*, it must be impossible to increase the output of one good without reducing the output of any other and in exchange, it must be impossible to increase the consumption of one household without reducing the consumption of some other.

For this state of Pareto efficiency or *Pareto optimality* to be achieved, there are three main requirements.

(a) *Efficiency in production.* This means that the economy must be employing all of its factors of production in efficient combinations so that it is on and not inside its production possibility frontier.

(b) *Efficiency in exchange.* This means that it must be impossible to reallocate a given stock of goods and services in such a way that benefits someone without at the same time harming someone else.

(c) *Efficient output mix.* This means that it must be impossible to change the actual combination of goods and services produced in such a way that will benefit someone without harming someone else.

In order to derive the main conditions for Pareto optimality, consider these three requirements in the context of a very simple model. To set up the model, the following assumptions are made.

(a) The economy is a barter economy where one good is simply exchanged for another and there is no international trade.
(b) There are only two goods, food and cloth.
(c) There are only two factors of production, capital and labour, which are fixed in supply.
(d) There are only two people, A and B, making up the society.

This model with its two goods, two factors and two individuals is sometimes called a 2 × 2 × 2 model. Obviously, it is highly unrealistic. It does, however, enable us to derive results which can be generalised to more realistic situations and it has the advantage that it can be analysed using graphs. Consider now the above three requirements for Pareto optimality in turn.

Efficiency in production

Recall that our simplified economy has fixed supplies of the two factors of production. Suppose that the total supply of labour is fixed at *OL* units per time period; this is said to be the country's *total endowment* of labour. Suppose further that the country's total endowment of capital is equal to *OK* units. These endowments are indicated on the axes of the graphs in Fig. 1. Fig. 1 (a) shows the isoquant map illustrating the production function for food and Fig. 1 (b) shows the isoquant map illustrating the production function for cloth. Since the production function for food is unlikely to be the same as the production function for cloth, the isoquant map for food (of which F_1, F_2, and F_3 are representative isoquants) is not likely to have the same shape as the isoquant map for cloth (of which C_1, C_2 and C_3 are representative isoquants).

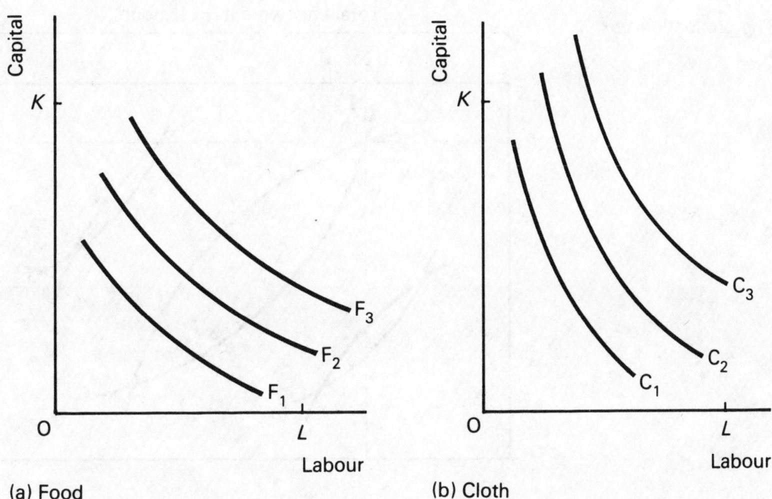

Fig. 1. Isoquant maps for food and cloth.

Suppose now that we turn upside down the graph showing the cloth isoquant map (Fig. 1 (b)), so that it looks like Fig. 2. Notice that Fig. 2 shows exactly the same information as Fig. 1 (b).

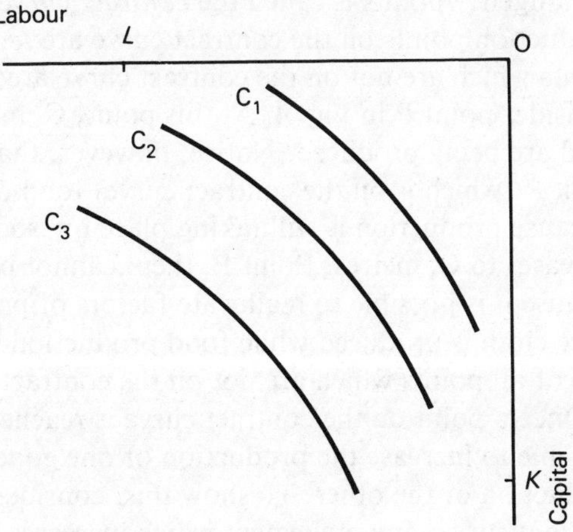

Fig. 2. The cloth isoquant map upside down.

Suppose further that we join the axes of the graphs in Fig. 2 and Fig. 1 (a) together so that they form a box, as shown in Fig. 3. This is the country's *Edgeworth-Bowley box diagram in production* (named after F. Edgeworth and A. Bowley). The food isoquant map is measured from the origin labelled O_F and the cloth isoquant is measured from the origin labelled O_C. The dimensions of the box are the country's factor endowments.

Any point in the box is a possible production point. Consider, for example, point P: if production takes place at this point, O_FK_1 units of capital and O_FL_1 units of labour are being used by food producers to produce F_2 tonnes of food and O_CK_2 units of capital and O_CL_2 units of labour are being used by cloth producers to produce C_2 metres of cloth. Although point P is a possible production point, we demonstrate shortly that it is not an efficient point.

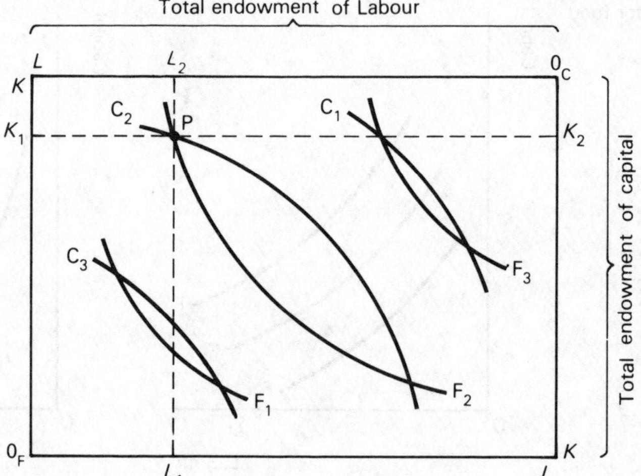

Fig. 3. The production box diagram.

Since the food isoquants in the box diagram are convex to the origin O_F and the cloth isoquants are convex to O_C, there must exist an infinite number of points at which food isoquants are tangent to cloth isoquants. We are particularly interested in these tangency points and three of them (labelled S, R and T) are illustrated in Fig. 4. The curve, $O_F\,O_C$, which joins together all the tangency points is called the *contract curve* and we can show that all the production points on the contract curve are *technically efficient*, whereas all points which are not on the contract curve are *technically inefficient*. Consider point P in Fig. 4. At this point, C_2 metres of cloth and F_2 tonnes of food are being produced. Notice, however, that by moving from point P to point R (which is on the contract curve) food output remains unchanged (because production is still taking place on isoquant F_2), but cloth output increases to C_3 metres. Point P, then, cannot be an efficient production point because it is possible to reallocate factors of production in such a way that more cloth is produced while food production remains unchanged. This is true of all points which are not on the contract curve.

Once a point on the contract curve is reached, however, it is no longer possible to increase the production of one good without reducing the production of the other. To show this, consider point R which is on the contract curve: any movement which increases food production (say, to point

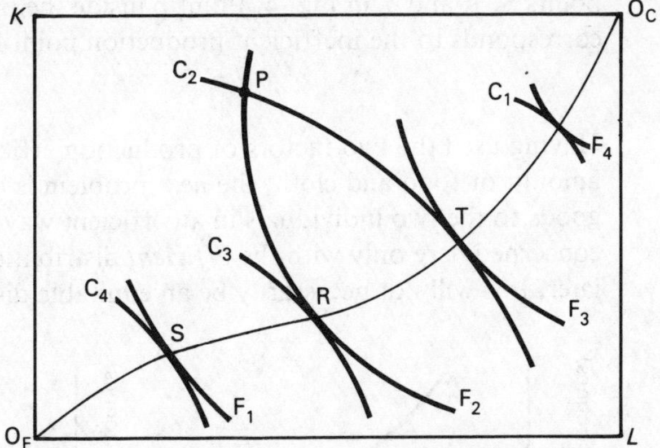

Fig. 4. The production box diagram and contract curve.

T) has the effect of reducing cloth production, and any movement which increases cloth production (say, to point S) has the effect of reducing food production.

The contract curve joins together all the points of tangency of food isoquants with cloth isoquants and all these points are technically efficient. Recall from Chapter 2 that the slope of an isoquant is equal to the *marginal rate of technical substitution* of capital for labour ($MRTS_{KL}$). It follows that *for efficiency in production, the $MRTS_{KL}$ in food production must be equal to the $MRTS_{KL}$ in cloth production.* More formally, we can write that, for efficiency in production, we require that:

$$(MRTS_{KL})_{food} = (MRTS_{KL})_{cloth} \qquad [1]$$

When this condition is not satisfied, it is possible to reallocate resources in such a way that more of at least one of the goods can be produced without having to reduce the output of either of the goods.

We should note at this point the relationship between the contract curve and the production possibility frontier (the graphical technique introduced in Chapter 1). Points on the contract curve can only be reached when the country is using all of its resources efficiently. It follows that these points must correspond to the points on the country's production possibility frontier. This is illustrated in Fig. 5, where points s, r and t correspond to the

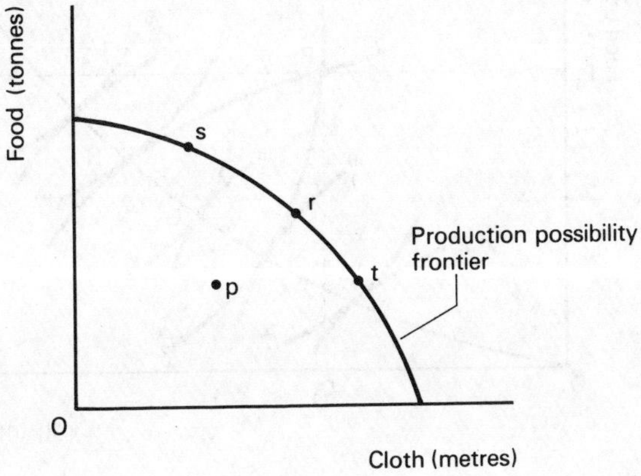

Fig. 5. The production possibility frontier.

points S, R and T in Fig. 4. Point p inside the production possibility frontier corresponds to the inefficient production point P in the box diagram.

Efficiency in exchange

Having used the two factors of production efficiently to produce a given amount of food and cloth, the next problem is how to distribute the two goods to the two individuals in an efficient way. Notice that we are concerned here only with the *efficient* distribution of the goods – as we show later, this will not necessarily be an equitable distribution.

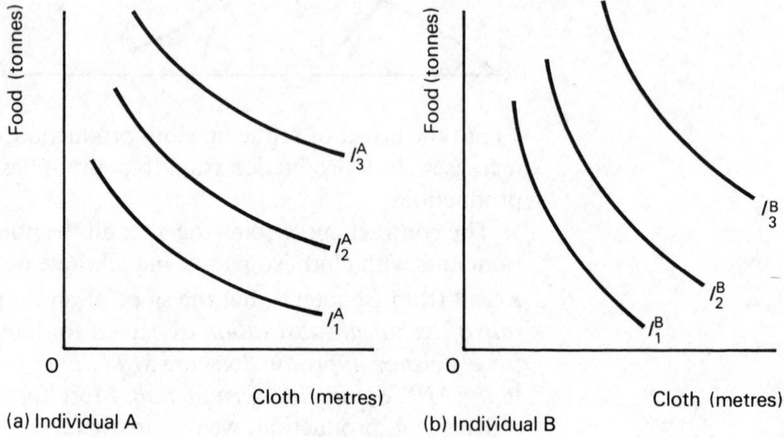

Fig. 6. The indifference maps for individuals A and B.

To derive a condition for efficiency in exchange, consider Fig. 6 (a) and (b) which shows the two individuals' indifference maps for the two goods. Since A and B are likely to have different preferences, the indifference maps have different shapes. As with the isoquant maps in the previous section, we can invert one of the indifference maps (in this case, B's) and join it on to the other one so that they form a box, as in Fig. 7. This is the *box diagram in exchange*. A's indifference map is measured from the origin labelled O_A and

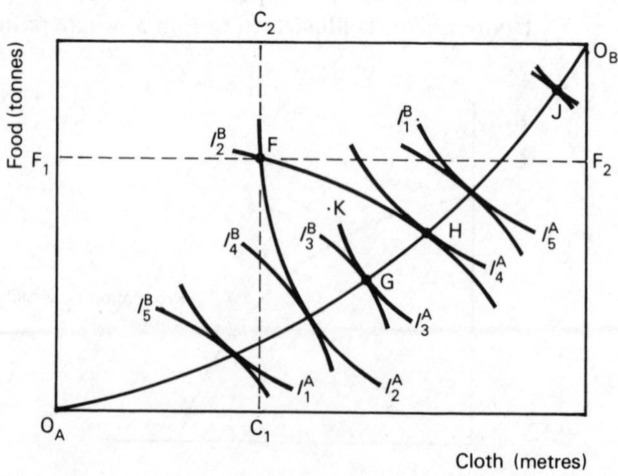

Fig. 7. The exchange box diagram.

B's is measured from the origin labelled O_B. The dimensions of the box are the quantities of food and cloth which the country has produced.

Any point in the box represents a possible allocation of the two goods to the two individuals. Consider, for example, point F. At this point, A consumes O_AF_1 tonnes of food and O_AC_1 metres of cloth, and B consumes O_BF_2 tonnes of food and O_BC_2 metres of cloth. Point F is inefficient because it is possible to move to another point, like G, in such a way that both individuals are made better off (that is, reach higher indifference curves) or at least to move to a point, like H, where A is better off and B no worse off.

As in the production box diagram, all the efficient points lie along a *contract curve* which this time joins together all the points of tangency between A's indifference curves and B's indifference curves. Once a point on the contract curve is reached, it is no longer possible to move to any other point without making at least one of the individuals worse off. As we showed in Chapter 4, the slope of an indifference curve is the *marginal rate of substitution* of one good for another (in this case, food for cloth). It follows that *for efficiency in exchange, the marginal rate of substitution of food for cloth (MRS_{fc}) for individual A must be equal to the MRS_{fc} for individual B.* More formally, we can write the condition for efficiency in exchange as:

$$(MRS_{fc})_A = (MRS_{fc})_B \qquad [2]$$

When this condition is not satisfied, it is possible to reallocate the two goods to the two individuals in such a way that at least one of them is made better off without making the other worse off.

Efficient output mix

When conditions (1) and (2) are satisfied, the economy will be producing at a point on its production possibility frontier and the two goods will be allocated to the two individuals in an efficient way. All the points on the production possibility frontier are efficient from a production point of view but they are not all equally efficient as far as the two consumers are concerned. For example, if both A and B prefer food to cloth, a movement along the production possibility frontier which increases food production at the expense of cloth production may make both consumers better off. The problem is to determine the point on the production possibility frontier from which it is impossible to move without making at least one individual worse off. It is found where the MRS_{fc} (equal for both individuals) is just equal to the *marginal rate of transformation* (MRT_{fc}). Recall from Chapter 1 that the MRT is the name given to the slope of the production possibility frontier. Formally, the condition for an efficient output mix can be written as follows:

$$MRS_{fc} = MRT_{fc} \qquad [3]$$

To show this, consider a simple numerical example where they are not equal. Suppose that the MRT is equal to $\frac{1}{4}$ and that the MRS_{fc} is equal to $\frac{1}{8}$ for both individuals. An MRT_{fc} equal to $\frac{1}{4}$ means that if 1 metre of cloth is sacrificed, an additional $\frac{1}{4}$ tonne of food can be produced. An MRS_{fc} equal to $\frac{1}{8}$ means that 1 metre of cloth can be taken from either individual and substituted for by $\frac{1}{8}$ tonne of food, leaving the individual at the same level of utility. Suppose, then, that 1 metre of cloth is sacrificed in production and an additional $\frac{1}{4}$ tonne of food is produced. Both individuals can now be made better off. For example, A will stay at the same level of utility if he gives up the metre of cloth in exchange for $\frac{1}{8}$ tonne of food. But an additional $\frac{1}{4}$ tonne of food has been produced, so the extra $\frac{1}{8}$ tonne can be allocated to the two individuals, raising them both on to higher indifference curves. This kind of reallocation is possible whenever MRT $\neq$ MRS. Only when MRT = MRS is no such reallocation possible.

Summary

We can say that in our very simple model the three conditions for economic efficiency in the Pareto sense are that:

(a) *the MRTS of one factor of production for another should be equal for all goods;*
(b) *the MRS for every pair of goods should be equal for all individuals;*
(c) *the common MRS should be equal to the MRT for all pairs of goods.*

We show in Chapter 9 that a perfectly competitive economy with no externalities (that is, one operating under the perfect conditions described in Chapter 7) satisfies the above three conditions for Pareto optimality.

A very important point to note at this stage, however, is that the satisfaction of these three conditions does not *necessarily* maximise social welfare. This is because no account is taken of equity considerations to which we now turn our attention.

Equity

The concept of equity is concerned with the allocation question of 'for whom to produce' and so belongs to normative rather than positive economics. This is because decisions about how the national income and national wealth *should be* shared out among the different members of society are necessarily based on value judgements. One can only argue subjectively about the existence of a '*socially desirable*' distribution of income and wealth and economists are as good as (though not necessarily better than) anyone else when it comes to making moral judgements concerned with equity. Indeed, it is true to say that there are no real experts on equity in society.

It follows that if the economist ignored equity considerations when giving his expert advice on economic policy, he may give the impression that he regarded economic efficiency as a more important criterion of social welfare than equity. Besides, there is a real danger that his advice on efficiency would be given greater weight by the policy-maker than society's vague views about the equitable distribution of income and wealth.

It has, therefore, become increasingly acceptable for the economist to judge social welfare in terms of both efficiency and equity. Clearly, most of his recommendations in the fields of international trade, taxation, government spending, industry and so on are bound to affect the distribution of welfare between individuals and different income groups. This means that the economist should have a sense of 'fairness' and 'economic justice'.

Equity criteria

In order to analyse welfare in terms of equity, it is necessary to develop some criteria for judging an equitable distribution of income and wealth. The following criteria have been suggested:

Egalitarian criteria These criteria stem from a belief in the equal worth of every human being in society. Thus, an egalitarian society is one which cares equally about every member.

Consider once again our simple economy with two individuals, A and B, and suppose that all income (say, £10,000) is earned by A while B is a sick man with no income. To ensure absolute equality, a 50 per cent tax rate would have to be imposed on A's income and the entire tax revenue transferred to B. Unfortunately, such a high tax rate may adversely affect A's willingness to work and so reduce total income (say, to £6,000). A lower rate of tax with less adverse effects on incentives to work would result in a larger total income for society (that is, more for both A and B). It follows that in order to maximise B's income, egalitarian criteria necessitates taking into account the effects that income transfers have on people's willingness to work, save and take business risks.

Egalitarian criteria may be criticised on the grounds that they assume that all individuals in a society have an equal capacity to enjoy. Utility, though, is a subjective concept and individuals may well differ in their abilities to experience satisfaction from a given amount of income. Furthermore, there are severe difficulties in measuring individual utilities and in adding up the utilities of individuals so as to be able to say whether society's welfare is greater in one situation than in another.

To overcome these difficulties, some economists have suggested a *social evaluation* approach. According to this, the total cost and benefit to society of a policy decision has to be estimated. As long as the social cost is less than the social benefit, the policy will increase society's welfare. This explains the growing importance of the cost-benefit approach to decisions in the public sector (see below, page 127).

'Social conscience' criteria These criteria are based upon the idea of the interdependence of individuals' utilities. A rich man's welfare may not only be dependent upon his own collection of goods and services but also upon the amount of goods and services available to a poor man. In other words, the rich man may have a 'social conscience' so that, once he has attained a certain level of welfare, he may enhance his own welfare by giving voluntarily to the less well off.

It follows that not all taxes are necessarily involuntary payments. A rich man might voluntarily contribute towards government programmes intended to reduce poverty levels. This helps to explain the existence of contributions to charities. According to these criteria, the 'social conscience' must be taken into account in determining whether or not a given distribution of income or wealth is equitable.

Raising the welfare of the lower income groups In this case, equity is judged by taking into account the relative share of the 'lower' income groups in the national income. Consequently, poverty levels have to be defined and the family incomes of those living below the poverty line have to be raised.

These criteria involve weights being assigned to the welfare of different income groups – it is by no means obvious how these weights could be devised.

Inter-generation equity criteria It is becoming increasingly realised that decisions about what and how to produce by one generation may affect, adversely or favourably, the welfare of future generations. When, for example, the present generation expedites the exploitation of irreplaceable natural resources and causes the destruction of part of the environment, this results in a loss of welfare for future generations. On the other hand, the future generation may experience a gain in welfare if they are bequeathed advances in science and technology and an accumulated stock of capital. An application of inter-generation equity criteria means taking into account temporal changes in the distribution of income and wealth.

Conflict between efficiency and equity

It is clear from the foregoing discussion that applying policies based on equity criteria means making some people better off and others worse off. Earlier in this chapter, however, we observed that judging society's welfare by efficiency criteria alone means dodging all questions of equity – efficiency criteria cannot be applied to a situation where a policy change benefits some people and harms others. It is nearly always the case that policy measures involve value judgements and thus some kind of interpersonal comparisons of welfare. It is impossible, therefore, to judge them on the basis of efficiency criteria alone because these dispense with both value judgements and interpersonal comparisons.

To illustrate the possible conflict between efficiency and equity, reconsider Fig. 7 which shows the exchange box diagram. All the points on the contract curve are efficient in the Pareto sense; they cannot all be described as equitable, however. At point J, for example, individual A has a very large quantity of both cloth and food while individual B has hardly any. It is impossible to make B any better off without making A worse off and so J is an efficient point, but it is still highly inequitable. Now consider point K: this is an inefficient point (off the contract curve) but, being in the centre of the box, represents a perfectly equal distribution of the two goods to the two individuals.

In practical terms, consider the following two examples of the conflict between efficiency and equity: (a) protecting jobs in the British Steel Corporation may be equitable but it is undoubtedly inefficient to prevent the movement of labour and capital from a declining industry into growing industries; (b) maintaining artificially high prices for farm products and thus higher welfare of the Common Market farmers may be equitable but such a policy is at the expense of the Community's taxpayers and it is inefficient to prevent the movement of labour and capital from agriculture to manufacturing industries.

Reconciling the conflict One way of reconciling the conflict between efficiency and equity is to choose from all the Pareto efficient points that one which is regarded as the most equitable and then attempt to reach it through

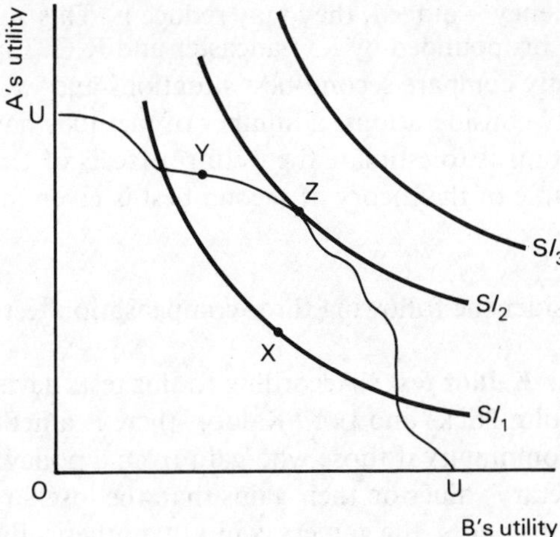

Fig. 8. The maximisation of social welfare.

redistribution policies. To illustrate this theoretically, consider Fig. 8 where the vertical axis measures A's utility and the horizontal axis measures B's utility. The curve UU is called the community's 'grand utility frontier' – every point on it is Pareto efficient (that is, all three marginal conditions are satisfied at every point). The 'grand utility frontier' shows all those combinations of utilities which can be attained when resource allocation is Pareto optimal – notice that since utility is assumed only to be ordinally measurable, the frontier cannot be drawn on a smooth curve. How can we decide which point is the most equitable and so maximise social welfare? One way is to return to the concept of a social welfare function in which the welfare of society depends on the utilities of the individuals, A and B. Such a function can be represented on the graph by a set of *social* indifference curves, three of which (SI_1 SI_2 and SI_3) are shown in Fig. 8. The one point on the grand utility frontier which maximises social welfare (that is, puts the community on its highest social indifference curve) is point Z, sometimes called a 'bliss point'.

The difficulty is how to reach point Z. Suppose that initially the community is at point Y. The imposition of taxes to change the distribution of income in an attempt to reach point Z may create an unwillingness to work hard and so reduce efficiency. It may, therefore, only be possible to reach a point like X, inside the grand utility frontier. In other words, there is likely to be a trade-off between efficiency and equity which makes point Z unattainable.

Changes in social welfare

The world is imperfect. The production, consumption and distribution of goods and services are neither efficient nor (most people believe) equitable. How, then, can we determine whether any given policy change will increase or decrease social welfare? Clearly, any change which causes all the marginal conditions for Pareto optimality to be satisfied will increase economic efficiency. Unfortunately, changes which cause only some and not all the marginal conditions to be satisfied do not necessarily improve efficiency – indeed, they may reduce it. This is the so-called *theory of second best,* propounded by K. Lancaster and R.G. Lipsey in 1957. Since we cannot directly compare second-best situations and we also want to take account of equity considerations, a number of methods have been devised to enable economists to estimate the welfare effects of changes in the economy. An example of the theory of second best is given in Chapter 12.

Compensation tests

Consider the following three compensation tests:

Hicks-Kaldor test According to this test, devised by the British economists Sir John Hicks and Lord Kaldor, there is a net improvement in the welfare of the community if those who gain from a policy measure place higher monetary values on their gains than the losers place on their losses. In these circumstances, the gainers could (hypothetically) compensate the losers and still have some gain left over. Note that this is a test of a potential improvement in welfare since compensation is rarely paid. A major criticism of this test is that it ignores equity considerations. If the test is satisfied, but the policy change affects the distribution of income in such a way that the rich become richer and the poor poorer, then overall there may be a decrease rather than an increase in social welfare.

The Scitovsky double test Tibor Scitovsky pointed out that where compensation is not actually paid, it is sometimes possible for the losers to 'bribe' the gainers to abandon the proposed change. This suggests that the change from the initial situation A to the new situation B and the reverse change from B to A would *both* satisfy the Hicks-Kaldor test. To cover this possibility, Scitovsky suggested a two-part test for a welfare improvement:

(a) confirm that the proposed change satisfies the Hicks-Kaldor test;
(b) confirm that the return to the initial position would *not* also satisfy the Hicks-Kaldor test. Notice that both sets of tests operate on an implicit value judgement and assume no actual payment of compensation. If compensation were paid, there would be a welfare improvement in the Pareto sense.

Little's test I.M.D. Little, in his book *A Critique of Welfare Economics* in 1957, pointed out several theoretical and practical shortcomings in the above two compensation tests. He thus devised the following stricter tests: first, apply the Hicks-Kaldor and Scitovsky tests; secondly, check that the policy proposal does not adversely affect the distribution of income of wealth. By arguing that explicit value judgements should be attached to what happens to the distribution of income following a change in policy, Little incorporated equity considerations into the social welfare function.

In practice, though, not all policy prescriptions have taken income distribution considerations explicitly into account. Instead, economists have frequently reverted to the Hicks-Kaldor test.

Cost-benefit analysis

This can be regarded as the practical illustration of the uses and limitations of compensation tests. As a technique, cost-benefit analysis is widely applied to public expenditure policies (for example, in transport, education, health and defence).

The underlying principle of the technique is to maximise social benefits in relation to social costs, both usually expressed in a common monetary unit. Social benefits include all those effects of a policy change that increase social welfare and social costs those that reduce social welfare. An increase in net social welfare can be written as equal to gross social benefits minus gross social costs.

Note that cost-benefit analysis involves the enumeration and monetary evaluation of the social costs and benefits associated with a public project. The streams of costs and benefits are generally unevenly spread over the life-time of the project; major costs are incurred almost immediately but benefits are more likely to accrue in the future. This necessitates computing *present values* by discounting the future streams of costs and benefits at a chosen rate of interest. The values obtained can then be expressed as a benefit-cost ratio: for example, discounted social benefits of £10 million and discounted social costs of £8 million would yield a benefit-cost ratio of 10/8 or 1.25. All those projects which have a ratio greater than 1 will result in a net increase in social welfare. For now, we leave a more detailed treatment of cost-benefit analysis until Chapter 12.

Conclusion

This chapter has discussed the complex factors on which social welfare depends. We have seen that for economic efficiency in the Pareto sense, certain marginal conditions must be met. However, social welfare maximisation also depends on equity considerations. But the simultaneous achievement of efficiency and equity poses problems in practice.

Further reading

Baumol, W.J., *Economic Theory and Operations Analysis*, Prentice Hall, New Jersey, 1977 (Ch. 21).

Koplin, H.T., *Microeconomic Analysis*, Harper and Row, New York, 1971 (Ch. 20 and 21).

Musgrave, R.A. and **Musgrave, P.B.,** *Public Finance in Theory and Practice*, McGraw Hill, New York, 1976 (Ch. 3 and 4).

Price, C.M., *Welfare Economics in Theory and Practice*, Macmillan, London, 1977.

Exercises

1. Review your understanding of the following terms:

social welfare function	egalitarian criteria
Pareto optimality	social conscience criteria
efficiency in production	inter-generation equity criteria

efficiency in exchange	social indifference curve
efficient output mix	'bliss point'
Edgeworth-Bowley box diagram	theory of second best
contract curve	Hicks-Kaldor test
marginal rate of technical substitution	Scitovsky double test
marginal rate of substitution	Little's test
marginal rate of transformation	cost-benefit analysis
equity	

2. Consider a country producing two goods (bread and ale), with two factors of production (labour and capital) and two individuals (Adam and Eve). Draw the box diagrams in production and exchange, showing clearly the contract curves. Explain why points off the contract curves fail to satisfy the marginal conditions (a) and (b) derived in this chapter. Suppose that the MRT of bread into ale is equal to 2 and that the common MRS of ale for bread is equal to 4. Suggest a reallocation which will make both Adam and Eve better off.

3. 'Pareto efficiency and equity are conflicting objectives.' What welfare policy could be used in the attempt to reconcile these conflicting objectives?

4. 'The rapid depletion of the Earth's natural resources by the present generation means that less is available for future generations.' Discuss this statement in terms of equity criteria. Comment on the applicability of compensation tests to this problem.

5. What variables might be included in the social welfare functions of: (a) the government of a developed country; and (b) the government of a less developed country? What problems might be encountered in the measurement of these variables?

6. Consider the proposal to introduce night flights into an airport which will result in noise disturbance to nearby residents. Discuss how the relevant authority might employ cost-benefit analysis and compensation tests to determine the desirability of implementing the proposal.

Private sector firms

9 Theory of the firm – I

Introduction

The theory of the firm is concerned with the analysis of firms' output and pricing decisions. Such decisions are influenced by the objectives that the firms set themselves and by the structure of the industries to which the firms belong. In this chapter, after examining the behaviour of firms' production costs in the short- and long-run, we consider price and output determination under conditions of *perfect competition,* assuming throughout that firms attempt to maximise their profits. We demonstrate the important result that *an economy characterised by perfect competition in all markets and with no externalities satisfies the marginal conditions for Pareto efficiency.*

The models of imperfect competition and alternatives to the assumption of profit maximisation are considered in Chapter 10.

Costs of production

It is important to note that economists base their estimate of production costs on the concept of *opportunity cost* which, as we saw in Chapter 1, is measured in terms of forgone alternatives. In this context, the opportunity cost to a firm of using resources in the production of a good is the revenue forgone by not using those resources in their next best alternative use.

In estimating opportunity costs, economists take a wider view of costs than accountants. In the economist's view, there is no necessary connection between the price originally paid for a factor of production and the cost of using that factor in production. Consider an extreme case of a firm that owns a specialised piece of machinery which can only be used in one production process, has no alternative use and no scrap value. The opportunity cost of using this machine in production is zero, whatever price was originally paid for the machine. If a firm buys a factor of production and uses it up entirely within the relevant production period, then the price actually paid is normally a good estimate of the opportunity cost. If, for example, a firm buys some fuel-oil for £1,000, the outlay of £1,000 represents the alternative resources that the firm has given up by spending that sum on fuel-oil. Similarly, if a firm hires the services of a factor (for example, labour), then the money cost of hiring that factor is a good estimate of opportunity cost.

In the case of factors owned outright by a firm, it is necessary to *impute* (or estimate) the opportunity cost. In this case, the estimate of opportunity cost is normally based on the amount for which the firm could hire out the services of the factor. If, for example, a firm uses money which it already owns, the cost is the interest given up by not lending that money to someone else at the market rate of interest. Analogously, an entrepreneur has the alternative of hiring out his labour services and working for another employer, who might pay him, say £10,000 per annum. Thus, in estimating production costs when the entrepreneur is in business on his own, he should include the sum of £10,000 per annum to reflect his own efforts.

Short-run costs

When we discussed production in Chapter 2, we distinguished between two production periods: the short- and long-run. Recall that the *short-run* was defined as that period of time over which the input of at least one factor of production cannot be increased. If the quantity of a factor cannot be increased in the short-run, it is called a *fixed factor*. A factor whose quantity can be increased in the short-run is known as a *variable factor*.

Corresponding to this division, total costs can be broken down into *fixed costs* and *variable costs*. As the firm has to pay the costs associated with the fixed factors whether or not the firm produces, these costs are called fixed costs. Examples are rents and rates on buildings, interest payments on loans, and licence fees contracted for manufacture under licence from a patent holder. It must be emphasised that fixed costs do not vary as the level of output varies: they are the same whether output is zero or a thousand units per week. Those costs that do change as the level of output varies are known as variable costs. Examples include the cost of raw materials, components, labour and power. Total variable costs increase as the level of output increases.

To summarise we have:

total costs = *total fixed costs* + *total variable costs,* or in symbols:

TC = TFC + TVC

Now consider the costs of a hypothetical firm producing good *X*, shown in Table 1. Suppose that labour is the only variable factor. Recall that, with a fixed capital stock, this firm will eventually encounter the law of diminishing returns and the average productivity of labour will begin to fall. Assuming that the firm buys its factors of production in perfectly competitive factor

Table 1. The costs of production of a hypothetical firm in the short run.

(1) Output (units)	(2) Total fixed costs (£)	(3) Total variable costs (£)	(4) Total costs (£)	(5) Average fixed cost (£)	(6) Average variable cost (£)	(7) Average total cost (£)	(8) Marginal cost (£)
0	5	0	5	∞	–	∞	–
1	5	4	9	5	4	9	4
2	5	7.5	12.5	2.5	3.75	6.25	3.5
3	5	10.8	15.8	1.67	3.60	5.27	3.3
4	5	13.8	18.8	1.25	3.45	4.70	3.0
5	5	17.0	22.0	1.00	3.40	4.40	3.2
6	5	20.5	25.5	0.83	3.42	4.25	3.5
7	5	24.3	29.3	0.71	3.47	4.18	3.8
8	5	28.6	33.6	0.63	3.57	4.20	4.3
9	5	33.5	38.5	0.56	3.72	4.28	4.9
10	5	39.0	44.0	0.50	3.90	4.40	5.5

markets, factor prices will be constant however much the firm buys. This implies that the eventual decline in the average productivity of labour must push up the average variable cost of production, as average variable cost and average labour productivity are opposite sides of the same coin.

In Table 1, column (6) is headed *average variable cost* (AVC). This is obtained by dividing total variable costs by the quantity produced, or in symbols:

$$\text{AVC} = \frac{\text{TVC}}{Q}$$

From Table 1 we see that AVC reaches a minimum when output is 5 units per production period. This is the level of output at which average productivity of labour is at a maximum. In other words, at this level of output, the proportions between the fixed factor and the variable factor are at an optimum.

At levels of output above 5 units, the variable factor has progressively less of the fixed factor to work with and its average productivity declines. This results in higher AVC as output increases. Conversely, AVC falls until output reaches 5 units because at low levels of output the variable factor has too much of the fixed factor to work with. Thus, if we plot AVC on a graph against output we obtain a U-shaped curve (see Fig. 1). Note that if a firm encountered diminishing returns as soon as it started production, it would have an upward-sloping AVC curve.

Column (5) is headed *average fixed cost* (AFC). This is obtained by dividing total fixed costs by the quantity produced, or in symbols:

$$\text{AFC} = \frac{\text{TFC}}{Q}$$

Clearly, AFC must decline continuously as output increases because the given level of fixed costs will be spread over a bigger level of output. The 'tooling-up' costs of establishing a car assembly line are an example. The tooling-up costs per car decline as the volume of output increases. This is sometimes described as 'spreading the overheads'.

Column (7) is headed *average total cost* (ATC). ATC is obtained by adding together average fixed costs and average variable cost, or in symbols:

$$\text{ATC} = \text{AFC} + \text{AVC}.$$

Alternatively, ATC can be obtained by dividing total costs by the level of output, or in symbols:

$$\text{ATC} = \frac{\text{TC}}{Q}$$

In Table 1, ATC declines until output reaches 7 units as the fixed costs are spread over a larger output and initially the firm benefits from increasing returns to the variable factor. Above the level of output of 7 units, ATC increases as the influence of diminishing returns which is pushing up AVC, outweighs the decline in AFC. Thus if we plot ATC on a graph against output, we obtain another U-shaped curve (see Fig. 1).

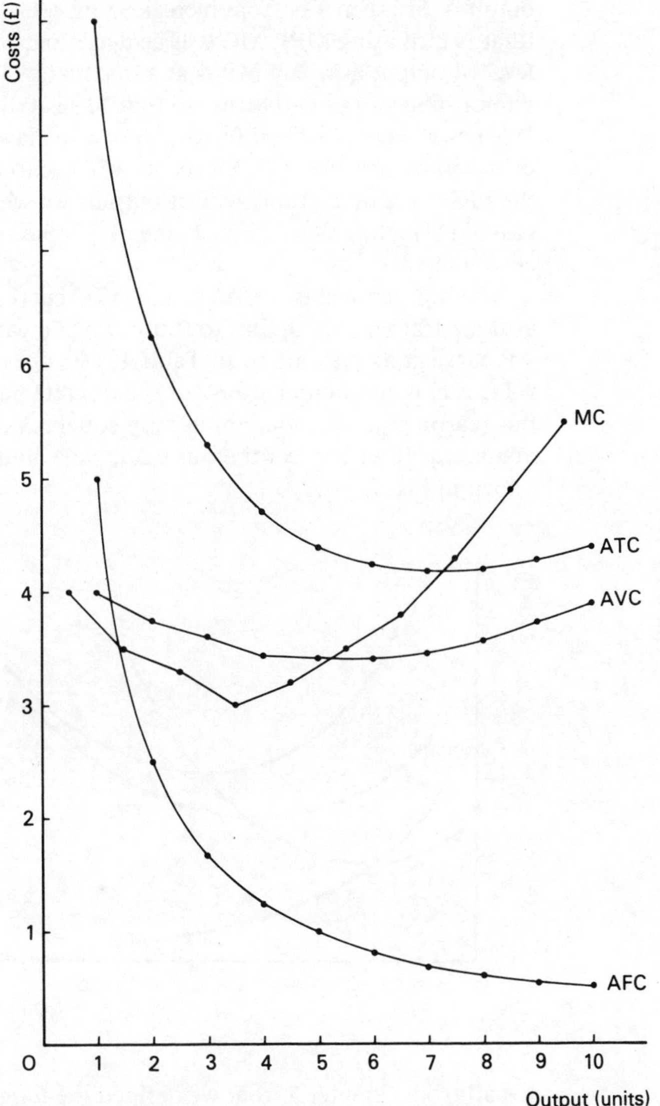

Fig. 1. Short-run cost curves plotted from Table 1.

Column (8) is headed *marginal cost* (MC). This is defined as *the change in total costs resulting from changing the level of output by one unit,* or in symbols:

$$MC = \frac{\triangle TC}{\triangle Q}$$

From Table 1, we see that producing 3 units of *X* costs £15.80, and producing 4 units costs £18.80. To work out the MC of producing the fourth unit, we have

$$MC = \frac{18.80 - 15.80}{1} = £3$$

The shape of the MC curve is related to the behaviour of the marginal product (MP) curve, which we encountered in Chapter 2. If at low levels of output a firm benefits from increasing marginal returns to the variable factor (that is increasing MP), MC will be declining. MC reaches a minimum at the level of output at which MP is at a maximum. When the firm encounters diminishing marginal returns, so that MP is falling, MC begins to rise. Whenever there is a fixed factor, so that the law of diminishing returns comes into operation, the MC curve will eventually start to rise. If we plot the MC curve on a graph against output, we see that it is a U-shaped curve (see Fig. 1). Note that in Fig. 1, the MC is plotted at the mid-point of the class interval.

The MC curve cuts the AVC and ATC curves at their minimum points for arithmetical reasons similar to those which meant that the MP curve cut the AP curve at its maximum. In Table 1, MC does not exactly equal ATC when ATC is at a minimum because of the discrete nature of the data. It is also for this reason that MC does not exactly equal AVC when AVC is at a minimum. If we had continuous data, we would obtain smooth cost curves as drawn in Fig. 2.

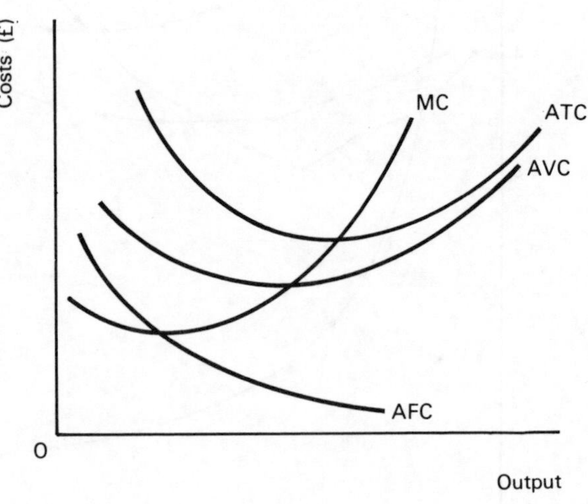

Fig. 2. Short-run cost curves for continuous data.

Long-run costs

Recall from Chapter 2, that we defined the *long-run* as that period of time over which the input of all factors of production can be varied. Thus, all factors are variable factors in the long-run. Recall also that profit-maximising firms will wish to minimise their costs of production.

Traditionally, when deriving the long-run average cost (LRAC) curve, elementary economic theory has assumed that a firm can build an infinite number of plants of different capacities. In some industries, this is clearly an unrealistic assumption; if only a limited number of plants of different capacities can be constructed, the firm's LRAC curve will not be continuously smooth.

The LRAC curve shows the lowest possible cost of producing different levels of output given the production function and factor prices, as reflected in the firm's isocost curves. Note that a cost-minimising firm will only produce at points along its *expansion path* as explained in Chapter 2. An LRAC curve is illustrated in Fig. 3. It indicates the minimum possible average cost of producing any level of output on the assumption that all factors are variable. Thus, the LRAC curve in Fig. 3 indicates the minimum average cost of production for each level of output, given that the plant of the appropriate capacity has been constructed. The minimum average cost of producing output Oq_1 is shown to be Oc_1.

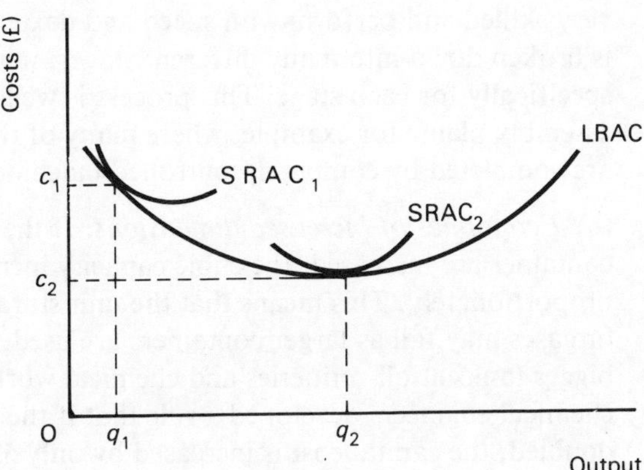

Fig. 3. Long-run average cost curve.

The LRAC curve reaches a minimum when Oq_2 units of output are produced. Up to this level of output, the LRAC curve is declining; the firm is experiencing *economies of scale*. Assuming fixed factor prices, this must be because the firm has increasing returns to scale. As output is increased above Oq_2, the LRAC curve rises, indicating that the firm is facing *diseconomies of scale*. With fixed factor prices, this is because at these levels of output the firm has decreasing returns to scale. If factor prices are constant and long-run average cost is also constant, the firm is said to have constant returns to scale.

Note that if, having built a plant appropriate to minimum long-run average cost at a given level of output, the firm varies its output, it will move along a short-run average cost (SRAC) curve. In Fig. 3 as the firm changes its level of output with the plant appropriate for minimum long-run average cost of production at output Oq_1, it moves along $SRAC_1$. There is an SRAC curve at a tangent at every point along the LRAC curve. Each SRAC curve lies above the LRAC curve except at the point at which it is at a tangent. For this reason, the LRAC curve is sometimes known as an envelope curve.

Now consider the factors which influence the shape of a firm's LRAC curve. The factors leading to declining long-run average cost (economies of scale) and to rising long-run average cost (diseconomies of scale) are discussed in turn.

Economies of scale

Economies of scale can be either internal or external.

Internal economies are those factors which bring about a reduction in average cost as the scale of production of the individual firm rises. Many types of production processes benefit from this phenomenon, particularly processing industries and certain manufacturing operations. Economies of scale can help to explain the trend towards larger production units in some industries. Consider the following internal economies.

Technical economies (a) *Increased specialisation.* The larger is the scale of production, the greater is the scope for the specialisation of both labour and machinery. By performing the same actions repeatedly, labour can become very skilled and perform with speed and dexterity. If the production process is broken down into many different stages, machines can be designed specifically for each stage. This process is well advanced in a modern car-assembly plant, for example, where many of the different stages in assembly are completed by computer-controlled machines.

(b) *Economies of increased dimensions.* If the external dimensions of a container are increased, the cubic capacity increases more than proportionately. This means that the unit storage or transport costs of liquids or gases may fall as larger containers are used. This has, for example, led to bigger tanks at oil-refineries and chemical works. C.F. Pratten reported that chemical engineers developed a rule that if the capacity of a chemical plant is doubled, the capital cost is increased by only 52 per cent and the average fixed cost falls by 24 per cent. An additional economy of increased dimensions has become more significant since the increase in energy costs. If the dimensions of a container holding heated material are doubled, the cubic capacity increases eight times, but the surface area only fourfold, resulting in a smaller heat loss per unit.

(c) *Factor indivisibility.* Certain pieces of capital equipment have to be of a certain minimum size or capacity to justify their manufacture. An automated car-assembly line, for example, is not a viable proposition for low volume manufacture as much of the capital would lie idle for long periods. By using indivisible pieces of capital, larger firms may be able to achieve lower average costs than small firms.

(d) *Principle of multiples.* If a production process involves the use of different types of machinery, a large firm can arrange to have more of the machines with a small output and fewer of the machines with a high output, thus achieving a high utilisation rate. A small firm, on the other hand, with only one of each type of machine would find the high capacity machines standing idle for much of the time.

(e) *Research and development.* A large firm may be able to support its own research and development programme which can result in cost-reducing innovations.

Financial economies Large firms are normally able to obtain finance at lower rates of interest than small firms. Large firms can often provide more collateral as security for loans and investors may be more likely to place money with a well-known, rather than with a small firm. The administrative costs of arranging a large loan will not be twice those of arranging a loan half as large. In addition, large companies have the option of making a new share issue on the stock exchanges. The expenses of a new share issue are such that it is not a practical proposition for raising small sums.

Marketing economies Marketing economies arise from the large-scale purchase of factors of production and from marketing and distributing the finished product in large quantities. A company selling a large volume may be able to use more expensive, but more cost-effective, advertising. Large companies often receive quantity discounts in the purchase of raw materials. An important user of a component is in a strong bargaining position as he can threaten to start production of the component himself. The distribution and administrative costs of an order for 1,000 units are unlikely to be ten times the costs of an order for 100 units.

Risk-bearing economies A large company that has diversified into several markets is likely to be better placed to withstand adverse trading conditions in one particular market. At the same time, other markets may have buoyant trading conditions. If a company is better able to withstand risks, this may mean that it becomes more willing to take risks than smaller companies. In recent years, many large companies have attempted to diversify their interests, such as the large tobacco companies.

A company has to hold stocks in order to meet fluctuations in orders. Stocks have to be financed and also incur storage costs. As the volume of orders increases because of an increased number of customers, the company will find that the required volume of stocks will increase less than proportionately, as individual changes in orders will tend to offset one another.

Diseconomies of scale

It has been argued that diseconomies of scale are unlikely to occur for purely technical reasons for if a company wishes to expand it can always duplicate its existing plant. As organisations become larger, however, managerial functions become increasingly difficult to perform effectively. In a large organisation, there are likely to be several departments so that more time and effort have to be devoted to communication and consultation. This may lead to delays in decision-making. In areas where consumers' tastes change rapidly, a small firm which can make decisions quickly may have an advantage over a larger firm.

If production is concentrated into one or more production units, the average transport costs of raw materials, components and the finished articles are likely to increase. Indeed, transport costs may place an effective limit on the concentration of production. There is some evidence that larger production units suffer from more strikes and other labour disputes. This may be because a worker in a large plant feels himself to be a 'cog in a machine' with no individual identity. A worker in a typical large manufacturing plant is likely to be far removed from the centre of decision-making and is unlikely to feel highly committed to the firm. A related problem with large integrated plants, such as a steelworks, is that an industrial dispute involving only a few key workers may lead to a complete halt in production, as all the stages in the production process are interdependent.

For these and other reasons, a feeling that 'small is beautiful' and in favour of small firms developed in some quarters in the 1960s and 1970s. It is, of course, true that in many markets small firms can compete effectively, particularly as they can respond quickly to the requirements of consumers. Competition amongst small firms can result in good service for consumers.

External economies of scale

External economies result from the simultaneous growth or interaction of a number of firms in the same or related industries. External economies are available to *all* firms in the industry no matter what their size. It can be noted that particular geographical areas often specialise in the production of particular products. Examples in the United Kingdom include the production of ceramics around Stoke-on-Trent and motor-vehicle production in the West Midlands. When an industry is concentrated in a particular area, all firms can benefit from the specialist services that develop. These include the specialist companies for supplying and repairing machinery, the provision of relevant training courses by local colleges and the facilities of the financial institutions. The specific labour skills developed in the industry will encourage new firms entering the industry to locate in the same region.

Typically, the expansion of an industry leads to the establishment of many firms specialising in particular stages of the production process. This is termed *disintegration.* The example of the textile industry is well known. By specialising in a particular operation, a firm can benefit from internal economies of scale and other firms in the industry can have this operation performed for them at lower cost. Note that external economies of scale are also referred to as externalities, which are considered in detail in Chapter 12.

Profit maximisation

Profits are defined as the difference between total revenue and total costs, or in symbols:

$$\pi = TR - TC$$

where π represents profits, TR total revenue and TC total costs. As total revenue is the income to the firm from the sales of its output, it is calculated by multiplying price (or average revenue) by the number of units sold (or quantity). Thus we have

$$TR = p \times q$$

where p is price and q quantity.

Recall that we assume that firms attempt to maximise their profits. How does a firm achieve profit maximisation? We can answer this question by utilising the concepts of *marginal cost* and *marginal revenue*.

When we considered a firm's marginal cost (MC) curve earlier, we saw that the short-run MC curve must eventually slope upwards because of the law of diminishing returns.

Marginal revenue is defined as *the change in total revenue resulting from altering the level of output by one unit.* The marginal revenue (MR) curve facing the firm is derived from the average revenue (or demand) curve. Assume for the moment that the firm faces a downward-sloping demand curve which, as we shall see in the next chapter, means that the firm also faces a downward-sloping MR curve, as in Fig. 4.

Consider whether the firm is maximising profits if it produces quantity Oq_1. It clearly is not, as at this level of output MR equals q_1A and MC is q_1B. As MR is greater than MC, by producing an additional unit of output, the firm will add more to revenue than to costs, and profit will increase. In general, we can state that if, for a profit-maximising firm, MR is greater than MC, the firm should increase output.

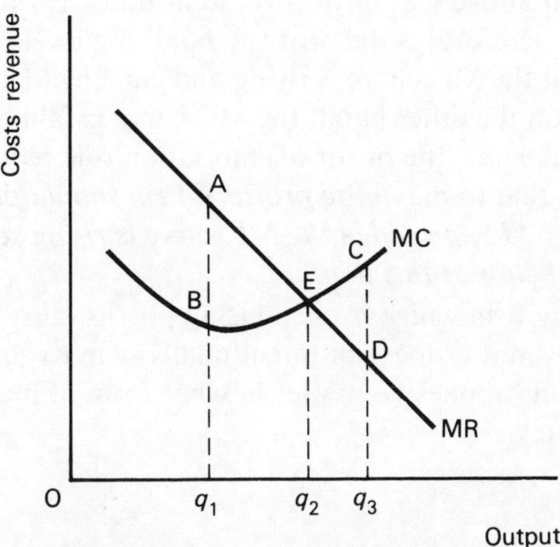

Fig. 4. Profit maximisation.

Now consider whether the firm is maximising profits if it produces output Oq_3. At this level of output, MC equals q_3C and MR is q_3D. As MC is greater than MR, by producing the last unit the firm has actually reduced profits. As long as MC is greater than MR, by producing less the firm can reduce costs more than revenue. Thus, in general, we can state that if MC is greater than MR, a profit-maximising firm should reduce output.

Taken together our two general statements imply that *in order to maximise profits, a firm should produce that quantity at which MC and MR are equal.* Referring back to Fig. 4, in order to maximise profits the firm should produce quantity Oq_2, at which point both MC and MR equal q_2E.

If we use the simple MC = MR rule for profit maximisation, what is the profit-maximising level of output in Fig. 5 where the MC curve cuts the MR

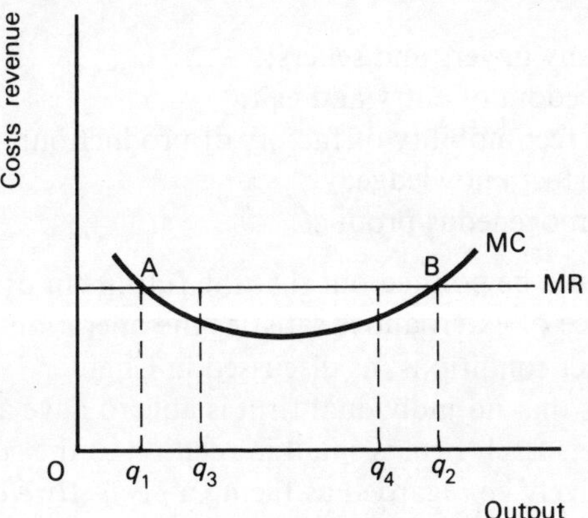

Fig. 5. Profit maximisation where MC cuts MR twice.

curve twice at points A and B? The simple MC = MR rule does not enable us to determine whether output Oq_1 or output Oq_2 is the profit-maximising level of output.

Consider output Oq_1: if the firm increased output to Oq_3, say, profit would increase as the MR of the additional units is greater than MC. Thus, output Oq_1 is clearly not the profit-maximising level.

Now consider output Oq_2: if the firm reduced output to Oq_4, say, profit would fall as MR is greater than MC. Conversely, if the firm increased output above Oq_2, profit would also fall as MC is greater than MR. Output Oq_2, therefore, is the profit-maximising level of output. At this level of output the MC curve is rising and cuts the MR curve from below. At output Oq_1, on the other hand, the MC curve is falling and cuts the MR curve from above. Thus, the profit maximisation rule requires some refinement. It now states that to *maximise profits a firm should produce that quantity at which MR = MC, provided the MC curve is rising so that it cuts the MR curve from below at this point.*

Any firm which is maximising profits must be producing where MR = MC even if it does not intentionally plan to equate MR and MC. The MR = MC rule applies no matter in what form of market structure the firm operates.

The model of perfect competition

Assumptions of the model

In a perfectly competitive market, no individual buyer or seller has any influence over the market so that market forces have full rein to determine price and output. Perfect competition is a theoretical market structure based on a number of assumptions. The fulfilment of these assumptions throughout the economy can be shown to lead to a Pareto optimal allocation of resources. As we saw in Chapter 8, in this situation it is impossible to make anyone better off without making someone else worse off.

Perfect competition is used by economists as a yard-stick against which other market structures are compared and evaluated. The model, however, cannot be realistically expected to exist in totality in everyday life. Nevertheless, some real world markets do contain a number of features of the perfectly competitive model as, for example, some agricultural markets.

The assumptions of the perfect competition model can be summarised as follows:

(a) many buyers and sellers;
(b) freedom of entry and exit;
(c) perfect mobility of factors of production;
(d) perfect knowledge;
(e) homogeneous product.

It should be pointed out that the fulfilment of these assumptions in the absence of externalities satisfies the operation of the price mechanism under ‘perfect conditions’ as discussed in Chapter 7. The existence of many sellers means that no individual firm is able to have a significant effect on the market. Each firm is small in relation to the size of the whole market and can effectively be regarded as facing a *perfectly elastic* demand curve for, at the ruling market price, it can sell whatever it produces. Such a firm is described as a *price taker*. If the firm tried to set a price above the ruling market price, it would sell nothing as, with their perfect knowledge, consumers would buy from the other producers. Similarly, the firm would not set a lower price as this would reduce its total revenue. Note that while the individual firm faces a perfectly elastic demand curve, the *market* demand curve for the product will normally be downward-sloping. The existence of many buyers means that no individual buyer has any influence over the market. Any collusion between buyers and/or sellers is also ruled out.

The assumption of freedom of entry and exit is almost self-explanatory. It means that there are no barriers to new firms entering the industry nor to existing firms leaving the industry. In addition to this mobility of firms, there is the assumption of perfect mobility of factors of production. It is assumed that land, labour and capital can switch immediately from one line of production to another.

We have already referred to the assumption of perfect knowledge on the part of both buyers and sellers. It is assumed that all participants in the market are perfectly well-informed about prices, quality, output levels and all other market conditions. As a consequence, there are neither advertising costs for sellers nor search costs for buyers. This assumption is a sharp reminder of the theoretical nature of perfect competition, as in reality the collection of information is often a costly and time-consuming chore.

The assumption of a homogeneous product implies that each unit produced is identical, so that buyers can have no preferences between different units. Perfect knowledge and a homogeneous product together imply that there must be a single market price for all units of output.

Prices and output determination in the short-run

Now consider the determination of price and output in the short-run for an individual perfectly competitive firm and for the whole industry, assuming profit maximisation. The equilibrium price is determined in the market for the good (say good *X*) by the interaction of supply and demand. Fig. 6 (a) shows the market demand curve (DD) and the market supply curve (SS) which intersect to give an equilibrium price Op_1 and an equilibrium industry output OQ_1.

Fig. 6 (b), drawn on a much bigger scale, illustrates the costs and revenues of a typical firm earning above-normal profit. The firm faces a perfectly elastic demand curve (dd), indicating that it can sell all that it produces at the ruling market price Op_1. The price the firm receives per unit is given by total revenue divided by the number of units produced, and is, therefore, the same as average revenue (AR). In symbols, we have:

$$p = \frac{\text{TR}}{q} = \text{AR}$$

As the firm receives a constant price Op_1, its AR is also constant. In addition, since an *extra* unit of output can always be sold without reducing price, MR must also be equal to price. Thus, in Fig. 6 (b) the demand curve facing the firm is labelled dd = AR = MR.

Fig. 6. Industry and firm in perfect competition earning above-normal profits.

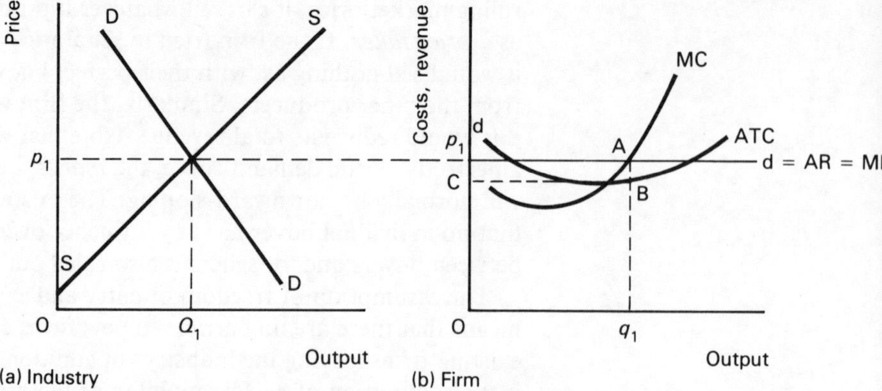

To find the equilibrium quantity that the firm will produce, we apply the MR = MC rule. The MR and MC curves in the diagram intersect at the point where MC cuts MR from below. The profit-maximising level of output, therefore, is Oq_1. Note that the equilibrium price Op_1 is equal to MC at the equilibrium level of output Oq_1. Since in perfect competition price and MR are equal, profit-maximising firms which equate MR and MC will also necessarily equate price and MC. The equality of price and MC is the most significant feature of perfect competition and its welfare implications are discussed below.

In Fig. 6 (b), average total cost at output level Oq_1 is q_1B. Total costs which are given by average total cost multiplied by quantity are thus represented by the rectangle Oq_1BC. The cost curves already incorporate an allowance for *normal profit*, which is the rate of return necessary to keep the factors of production in their present use.

At the equilibrium level of output, total revenue is represented by the area of rectangle Op_1Aq_1. Thus, this firm is earning revenue in excess of total costs. It is said to be earning *above-normal profits* equal to the area of rectangle p_1ABC. In the long-run, the high level of profits in this industry will attract new firms to enter the industry. The increased production will eventually push down the price of the output, thus eliminating the above-normal profits.

Firm making a loss Consider now another perfectly competitive firm whose situation is illustrated in Fig. 7.

Fig. 7 (a) again illustrates the determination of the equilibrium price (Op_1) in the market. The cost and revenue curves of a typical firm are illustrated in Fig. 7 (b). Note that the ATC curve lies completely above the AR curve, indicating that this firm cannot cover its full opportunity costs. The intersection of the MR and MC curves at point A now indicates that the *loss-minimising* level of output is Oq_1. At this output, ATC equals Bq_1, which is greater than AR (= price) or Aq_1. The loss per unit of output is equal to BA so that the total loss is represented by the area of rectangle p_1DBA.

As the price is above average variable cost (AVC) at output Oq_1, the firm will continue to produce in the short-run, as it thereby minimises its losses. If it shut down production entirely, its loss would be equal to its total fixed

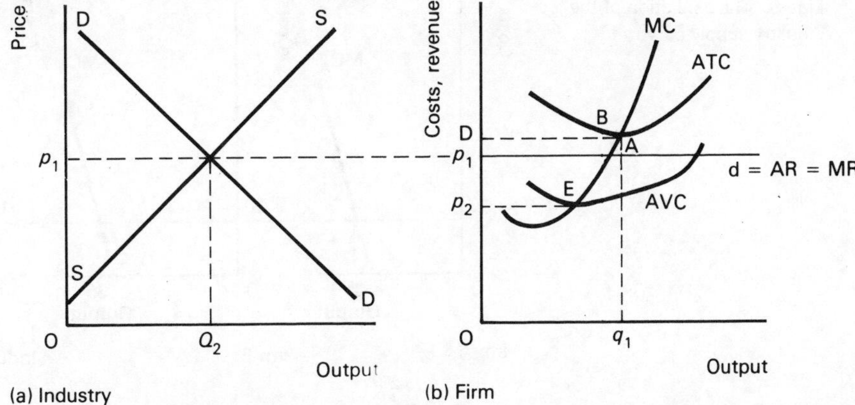

Fig. 7. Industry and firm in perfect competition making a loss.

(a) Industry (b) Firm

costs. By producing and selling output Oq_1 at price Op_1, the firm more than covers its variable costs and can pay for part of its fixed costs.

The firm's short-run supply curve

We can note from the foregoing analysis that the perfectly competitive firm which aims to maximise profits produces at the intersection of its horizontal MR curve with the MC curve provided this is above the shut-down point. This is illustrated for different prices in Fig. 8. For example, the firm offers for sale quantity Oq_2 at price Op_2. If price rises to Op_3, the quantity supplied by the firm increases to Oq_3. We can see that the short-run supply curve of the perfectly competitive firm is its MC curve above the intersection with the AVC curve.

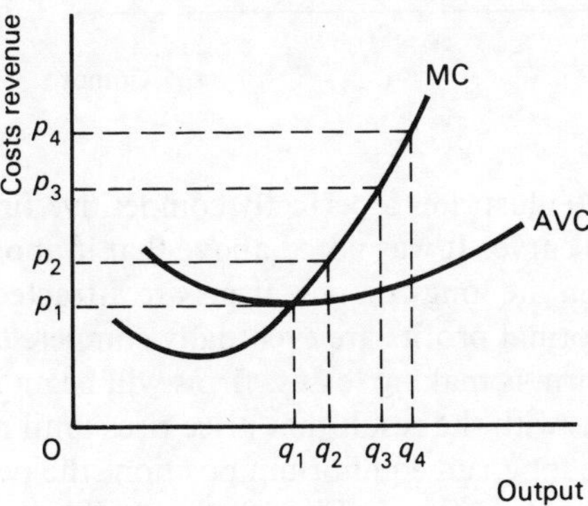

Fig. 8. A firm's short-run supply curve.

The short-run *industry* supply curve is obtained by the horizontal summation of the MC curves of the firms comprising the industry. This is illustrated in Fig. 9 for an industry containing only two firms.

The two left-hand diagrams illustrate the MC curves of firms A and B respectively. At a price of £10, firm A produces 25 units and firm B 35 units of output per time period. Industry output at this price, therefore, is 60 units and A is one point on the industry supply curve. Summing the firms' outputs at other prices enables the industry short-run supply curve, SS, to be derived. This is the supply curve which (together with the market demand curve for

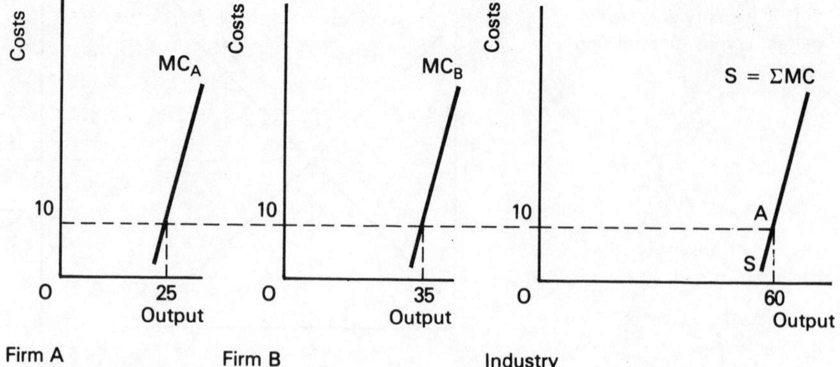

Fig. 9. The derivation of the industry supply curve.

the good) determines the market price which all the individual firms have to take as given.

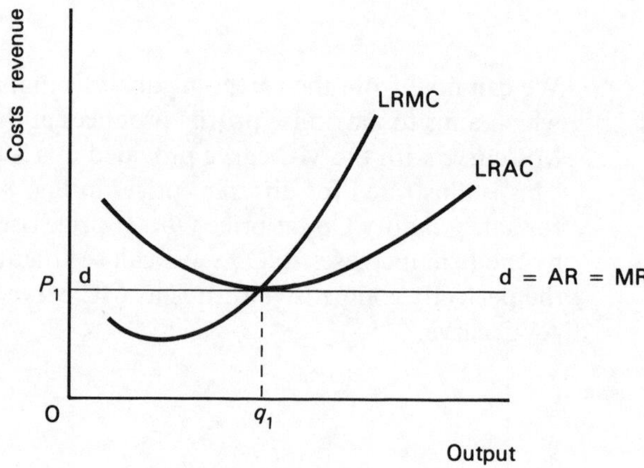

Fig. 10. The long-run equilibrium of a perfectly competitive firm.

The long-run equilibrium of the perfectly competitive firm

Figure 10 illustrates a perfectly competitive firm's long-run average cost (LRAC) curve. It was noted above that if above-normal profits can be earned, in the long-run new firms are attracted into the industry, so that the above-normal profits are eventually competed away. Conversely, if the typical firm is making losses, firms will begin to leave the industry in the long-run, with the result that price rises until normal profits are restored.

In the long-run equilibrium position, the perfectly competitive firm earns only normal profits. In Fig. 10, the equilibrium price is Op_1 and the equilibrium output is Oq_1. Note that in this situation, production is carried on at the lowest point on the LRAC curve. Price equals both marginal cost and average cost. The firm is earning sufficient revenue to cover its full opportunity costs. There exists no incentive for firms to enter or to leave the industry.

Perfect competition and welfare

One of the arguments in favour of a competitive market structure is that perfect competition leads to an efficient, or Pareto optimal, allocation of resources. Indeed, it can be demonstrated that an economy with perfect competition in all markets and with no externalities satisfies all three of the marginal conditions for Pareto optimality that we derived in Chapter 8.

Assume once again that we are dealing with an economy with only two goods (food and cloth), two factors (capital and labour) and two individuals (A and B). Consider the three marginal conditions in turn.

Fig. 11. A firm's least-cost combination of factors.

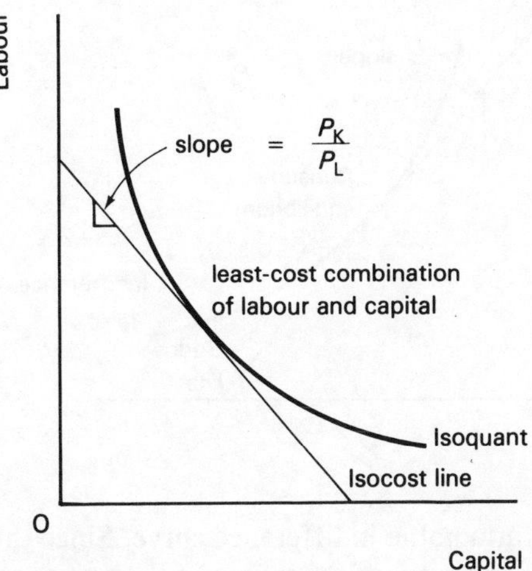

The MRTS of one factor of production for another should be equal for all goods Recall from Chapter 2 that a profit-maximising firm will choose that combination of factors at which the firm's isocost line is tangent to an isoquant, as illustrated in Fig. 11: this ensures that the chosen output level is produced at minimum cost. Since the slope of the isocost line is equal to the ratio of the prices of the two factors and the slope of the isoquant is the MRTS, we can say that if the food producers are profit-maximisers, they will employ that combination of factors at which

$$\text{MRTS}_F = \frac{P_K}{P_L}$$

where MRTS_F is the MRTS in food production, P_K is the price of capital and P_L is the price of labour.

Similarly, if the cloth producers are also profit-maximisers, they will employ that combination of factors at which

$$\text{MRTS}_C = \frac{P_K}{P_L}$$

where MRTS_C is the MRTS in cloth production.

In perfect competition, all firms face the same prices for capital and labour, so it must follow that

$$\text{MRTS}_F = \text{MRTS}_C$$

and the first condition is satisfied.

The MRS for every pair of goods should be equal for all individuals Recall from Chapter 4 that a utility-maximising consumer will choose that combination of goods at which his budget line is tangent to an indifference curve, as illustrated in Fig. 12: this ensures that the consumer is on his highest attainable indifference curve. Since the slope of the budget line is equal to the ratio of the prices of the two goods and the slope of the indifference curve is the MRS, we can say that if A is a utility-maximising consumer, he will allocate his income in such a way that

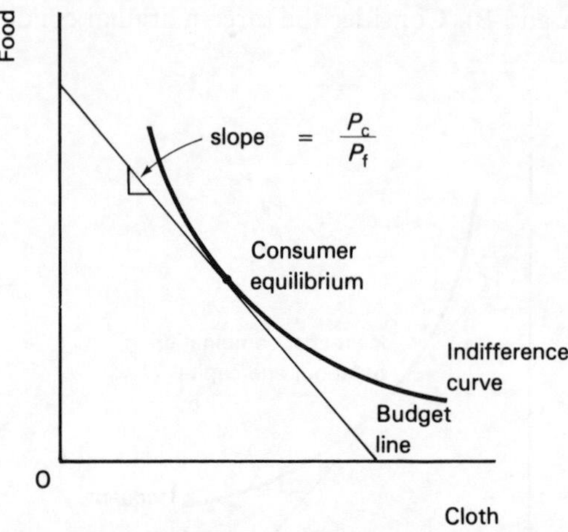

Fig. 12. Consumer equilibrium.

$$MRS_A = \frac{P_c}{P_f}$$

where MRS_A is consumer A's MRS, P_c is the price of cloth and P_f the price of food.

Similarly, if B is also utility-maximising consumer, he will allocate his income in such a way that

$$MRS_B = \frac{P_c}{P_f}$$

where MRS_B is consumer B's MRS.

Assuming, as *we must do* in perfect competition, that both A and B face the same prices for food and cloth, it follows that

$$MRS_A = MRS_B$$

so that the second condition is satisfied.

The common MRS should equal the MRT for all pairs of goods We have seen that each consumer's MRS will be equal to the ratio of the goods' prices. That is,

$$MRS_A = MRS_B = \frac{P_c}{P_f} \qquad [1]$$

Recall that the marginal rate of transformation (MRT) is given by the slope of the production possibility frontier. As such, it can also be regarded as the ratio of the marginal costs of producing the two goods. That is,

$$\text{MRT} = \frac{\text{MC}_c}{\text{MC}_f} \qquad [2]$$

This result is illustrated in Fig. 13 where, in making a small movement along the frontier from A to B, $\triangle c$ of cloth is given up in order to produce $\triangle f$ of extra food. Since moving along the frontier leaves total cost unchanged (because *all* resources are fully employed at every point), it must be true that

$$\triangle c \times \text{MC}_c = \triangle f \times \text{MC}_f$$

$$\text{Slope of frontier} = \frac{\triangle f}{\triangle c} = \frac{\text{MC}_c}{\text{MC}_f} = \text{MRT}$$

From [1] and [2] above, we can say that for MRS to be equal to MRT, it is necessary that

$$\frac{P_c}{P_f} = \frac{\text{MC}_c}{\text{MC}_f}$$

In perfect competition, where the food-producing and cloth-producing firms set their prices equal to their marginal costs of production, this condition must be satisfied.

We can conclude from the above that an economy with perfect competition in all markets and with no externalities will be efficient in the Pareto sense. Of course, this does not necessarily mean that such an economy will have an equitable distribution of income.

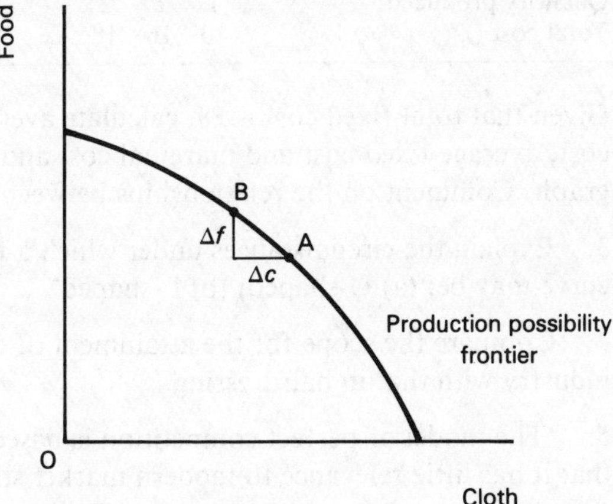

Fig. 13. The production possibility frontier and the marginal rate of transformation.

Conclusion

In this chapter, we have discussed the behaviour of firms' costs of production in the short- and long-runs and examined the factors determining price and output in perfect competition. Finally, we have outlined the welfare implications of a competitive market structure. In the next chapter, we see that imperfect competition will normally result in a Pareto suboptimal allocation of resources, and in Chapters 11–14 we examine the role of the public sector in its attempt to achieve both efficiency and equity.

Further reading

Koplin, H.T., *Microeconomic Analysis*, Harper and Row, New York, 1971 (Ch. 9 and 10).
Lancaster, K., *An Introduction to Modern Microeconomics*, Rand McNally, Chicago, 1974 (Ch. 5 and 6).
Ryan, W.J.L. and **Pearce, D.W.**, *Price Theory*, Macmillan, London, 1977 (Ch. 4, 5 and 12).

Exercises

1. Review your understanding of the following terms:

opportunity cost	economies of scale
fixed costs	diseconomies of scale
variable costs	internal economies
average variable cost	external economies
average fixed cost	marginal revenue
average total cost	profit maximisation
marginal cost	perfect competition
long-run average cost	price taker
expansion path	normal profit

2. Consider the following data on a firm's total costs of production.

Quantity produced:	1	2	3	4	5	6
Total cost (£):	10	16	18	28	45	66

Given that total fixed cost is £8, calculate average total cost, average variable cost, average fixed cost and marginal cost and plot them all on the same graph. Comment on the relationships between the four cost curves.

3. Explain the circumstances under which a firm's long-run average cost curve may be: (a) U-shaped; (b) L-shaped.

4. Compare the scope for the attainment of economies of scale in the steel industry with that in hairdressing.

5. 'The model of perfect competition is based on such unreal assumptions that it has little relevance to modern market structures.' Discuss.

6. Outline the factors that determine the level of normal profits in a perfectly competitive industry. Under what conditions will a perfectly competitive firm close down: (a) in the short-run; (b) in the long-run?

10 Theory of the firm – II

Introduction

In the previous chapter, we considered the model of perfect competition under the traditional assumption of profit maximisation. Perfect competition can be thought of as being at one end of the spectrum of market structures with pure monopoly (in which an industry is dominated by a single firm) at the other end. Between these two extremes, there is an infinite number of market structures with differing degrees of competition. In this chapter, we first consider the price and output determination of a profit-maximising monopolist. Secondly, we consider two of the intermediate forms of market structure – monopolistic competition and oligopoly. Finally, we examine alternatives to the assumption of profit maximisation and briefly outline some of the views of the American economist, J.K. Galbraith.

Monopoly

Definition: ***A pure monopolist is a single supplier of a good or service for which there is no close substitute.***

Problems of defining a monopoly

In general terms, we can say that the cross-elasticity of demand between the monopolist's product and all other products is low – in other words, a rise in the price of the monopolist's product leads to no significant increase in the demand for any other product. The definition of a 'close substitute' is, however, somewhat arbitrary. For example, are gas and oil close substitutes for coal? The answer is likely to depend on the use to which the fuel is put. In the United Kingdom, the National Coal Board has a monopoly in the supply of coking coal for steel production, but faces stiff competition from gas and oil in the heating market.

Pure monopoly can best be regarded as a theoretical model as it is unusual to find a single firm with a 100 per cent market share. In the United Kingdom, the Monopolies and Mergers Commission can be asked to investigate a monopoly to determine whether or not it is operating in the public interest; for this purpose, a monopoly is defined as a single firm or interrelated group of firms controlling 25 per cent or more of a market. The United Kingdom policy towards monopoly is discussed fully in Chapter 14.

It is possible for a group of firms or countries to engage in collusion over prices or production levels and hence act as a monopolist. Such a situation is described as a *cartel*. Examples of cartels in the United Kingdom include the Milk Marketing Board and the Potato Marketing Board. Similarly, the Organisation of Petroleum Exporting Countries (OPEC), which forced up oil prices in the 1970s, is an example of an international cartel. In what follows, we confine our attention to a single-firm monopoly.

The monopolist's demand curve

As the monopolist is the sole supplier of a good, he is, in effect, the industry. He thus faces the *market* demand curve which is normally downward-sloping from left to right. This demand curve tells us the prices at which the producer can sell different levels of output.

Recall that average revenue (AR) is equal to total revenue (TR) divided by the quantity sold and so is also equal to the price of the good. The demand curve can, therefore, also be called the AR curve. Faced with a downward-sloping AR curve, the monopolist has to reduce the price of all units sold in order to sell an extra unit of output. This means that marginal revenue (MR), which is the revenue earned by selling an extra unit, must be less than AR (or price).

Consider the data in Table 1. Columns (1) and (2) represent the demand schedule for the product of a monopolist, say good *X*. Column (3) shows total revenue, obtained by multiplying together columns (1) and (2). Column (4) shows marginal revenue and it can be seen that MR falls faster than and is less than AR over its entire length. The monopolist's AR and MR curves are plotted in Fig. 1 which illustrates graphically the result that whenever a firm's AR curve is downward sloping, the MR curve lies below the AR curve.

From Table 1, we can see that at first as the monopolist sells more, TR increases and reaches a maximum of £91 when seven units are sold. Beyond this level of output, TR begins to fall and MR becomes negative. Clearly, a profit-maximising monopolist would never produce where MR was negative, unless MC were also negative – a highly unlikely event.

Table 1. The revenue of a monopolist.

(1) Quantity	(2) Price (= average revenue) (£)	(3) Total revenue (£)	(4) Marginal revenue (£)
1	25	25	25
2	23	46	21
3	21	63	17
4	19	76	13
5	17	85	9
6	15	90	5
7	13	91	1
8	11	88	−3
9	9	81	−7
10	7	70	−11

Output and price determination of a profit-maximising monopolist

As with any other profit-maximising firm, the monopolist will equate MC with MR. This is illustrated in Fig. 2 where the monopolist is producing quantity OQ_1 and charging a price of OP_1 ($= AQ_1$). This monopolist is making above-normal profits. Total revenue is given by the area of the rectangle OP_1AQ_1. Total costs are given by the area of the rectangle $OCBQ_1$. Thus, the smaller rectangle CP_1AB represents the above-normal profits.

Fig. 1. The monopolist's revenue curves.

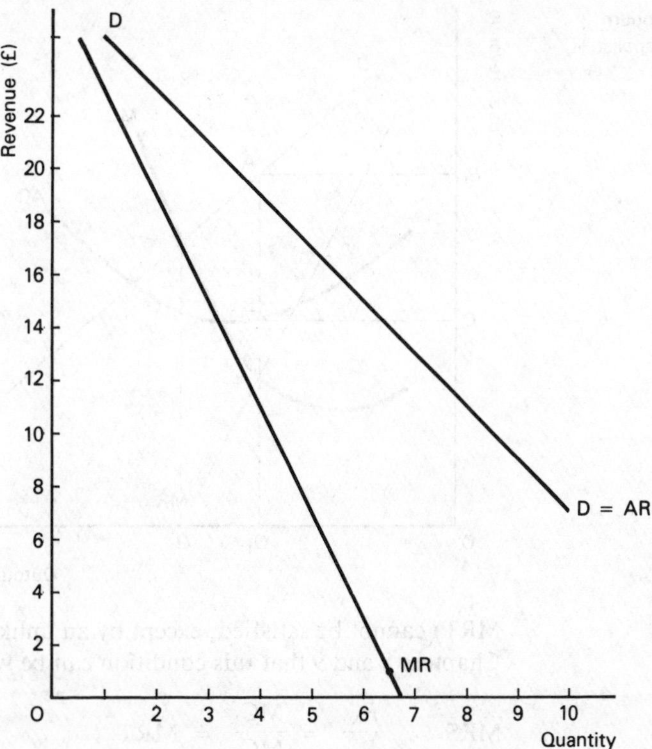

Welfare implications and criticisms of monopoly

Note from Fig. 2 that the price (AQ_1) is greater than MC which is equal to Q_1D. This underlies the charge that monopoly leads to a *Pareto sub-optimal allocation of resources.* The following rationale can be given for this charge of resource misallocation. The demand curve DD tells us the consumers' valuation of marginal units of the monopolist's product. Thus, consumers place a value of AQ_1 on the last unit of good *X* actually produced. The MC curve can be viewed as the consumers' valuation of the alternatives forgone as a result of producing good *X*. Thus, they place a value of Q_1D on the marginal unit of the forgone alternative. It can be seen, then, that at the level of output OQ_1, consumers value marginal units of the monopolist's output more highly than marginal units of the forgone alternative.

The implication of this is that consumers would prefer the monopolist to produce extra units of output, up to the point of the intersection of the demand curve with the MC curve. It is output OQ_2, therefore, that maximises society's welfare because at this output level, marginal benefit (given by the demand curve) is equal to MC. Here we are judging welfare by efficiency criteria alone and are ignoring equity questions. We are also assuming that the firm's MC curve accurately reflects marginal *social* cost – that is to say, no externalities are present.

We saw in Chapter 9 that, with no externalities, Pareto optimality would result under perfect competition where price is equal to MC. In monopoly, though, output is restricted and price is set above MC. This means that the third marginal condition for Pareto optimality (that MRS should equal

Fig. 2. The equilibrium position of a monopolist.

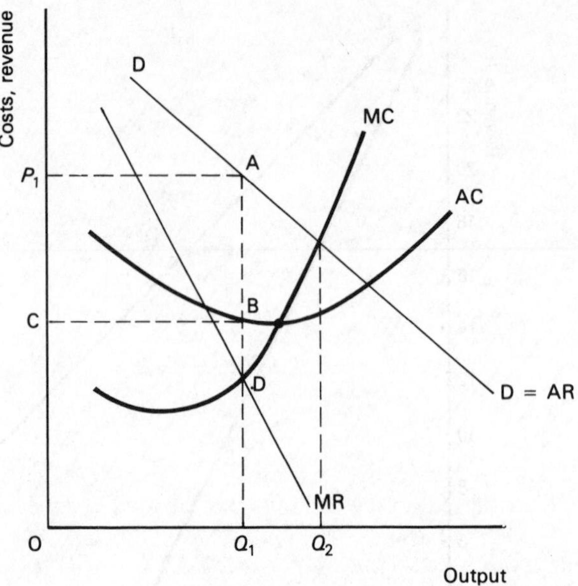

MRT) cannot be satisfied, except by an unlikely coincidence. Recall from Chapters 8 and 9 that this condition can be written as follows:

$$\text{MRS} = \frac{P_X}{P_Y} = \frac{\text{MC}_X}{\text{MC}_Y} = \text{MRT}$$

where *X* and *Y* represent any pair of goods. Clearly, if both the *X* and *Y* industries are perfectly competitive, so that $P_X = \text{MC}_X$ and $P_Y = \text{MC}_Y$, the condition must be satisfied. But if the *X*-industry is a monopoly, so that $P_X > \text{MC}_X$, the condition will not be satisfied and a misallocation of resources will result. Only if both industries are monopolised to exactly the same extent and in such a way that P_X exceeds MC_X by the same proportion as P_Y exceeds MC_Y, will the condition be satisfied in the absence of perfect competition: this is highly unlikely.

Our analysis leads to the prediction that if a perfectly competitive industry is taken over by a profit-maximising monopolist, and production costs do not change, output will fall and price will rise. This result is illustrated in Fig. 3. For simplicity, we assume constant average and marginal production costs. Price and output in perfect competition are OP_c and OQ_c respectively, as determined by the intersection of the demand curve DD and the industry supply curve which, in this case, is horizontal. Consumer surplus is represented by the triangle ABP_c. Now suppose that the industry is taken over by a monopolist and that costs do not change so that the industry supply curve becomes the monopolist's MC curve. To maximise profits, the monopolist will equate MR and MC and so produce the lower quantity OQ_m at the higher price OP_m. Consumer surplus falls to the triangle ACP_m. Part of the original consumer surplus (rectangle P_cP_mCE) is the monopolist's gain, but the triangle CBE represents a net fall in welfare and is sometimes called the 'deadweight loss' of the monopoly. Representing the welfare loss in terms of the triangle CBE is, however, a little misleading as it ignores the equity aspects of the redistribution of income from consumers to the monopolist.

Fig. 3. The welfare loss under monopoly.

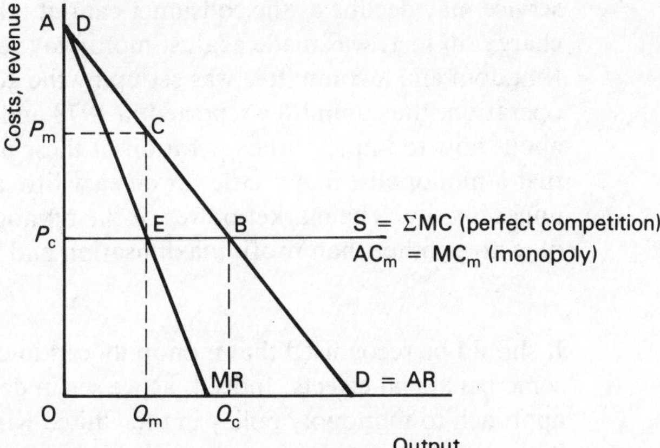

Long-run profits resulting from barriers to entry A monopolist may be criticised on the grounds that he may be able to maintain above-normal profits in the long-run because of barriers to the entry of new firms. As we have seen, this might result in a redistribution of income that is not desirable on equity grounds. There are several entry barriers which may have the effect of preventing the emergence of competitive firms. Consider the following.

(a) *High entry costs.* An existing monopolist, producing a large volume of output, may be benefiting from economies of scale. This may mean that a new competitor, probably producing a low volume of output, would be faced with higher per unit production costs and so would not be able to compete effectively in the market. If the new firm were faced with heavy initial losses, it might never be able to produce at a volume sufficient for it to enjoy comparable economies of scale.

(b) *Legal monopolies.* In some cases, the state has created monopolies by law as, for example, with the Post Office in the United Kingdom. In cases like these, it is illegal for rival firms to enter the industry.

(c) *Patents and copyrights.* A monopoly may result from the holding of a patent on an invention or innovation. A patent confers sole production rights for a given time period on those who have invested in research and development to enable them to earn a return on their investment. A copyright restricts the reproduction of printed or recorded material in a similar way.

(d) *Ownership of natural resources.* The monopolist may be the sole owner of a natural resource. Unless new supplies of the resource are discovered, there will be no possibility of new firms entering the industry. Consequently, the monopolist will have effective control over the supply of the resource and over the supply of any manufactured products derived from the resource. In recent years, the oil exporting nations formed OPEC (the Organisation of Petroleum Exporting Countries) in order to act as a cartel and so drive up the price of oil.

Increased costs Another possible criticism is that because a monopolist is not subject to conventional competitive pressures, the quality of the good or service may decline as the consumer cannot take his custom elsewhere. This charge, in fact, was made against motorway service areas in the United Kingdom and a committee was set up by the government to investigate their operation: the committee reported in 1978 and made a number of suggestions about how to improve the operation of these areas. It can further be argued that a monopolist may 'settle for an easy life' and allow costs to rise unnecessarily. The market power of the monopolist enables him to pursue objectives other than profit maximisation and still survive in the long-run.

Possible benefits of monopoly

It should be recognised that monopoly can in certain circumstances have some beneficial effects. Indeed, as we see in detail in Chapter 14, the approach to monopoly policy in the United Kingdom is to judge each case on its merits. So consider now the following possible advantages of monopoly.

Economies of single ownership As we have seen, the standard prediction that a monopolist restricts output and raises price rests on the assumption that costs remain unchanged when a perfectly competitive industry is taken over by a monopolist. It is most unlikely, however, that costs would remain unchanged in such a situation. A monopolist may be able to benefit from economies of scale that are not attainable by the individual perfectly competitive firms. It is even possible for costs to fall so much that price will actually fall and output rise in the new monopoly situation.

This is illustrated in Fig. 4. The supply curve under conditions of perfect

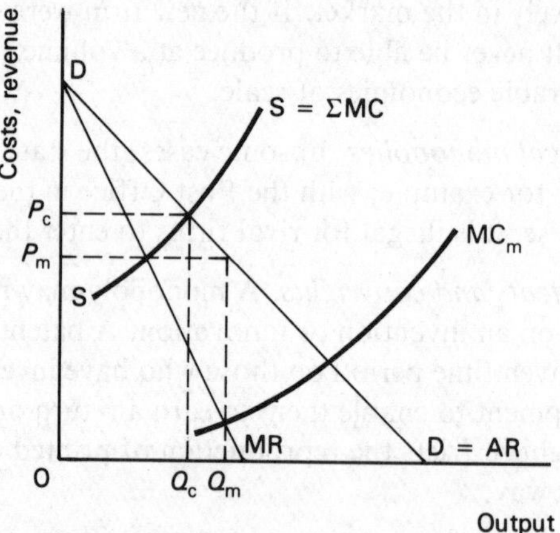

Fig. 4. The case of a monopolist reducing price and increasing output.

competition (SS) is the sum of the individual firms' marginal cost curves. Competitive price is OP_c and output OQ_c. After the industry is taken over by the monopolist, the monopolist's marginal cost curve is MC_m and lies below the competitive supply curve. As a result of equating MR with MC, the monopolist will produce the larger quantity OQ_m and charge the lower price Op_m. It can thus be argued that the monopolisation of the industry benefits the consumer in this instance; the misallocation of resources still remains, however, as price is greater than the new MC.

As mentioned in Chapter 7, the economies of scale are so large in the cases of some public utilities that monopoly is the natural production unit. These are described as *natural monopolies*. There would clearly be an unnecessary duplication of resources if two gas companies served the same district with two sets of pipes under each road. In the case of two separate telephone systems serving the same district, there would be a similar waste of resources with two sets of cables side by side, and with the added complication that in order to be able to contact all telephone subscribers, one would need to hire two telephones! With natural monopolies, the United Kingdom approach has generally been to place them in public ownership (see Ch. 14). An alternative approach (more common in the United States) is to allow the existence of a private monopoly, but to establish a regulatory agency to monitor and control the monopolist's prices and profits.

Technical progress It has been claimed that the existence of high profits and larger resources allows the monopolist to devote a large amount of expenditure to research and development. This may be beneficial to society as it can lead to an increased rate of technical progress and thus economic growth. The monopolist's position is often more secure than that of a competitive firm and he is thus able to devote more resources to innovative activity over a long period.

Schumpeter was a notable proponent of the view that the dynamic gains to society from monopoly through increased technical progress outweighed the costs of resource misallocation. Whether or not monopoly actually does lead to increased technical progress, however, is not clear. Studies for the United Kingdom have found no conclusive evidence of a link between the levels of concentration and the rate of innovative activity.

Discriminating monopoly

A monopolist may be able to charge different prices to different consumers of similar goods and services *in different markets* and in this way increase total profits. The markets may be separated from each other in a number of different ways. First, they may be separated *geographically*, as when an exporter charges a different price in the overseas market than in the home market. Secondly, the markets may be separated by the *type of demand*, as in the market for milk where the household demand for liquid milk differs from the industrial demand for milk for cheesemaking. Thirdly, they may be separated by *time*, where typically a lower price is charged in off-peak periods – this is the case in the electricity, telephone and travel industries. Finally, they may be separated by the *nature of the product*, as with medical treatment where if one person is treated he is unable to resell that treatment to another. The important point is that, for successful price discrimination, the monopolist must be able to prevent resale of the product, otherwise the purchasers at the lower price might sell directly to other customers.

As an example, consider the profit-maximising outputs and prices of a discriminating monopolist who operates in two completely independent markets. In Fig. 5 (a), AR_A and MR_A are the relevant average and marginal revenue curves in market A. Similarly, Fig. 5 (b) illustrates the monopolist's average and marginal revenue curves in market B. Notice that, at given prices, the elasticity of demand is greater in market B than in market A – this is, therefore, a situation in which price discrimination can be profitable to the monopolist. Fig. 5 (c) shows the combined marginal revenue curve for both markets (MR_{TOTAL}): this is obtained by summing MR_A and MR_B horizontally.

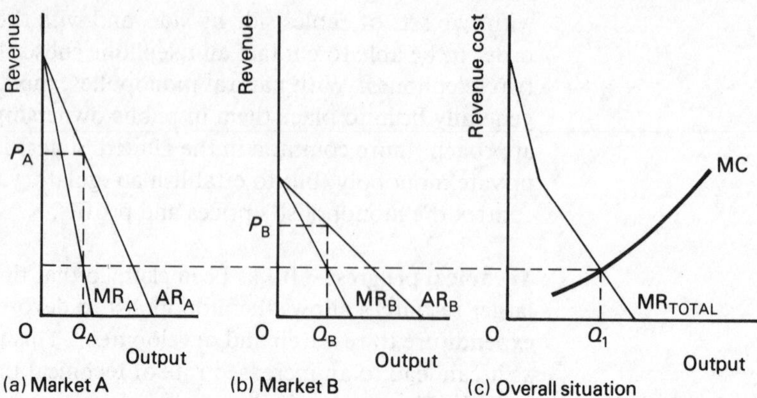

Fig. 5. Price discrimination in two separate markets.

For profit maximisation, MR_A and MR_B *must be equal*. If this were not so, then profits could be increased by selling extra units of output in the market with the higher marginal revenue. As is usual, the profit-maximising level of output, OQ_1, is found where the common MR is equal to marginal cost. This output is then divided between the two markets with OQ_A being sold in market A at price OP_A, and OQ_B being sold in market B at price OP_B. Notice that $OQ_A + OQ_B = OQ_1$.

Price discrimination is sometimes criticised on the grounds that it confers on the monopolist the power to decide which groups of consumers should pay higher prices. Also, in terms of the welfare criteria outlined in Chapter 8, we can say that, since with price discrimination all consumers do not face the same prices, it must follow that the first marginal condition for Pareto optimality (that the marginal rates of substitution should be equal for all pairs of individuals) will no longer be satisfied.

Monopolistic competition

The model of monopolistic competition was originally developed by E.H. Chamberlin in his book *The Theory of Monopolistic Competition* in 1933. The assumptions of the model are similar to those of perfect competition with one exception. It is assumed that there are a large number of producers of similar, but *differentiated*, products. An example might be food retailing where a large number of competing stores offer a similar range of goods, but differ as regards location and service. Within the model, there is freedom of entry and exit for firms.

The differentiation of the product offered by individual producers implies that whilst each firm is likely to face a relatively elastic demand curve, it will not face a *perfectly* elastic demand curve. This is because if a single firm should raise its price, it would not lose all of its sales, as would be the case in perfect competition. Some customers would continue to buy the product because of the qualities that differentiate it from the competing products. In other words, brand loyalties exist.

Short-run equilibrium

Consider now the short-run equilibrium position of a firm operating in monopolistic competition. This is illustrated in Fig. 6. The curve dd = AR is the demand curve facing the firm on the assumption that all other firms hold their prices constant. To achieve maximum profits, the firm will equate MC with MR and so produce quantity OQ_1 and charge a price of OP_1. The firm is making above-normal profits in the short-run equal to the area of the rectangle P_1ABC. The firm may try to retain or increase its above-normal profits by engaging in some form of non-price competition – this might include advertising or further expenditure on packaging to make the good appear more attractive to consumers.

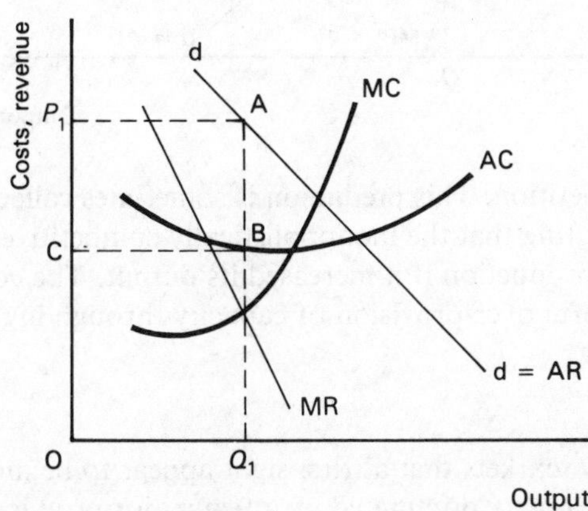

Fig. 6. Short-run equilibrium of a firm in monopolistic competition.

Long-run equilibrium

As long as the monopolistically competitive firms are earning above-normal profits, there exists an incentive for new firms to enter the industry. If we assume that the total demand for the product does not change, this implies that the demand for any single firm's product will fall. The demand curve will shift to the left until the above-normal profits are eliminated, at which point there will exist no further incentive for new firms to enter the industry. The long-run equilibrium position of a firm in monopolistic competition is illustrated in Fig. 7. Notice that the above-normal profits are completely eliminated when the demand curve facing the firm is tangential to the long-run average cost curve. As the demand curve is not perfectly elastic, this point of tangency must be above the lowest point on the LRAC curve (it is at point A in Fig. 7). Equating MR with MC, the firm produces quantity OQ_1 and sells it at price OP_1. Since AR and AC are equal, only normal profits are earned in the long-run.

Welfare implications

The model of monopolistic competition clearly does *not* lead to an optimal allocation of resources. As can be seen from Fig. 6 and Fig. 7, price exceeds marginal cost in both the short-run and the long-run. We have discussed the ensuing misallocation of resources earlier in this chapter.

As we noted above, production in monopolistic competition is conducted above the minimum point on the LRAC curve. This means that the consumer pays a higher price relative to that paid in the long-run in perfect

Fig. 7. Long-run equilibrium of a firm in monopolistic competition.

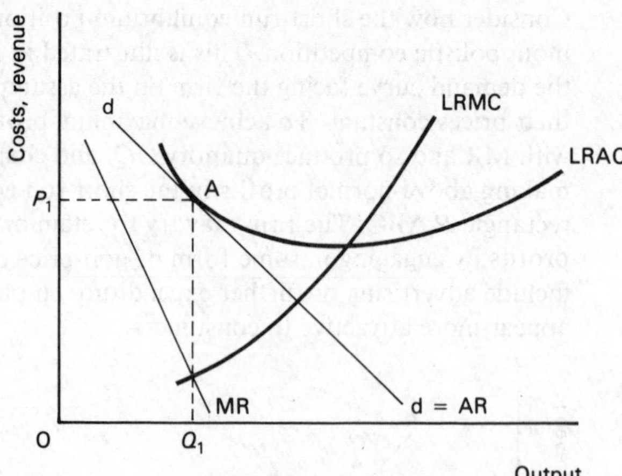

competition. This prediction is sometimes called the *excess capacity theorem*, indicating that the monopolistically competitive firm could achieve lower-cost production if it increased its output. The consumer has to pay for the wasteful over-provision of capacity through higher prices.

Oligopoly

Many markets that at first sight appear to be monopolistically competitive are in reality dominated by a few major producers who each manufacture a large number of different brands. These markets can best be described as *oligopolies*. In an oligopoly, the number of firms is small enough for each seller to take account of the actions of other sellers in the market. Sellers realise that they are mutually dependent. The model is sometimes called 'competition among the few' and is relatively common in manufacturing industries, such as automobile production and the tobacco industry. The special case of a market dominated by two firms is called a *duopoly*.

The recognition of interdependence between oligopolists means that a comprehensive theory of oligopoly would have to take account of the oligopolist's view of how his rivals would react to any price or production change. Because of the uncertainties involved, there is no satisfactory comprehensive theory of oligopoly. Nevertheless, many models of oligopolistic behaviour have been developed, including 'market sharing' and 'dominant firm' models.

P. Sweezy developed a model in 1939 to explain the relative stability observed in the pricing policies of oligopolists. To illustrate this, consider a single firm operating in a market in which there are also several rival firms producing similar products. Suppose that, as shown in Fig. 8 (a), the oligopolist is selling quantity Oq_1 at a price of Op_1. Based on past experience, the oligopolist might believe that if he lowered his price, the rivals would also reduce their prices in order to maintain their market shares. Thus, for prices below Op_1, the oligopolist believes that he is effectively facing a relatively *inelastic* demand curve, as indicated by the segment AD_1. The line D_1D_1 is the demand curve facing the oligopolist when his rivals match his price changes. (MR_1 is the associated marginal revenue curve.) The line D_2D_2, on the other

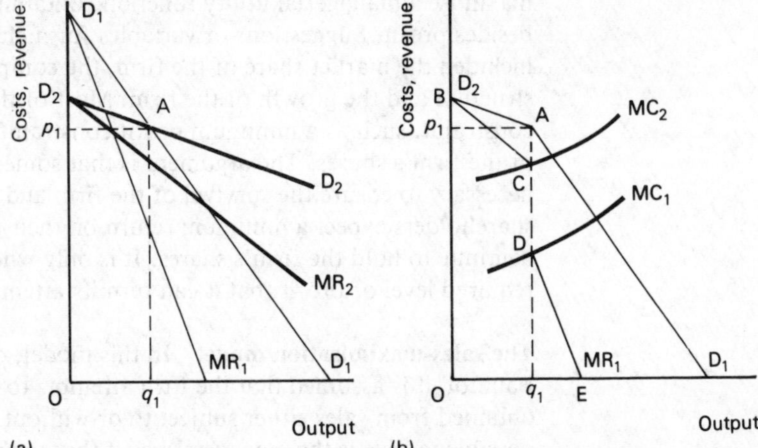

Fig. 8. The oligopolist's kinked demand curve.

hand, is the demand curve facing the oligopolist if his rivals do not match his price changes. (MR_2 is the associated marginal revenue curve.) If the oligopolist believes that when he increases his price, the rivals will keep their prices constant to increase their market shares, he will believe that he is effectively facing the demand curve D_2A at prices above Op_1.

For simplicity, the demand curve that the oligopolist thinks he is facing is reproduced in Fig. 8 (b). It is D_2AD_1 and because it has a kink at point A, it has been called the oligopolist's *kinked demand curve.* Also transferred to Fig. 8 (b) is the effective marginal revenue curve that the oligopolist faces. It is given by the curve BCDE, with a discontinuity at CD. Since the firm's profit-maximising price and output are Op_1 and Oq_1 respectively, it must be true that the marginal cost curve must cut the marginal revenue curve somewhere in this area of discontinuity. It follows that quite large changes in the firm's marginal costs are possible (from MC_1 to MC_2 in fact) which will *not* induce the firm to change either its price or quantity.

Whilst this theory may help to explain the relative stability of prices in oligopoly, it is of limited value. It does not explain what factors determine the profit-maximising price and output initially. Indeed, we need to know the profit-maximising price and output in order to find the kink in the demand curve.

Alternatives to profit-maximisation

Managerial models

In perfect competition, profit maximisation is a necessary condition for survival in the long-run. However, once we turn to other models in which firms do not face a perfectly elastic demand curve, an area of discretion becomes available to firms in their behaviour. The growing recognition of the possible divergence of interest between the owners of large companies (the shareholders) and the day-to-day controllers (the managers) was remarked upon in Chapter 2. The awareness that managers may be interested in maximising variables other than profits has led to the development of several managerial models of the firm.

These models implicitly or explicitly assume that the managers aim to maximise a managerial utility function containing at least one variable besides profit. Suggestions of variables for inclusion in this function have included the market share of the firm, the complexity of the corporate structure and the growth of the firm. Most of the models specify a constraint, such as a minimum profit constraint or a constraint on the value of the firm's shares. The argument is that some minimum level of profit is necessary to ensure the survival of the firm and its managers because shareholders expect a minimum return on their investment if they are to continue to hold the firm's shares. It is only when the firm has earned this required level of profit that it can turn its attention to other objectives.

The sales-maximisation model In this model, originally developed by Baumol, it is assumed that the firm attempts to maximise the revenue obtained from sales either subject to or without a profit constraint. A possible motive is the managers' belief that their salaries are related to the size of the firm.

In Fig. 9, the total cost and total revenue curves of a firm are shown. From these, the total profit curve is derived and it can be seen that the profit-maximising level of output is OQ_1. If the firm should attempt to maximise sales revenue without any profit constraint, it would produce quantity OQ_3, which is bigger than OQ_1. Now assume that the firm attempts to maximise sales revenue subject to a minimum profit constraint of OZ. The sales-

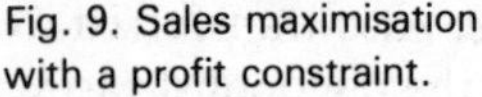
Fig. 9. Sales maximisation with a profit constraint.

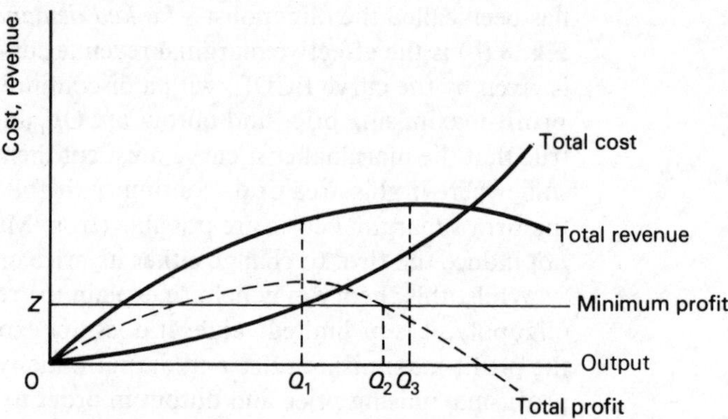

maximising quantity OQ_3 does not meet the profit constraint and so output has to be reduced to OQ_2, the largest volume of output that meets the constraint. Notice that in general the sales-maximising level of output is greater than the profit-maximising level. The two output levels would be identical only in the exceptional case where the maximum attainable level of profits was just equal to the profit constraint.

The sales-maximising model subject to a profit constraint leads to a prediction about a firm's reaction to an increase in fixed costs different from that of the profit-maximising model. In the profit-maximising model, as an increase in fixed costs does not affect marginal cost, the firm's equilibrium output remains unchanged. But now reconsider the firm in Fig. 9 which is maximising its sales revenue at output OQ_2, subject to the profit constraint OZ. If fixed costs increase, profits will fall, so that in the diagram the total profit curve will shift downwards. The firm will now have to reduce output to meet the profit constraint.

An unresolved problem with this model is what determines the minimum acceptable level of profit. Indeed, one might ask why, in the face of the increase in fixed costs in the above example, the minimum acceptable level of profit was not reduced to accommodate the new situation.

Behavioural models

The behavioural school emphasises that the internal organisational structure of firms is likely to influence their behaviour. Behavioural models, such as those of Cyert and March, suggest that the decision-making process within the firm results in the pursuit of a number of objectives. Each objective acts as a constraint on the future activity of the firm.

The behavioural approach points out that decision-making results from a bargaining process among members of the firm (or *coalition*); the bargaining process is conducted between individuals and groups (for example, managers, workers, trade unions and shareholders) with differing viewpoints, bargaining strengths and conflicting interests.

The decision-making process takes place with limited information and subject to a background of uncertainty. A number of objectives for the firm emerge from this process, of which the most important is the survival of the firm. It is possible for two or more of the objectives to conflict with each other and, in this case, the objectives may be given priority in turn or the firm may aim for satisfactory levels of attainment of each objective. This latter process has been described as *satisficing*. Thus, the concept of the firm maximising a single objective is replaced by the concept of the firm attempting to achieve a satisfactory level of performance with respect to multiple objectives. In addition to survival, other objectives include target levels of profit, sales, rate of return on capital, growth and market share.

The target level of attainment of these objectives is influenced by both the past level of attainment and by what is thought to be currently attainable. If the target level is achieved too easily, it is subsequently raised; if it proves impossible to reach, it is lowered. If a target level is not achieved, the firm may pursue problem-oriented search procedures. Information is gathered and alternative courses of action are considered sequentially, beginning with alternatives that involve a small change from existing policies. If the target level is still not achieved, strategies that involve greater changes may be introduced.

As an example, consider a firm which has a minimum market share as one of its objectives, but which is no longer achieving its desired target. The firm may conduct market research to find out why consumers are turning away from its products. It may also increase its advertising expenditure and search for information on what new products may help to restore the market share. It may analyse carefully the products of its competitors to see if they include features popular with consumers. In addition, the firm may instigate a long-run research programme to develop possible new products. Search procedures are satisficing rather than maximising, so that the first satisfactory course of action is selected.

Another feature associated with the behavioural models is the concept of *organisational slack*. Members of the coalition receive side-payments in the form of monetary awards or as commitments to specific policies. Typically, the level of side-payments distributed exceeds that necessary to maintain the coalition and this gives rise to the concept of organisational slack.

Whilst behavioural models provide useful insights, they are of limited value at present as detailed knowledge of the internal bargaining process of the firm is required in order to derive precise predictions. This is an area where economics comes into close contact with the disciplines of psychology and sociology. Indeed, recent progress has been recognised by the award of the Nobel Prize for economics to H.A. Simon in 1978 for work in this field.

Cost-plus pricing

An attack on the profit-maximisation theory resulted after a number of surveys reported that many businessmen did not employ, or were not familiar with, the concepts of marginal cost and marginal revenue. How then, it was argued, could these businessmen achieve profit maximisation? It was claimed that in practice *cost-plus* (or *full cost*) pricing was pursued. According to this approach, businessmen request their accountants to estimate the full cost of production per unit of output (including both fixed and variable costs). The final price is then determined by adding on a mark-up to ensure the achievement of the required profit level.

A possible explanation for this procedure is that the typical firm may be unable to estimate its demand curve (and hence its marginal revenue curve) accurately. Similar problems of estimating marginal cost also arise. Moreover, it has been claimed that cost-plus pricing using a flexible mark-up can result in relatively infrequent price changes which will appeal to customers. If price is held constant and costs vary, this implies a variable profit margin.

Later observers have pointed out that the survey results were not necessarily a challenge to the traditional theory of the firm which does not claim to predict how prices are actually fixed. The MR = MC rule for profit maximisation does not imply that businessmen must consciously calculate and equate the two variables. Indeed, cost-plus pricing could result in the same price and output decisions as profit maximisation. This possibility is highlighted by some of the businessmen questioned who stated explicitly that the actual size of the mark-up is determined with reference to the state of competitive pressures. In those cases where the size of the mark-up is rigid and is not varied in response to competition, however, the outcomes are likely to differ from those derived in the traditional theory.

Some critics have questioned whether the cost-plus approach does constitute a theory. A theory is expected to yield testable predictions, but the cost-plus approach does not appear to result in predictions that can be subjected to empirical tests.

The economics of J.K. Galbraith

One of the most controversial figures in modern economics is the American economist, John Kenneth Galbraith. His ideas, particularly those on the role of large companies, have been influential with the general public. His critics, though, argue that he acts like a disciple in propagating his ideas, without any regard as to whether there exists any evidence to support his theories. Galbraith is certainly one of the most literate economists and he has introduced several striking phrases into the literature, such as *countervailing power.* This expresses the idea that any power centre is eventually likely to come against another power centre that may have grown up in response to the initial exercise of power. An example is a large company faced with the countervailing power of the trade unions.

In his later writings, Galbraith analysed the consequences of the concentration of economic activity in the hands of large companies. He argued that large companies are not subservient to market pressures. By generating internal funds for investment, they are no longer subject to the disciplines imposed by the capital market and to a large extent, they can create markets for their products through advertising, so that consumers are no longer 'sovereign'.

The large company is controlled by what Galbraith calls the *technostructure* – that is, the groups of specialists whose skills and information are vital to the continued functioning of the company. The technostructure includes technologists, scientists, computer programmers, accountants and managers. The technostructure aims to ensure the stability of the company and, therefore, of itself. Thus, the resources of the company are not used to maximise profits, but to promote growth and stability. Galbraith argues that the large company is forced to plan and in this way performs society's planning function.

As mentioned earlier, the ideas of Galbraith have been subjected to much criticism. It has often been pointed out that in contrast to the Galbraithian model, large companies are indeed subject to market pressures. Examples of United Kingdom companies that hit major crises in the 1970s include Rolls-Royce, Burmah Oil, Chrysler (now Talbot) UK and British Leyland. Similar crises have been experienced by companies in Europe and the United States. The Galbraithian idea that the technostructure controls the large company has also been challenged. It is argued that in many cases large shareholders or those in control of the shareholders' votes are in effective control. In addition, many top executives have large shareholdings in their company which might act as a powerful incentive towards profit maximisation (and consequently large dividends for the executives) rather than towards the stability of the company.

Galbraith has admitted that market pressures do operate effectively in those parts of the economy where small businesses predominate, such as hairdressing, agriculture, household and personal services: this is the *market sector*. The world of the large companies is the *planning sector.* Where the dividing line between the two should be drawn is not made clear. To ensure a compatible level of economic development, not only in the market and planning sectors but also in the public sector, Galbraith is in favour of a high level of public expenditure. Because of the relatively low level of public expenditure in the United States, Galbraith has pointed to the contrast between 'private affluence and public squalor': by this, he is referring to the waste of resources in the affluent private sector and the consequent underprovision of public services required to deal with pressing social needs. It is because Galbraith favours more government intervention that he has been widely criticised by right-wing economists who favour the operation of the market mechanism in as many fields as possible.

Conclusion

In this chapter, we demonstrated the misallocation of resources resulting from imperfect competition under the assumption of profit maximisation. We then turned our attention to the alternatives to profit maximisation and considered managerial and behavioural models of the firm. We saw that these models can give rise to price and quantity predictions which conflict with the traditional theory of the firm.

Further reading

Ryan, W.J.L. and **Pearce, D.W.**, *Price Theory*, Macmillan, London, 1971 (Ch. 13, 14 and 16).
Koplin, H.T., *Microeconomic Analysis*, Harper and Row, New York, 1971 (Ch. 11–14).
Lancaster, K., *An Introduction to Modern Microeconomics*, Rand McNally, Chicago, 1974 (Ch. 6).

Exercises

1. Review your understanding of the following terms:

monopoly	oligopoly
cartel	kinked demand curve
resource misallocation	sales maximisation
barriers to entry	satisficing
natural monopoly	cost-plus pricing
price discrimination	countervailing power
monopolistic competition	technostructure
product differentiation	

2. The following data represent the cost and revenue schedules of a pure monopolist.

Quantity	Total revenue (£)	Total cost (£)
5	500	350
10	900	550
15	1,200	675
20	1,400	800
25	1,500	1,125
30	1,500	1,800
35	1,400	2,800

(a) Calculate AR, MR, ATC and MC.
(b) Plot the AR, MR, ATC and MC schedules on the same graph and

estimate the profit-maximising price and quantity.
(c) Estimate the firm's total profit.

3. Explain why a profit-maximising monopolist is unlikely to operate on the inelastic part of the demand curve facing him.

4. Consider the scope for price discrimination in the following cases:
(a) British Rail; (b) a single wheat farmer; (c) the Milk Marketing Board; (d) a doctor with private patients.

5. 'Monopolistic competition provides a wide variety of products for consumers at the cost of some resource misallocation.' Discuss.

6. Consider the view that an oligopolistic market structure provides a higher incentive to innovate than other market structures.

7. What criticisms can be levelled against the assumption of profit maximisation in the traditional theory of the firm? Describe two alternative models that have been developed in response to these criticisms.

The public sector

11 Introducing the public sector

Introduction

The aim of the next four chapters is to consider the role of the public sector in an economy. By the term 'public sector', we mean that part of the national economy for which the government has some direct responsibility; it includes both central and local government, public corporations and other public enterprise activities. Economists are interested in the behaviour of the public sector because the government's decisions affect individuals and institutions in many different ways. The most important decisions are concerned with public spending, taxation and various rules and regulations that have an influence on social welfare. It is appropriate, therefore, that we should examine the basis of these decisions and indicate the principles of state policy on welfare.

Our major task in the present chapter is to highlight the objectives of the public sector, to examine the 'optimum' size of the public sector and to indicate the difficulties associated with measuring state activity. In this connection, we consider the structure and growth of public expenditure and taxation in the United Kingdom and other selected countries; we also outline some of the theories of the growth of public expenditure.

A fundamental point that must be made at the outset is that the public and private sectors in an economy constantly interact. This process of interaction tends to increase with imperfections in the market mechanism as public action is frequently called for to compensate for market failure. It is hardly surprising to note that in most of the present-day major western industrial nations, about 30 per cent (and in many cases, including the United Kingdom, more than 30 per cent) of the gross national product is made up of public sector activity. Note that the gross national product (or GNP) can be defined as the total monetary value of a country's annual output of final goods and services. The related measurement of gross domestic product (or GDP) is equal to gross national product minus property income from abroad.

Why do we need a public sector?

In a national economy, the market mechanism cannot perform all those functions required to attain an efficient and equitable allocation of resources. There are a number of reasons, therefore, why a public sector may be needed. Consider the following.

To promote competition The claim that the pricing system leads to an efficient use of resources depends on a most important condition: that there should be competition in the markets for both resources and finished goods.

This means that there should be no restrictions on the free entry of firms into industries and consumers and producers should have complete information about prices and profit-making opportunities. To promote competitive conditions and to prevent potential abuse of monopoly power, government measures such as taxes, subsidies and rules and regulations may be used.

To ensure the provision of goods not adequately provided by the private sector Even if we had perfect markets, there are certain types of goods which could not be provided adequately by private firms. For example, in Chapter 7 we noted that *public goods* (like defence and lighthouses) and *natural monopolies* (like gas, electricity and telecommunications) would lead to an inefficient use of resources if production were left to private enterprise.

To tackle externalities Connected with market failure are the problems of externalities, such as noise and pollution, which require public action. Generally, private sector decisions take into account only the private costs and benefits connected with production and consumption and in this way ignore the wider implications of such decisions for others in society or for future generations. A public sector can weigh the benefits and costs of the future, and take a wider view of the effects of producers and consumers on others.

To enforce contracts To make the market mechanism work, government rules and regulations are required to enforce contracts entered into between buyers and sellers of goods and resources.

To redistribute income and wealth Given that the government's goal is to maximise social welfare, public policy may be required in the attempt to achieve a more equitable distribution of income and wealth.

To promote macroeconomic objectives Public policy may be required in market economies where the pricing system is prone to high unemployment, inflation and balance of payments difficulties. In such economies, governments are concerned to implement policies designed to achieve a high level of employment, a low rate of inflation, a satisfactory balance of payments position, a desired rate of economic growth and balanced regional development. In this part of the book, we are concerned only with the government's microeconomic policy objectives. Macroeconomic theory and policy are dealt with from Chapter 17 onwards.

The microeconomic objectives of government

Governments are primarily concerned with maximising social welfare and in seeking to achieve this, they aim to influence both the allocation and distribution of resources. Microeconomic policies, then, may be said to have an allocation function and a distribution function. Consider these in turn.

The allocation function In its allocation function, the major objective of the public sector is to achieve Pareto efficiency in resource allocation. In order to implement public decisions about allocation, the government's *budget* (that is, its receipts and expenditures) plays an important role in switching resources from private to public consumption and *vice versa*. Budgetary policy, in fact, is at the heart of the government's allocation function. For example, it is through its budget that a government is able to ensure the provision of public goods, like defence and law and order. However, to make the market mechanism work, we mentioned above that the government also lays down rules and regulations (such as anti-pollution and anti-monopoly legislation); these must be regarded as part of the state's allocation function as well.

It is important to distinguish between the state *production* and the state *provision* of goods. Some goods (for example, gas, electricity, rail, air travel and municipal transport) are actually produced by state agencies and rationed through prices. Such state production in many western European countries and in the United States and Canada accounts for between 15 and 25 per cent of GNP. Public provision refers to those goods and services generally produced by private firms, but financed through the budget and paid for indirectly by the community in the form of taxation. Examples of publicly provided goods in the United Kingdom include pharmaceutical supplies to the National Health Service and defence equipment to the armed forces.

The distribution function In its distribution function, the overriding aim of the state is to promote equity – that is to say, to achieve a 'fair' distribution of income and wealth. For this purpose, budgets are usually designed to impose higher rates of taxation on higher incomes and to try and secure a fair distribution of tax burdens in the community. On the expenditure side of the budget, spending can be channelled into those areas (such as health, education and social security benefits) which directly benefit the lower-income groups.

Difficulties arise, however, in deciding whether income, spending power or wealth is the most equitable base for taxation. Added to this is the problem of defining income, capital and wealth and the difficulty of valuing assets.

Conflict of objectives

It is argued that the public sector's objectives cannot all be attained simultaneously. Conflicts arise partly because, unlike private individuals, governments strive to achieve a multiplicity of objectives. For example, the policy of maintaining low council house rents on equity grounds results in long waiting lists; this may be undesirable on efficiency grounds as it acts as a barrier to labour mobility and this in turn may increase unemployment. Likewise, policies to combat inflation might call for a cut in public expenditure which in the short-run may lead to a higher rate of unemployment and a less equitable distribution of income and wealth.

The size of the public sector in theory

Since the government plays such an important role in a mixed economy, the next question we must ask is what size of public sector will maximise social welfare, a question which concerns both economic efficiency and equity.

There are two main ways of illustrating conceptually the most efficient and equitable size of the public sector. These are (a) by identifying the social welfare maximising point on the production possibility frontier; and (b) by determining the *optimum-size fiscal community*. Consider these in turn.

Identifying the social welfare maximising point This approach starts from the division of the given stock of a country's resources between the private and public sectors. The resources allocated to the public sector have to be determined by the political process as there exists no market mechanism by which people can express their preferences for goods for collective consumption. On the other hand, the resources used for private goods are allocated by the price mechanism where consumers bid for those assortments which they want most.

When resources have been divided between the two sectors in such a way that enables the community to reach its highest attainable community indifference curve, then that community can be said to have reached a Pareto optimal intersectoral allocation of resources. This is illustrated in Fig. 1, where AB is the production possibility frontier and CIC_1 and CIC_2 are two of the community indifference curves drawn on the assumption of a given socially desired distribution of income. CIC_2 is the highest attainable community indifference curve; point Z is the social welfare maximising point and OT is the most efficient and equitable size of the public sector.

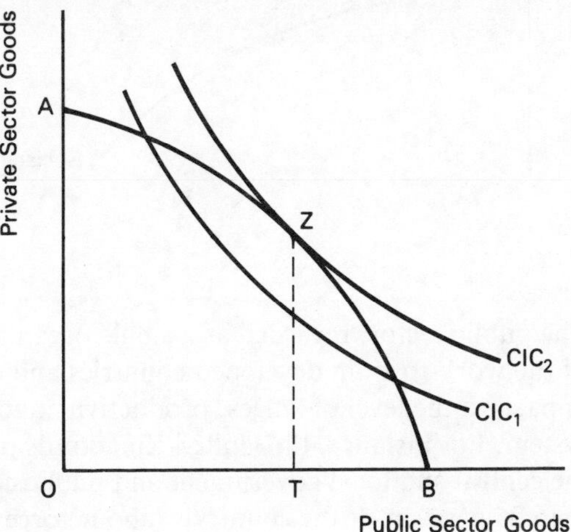

Fig. 1. The choice between public and private goods.

The optimum-size fiscal community The phrase 'optimum-size fiscal community' refers to that level of government activity at which the social marginal benefit from public spending is equal to the social marginal cost imposed on the community by taxation. The social marginal benefit from public spending can be defined as the extra utility to society resulting from each additional pound spent by the government; assuming that it obeys the law of diminishing marginal utility, we can expect it to fall as government activity increases. The social marginal cost of taxation, however, which includes both the loss of command over purchasing power and such things as disincentives to work and save, is likely to increase as government activity (and therefore taxation) increases.

These relationships are illustrated in Fig. 2 where government expenditure and taxation are measured along the horizontal axis (labelled 'size of the fiscal community'). Notice that the quadrant in which the social marginal cost of taxation is plotted has been inverted for ease of comparison. Assuming that government expenditure and taxation are kept equal, the optimal scale of government activity is shown by OB, where AB = BC. Points to the left of B would call for an expansion of government activity because such an expansion would increase total benefit to society by more than it would increase total cost. For the opposite reason, points to the right of B would call for a contraction of government activity. OB, then, is called the optimum-size fiscal community.

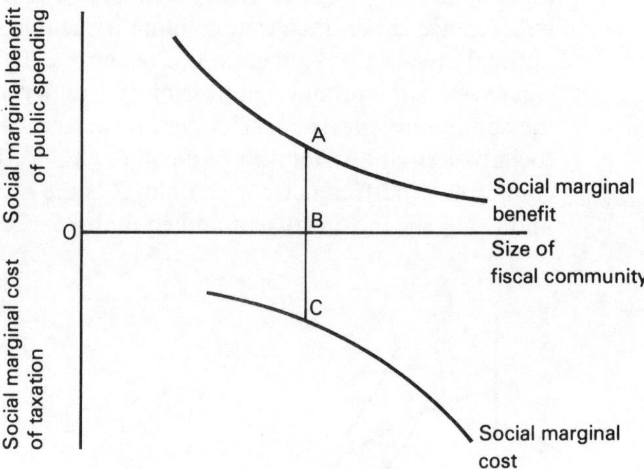

Fig. 2. The social marginal benefit and cost of state activity.

The size of the public sector in practice

Measuring the size of the public sector

The public sector, regarded as a single organisation, is the largest employer of the work-force in developed countries and can thus have a considerable impact on the level of wages, productivity and investment in the economic system. For instance, the United Kingdom's public sector (defined to include the central and local government and public corporations) employed more than 25 per cent of the country's labour force in 1975. However, the most frequently applied measures of the size of a country's public sector are total public expenditure and taxation expressed as ratios of gross national product. As will be seen below, these measurements pose a number of conceptual and statistical problems. Notwithstanding these problems, the most general point to make at this stage is that in both the industrially advanced nations and the less developed countries, the share of the public sector has increased both relatively as a proportion of GNP and absolutely over time.

In Britain, as in other countries, attempts are often made at international comparisons of the relative size of the public sector. Table 1 shows the relative size of the United Kingdom's public sector compared with Germany, France, Italy, the Netherlands, Sweden, the United States, Japan and Australia in 1967–69 and 1974–76. One conclusion that can be drawn from the figures is that the relative size of the United Kingdom's public sector is not very different from other industrially advanced countries. Consider, for example, total government expenditure as a percentage of gross domestic product (GDP) in the period 1974–76 (line 1): the figure of 44.5 per cent for the United Kingdom is similar to Germany's 44.0 per cent and is not a great deal out of step with France (41.6 per cent) and Italy (43.1 per cent). Even the United States, which has not yet reached the European standards of welfare schemes, has passed the 30 per cent mark, reaching 35.1 per cent in 1974–76. Japan had the lowest ratio (25.1 per cent). At the other end of the scale, the Netherlands and Sweden had the highest expenditure ratios (53.9 and 51.7 per cent respectively).

Table 1. Total government expenditure and total taxes as percentages of GDP in the United Kingdom and other advanced countries, 1967–9 and 1974–76.

	United Kingdom	Germany	France	Italy	Netherlands	Sweden	USA	Australia	Japan
1967–69									
1. Total expenditure[a]	38.5	33.1	39.4	35.5	42.6	41.3	31.7	26.4	19.2
2. Total taxes[b]	34.1	33.6	36.2	30.2	38.4	38.8	29.1	23.9	18.8
1974–76									
1. Total expenditure[a]	44.5	44.0	41.6	43.1	53.9	51.7	35.1	32.8	25.1
2. Total taxes[b]	36.0	38.3	37.2	31.8	46.2	47.0	27.5	29.0	22.1

Source: National Accounts of OECD Countries, Public Expenditure Trends, Paris, June 1978.
[a] Includes transfers to the rest of the world and purchases of land.
[b] Excludes fees, fines and penalties.
All the figures are three-yearly averages.
The figures in this table have been standardised for purposes of international comparison and so exclude certain items which are included in the figures in Table 2.

Now consider the taxation ratios (line 2) as a measure of the size of the public sector: the United Kingdom government raised 36.0 per cent of GDP in taxes in the period 1974–76. The Netherlands, Sweden, Germany and France took away higher amounts (46.2, 47.0, 38.3 and 37.2 per cent respectively). All the other countries in the Table had lower taxation ratios, with Japan having the lowest (22.1 per cent).

Conceptual and statistical problems of measurement

We see in Chapter 17 that a major difficulty arises in estimating the GNP: this is that only goods which are subject to the measuring rod of money are included. So, for example, leisure, pollution, noise and the domestic services of housewives are excluded. As far as international comparisons are concerned, the differing needs and tastes of different income groups within and between nations are not taken into account.

When we turn to public expenditure, the main difficulty is whether or not to include transfer payments – that is, payments for which no direct service is rendered (for example, pensions and social security payments). On the one hand, it can be argued that transfers do not result in the direct absorption of resources by the government. On the other hand, they do help to redistribute incomes and so are part of the government's distribution function. A more important difficulty arises from the fact that transfer payments are always excluded from GNP; if they were included in the measurement of public expenditure, the ratio of total public expenditure to GNP (or GDP) would tend to overstate the size of the public sector.

A number of problems also arise in using taxation as a measure of government activity. First, should social security contributions (called national insurance contributions in the United Kingdom) be included as taxes? If a tax is defined as a compulsory payment without direct benefit to the payer, then social security contributions are not taxes because they confer entitlements to direct benefit. Secondly, it can be argued that it is the taxable capacity of a taxpayer (that is, his ability to pay and not the actual tax payment) that most reflects the tax effort of the community. Such a tax effort may be judged by the extent to which a community is capable of earning, accumulating or spending its income and wealth. Finally, using the taxation ratio alone would tend to hide the extent to which a government borrows money to finance a budget deficit.

We can conclude from this section that public expenditure and taxation expressed as ratios of GNP or GDP are but crude measures of the impact of public sector decisions on the economy.

The growth of public expenditure in the United Kingdom

In the 1880s, the German economist Adolph Wagner advanced his *law of ever rising public expenditures*, basing his observations on a statistical study of major European countries, including Britain. He maintained that, with industrialisation giving rise to 'social progress', there would be greater public pressure for increased public expenditures over the next fifty to a hundred years. The long-term trend would be one of an increase in public spending at a faster rate than the increase in GNP. Has this law been borne out by United Kingdom data?

Table 2 shows that public expenditure in the United Kingdom has risen both in absolute terms and in relative terms (as a ratio of GNP) since 1968. Line 1 shows that between 1968 and 1978, government expenditure in current prices rose by almost fourfold. This, however, is not a very useful way of looking at the growth in public expenditure because the general level of prices more than doubled during the same period. Line 2 shows the rise in government spending in *constant* (1975) prices and line 4 shows the rise in government spending as a percentage of GNP. Both confirm that public expenditure rose significantly in the ten year period.

It is instructive to note that there has been an *upward long-term trend* in total government expenditure in most industrialised countries and in less

Table 2. The growth of public expenditure in the United Kingdom, 1968 – 78.

	1968	1978
1. Total government expenditure in current prices (£m.)	18,289	71,351
2. Total government expenditure in constant prices (£m.)	21,516	29,729
3. GNP at factor cost in current prices (£m.)	37,890	142,835
4. Total government expenditure as a percentage of GNP in current prices	48.3	50.0

Source: National Income and Expenditure, 1979.

developed countries. Peacock and Wiseman undertook a major statistical study of the growth of public expenditure in the United Kingdom for the period 1890–1955. The study showed that total public expenditure in current prices rose from 8.9 per cent of GNP in 1890 to 36.6 per cent of GNP in 1955. This indicates a considerable increase in the relative size of the United Kingdom's public sector since 1890. Additionally, Peacock and Wiseman observed a marked change in the composition of government expenditure. In particular, they pointed to the growing share of expenditure on education, health and transport and the growing importance of transfers, such as social security payments, subsidies and debt interest.

There is a major difficulty in trying to draw worthwhile conclusions from secular increases in total government expenditure. This difficulty stems from the problem of maintaining a consistent definition of public expenditure. Definitions tend to change over time. In the United Kingdom, for instance, the official definition of 'total public expenditure' included the entire capital expenditure of nationalised industries and other public corporations for many years. But part of the capital expenditure of nationalised industries was financed from internal surpluses and from domestic and overseas borrowing. This meant that the definition overstated the extent to which the government had to finance the activities of the public sector by taxation and through its own borrowing requirement. Consequently, a new definition of public expenditure was adopted in 1976 which included only loans and grants by the public sector to the nationalised industries and other public corporations.

The composition of public expenditure

Table 3 shows the composition of public expenditure in the United Kingdom in 1968 and 1978. Consider the various categories of expenditure in turn.

Total final expenditure on goods and services (line 1) is by far the biggest item and rose from 41.8 per cent of the total in 1968 to 45.8 per cent in 1978. This category includes spending on the wages and salaries of the armed forces, the police, teachers and civil servants as well as the supply of provisions to the armed forces, schools and hospitals.

Total capital expenditure (line 2) dropped from 15.8 per cent of the total in 1968 to 9.1 per cent in 1978. This category is in fact subject to quite large fluctuations over time largely because changes in capital expenditure are politically less unpopular in response to the call for demand-management policies. Examples of capital expenditure include spending on roads, bridges, hospitals and school buildings.

Note that these first two categories of public expenditure (lines 1 and 2) are the real resource-using expenditures of the public sector. Resources used to produce goods like roads, education and defence are no longer available for the production of goods and services by the private sector. It might be argued, however, that some of the real resource-using public expenditures provide goods which are complementary to those provided by the private sector. For example, government expenditure on roads, traffic lights and street lighting complement private sector goods, such as cars and bicycles. Similarly, education, defined as investment in 'human capital', can be regarded as being complementary to investment in plant and machinery by the private sector.

Subsidies (line 3) represent unrequited payments by both central and local government to the nationalised industries, other public corporations and private firms.

Table 3. The composition of government expenditure in the United Kingdom, 1968 and 1978.

	1968		1978	
	£m.	% of total	£m.	% of total
1. Total final expenditure on goods and services	7,640	41.8	32,693	45.8
2. Total capital expenditure	2,899	15.8	6,500	9.1
3. Subsidies	895	4.9	3,598	5.1
4. Grants to personal sector	3,678	20.1	17,853	25.0
5. Grants abroad	179	1.0	1,700	2.4
6. Debt interest	1,794	9.8	7,302	10.2
7. Net lending	1,204	6.6	1,705	2.4
Total government expenditure	18,289	100.0	71,351	100.0

Source: National Income and Expenditure, 1979.

Grants to personal sector (line 4) include pensions, unemployment benefits and other social security payments. This is a growing category of public expenditure in the United Kingdom and rose by almost a quarter from 1968 to 1978. Indeed, this category is one of the most important indicators of the extent to which the government is attempting to carry out its redistribution function.

Grants abroad (line 5) include mainly development aid to the less developed countries.

Debt interest (line 6) represents payment of interest on the national debt, including interest on the amount of money borrowed annually to cover any budget deficit. The increase in debt interest during the period 1968–78 was largely due to budget deficits having to be financed by borrowing.

Net lending (line 7) includes lending to private firms, overseas governments and international lending bodies, including the specialised agencies of the United Nations. This item was curtailed during the period

1968–78 mostly because of the persistent economic recession at home during the 1970s.

It should be noted that the public expenditure categories from lines 3 to 7 differ from those in lines 1 and 2. The items in lines 3 to 7 do not involve the absorption of real resources by the public sector itself. Spending on these items rose from about a third of the total in 1968 to nearly a half by 1978.

The composition of the public sector's revenues

It can be seen from Table 4 that taxes on incomes make the largest contribution to the government's total revenues in the United Kingdom. Taxes on expenditure and national insurance and health contributions are the second and third largest contributors respectively. Notice the marked rise in national insurance and health contributions during the period 1968–78 and the decline in the relative importance of rates as a means of raising revenue. The financial receipts shown in line 8 represent the amount of money which the government has had to borrow to finance the public sector's budget deficits – that is to say, the shortfall in tax revenues (lines 1–7 in Table 4) required to finance total public expenditure (lines 1–7 in Table 3) is made up through borrowing. In the 1970s, the public sector became increasingly dependent upon borrowing as an additional method of financing its spending.

Table 4. The composition of total government revenue in the United Kingdom, 1968 and 1978.

	1968		1978	
	£m.	% of total	£m.	% of total
1. Taxes on income	5,846	31.9	22,321	31.3
2. Taxes on capital	437	2.4	898	1.3
3. Taxes on expenditure	5,261	28.8	17,545	24.6
4. Rates	1,548	8.5	5,693	8.0
5. National insurance and health	2,161	11.8	10,023	14.0
6. Total taxes	15,253	83.4	56,480	79.2
7. Government property income	1,613	8.8	6,382	8.9
8. Financial receipts	1,423	7.8	8,489	11.9
Total government revenue	18,289	100.0	71,351	100.0

Source: National Income and Expenditure, 1979.

The amount of money which the public sector intends to borrow during a given financial year is called the *public sector borrowing requirement* (PSBR). The size of the PSBR is determined by the following factors:

(a) the size of the deficit of the central and local governments;
(b) the size of the deficit of the nationalised industries and other public corporations;
(c) the amount of net lending to the private sector and overseas;
(d) the public sector's receipts from the sale of financial assets and other financial transactions.

Causes of the growth of public expenditure

The foregoing account of public expenditure and taxation ratios has shown a rise in the relative size of the public sector in many countries. But why has public expenditure risen? One of the main reasons has undoubtedly been the social and political changes which have taken place in western industrialised countries during the last seventy years. These changes have led to the development of social and welfare services by the state and hence growth in public expenditure. In the United Kingdom, the Beveridge Plan of 1944 marked the beginning of a comprehensive social security system. Public expenditure on transfer payments increased as a result, and since the early 1970s, the index-linking of pensions and certain other benefits has further increased public expenditure in the United Kingdom.

A number of theories have been put forward in the attempt to explain why public expenditure has increased. We have already briefly considered Wagner's law. In addition, consider the following theories.

Peacock and Wiseman's social disturbance hypothesis This hypothesis is based on Peacock and Wiseman's statistical study of the growth of public expenditure in the United Kingdom during the period 1890–1955. It starts from the premise that decisions about public expenditure are taken politically with the popular support of the electorate. Citizens' ideas about desirable levels of expenditure, however, do not coincide with their ideas about tolerable levels of taxation. This divergence is narrowed, though, by major social disturbances, such as wars and national crises, which create a 'displacement effect' and lead people to expect higher levels of both public spending and taxation. The Boer War, the First World War, the Great Depression and the Second World War created such 'displacement effects'. During these social disturbances, voters become used to the higher levels of taxation and spending with the result that, after the disturbance, public spending settles on a plateau, well above the pre-disturbance level. This explanation is concerned with the time pattern of public spending, whereas Wagner was principally interested in the long-run trend. However, Peacock and Wiseman's hypothesis apparently fails to explain the record peacetime growth of public spending after 1955.

Buchanan and Tullock's oversupply hypothesis According to this hypothesis, voters derive utilities from state provisions, whilst politicians strive to maximise their stay in office. This means that politicians carry out electorally popular programmes which will ensure their return to office at the next general election. Assuming that taxes imposed on the entire community are used to finance expenditure proposals which benefit only a small part of the population, the chances are that there would be an oversupply of local and sectional benefits as voters are likely to view such spending as costless. Similarly, when a budget deficit is financed by borrowing, voters may view the growth in public expenditure as costless and this will result in the oversupply of public goods. Correlation between economic booms and elections in postwar Britain seems to support this hypothesis. However, it is difficult to accept that defence, national health and education spending benefit only sectional interests.

In opposition to Buchanan and Tullock, other economists have argued that, despite the growth of public spending, there may still be an *undersupply* of public provision relative to private provision. Pigou, for example, has suggested that this arises because private producers take account only of their private costs and benefits while public producers have to take account of all external costs and benefits as well. Where external costs exceed external benefits, there results an overallocation of resources to the private sector and an underallocation to the public sector. As mentioned in Chapter 10, J.K. Galbraith has taken this argument further. He points out that the consumer is subjected to an intensive advertising campaign by private producers and this diverts attention from 'social needs', so resulting in a smaller public sector than is socially desirable.

The role of the public sector in less developed countries

The market mechanism in less developed countries operates in far less perfect conditions than that in industrially developed countries. In particular, the price incentives which might otherwise be engendered by demand and supply conditions in the markets for goods and services are usually hampered by such factors as the lack of developed means of communications, lack of specialisation and exchange, customs and traditions and general inertia on the part of producers and consumers. This places the public sector in a position to initiate and influence the pattern of economic development through its expenditure and taxation policies. For example, government budgets can help to break the 'vicious circle' of poverty by stimulating investment and developing the infrastructure. Thus, investment in health, education, transport and the development of natural resources very often falls into the 'social overhead' investment category which becomes the spearhead of budgetary policy.

As regards the financing of economic development, the budgets are frequently deficit-financed by borrowing or printing money because the revenue side of the budget has only meagre taxation income. Furthermore, unlike developed countries where progressive income taxes are a principal instrument for redistributing incomes, less developed countries depend mainly on selected indirect taxes, such as import and export duties and sales taxes, with the result that the development objective takes precedence over the distribution and other objectives. Note that a broadly-based indirect tax is difficult to apply in less developed countries because of the problem of identifying the origins and destinations of many goods since many firms keep incomplete records of their accounts. In addition, the subsistence level of income and the absence of an efficient administrative machinery to discover incomes above the subsistence level mean that it is extremely difficult to put into practice an equitable system of progressive income taxation.

Conclusion

This chapter has attempted to show why a community needs a public sector and has explored the principles according to which the public sector must operate so as to maximise social welfare. We have also examined the size of the public sector in the United Kingdom and other selected countries.

Because the size of the public sector is limited, it is the nature and composition of the budget which, at any time, will be the arbiter of social welfare.

Further reading

Haveman, R.H., *The Economics of the Public Sector*, J. Wiley and Sons, London, 1976 (Ch. 4 and 5).
Brown, C.V. and **Jackson, P.M.**, *Public Sector Economics*, Martin Robertson, Oxford, 1978 (Ch. 6 and 7).
Musgrave, R. and **Musgrave, P.**, *Public Finance in Theory, and Practice*, McGraw-Hall, New York, 1976 (Ch. 5 and 6).
Carter, H. and **Partington, I.**, *Applied Economics in Banking and Finance*, Oxford University Press, Oxford, 1979 (Ch. 9).
Peacock, A.T. and **Wiseman, J.**, *The Growth of Public Expenditure in the United Kingdom*, Allen and Unwin, London, 1958.

Exercises

1. Review your understanding of the following terms:

public sector	government revenue
allocation function	optimum-size fiscal community
distribution function	Wagner's 'law'
state production	'social disturbance' hypothesis
state provision	oversupply hypothesis
government expenditure	public sector borrowing requirement

2. Consider the following data on the United Kingdom's public sector borrowing requirement (PSBR):

1975–76	£10.6 billion
1976–77	£8.5 billion
1977–78	£5.6 billion
1978–79	£9.3 billion

Source: *Financial Statistics*, January 1980.

(a) Explain what is meant by the PSBR.
(b) Suggest reasons for the size of the PSBR in these years.
(c) In what ways might changes in the PSBR affect the level of government expenditure?

3. Discuss the meaning of the 'optimum size' of a country's public sector. What conditions should be satisfied before a public sector can be described as being of 'optimum size'?

4. Discuss the main difficulties which arise in attempting to measure the size of a country's public sector and in comparing it with that of other countries.

5. Which, in your view, is the most plausible explanation of the growth of public expenditure in the United Kingdom?

6. What theoretical and practical arguments are there in favour of reducing the size of a country's public sector?

12 Public goods and externalities

Introduction

The aim of this chapter is to explore the basis of public expenditure policies concerned with public goods and externalities. Economists have striven to explain public expenditure decisions in terms of the concepts of public goods and externalities because these form the basis of many government decisions about the size and composition of public expenditures. We propose in this chapter, after establishing certain definitions, to focus attention on the following areas: (a) the nature of public goods; (b) the links and differences between public goods and private goods; (c) the nature and causes of externalities and some suggested solutions; (d) the cost-benefit analysis of public expenditure decisions; (e) the role of cost-benefit analysis in less developed countries.

Public goods, private goods, mixed goods and externalities

Definition: ***A pure public good is a good or service, such as defence, the consumption of which by one person does not reduce its benefit to others in society.***

If we let Y denote the total quantity of a pure public good, Y_A the quantity consumed by individual A and Y_B the quantity consumed by individual B, then we can write: $Y = Y_A = Y_B$. The equality signs show that there is no extra cost in supplying a given quantity of a public good to additional people – although, of course, the production of additional units of such a good would involve extra cost.

From the standpoint of the goal of maximum social welfare, a public good with a zero marginal cost of supply to an extra individual should be made

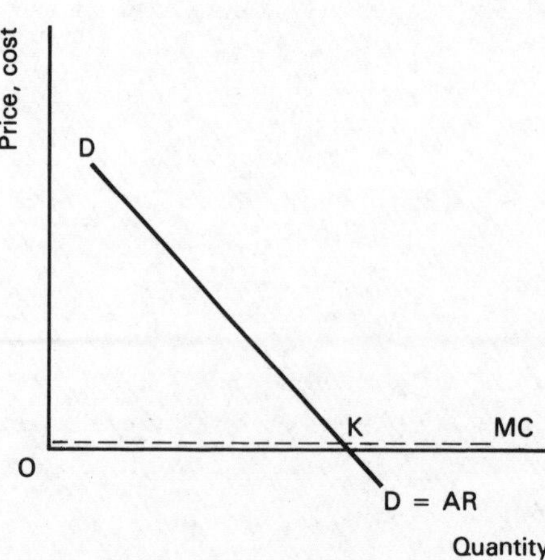

Fig. 1. Determination of the welfare maximising quantity of a pure public good.

available free of charge to all, as shown in Fig. 1. This zero marginal cost of supply to an extra individual is indicated on the graph by the dotted line which coincides with the horizontal axis and intersects the demand curve DD at point K. Assuming that the marginal conditions for Pareto optimality are satisfied in the rest of the economy, social welfare is maximised in the Paretian sense by producing OK units of the public good; that is, where the supply of the public good equals its consumption at zero price. As there is a positive cost of producing a public good, this raises the practical problem of whether to finance its production through taxes or borrowing.

Definition: ***A private good is a good or service whose consumption by one individual results in the reduction of its supply to others.***

The more bread is consumed by one individual, the less is left for others to consume; the more petrol this generation uses, the less it leaves for future generations. If we let Z denote the total supply of a pure private good, we can write: $Z = Z_A + Z_B$, where Z_A is the amount consumed by individual A and Z_B is the amount consumed by individual B. The marginal cost of a private good, unlike that of a public good, will be positive and will eventually increase as more and more units are produced.

Definition: ***A mixed good is a good or service which has both private and public good content.***

In real life, there are few *pure* public or private goods. A public good may have some private good content: for example, a motorist crossing a bridge in peak-hour traffic affects the supply of bridge-crossings to other motorists by contributing to congestion and delays; in this case, the marginal cost of supply is zero for low levels of use, but exceeds zero for higher levels. Similarly, a private good may have some 'publicness': for example, watching a television at home (basically, a private good) has some public good content as neighbours and friends may also be invited to watch. Such observations of real life situations show that there are a whole range of mixed goods, whereas pure public and pure private goods are but extremes of these situations. Producers depend upon other producers and upon consumers in their attempts to maximise their profits and thus their behaviour can hardly be described as completely private. Consumers depend upon other consumers and producers in the attempt to maximise their utilities and so their behaviour is not completely private either.

It is because of the interdependence of the behaviour of consumers and producers that considerable interest has been stimulated in the analysis of externalities.

Definition: ***Externalities are those gains and losses which are sustained by others as a result of actions initiated by producers or consumers or both and for which no compensation is paid.***

Externalities are sometimes called 'third party effects', 'neighbourhood effects' or 'spillovers'. Alfred Marshall, the Victorian economist, used the phrases 'external economies' and 'external diseconomies'. As an example of an externality, consider a chemical firm which discharges noxious wastes into a river estuary, killing all the fish and resulting in the loss of livelihood of a fisherman: no compensation is paid for this loss. Similarly, the discharge of unclean water from an industrial city into a river may result in the loss of recreational activities like swimming, boating and angling. Yet no compensation is claimed for the loss of these pleasures, nor are these external costs included in the cost calculations of the polluting firms and other agents.

As we shall see, the most important externalities are those which affect the environment within which mankind seeks to satisfy his economic and biological needs. The most important point to emphasise at this stage, though, is that externalities can arise from *both* production and consumption. Following Buchanan and Stubblebine, a *consumption externality* may be explained in the context of a two-person, two-good economy using the following functional notation:

$$U_A = f(a_1, a_2, \dots a_n; b)$$

where U_A denotes the total utility of individual A; a_1 to a_n denote the activities from 1 to n which are directly under the control of individual A; and b denotes the activity of individual B. The equation asserts that A's utility is not only dependent on his own activities, but also on the activity of individual B. For example, an individual's enjoyment of peace and quiet depends not only on what he does, but also on his neighbours' activities.

It must be noted that interdependence alone is not sufficient to constitute an externality. It must also be shown that there has been a failure to pay for or to receive payment on account of any gains or losses. Thus, a consumption externality exists where there is interdependence coupled with an absence of any form of compensation or price paid by the gainers.

A *production externality* can similarly be defined using the following functional notation:

$$P_C = f(c_1, c_2, \dots c_n; d)$$

This states that firm C's profits (P_C) depend on the n activities of firm C (that is, c_1 to c_n) and on the activity d of a second firm. Thus, a production externality exists where there is some interdependence among the activities of firms coupled with an absence of any form of price or compensation paid on account of the loss or gain.

The nature of public goods

Pure public goods have two main identifiable characteristics.

(a) *Non-rivalness in consumption.* If a public good is supplied to one individual, it is at the same time made available to others at zero cost. This is true of defence, lighthouses and police protection. Such goods are indivisible in the sense that the benefits that each user derives from them cannot be measured, nor can the actual number of users of such goods be identified.

(b) *Non-exclusion.* Once a public good is supplied to individual A, individual B cannot be excluded from consuming it, whether he wants to or not. This implies that public goods are impossible to reject: a pacifist, for example, cannot fail to be affected by defence provided to other members of society. Note that this characteristic of non-exclusion can also be applied to externalities where, as we noted above, other members of a group cannot be excluded from suffering a loss or deriving some benefit as a result of the action of a producer or consumer.

Only *pure* public goods will exhibit both of the above characteristics. The degree of 'publicness' of other public goods can be restricted by either spatial or capacity limitations. Consider these in turn.

(a) *Spatial limitations.* The degree of 'publicness' may depend on the geographical area which a given public good is able to benefit. For example, fire protection is likely to be non-rival in a compact geographical area, but once the area is enlarged the 'publicness' element disappears. Similarly, the Blackpool illuminations are non-rival only when one is on or near the promenade and certainly not when one is in London.

(b) *Capacity limitations.* The number of people able to enjoy a public good is dictated by the limits of its capacity. For example, a road bridge has a given traffic-carrying capacity beyond which it would become congested and lose its non-rival characteristic.

Links between public and private goods

Mixed goods exhibit some of the characteristics of both private and public goods. The possible linkages between private and public goods are summarised in Table 1, where the following four cases are identified.

Case 1 (rival and excludable) is a clear-cut example of a pure private good, such as a loaf of bread whose consumption by individual A necessarily reduces its supply to individual B. When A pays the price for the loaf, this entitles him to exclude B from consuming it.

Table 1. Linkages between private and public goods.

	Excludable	Non-excludable
Rival	Case 1	Case 2
Non-rival	Case 3	Case 4

Case 2 (rival and non-excludable) illustrates the case of a private good with some public good content. As an example, consider a bee-keeper and a flower grower: the bee-keeper is unable to select which flowers his bees will pollenate and the flower grower is unable to choose which bees should get the nectar for honey (non-exclusion in both cases). Once a given swarm of bees is engaged in pollenating the nursery of one flower grower, however, they cannot at the same time be expected to benefit another nursery (rival consumption).

Case 3 (non-rival and excludable) illustrates a situation of the private provision of goods which have a public good content and the public provision of goods with a private good content. As an example, consider a football stadium with a capacity crowd of 60,000 spectators. Up to this capacity, watching a match is non-rival. It is made excludable by fencing the ground so that entry can only be gained by payment or by ticket. The same argument applies to theatres and cinemas. As an example of a good provided by the government but which has a private good content, consider the

National Health Service: this is non-rival up to its capacity, but excludable in the sense that the beneficiaries of medical care can be identified – this means that the government is able to choose to some extent who shall benefit from the service.

Case 4 (non-rival and non-excludable) typifies a pure public good, like defence and lighthouses, as discussed above.

Differences in the demand for private and public goods

Demand for a private good Since consumers of private goods buy different quantities but normally pay the same price, the market demand curve for such a good is obtained by summing the individual demand curves *horizontally*.

Figure 2 shows the derivation of a market demand curve for good X in a simple two-person economy, with the two individuals A and B. The curve D_AD_A represents A's demand curve for X and the curve D_BD_B represents B's demand for the same good. At price OP, A's demand for X is equal to Oq_A and B's demand is equal to Oq_B: the total market demand at price OP must be $Oq_A + Oq_B = Oq_M$. The market demand curve, D_MD_M, is found by adding A's and B's demands together at every price – in other words, by horizontal summation.

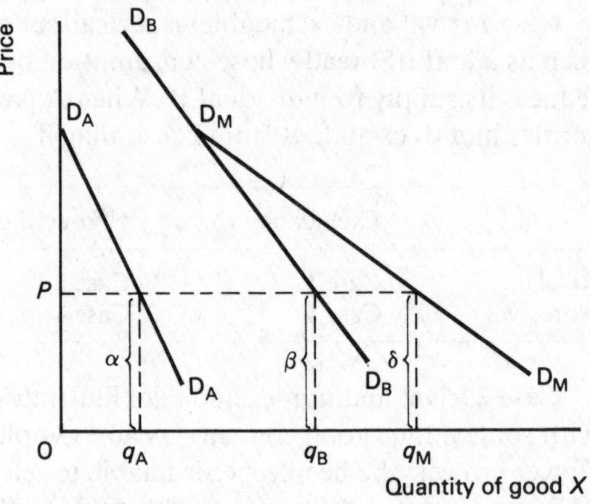

Fig. 2. Horizontal summation of individual demand curves.

Notice also that the marginal benefits derived by the two people are the same, indicated on the graph by α and β, and that these in turn are equal to the market marginal valuation δ. These marginal benefits are all equal to the prevailing price OP.

Demand for a public good Since each additional unit of a public good benefits everyone, we must add all the individuals' valuations placed on extra units of such a good in order to obtain its market demand curve. To find society's *willingness to pay*, the price each individual would be willing to pay if he revealed his true preferences must be added. Graphically, this means that individual demand curves must be summed *vertically*, as shown in Fig. 3. The graph again portrays an economy with two persons, A and B. The curves D_AD_A and D_BD_B represent the two individuals demand curves for the public good *Y*. The market demand curve is represented by D_MD_M. Consider the quantity OQ: individual A is willing to pay the price OP_1 for this quantity and B is willing to pay the price OP_2. The marginal benefits derived from the good by the two individuals differ. Thus, the price which society as a whole is prepared to pay for the quantity OQ is $OP_3 = OP_1 + OP_2$.

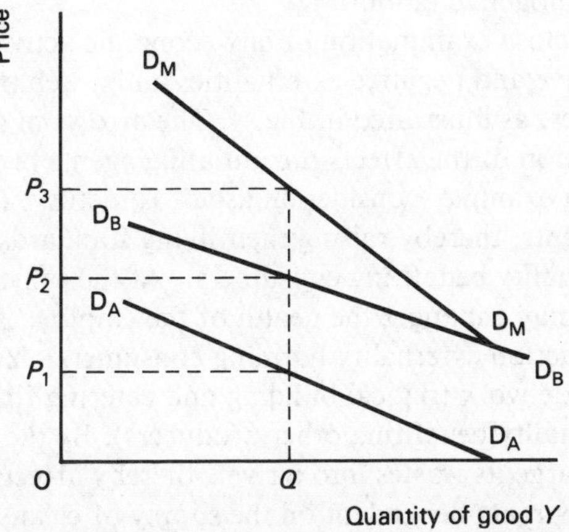

Fig. 3. Vertical summation of individual demand curves.

The number of people participating in the enjoyment of non-excludable and non-rival consumption goods is generally very large. As a result, each individual has little incentive to reveal his true preference for public goods. Members of large groups are aware that it is impossible to exclude them from enjoying the benefits of public goods and so they may try to be *free riders* and avoid payment. The potential existence of free riders makes the estimation of the market demand for public goods exceedingly difficult. Furthermore, unlike most private goods whose quantities demanded are measurable, there exists no identifiable unit of measurement for many public goods. For example, defence is not a single concept, but is made up of disparate elements of men, equipment and strategy. The same is true of the police, education and health.

One important policy conclusion emerging from our discussion of the demand patterns of the two types of goods is worth noting. Given the goal of social welfare maximisation, it must be determined whether the most efficient unit of supply of public goods is the central government, a local authority, a public corporation or any other autonomous public body. For example, street lighting, sewage disposal and public parks are probably most efficiently supplied by local authorities: they are in a better position to estimate the demand for these amenities and can more easily compare the relevant costs and benefits. Where the benefits are diffused and widespread, however, the most efficient unit of supply may be the central government: this is so in the cases of external security, space exploration and nuclear energy development, for example.

Externalities – public goods and public bads

The nature of externalities

Externalities can be classified as either *positive* or *negative*. Most of the foregoing discussion about public and private goods has centred around positive externalities. In addition to these, though, all economic systems, irrespective of their state of development, are characterised by negative externalities of differing degrees of severity. Negative externalities are *public bads*, the opposite of public goods. Examples include international tension resulting from a doubling of defence spending by one country; smoke and noise from vehicles, aeroplanes and factories creating air pollution and discomfort; nuclear tests polluting the environment and exposing human life to radioactive fallout.

A close examination of any economic activity is likely to reveal both positive and negative externalities and a web of initiating agents and affected parties, as illustrated in Fig. 4. The arrows in the diagram indicate the direction of the effects the initiating agents produce on firms or consumers. As an example, consider an asbestos factory. It may provide jobs to local residents, thereby raising their living standards (a positive production externality benefiting consumers). At the same time, the emission of asbestos dust may endanger the health of the employees and local residents (a negative production externality harming consumers). Yet again, the factory may provide work to local building and catering firms (a positive production externality benefiting other producers). By the same token, the factory may discharge its wastes into a river, thereby affecting the profit levels of firms downstream dependent on the supply of clean water from the river (a negative production externality harming producers).

Fig. 4. Externalities.

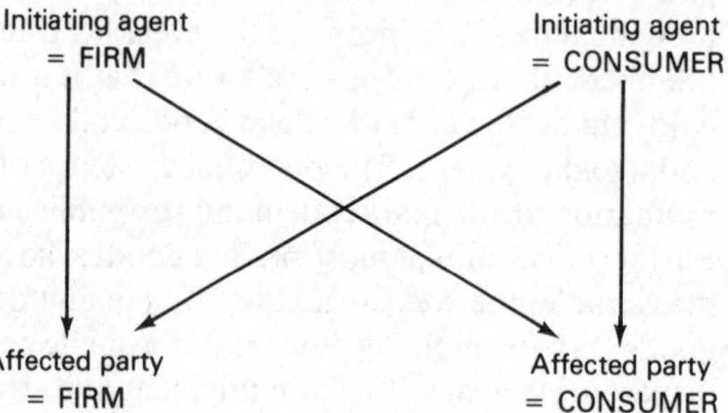

We note from this that externalities, positive or negative, can run from production to production and from production to consumption. In addition, they can run from consumption to production and from consumption to consumption.

An important problem is how to determine whether a given externality-generating activity is one of net external costs (that is, a negative externality) or net external benefits (that is, a positive externality). Broadly speaking, if the externality leads to a net increase in the total of consumer and producer surplus, it can be said to be a positive externality and, in that case, state action might be called for to encourage it. Conversely, if the externality leads to a net reduction in the total of consumer and producer surplus, government action may be called for to curtail it or even to ban it completely.

The divergence between private and social costs

Where there is a negative externality, we can say that there exists a divergence between private and social costs. To illustrate this graphically, consider a firm which is polluting a river with noxious chemical wastes. This pollution creates an *external* marginal cost which is imposed on society, but which is not included in the firm's own *private* marginal cost. This is shown in Fig. 5. The *social* marginal cost curve (SMC) represents the extra cost to society of producing an additional unit of the good; it lies above the private marginal cost curve (PMC) because private producers fail to take account of the external marginal cost (EMC). Notice that the infinitely elastic demand curve facing the firm, DD, implies that the market is assumed for convenience to be perfectly competitive. It can be seen that Oq_1 is the Pareto optimal level of output where SMC intersects DD at point h. A profit-maximising firm, however, will produce the larger quantity Oq_2 at which point social marginal cost (equal to q_2j) exceeds private marginal cost (equal to q_2g). Thus, the good in question may be said to be *oversupplied*.

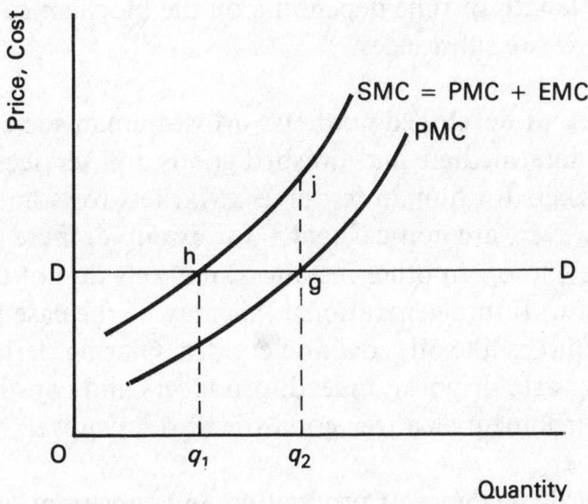

Fig. 5. The divergence between private and social costs.

Causes of externalities

Consider the following four possible reasons for the existence of externalities.

Interaction between the economic system and the environment A most important reason for the existence of externalities is that every economic activity begins and ends with the environment. All initiating agents draw resources, such as air, water and raw materials, from the environment. They then transform these resources partly directly into consumption, and partly into the production of intermediate and finished goods. The resources are then returned to the environment as wastes - for example, in the form of polluted air, unclean water, empty tins and bottles. This constant interaction between the economic system and the environment is illustrated in Fig. 6. The direction of the arrows indicates flows to initiating agents in the top half of the diagram. The bottom half of the diagram shows the waste disposal flows from initiating agents into the environment which then recycles these flows back to producers and consumers. The recycling process is shown by the dotted arrows from the environment as a waste sink.

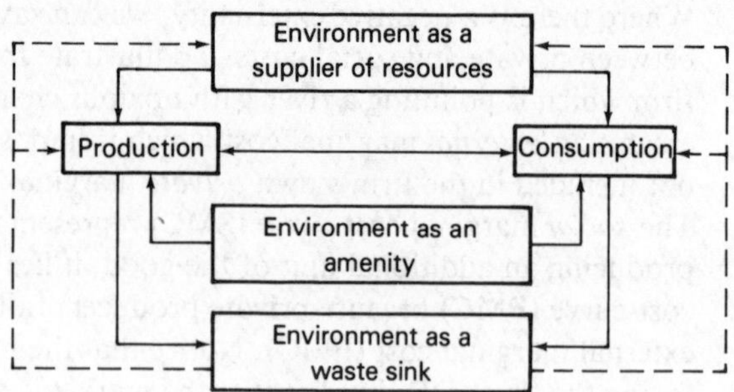

Fig. 6. The economic system and the environment.

Externalities arise because the environment has only a limited *assimilative capacity* as a waste disposal sink. Given the existing state of technological knowledge, the environment has a zero assimilative capacity for certain types of wastes – for example, cumulative pollutants such as cadmium and mercury. For wastes like polluted water, the assimilation process takes time, the length of time depending on the biochemical and organic composition of the waste substances.

Lack of developed markets Most human societies have developed markets for intermediate and finished goods and services. They also have labour markets for human resources. Markets for some environmental resources, however, are non-existent – for example, there can be no market for fresh air (see Ch. 6). In other instances, markets do not take account of the full social cost to future generations: this may be the case in markets for non-renewable resources like oil, coal and copper. Glaring deficiencies exist in the markets for waste disposal; indeed, producers and consumers often regard the environment as a free good for waste disposal.

Interdependence of production and consumption Even if the economic system could be completely isolated from the environment, the interdependence of production and consumption activities by itself would generate potential externalities (see Fig. 4 above).

Incomplete property rights Since human societies have less developed private and communal property rights over resources like land, air, space and water than over other goods, both positive and negative externalities can arise. It is because these resources cannot easily be owned that firms and consumers are not excluded from using them in ways which affect third parties.

Methods of dealing with externalities

A number of methods have been suggested for dealing with externalities. Consider the following.

Pigou's tax-subsidy solution Pigou suggested that a *tax* be imposed on generators of negative externalities and a *subsidy* be given to generators of positive externalities.

First, consider the tax solution to a negative externality such as river pollution caused by a perfectly competitive chemical industry, as shown in Fig. 7. DD is the market demand curve and SS is the supply curve for the industry's product, reflecting only the industry's private marginal costs (Σ PMC). The price O*P* and quantity O*Q* are determined by market forces. Suppose, however, that the industry's production imposes an external marginal cost on society in the form of river pollution, shown by the EMC curve in the graph. Thus, at output O*Q*, the external marginal cost is equal to *Q*A. To allow for this, the government can impose an excise tax equal to EMC at each level of output, which shifts the supply curve upwards from SS to S + T. This induces the industry to reduce its level of activity to the optimal level OQ_1, where price equals social marginal cost (SMC). Notice that this method of pollution control is generally one of reducing the level of pollution rather than eliminating it completely. This is shown in Fig. 7 where the post-tax EMC, equal to Q_1B is less than the pre-tax EMC, *Q*A.

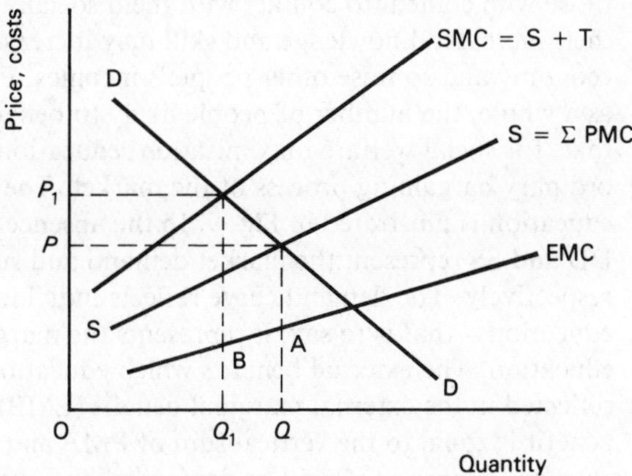

Fig. 7. Tax solution to a negative externality.

The tax remedy, however, is not entirely satisfactory when we come to consider the scale of activity of a firm under conditions of *imperfect competition*. To show this, consider Fig. 8 which illustrates a monopolistic firm maximising its profits (where MR equals PMC) by producing output O*Q* at price O*P* before any tax is imposed. The Pareto optimal price and output, though, are found where price equals social marginal cost – that is, price OP_1 (lower than O*P*) and output OQ_1 (greater than O*Q*). The imposition of an excise tax which shifts the firm's PMC curve upwards to PMC + T, causes the firm to produce a reduced quantity OQ_2 and charge a higher price OP_2. In this case, therefore, the tax causes the firm to move in the opposite direction to that required to achieve a Pareto optimum. The reason for this is that the negative externality causes overproduction which tends to offset the profit-maximising monopolist's restriction of output. Notice that this is a clear example of the *theory of second best* because there are two imperfections and even after tackling the externality, the market imperfection persists.

Now consider the subsidy solution to a positive externality and take the external benefits of *education* as an example. Education directly increases the

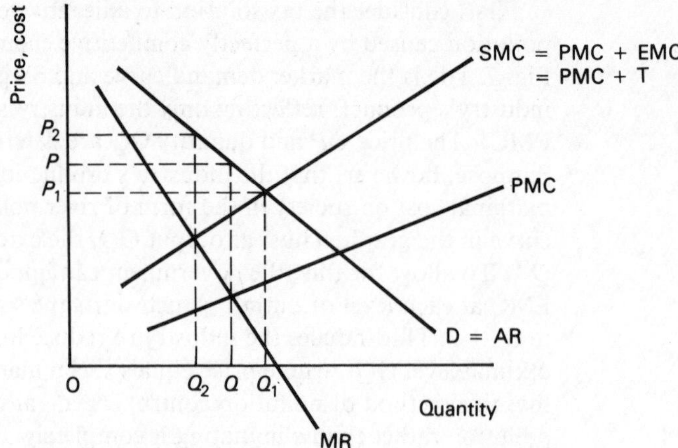

Fig. 8. The tax solution in an imperfect market.

earning power of those individuals who receive it and they in turn benefit those who come into contact with them socially and at work. For example, their increased knowledge and skill may increase the productivity of the economy and so raise other people's incomes. From the standpoint of society as a whole, the number of people likely to benefit is large and this means that, for social welfare maximisation, education cannot be left to the ordinary bargaining process of the market. The case for subsidising education is illustrated in Fig. 9. In the absence of government intervention, DD and SS represent the market demand and supply curves for education respectively. The demand curve reflects individuals' valuation of education – that is to say, it represents the marginal private benefit (PMB) of education. The external benefits which education provides for society are reflected in the external marginal benefit (EMB) curve. Total social marginal benefit is equal to the vertical sum of PMB and EMB. In the absence of any subsidy, quantity O*Q* will be demanded and supplied at price O*P*. Now suppose the government gives a subsidy which mirrors EMB. This subsidy might take the form of vouchers to be spent on education and so will shift the demand curve for education upwards by the full amount of the subsidy

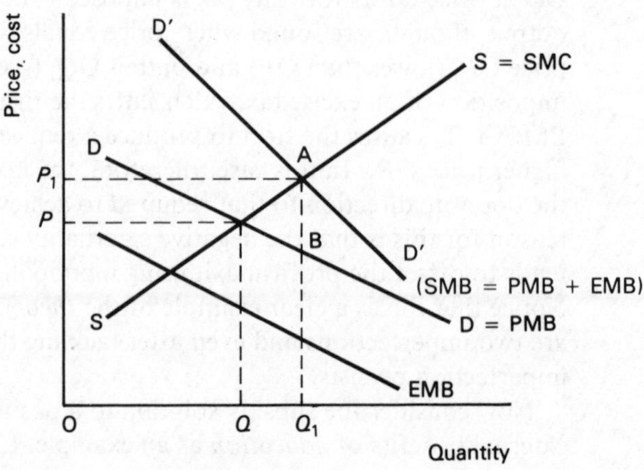

Fig. 9. A subsidy on education.

(to D′D′). The equilibrium quantity will now be increased to the Pareto optimal level of OQ_1, at which point social marginal cost is equal to social marginal benefit. At this point, the subsidy paid is equal to AB.

If society considered that the external benefits of education outweighed the private benefits, then the government may decide to subsidise the entire quantity, making it available free of charge to all, as with compulsory education in the United Kingdom. In that case, it would become analogous to a pure public good benefiting large groups of people.

Bargaining solution in small groups Bargaining is another method of dealing with an externality, applicable where only small groups are involved. Consider the external cost of pollution where there are only two parties involved: the profit-maximising producer and polluter (P) and the sufferer (S). If P has the prior right to pollute the environment, S can negotiate and bargain with P to reduce the level of pollution. Conversely, if S has the prior right to enjoy an uncontaminated environment, P can offer S compensation. Thus, the question of whether to bribe P to reduce the pollution or to compensate S for his suffering is determined to a large extent by the existence of property rights. Such a bargaining solution is generally only appropriate where small numbers of people are involved, otherwise the transaction and administration costs may be so high that they outweigh the benefits of bargaining.

Merger solution Where one firm imposes an external cost on another, it may be possible to *internalise* the externality by merging the two firms into one. Consider two competitive firms, A and B, where A imposes a negative externality on B. This effectively means that A's social marginal cost of production exceeds its private marginal cost, as shown in Fig. 10. DD is the demand curve for firm A's product. Before the merger, A will be producing output OQ, ignoring the external cost which it is imposing on B. After the merger, though, the combined management of A and B will reduce the level of output of firm A to OQ_1, the Pareto optimal quantity. This is so because what was previously an external cost to firm A has become a private cost to

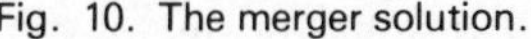
Fig. 10. The merger solution.

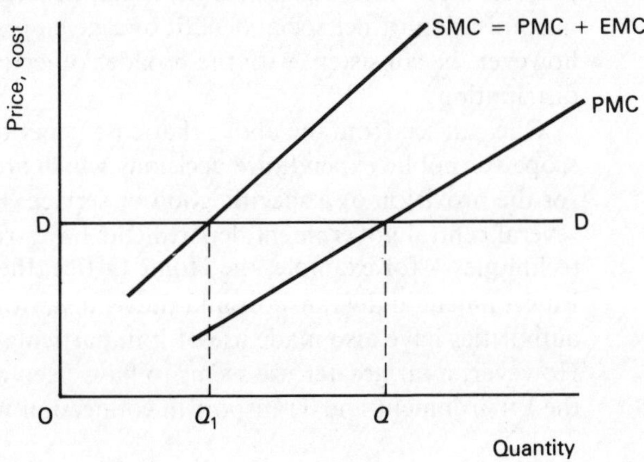

the larger, merged firm and must, therefore, be taken into account in determining the profit-maximising output level.

Legislation to impose minimum standards This method of dealing with externalities belongs to the wider field of legal rules and regulations. For instance, factory owners could be legally obliged to raise the height of their chimneys or to install noise abatement equipment. Motor-car manufacturers may be compelled to fit exhaust systems that reduce emissions from vehicles and to develop petrol-economy engines. Aeroplanes might be required to fly at certain minimum heights over residential areas.

It can be seen that these methods stipulate environmental standards of minimum desirable quality. There are, however, major difficulties associated with ascertaining the costs of pollution control and measuring the benefits from pollution control. There are as yet no precise measurements of the extent of damage caused by environmental pollution.

The cost-benefit analysis of public expenditure decisions

The nature of cost-benefit analysis

Cost-benefit analysis is a practical method of evaluating individual public projects concerned with the provision of specific goods and services, such as education, health, transport and civil amenities. A public body aiming to maximise social welfare will take account of the *social* costs and benefits of individual projects, as opposed to a private firm which takes account only of its private costs and benefits. The cost-benefit technique attempts to identify the social costs and benefits associated with a scheme over a long period of time and tries to quantify them by expressing them in a common monetary unit. Consider, for example, the building of a motorway. Its social costs include construction and maintenance costs, noise, pollution from dirt and exhaust fumes, loss of landscape and general disfigurement of the environment. Its social benefits include savings in journey time to existing and new road users, possibly fewer accidents and deaths and a smaller fleet of commercial vehicles needed to meet the same demand.

Viewed in this way, cost-benefit analysis is an alternative technique for resource allocation in the public sector to that of allocation by the market mechanism. It enables the decision maker to choose from the alternative projects that which maximises net social benefit. This narrow objective of the maximisation of net social benefit of a given project should in principle, however, be consistent with the broader objectives of allocation and distribution.

One can see from the above that cost-benefit analysis provides a wide scope for public expenditure decisions which are not made in aggregate but for the provision of a specific good or service. In the United Kingdom, several central government departments have tried to apply cost-benefit techniques – for example, the Home Office, the Departments of the Environment and Transport and the Ministry of Defence. Some local authorities have also made use of it in particular fields of expenditure. However, a far greater use seems to have been made by the Departments of the Environment and Transport in connection with town planning, urban transport, commuter train closures and the siting of the proposed third London airport.

Shadow pricing

The existence of externalities and monopolistic elements in the market mechanism means that prevailing market prices do not reflect the true social marginal cost of resources in alternative uses. This leads the cost-benefit practitioner to resort to the device of using *shadow prices* which are imputed prices designed to reflect the 'true' social costs and benefits of a project. For instance, the journey time saved by motorists as the result of the building of a motorway may be valued at an appropriate average hourly wage rate. Similarly, savings from a reduction in the number of accidents can be estimated in terms of the reduced cost of medical treatment. The foreign exchange costs of a project can be imputed if, for example, the prevailing exchange rate in the market overvalues the domestic currency, perhaps because of government reluctance to devalue.

The discounting process

The costs and benefits of a project, once given monetary values through shadow pricing, must be *discounted* before the *present worth* of the project can be determined. This is necessary because people generally prefer present consumption to future consumption. A sum of £100 received today, for example, is worth more to a person than the same sum received in two years' time: this is because by investing the £100 at, say, a 10 per cent rate of interest compounded annually, both the principal (£100) and the accumulated interest (£21) would be received at the end of the two year period. Reversing this process, we can say that the present value of £121 to be received in two years' time (given a current rate of interest of 10 per cent) is £100. The same discounting process has to be applied to the costs and benefits of a capital project.

There are two well-known rules for discounting the costs and benefits associated with a project. These are the net discounted present value (NDPV) rule and the internal rate of return (IRR) rule. Consider these two rules in turn.

The net discounted present value rule This refers to the process of discounting back to the present the streams of costs and benefits associated with a project during its lifetime. According to this rule, *a project is acceptable if the NDPV is greater than zero*. The NDPV can be calculated by applying the following generalised formula:

$$\text{NDPV} = \left[\frac{B_1}{(1+i)} + \frac{B_2}{(1+i)^2} + \ldots + \frac{B_t}{(1+i)^t}\right] - \left[\frac{C_1}{(1+i)} + \frac{C_2}{(1+i)^2} + \ldots + \frac{C_t}{(1+i)^t}\right]$$

where $B_1, B_2, \ldots, B_t$ and $C_1, C_2, \ldots, C_t$ are the gross benefits and costs accruing in years 1 to t, and i is the rate of interest.

As an example, consider a hypothetical project which has a useful life of two years. Suppose for simplicity that it has no maintenance costs and no scrap value at the end of its life, so that all costs are incurred at the initial stage. Suppose in fact that the initial capital outlay is £10 million and that benefits of £6 million and £7.25 million accrue in years 1 and 2 respectively. Applying the above formula with a rate of discount of 10 per cent, we have:

$$\text{NDPV} = \left[\frac{6\text{ m.}}{1 + 0.1} + \frac{7.25\text{ m.}}{(1 + 0.1)^2}\right] - 10\text{ m.}$$

$$= £1.4\text{ m.}$$

Since the NDPV > 0, the project is acceptable.

The internal rate of return rule The IRR is the estimated rate of return achieved by investing in the project. Since both costs and benefits are involved, it can be calculated as that rate of discount which equates the present value of the project's benefits with the present value of the project's costs. The project can then be regarded as acceptable *if the IRR exceeds the current market rate of interest*. In terms of a generalised formula, the IRR is that rate of discount, r, which solves the following equation:

$$\left[\frac{B_1}{(1 + r)} + \frac{B_2}{(1 + r)^2} + \ldots + \frac{B_t}{(1 + r)^t}\right] - \left[\frac{C_1}{(1 + r)} + \frac{C_2}{(1 + r)^2} + \ldots + \frac{C_t}{(1 + r)^t}\right] = 0$$

Applying this to the above example of a project which has a present cost of £10 million and benefits of £6 million after one year and £7.25 million after the second year, we have

$$\left[\frac{6\text{ m.}}{(1 + r)} + \frac{7.25\text{ m.}}{(1 + r)^2}\right] - 10\text{ m.} = 0$$

$$r = 0.2 \text{ or } 20 \text{ per cent.}$$

Thus, the IRR is 20 per cent which is greater than the rate of interest of 10 per cent. So the project proves to be acceptable by this rule too.

The NDPV rule versus the IRR rule An important question is which of these rules should be applied in determining whether or not a given project is economically viable. As the above examples suggest, a capital project which passes the NDPV test will also pass the IRR test and one which fails the NDPV test will also fail the IRR test; so in that sense, the two rules are consistent.

However, a conflict can arise between the two rules when they are used to compare *alternative* projects both of which may be economically viable. This is illustrated in the example summarised in Table 2, where the initial costs of projects A and B are the same (£100 m.), but project A is a more capital-

Table 2. Conflict between the IRR and NDPV rules in comparing two projects.

	Present cost	Benefits Yr I	Benefits Yr II	IRR	NDPV (i = 10%)
Project A	£100 m.	£2 m.	£125 m.	12%	£5 m.
Project B	£100 m.	£110 m.	£4 m.	14%	£3 m.

intensive project so that only £2 million of benefit accrues in year I, but £125 million accrues in year II. Project B is a less capital-intensive project so that bigger benefits accrue in year I (£110 m.) and smaller benefits accrue in year II (£4 m.). With an interest rate of 10 per cent, the NDPV rule favours project A, but the IRR rule favours project B.

In cases of conflicting results, the appropriate solution is to apply the NDPV rule. This rule produces the conceptually 'correct' result. The IRR rule is deemed to be less appropriate because it discriminates against capital-intensive projects which yield benefits in the more distant future. Public sector projects, of course, are typically of this type.

Limitations of cost-benefit analysis

The technique attempts to measure the social costs and benefits of a project, but fails to take account satisfactorily of income distribution effects and 'intangibles'. Consider the following limitations.

(a) Some studies ignore the income distribution effects in that they avoid the crucial issue of the actual distribution of the gains and losses of the projects under consideration. This is partly because the technique itself depends upon the Hicks-Kaldor hypothetical compensation test initially devised to preserve the notion of a Pareto improvement. Pearce and Nash showed, in connection with the Portswood Link Urban Motorway (Southampton), that although total benefits exceeded total costs, the analysis ignored the question of the distribution of gains and losses. One way to overcome this problem might be to give different weights to the gains and losses of different income groups in the population: the main problem with this, though, would be the difficulty of devising appropriate weights. Alternatively, the gains and losses accruing to different groups may be shown separately (as in the Roskill Commission Study of the siting of the third London airport), leaving the final decision to the policy maker.

(b) The forecasting of the flows of benefits and costs during the lifetime of a project is an extremely hazardous business. It requires predictions of supply and demand patterns over a period of perhaps twenty or thirty years, estimates of future rates of inflation, population growth and spatial movements of population, all of which are extremely difficult to assess accurately.

(c) Intangibles, such as pollution and the general disfigurement of the landscape, are difficult to measure. For example, the environmental damage caused by a motorway in an area of scenic beauty is impossible to evaluate objectively.

(d) Cost-benefit analysis aids decision makers to choose between different methods of achieving a *particular* objective, but not to choose between different objectives. For example, if the objective is to reduce traffic congestion in a city, the technique helps the decision makers to choose between, say, an urban motorway system and an underground railway system. The technique does not, however, help the government to choose between, say, education projects and defence projects.

Cost-benefit analysis in less developed countries

The application of cost-benefit analysis to resource allocation is important in less developed countries since public investment plays a key role in the development process – for example, in health, road transport and irrigation schemes. Moreover, the governments of many of these countries provide Pigovian type subsidies directly to private investment. The purpose of public investment and the government support for private investment is to generate widespread external benefits and thus try to overcome the problem of structural imbalances.

However, the scarcity of foreign exchange, domestic savings, technical knowledge and entrepreneurial abilities imposes severe limits on the speed of the development process. By the same token, markets may not reflect the true social cost of resources. For instance, market prices tend to overvalue labour if there is widespread unemployment so that the market wage rate exceeds the social opportunity cost of labour.

It follows that in order to allocate scarce resources amongst the competing claims of different sectors, it is necessary for economic planners to use shadow prices when engaged in estimating the social costs and benefits of development projects. More importantly, it is necessary that in the design of development plans the distribution of gains and losses is given explicit consideration, for the basic philosophy of planned development is to increase the welfare of the individual members of a group by raising their incomes and thus their living standards.

Conclusion

This chapter has shown that in modern times, many public expenditure policies can be explained in terms of public goods and externalities. The discussion of these two concepts has shown that public expenditure makes a positive contribution to society's goal of welfare maximisation. Externalities are all-pervasive since production and consumption activities begin and end with the environment. It is for this reason that a number of policy measures have been devised to deal with the problem of externalities.

In the final part of the chapter, we considered the technique of cost-benefit analysis as a method of evaluating public sector projects where narrow financial investment appraisal techniques are inappropriate. Cost-benefit analysis attempts to take account of *all* relevant social costs and benefits.

Further reading

Musgrave, R. and **Musgrave, P.**, *Public Finance in Theory and Practice*, McGraw Hill, New York, 1976 (Ch. 3).

Pearce, D.W., *Environmental Economics*, Longman, London, 1976.

Pearce, D.W., *Cost-benefit Analysis*, Macmillan, London, 1971.

Brown, C.V. and **Jackson, P.M.**, *Public Sector Economics*, Martin Robertson, Oxford, 1978 (Ch. 3, 4 and 8).

Exercises

1. Review your understanding of the following terms:

public good	initiating agents
private good	affected parties
mixed good	social cost
positive externality	private cost
negative externality	external cost
consumption externality	cost-benefit analysis
production externality	shadow pricing
non-rivalness	IRR rule
non-exclusion	NDPV rule

2. Consider two individuals, A and B, who have truly revealed their preferences for a particular *public* good. The following data represent the two demand schedules:

Price (£):	10	20	30	40	50	60
A's demand:	50	45	40	35	30	25
B's demand:	20	18	16	14	12	10

(a) Draw the two demand curves on a graph.
(b) Aggregate them and draw the total demand curve for the public good on the same graph.
(c) Now draw the total demand curve on the assumption that the good is a pure private good.

3. 'Education cuts can be criticised because education is a public good.' 'Increases in tuition fees can be justified because education is a private good.' Discuss these two statements.

4. To what extent is an open-air pop concert a public good in the same sense as defence and police protection?

5. How do externalities arise? Suggest methods for dealing with: (a) environmental pollution; and (b) the benefits of a national health service.

6. Consider two neighbours, one of whom has a garden which is unattended and unsightly, thereby imposing a negative externality on the other, whose garden is well-stocked with flowers. In what ways might the two neighbours bargain with each other to overcome the externality? What other solutions are possible?

7. Discuss the problems involved in using cost-benefit analysis to evaluate the construction of a tunnel under the English Channel.

13 Financing the public sector

Introduction

This chapter is concerned with investigating the major sources of the public sector's revenues. Like private individuals, governments need money to finance their spending. But unlike private individuals who, given their incomes and tastes, try to maximise their own utility, the public sector raises revenues to spend in a way that maximises the welfare of society as a whole. Revenues are collected not merely to meet the public expenditure requirements, but also to serve many other objectives. For example, as pointed out in Chapter 11, taxes are levied on the community by the state to perform its allocation function, to assist its redistribution function, and to implement macroeconomic objectives.

After establishing a definition of taxation, the focus of attention in this chapter is on the following areas: (a) the principles of taxation; (b) the concepts of tax incidence and excess burden; (c) the allocational efficiency and equity of direct and indirect taxes; (d) the structure of taxation in the United Kingdom; (e) the financing of government spending by user charges; (g) the financing of government spending by borrowing and the printing of money.

A major emphasis is placed on taxation because most governments in western industrialised countries obtain a substantial proportion of their income from *taxes* (T). The remaining sources from which governments derive revenue are *borrowing* (B), *printing money* ($\triangle M$) and *state trading activities*. Strictly, the profits earned from state trading activities are in the nature of a tax on the community and for the purposes of this chapter are included in taxation. It follows that the methods of financing the public sector can be expressed conveniently by the following identity:

$$G - T \equiv B + \triangle M$$

This tells us that the difference between the level of government expenditure (G) and taxation is met from borrowing and printing money.

Definition of taxation

Definition: ***Taxes are compulsory transfers of money from private individuals, groups or institutions to the government.***

Broadly, *direct taxes* are levied on income, wealth or spending power, or any combination of these three tax *bases*: most tax systems in practice combine the three bases to differing degrees. *Indirect taxes* are levied on goods and services; in this case, the tax base is the good or service itself and the taxes may be applied *ad valorem* (that is, as a percentage of value), at a specific rate (that is, so much per unit sold), or at a flat rate (that is, a lump sum which does not vary with the quantity or value of the good or service).

Taxes can be *proportional, progressive* or *regressive.* With a proportional tax, the percentage of income paid in tax remains constant as income rises. With a progressive tax, the percentage of income paid in tax increases as income rises. With a regressive tax, the percentage paid falls as income rises. These three cases are illustrated in Fig. 1. Notice from the graph that the *average rate of tax* (that is, tax divided by income, T/Y) and the *marginal rate of tax* (that is, the increase in tax brought about by a one pound increase in income, $\triangle T/\triangle Y$) are both constant for proportional taxes, rise as income rises for progressive taxes, and fall as income rises for regressive taxes. For a lump-sum tax, which is fixed in amount whatever the level of income, the marginal rate of tax is zero and the average rate of tax falls as income rises. Lump-sum taxes are, therefore, regressive in nature.

Fig. 1. Proportional, progressive and regressive taxes.

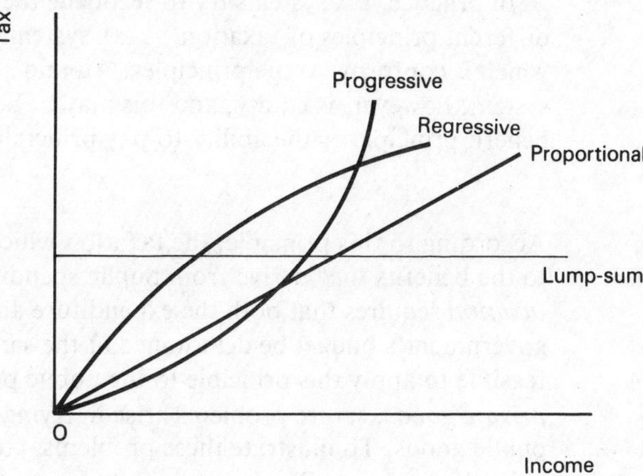

Principles of taxation

In his book, *The Wealth of Nations*, Adam Smith stated four principles which he called the 'canons of taxation'. These were (a) that people should pay taxes according to their abilities (a principle which modern economists have subjected to two interpretations – the *benefit principle* and the *ability-to-pay principle*); (b) that the payment of taxes should be *clear* and *certain* to the taxpayer and the taxman; (c) that the method, manner and time of payment should be *convenient* to the taxpayer; and (d) that the cost of collection in relation to the tax-yield should be minimal.

Initially, Smith's canons were propounded to enable governments to raise money to meet their expenditures. In view of the more diverse aims of taxation of modern governments, there are additional criteria by which a tax system should be judged. Consider the following desirable characteristics of a modern tax system.

(a) The finance minister (or Chancellor of the Exchequer) must be able to estimate the *yield* of individual taxes accurately. This will assist the government to control the economy and to plan its future expenditures.

(b) The finance minister must be certain of the distribution of the tax burden. That is, he should know with some accuracy the different income groups that will bear the burden of the tax. This will assist the government to achieve its equity objective.
(c) Except for equity reasons, taxes should not discriminate between different income groups. Similarly, in the absence of market imperfections, taxes should not distort people's choices between goods or occupations, or reduce the willingness to work and take business risks. Thus, to achieve the efficiency objective, taxes should be *neutral*.
(d) Taxes should have built-in flexibility or automatic adjustment. This is the case with a progressive income tax system where, as incomes rise, taxes increase more than proportionately, thereby having a dampening effect on total demand in the economy. This means that less frequent changes in the budget are required to achieve the macroeconomic objectives.

In practice, tax systems try to reconcile the conflicting aims of these different principles of taxation. A tax system can be judged by the extent to which it conforms to the principles. An underlying objective of any tax system, however, is equity, and this may be achieved by applying either the benefit principle or the ability-to-pay principle.

The benefit principle

According to this principle, the taxation which people pay should be related to the benefits they derive from public spending. The application of *benefit taxation* requires that both the expenditure and taxation sides of the government's budget be determined at the same time. Whilst it may be feasible to apply this principle to the public provision of certain *excludable private goods*, severe problems arise in trying to apply it to the provision of public goods. To illustrate these problems, consider an economy of two individuals, A and B, who are willing to pay taxes for the supply of a public good, such as defence. The two individuals' demand curves for the public good, D_AD_A and D_BD_B, are shown in Fig. 2 together with the cost line CC which shows the cost of producing each unit of the good. To simplify matters, the average and marginal costs are assumed to be constant.

The demand curves, D_AD_A and D_BD_B, measure the different valuations which A and B put on different levels of output. The market demand curve (the vertical summation of the two individual demand curves) is shown as D_MD_M. In the graph, there is only one output level (O*Q*) at which the sum of

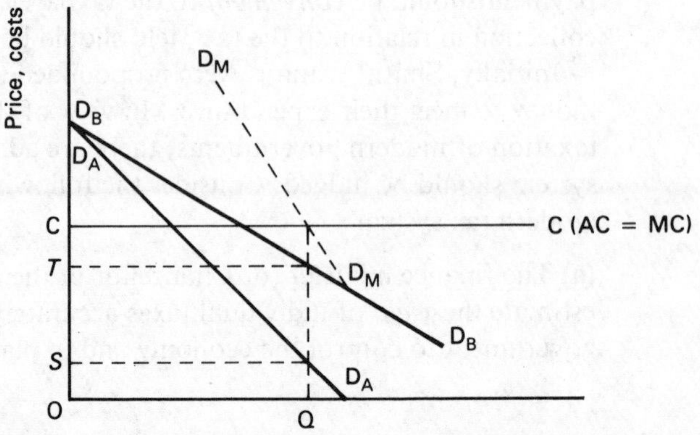

Fig. 2. The determination of tax shares by the benefit principle.

the amounts the two individuals are willing to pay is just equal to the average and marginal cost of providing the public good. At any other output level, the total amount that they are willing to pay either exceeds or falls short of this cost. Applying the benefit principle, when O*Q* units are supplied, A should pay O*S* per unit in taxes and B should pay O*T* per unit. In spite of the fact that the public good is equally available for both to enjoy, B pays more than A because, given his tastes and income, he derives more benefit from it. The two individuals would only pay equal tax shares if they had identical demand curves for the good – a highly unlikely event.

For such a system to be put into practice, it is necessary that taxpayers should in some way reveal their preferences fully and truthfully for public goods and that they should have equal bargaining skills. Where only a small number of people are involved, this may be possible. In an economy consisting of millions of taxpayers, however, such honest preference revelations are highly unlikely. Indeed, as we saw in Chapter 12, it would pay people to understate their preferences. Furthermore, any changes in individuals' tastes, incomes or the prices of other goods will shift the demand curves and so alter the tax shares. It would be impossible to take account of these changes in practice.

The same difficulties apply, though to a lesser extent, to government expenditure on education, health and other social services. The people who receive these services directly are not the only ones to benefit from them. Such services give rise to *external* benefits which cannot easily be evaluated in money terms. More important, in performing its redistribution function, a government may decide to levy taxes on the rich regardless of direct benefits to them. Only in specific instances where the government supplies *excludable private goods* (with few externalities) is the benefit principle applicable. Water rates and social security contributions reflect the application of benefit taxation.

The ability-to-pay principle

According to this principle, tax revenues should be raised in such a way that the tax burden is distributed among individuals according to their *abilities to pay* (or their taxable capacities). The principle shifts the emphasis from taxing individuals on the basis of the benefits they receive from public spending to the basis of how much each individual can afford to pay. Such a 'just' distribution of the tax burden is taken to mean *equality of sacrifice*, where the 'sacrifice' refers to the loss of utility by the taxpayer. This does not necessarily mean that each person should pay the same amount of tax: clearly, a rich man can afford to pay more tax than a poor man and yet suffer the same loss of utility.

The equality of sacrifice is by no means an unambiguous concept and has been subjected to three interpretations: (a) *taxes of equal absolute sacrifice* which impose the same loss of total utility on all taxpayers; (b) *taxes of equal proportional sacrifice* which impose a loss of the same fraction of utility to total utility; (c) *taxes of equal marginal sacrifice* which minimise the loss of total utility to the community by reducing every taxpayer's income to the point where the marginal utility of income of every taxpayer is the same. Consider these in turn.

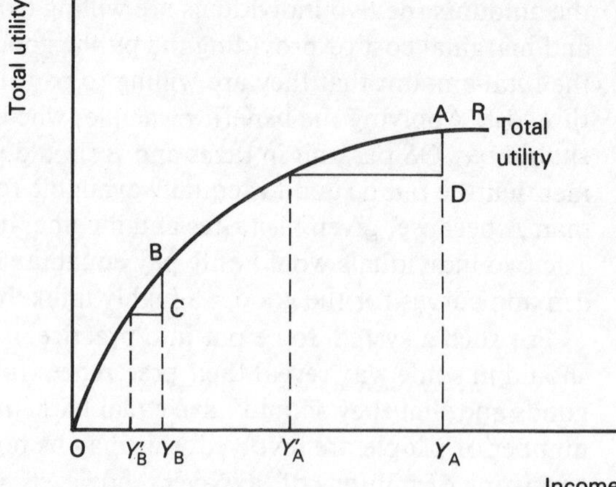

Fig. 3. Taxes of equal absolute sacrifice.

Equal absolute sacrifice To illustrate this, consider an economy of two individuals, A and B, who both have equal preferences so that they have the same total utility function, represented by OR in Fig. 3. Notice that as income rises, total utility rises but at a decreasing rate. This means that the marginal utility of income (given by the slope of the total utility curve) falls as income rises. Now suppose that individual A is a rich man with a pre-tax income of OY_A and that that individual B is a poor man with a pre-tax income of OY_B. A tax which imposes an equal absolute sacrifice is one which reduces both individuals' total utilities by the same amount. An example of such a tax is one which reduces A's income to OY'_A and B's income OY'_B. Although A pays more tax than B, they both suffer the same loss of utility (BC = AD). Nothing conclusive, however, can be said about whether this requires a progressive, proportional or regressive tax. The choice of the rate structure depends on the rate of decline of the marginal utility of income.

Equal proportional sacrifice The idea behind this rule is that the tax should have an equal impact on the total utilities of all taxpayers. In terms of the two individuals, A and B, the fraction of total utility lost because of the tax should be the same. This is shown in Fig. 4 where the tax reduces A's income

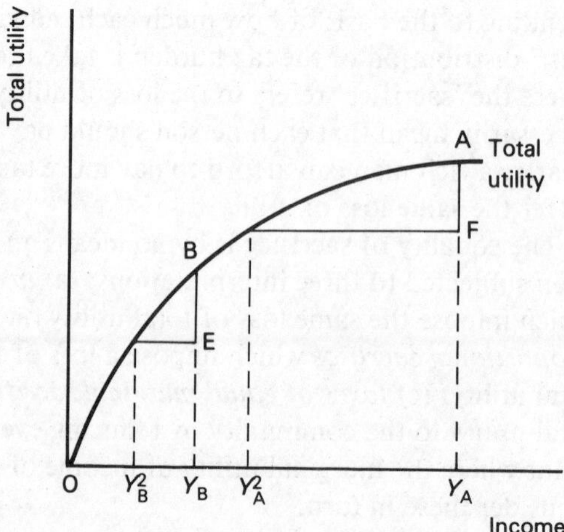

Fig. 4. Taxes of equal proportional sacrifice.

to OY_A^2 and B's income to OY_B^2 in such a way that $AF/AY_A = BE/BY_B$. Once again, the choice of rate structure depends on the marginal utility of income schedule.

Equal marginal sacrifice Since the slope of the total utility schedule represents the marginal utility of income, it follows that, in our example, to tax individuals A and B in such a way that equalises their marginal utilities of income, a *progressive* tax has to be imposed which equalises the post-tax incomes. This is shown in Fig. 5, where both individuals' post-tax incomes are equal to OY_1.

Fig. 5. Taxes of equal marginal sacrifice.

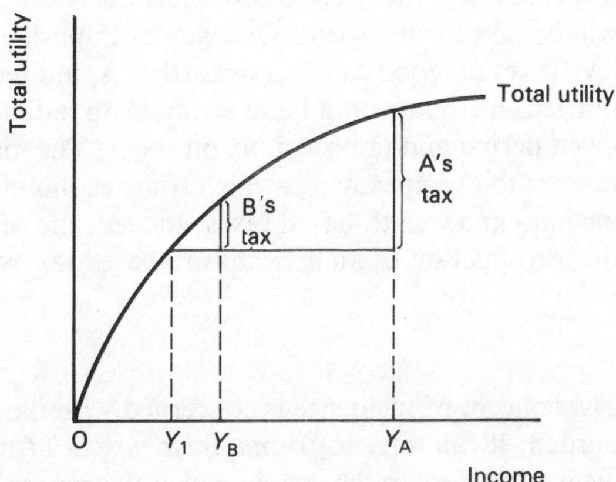

Apart from the problem of deciding which of the three possible interpretations of equality of sacrifice to adopt, there are a number of practical and conceptual difficulties associated with the ability-to-pay principle: (a) there are severe problems in trying to measure utility; (b) it is by no means certain that the marginal utility of income declines as income rises, nor is it at all clear why income should be the main determinant of utility; and (c) the principle calls for inter-personal comparisons of utility which depend upon cardinal utility measurement.

In seeking to achieve the objective of equality of sacrifice, governments have to decide whether income, wealth or spending power is the appropriate index of ability-to-pay. Consider these in turn.

Income-based taxes best serve the objective of equality of sacrifice when income is defined broadly in the 'total accretion' sense. This means taking into account income (monetary and non-monetary) from all sources – for example, income from work, gifts, inheritance and life-time savings; in other words, the increase in net worth valued at market prices during a given tax period. Such a broad definition of income poses many practical difficulties of measurement. Equality of sacrifice also requires the choice of an appropriate *tax period*; for example, should tax liabilities be calculated on a one year, five year or life-time basis? The timing of the assessment will affect different taxpayers in different ways. For instance, an individual earning £15,000, £15,000, £10,000 and nothing in four successive years will pay more tax than another individual who earns a steady £10,000 per year if the tax period and tax allowances are annually-based.

Wealth-based taxes are sometimes advocated as a way of achieving a more equitable distribution pattern because statistical studies of western industrial societies show that wealth (that is, accumulated assets) tends to be more unevenly distributed than income. It may be objected, however, that wealth-based taxes are unlikely to provide adequate revenues. Furthermore, difficulties arise: (a) in valuing assets to assess tax liability; (b) in adjusting asset values for inflation; and (c) in defining the tax-paying units as wealth may be held in joint names.

Expenditure-based taxes define ability-to-pay in terms of what a person spends rather than in terms of what he owns or earns. The use of such taxes dispenses with the need to distinguish between income and wealth since both will be taxed when spent. One way of imposing an expenditure-based tax is to levy taxes on goods and services (that is, indirect taxes). Another (as yet, untried) method would be to estimate an individual's expenditures during a given period and impose a tax on those. The main idea of expenditure-based taxes is to exempt savings which some economists argue are penalised by income- and wealth-based taxes. Indeed, the Meade Report in 1978 favoured the introduction of an expenditure-based tax system in the United Kingdom.

Incidence and excess burden

The concept of incidence is concerned with the question of who bears the tax burden. It can refer to *formal incidence* or *effective incidence.* Formal incidence refers to the way in which the money burden of a tax is statistically distributed among the tax-paying units. For example, the formal incidence of income tax is on the person who pays the tax, and that of excise duties on tobacco is on smokers in proportion to the value of their purchases. It is possible to calculate the distribution of revenues from all taxes to arrive at the formal incidence of the entire tax system on the community. This shows the money burden on different income groups and is of importance from the standpoint of government policy since it is directly connected with the question of the redistribution of income.

Effective incidence refers to the way a tax change affects the behaviour of the taxpayer: that is to say, how it affects the taxpayer in terms of working, spending, saving and investing in risky businesses. Ideally, the statistical calculation of effective incidence should tell us whether society is better or worse off under different tax systems. Such a statistical measure is, however, difficult to obtain because of the complex social and psychological factors involved.

Where a taxpayer also incurs costs of adjusting to a change in tax, he is said to bear an *excess burden*. This can be defined as the loss of consumer surplus arising from the imposition of the tax over and above the formal incidence of the tax. This is illustrated in Fig. 6 where D_XD_X is the demand curve for good *X* and S_X is its supply curve (assumed perfectly elastic for simplicity) before any tax is imposed. Suppose now that a tax is imposed on the supply of *X*, shifting the supply curve to $S_X + T$ with the result that the quantity consumed falls from OQ_1 to OQ_2. The tax revenue (or formal incidence) is ABCD. The loss of consumer surplus over and above that,

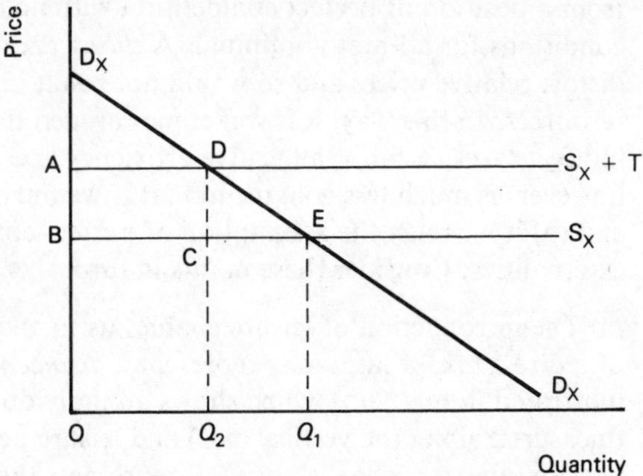

Fig. 6. Excess burden.

DCE, is the excess burden. Notice that the excess burden will be greater, the more elastic is the demand for the good.

Taxation and the allocation of resources

The excess burden of an indirect tax illustrated in Fig. 6 results from the distortion of relative prices following the imposition of the tax and it highlights the inefficiency (or misallocation of resources) which results from imposing such a tax. This inefficiency is further illustrated in general equilibrium in Fig. 7. The pre-tax Pareto optimal equilibrium position is at point E where the community indifference curve CIC_1 is tangential to the production possibility frontier, AB. This position will be achieved, with the pre-tax price ratio given by the slope of PP, under conditions of perfect competition with no externalities. If an indirect tax is imposed on good *X*, its price to *consumers* will rise relative to *Y*, shifting the price line to consumers to P_2P_2, say. However, producers' revenues are *exclusive of tax* so that they face the less steep price line P_1P_1. Production will shift to point F and the community will move on to the community indifference curve CIC_2, lower than CIC_1.

We can conclude from the above analysis that an indirect tax, starting

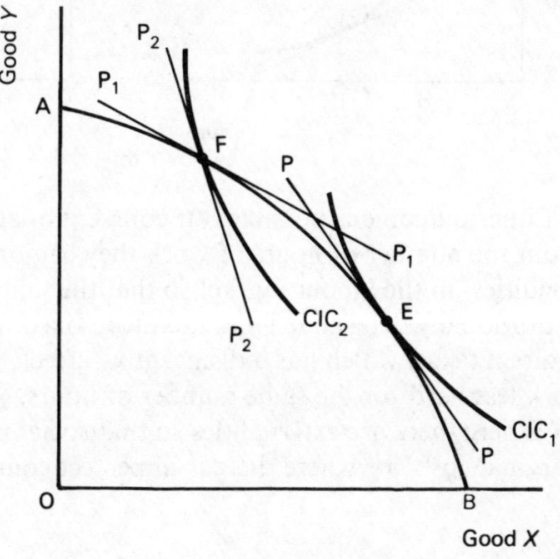

Fig. 7. The welfare loss from an indirect tax.

from a position of perfect competition with no externalities, spoils the conditions for a Pareto optimum. A *direct tax,* on the other hand, would not distort relative prices and so would not result in such a misallocation of resources. In this way, it is sometimes argued that direct taxes are superior to indirect taxes so far as allocative efficiency is concerned. This argument, however, is much less convincing: (a) if we introduce *leisure* into the analysis; and (b) if we relax the assumption of perfect competition with no externalities. Consider these points in turn.

(a) The introduction of leisure enables us to analyse a possible disadvantage of a direct tax – that it may represent a *disincentive to work*. This is illustrated in Fig. 8 (a) which shows an individual's choice between income (measured along the vertical axis) and leisure per day (measured along the horizontal axis). The distance OB represents the maximum amount of leisure possible – that is, twenty-four hours. Before any tax is imposed, the individual's budget line is AB and he maximises his utility by choosing point E_1 which puts him on his highest attainable indifference curve I_1. At this point, he is offering HB hours of work per day and taking OH hours of leisure per day. Now suppose that a 50 per cent income tax is imposed shifting the budget line to CB, so that OC = CA. The individual will now choose point E_2, offering only H_1B hours of work and taking OH_1 hours of leisure. The tax in this case is a disincentive to work and so cannot necessarily be regarded as superior to an indirect tax so far as allocative efficiency is concerned. But now consider Fig. 8 (b) where the individual has a different preference pattern between income and leisure. In this case, the direct tax induces him to offer *more* hours of work (H_1B hours as opposed to HB).

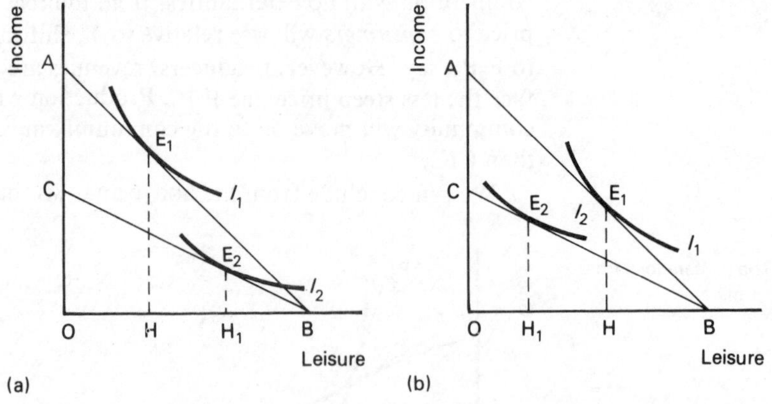

Fig. 8. The effect of a direct tax on the incentive to work.

Either outcome is possible. Of course, not all workers have much choice about the number of hours of work they can offer. Where there are 'rigidities' in the labour market so that the number of hours worked is institutionally determined and therefore fixed for an individual, an increase in direct taxes, which has a disincentive effect, may cause the individual to work less hard for the same number of hours.

(b) Where there are externalities so that social marginal costs exceed private marginal costs, or where there is imperfect competition, it is possible for the imposition of indirect taxes to improve the allocation of resources (as was demonstrated in the case of Pigou's tax solution to externalities in Chapter 12). In a second-best situation such as this, indirect taxes may be superior to direct taxes so far as the allocation of resources is concerned.

The structure of taxation in the United Kingdom

In the United Kingdom, as in other countries, the tax system is a mixture of direct and indirect taxes. The main direct taxes are personal income tax, corporation tax, capital gains tax and capital transfer tax. The indirect (or outlay) taxes are imposed on goods and services and take the form of value-added tax, customs and excise duties, car tax, petrol and oil taxes, betting tax, community land tax and local rates.

If we look at the relative contributions of direct and indirect taxes to total tax receipts, we see that direct taxation has always been the major contributor in the United Kingdom. For instance, in the financial year 1978–79, of total tax receipts of £57,471 million, direct taxes, including national insurance contributions, brought in £33,025 million – that is, about 57 per cent of the total. In general, the smaller share of indirect taxes may be justified on equity grounds since these taxes are usually levied at flat rates and so are normally regressive. They fail to take into account the personal circumstances or taxable capacities of taxpayers. The larger share of direct taxes, on the other hand, may be justified on the grounds that these taxes reflect the ability-to-pay principle and have enabled the authorities to introduce a certain degree of progression into the tax system.

Of the direct taxes, personal income tax including national insurance contributions brings in more than half of the total revenues. Of the indirect taxes, value-added tax and excise duties are the largest revenue raisers. We turn now to a description of the major direct and indirect taxes in the United Kingdom.

Direct taxes

Personal income tax In the United Kingdom, personal income tax applies to taxable income bands, as shown in Table 1. These rates and income bands illustrate the principle of progression. Taxable incomes are calculated net of reliefs and allowances under Schedule E if tax is payable under the pay-as-you-earn scheme, and under Schedule D for self-employed workers. Schedule D is more generous in terms of reliefs and allowances than Schedule E. As can be seen from the Table, the tax rate rises from 30 per cent in five steps to

Table 1. Income tax rates in the United Kingdom, 1979–80.

Taxable income bands (£)	Tax rate (%)
0–11,250	30
11,251–13,250	40
13,251–16,750	45
16,751–22,250	50
22,251–27,750	55
Over 27,750	60

the top rate of 60 per cent on earned income over £27,750 per year. In addition, there is a flat rate investment income surcharge of 15 per cent on unearned income over £5,500.

One of the major effects of the rapid inflation in the 1970s and 1980s in the United Kingdom has been a substantial increase in the real burden of income tax. This is because with a progressive tax system, rising money incomes 'drag' some people into the tax net for the first time and others into the higher tax bands (even though their real incomes may be unchanged). Thus, inflation distorts the distribution of the tax burden among different groups of taxpayers and so may undermine the notion of equality of sacrifice in the ability-to-pay principle. It was in an attempt to overcome this problem that the 1977 Finance Act index-linked the personal allowances to the Retail Price Index.

Corporation tax This was introduced in 1966 and is levied on the whole of a company's profits net of interest payments and depreciation allowances. The philosophy of the tax is to favour the retention of and to penalise the distribution of profits. This is intended to enable companies to buy plant and capital equipment from their own internal sources of funds. Thus, the tax is designed to encourage a greater volume of investment to be financed from a company's own savings. Statistical studies have, however, failed to show any causal connection between the rate of company savings and the growth of investment.

Since 1973, the imputation form of corporation tax has been introduced. In this, tax is payable in two parts: (a) advance corporation tax; and (b) mainstream corporation tax. The combined payments add up to the standard rate of 52 per cent of taxable profits, but partial relief is given to shareholders against their personal income tax liability. Advance corporation tax is paid at the rate of $\frac{3}{7}$ of the dividend (the fraction $\frac{3}{7}$ being determined by the basic income tax rate) and is credited to shareholders who become, in turn, entitled to equivalent relief against their personal income tax. Mainstream corporation tax is calculated on all profits at 52 per cent for the accounting period, less advance corporation tax already paid. However, the very high rates of inflation in recent years have made it necessary for the government to give generous reliefs to companies on stock appreciation caused by rising prices and this has virtually wiped out the mainstream part of corporation tax.

Capital gains tax The Finance Act of 1965 introduced a comprehensive capital gains tax which applies to gains accruing from the sale of assets, including gifts and trusts. The tax is payable when assets are disposed of and not when gains actually accrue. At the time of writing, the first £3,000 of net gains are exempt; thereafter, where the net gains exceed £3,000, a rate of 30 per cent is applied. Important exemptions from capital gains tax include owner-occupied houses, national savings certificates, life assurance policies, betting winnings, gifts to charities and government securities.

Capital transfer tax The Finance Act of 1975 introduced capital transfer tax to replace estate duty which, under certain circumstances, could be avoided by gifts and bequests. Capital transfer tax applies to life-time gifts, bequests and property held in trust. The tax rates rise progressively from zero (on the first £50,000) to a top rate of 75 per cent which applies to the capital values of property over £2 million. The tax rates on transfers on death are steeper than those on life-time transfers. Important exemptions include gifts between husband and wife, and gifts to charities and political parties.

Development land tax This tax was introduced in 1976 and applies to development gains from land over £50,000. Every individual with an interest in land who materially benefits from development is liable to the tax.

Indirect taxes

Value-added tax Value-added tax was introduced in 1973 to replace purchase tax and selective employment tax. It can be described as a tax levied on businesses at every stage of production and distribution on the value they add to their purchases of raw materials, fuels and capital goods. It can, therefore, be regarded as a general *turnover* tax on consumption.

To show how it can be calculated, let VA denote value-added, Q the value of output and I the value of inputs (that is, intermediate goods and capital goods). We can write:

$$VA = Q - I$$

Each firm has to calculate its gross tax by applying the appropriate tax rate to its total sales and against this set the tax already paid by supplying firms. This is facilitated by the 'invoice method' which compels each buying firm to insist on the presentation of tax receipts made out to the previous suppliers. The tax applies to a wide range of goods and services, including imported goods but not imported services. Its comprehensive coverage minimises the distortion of choices – that is, it has substantially neutral effects on relative prices. Its wide coverage also means that there is only limited scope for substitution of non-taxed goods and this makes it possible for businesses to shift the tax forward to final consumers.

At the time of writing, the rate of value-added tax is 15 per cent. In addition, some goods are zero-rated and others are exempt. The former are those goods which are basic essentials (such as bread, milk, fresh food, electricity, coal, new houses, books and children's clothes) and all exports: on these goods, complete tax relief is given and any tax paid on supplies is refunded. The exempt category includes traders with an annual turnover of £15,000 or less and all banking, insurance and stock-broking firms: businesses in this category do not have to charge value-added tax, but they are not entitled to a refund of tax paid on supplies obtained from other firms.

Customs and excise duties Customs duties (or tariffs) are imposed on certain imported goods from all countries. Note, however, that all trade with Common Market countries is tariff-free and certain preferential rates apply to some products imported from Commonwealth and certain less developed countries. Excise duties are generally imposed on goods which are not subject to value-added tax: in particular, goods such as tobacco, beers, wines and spirits are affected.

Proposed negative income tax

It has been suggested that the existing tax system could be used in reverse to provide income maintenance for the poor. This could either be supplementary to or a substitute for the present social security system. The name given to such a system is negative income taxation. To implement it, a level of minimum taxable income has to be determined. Income earners above this level then pay positive taxes in the normal way, but income earners below it 'pay' negative taxes (that is, receive positive transfers). To illustrate this, consider a simple example where the minimum taxable income for an individual is set at £2,000 per year and the positive and negative rates of tax are equal at 40 per cent. An income earner with a gross income of £4,000 will pay £800 in tax (that is, 40 per cent of £2,000 over the minimum taxable income) and an income earner with a gross income of only £1,200 will receive a transfer of £320 (that is, 40 per cent of the £800 below the minimum taxable income). This is illustrated in Fig. 9.

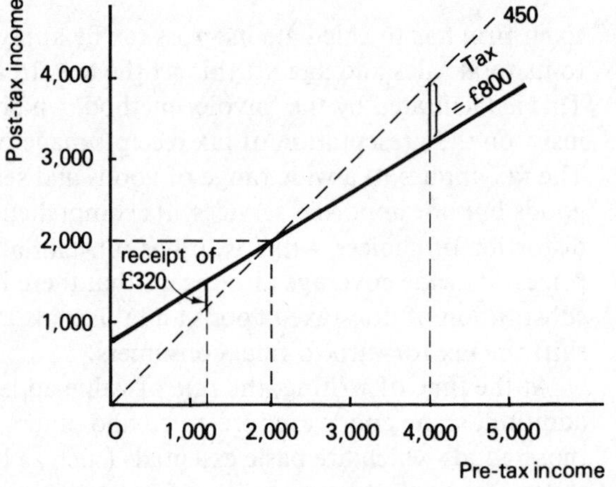

Fig. 9. A negative income tax.

Before adopting such a system, however, we should show that the present social security system is unsatisfactory. Consider the following defects.

(a) Certain benefits, such as child benefits, are available to both the rich and poor and so do nothing to reduce the disparities between them.
(b) The system is a bundle of grants and allowances topped up by supplementary benefits and the family income supplement and, to the layman, this results in a bewildering complexity of benefits and hence, in many cases, low take-up rates.
(c) The system may create disincentives to work: when income from work is less than social security benefits, some people may prefer to stay at home rather than work.
(d) There are administrative complexities with overlapping benefits, such as

unemployment benefit, supplementary benefit, family income supplement, rate and rent rebates.

In contrast, negative income taxation is simpler to operate and so would create considerable administrative savings. It tries to preserve incentives to work and concentrates the benefits on the needy via selectivity. It also minimises ignorance about benefit entitlement. Negative income taxation does have its disadvantages, however. For example, it may itself have disincentive effects, though these will depend on the type of scheme. Furthermore, the problems of coverage could be very severe – for example, the adoption of a comprehensive negative income tax system in the United Kingdom may mean a drastic reduction in the state provision of the health service, the education system and welfare benefits in cash and kind. Such a system may, therefore, only have limited scope in countries which already have advanced welfare services.

User charges

Broadly, the term 'user charge' refers to the price charged to an individual user of a facility provided by the public sector and has its origin in the benefit principle of taxation. User charges, then, are an alternative to taxation as a means of financing public spending.

Supporters of user charges maintain that, according to the benefit principle, it is inequitable to raise taxes to finance those social services which benefit identifiable groups. Such social services may include education, health services, water supply, civic amenities, sewage disposal, social work and council housing. The supporters go on to allege that governments, local authorities and other public bodies are encouraged to oversupply 'high cost' social services at almost zero prices. In the absence of a price, there is no effective constraint on demand so that queueing, delays, staff shortages and a general deterioration in the standards of these facilities may result. As an example, consider the National Health Service in the United Kingdom: it is argued that tax-financed medicine is less efficient than market-financed medicine since only market-financed medicine reflects the true choices of consumers – tax-financed medicine may result in the overconsumption of particular medical services because the consumer-patient does not take into account the full costs of supply.

The main arguments against applying user charges in the fields of education and health are as follows:

(a) The demand for these services may become elastic if high charges are imposed; an individual may find himself in the onerous position of having to choose between his own health and his children's education.
(b) As far as the National Health Service is concerned, the costs of administering charges may exceed the revenues.
(c) Some medical and educational expenditures are wealth-producing for the economy as a whole; for example, they help to create a healthy and educated labour force. Also, medical expenditure on infectious diseases must be tax-financed because of externalities.

(d) Free education and medical care may be justified on equity grounds as a means of redistributing income and wealth.

Other sources of public sector finance

Borrowing

It is possible for a government to spend more than its tax receipts, covering the resulting *deficit* by borrowing. In the postwar years, loan finance has become one of the major instruments which governments use in connection with their micro- and macroeconomic objectives. This is a marked departure from the classical view that the government's budget should be balanced.

Public sector borrowing involves an issue by the government of some sort of security (for example, a treasury bill, a gilt-edged security or a consol). The total amount of securities issued is called the *national debt*. In the United Kingdom, the national debt dates back to 1694 when the Bank of England was established to lend money to the government to wage war against France. In fact, government borrowing over the centuries has been mainly associated with war finance. Borrowing to finance government expenditure for other purposes has been largely a postwar phenomenon.

There is a popular misconception that government borrowing increases the national debt and therefore 'impoverishes' the nation. But if the debt is *internal,* so that the holders of the government securities are the country's own citizens, then increasing the debt is unlikely to have a significant effect on economic welfare. One effect will be to change the distribution of income as interest payments on the debt are financed from taxation. Another effect may be to reduce the availability of funds for the private sector, but this will only result in a welfare loss if the return on the funds used in the private sector is greater than in the public sector. If the loan is *external*, there is a potential loss of social welfare because then its repayment and interest charges mean that society has to consume less than it has produced. Even so, if external borrowing is used to create assets which expand the economy's productive capacity, then in the long-run, there may be a gain rather than a loss of social welfare.

From the standpoint of equity, if larger government borrowing means less taxation, then it depends upon whether it is direct or indirect taxes which are reduced. Assuming that indirect taxes are regressive and direct taxes progressive, a reduction in indirect taxes will benefit the poor while a reduction in direct taxes will benefit the rich. The financing of interest payments from taxation, however, will represent a transfer of purchasing power from all taxpayers to the richer members of society who own the securities. This effect will be reduced if some part of the interest payments are themselves financed from borrowing.

Finally, government borrowing may be more inflationary than tax finance. This is because, as we see in Chapter 19, raising taxes has the effect of reducing disposable incomes and so curbs consumption spending which offsets to some extent the rise in government spending. Financing government spending by borrowing does not have this offsetting effect.

Printing money

This method of financing public expenditure is as old as a country's central bank – in the case of the United Kingdom, the Bank of England. It has all the characteristics of loan finance discussed above. The issue department of the central bank is in charge of note issue in exchange for government securities which earn interest. Thus, any increase in note issue means an equal increase in the stock of government securities at the issue department. This apparently painless method of finance has ruined many governments in the past through over-issue of notes resulting in a loss of public confidence in the currency in question and serious inflationary consequences. A judicious use of the government's power to print money is necessary for the nation's financial stability.

Conclusion

We have seen that the main method of financing government spending is by raising taxes. In this chapter, we have discussed the principles of taxation, considered the resource allocation effects of direct and indirect taxes and set out the main types of taxes levied in the United Kingdom. We have also considered briefly the other methods of financing the public sector – through user charges, borrowing and printing money.

Further reading

Kay, J.A. and **King, M.A.**, *The British Tax System*, Oxford University Press, Oxford, 1978.
Prest, A.R. and **Barr, N.A.**, *Public Finance in Theory and Practice*, Weidenfeld and Nicolson, London, 1979 (Ch. 3–5, 9 and 19).
Brown, C.V. and **Jackson, P.M.**, *Public Sector Economics*, Martin Robertson, Oxford, 1978 (Ch. 3, 9, 11, 13 and 16).

Exercises

1. Review your understanding of the following terms:

taxation	equality of sacrifice
ad valorem tax	'neutral' taxes
specific tax	income-based tax
proportional tax	wealth-based tax
progressive tax	expenditure-based tax
regressive tax	formal incidence
average tax rate	effective incidence
marginal tax rate	tax burden
benefit principle	negative income tax
ability-to-pay principle	user charges

2. An individual's income rises from £5,000 to £5,200. Calculate his marginal tax rate and his original and final average tax rate if the amount of tax he pays changes: (a) from £1,000 to £1,050; (b) from £500 to £510; (c) from £1,000 to £1,250; (d) from £2,500 to £2,600. Comment on the relationship between the marginal and average rates of tax in these examples.

3. What principles should govern the design of an efficient and equitable tax system in a country?

4. Consider the view that the most efficient way to increase government revenues is to increase the rate of income tax rather than to increase the rate of tax on spending.

5. In what ways might wealth be regarded as superior to income as a measure of ability-to-pay?

6. Discuss the advantages and disadvantages of financing government expenditure by: (a) taxation; (b) borrowing; (c) printing money; and (d) user charges.

7. Discuss the arguments for and against the introduction of a negative income tax in the United Kingdom.

14 Issues of public policy

Introduction

The purpose of this final chapter on the public sector is to consider some selected elements of British government policy towards: (a) firms and industry in the private sector and (b) the nationalised industries.

One of the aims of the public sector's policies towards the private sector is to improve allocational efficiency. In Chapter 9, we showed that perfect competition with no externalities ensures economic efficiency because firms equate their prices with marginal costs. In contrast, we saw in Chapter 10 that monopolies and firms in other imperfect market structures, such as oligopoly, normally fail to equate prices with marginal costs and so create a misallocation of resources. Such imperfect market structures may therefore adversely affect society's welfare.

In addition to imperfect markets for goods, there are imperfect markets for the nation's resources of labour, capital and land. Also, the rules governing the tendering for government contracts (such as defence contracts and contracts for medical supplies) are by no means competitive. We propose in the first part of this chapter to focus attention on the legal regulation of markets for goods and services (called *negative public policy*). Secondly, we consider those measures designed to encourage firms, through financial assistance or 'planning agreements', voluntarily to change their present and future investment and output decisions (called *positive public policy*). Finally, we examine the pricing and investment policies of nationalised industries.

Negative public policy

By the phrase 'negative public policy', we mean that set of government measures which is intended: (a) to promote competition and (b) to control monopolies, mergers and restrictive practices. Such measures have developed at a time when British industry has been becoming more and more concentrated. A study by S.J. Prais in 1976 revealed that the share of the 100 largest manufacturing firms in Britain, measured in terms of net output, rose from only 16 per cent in 1909 to over 40 per cent in 1968. There is also evidence to show that British industry is more highly concentrated than that in the United States, France and Germany.

It is noteworthy that postwar competition policy in Britain has been built step-by-step through a series of Acts of Parliament. There has thus been no consistent general policy to promote competition. There has, though, been a presumption that competition is 'good' and monopoly is 'bad'. Assuming that the utility-maximising consumer is the best judge of his own interests, competition policy can broadly claim the following benefits to the community:

(a) greater economic efficiency;
(b) wider consumers' choices;
(c) an improved system of information about prices in the markets for goods and resources;
(d) greater incentives to innovate and to develop new products and processes.

However, if we accept that the individual is not always the best judge of his own interests, then it is possible to argue that monopolies are not 'bad' *per se*. Indeed, some private sector monopolies and conglomerates may be allowed to operate because they confer special benefits which competition is unable to provide. In the same way, some public sector monopolies, such as gas, electricity, health and education, may be justified on the grounds that the private individual's interests do not always coincide with the interests of society. As a result, state monopolies may increase society's welfare whilst competition, if permitted in these spheres, may reduce social welfare.

We discussed the main possible advantages and disadvantages of monopolies in Chapter 10. Recall that advantages might accrue from the monopolist's ability *to reduce costs by benefiting from economies of single ownership* and *to undertake extensive research and development*. The main disadvantages are that the monopolist is likely to set a *higher price* and produce a *lower output* than would be the case under competition and may be able to maintain *above-normal profits in the long-run* because of barriers to the entry of new firms.

Evolution of the control of monopolies, mergers and restrictive practices

In its negative aspect, British government policy is characterised by a series of anti-monopoly legislation designed to curb the disadvantages of monopolies and mergers. The major provisions of some of the more notable Acts of Parliament are outlined below.

The Monopolies and Restrictive Practices (Inquiry and Control) Act 1948 This was the first piece of legislation to encourage competition and curb monopoly in the United Kingdom. The Act established a Monopolies Commission charged with the responsibility for *investigating* and *reporting* on monopoly situations. The Commission was required to determine whether or not a particular monopoly was in the 'public interest'. The Act defined a monopoly as a single firm or group of linked firms controlling one third or more of the market. In course of time, the Commission focused attention on the *market behaviour* of firms more than the *structure*. It found evidence to show that collective restrictive practices were widespread in British industry and this led to the enactment of legislation intended to curb such agreements in 1956.

The Restrictive Trade Practices Act 1956 This established the Restrictive Practices Court charged with the responsibility for supervising agreements between firms and determining whether or not such agreements were contrary to the public interest. The Act required firms to register restrictive agreements between two or more firms carrying on business in the production or supply of goods. In particular, the agreements required to be registered included the following: (a) those in which the parties accepted restrictions in respect of the prices to be charged or the terms and conditions of sale; (b) those in which the parties accepted restrictions in respect of the quantities or types of goods to be produced or the persons or areas to be supplied.

It can be noted that the major emphasis of the Act is on the behaviour of firms. However, the Act did specify some 'gateways' on the basis of which the parties could justify to the Court the continuation of an agreement. According to these gateways, an agreement may be upheld if it can be shown that:

1. the agreement is necessary to protect the public against injury;
2. removal of the restriction would result in the loss of specific and substantial benefits to the public;
3. the restriction is necessary against a person or firm not party to the agreement trying to restrict competition;
4. the restriction is necessary to negotiate reasonable and fair terms with another supplier or buyer;
5. removal of the restriction would result in higher unemployment in areas where the industry in question is heavily concentrated;
6. removal of the restriction would cause a substantial loss of exports;
7. the restriction is necessary to support some other agreement which the Court finds acceptable.

The Restrictive Trade Practices Act 1968 added an eighth gateway: that an agreement may be acceptable if it does not restrict competition. It should be emphasised that even if an agreement can be shown to satisfy one of the gateway conditions, the Court still has to be convinced that the benefits of the agreement outweigh its disadvantages. The most important cases heard by the Court have been allowed under gateways (2) and (5). For instance, in 1961, the Court accepted the argument of the Cement Makers Federation under gateway (2) that an agreement which restricted competition reduced the risks facing its members and so enabled them to charge lower prices: in making this decision, the Court took into account the efficient performance of the industry prior to the investigation. In 1959, the Court also accepted the arguments of the Yarn Spinners Association under gateway (5), but refused to uphold the agreement after taking into consideration the industry's inefficient performance.

It is interesting that many of the agreements that were registered were in fact voluntarily abandoned or modified. Few agreements actually came before the Court and of these less than a third were upheld.

The Resale Prices Act 1964 The 1956 Act banned collective resale price maintenance (RPM), but made individual RPM legally enforceable. This in turn had adverse effects on the growth of multiple retailers, who were keen to reduce prices in order to achieve a higher volume of turnover. The Resale Prices Act 1964, was, therefore, passed to ban individual RPM in all forms unless the firm could justify it to the Restrictive Practices Court. RPM could be maintained where its abandonment would result in: (a) loss of quality; (b) a substantial reduction in the number of shops; (c) price increases in the long-run; (d) loss of necessary service; (e) danger to health. Even if allowed on any of these grounds, the firm had to show further that the advantages of RPM were in excess of its disadvantages. In course of time, only publishers of books and maps and some manufacturers of drugs and medicines were able to satisfy the Court in this respect.

The Monopolies and Mergers Act 1965 This was passed to deal with the rising industrial concentration caused by mergers and takeovers. The Act gave power to the then Board of Trade to scrutinise and, if thought fit, refer to the Monopolies Commission two categories of mergers: those in which the assets to be acquired exceeded £5 million and those which created or strengthened a monopoly. The Act also empowered the Monopolies Commission to investigate monopolies in *service* industries.

The Fair Trading Act 1973 This Act created the Office of the Director-General of Fair Trading (DG) with wide powers to protect consumers' interests and to maintain supervision over and to collect information on all types of trading practices in relation to the supply of goods and services.

The Act had the following main provisions:

1. It changed the definition of a monopoly from a firm or group of linked firms controlling one-third of the home market to a firm or group of linked firms controlling *one-quarter* of the home market.
2. The DG was given wide powers to refer monopolies to the new Monopolies and Mergers Commission. However, the minister responsible for prices and consumer protection may also initiate a reference to the Commission. Merger references, though, could only be made by the minister.
3. The provisions of the 1956 Act were extended to cover firms supplying services, such as hairdressers, estate agents and travel agents, requiring them to register their agreements relating to prices, persons and areas with the Office of Fair Trading.
4. If dissatisfied with the methods of operation of a firm, the DG should refer the matter to a new body, the Consumer Protection Advisory Committee. The Committee determines whether or not the firm's trading operations are against the public interest and the minister then makes an order on the basis of the Committee's recommendations. Also, the DG may refer a registered agreement, if considered to be in restraint of competition, to the Restrictive Practices Court for adjudication.
5. The DG can receive complaints from the public and investigates any alleged business malpractices through the Consumer Protection Advisory Committee.

Assessment of negative public policy

Overall, government measures dealing with restrictive practices have been more successful than monopolies and mergers controls. Following the 1956 Act, over 3,000 restrictive agreements were registered in the next two decades and many were voluntarily abandoned. The Monopolies and Mergers Commission's impact on 'dominant firms' has, however, been less significant. This is partly because the implementation of its reports and recommendations is a political decision lying with the relevant minister. In the past, the minister concerned has frequently bypassed the Commission, contenting himself with assurances and undertakings of good behaviour from dominant firms. For instance, the merger between the General Electric Company and Associated Electrical Industries was allowed without reference to the Commission.

Even where the Commission has been active in the field of monopolies and mergers, competition policy has been lacking well-defined objectives. This is because the Commission bases its ultimate judgement on the application of statutory criteria to situations of monopolies and mergers on the vague concept of the 'public interest'. Thus, the proposed merger between Lloyds, Barclays and Martins Banks (1968) was not allowed as the Commission was unable to find substantial benefits from economies of scale and so believed the merger to be against the public interest. Similarly, the proposed mergers of Ross and Associated Fisheries (1966), and British Sidac and Transparent Paper (1970) were disallowed on the grounds that they were unable to show that they would result in the elimination of excess capacity and waste. In contrast, the Commission found the activities of the London Brick Company, though a monopolist, *not* to be against the public interest. When it considered the pricing policy of the Company in 1976, the Commission found that the Company was charging reasonable prices and had made no excess profits.

It can, however, be argued that monopolies and mergers confer power without responsibility and so may abuse the public interest. This may in turn lead to higher than competitive prices, less than competitive levels of output, resulting in excess capacity and loss of social welfare. In addition, monopolies may have little incentive to innovate which may mean loss of technical progress. The extent to which the Commission attaches importance to technical progress is illustrated by the proposed merger between Boots and Glaxo (1972). This was disallowed on the grounds that each unit was large enough to conduct research and development efficiently. The Commission felt that the merger would reduce the incentive to innovate.

It is worthwhile pointing out that up to 1965, the Commission was mainly concerned with the *deviant behaviour* of firms with monopoly power. In other words, between 1948 and 1965, dominant firm monopolies were the major preoccupation of the Commission and it tended to ignore the increasing concentration in the industrial structure of the United Kingdom. Following the 1965 Act, however, the Commission also became concerned with the structure of industry. Between 1965 and 1978, over 1,500 proposed mergers were considered by the Mergers Panel, of which 43 were referred to the Commission. Only 13 of these were found to be against the public interest.

The 1973 Act gave the DG the power to initiate action against unfair trading practices and the Act included the activities of trade unions and nationalised industries as possible candidates for investigation. If unions are treated in the market for labour in the same way as monopolies in the market for goods, then a reference might be made to the Commission where a single union or group of linked unions: (a) controlled one-quarter of a market's supply of labour; or (b) proposed a merger resulting in either a one-quarter share of a particular labour market or where the value of the assets involved exceeded £5 million. Similarly, 'free collective bargaining' and 'closed shops' might be considered as practices in 'restraint of trade', restricting consumers' choice and adversely affecting the allocational efficiency of resources. No such activities of unions have, as yet, been investigated. Even if a reference were made in this field or in other fields of business behaviour and industrial concentration, the final decisions about the recommendations of the Monopolies and Mergers Commission are bound to be based on the political judgement of the government of the day.

Positive public policy

By the phrase 'positive public policy', we mean those sets of government measures which are designed to promote faster economic growth through: (a) greater economic efficiency; and (b) the restructuring of British industry. In the 1970s, the term 'industrial strategy' was used in relation to the planning of key sectors of the British economy. This strategy referred, first, to those government measures concerned with providing financial assistance to private firms and secondly, to consultations between the government, the Confederation of British Industry and the trade unions as regards the key sectors of the economy. Many of the tripartite consultations took place under the aegis of the National Economic Development Council and resulted in the formation of a number of sector working parties. In order to put the industrial strategy into effect, the government took powers under the Industry Acts of 1972 and 1975.

The Industry Act of 1972 outlined the pattern for regional assistance, with a view to increasing industrial efficiency and protecting jobs. The Act also strengthened the financial help being given already to private firms under previous legislation.

The Industry Act of 1975 established the National Enterprise Board (NEB) with access to funds to enable it to acquire holdings in private firms. It took over existing government holdings in, for example, British Leyland, Rolls-Royce and Ferranti and it acquired stakes in a number of small companies. The NEB's major role is to promote investment in the key economic sectors and to encourage rationalisation into fewer but more efficient units. *Voluntary planning agreements* were another notable feature of the 1975 Act which stipulated that companies should discuss with the government plans concerning their future operations. Progress was slow on this front and only two planning agreements were made (with Chrysler UK and the National Coal Board). However, the government drew up schemes to improve the performance of individual industries, such as ferrous foundries, machine tools and textiles.

Why should public money be given to the private sector?

The over-riding objective of the Industry Acts of 1972 and 1975 was to enable the government to provide financial assistance to private firms. Clearly, government 'cash handouts' to private firms contradict the philosophy of competition that businesses should stand on their own feet and that 'lame ducks' should be left to market forces so that the incentive to be efficient is strengthened.

However there are several arguments in favour of state support to private firms. Consider the following:

(a) Efficiency in resource allocation requires that firms set price equal to marginal cost. However, in a decreasing cost industry, this will result in a loss. Efficiency may require a government subsidy to enable the industry to set price equal to marginal cost.
(b) Temporary financial assistance may be justified to protect employment in an industry that would otherwise contract or close down, creating serious structural unemployment. In this way, the government will gain time to institute retraining schemes and attract new industries into the affected area.
(c) If there are externalities present in the pricing system, a state subsidy may improve the market performance of firms. For instance, financial help to the British aircraft industry to develop new technology benefits other sectors of private industry, such as electronics, radar, radio and digital computing.
(d) Government financial assistance may be justified to promote exports and save imports, and to strengthen defence. All of these confer external benefits on other firms.

There are, however, counter-arguments about the flow of public money to the private sector. Consider the following:

(a) State support to private firms has an opportunity cost in terms of the foregone benefits in alternative sectors of British industry.
(b) Financial help encourages the growth of inefficient industries, resulting in a waste of the nation's scarce resources. Such help hinders the outflow of resources from inefficient industries into more productive ones.

Some critics of financial assistance to private firms believe that the market mechanism leads to an efficient allocation of resources and that, therefore, government intervention should be minimised.

Public sector firms

It is not always easy to determine what is and what is not a public sector firm because there are no well-defined criteria for judging whether a particular enterprise forms part of the private or public sector of the United Kingdom economy. However, we shall define a public sector firm as being a *nationalised industry*. Such an industry is owned by the state and has its own board of directors which is appointed by the minister concerned. In turn, the minister is responsible to Parliament for the efficient operation of the industry. In practice, ministerial interference in the running of nationalised industries has been much more frequent than was envisaged by the original statutes which created these industries.

Historically, the nationalised industries have been brought under public ownership and control during the twentieth century. For instance, the Port of London Authority was formed in 1908 and the Central Electricity Board was set up in 1926, whilst the London Passenger Transport Board was established in 1933. During the period 1945 – 51, a large number of industries were nationalised by the Labour government, including the railways, the Bank of England and the coal and gas industries. The iron and steel industry was nationalised in 1951, denationalised by the Conservative government in 1953 and renationalised by the Labour government in 1967.

The nationalised industries play a key role in the United Kingdom economy. In the 1960s, their investment was approximately equal to the whole of that for manufacturing industry. In 1975, their share of the United Kingdom's total final investment was 19 per cent. Besides their importance in terms of investment, they contributed 11 per cent to total output in 1975 and employed 8 per cent of the total labour force. Table 1 shows the individual contributions of these industries in terms of investment, output and employment in 1975.

Table 1. United Kingdom public corporations – shares in United Kingdom economy, 1975, percentage of United Kingdom total.

	Fixed investment	Output	Employment
British Airways	0.4	0.3	0.2
British Gas	1.7	0.8	0.4
British Rail	1.0	1.2	1.0
British Steel Corporation	2.0	0.8	0.9
Electricity (England and Wales)	2.9	1.5	0.7
National Coal Board	0.9	1.5	1.2
Post Office	4.5	2.8	1.8
National Bus	0.1	0.2	0.3
National Freight Corporation	...	0.2	0.2
Nine major nationalised industries	13.6	9.2	6.7
Other nationalised industries	0.8	0.4	0.2
Other public corporations	4.6	1.4	1.1
Total	19.0	11.0	8.0

Source: A Study of UK Nationalised Industries, NEDO, 1976.
Note: Individual shares do not sum to totals, due to rounding.

These figures suggest that the nationalised industries are more important in terms of their share of investment than their shares of output and employment. This implies that they tend to be more capital-intensive than the economy as a whole; indeed, their investment/output ratio was estimated to be 38 per cent in 1975, while for the economy as a whole, this ratio was estimated to be only 22 per cent. Clearly, with such a large share of investment, it is important that their investment choices be made efficiently because inefficient resource allocation between and within the public and private sectors would mean a loss of social welfare.

Reasons for nationalisation

Consider the following reasons for nationalisation.

Economic planning Some economists believe that planning and control of the economy is best achieved through public ownership. In some European countries and many developing countries, this has been an important factor. In the United Kingdom, though, the process of nationalisation cannot be explained solely in terms of economic planning.

Ideology In many western European countries, including the United Kingdom, the nationalisation movement gathered momentum after the Second World War. By and large, the movement seems to have been sparked off by a desire to achieve certain social and political objectives. It was increasingly believed by democratic socialists that nationalisation was an effective method of achieving the transition from capitalism to socialism.

Natural monopolies Economies of scale may result in an industry becoming a natural monopoly in which case the public interest may be best served by putting such a monopoly into public ownership rather than leaving it to private enterprise. Some state monopolies control natural resources, such as water and energy; others are sole producers of goods or services, such as telecommunications. If these industries were left to private enterprise, this might result in the abuse of monopoly power.

'Lame ducks' Most economists would agree that free market forces do not enable some industries to adjust themselves quickly to changes in tastes, incomes and technology. Given the public sector's macroeconomic objective of full employment, the government may decide that it is socially desirable to nationalise wholly or partly some such industries in order to protect jobs. This was one of the motives for the nationalisation of the ship-building industry in the United Kingdom in 1977.

Objectives of nationalised industries

The statutes which created these industries gave them two types of obligations: first, to operate in the public interest in the sense that they must respond to the needs of the community; secondly, to achieve resource allocational efficiency through their pricing and investment policies. In seeking to discharge these obligations, it was possible for the nationalised industries to sustain losses. The only statutory requirement was to break even taking one year with another. The statutes were vague about the ways in which losses, if sustained, should be covered.

More specific guidance on pricing and investment policies was given to the nationalised industries with the publication of two White Papers in the 1960s. The first one was entitled *The Financial and Economic Obligations of the Nationalised Industries* (1961) and the second *A Review of Economic and Financial Objectives* (1967). The 1961 White Paper emphasised that nationalised industries should act as commercial concerns, earning a commercial rate of return on their gross assets: this implied that they should earn a surplus over costs net of interest payments. Such a surplus came to be called a 'target rate of return' which had to be achieved on average over a five-year period. This meant that an industry failing to achieve the required surplus in a particular year was required to make up the deficit over the remainder of the five-year period.

Note that the target rate of return corresponds to the familiar notion of profits earned by a private firm. In fact, many nationalised industries failed to reach their target rates of return. It also became increasingly clear that the financial criteria of the 1961 White Paper were inadequate as they did not provide sufficient guidance on the practical application of investment and pricing policies. In particular, this White Paper did not clearly separate the statutory social responsibilities of the nationalised industries from their commercial operations.

The 1967 White Paper attempted to remedy some of these weaknesses. The public interest role was to be analysed by the government using a cost-benefit approach and thus to be separately accounted for. This meant that the government had to compensate the enterprise concerned for any losses sustained in discharging its social responsibilities. Secondly, the White Paper formulated strict criteria for investment and pricing policies in pursuit of the objectives of efficiency and profitability.

The 1978 White Paper (entitled *The Nationalised Industries*) broadly reinforced the objectives of the nationalised industries outlined above, as well as the principles laid down in the 1961 and 1967 White Papers for the achievement of these objectives. This White Paper held out greater promise of less frequent ministerial interference in the day-to-day running of the nationalised industries. It also promised greater freedom from the minister in the industries' pricing and investment policies. A major feature of the White Paper was to shift emphasis away from the nationalised industries towards the taxation and social security systems as means of subsidising the less well-off sections of the community.

Financial resources and control

In order to finance their capital projects, the nationalised industries have two main sources of funds: (a) internal funds; (b) borrowing from the Treasury, including subsidies.

During the 1960s, their internal sources varied between 25 per cent and 45 per cent of their total capital requirements and, in some cases, especially in the 1970s, their self-finance dwindled to 17 per cent. This decline was due in part to the government's 'price restraint' policies which prevented the nationalised industries from achieving adequate trading surpluses. One result of this was an increased dependence of the nationalised industries on borrowing from the Treasury: about £1,600 million in 1974 and over £2,000 million in 1975. This, in turn, enabled the Treasury to exercise considerable control over the industries' investment decisions.

Such control comes about in the following way. Each year, there is an 'investment review', the purpose of which is to approve totals for investment expenditure for every industry in each of the following five years. But the spending totals for the first two years are already committed by past investment decisions and the estimates of the last two years are tentative, so that effectively serious consideration is given only to the third year ahead. Thus, the review period provides an opportunity for the Treasury to examine carefully the industry's assumptions about demand forecasts, technology, prices and the government's broad economic policy. However, the Treasury, because of insufficient information about the details of planned investment, is unable to evaluate specific investment plans. This means that if it is desired to make cuts in capital expenditure in order to accommodate them all within a given total, then the Treasury has to suggest equal percentage cuts all round, leaving each industry to make up its own mind about which capital spending to prune or to postpone.

As part of the control technique, the Treasury may also set limits on the short-term borrowing of the nationalised industries. This enables the government to have an advance warning of a possible deterioration in their current operations since exceeding the set limit requires government approval. Furthermore, the Treasury's decision about a capital write-off and compensation is both a source of funds to finance capital projects and a means of controlling the industries' investment decisions. This is so because the smaller the size of the repayment of a loan, including interest, to the Treasury on account of a capital write-off, the larger is the internal source of funds available for capital expenditures.

Investment and pricing policies

A pricing policy entails setting price at a level that makes full use of the industry's productive capacity. We saw in Chapers 9 and 10 that setting *price equal to marginal cost* would result in an efficient level of output, provided perfect competition prevails in the rest of the economic system with no externalities. Under these conditions, the price consumers have to pay is equal to the cost of resources employed in the production of one additional unit of output.

The 1967 White Paper introduced the principle of marginal cost pricing for nationalised industries. We may, however, distinguish between *short-run* and *long-run* marginal cost pricing. In the case of short-run marginal cost pricing, the relevant costs are the *variable* costs of labour, fuel and raw materials, and *not* the costs of capital assets which are fixed in the short-run. As an example, consider the electricity industry. Its capital assets, such as the electric power generating stations, electric cables and so on, are fixed in meeting a given demand for electricity consumption. The only costs it can vary in the short-run are the manning levels of the power stations, supplies of oil, coal and water.

The rule of equating price with short-run marginal cost is illustrated in Fig. 1, where SMC is the industry's short-run marginal cost curve and DD is the market demand for electricity consumption. The short-run marginal cost price per unit is O*P* and O*Q* is the efficient output level.

It can be seen that at price O*P*, the industry is producing that level of

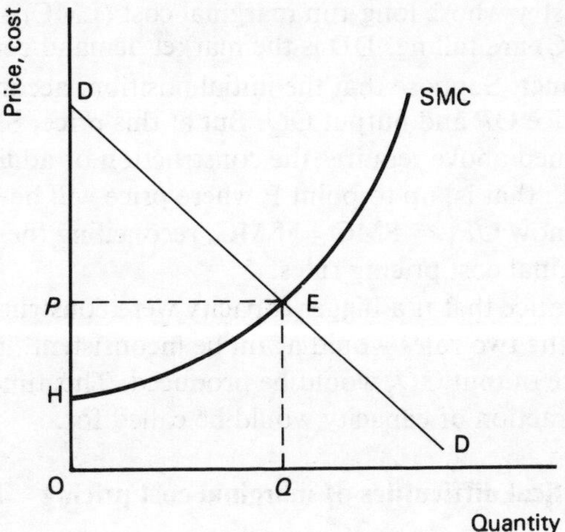

Fig. 1. Short-run marginal cost pricing.

output at which total benefits (measured by the area under the demand curve, DD) minus total costs (measured by the area under the supply curve, SMC) is maximised. This maximum net benefit is equal to the sum of consumer surplus, *P*DE and producer surplus, H*P*E. Output O*Q*, then, is the efficient level of output which maximises net social benefit.

However, where the price is unrelated to the costs of capital assets, as in the above analysis of short-run marginal cost pricing, the managers of a nationalised industry are left with an unresolved problem. That is, when should the industry invest in additional productive capacity? The resolution of this problem depends upon whether the existing capacity is larger or smaller than that required to meet future demand at minimum cost. The industry cannot change its capacity in the short-run, but can undoubtedly increase or decrease capacity in the long-run by changing the volume of investment.

Thus, in the long-run, marginal cost is the *cost of adding to capacity* and, from the point of view of efficiency, prices should be set equal to long-run marginal cost, rather than short-run marginal cost. This gives rise to the basic question: do the two rules (P = SMC and P = LMC) contradict each other? The answer is that they will be consistent so long as the industry is operating at its 'optimum' productive capacity – that is, that capacity at which the given demand can be satisfied at least cost. This is because *when optimum capacity is reached, then prices equal to SMC will also equal LMC.* In that case, the managers of a nationalised concern would find that the cost of increasing output by using existing capacity marginally more intensively equals the cost of expanding output by additions to capacity.

When the industry is not operating at its optimum productive capacity, the two rules will not be consistent. They can, however, be reconciled once again if a particular nationalised industry complies with the following requirement: *where SMC exceeds LMC, construct new productive capacity; where LMC exceeds SMC, cut back on investment and reduce capacity.* In both cases, the investment or disinvestment should be continued until SMC and LMC are equal. The policy of disinvestment and curtailment of capacity is illustrated by the proposed closures of plants by the loss-making British Steel Corporation.

The policy of investment and disinvestment is illustrated in Fig. 2 for an industry whose long-run marginal cost (LMC) and long-run average cost (LAC) are falling. DD is the market demand curve for the industry's product. Suppose that the initial position, according to the P = SMC rule, is at price O*P* and output O*Q*. But at this price, SMC exceeds LMC. The rule outlined above requires the construction of additional capacity until SMC = LMC: that is, up to point E where price will be OP_1 and output OQ_1. Notice that now OP_1 = SMC = LMC, reconciling the short-run and long-run marginal cost pricing rules.

Notice that if a bigger capacity were constructed, LMC would exceed SMC and the two rules would again be inconsistent. This is the case at point F where output OQ_2 would be produced. This time, disinvestment and contraction of capacity would be called for.

Practical difficulties of marginal cost pricing There are several difficulties

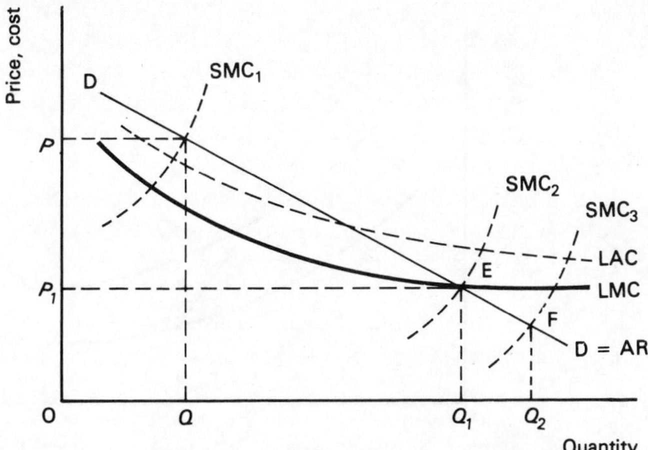

Fig. 2. Investment and pricing policy in a decreasing cost industry.

in implementing marginal cost pricing. First, the rule fails to take into account changes in demand: in particular, the demand patterns for gas, electricity, telecommunications and transport vary daily, weekly and from season to season. For example, commuter trains are crowded during rush-hours, but have few passengers during the rest of the day: at peak periods, to carry an extra passenger might require an extra train service, whilst at off-peak periods, the marginal cost of carrying an extra passenger is virtually zero. Such variations in demand make it difficult to estimate marginal cost realistically.

Secondly, in integrated systems of production, such as the electricity industry, marginal cost is exceedingly difficult to identify. For example, an increase in the price of oil which raises the marginal cost of generating electricity in oil-fired power stations by, say, 10 per cent does not enable the industry to increase price by exactly 10 per cent. This is because a single consumer, through the grid system, might be consuming electricity generated in nuclear or coal-fired power stations where marginal costs are unchanged. The problem facing the industry is to estimate the overall increase in the marginal cost of the system.

Thirdly, as shown in Fig. 3, marginal cost pricing may cause an industry with decreasing long-run costs to encounter financial deficits. Inspection of Fig. 3 shows that at price O*P*, the enterprise sustains a total loss equal to the area *P*TJE.

The loss arises because the enterprise charges a price below long-run average cost and so is unable to generate sufficient revenues to replace worn out plant and equipment. If the deficit were financed by taxes (other than lump-sum taxes), this would distort allocation efficiency in other sectors of the economy and result in a redistribution of income from taxpayers to the consumers of the product of the nationalised industry.

Fourthly, the marginal cost pricing rule is designed to achieve Pareto efficiency in the allocation of resources in the private and public sectors of the economy. But when there are externalities or monopoly elements in the private sector, these will spoil the Pareto 'first best' conditions. Consequently, from the theory of second best, it cannot be concluded

Fig. 3. Marginal cost pricing and decreasing costs.

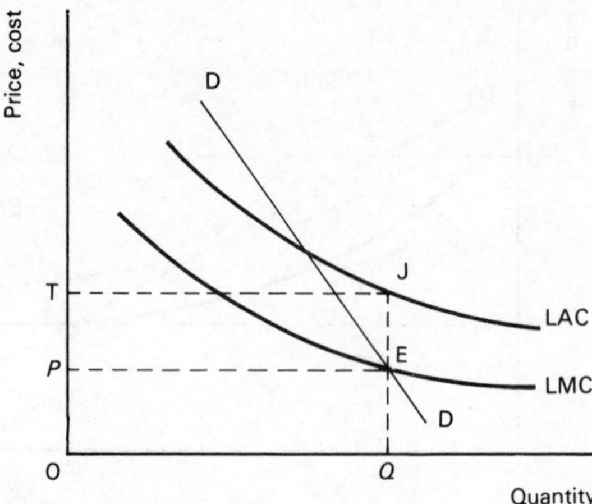

whether marginal cost pricing in the public sector will improve or worsen the allocation of resources.

In the light of the difficulties associated with calculating marginal cost, the 1978 White Paper suggested that nationalised industries should set their prices equal to *average incremental cost* (AIC). This can be regarded as an approximation of marginal cost and yet is much easier to calculate. As an example, suppose that the coal industry decides to produce 1,000,000 extra tonnes of coal per week and that this costs an additional £50 million (including the extra labour costs, interest costs and depreciation). We can write

$$\text{AIC} = \frac{\triangle \text{TC}}{\triangle Q} = \frac{50 \text{ m.}}{1{,}000{,}000} = £50.$$

The coal industry should set a price of £50 per tonne. The main advantage of AIC pricing is its ease of computation. It will, of course, be closer to marginal cost pricing, the smaller is the increase in output and the nearer the industry is to constant returns to scale.

Conclusion

This chapter concludes our microeconomic analysis of the public sector. In the last four chapters, we have seen that the role of the public sector in a mixed economy is wide-ranging and of crucial importance to social welfare. It has been shown that most of the public sector's decisions are normative in nature because, of necessity, they are based on value judgements. This final chapter on the microeconomic aspects of the public sector has highlighted the practical difficulties of applying the principles of positive economics to complex policy problems.

Further reading

Grant, R.M. and **Shaw G.K.**, (eds), *Current Issues in Economic Policy*, Philip Allan, Oxford, 1980 (Ch. 2 and 3).

Hartley, K., *Problems of Economic Policy*, Allen and Unwin, London, 1977 (Ch. 9 and 10).
George, K.D. and **Shorey, J.**, *The Allocation of Resources*, Allen and Unwin, London, 1978 (Ch. 4).
Prest, A.R. and **Coppock, D.J.**, (eds), *The UK Economy: A Manual of Applied Economics*, Weidenfeld and Nicolson, London, 1978 (Ch. 4).

Exercises

1. Review your understanding of the following terms:

negative public policy
positive public policy
restrictive practice
the eight 'gateways'
resale price maintenance
deviant behaviour
dominant firm monopoly
industrial strategy
planning agreements
nationalised industries
'lame duck'
target rate of return
short-run MC pricing
long-run MC pricing
average incremental cost

2. Suppose that a nationalised industry faces the long-run cost and revenue curves shown in Fig. 4. Indicate on the graph the price, output and profit levels consistent with: (a) long-run marginal cost pricing; (b) long-run average cost pricing; and (c) long-run profit maximisation.

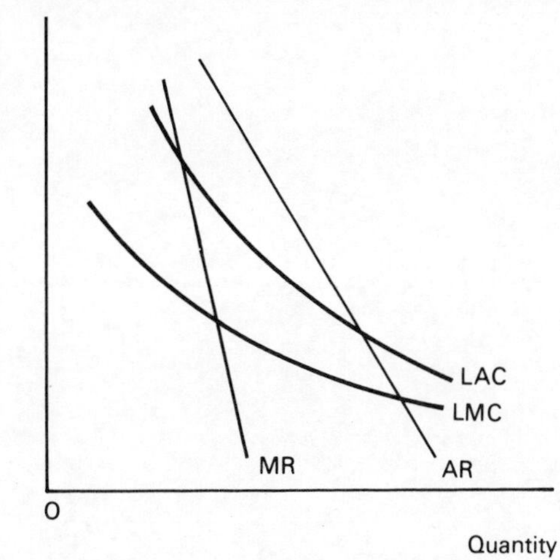

Fig. 4. The long-run cost and revenue curves of a nationalised industry.

3. Illustrate the arguments that might lead the Monopolies and Mergers Commission to decide that a particular monopoly is operating in the 'public interest'.

4. Suggest reasons why the United Kingdom government found it difficult to get planning agreements widely accepted by industry following the passing of the Industry Act 1975.

5. 'Monopolies are harmful and should be banned!' Discuss.

6. Discuss the case for and against financial help to private industry from the state.

7. Discuss the problems of identifying short- and long-run marginal costs in a nationalised industry which faces demand fluctuations according to the season and the time of day.

Theory of distribution

15 The determination of wages

Introduction

In Chapters 15 and 16, we are concerned with a vitally important topic – the distribution of income among the members of a society. We analyse the factors determining how the output of an economy is divided up, and shared out among the groups and individuals that comprise that society.

We have seen already in Chapter 7 that one method of determining the relative incomes of the factors of production is through a central planning agency. This system operates in a planned or command economy. In a market economy there are two basic factors influencing the distribution of income to the owners of the factors of production. One is clearly the pattern of ownership of the factors of production; the second is the prices at which the services of the factors of production sell in the factor markets.

The ownership of factors of production can be regarded as given, so that we concentrate on the determination of factor prices. Strictly, it is the determination of the prices of the *services* of the factors that is important as some factors, such as labour, are not used up during the production period. But conventionally, reference is made to the determination of factor prices and we follow that convention.

In a market economy the major influences on the determination of factor prices are the demand and supply conditions of the factors. In this chapter, we concentrate on labour and examine the variables which influence the determination of wages. But much of what we say can be adapted to the determination of other factor prices. The marginal productivity theory of the demand for a factor of production is, for example, a general theory of the demand for any variable factor. In Chapter 16, we turn specifically to the returns to capital and land.

The demand for a factor

It is important to bear in mind that the demand for a factor of production is a *derived demand*: it is necessarily derived from the consumers' demand for the products which the factor helps to make. For example, the demand for the services of ice-cream salesmen is derived from the consumers' demand for ice-cream. We start this section by considering a single firm's demand for labour, assuming that labour is a variable factor of production and that all other factors are fixed. This analysis then enables us to determine the total demand for labour of an entire industry.

The demand for labour of a single firm

In Chapter 9, we saw that a firm maximises profits by producing up to the point at which the last unit produced adds just as much to revenue as to costs

– that is, at which marginal revenue equals marginal cost. An implication of this is that a firm will hire units of its variable factors of production until the last unit hired adds just as much to revenue as to costs. This result brings us to the important concepts of *marginal revenue product, the value of the marginal product* and *marginal factor cost.*

Definition: ***The marginal revenue product (MRP) of a variable factor is the change in total revenue resulting from the employment of one more or one less unit of the variable factor. It is equal to the marginal physical product of the variable factor (MPP) multiplied by marginal revenue (MR):***

MRP = MPP × MR

Note that the term 'marginal physical product' is used in place of marginal product. This is to emphasise that it is measured in *physical* units and to distinguish it from the *value* of the marginal product.

Definition: ***The value of the marginal product (VMP) of a variable factor is the market value of the marginal physical product of the variable factor. It is equal to the marginal physical product multiplied by the price of the final product (P):***

VMP = MPP × P

Definition: ***Marginal factor cost (MFC) is the change in total cost resulting from the employment of one more or one less unit of the variable factor.***

Notice that if the firm is selling its product in a perfectly competitive market, so that $P = \text{MR}$, then it must also be true that MRP = VMP.

It should be clear from the above definitions that *a profit-maximising firm selling its product in a perfectly competitive market will hire additional units of its variable factor of production up to the point at which MRP (VMP) is equal to MFC.* This is the *theory of marginal productivity.* If, in addition, we assume that *labour* is the variable factor and that the firm purchases it in a perfectly competitive labour market then MFC will be the (given) wage rate. The theory of marginal productivity then states that the firm will hire additional units of labour up to the point at which *the wage is just equal to the value of the marginal product of labour.*

To illustrate this, consider the numerical example set out in Table 1. The example is that of a wheat farmer who is operating in perfectly competitive factor and product markets and whose only variable factor of production is labour.

Notice that columns (1) and (2) are reproduced from Table 1 of Chapter 2. They illustrate the 'law of diminishing returns' because as more and more workers are employed, the marginal physical product of labour eventually declines. Suppose now that the price of wheat is given as £2 per tonne: this enables us to calculate the MRP (= VMP). This is shown in column (3) and, since the wage is constant, it follows that this must also eventually decline as more and more workers are hired.

We can state the following general rule for profit-maximisation: *profit-maximising firms will hire additional units of the variable factors up to the point at which the last unit hired adds just as much to revenue as to costs;*

Table 1. Derivation of marginal revenue product.

(1) No of men	(2) MPP (tonnes of wheat per week)	(3) MRP = VMP (of labour) (£)
1	4	8
2	10	20
3	11.5	23
4	14.5	29
5	20	40
6	12	24
7	5	10
8	3	6
9	1	2
10	−6	−12

that is until the factor's marginal revenue product is equal to its marginal factor cost. The equilibrium *condition* for a profit-maximising firm is

Marginal Revenue Product = Marginal Factor Cost

This condition must be fulfilled for *all* variable factors employed if the firm is to maximise its profits.

If a firm purchases its variable factor in a *perfect factor market*, so that it can purchase any quantity without influencing price, the marginal factor cost will be equal to the price of the factor. In this case the equilibrium *condition* becomes

Marginal Revenue Product = Price of Factor

The analysis implies that a firm's MRP curve is its demand curve for a variable factor on the assumption that all other factors of production are held constant.

Suppose now that labour is the only variable factor and is sold in a perfect market. A profit-maximising firm will employ additional workers up to the point at which the wage rate equals the marginal revenue product of labour. Consider Table 1 again. If the weekly wage is £24, the farmer will maximise profits by employing six men, as the MRP of the sixth man is just equal to £24. The farmer would not hire a seventh man, as he would add only £10 to revenue, but £24 to costs, thus reducing profits by £14.

Now assume that the weekly wage falls to £6. In this situation, the farmer would employ eight workers, once again equating MRP with the wage rate. Consider a diagrammatic representation of the above argument.

Figure 1 illustrates the MRP (= VMP) curve of a profit-maximising firm that sells its product in a perfect market. Assume that labour is the only variable factor and that the firm is able to hire any number of workers at the market wage, so that it faces a perfectly elastic supply curve of labour (S_1S_1) at the market wage (OW_1).

To maximise profits the firm will hire OL_1 units of labour, as that equates MRP and the wage. If the firm hired fewer than OL_1 units of labour, it could increase profits by hiring additional workers, for MRP would be greater than the wage. Conversely, if the firm hired more units of labour than OL_1, it could increase its profits by hiring less labour, for MRP would be less than

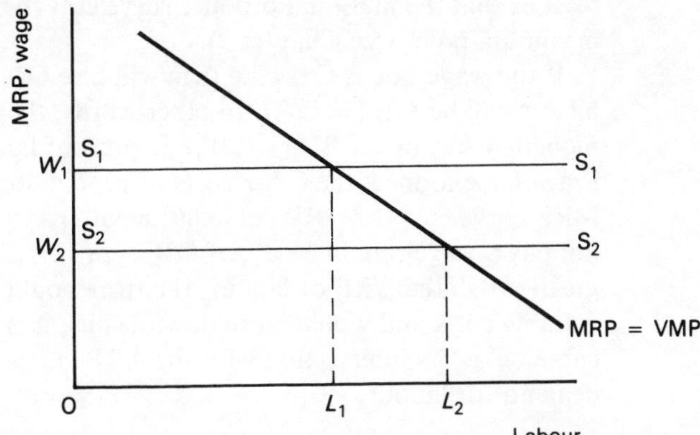

Fig. 1. The MRP equals VMP curve of a firm that sells its product in a perfectly competitive market.

the wage. Profits are only maximised if the MRP of labour equals the wage rate.

Now consider the quantity of labour the firm will hire if the wage falls to OW_2 so that the perfectly elastic supply curve shifts down to S_2S_2. With OL_1 men employed, MRP is now greater than the wage rate, so that the firm will hire additional workers. The MRP and the wage rate are equated if the firm now employs OL_2 units of labour. For this firm we have seen that its MRP (= VMP) curve represents its demand for labour curve.

If the producer is selling the product in an imperfect market, he will face a downward-sloping demand curve; in order to sell extra units the producer has to accept a lower price. Thus, in this case the increase in revenue from selling an additional unit of output (MR) is less than its price (= AR), as the producer has to reduce the price on all other units sold. In the case of an imperfect competitor MRP must be less than VMP.

It is in fact only the downward-sloping section of the MRP curve that represents the demand for labour. Consider Fig. 2 which shows a perfectly competitive firm's MRP curve together with the associated average revenue product curve. The average revenue product (ARP) of labour is obtained by multiplying the average product of labour by the price of the product. Note that both MRP and ARP rise at first but eventually decline because of diminishing returns. MRP cuts ARP at its maximum point for the same

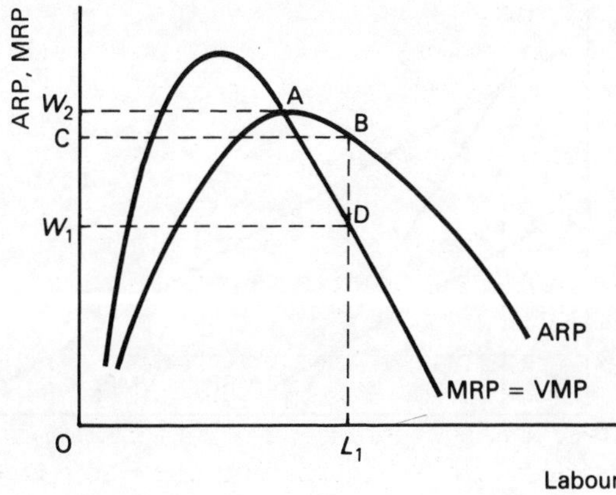

Fig. 2. The firm's demand curve for labour.

reasons that the marginal product curve cuts the average product curve at *its* maximum point (see Chapter 2).

If the wage rate is OW_1 the firm will hire OL_1 units of labour. The ARP of labour will be L_1B (= OC). In other words, the firm benefits from a monetary surplus of BD ($=CW_1$) per unit of labour employed. This surplus is available to meet the other costs of production, including fixed costs. The MRP curve cuts the ARP curve at the latter's maximum at A. The firm will not pay a wage rate in excess of OW_2, for if it did so, the wage would be greater than the ARP of labour; the firm would then be unable to cover its variable costs and would close down. Thus, it is only the section of the MRP curve below its intersection with the ARP curve that represents the firm's demand for labour.

The industry's demand for labour

We have established that a firm's MRP curve represents its demand for labour when only one factor is variable. In establishing this proposition, we adopted a partial approach assuming *ceteris paribus*, so that when the individual firm increased its output, all other firms held their outputs constant.

However, when considering the demand for labour by the industry as a whole, it has to be recognised that a change in the wage rate will affect each firm's hiring of labour and, therefore, total production. A fall in the wage rate, for example, will induce all firms in the industry to hire more labour, so that total production will increase and the supply curve of the good will shift to the right. With a downward-sloping demand curve, the price of the product will decline. This means that the typical firm's MRP curve will shift towards the origin.

Consider Fig. 3 where initially the wage rate is OW_1 and the firm operates at point A, hiring OL_1 units of labour. MRP_1 is the firm's demand curve for labour on the assumption that the price of the product is fixed.

If there is an exogenous fall in the wage rate to OW_2, the firm hires additional units of labour (L_1L_2) until the wage rate and MRP are again equal. However, as all firms hire more labour, total production increases and

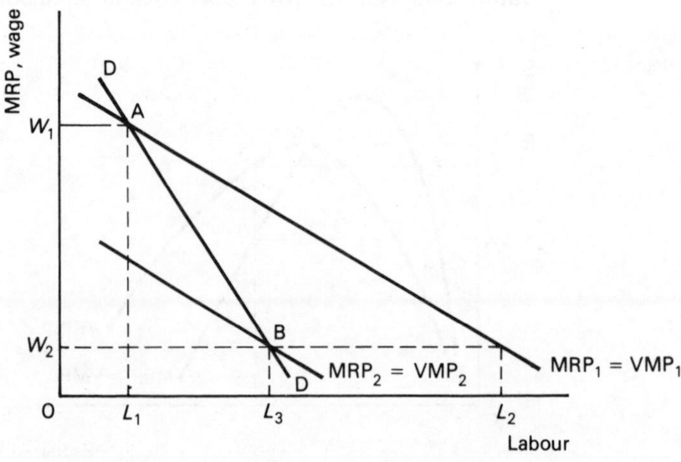

Fig. 3. A firm's demand for labour allowing for changes in the price of the product.

the price of the product falls. This causes the firm's MRP curve to shift down to MRP_2. From the new MRP curve it can be seen that with a wage rate of OW_2 the firm operates at point B and will hire OL_3 units of labour. By joining points such as A and B we derive the demand curve DD which is steeper than the firm's MRP curve. To obtain the industry's demand curve for labour, allowing for industry-wide changes in wage rates, we must add together horizontally the DD curves of all the firms in the industry. This industry demand curve will normally, therefore, be downward-sloping.

The limitations of the marginal productivity theory

The analysis outlined above is sometimes referred to as the *marginal productivity theory* of the demand for a variable factor. Since this theory ignores the supply side, it cannot be regarded as a complete theory of factor pricing. Furthermore to obtain a determinate equilibrium position we assumed that labour is a homogeneous factor, which sells for a single price in a perfectly competitive labour market. In reality, of course, labour is not a homogeneous factor because of differing innate characteristics and skills and labour markets are by no means perfectly competitive.

It was also pointed out earlier that the theory is based on the assumption that firms attempt to maximise profits. We saw in Chapter 10, however, that private firms may have other objectives; for example, public corporations do not normally attempt to maximise profits. In such cases the theory is unlikely to be an adequate explanation of the demand for labour.

The theory also assumes that wage levels and labour productivity are independent. This is not necessarily valid. Increased wages may call forth extra effort from the labour force, so that productivity increases. It is also possible that higher wage costs induce managers to exercise their supervisory function more effectively, which could also result in extra output. Finally, in some countries it is possible that higher wages, which lead to improved nutritional standards, may result in more productive workers in the long-run. Such changes in productivity increase the MPP of labour, and thus shift a firm's MRP curve to the right.

The marginal productivity theory is sometimes criticised on the grounds that firms do not actually sit down to calculate a factor's MRP, perhaps because of insufficient information about the productivity of marginal workers. This criticism, however, is missing the point to some extent; it comes back to the question: is the firm maximising profits? If the answer is in the affirmative, then the firm must be paying factors their marginal revenue products, regardless of whether the firm has specifically set out to calculate the marginal revenue product.

The supply of labour

The total supply of labour in an economy depends on such factors as the size of the population, the age composition of the population and many institutional and social factors. The school-leaving age is one such institutional factor. In the early 1970s in the United Kingdom, for example, the minimum school-leaving age was raised from fifteen to sixteen years. This change clearly reduced the potential labour supply. Currently in the

United Kingdom, there is some pressure to reduce the normal retirement age from sixty-five for males and from sixty for females. If the retirement age is reduced, this will also reduce the supply of labour.

Other institutional factors, such as the length of the average working week and of holidays, are also of significance. The participation rate (the percentage of the potential work-force working or actively seeking work) is influenced by many factors, such as the level of unemployment benefits relative to wage levels and social attitudes towards the participation of women in the work-force.

The elasticity of the supply of labour

Clearly, the *total* supply of labour is not perfectly inelastic as higher wage rates are likely to draw extra workers into the labour force (for example, students and married women) and will induce some workers to work longer hours.

If we ask what induces the owners of factors of production to allocate them to *particular* uses, the hypothesis of equal net advantage is relevant. This states that the owners of factors of production will move them between different uses until there is no further advantage, monetary or otherwise, in another move. For the owners of *non-human* factors of production, monetary advantage will be of overwhelming importance.

This is not, however, the case with labour, where non-monetary advantages will also be very important. Consider two jobs requiring a similar skill which pay the same rate, but where the working conditions for job A are clean and pleasant whilst job B means working in hot and dirty conditions. Most individuals will require higher monetary rewards to accept job B in order to compensate them for the non-monetary advantages of the unpleasant working conditions.

The supply of labour to a single industry, then, is likely to be elastic as an increase in the industry's wage rate will induce some workers to transfer from other industries. This elasticity, though, will vary with the length of the time period considered. The longer the time period, the greater will be the elasticity of supply. This is largely because there are barriers to the mobility of labour. These barriers, which may be quite strong in the short-run, can be discussed in terms of occupational and geographical immobility.

Occupational immobility Workers are clearly not homogeneous so that natural ability may be a barrier to movement between jobs. Some jobs require an innate ability, such as nimble fingers or an analytical mind, which some workers just do not possess. Many jobs require a period of training, so that a redundant steel-worker cannot become a television repairman overnight. Workers may be reluctant to undertake retraining as it normally involves a period of low income and starting again at the bottom of the job ladder.

In some cases, artificial barriers to the mobility of labour are erected which have the effect of benefiting special interest groups. In some industries there are *'closed shop'* agreements which require all workers to be members of a trade union. Similarly membership of some professional bodies, such as the British Medical Association and Law Society, is restricted by high entry requirements.

In the long-run, these barriers to occupational mobility are not likely to be as significant, as new workers enter the labour force and existing workers can be retrained.

Geographical immobility There are several factors which can deter a worker from moving to a job in another part of the country, even if he is unemployed. Social ties to family and friends may be strong. There may be problems in obtaining suitable housing in the new location and the monetary costs of transferring a home are significant. A move is also likely to be disruptive to children's education.

Despite the efforts of the Manpower Services Commission in the United Kingdom, it is often difficult to obtain information about vacancies, job conditions and wages in other parts of the country. To help the problem of geographical immobility the Department of Employment operates a scheme by which unemployed workers can obtain help with fares to attend job interviews and grants towards the cost of moving home. One problem in the United Kingdom is that many workers prefer to remain in their own region even when unemployed and when jobs are available in other regions.

The individual's supply of labour

When we consider an individual's supply of labour, we have to take into account the possibility of a backward-bending supply curve. Consider Fig. 4 which shows an individual's indifference map between work and pay. The horizontal axis measures hours of work per day and the vertical axis measures the daily wage. The maximum number of hours the individual is prepared to work is given by OH_m hours. The individual regards his wage as a 'good' and so derives utility from it. However, he regards work as a 'bad' and so derives disutility from it.

Each indifference curve joins together those combinations of the daily wage and hours worked per day which yield the same amount of utility to the

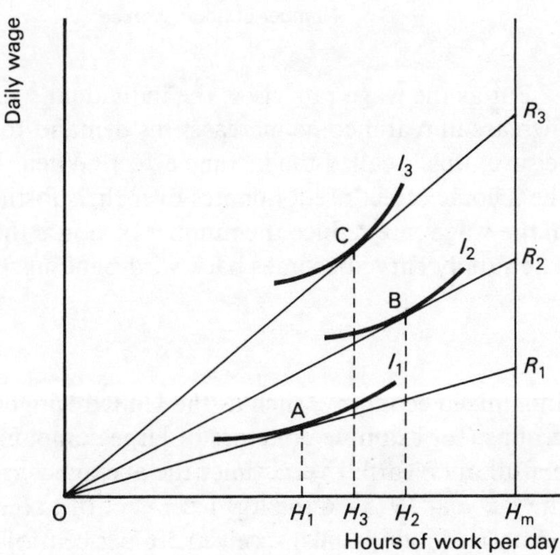

Fig. 4. Individual's choice between work and leisure.

individual. Clearly, for the individual to stay at the same level of utility, as he works more hours he must receive a higher daily wage. This means that the indifference curves must slope upwards from left to right. It also follows that the higher the indifference curve, the greater the level of utility.

Consider the rays OR_1, OR_2, and OR_3, whose slopes represent different wage rates. The slope of OR_1 represents a wage rate equal to £AH_1 / OH_1 per hour. At this wage rate, the individual maximises his utility by supplying OH_1 hours of work. This puts him at point A on the highest attainable indifference curve, I_1. The slope of OR_2 (equal to £BH_2 / OH_2 per hour) represents a higher wage rate than OR_1 and the individual will maximise his utility by supplying OH_2 hours of work. This puts him on the indifference curve I_2 at point B. Finally, consider the wage rate OR_3 (equal to £CH_3 / OH_3 per hour) which is higher than OR_2. At this wage rate, the individual maximises utility at point C and offers OH_3 hours.

If we now plot the individual's supply of labour against the different wage rates, we obtain the backward-bending supply curve, SS, illustrated in Fig. 5. As the wage rate increases from OR_1 to OR_2, the individual offers to work more hours. As the price of labour rises, leisure is becoming more expensive relative to working. The worker substitutes extra hours of work for leisure; this is called the substitution effect.

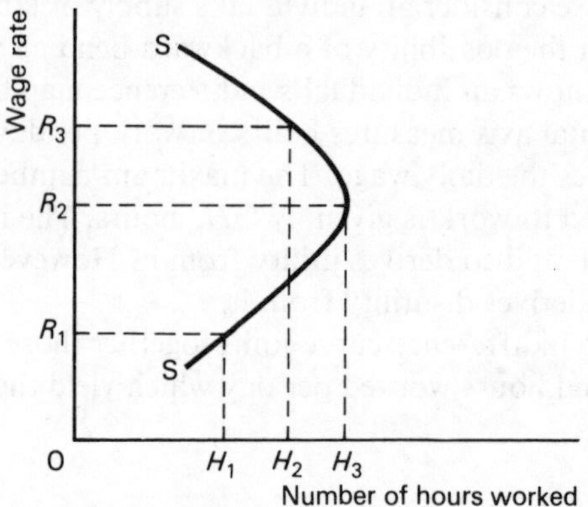

Fig. 5. Individual's backward-bending supply curve of labour.

But as the wage rate rises, the individual's real income also increases. The increase in real income increases his demand for normal goods, including leisure; this is called the income effect. When the wage rate rises above OR_2 the income effect predominates over the substitution effect, so that increases in the wage rate reduce the number of hours the individual offers to work. The supply curve becomes backward-bending.

Wage differentials

In a mixed economy, such as the United Kingdom, it is well-known that some groups (for example directors of large companies, judges and hospital consultants) earn several times the average wage. In the United Kingdom in the tax year 1975–76 the top 1 per cent of tax units (married couples or unmarried individuals) received 5.6 per cent of total pre-tax income. Their corresponding share of post-tax income was 3.6 per cent. We should not be surprised that such income differentials exist. One might ask under what conditions would the wages for all jobs be equal? An impressive list of conditions would have to be fulfilled. All workers would have to be homogeneous; all jobs would have to display identical non-monetary advantages and disadvantages; there would have to be perfect knowledge and perfect mobility of labour.

If this demanding list of conditions were fulfilled, wages in all occupations would be equalised. If the wage rate in one industry rose temporarily above the common wage rate, there would be a massive switch by workers who would want to transfer to that industry. The excess supply of labour in the industry would drive down the industry wage rate to that in the other industries. Conversely, if the wage rate in a single industry fell below the general level, there would be a transfer of workers into other industries, resulting in an excess demand for labour in this industry. This would force the industry wage rate up to the level prevalent in the economy as a whole.

It should be recognised that the conditions necessary for the equalisation of wage rates are not fulfilled in practice. In reality workers are not homogeneous because of differences in natural ability, skills and training. As mentioned above, a steel-worker cannot switch to being a television repairman overnight. Some people do not have the physical requirements or the natural ability required for particular jobs. A policeman, for example, has to be of a minimum height; a lifeguard requires a good swimming ability. Consequently, it can be argued that the labour market is separated into many distinct markets, so that workers can be viewed as comprising 'non-competing groups'.

Additionally, jobs do not offer identical non-monetary advantages and disadvantages. Some jobs mean working in pleasant conditions with convenient hours of work, as for example, a university professor. Other jobs require working in dirty and unpleasant conditions, perhaps at unsocial hours, as for example, a coal miner.

We know that in practice neither employers nor employees are perfectly well-informed about conditions of service and pay in all occupations. Workers often do not know of all job opportunities that are available particularly in other areas. This point is further developed below in the section on the 'theory of search'.

Finally, we saw earlier that there are several barriers to the mobility of labour, both geographical and occupational. These may take the form of workers not being willing to move to another part of the country; or barriers may exist because of the differing skill requirements of different jobs. We also saw that trade unions and professional associations sometimes erect entry barriers, perhaps through the requirement of a long apprenticeship or period of training.

Factors such as those outlined above help to explain the differentials that exist between the wages earned in different occupations. But why do certain talented people such as pop-stars and other entertainers earn very high incomes? It all comes back to supply and demand. There is a large demand for the services of 'star' entertainers like Elton John. On the supply side, of course, there is only one Elton John with his particular talents.

As pointed out above, certain jobs and professions require several years' training. Examples include the jobs of doctors, scientists and computer programmers. The above-average earnings of these groups can partly be explained by a scarcity of supply.

Imperfections in labour markets

Labour markets are remarkably imperfect. On the demand side, there are product monopolies, monopsonies (that is, monopoly buyers of labour) and 'collusive oligopsonies' (that is, employers' organisations collectively negotiating wages and conditions of employment on behalf of member firms). Some large firms may even form labour markets in their own right. On the supply side, there are trade union monopolies which have developed the well-known institution of collective bargaining.

In considering such imperfect markets, the essential point to note is that traditional analysis is merely an extension of the principles of the marginal productivity theory. By comparing the wage rates and levels of employment that would prevail in perfect and imperfect labour markets, we can draw conclusions about the welfare implications of different market structures.

In the following sections, we examine the case of a product monopolist and that of a monopsonistic buyer of labour. On the supply side, we consider the influence of trade unions and collective bargaining.

The hiring policy of a profit-maximising product monopolist

A product monopolist faces a downward-sloping demand curve for the good he is producing. This means that if he employs additional workers, he must lower the product price to sell the additional output. As shown in Fig. 6, the MRP curve lies below the VMP curve for the same reasons as the monopolist's marginal revenue (MR) curve lies below the average revenue (AR) curve (see Ch. 9).

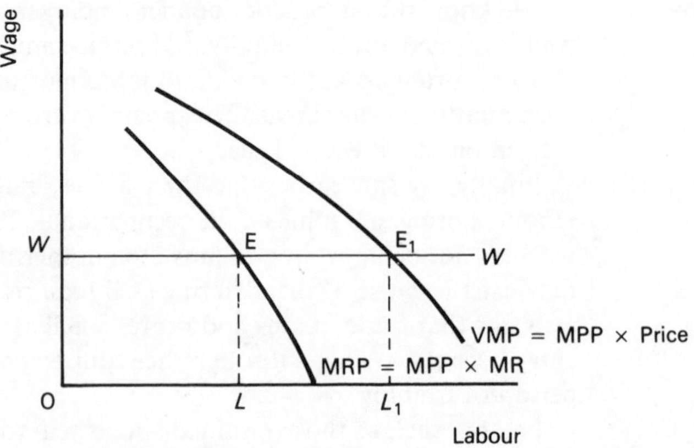

Fig. 6. A product monopolist's demand for labour.

Assume that the monopolist is operating in a perfectly competitive labour market and so faces an infinitely elastic supply curve of labour WW paying a fixed wage rate O*W* per hour as in Fig. 6. Then, such a monopolist will employ O*L* units of labour as indicated by the intersection of MRP with WW at point E. Employment of extra units of labour beyond OL would mean that the wage bill would increase by more than the increase in total revenue so reducing profits.

Implications for social welfare The Pareto efficient level of output requires that the level of employment should be pushed up to OL_1 where VMP intersects WW at point E_1: this is the level of employment which would be achieved under conditions of perfect competition in all markets. It can be seen that a monopolist employs less labour than a perfect competitor. This arises from the monopolist's restriction of output to a level below that required for Pareto efficiency.

The hiring policy of a monopsonistic buyer of labour

Now consider the case of a monopsonist who sells his finished product in perfect competition. By definition, a monopsonist is the only buyer of labour in a particular market and (unlike the product monopolist or perfect competitor) is in a position to influence the prevailing wage rate and level of employment. The monopsonist's equilibrium level of employment will be influenced by the marginal cost of labour (MC_L) and the marginal revenue product of labour (MRP = VMP). The marginal cost of labour has two components. First, being a monopsonist, he can hire additional workers only by offering a higher wage rate. Second, assuming that all workers are paid the same wage, any higher wage offered to attract additional workers will have to be paid to the existing work-force. Thus the marginal cost of labour exceeds its average cost.

In Fig. 7 the upward-sloping supply curve SS is in fact the average cost of labour curve: it shows the wage rate that has to be offered to attract a given supply of labour. Given that the monopsonist is a profit-maximiser, then the number of workers he is able and willing to employ will be determined by the intersection of the MC_L curve with the MRP = VMP curve. Inspection of Fig. 7 shows that the monopsonist employs OL units of labour (as indicated by the intersection of MC_L with MRP at point E). The wage rate OW, however, is given by the intersection of the line EL with SS at point F. Contrast this outcome with the perfectly competitive case where a higher wage rate OW_1 and level of employment OL_1, would prevail.

Fig. 7. Monopsonist's demand for labour.

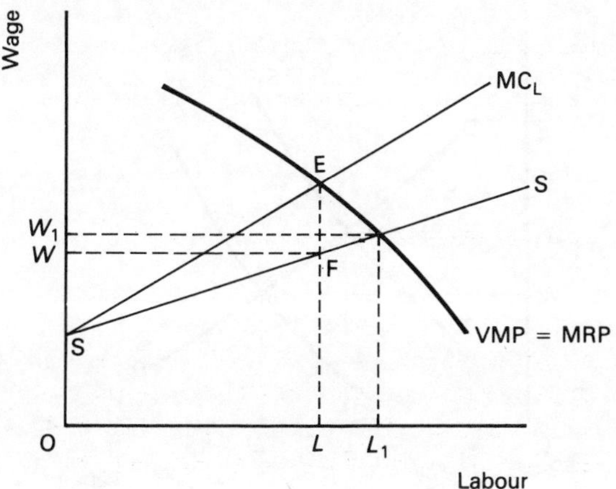

Implications for social welfare It can be concluded that the monopsonistic buyer of labour pays a wage less than the value of the marginal product of labour. He thus employs a smaller work-force than that required for Pareto efficiency.

The influence of trade unions and collective bargaining on wages and jobs

The institutions of trade unions and collective bargaining play a central role in setting wage levels and determining conditions of service in industrialised countries. In the United Kingdom, for instance, 462 unions with about twelve million members (constituting nearly 50 per cent of the total labour force) set the pace for wages and conditions of service for other groups of workers in the economy.

Typically, wage bargaining processes are characterised by bilateral monopolies in many trades, occupations and industries. Negotiations are conducted between union representatives and representatives of employers' organisations, as for example in the case of pay negotiations between the Amalgamated Union of Engineering Workers and the Shipping Employers' Federation.

A union has a few well-defined objectives when bargaining with employers. Consider the following:

(a) to restrict the supply of labour via closed shops and long apprenticeship periods;
(b) to keep all its members employed;
(c) to raise the basic wage for all its members;
(d) to improve conditions of service including holidays, pensions and hours of work.

In practice, unions are seldom able to attain these objectives simultaneously in every round of pay negotiations. At any given time, the choice of objectives is likely to be influenced by such factors as the government's counter-inflation policy, the level of economic activity and the relative bargaining power of the union in question. However, these objectives have different implications for wages and jobs.

Suppose, for example, a union pursues objective (a) and as a result,

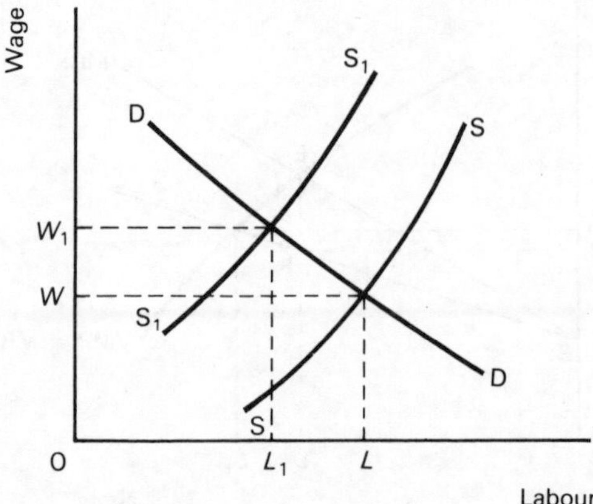

Fig. 8. Effects of restriction of labour supply on wages and employment.

succeeds in the restriction of the labour supply to a particular occupation or industry. In Fig. 8, DD represents the market demand for labour. The restriction of the labour supply leads to the inward shift of the supply curve SS to S_1S_1. This results in a rise in the wage rate from OW to OW_1 with a fall in the number of workers employed from OL to OL_1.

If, however, the objective is to maintain employment of all its members and total membership is equal to OL as in Fig. 8, then the union will have to settle for a lower hourly wage rate than OW_1. Any wage rate higher than OW would lead to a cut in the quantity of labour demanded.

Unions may succeed in getting all employers to agree to pay not lower than the basic minimum wage OW_1 as in Fig. 9 in which case the minimum wage line (W_1W_1) becomes parallel to the horizontal axis. If, as is likely, such a wage rate is set above the equilibrium wage level OW, as shown in the diagram, the part of the SS curve below J becomes irrelevant. Instead, the supply curve becomes W_1JS intersecting the DD curve at E_1 with OL_1 units of labour employed. This means that some people willing to work at less than OW_1 wage rate are prevented by the union agreement and therefore remain unemployed.

Fig. 9. Effects of basic minimum wage.

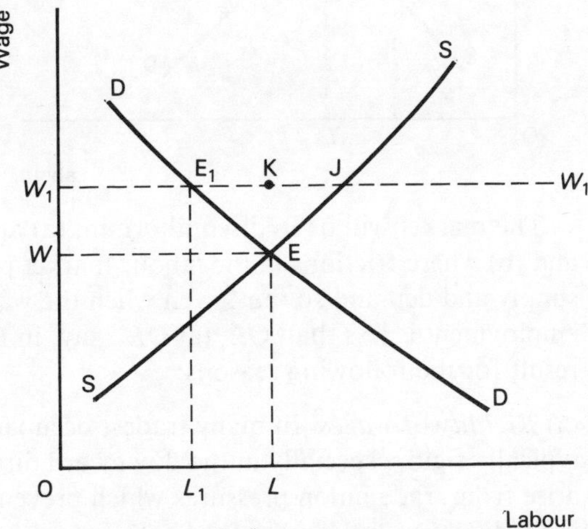

This also explains the view of the opponents of minimum wage legislation that it tends to cause inflation and unemployment. On the other hand, the supporters of the argument for a high-wage economy (which include some unions) maintain that raising wage rates above the competitive equilibrium level will ultimately lead to an increase in the productivity of labour. If this happens the demand for labour will increase resulting in a higher level of employment and a higher wage rate.

Finally, a union may attempt to force an employer 'off' his demand curve in order to achieve a wage increase without any reduction in employment. In this case the union would be aiming for point K in Fig. 9. This strategy is more likely to be successful if the firm is highly profitable.

Disequilibrium in the labour market

The marginal productivity theory of wages is clearly an oversimplification of reality. It asserts that an equilibrium wage rate will be established in the markets for particular grades of labour, skills and occupations. However, labour markets in practice are unlikely to be in equilibrium. The average worker has a narrow view of the market. He is not an alert participant in the market able to take advantage of any variations in wage rates.

Consider Fig. 10 which shows the demand and supply curves for a particular type of labour. Equilibrium in this market requires that the wage rate be established at OW_1 and actual employment be OL_1 units of labour.

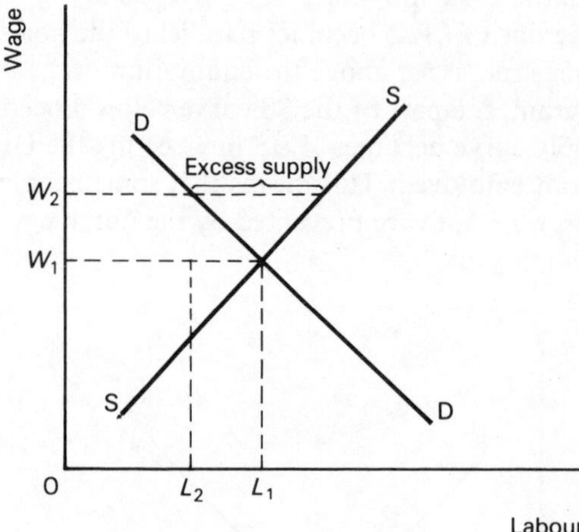

Fig. 10. Disequilibrium in a labour market.

The market will be in disequilibrium: (a) at any wage rate other than OW_1, and (b) where frictions in the labour market prevent the matching up of supply and demand so that, even when the wage rate is OW_1, actual employment is less than OL_1 (at OL_2, say, in Fig. 10). Such disequilibria may result for the following reasons:

(a) *Rigidity of wages.* In many trades, occupations and industries, wages are typically rigid, especially in the downward direction. Wage rigidities may arise from trade union pressures which prevent workers from bargaining individually with their employers. Suppose, for example, a wage rate of OW_2 is established in Fig. 10 which creates an excess supply of labour. Trade unions may use their monopoly power to resist any cut in wages, so that the disequilibrium persists.

(b) *Labour as a heterogeneous factor.* Labour is a collection of differing skills, education, training and experience, and so consists of 'non-competing groups'. For instance, mathematics teachers and English teachers are dissimilar in the sense that they do not compete for the same jobs. Even two doctors may differ in their abilities and specialisms, so creating non-competing groups within the medical profession. Consequently, even if the total demand for and supply of doctors are equal, there may be an excess supply of obstetricians at the same time as a shortage of anaesthetists.

(c) *Internal labour markets.* Examination of modern methods of hiring shows that some firms have their own internal labour markets, more or less insulated from outside influences. They generally recruit non-craft and semi-skilled workers at the bottom of the job ladder and employees progress to higher grade jobs by a system of internal training and promotion based on seniority and ability. Clearly, such a recruitment policy hinders labour mobility since workers can only enter this firm in the lower grades. In addition, these firms develop their own complex methods of job evaluation for the structure of wage differentials. Thus, there are different rates of pay for the range of jobs to be performed within the firm and this makes it difficult for workers to draw comparisons with those of other firms and industries.

(d) *Information costs.* Seeking information about wages and jobs imposes monetary and non-monetary costs on both firms and workers. To obtain a job, an unemployed worker might have to spend a considerable amount of money and time collecting information about job vacancies from newspapers, official employment exchanges, private employment agencies and even by word of mouth. This important point is further developed in the section below on the theory of search.

The theory of search

This theory maintains that given disequilibrium in the labour market, workers and employers engage in a process of search to strike the best possible bargains about wages, terms and conditions of employment including 'fringe benefits'. The longer the process of search for information about wages and job prospects in various firms and industries, the greater are the costs to buyers and sellers of labour. Such costs of search and information gathering have been ignored by the marginal productivity theory of wages which assumed that such activities as bargaining, information collection and labour mobility were costless.

Consider, for example, an employer of labour. On top of the usual wages paid to workers, the hiring transaction includes several costs. The employer has to incur the costs of recruitment which include advertisement costs, employment agency costs, the cost of screening applications and the costs of training workers. In some cases, employers may have to offer inducements to obtain suitably qualified workers. The costs of hiring skilled workers (such as executives and senior managers) will be proportionately higher than the costs of recruiting unskilled and semi-skilled workers. This is because a much more intensive search is called for in order to attract suitable applicants for specialised jobs. In addition, the costs of search are likely to be higher if there are competing firms which are offering terms with considerable variations for more or less similar jobs. The unsuccessful firms may have to re-advertise, reassess their relative bargaining positions, improve upon the initial wage offers and lower recruitment standards.

On the other hand, to the seller of labour, the most important cost is the *opportunity cost* of the search. Consider, for example, an unemployed worker with several job offers in hand. Clearly, he is not likely to strike the best possible bargain, if he accepts the first offer. It may be that he can obtain much better terms if he intensifies his search for better pay and conditions of work, or it may be that he has some ideas beforehand about the minimum acceptable pay. The further he intensifies the search, however, the higher is the opportunity cost in terms of the forgone income he could have otherwise earned. Note that the forgone income is measured net of unemployment benefits.

To a dissatisfied worker, who, though already employed, is looking for a job elsewhere, the *loss of leisure time* is the most important cost. Like an unemployed worker, he may also have pre-conceived ideas about the lowest acceptable wage, which he may revise upwards or downwards in the light of experience and information gained from continued search. The higher the level of unemployment, the higher is the cost of search because the worker may have to search for much longer before he receives an offer. At the same time there are greater risks involved in search because if he does not accept the first offer promptly, he may find that it has been taken by someone else. The rising cost of search tends to support the 'discouraged worker hypothesis', according to which searching for work and pay during a period of unemployment could be so disheartening that some of the unemployed may give up looking for work and withdraw from the labour market. A decision to give up the search for a job is obviously influenced by the level of unemployment benefits and the availabilities of such non-market activities as part-time education, sports and recreation facilities, and other social and cultural pursuits.

Equal pay for women

In the United Kingdom, the Equal Pay Act 1970 and the Sex Discrimination Act 1975 are the major legislative measures designed to achieve pay parity between the sexes and to provide equal opportunities to males and females in the areas of recruitment, training, promotion, overtime and shift work. Similar legislation has been enacted in other industrialised countries, such as the United States, Australia, New Zealand and Japan.

Since the Second World War, there has been a considerable increase in the overall activity rate of women in the labour force in all the major industrial countries. In the United Kingdom, as in other countries, a large proportion of this increase is in the activity of married women in the age group forty years and over. This is because married women are returning to the labour force in increased numbers after bringing up their children. The employment of married women in the United Kingdom rose from about 30 per cent of the female occupied population in 1951 to about 63 per cent in 1971. By the end of the century, it is estimated that married women will comprise over 75 per cent of the female occupied population. In 1975, the absolute size of the female labour force of nearly nine million represented about 32 per cent of the total occupied population. It must be noted, however, that about 40 per cent of women employed in 1976 were in part-time employment.

Causes of differences in rates of pay between men and women In spite of the increase in the female labour force in the occupied population, differences in rates of pay and conditions of service between men and women have persisted. In 1977, the median earnings of full-time women workers in the United Kingdom were 65 per cent of the median earnings of full-time men (up from 54% in 1970). Consider the following reasons for these differences.

(a) Women have become concentrated in certain industries and occupations, many of which are not covered by collective agreements and especially where trade union organisation is weak (for example, clothing, footwear and service industries).

(b) Traditional attitudes of women's work and men's work have created non-competing groups within the labour force. Similarly, these traditional attitudes are reflected in the education, guidance and training of the sexes in schools, colleges and universities as exemplified by girls' subjects and boys' subjects. Consequently, male occupations have often meant high levels of skills, wages and employment mobility with good promotion prospects; female occupations have typically meant low skills, low wages, poor promotion prospects and high labour turnover.

(c) Looking upon the training of male and female labour as an investment in human capital, employers are more likely to invest in the training of those workers expected to remain with the firm after the completion of training. A high labour turnover would reduce the rate of return to the firm. This is because the returns in the early years after training are given much greater weight via the discounted cash flow technique than the returns in later years. But it is during these early years that many married women may leave the labour force to have children. In addition, women in the younger age groups may be unwilling to undertake the long period of training associated with high levels of skills and pay.

Effects of equal pay legislation The Equal Pay and Sex Discrimination Acts were passed to equalise some of the differences in pay and job opportunities between men and women in the United Kingdom. Consider the following possible effects. Removing barriers to the employment of women may lead to an increase in female employment and an increase in female pay. Fearing rising labour costs and bankruptcies, firms may take measures to counter the effect of the equal pay legislation through regrading the women's jobs in the attempt to justify lower pay. Alternatively, male employees and employers may seek to maintain wage differentials over women through other means, such as increases in overtime pay and shift allowances or through negotiating lower rates for part-time work.

Obstacles to implementation of equal pay legislation These Acts may succeed in narrowing wage differentials, but it is doubtful if they will succeed in bridging totally the earnings gap between the sexes. The Acts stipulate equal rates for work of equal value. However, disagreements may arise as to what constitutes 'work of equal value'. Similarly, there are no reliable measures of job content and job comparability. Even where jobs are separated through job evaluation the result may be to place women in a lower grade or 'light work category' with low pay.

Employers may be reluctant to accept the principle of equal pay because they believe that female productivity tends to be lower since women have higher rates of labour turnover. In turn, this may mean continued discrimination against female employment, particularly during periods of recession when an enforcement of equal pay may mean the creation of additional female unemployment.

Conclusion

This chapter has investigated the forces underlying the process of wage determination in a market economy. We demonstrated the operation of the labour market under conditions of perfect competition and imperfect competition and considered the implications for social welfare. We analysed the reasons for disequilibrium in labour markets and finally considered the effects of equal pay legislation.

Further reading

Laidler, D., *Introduction to Microeconomics*, Philip Allan, Deddington, 1974 (Ch. 17–19).
Mulvey, C., *The Economic Analysis of Trade Unions*, Martin Robertson, Oxford, 1978.
King, J.E., *Labour Economics*, Macmillan, London, 1972.
Hunter, L.C. and **Robertson, D.J.**, *Economics of Wages and Labour*, Macmillan, London, 1969.

Exercises

1. Review your understanding of the following terms:

derived demand	monopsony
marginal revenue product	geographical immobility
marginal physical product	occupational immobility
value of the marginal product	internal labour market
marginal factor cost	search period

2. Given that the price of wheat is £15 per tonne and the information below about a profit-maximising farmer's output of wheat, calculate the marginal physical product of labour and the marginal revenue product of labour. How many men will be employed if the wage rate is £150 per week? How many men will be employed if the wage rate falls to £120?

No. of men	1	2	3	4	5	6	7
Total product (tonnes of wheat per week)	10	24	34	42	45	46	46

3. Explain in terms of the income and substitution effects the circumstances under which the individual's supply curve of labour will be 'backward-bending'.

4. Discuss the view that a trade union pushing for higher wage rates will inevitably increase the level of unemployment.

5. Discuss the factors influencing the length of the 'search' period during which an unemployed worker is engaged in seeking employment.

6. 'Imperfect competition in labour markets spoils the marginal conditions for Pareto efficiency.' Discuss with reference to: (a) a monopsonistic buyer of labour; (b) a product monopolist and; (c) a trade union.

16 Rewards to factors of production

Introduction

In the last chapter, we looked at the labour market in isolation and considered how wages are determined in a modern market economy. Our intention in this chapter is to investigate in greater detail the determination of the *relative* shares of the total national income going to the respective owners of the three factors of production: labour, land and capital. Economists are interested in these distributive shares because they represent the most important measures of the welfare of the owners of factors. For instance, a 10 per cent increase in profit income and a corresponding 10 per cent decrease in wage income may mean a redistribution of the total national income from the lower to higher income groups which in turn may represent a deterioration in society's welfare.

First, we shall develop a general theoretical approach to distribution. Then, with the help of this approach, we consider the particular rewards going to land and capital. The general theoretical approach focuses attention on: (a) Ricardo's theory of distribution; (b) the marginal productivity theory of distribution; (c) the relation between distributive shares and technical progress. In the final part of the chapter, we investigate theories of rent and interest, consider the controversy between the two Cambridges over the reward to capital, and finally examine the Ricardian and Marxian views of the falling rate of profit.

Note, however, a most important point. There is no universally accepted view of why different factors of production get what they receive in payment. This is so because the total value of goods and services produced is a result of the collaboration and co-operative effort of all productive resources. The rewards to factors, therefore, are explicitly or implicitly mingled with property rights which, in turn, are institutionally determined. As a result, a Pareto efficient distribution of income based on *given* property rights may not be the income distribution pattern which maximises society's welfare. As noted earlier, a Pareto efficient allocation of resources can co-exist with large-scale poverty which, from the standpoint of social welfare maximisation, may be judged to be undesirable.

Economists have developed two main approaches to distribution: a *functional* distribution approach and a *personal* distribution approach. According to the former, like the price of any ordinary commodity, the price of a factor of production is determined by the forces of supply and demand; the marginal productivity theory has sprung from this approach. In the second approach, emphasis is placed on the actual size of the income accruing to individuals and families and so is concerned with measuring the inequalities of income and wealth. This aspect of the problem of distribution is dealt with in Chapter 30.

Theories of distribution

Ricardo's theory of distribution

David Ricardo (1772–1823) identified three classes in society – landlords, labourers and capitalists who receive rents, wages and profits respectively. Rents and wages, according to Ricardo, are part of the costs which capitalists must meet so as to be able to carry on production; whatever is left over is the capitalists' profits. In other words, profits are a *residual.*

The central idea of Ricardo's theory is that the demand for investment in the production of commodities comes from the capitalist and is stimulated by the desire to earn profits. Any increase in investment, though, increases the demand for labour and, through competition, pushes up the wage rate above what Ricardo called its 'subsistence level'. This subsistence wage level was defined by Ricardo as that which provided the labourers with their customary standard of living. An increase in wages above the subsistence level encourages the population to grow faster through earlier marriages and the resulting increase in the labour supply depresses wages back to the subsistence level. So, in Ricardo's model, the share of wages in the total national income can in the long-run be no higher than that required for mere subsistence.

It also follows that with a rising population (which keeps wage rates down) the demand for land will increase and so tend to raise landlords' rents. Payment of these rising rents by capitalists will squeeze their profits. Since, in the long-run, wages are kept equal to the subsistence level, it follows in Ricardo's model that capitalists will experience *a falling rate of profit* because of ever-rising rents.

The marginal productivity theory again

We saw in the previous chapter that in perfectly competitive markets factors of production would be paid the value of their marginal products as a reward for their services by profit-maximising firms. The neo-classical or so-called 'marginalist' school of economics argued that all factors made some contribution to production and that it was 'just' that they should receive payments equal to their marginal contributions. This, of course, was quite different from the views of Karl Marx who believed that labour was the source of all production and so should receive the total value of output as payment: anything less he regarded as capitalist 'exploitation' of labour.

The 'marginalist' school owes much to the work of the American economist, John Bates Clark. To outline his views, consider an aggregate production function with only two factors of production, labour (L) and capital (K), which we can write in the following general form:

$$Q = f(L, K)$$

Clark's views can be summarised in terms of the following propositions.

(a) With perfect competition and no externalities, both labour and capital will be paid the values of their marginal products. For example, as we showed in Chapter 15, profit-maximising firms will go on employing labour up to the point where the marginal product of labour is equal to the real wage (that is, $\triangle Q/\triangle L = W/P$). If the marginal product of labour exceeded the real wage, it would pay the firm to hire more workers; if the marginal product was less than the real wage, it would pay the firm to lay off some workers.

(b) Payments equal to the value of marginal products represent 'fair' and 'just' rewards to factor owners. This is clearly a value judgement based on the belief that *all* factor units should be paid the value of the contribution made by the last unit employed (which is likely to be the least productive unit).
(c) Paying all factors the value of their respective marginal products will just exhaust the value of total output and there will be no residual left over to be seized by the capitalists or by anyone else. This proposition was eventually proved by Leonhard Euler who showed that for a production function ($Q = f(L, K)$) which exhibits *constant returns to scale,*

$$Q = MP_L . L + MP_K . K$$

In other words, the total product is exactly used up in making payments to factor owners on the basis of their marginal products. This has become known as *Euler's Theorem.*

Critics of the marginal productivity theory have emphasised that the neo-classical views about the rewards to factors hold true only under the restrictive assumptions of constant returns to scale and perfect competition with no externalities.

Testing the marginal productivity theory empirically In the inter-war years, the economists R.W. Cobb and P.H. Douglas attempted to measure the shares of wages and profits in the total national income of the United States using a production function of the form $Q = AL^{\alpha}K^{1-\alpha}$, where A is a constant and α represents the share of labour and $1-\alpha$ the share of capital in the total product. This has become known as a Cobb-Douglas production function. They found a remarkable constancy in the share of labour and capital for many years. Their empirical results gave a value for α of about 0.75 and a value for $1-\alpha$ of about 0.25. Subsequently, empirical studies for other western industrial countries gave similar results.

A major implication of this is that workers as a whole are powerless to raise their share in the total national income. Any attempt by workers to increase wages will lead capitalists to cut back on their labour force so as to maintain their share of profits.

In the postwar years, however, there has been a tendency for the share of wages to rise without severe unemployment resulting. Robert Solow, a supporter of the neo-classical theory, has maintained that the explanation for this is capital accumulation which has increased the amount of capital per head of the labour force and so increased labour productivity. Other possible explanations of the rising share of wages are as follows.

(a) There has been an increase in the size of countries' public sectors in the postwar years. Public sector capital investments (for example, on roads, schools and hospitals) are estimated at cost – that is, they do not include a profit component in the calculation of national income.
(b) There has been a secular decline in the number of self-employed workers. Ceasing to be self-employed and working instead for an employer increases the share of wages.
(c) Technical progress has tended to make the price of capital lower relative

to the price of labour. Most technical progress is labour-saving and so increases the productivity of labour.

An assessment of the marginal productivity theory The theory as a whole is an oversimplification of the determination of distributive shares. For one thing, the total income of a factor depends on both its quantity and its marginal productivity; it is by no means easy to identify those changes in income which result from changes in its quantity and those which result from changes in marginal productivity.

Secondly, the theory assumes that all units of factors are homogeneous and are, therefore, capable of being measured; labour, for instance, could be measured in man-hours provided differences in grades and quality were ignored. As we saw in Chapter 15, however, ignoring differences between grades of labour is a serious oversight. The same goes for capital – the quantity of capital can be measured on the basis of what it costs at the time of purchase (that is, its historic cost), but such costs have little bearing on the current value of the capital. Besides, it can be argued that although machines and equipment are productive, it does not follow that the owners of the capital are equally productive.

Technical progress and income distribution

Economists have argued that when technological changes occur in society, these changes can bring about alterations in the relative shares of land, labour and capital. For instance, Marx was one of the first economists to argue that labour-saving technology (for example, automation) would lead to rising unemployment, a decline in the share of wages and conflict between labour and capital.

Broadly speaking, technical progress can be either *neutral* or *non-neutral*. Ignoring land to simplify the argument, neutral technical progress is that which leaves the ratio in which labour and capital are employed unchanged and so does not alter the wage-profit ratio. Non-neutral technical progress, on the other hand, takes the form of a new invention or the development of a new technique of production which is either *labour-saving* or *capital-saving*. It is often argued that labour-saving technical progress tends to lower the share of labour in the national income, whilst capital-saving technical progress tends to lower the share of capital.

An important point must be made here. It is that a labour-saving innovation, instead of raising the share of profits, may actually depress the share of profits and raise the share of wages via the law of diminishing returns. This is possible because, as industries become more capital-intensive, larger units of capital per head of the labour force are employed. This implies greater labour productivity and a decline in the marginal productivity of capital. As a result, we should expect a rise in wages and a fall in profits.

Unfortunately, it is difficult in reality to distinguish changes in output which are due to changes in the capital – labour ratio brought about by technical progress from those which are due to increases in capital and labour (keeping the capital-labour ratio constant). This is because in practice technical progress is inevitably associated with increases in capital. For example, the introduction of jet engined technology required investment in new aircraft. Consequently, the empirical evidence on the effects of technical progress on the shares of wages and profits is inconclusive.

We turn now to an examination of the rewards to specific factors. Chapter 15 has already dealt with the special problems connected with the reward to labour. In the remainder of this chapter, we focus our attention on the issues associated with the rewards to land and capital.

Rent – the reward to land

A most important point to note in understanding the economist's conception of rent is that its meaning differs substantially from that in ordinary usage. To the economist, rent is the reward for the use of the services of land; in addition, as we see below, it is a term used for any payment in excess of that needed to keep a particular factor in its current use, whether that factor be land, labour or capital. Whenever rent is used in this second sense, we shall refer to it as *economic rent*. This should be distinguished from the common usage of the term 'rent' which is a payment for the use of property (that is, houses, factories, offices and shops) and which includes a payment for the use of the land, capital and certain labour (for example, for repair and maintenance work). Clearly, this usage of the term 'rent' is much broader than the economist's conception of rent.

Ricardo's theory of rent

Ricardo saw rent as a payment for the 'original and indestructible qualities of the soil' on the assumption that land had only one use: that of growing foodstuffs. He pointed out that, from the standpoint of society, the supply of land is fixed – its supply price is zero in the sense that it is there whether or not it receives any payment. By the same token, it is the community's demand for foodstuffs that determines the demand for land. In other words, the demand for land is a derived demand.

Figure 1 illustrates the perfectly inelastic supply of land, SS, intersecting the community's demand for land, DD. The equilibrium rent is O*R*. Now

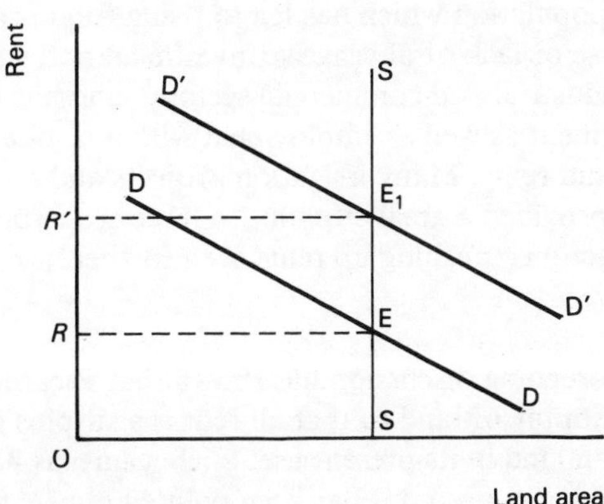

Fig. 1. The determination of rent.

suppose that a growing population leads to an increase in the demand for land use in general to D′D′. This raises the equilibrium rent from O*R* to O*R*′. We can say that, given the fixed supply of land, rent is demand-determined.

Henry George, in his most celebrated book *Progress and Poverty* (1880) popularised the notion that rising rents represent 'unearned increments'. From the standpoint of equity, he argued, there is no justification for a few landlords being permitted to receive such 'unearned increments' which arise from the general progress of society and without any effort on the part of the landowners. He therefore campaigned for a 'single tax' system in which land rent regarded as a surplus could be taxed without any adverse effects on incentives. For example, in Fig. 1, starting at the equilibrium point E_1, a tax could be imposed which took away from the owners of land the rent equivalent to *RR*′. Landowners would obviously be made worse off but the demand curve, the supply curve and the equilibrium position would all be left unchanged.

Site rents The above argument applies equally well to different amounts of rent paid for urban sites. Two urban sites may be equally good in all respects other than location and yet command different rents on account of these differences in location. For example, sites in the centre of a city command higher rents than sites on the outskirts of a city. Shops and offices in Oxford Street in London have higher rents than those on the outskirts of London because sites in the centre of London have inelastic supplies in relation to the demand for them.

Assessing Ricardo's theory of rent It may be objected that land does not have original and indestructible powers so that rent cannot be regarded as purely demand-determined. Good quality land, after constant cultivation, can lose its fertility considerably. Likewise, natural resources like oil, gas and coal can become permanently exhausted. Furthermore, it is unrealistic to assume that land has only one use. Instead, it has many alternative uses so that the supply of land to a particular use cannot be regarded as perfectly inelastic.

The theory is, however, helpful in understanding the reasons for the rapid rise in rents in developing countries. Most of these countries suffer from over-population which has led to rising food prices and rising rents. Also, because of lack of alternative investment and employment opportunities in the industrial and commercial sectors, land has become a major source of investment as well as employment with a resultant steep rise in land prices and land rents. Many irrigation projects and housing development schemes have provided a great stimulus to large-scale speculative activity in land transactions, pushing up rents even further.

Economic rent and transfer earnings

The foregoing discussion has shown that Ricardo's theory of rent assumes a fixed supply of land so that all rent is a surplus over and above the cost of keeping land in its present use. Such a surplus has become known as 'economic rent' and it has been pointed out that this concept can be applied not only to land, but also to labour and capital. We now define 'economic rent' and the related concept of 'transfer earnings'.

Definition: ***Transfer earnings are the payment required to keep a factor in its present use.***

Definition: ***Economic rent is any payment in excess of transfer earnings.***

Consider a doctor employed in private sector medicine and who earns £15,000 per annum. If he would be paid £12,000 per annum in the National Health Service and assuming that all other conditions of service were identical to those in his present post, his transfer earnings would be £12,000 per annum, because this is the payment necessary to keep him in the private sector. The doctor can be regarded as earning an economic rent of £3,000 per annum.

As pointed out above, in the case of perfectly inelastic supply of a factor, all of its earnings are economic rent. This situation was illustrated in Fig. 1 in which SS represented the inelastic supply of land. Given the demand curve DD, the factor's earnings (given by O*R*ES) are all economic rent.

In the case of an upward-sloping supply curve of a factor, part of its earnings are transfer earnings and part economic rent. Given the demand curve DD and the supply curve SS in Fig. 2, the equilibrium price and quantity are OP_1 and OQ_1 respectively. Total earnings of the factor are thus given by the area of OP_1EQ_1. The price paid for the marginal unit of the factor supplied ($OP_1 = Q_1E$) is just equal to the transfer earnings of this unit. All previous units supplied are therefore receiving an economic rent. The area $OSEQ_1$ represents the total transfer earnings of the factor. The remainder of the factor's earnings, that is the area between the supply curve and the line P_1E (triangle SP_1E) represents economic rent.

Fig. 2. The distinction between transfer earnings and economic rent.

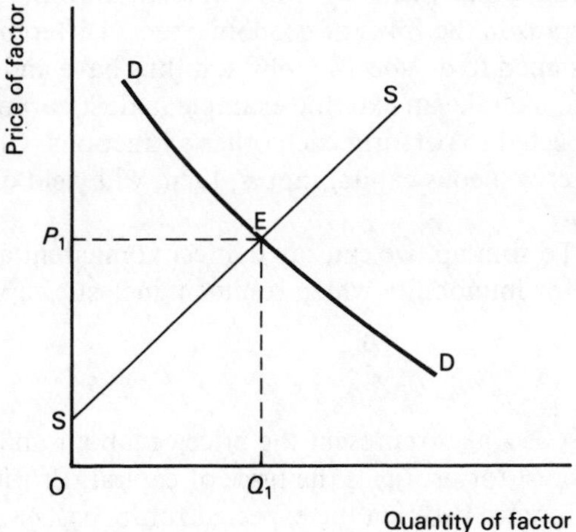

In some cases all of the earnings of a factor can represent transfer earnings. Consider the case of a firm that buys a factor in a perfectly competitive market so that it faces a perfectly elastic supply curve. This is represented by the line SS in Fig. 3. The factor's total earnings (represented

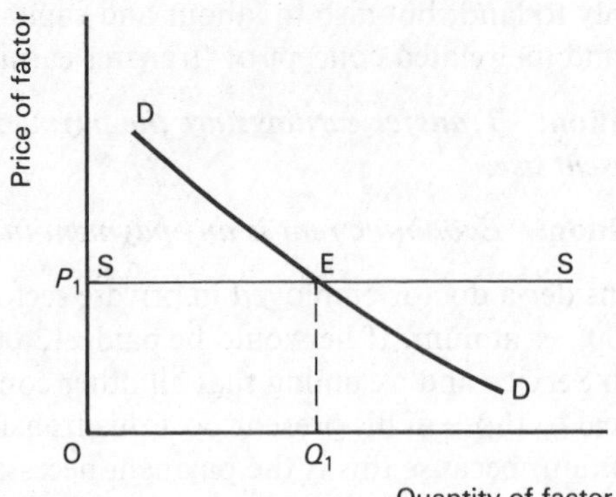

Fig. 3. Case in which all of factor's earnings represent transfer earnings.

by the area OP_1EQ_1) are purely transfer earnings because if the firm offered any price below OP_1 it would be unable to purchase any of the factor.

Like land, labour and capital are heterogeneous factors of production – for instance, different grades of workers (teachers, doctors and nurses) have different training and skills. Such grades have an inelastic supply, at least in the short-run. A sudden increase in the demand for doctors cannot be met overnight so existing doctors will earn an economic rent.

Marshall called rent which disappears in the long-run 'quasi-rent'. As an example, consider a machine with only one use, so that in the short-run its transfer earnings are zero and all of its earnings represent economic rent. In the long-run, the machine will depreciate and will only be replaced if it earns a sufficient return to make it worthwhile to the owner. Thus, part of its earnings (regarded as economic rent in the short-run) becomes transfer earnings in the long-run.

In general, because factors of productions are heterogeneous, any grade of factor which becomes scarce in relation to the demand for it will earn a surplus in the form of economic rent. Different machines, for example, are designed to do specific jobs and thus have an inelastic supply in the short-run. To take an extreme example, a dust-cart and a computer cannot be expected to perform each other's functions. Changes in the demand for heterogeneous capital inputs, then, will yield differing amounts of economic rent.

To sum up, we can say that economic rent accrues to factors because of factor immobility which results in inelastic supply.

Interest or profit – the reward to capital

Just as wages represent the price of labour and rent is the price of land, so interest (or profit) is the price of capital. Profit can be regarded as the difference between the expected future costs and the expected future returns on investment. Profit is, therefore, the usual term for the reward to capitalists. Interest, on the other hand, represents the cost of capital – if money has to be borrowed to finance an investment, interest has to be paid on it; if a firm uses its own money to finance investment, the interest that could have been earned by lending the money is an *opportunity* cost. In the neo-classical model with perfect competition and perfect foresight, both the cost of capital and the reward to capitalists are equal to the value of the marginal product of capital and there is no surplus. It follows that the terms interest and profit can be used interchangeably in that model.

The nature of capital Capital can be regarded as a heterogeneous collection of machines, buildings and equipment all with different life-spans. Because of this, economists disagree about whether it is justifiable to use a single concept, like interest, as the reward to capital. Economists at the University of Cambridge (England) have led an attack on neo-classical economists who believe that the principles of marginal productivity apply to the reward to capital in the same way as it does to land and labour. The results of the marginal productivity theory, however, can only apply if the stock of capital is assumed to be composed of homogeneous units – given the apparent heterogeneity of capital, the marginal productivity theory is on a shaky foundation.

Economists at the Massachusetts Institute of Technology (Cambridge, USA) however, have upheld the marginal productivity theory, maintaining that there is no better explanation of how capital is rewarded. They contend that the *neo-classical theory of interest* (in which, as we see below, the demand for investment goods is determined by the marginal productivity of capital) is the most satisfactory explanation of the reward to capital. Furthermore, they claim that, in the long-run, capital is more malleable and flexible and so not so heterogeneous as people think.

First, then, we outline the neo-classical theory of interest. Then, we set out the main criticisms levelled against it by the Cambridge (England) economists.

The neo-classical theory of interest

The central proposition of this theory is that interest is the reward for waiting. Such waiting involves the postponement of current consumption to some future date. The longer the period of waiting, the higher the rate of return on capital because it enables investors to adopt capital-using techniques of production.

According to the neo-classical theory of interest, the price of capital (that is, the interest rate) is determined by the total demand for and the total

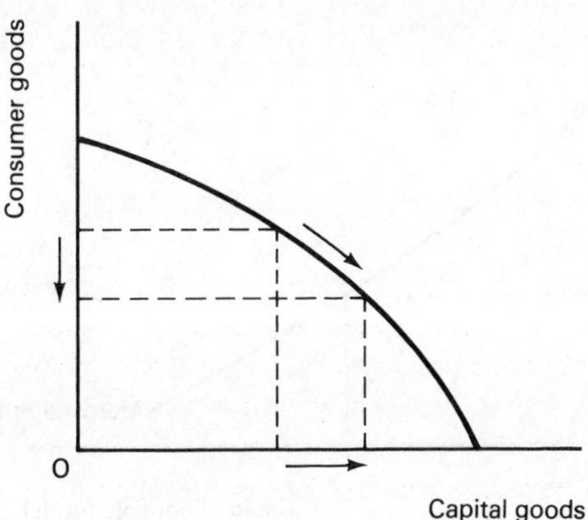

Fig. 4. The choice between capital goods and consumer goods.

supply of funds for spending on capital goods. As illustrated in Fig. 4, using more resources to produce capital goods means giving up some quantity of consumer goods in the present period. In other words, capital accumulation (or investment) necessitates *refraining from some current consumption* (or saving). In the neo-classical model, savings are seen as providing the supply of loanable funds and releasing resources from the production of current consumer goods into the production of capital goods. Investment, on the other hand, is seen as providing the demand for loanable funds.

The higher the rate of interest, the more willing households and individuals will be to save and so sacrifice some present consumption for (uncertain) future consumption. This implies that the supply of loanable funds plotted against the rate of interest will yield a curve which slopes upwards from left to right as shown in Fig. 5.

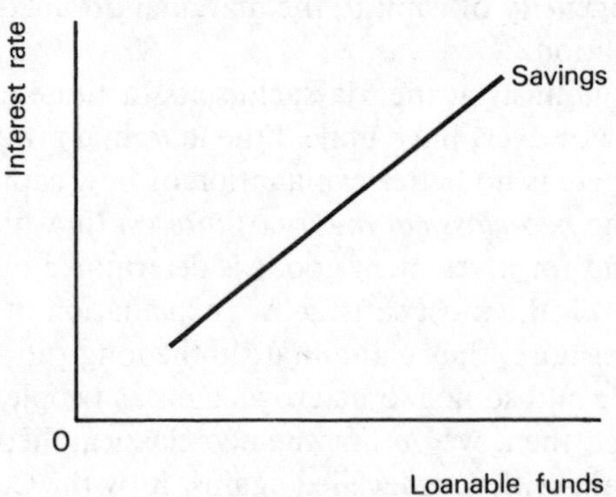

Fig. 5. The supply of loanable funds.

The total demand for loanable funds is the sum of all individual firms' demands for capital at different interest rates. It is here that the marginal productivity of capital comes into the analysis. Given perfect competition, the interest rate facing a single firm can be taken as given. To determine how much investment to undertake, therefore, a firm must estimate the marginal productivity of a capital project and compare it with the project's real cost. One way is to estimate the project's *expected internal rate of return* and then compare this with the prevailing market rate of interest, as was shown in

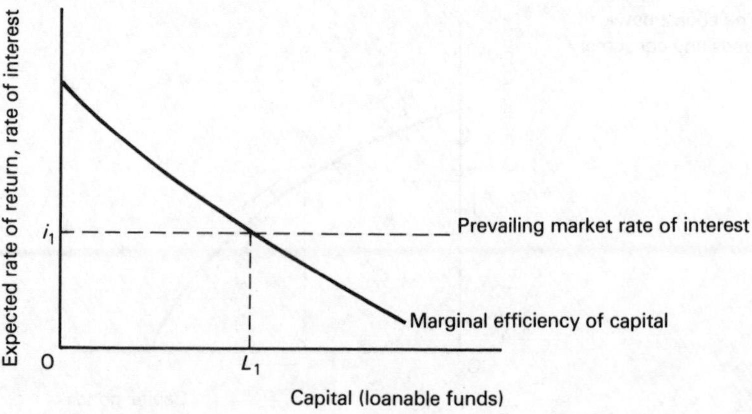

Fig. 6. A single firm's demand for capital.

Chapter 12. Since a firm will undertake the most profitable capital projects first, the expected rate of return will decline as more and more units of capital are employed (because of diminishing returns). This is illustrated in Fig. 6 where the firm in question will invest in capital projects up to OL_1 where the expected rate of return is just equal to the market rate of interest Oi_1. The curve in Fig. 6 is sometimes called the *marginal efficiency of capital* curve and can be interpreted as the firm's demand for capital.

Aggregating all firms' demands for capital and drawing the total demand curve against the rate of interest on the same graph as the total supply of loanable funds, we obtain the graph shown in Fig. 7. The equilibrium rate of interest (or equilibrium price of capital) is determined at the point where the two curves intersect and is denoted by Oi_1 in the graph.

Fig. 7. Determination of the equilibrium price of capital.

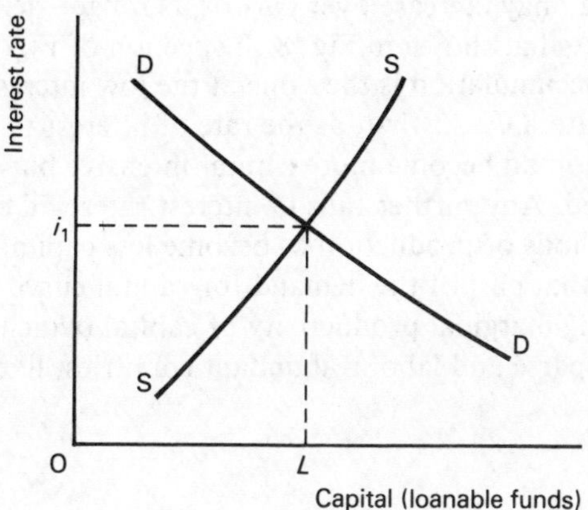

Figure 7 suggests that if, for some reason, there were an autonomous increase in savings, shifting the supply curve to the right, this would depress interest rates and so reduce the cost of additional investment. Since additional investment yields diminishing returns, a conclusion of the neo-classical theory of interest is that such investment will only be undertaken under conditions of falling interest rates.

Assessing the neo-classical theory of interest Several criticisms can be levelled against the theory. Consider the following.

(a) It ignores the possibility that savers may have a given purpose for which they are saving – to buy a new car or pay for a holiday, for example. In such a case, a higher interest rate may actually reduce savers' willingness to save because rising interest rates raise real incomes and so reduce the amount of saving necessary for the given purpose.
(b) A substantial amount of saving in modern industrial societies is done as a matter of habit and custom, independently of interest rate levels.
(c) On the capital side, severe problems arise in measuring the capital stock in a country, making it difficult to identify and measure the reward to capital.
(d) A basic conclusion of the neo-classical theory of interest is that a falling interest rate will induce greater investment to take place and so cause a shift from less capital-intensive to more capital-intensive methods of production.

Economists at the University of Cambridge (England) have pointed out that this conclusion may not hold – in particular, they point to the possibility of *reswitching*, a phenomenon which is explained in the next section.

The phenomenon of reswitching (the 'two Cambridges' controversy)
According to the neo-classical theory, a falling interest rate will cause a 'switch' from less capital-intensive to more capital-intensive methods of production and this is the view supported by economists at Cambridge (USA), led by Solow and Samuelson. They maintain that the marginal productivity of capital will decline as the capital stock expands, yielding the demand for capital curve shown in Fig. 7.

Economists at the University of Cambridge (England) led by Joan Robinson and Lord Kaldor, though, maintain that the marginal productivity of capital may increase over part of its range, yielding a demand for capital curve like that shown in Fig. 8. Inspection of Fig. 8 shows that the rate of capital accumulation is the same at the low interest rate, Oi_1, as it is at the higher rate, Oi_2. At first, as the rate of interest falls from Oi_2, methods of production do become more capital-intensive but only until interest rate Oi_3 is reached. Any further falls in interest rates will cause a 'reswitch' to occur and methods of production to become less capital-intensive again. We are now on that part of the demand for capital curve which exhibits an increasing marginal productivity of capital (which is a distinct possibility in capital-sparse and labour-abundant countries, like India).

Fig. 8. Backward-bending demand for capital curve.

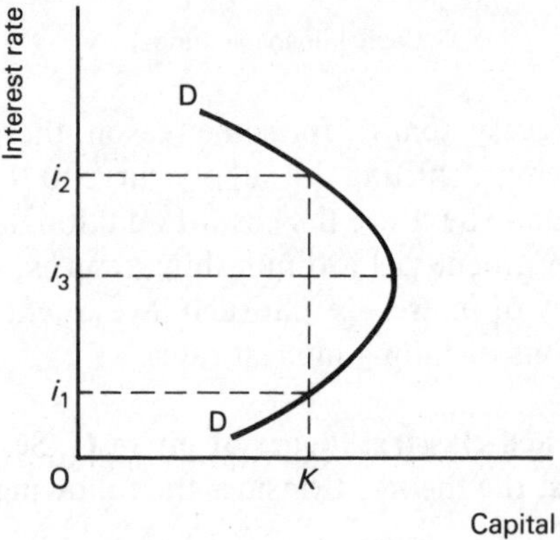

The tendency of the falling rate of profit

We have already noted how Ricardo perceived the falling rate of profit in his theory of distribution. Marx also made a major contribution to the ideas of Ricardo and to those of other economists of his time.

Basically, the falling rate of profit is associated with the process of industrialisation. When total production expands, the total amount of profit increases but the rate of profit per unit of output falls. Ricardo's theory of distribution demonstrated this tendency. The smaller the rate of profit, the weaker the incentive for capitalists to invest more money in plant and equipment. Eventually, investment may cease completely so that the expansion of output comes to an end. Then, the economy is said to have reached a 'stationary state'.

Marx, however, pursued a different line of argument. The heart of his argument is that labour is the sole producer of value, but the workers providing the labour are paid no more than a subsistence wage which is less than the full value of their produce. The *surplus* over and above the workers' subsistence requirements is the profit expropriated by the capitalists. By the phrase 'subsistence wage', Marx, like other economists of his time, meant a wage which was just enough to maintain a customary standard of living. The capitalists' desire to earn profit and thus to accumulate capital leaves the workers with no independent means of livelihood - they have to seek employment from the capitalists at the subsistence wage. Yet capital itself is not productive unless aided by labour.

Marx further points out that profits are calculated net of the costs of labour, raw materials and depreciation. Because of forceful competition, though, capitalists are pushed to improve their methods of production - for example, by installing new and better machines and equipment. This means an increase in depreciation costs which in turn adversely affects the rate of profit.

Capitalists can increase their profits by increasing work-hours or by direct wage cuts, either of which might be resisted by the working classes. Alternatively, capitalists may reduce the cost of capital and of raw materials via technical progress, or by finding newer and cheaper sources of raw materials and establishing markets overseas for finished products. It is possible, though, that rivalry between different capitalist powers may lead to conflict and wars.

Marx maintains that even if these counteracting tendencies succeed at first, they will not prevent the inevitability of falling profits. Such low profit rates will then lead to frequent crises - for example, strong businesses taking over weaker rivals, sudden lay-offs of workers by firms in search of bigger profits. Unemployment may be deliberately created to force workers to accept the capitalists' terms and conditions of employment.

Note that all the foregoing outcomes are the result of the forces of competition and of the profit-maximising behaviour of capitalists because production is organised to satisfy the profit motive and is not directly concerned with the satisfaction of the community's wants.

Conclusion

In this chapter, we have considered the forces underlying the rewards to land and capital. We have also examined some difficult and controversial questions relating to the theory of distribution. In an introductory treatment, however, it is not possible to give more than a cursory account of the complex issues involved in, for example, the 'Cambridge controversy' of capital theory and the Marxian 'law' of the tendency of the falling rate of profit. Interested readers are directed to the further reading listed below.

Further reading

Pen, J., *Income Distribution*, Penguin, Harmondsworth, 1971.
Baumol, W.J., *Economic Theory and Operations Analysis*, Prentice Hall, Englewood Cliffs, 1977 (Ch. 24 and 26).
King, J. and **Regan, P.**, *Relative Income Shares*, Macmillan, London, 1976.
Robinson, J. and **Eatwell, J.**, *An Introduction to Modern Economics*, McGraw Hill, London, 1973.
Blaug, M., *The Cambridge Revolution: Success or Failure*?, Hobart Paperback No. 6, I.E.A., 1975.

Exercises

1. Review your understanding of the following terms:

functional distribution	rent
personal distribution	economic rent
marginal productivity	transfer earnings
aggregate production function	quasi-rent
Euler's theorem	Cambridge controversy
Cobb-Douglas production function	reswitching
neutral technical progress	subsistence wage
non-neutral technical progress	falling rate of profit

2. Consider the following demand and supply schedules per time period for a homogeneous type of labour

Wage rate (£)	100	110	120	130	140	150
Quantity demanded	1,000	800	600	400	200	0
Quantity supplied	0	300	600	100	1,200	1,500

(a) Plot the demand and supply curves on the same graph and identify the equilibrium wage rate.
(b) Calculate the total wage income at the equilibrium and find the total amount of economic rent and transfer earnings.

3. Discuss the view that since capital is not itself productive and labour is the sole producer of value, the total value of output should be received by labour.

4. Consider the problems involved in measuring a country's capital stock. How do these problems affect the conclusions of the marginal productivity theory of distribution?

5. Explain why office rents are lower in the provinces than in the centre of London.

6. Discuss the effect on the distribution of income of a 20 per cent tax on all land in the UK. What would the effect be if the tax were only imposed on land in the City of London?

Introduction to the economy as a whole

17 Introducing macroeconomics

Introduction

We now start our study of the economy as a whole and in the remainder of the book we consider many of the world's most pressing macroeconomic problems - problems like persistent unemployment, rapid inflation, balance of payments difficulties, economic stagnation and unequal distributions of income and wealth. In order to analyse these problems, though, we must first identify, measure and consider the determinants of the main *aggregates* in the economy. The most important aggregates we examine are: (a) the economy's total output of goods and services; (b) the total demand for this output; (c) total employment and unemployment; (d) the general price level; (e) the balance of payments; (f) the rate of economic growth. To begin with, it is important to gain a good understanding of the meaning of these aggregates. Defining and explaining them and showing how they may be measured are the major objectives of this and the following chapter. In this chapter, we concentrate on the meaning and measurement of an economy's total output and the total demand for that output. The other main aggregates are dealt with in the next chapter where the major macroeconomic policy objectives are discussed.

All aggregates are made up of their constituent parts - for example, we see later that the total demand for the economy's output consists of the sum of individual demands and can be written as follows:

$$AD = C + I + G + X$$

where AD is total (or aggregate) demand, C is the sum of all individual consumers' demands for domestic goods and services, I is the sum of all individual firms' demands for investment goods, G is the government's demand for goods and services and X is the total foreign demand for the country's exports. To analyse the main determinants of aggregates like this, it is necessary first to have an understanding of the behaviour of the individual economic agents. This means that we must be aware of the microeconomic theories of consumer behaviour, of the firm, of public sector activity and of distribution. For this reason, we started the book with microeconomics and only now turn to the study of macroeconomics. Micro- and macroeconomics are intimately linked and, where appropriate, we shall point out the microeconomic foundations of the macroeconomic analyses that we develop and apply.

The problems of aggregation

Problems arise in aggregation largely because of the difficulty of finding an appropriate unit of measurement. In adding up the total output of the United

Kingdom, for instance, there is no single physical unit of measurement that can be used: the millions of different types of goods and services are all measured in different units – for example, steel is measured in tonnes and cloth is measured in metres and it is, of course, impossible to add tonnes to metres. The problem is overcome, at least partially, by using money as the unit of measurement – this greatly simplifies the adding up, but it gives rise to the problem of distinguishing between real and nominal values.

If the *value* of total output should double from, say, £10 billion to £20 billion, this does not necessarily mean that total output itself has doubled: part of the increase may indeed be due to an increase in physical output, but part may be due to an increase in *prices.* The problem with value measurements is that they necessarily have a price and quantity component and it is not always easy to separate the two. To estimate *real* output, it is necessary to deflate the value of total output by an appropriate price index. This converts total output measured in *current* prices to total output measured in *constant* prices. (The actual way in which this calculation is done is illustrated later in this chapter.) There is, however, the problem of deciding which price index to use. In the United Kingdom, two main price indices are calculated: the Index of Retail Prices and the Wholesale Price Index. Each one is a weighted average of the prices of a number of selected goods – neither provides a completely true average price of all the goods and services included in the country's total output. Changes in the deflated total output figures, therefore, can really only give us an estimate of the true changes in the nation's physical output.

Another problem with aggregates is that they hide their constituent elements. For example, an increase in the economy's total output tells us nothing about who receives that output. Indeed, as we shall see later, a rise in total output accompanied by a change in the distribution of income which makes some people better off and others worse off cannot necessarily be interpreted as an improvement in the country's living standards. Distributional factors should always be borne in mind when considering the effects of changes in aggregate variables.

Total output: national product, national expenditure, national income

In principle, the value of an economy's total output can be measured in three ways. These can be seen by examining Fig. 1 which shows the *flow* of income and spending in a simple model of an economy. The two main economic agents in the flow diagram are households and firms. The households can be thought of as the owners of factors of production, the services of which they sell to firms in exchange for income (in the form of wages, salaries, interest, rent and profit). Note that, in the model, all profits are assumed to be distributed to households and not retained by the firms. The firms use the factors of production to produce the many different types of goods and services which they then sell to households (whose spending is called consumption), the government, foreigners (who buy exports) and other firms (whose spending on capital goods is called investment). The diagram also shows that the part of household income which is not spent on consumption is either saved, spent on imports or is taken in taxes by the government. The

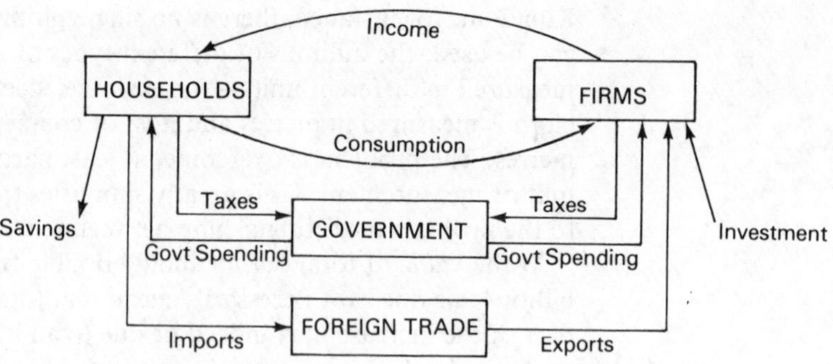

Fig. 1. The circular flow of income and spending.

government itself uses its tax revenue (as well as money from other sources – see Ch. 13) to finance government spending, including transfer payments (such as pensions, unemployment benefits and student grants).

Before proceeding, we must define the terms consumption, investment and savings more fully.

Definition: ***Consumption can be regarded as total expenditure by households on goods and services which yield utility in the current period.***

Definition: ***Savings are that part of disposable income (that is, total income less taxes) which is not spent in the current period. It follows that disposable income minus savings equals consumption.***

Definition: ***Investment is the production of or expenditure by firms on goods and services which are not for current consumption: that is, real capital goods, like factories, machines, bridges and motorways, all goods which yield a flow of consumer goods and services in future periods.***

The three ways of measuring the annual value of total output in an economy are by calculating its *national product, national expenditure* and *national income.* Consider these in turn.

National product This is found by adding up the value of all final goods and services produced by firms during the year. Note that *all* final goods and services produced must be included, whether they are to be sold to consumers or to the government, whether they are to be sold abroad as exports, or whether they are capital goods to be sold to other firms. It is, however, important to include only *final* goods and services: all intermediate goods must be excluded so that double-counting is avoided. For example, in the production of a woollen coat, only the value of the final coat should be counted. The values of the raw wool and the woollen cloth are included in the value of the coat. If we were to count them as well we should be guilty of double - or even triple-counting. If all intermediate goods were included in the calculation of the national product, therefore, we would seriously overestimate the value of the country's total output.

National expenditure This is found by adding up all the spending on the final goods and services produced by firms. Such an aggregate, though, will only equal the value of total output if those goods which are produced but not sold are also included – this item, which is called 'net changes in stocks and work in progress', is normally counted as part of firms' investment spending (which is logical since such goods are for future rather than current consumption). National expenditure, then, is the sum of consumption of domestically produced goods, investment (including changes in stocks and work in progress), government expenditure and exports. Notice that, as before, in order to avoid double-counting, only spending on *final* goods and services is included.

National income It is because goods and services are produced by factors of production that income is created in an economy, so another way of calculating the value of total output is to add up all the incomes paid out to the owners of factors of production. Moreover, it comes to the same thing to add the *values-added* by all firms at the different stages of production. To illustrate this, consider a simple example in which producing a woollen coat involves the following three stages of production.

1. A sheep farmer produces raw wool and sells it to a mill for £10. This represents an income of £10 for the farmer. *Value-added* = £10.
2. The mill uses the raw wool to produce cloth which it sells to a coat factory for £21. This represents income (including profit) of £11 for the mill – remember that £10 has had to be paid for the raw wool. *Value-added* = £11.
3. The coat factory produces the coat and sells it for £40. This includes £21 to cover the cost of the cloth and £19 to pay incomes, including profits. *Value-added* = £19.

The total value-added in this example (£40) is just equal to the value of the final coat; it is also equal to the sum of all incomes paid at each stage of production. The value of a country's total output can, therefore, be found either by adding the values-added by all firms or by adding up the incomes (that is, wages, salaries, interest, rent and profits) of all factors of production, those producing intermediate goods as well as those producing final goods. In either case, double-counting will be avoided. It is important in using this method, though, to exclude all transfer payments as these represent nothing more than a redistribution of income from taxpayers to the transfer recipients; including them, therefore, would involve double-counting.

Assuming: (a) that all three measures are calculated accurately; (b) that only *final* goods and services are counted in the national product and national expenditure figures; (c) that any changes in unsold stocks are included in the national expenditure figures; and (d) that *all* incomes, including profits but excluding transfer payments, are counted in the national income figures, then it must follow that all three measures will provide an identical figure for the value of the country's total output. That is,

National product ≡ National expenditure ≡ National income

In principle, then, these three aggregates simply represent different ways of measuring the flow of output or income being created in an economy over a period of time.

Complications

In the attempt to calculate a country's total output using the above methods, a number of complications arise. For example, how to deal with capital depreciation and stock appreciation; whether to value output at market prices or at factor cost; whether to include net property income from abroad. Consider these problems in turn.

Depreciation When investment takes place during a year, new capital is created and it is correct that this should be included in our calculation of the value of total output for that year. Some investment occurs, though, simply to replace capital which has worn out during the year – such 'wearing out' of capital is called 'depreciation' or 'capital consumption'. Where no allowance is made for this depreciation in the calculation of investment, the resulting figure is called *gross* investment. When depreciation is deducted from gross investment, we have what is called *net* investment and it is this which measures the true addition to the country's capital stock during the year. Where no allowance is made for depreciation in calculating the value of total output, the resulting figures are also referred to as gross. Thus, we have:

$$\left.\begin{array}{l}\text{Gross National Product}\\ \text{Gross National Expenditure}\\ \text{Gross National Income}\end{array}\right\} - \text{depreciation} = \left\{\begin{array}{l}\text{Net National Product}\\ \text{Net National Expenditure}\\ \text{Net National Income}\end{array}\right.$$

For two main reasons, economists are usually quite happy to work with 'gross' rather than 'net' figures: first, depreciation tends to change only slowly over time so that the 'gross' and 'net' figures move closely together over any period of a few years; and secondly, depreciation figures are notoriously difficult to estimate with any accuracy.

Stock appreciation We have noted before that all three measurements of total output include the value of the net change in stocks of unsold goods. If prices are rising, the value of firms' stocks will be rising even if there are no net physical additions to them. To take account of this so-called 'stock appreciation', it is necessary to subtract an appropriate amount in computing the national income.

Market prices and factor cost When national expenditure is computed, it is measured initially in market prices – for example, the total spending on beer is equal to the quantity of beer bought times its average market price. Unfortunately, many market prices are distorted by indirect taxes and subsidies: indirect taxes have the effect of raising the prices of goods above what would otherwise have been set, while subsidies lower such prices. National income and national product, however, are both measured at 'factor cost' – that is, in terms of the sums paid out to the owners of factors of production – and this excludes indirect taxes and subsidies. To ensure that national expenditure is the same as national income and national product, it is necessary to convert market prices to factor cost by *subtracting* indirect taxes and *adding* subsidies. In other words, we can write:

$$\begin{array}{l}\text{National Expenditure at}\\ \text{Market Prices}\end{array} - \begin{array}{l}\text{Indirect}\\ \text{Taxes}\end{array} + \text{Subsidies} = \begin{array}{l}\text{National Expenditure}\\ \text{at Factor Cost}\end{array}$$

It is preferable (and usual) to measure the value of total output at factor cost rather than in market prices, otherwise an increase in indirect taxation or a reduction in subsidies would have the effect of raising the estimate of total output even when no greater quantity of goods and services was being produced.

Net property income from abroad Some of the output produced within a country, for example, the United Kingdom, is actually produced by firms which are owned by overseas residents. Similarly, some output produced overseas is produced by firms owned by United Kingdom residents or United Kingdom companies. Whether this should be taken into account or not in calculating the value of total output depends on whether we require a measurement of the domestic output of the United Kingdom or a measurement of the output produced by all the factors of production owned by United Kingdom residents. In the former case, we need make no adjustment but the figures are renamed *domestic* product, income and expenditure. In the latter case, 'net property income from abroad' has to be added, where the term 'net property income from abroad' is equal to that income received by United Kingdom residents from the production of output by firms overseas *minus* that income paid to overseas residents from the production of output by domestic firms. We can thus write:

$$\left.\begin{array}{l}\text{Domestic Product}\\ \text{Domestic Income}\\ \text{Domestic Expenditure}\end{array}\right\} + \begin{array}{c}\text{Net Property Income}\\ \text{from Abroad}\end{array} = \left\{\begin{array}{l}\text{National Product}\\ \text{National Income}\\ \text{National Expenditure}\end{array}\right.$$

The United Kingdom accounts

A detailed breakdown of the national product, national expenditure and national income figures for the United Kingdom in 1978 are shown in Tables 1, 2 and 3. All the terms used have been explained in the previous section with the exception of the *residual error*. This is a figure included to ensure that all three methods yield identical results which, of course, they should do in principle, but which they invariably fail to do in practice because of errors and omissions which arise through imperfect data collection.

Since we now have three different measures for the value of a country's total output, we also have three different names which we could use to describe that output. In the remainder of the book, we follow convention and use the term *national income*. It will be understood that when this term is used, the terms national product and national expenditure could have been used equally well.

The 'black' economy

It should be pointed out that official statistics tend to underestimate the actual volume of economic activity that occurs. This is because of the operation of the so-called 'black' or underground economy. The black economy refers to those unrecorded economic transactions conducted on a cash basis with a view to illegal evasion of tax. In 1979, the chairman of the Inland Revenue board estimated that the black economy accounted for about

Table 1. Gross and net national product for the United Kingdom, 1978.

	£ million
Agriculture, forestry, fishing	3,715
Mining and quarrying	4,467
Manufacturing	40,690
Construction	8,610
Gas, electricity, water	4,772
Transport, communications	11,688
Distributive trades	14,687
Insurance, banking, finance and business services	5,170
Ownership of dwellings	8,578
Public administration, defence	10,197
Public health, education	9,674
Other services	18,680
Total	140,928
Residual error	1,071
Gross Domestic Product	141,999
Net property income from abroad	836
Gross National Product	142,835
Depreciation	− 18,310
Net National Product	124,525

Source: National Income and Expenditure, 1979.

Table 2. Gross and net national expenditure for the United Kingdom, 1978.

	£ million
Consumers' expenditure	96,086
General government final consumption	32,693
Gross domestic fixed capital formation	29,218
Value of physical increase in stocks and work in progress	1,528
Total domestic expenditure at market prices	159,525
Exports of goods and services	47,636
Imports of goods and services	− 45,522
Taxes on expenditure	− 23,238
Subsidies	3,598
Gross domestic expenditure at factor cost	141,999
Net property income from abroad	836
Gross national expenditure	142,835
Depreciation	− 18,310
Net national expenditure	124,525

Source: National Income and Expenditure, 1979.

Table 3. Gross and net national income for the United Kingdom, 1978.

	£ million
Income from employment	98,156
Income from self-employment	13,245
Gross trading profits of companies	17,055
Gross trading surplus of public corporations	5,412
Gross trading surplus of government enterprises	184
Other incomes	11,125
Total domestic income	145,177
Stock appreciation	− 4,249
Residual error	1,071
Gross domestic income	141,999
Net property income from abroad	836
Gross national income	142,835
Depreciation	− 18,310
Net national income	124,525

Source: National Income and Expenditure, 1979.

7.5 per cent of national income. The Central Statistical Office in 1980, however, estimated that the black economy represented only about 3.5 per cent of national income. It appears that in the case of many consumer services (like plumbing, decorating and electrical repairs), it is common for two prices to be quoted. The lower price is quoted on the understanding that payment will be made in cash and that no receipt or other record of the transaction will be issued. The existence of a black economy is, of course, not confined to the United Kingdom. It has been widely reported that in Italy, for example, whole industries operate outside the officially recorded economy.

The borderline between the officially recorded economy and the black economy is not always clear-cut. If a painter decorates his own house, nobody would argue that he should pay tax on the non-existent earnings; but what if he decorates a friend's house in return for some help with fixing his car? Or what if the painter works for other people in his free time in return for cash? Many would exclude the second example, but would include the third example in a definition of the black economy. By its very nature it is impossible to quantify exactly the extent of the black economy. There is some partial evidence of its existence as the expenditure estimates of gross national product (based on the Family Expenditure Survey) regularly exceed the estimates from the income side. Indeed, some estimates have suggested that if the Exchequer received all the tax due to it from the black economy, the basic rate of income tax might be cut by 10 per cent.

National income and economic welfare

Since the national income of a country is a measurement of the output of the final goods and services produced by that country in a year, can we conclude that if national income rises from one year to the next, economic welfare must also rise? We certainly can make no statements about economic welfare unless we first convert national income into *real* national income *per capita*. In this section, we first show how this is done and secondly, we consider under what circumstances a rise in real output per capita can be interpreted as an *actual*, *potential* or *pseudo* improvement in economic welfare.

National income and real output per capita To convert national income into real output per capita, it is necessary to make two adjustments: (i) national income must be deflated by an appropriate price index to convert it to real terms; (ii) the figure must then be divided by the population to convert it to per capita terms. To show how these adjustments are made, consider a simple numerical example. Examine the figures in Table 4 where the two years 1975 and 1980 are being compared for a hypothetical economy. Notice that money national income has increased by 100 per cent during the period, but prices have risen by 20 per cent from the base year figure of 100 in 1975 to 120 in 1980, and population has risen by $33\frac{1}{3}$ per cent from 3,000 to 4,000 inhabitants.

Table 4. Comparing national income figures.

	1975	1980	
National income	£12 m.	£24 m.	
Price index	100	120	
Real national income (1975 prices)	£12 m.	£20 m.	(24 m. × 100/120)
Population	3,000	4,000	
Real output per capita	£4,000	£5,000	

The first step is to *deflate* the national income figures to eliminate the effects of the rise in prices. As 1975 is the base year, the money value and the real value of national income are the same in that year. In 1980, though, the price index is 120 and this means that part of the increase in national income is a result of the rise in prices rather than the rise in physical output. The rise in prices is eliminated from the figures by dividing national income by the price index and multiplying by 100. This calculation is called deflating the national income. Comparing the deflated figures, we see that real national income (or national income in constant prices) has increased by $66\frac{2}{3}$ per cent during the period.

The next step is to take account of the increased size of population because, although real national income has risen, it has to be shared out among more people. Dividing the real national income figures by population for the two years, we obtain a figure for 'real output per capita' of £4,000 in 1975 and £5,000 in 1980, an increase of 25 per cent. So, in this example, although money national income rose by 100 per cent, real output per capita rose by only 25 per cent. We can conclude that an increase in national income will only be equivalent to an increase in real output per capita if both prices and the population remain unchanged. Since prices and populations generally change over time, it is crucially important to compare real output per capita figures rather than money national income figures, before coming to any conclusions about changes in economic welfare.

Actual, potential and pseudo improvements in economic welfare Even if real output per capita rises, it is not necessarily true that *actual* economic welfare will have improved. If changes in the distribution of income have also occurred, the improvement may only be a *potential* one. The improvement may only be apparent (or *pseudo*) if, in addition, the increase in real output per capita is accompanied by negative externalities or is caused by increased production of goods and services which are not for current consumption. Consider now these three types of 'improvements' in turn.

An actual improvement. In Chapter 8, where welfare economics was introduced, we stated a very important condition for an increase in economic welfare. This was the Pareto condition that at least one consumer must be made better off without at the same time any others being made worse off. Adopting this condition, we can only interpret an increase in real output per capita as an actual improvement in economic welfare if no distributional changes occur which make any individuals or groups worse off.

A potential improvement. Unfortunately, increases in real output per capita often do leave some individuals or groups in society worse off. For example, suppose that there were a big new discovery of a fuel, like oil, whose production considerably boosted a country's real national income. An unfavourable side-effect of this may be a reduction in demand for some other fuel, like coal. Some coal-workers may then lose their jobs or be put on short-time. These people will have been made worse off by the oil discovery which, on average, increased real output per capita, making many other people better off. By applying the Pareto condition, we cannot say that the oil discovery improves actual economic welfare. What we can do in cases like this is to apply the Hicks-Kaldor condition for a *potential* improvement. Recall from Chapter 8 that, according to the Hicks-Kaldor condition, if any change occurs which redistributes income in such a way that the gainers can potentially compensate the losers and still be better off than they were before, then we can conclude that potential economic welfare has increased. Clearly, when real output per capita rises, it must be theoretically possible for the gainers to compensate any losers, but this could only be interpreted as an actual improvement if full compensation were actually paid. Since workers made unemployed in general find themselves worse off receiving unemployment benefits than they were when working, we can say that only very rarely is full compensation ever paid.

A pseudo improvement. An increase in real output per capita may not even increase potential economic welfare if it is accompanied by negative externalities, an increase in the number of hours worked or increased production of investment goods at the expense of consumer goods.

Some *negative externalities,* in the shape of pollution, congestion and less pleasant working conditions, are likely to arise as output expands and these factors will tend to offset the effects of any increase in average income. So although consumers may on average be better off so far as their spending power is concerned, they may be worse off overall when environmental factors are taken into account. As an example, consider the building of a large chemical factory in the heart of the countryside: the extra production may increase real output per capita in the United Kingdom, but the factory may pollute the air and water and cause severe visual pollution in an area of natural beauty. If these external costs offset the increase in real output per capita, then any overall improvement in economic welfare would only be apparent and not real. We call this a *pseudo* improvement.

The same argument applies if output has been increased only through the work-force taking fewer hours of leisure and putting in *more hours of work*. Again, the improvement in welfare resulting from increased spending power may be offset by a reduction in welfare resulting from loss of leisure. Overall, there may be no real improvement in welfare.

Finally, if the rise in real output per capita is caused by an expansion of investment goods industries and public sector expenditures on the civil service and defence, while at the same time there is a decline in consumer goods industries, then current economic welfare may fall rather than rise. The reason for this is that economic welfare stems from the activity of consumption. The production of investment goods does not in itself add to welfare in the current period, though it should do so in future periods.

Other uses of the national income statistics

We can conclude from the previous section that a change in national income (even when adjusted for price and population increases) can only be used as an *indicator*, and not an accurate measure, of a change in economic welfare. There are two other possible uses of the national income figures that we should mention.

Making international comparisons Great care should be taken in using real output per capita figures to compare different countries' standards of living. First, a further adjustment is necessary to convert the figures to the same currency using a rate of exchange. This poses problems because the market rate of exchange is not necessarily the ideal measure of the relative values of the goods and services consumed in each country. Secondly, different countries have different needs and tastes which cannot easily be taken into account in making comparisons.

Government planning We shall see later that there is a close connection, at least in the short-term, between real national income and the level of employment in an economy. A rising real national income with a fairly constant capital stock will generally be associated with a fall in unemployment. Since governments have 'full employment' as one of their major policy objectives, it is important for them to have accurate national income statistics. A rising national income in the long-run is called economic growth and this is yet another policy objective of governments. We can conclude that the national income figures play an important role in the planning of both short- and long-run government policies.

Macroeconomic equilibrium

Aggregate demand As we mentioned at the beginning of this chapter, aggregate demand is the total demand for all final goods and services in an economy over a period of time and consists of the sum of the demands of consumers, firms, the government and foreigners. At first sight, it may appear that the value of aggregate demand for a country should be the same as its national expenditure. This, however, is not necessarily so. National expenditure is the *actual* amount of money spent on goods and services over a given period of time, whereas aggregate demand is the total value that households, firms, the government and foreigners *plan* to spend out of their respective incomes over that time period: in other words, it is the total amount they are willing and able to spend. National expenditure, then, can be called *actual expenditure,* while aggregate demand can be called *planned* expenditure. The actual and planned measurements will differ if total output should fall short of or exceed total demand – in the former case, some demand will be unsatisfied because insufficient goods have been produced; in the latter case, some net addition to stocks will occur since too many goods have been produced.

The equilibrium level of national income In the microeconomic market for a single good, an equilibrium is said to exist when the demand for the good is equal to the supply of it. Similarly, in macroeconomics, we can say that the equilibrium level of national income has been reached when there are no economic forces operating to change the level of national income. This occurs when the total demand for all goods and services (aggregate demand) is equal to the total supply of these goods and services (aggregate supply). That is, for the equilibrium level of income to be achieved, we require that:

Aggregate demand = Aggregate supply

Only when this condition is satisfied can we say that the total value of goods and services that households and the other economic agents want to buy is equal to the total value that firms want to produce. Note that aggregate supply cannot strictly be regarded as being the same as national income. National income is the value of the actual amount produced and so is necessarily equal to the national product and expenditure. Aggregate supply, on the other hand, is the amount that firms want to produce given the general level of wages and prices. The two will only be equal: (a) if wages and prices are such that firms plan to produce what is currently being produced; and (b) if firms are able to implement their production plans successfully.

Conclusion

In this chapter, the notion of national income accounting has been introduced and the equivalence of national income, product and expenditure demonstrated. We highlighted the problems of using national income as an indicator of economic welfare. Finally, we considered briefly the meaning of an equilibrium in macroeconomics.

The determination of the equilibrium level of national income is of central importance in macroeconomic analysis because it is this which determines to a large extent the level of employment in the economy. It is the debate about the forces which determine this equilibrium which fundamentally separates the various schools of thought in macroeconomics. We consider this debate in Chapter 19 after discussing the major macroeconomic policy objectives in Chapter 18.

Further reading

Beckerman, W., *National Income Analysis*, Weidenfeld and Nicolson, London 1976.

Brooman, F.S., *Macroeconomics*, Allen and Unwin, London, 1977 (Ch. 1-3).

Black, J., *The Economics of Modern Britain*, Martin Robertson, Oxford, 1979 (Ch. 2).

Prest, A.R. and **Coppock, D.J.**, *The UK Economy: A Manual of Applied Economics*, Weidenfeld and Nicolson, London, 1978 (Ch. 1).

Exercises

1. Review your understanding of the following terms:

economic aggregate	market prices
current prices	factor cost
constant prices	net property income from abroad
national product	gross domestic product
national expenditure	gross national product
national income	residual error
consumption	black economy
savings	actual expenditure
investment	planned expenditure
value-added	aggregate demand
depreciation	aggregate supply
stock appreciation	equilibrium level of income

2. The following data show the national income figures, price indices and population for a hypothetical country in 1978 and 1981:

	1978	*1981*
National income	£5,000 m.	£7,200 m.
Price index (1975 = 100)	120	160
Population	10 m.	11 m.

(a) Calculate real national income in both years.
(b) Find real national income per capita in both years.
(c) Comment on the change in potential economic welfare. What other data would be useful in determining the change in economic welfare?

3. Consider the problems involved in using national income statistics to make international comparisons of living standards.

4. Use the following figures to compute national income (that is, net national product at factor cost):

Value of physical increase in stocks and work in progress	£400 m.
Imports of goods and services	£37,000 m.
General government final consumption	£27,000 m.
Gross domestic fixed capital formation	£23,000 m.
Exports of goods and services	£35,000 m.
Depreciation	£14,000 m.
Taxes on expenditure	£17,000 m.
Net property income from abroad	£1,000 m.
Consumer expenditure	£74,000 m.
Subsidies	£3,000 m.

5. Explain the distinction between microeconomics and macroeconomics. Give examples of economic problems that have both microeconomic and macroeconomic dimensions.

18 Macroeconomic policy objectives

Introduction

The main macroeconomic policy objectives which modern governments strive to achieve are: (a) a high level of employment; (b) stable prices; (c) balance of payments equilibrium; (d) a high rate of economic growth; (e) an equitable distribution of income and wealth. The purpose of this chapter is to discuss generally these objectives in turn, explaining at the same time the main economic aggregates involved and showing briefly how they are measured in the United Kingdom.

One very important consideration which we have to bear in mind throughout is that, in many cases, *policy conflicts* arise. For example, we see in later chapters that a government's attempts to reduce the rate of inflation may worsen the level of unemployment and vice versa. Because of these conflicts, most countries have found it impossible to achieve all five objectives to their complete satisfaction and so have had to decide on their priorities. The list of priorities for a country can change over time, though, depending on economic circumstances and on the political party in power. In the United Kingdom, for instance, throughout the 1960s full employment was the major objective (though at times this had to play second fiddle to the balance of payments objective). In the 1970s, however, when the rate of inflation rose at times to over 20 per cent, the government's stated priority was to reduce the rate of inflation.

Although each objective is considered separately in this chapter, the reader should bear in mind that no single objective could ever be achieved through government policy without at the same time the other objectives being affected in some way. Consider now the five policy objectives in turn.

High level of employment

Unemployment is often extremely demoralising to the unemployed, can result in poverty or even starvation and means that the economy as a whole is producing less than its potential output. Unfortunately, unemployment has been a recurring feature of western industrial societies and its eradication has become a major policy objective.

The rate of unemployment is found by applying the following formula:

Rate of Unemployment $= U / L \times 100\%$

where U is the number of people registered as unemployed with an official agency and L is the total labour force (that is, the sum of the numbers employed, self-employed and unemployed). Unemployment figures are not entirely reliable because of problems of measurement – for example, many people who are not registered as unemployed may actually be seeking jobs, particularly those married women in the United Kingdom who are not eligible for unemployment benefit.

Table 1 shows the average rates of unemployment, the actual numbers unemployed and the numbers of vacancies in the United Kingdom for the years 1972–80. It is clear from the table that unemployment does not remain a constant proportion of the labour force – instead, it fluctuates from one year to the next. At times, the number of unemployed and the number of vacancies are close; at other times, there is an enormous gap between them. In the Great Depression of the early 1930s, the rate of unemployment went over 30 per cent in the United States and rose to over 25 per cent in the United Kingdom, extremely high rates of unemployment which created a great deal of misery and poverty. It was just after this depression that the famous economist John Maynard Keynes (in his book *The General Theory of Employment, Interest and Money,* 1936) argued that unemployment may be caused involuntarily by a general deficiency of aggregate demand. We turn now to a discussion of the main *types of unemployment* under two headings: 'natural' unemployment and demand-deficient unemployment.

Table 1. Unemployment and vacancy statistics for the United Kingdom 1972–79.

Year	Rate of unemployment (%)	Number of unemployed (000s)	Number of vacancies (000s)
1972	3.7	854.9	147.3
1973	2.6	611.0	307.0
1974	2.6	599.7	301.6
1975	3.9	929.1	148.1
1976	5.3	1,269.5	119.7
1977	5.7	1,378.0	155.8
1978	5.7	1,376.5	210.4
1979	5.4	1,304.0	241.6
1980	6.8	1,645.8	143.0

Source: Economic Trends, Feb. 1980.

'Natural' unemployment 'Natural' unemployment may be defined as that which exists even when the overall demand for labour in the economy is equal to its supply at the prevailing level of real wages. In other words, it is that unemployment which exists when the labour market is in equilibrium. Such unemployment persists because of *frictions* in the economy which prevent some of the suppliers of labour from taking up the available jobs. 'Natural' unemployment is illustrated in Fig. 1 where DD is the demand curve for labour and SS is the supply curve of labour. The curve EE shows the actual numbers employed at different wage rates and, because of frictions in the economy, always falls short of the demand for and supply of labour. At the real wage Ow_1, the demand for and supply of labour are just equal at OL, but actual employment is only OA. The number of people unemployed and the number of job vacancies available are equal to AL. This is 'natural' unemployment and its size depends on *structural* and *institutional* factors in the economy. Consider the following categories of unemployment, all of which can be described as 'natural' in the sense that they can exist when the demand for and supply of labour are equal.

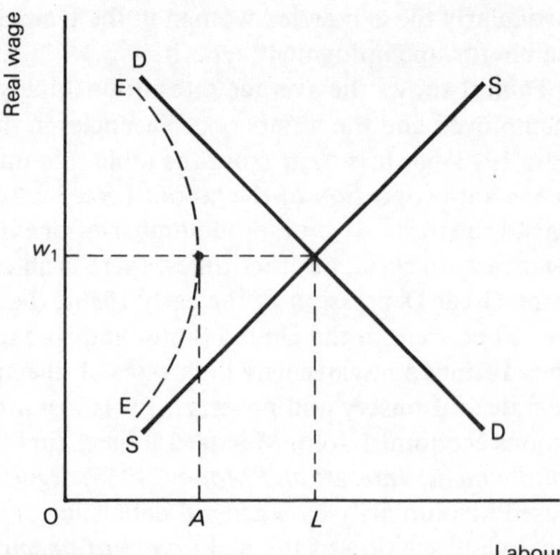

Fig. 1. The labour market and the 'natural' level of unemployment.

(a) *Frictional unemployment.* This occurs when the unemployed are in different geographical locations from the available vacancies or are skilled in different occupations from those being demanded. It persists because of the geographical and occupational immobility of labour. Reasons for such immobility include the high cost of moving or retraining, unwillingness to leave relations and friends and prejudice against new areas. Generally, older people tend to be less mobile than younger ones.

(b) *Structural unemployment.* This is a severe form of frictional unemployment which results from a long-term change in the structure of a country's industries. For example, in the United Kingdom, the decline of the ship-building and textile industries has created localised structural unemployment (or regional unemployment) in the north-west and north-east of England and in parts of Scotland. Again, such unemployment persists because of the immobility of factors of production.

(c) *Seasonal unemployment.* This is common in industries like building and tourism where demand for workers is high in certain weather conditions or at certain times of the year, but is low at other times.

(d) *Transitional unemployment.* Some unemployment must always exist because of people changing their jobs. The job search for an individual may take a few days or a few weeks depending on the availability of information about local vacancies.

(e) *Residual unemployment.* This includes those people with physical and mental disabilities who consequently have a very limited choice of jobs open to them.

To reduce these types of unemployment requires changes in the structure of industry or in the institutional framework of the economy. For example, the following policies may be helpful: improvement of information services provided by employment offices; setting up of retraining schemes and provision of financial help for those prepared to move to high-employment areas; giving grants or tax concessions to firms who locate in depressed areas. Such policies, however, will not help to reduce the second main type of unemployment – demand-deficient unemployment – to which we now turn our attention.

Demand-deficient unemployment This is that unemployment which exists when the general level of demand in the economy is not sufficient to enable everyone who is seeking work to be employed. Although it is possible that certain industries will suffer more than others, no sector of the economy is safe from demand-deficient unemployment. It is a general form of unemployment and policies to reduce it must be policies which influence the economy as a whole – that is, policies which will in some way expand the level of aggregate demand for all goods and services.

Demand-deficient unemployment is often associated with the depression phase of the trade cycle. A typical trade cycle is illustrated in Fig. 2. It is in the depression or slump that aggregate demand is at a low level, so low in fact that firms find their inventories of unsold goods rising to unsatisfactorily high levels and eventually lay off workers so that unemployment is created. We see in the next chapter that 'classical' economists denied the existence of such unemployment, believing that, given competition, 'full' employment would always be assured. It was Keynes in 1936 who argued that demand-deficient unemployment was a severe problem which governments should seek to remedy. Indeed, despite 'neo-classical' challenges, Keynesian economics was the basis of most governments' employment policies for many years after the Second World War.

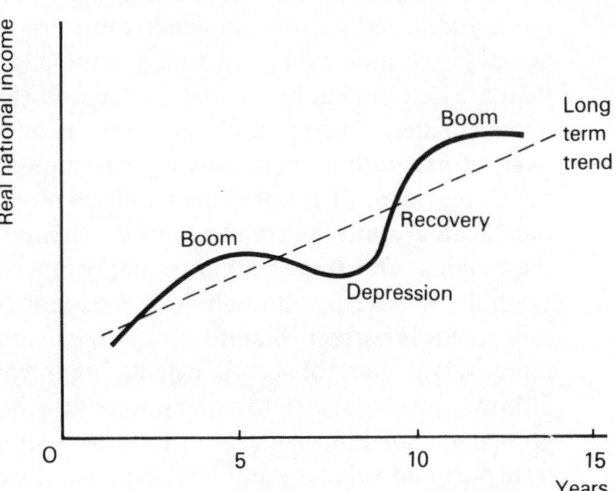

Fig. 2. A typical trade cycle of the nineteenth century.

Finally, how can we distinguish between 'natural' and demand-deficient unemployment? One way would be to say that where the number of vacancies is equal to the number of unemployed, then all unemployment is 'natural' because at that point the demand for labour is just equal to the supply of labour. Where the number of unemployed exceeds the number of vacancies, some demand-deficient unemployment must also exist. In principle, this may be a satisfactory means of distinguishing between them. In practice, there are measurement problems: we have already mentioned some of the problems associated with the unemployment figures; the 'number of vacancies' figure is even more likely to be unreliable since not all vacancies are notified to the Department of Employment; consequently, the official figure probably underestimates the true number of jobs available.

Stable prices

In this section, we are concerned with the policy objective of maintaining a low rate of inflation. But what is inflation and how is the rate of inflation measured? Inflation has to be carefully defined. It is not simply 'rising prices' for as the prices of some goods rise, others may fall, leaving the general level of prices unchanged. Nor should inflation be defined simply as 'an increase in the general price level' for an increase one month may be offset by a decrease the next. For inflation to be taking place, it is necessary that the general price level be rising continuously over a fairly long period of time (for example, several months or a year). In this book, we define inflation as *a persistent tendency for the general price level to rise.*

The next question is: which measure of the general price level should be used to calculate the rate of inflation? The general price level can be estimated in different ways: in the United Kingdom, for example, there are wholesale price indices and a retail price index. The retail price index is undoubtedly the most commonly quoted and in this book we define the *rate* of inflation as *the percentage increase in the retail price index over a period of one year.*

Consider now how the United Kingdom Retail Price Index is calculated. The Index is a measure of the changes in the average price of a basket of those goods and services on which most households spend their income. The actual goods and services included in the basket and the weights given to each item are determined by the Family Expenditure Survey in which approximately 7,000 households a year provide a record of their spending over a fortnightly period. Having determined the composition of the basket, the Department of Employment collects monthly price quotations from retail outlets all around the country and a *weighted* average of these is calculated, the weights reflecting the relative importance of the items in the basket. For example, the average household spends more on food than it does on tobacco: it is correct, therefore, that the average price of food should have more weight than tobacco in calculating the overall average price level. Table 2 shows the actual weights which were attached to the major expenditure groups included in the index in 1977. As can be seen from the Table, food, transport and vehicles, and housing have the biggest weights. Finally, the average is expressed, not in pounds and pence, but as an index showing the percentage changes in prices from a selected reference base (which at present is January 1974). The price of the basket is set equal to 100 in the base period and the current index (say, 140) indicates the change in prices since that period (that is, 40 per cent). The index can also be used to estimate the percentage change in prices between any two months.

We see in greater detail in Chapter 27 that a high rate of inflation can have some adverse effects on an economy; in particular: (a) some individuals and groups in society who have fixed or only slowly rising incomes will suffer at

Table 2. Group weights used in the Retail Price Index in 1977.

Groups	Weights
Food	247
Alcohol	83
Tobacco	46
Housing	112
Fuel and light	58
Durable household goods	63
Clothing and footwear	82
Transport and vehicles	139
Miscellaneous goods	71
Services	54
Meals out	45
	1000

the expense of those who can gain full compensatory wage increases; and (b) the international competitiveness of the country's exports will be reduced leading to exchange rate or balance of payments problems. Reducing the rate of inflation to a tolerable level, then, has been a major policy objective of governments. Note that by 'stable prices', we do not normally mean a zero rate of inflation – prices tend to be inflexible downwards so that for the price mechanism to work effectively, the prices of goods and services have to rise at different rates, resulting in an overall positive rate of inflation. A desirable rate of inflation is one at which the price mechanism works effectively and at which the costs of inflation are minimised.

Balance of payments equilibrium

Before discussing why governments seek to achieve a balance of payments equilibrium, or in many cases a small surplus, we should first define the balance of payments, show its components in general terms and outline a set of United Kingdom accounts.

Definition: ***The balance of payments is the set of accounts which shows all the economic transactions which take place between the residents of one country and the residents of all other countries during a given time period, usually one year.***

In general terms, a country's balance of payments can be described under two main headings: the current account and the capital account.

The current account This account includes both 'visible' and 'invisible' items. The 'visible' imports and exports consist of physical merchandise of all kinds, whereas the 'invisible' imports and exports are mainly services and come under the following major headings: net income from services rendered by residents to non-residents (this includes tourism, shipping and various financial services like insurance and banking); the balance of gifts and the transfer of migrants' funds; net grants by the government to other countries; interest, profits and dividends. All inflows of money, which result from 'visible' and 'invisible' *exports*, are recorded as *credit* items in the accounts.

All outflows of money, which result from 'visible' and 'invisible' *imports*, are recorded as *debit* items in the accounts. It follows that an excess of imports over exports will give rise to a current account *deficit* and an excess of exports over imports will give rise to a current account *surplus.*

The capital account This account includes both long-term and short-term capital movements between the home country and all other countries. The long-term capital movements include *direct investments* (which involve the actual setting up and controlling of an enterprise in a foreign country), *portfolio investments* (which involve the purchasing of the securities of a foreign company or government) and *inter-governmental loans.* The short-term capital movements include all forms of short-term private lending and short-term investments many of which are designed to exploit international interest rate differentials.

The capital account also includes the *official financing* required to cover any overall deficit or surplus in the rest of the accounts. The official financing transactions include 'net changes in the country's reserves', net transactions with the International Monetary Fund (IMF) and other monetary authorities and 'foreign currency borrowing'. Since the 'official financing' transactions are included in the accounts, it must be true that the balance of payments will always balance in an accounting sense. However, this does not mean that the balance of payments is always in equilibrium. If we describe the 'official financing' items as *accommodating* (because they are in existence only because of a deficit or surplus in the rest of the accounts) and all other current and capital account items as *autonomous* (because they occur independently of other items in the accounts), then we can define a deficit and surplus on the balance of payments in the following ways:

Definition: ***A deficit exists when the value of autonomous debit items exceeds the value of autonomous credit items.***

Definition: ***A surplus exists when the value of autonomous credit items exceeds the value of autonomous debit items.***

Unfortunately, it is not always easy to decide whether a particular item is autonomous or accommodating. For example, if a deficit country decides to raise domestic interest rates to attract capital inflows, are these short-term

Table 3. Summary balance of payments for the United Kingdom 1978.

		£ million
Current account	+	1,032
Investment and other capital transactions	–	2,931
Balancing item	+	773
Balance for official financing	–	1,126
Official financing:		
Net transactions with overseas monetary authorities	–	1,016
Net foreign currency borrowing	–	187
Official reserves (drawings on +, additions to –)	+	2,329
		1,126

capital movements autonomous or accommodating?

Now consider Table 3 which shows the summary balance of payments accounts for the United Kingdom in 1978. Notice that there is a current account surplus of £1,032 million and a deficit on the 'investment and other capital transactions' account of £2,931 million. The 'balancing item' is the net total of errors and omissions and accounts for the difference between the official financing balance and the overall balance on the current and investment accounts. There was an overall deficit on the United Kingdom Balance of Payments in 1978 of £1,126 million and this resulted in large drawings on the country's official reserves.

Why is a deficit undesirable?

A country with a deficit is experiencing a net outflow of currency. To finance deficits, countries maintain reserves of foreign currencies and are also able to borrow from the IMF or from other countries. Given these sources of finance, short-term deficits are not serious – any loss of reserves one year, for example, can be made up by surpluses in future years. Reserves are not infinite, however, and no country can go on borrowing from other countries or from the IMF indefinitely. A country with a persistent deficit (that is, one lasting for several years) will eventually have to adopt some policy to restore equilibrium. Such a policy might be one of reducing aggregate demand at home (and possibly creating some unemployment) or of changing the exchange rate. These policies, as well as the arguments for and against fixed and flexible exchange rate systems, are discussed in Chapter 28.

Finally, note that a large surplus is not particularly desirable either. A surplus means that the country's reserves are being increased, but at the same time, this may mean that the country is selling overseas a greater value of goods and services than it is receiving in imports. In other words, the country is actually consuming a smaller value of goods and services than it is producing. The standard of living, therefore, may be lower than it would be if the country had a balance of payments equilibrium.

A high rate of economic growth

Reconsider the illustration of a typical trade cycle in Fig. 2. At times, real national income is rising and at other times, it is falling. The overall long-term trend, though, is one of rising real national income and this is what is meant by economic growth. It is important to remember that economic growth is a long-run concept and occurs because of an overall expansion of the economy's productive capacity. Economic growth can be illustrated as an outward shift in the production possibility frontier. A growing economy is able, through an expansion of its factors of production or because of technological progress, to produce bigger and bigger combinations of goods and services. This is shown in Fig. 3 where AB is a country's production possibility frontier before growth and A′B′ is the production possibility frontier after economic growth has occurred.

Definition: ***Economic growth is equivalent to an increase in an economy's productive capacity and is measured as a percentage rise in annual real***

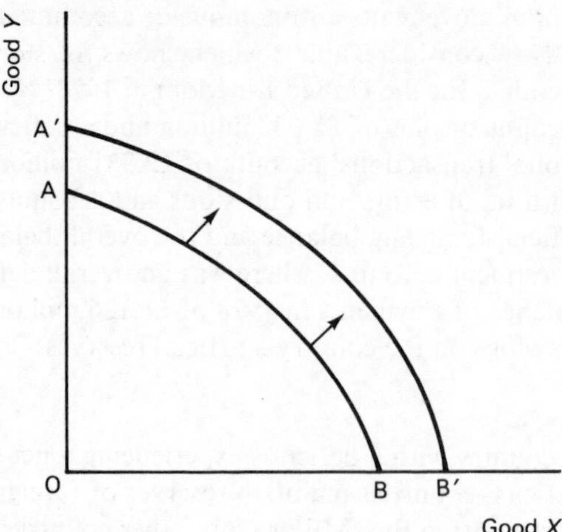

Fig. 3. A shifting production possibility frontier.

national income, averaged out over a period of years so as to eliminate cyclical variations.

Now consider the following reasons why most governments have a high rate of economic growth as a major objective:

(a) *It leads to an increased standard of living.* So long as economic growth results in a rising real income *per head,* then this should mean that a greater quantity or better quality (or both) of goods and services is made available for each person to consume. Recall from the last chapter, however, that this may not result in an actual improvement in economic welfare – it may only be a potential or pseudo improvement.

(b) *It can eliminate poverty.* The view that economic growth enables economies to eliminate poverty is debatable and depends upon whether poverty is a relative or absolute term. If it is a relative term, then it will always exist (given a constant distribution of income and wealth) whether economic growth occurs or not. For example, if everyone enjoys a 10 per cent rise in income, the poor remain in exactly the same relative position as before and so are still poor. It should be noted that the poor (who are often pensioners and the unemployed) depend for their incomes on what the government gives them and so are the least likely members of society to benefit directly from economic growth.

(c) *It can redistribute income without making anyone worse off.* It must be emphasised that economic growth itself does not necessarily improve the distribution of income. However, it is possible, when economic growth is taking place, to change the distribution of income in an attempt to achieve greater equity without having to make anyone worse off in absolute terms.

Economic growth also imposes some costs on society which has made some modern economists doubtful as to its continued desirability. Consider the following:

(a) *Growth involves change which benefits many but may harm some.* For example, technological progress may create many new jobs but at the same time may make current jobs obsolete and therefore lead to some redundancies. The need to move to another area or to retrain in order to take up a new job imposes significant costs on those affected.

(b) *Growth has an opportunity cost.* Where economic growth is created by investment of resources in capital goods, the opportunity cost of growth is the current consumption which could otherwise have been enjoyed. The more resources a country devotes to the production of investment goods, the faster the rate of economic growth it can expect to attain and the greater the quantity of consumer goods it can expect to enjoy in the future. So, in effect, current consumption is being sacrificed in order to achieve a higher rate of consumption in the future. Whether or not the sacrifice is worthwhile depends on the amount of extra consumer goods produced in the future and how long it takes to make up for the sacrificed goods.

(c) *Continued growth may not be possible for much longer.* Resources on the Earth are finite and largely irreplaceable. It is argued that at some critical date in the future, economic growth must cease. No matter what new discoveries are made, resources must eventually run out and so the greater the rate of economic growth today, the sooner that critical date will be reached. It is possible, therefore, to argue in favour of a reduced rate of economic growth because this will reduce the rate at which our resources are being used up.

(d) *Growth causes negative externalities.* As pointed out in the previous chapter, a rising real national income may impose costs on society in the form of pollution, noise and increased congestion. If these costs could be properly evaluated and included in the estimates of real national income, present estimates would be shown to overstate the benefits of economic growth.

Most governments aim for a high rate of economic growth because of the higher standard of living which they expect it to create in their countries and possibly also because of their desire for national prestige. As economists, however, we must bear in mind that growth can impose costs as well as benefits on society and these must be taken into consideration in evaluating the desirability of growth.

An equitable distribution of income and wealth

This may be regarded as both a micro- and macroeconomic policy objective. In the first half of the book, we discussed equity at some length and showed how subsidies and progressive taxes might be used to create a more equitable distribution pattern. The use of such microeconomic policies will, of course, impose a constraint on the macroeconomic policy-maker who may, for example, want to reduce the overall level of taxation to combat unemployment. If progressive taxes are reduced, the gap between rich and poor will be widened, whereas if regressive taxes are reduced, the gap will be narrowed. So the equity objective cannot be ignored in macroeconomic policy making.

Earlier in this chapter, we described structural unemployment and pointed out that this may be localised and so lead to regional unemployment. A country which has some areas of high employment and others of high unemployment will be suffering from an unequal *spatial* distribution of income and wealth. So balanced regional development is another macroeconomic policy objective which modern governments strive to achieve.

The problem of economic inequality and a discussion of the possible ways in which the distribution of income and wealth may be measured statistically are topics dealt with in Chapter 30.

Conclusion

We have seen in this and the last chapter that macroeconomics is concerned with: (a) determining the broad aggregates in the economy, particularly the level of real national income and employment; and (b) devising appropriate policies to meet the employment, inflation, balance of payments, growth and distribution objectives. In the next seven chapters, we are concerned with basic macroeconomic theory which deals with the determination of economic aggregates, and in the remaining five chapters, we deal in greater detail with the major macroeconomic policy issues.

Further reading

Black, J., *The Economics of Modern Britain*, Martin Robertson, Oxford, 1979 (Ch. 3, 18, 24).

Brooman, F.S., *Macroeconomics*, Allen and Unwin, London, 1977 (Ch. 4).

Prest, A.R. and **Coppock, D.J.,** *The UK Economy: A Manual of Applied Economics*, Weidenfeld and Nicolson, London, 1978 (Ch. 1 and 3).

Mishan, E.J., *The Economic Growth Debate: An Assessment*, Allen and Unwin, London, 1977.

Exercises

1. Review your understanding of the following terms:

policy conflicts
rate of unemployment
'natural' unemployment
frictional unemployment
structural unemployment
seasonal unemployment
transitional unemployment
residual unemployment
demand-deficient unemployment
price index
rate of inflation
balance of payments
accommodating transactions
autonomous transactions
rate of economic growth

2. Using the figures from Table 4: (a) calculate GDP at factor cost in 1975 prices; and (b) compare time-series graphs for unemployment and real GDP for the period 1969–79.

3. 'Full employment is achieved when the number of people unemployed is equal to the number of job vacancies.' Discuss.

Table 4. GDP at factor cost, retail prices and unemployment in the United Kingdom, 1969–79.

Year	Gross domestic product at factor cost (£m.)	Retail Price Index (1975 = 100)	Unemployment (excl. school-leavers) (000s)
1969	39,579	51.0	566.3
1970	43,466	54.2	602.0
1971	49,351	59.3	775.8
1972	55,101	63.6	854.9
1973	63,941	69.4	611.0
1974	73,953	80.5	599.7
1975	93,592	100.0	929.1
1976	110,087	116.5	1,269.3
1977	124,528	135.0	1,376.8
1978	141,606	146.2	1,376.2
1979	159,090	165.8	1,303.4

Source: Economic Trends, 1978–80.

4. Discuss the problems of distinguishing between accommodating and autonomous transactions on the balance of payments. What policy conflicts might arise in trying to eliminate a balance of payments deficit?

5. 'The current world energy crisis is a result of the high rate of economic growth in the postwar years.' Discuss.

6. Is a high rate of economic growth necessarily desirable?

Macroeconomic theory

19 National income and employment

Introduction

In this chapter, we are concerned with the very important question of what determines the level of national income and the level of employment in an economy. We start with a brief summary of the 'classical' economics which J.M. Keynes attacked in his book, *The General Theory of Employment, Interest and Money* in 1936. Secondly, we outline what has become known as the Keynesian theory of national income determination. Thirdly, we develop two extensions of the Keynesian model: the multiplier and gap analysis. Finally, we point out the main limitations of the theory and briefly introduce the more recent 'neo-classical' resurgence in the shape of 'monetarism'.

The classical theory of full employment

A basic result of classical economics was that, given flexible wages and prices, a competitive market economy would operate at full employment. That is, economic forces would always be generated to ensure that the demand for labour would always equal its supply.

The equilibrium levels of income and employment were believed to be determined largely in the labour market. The demand curve for labour shows the relationship between the real wage (equal to the value of the marginal product of labour in a competitive economy) and the demand for labour by employers. This relationship is indirect: the lower the real wage, the more workers employers will want to employ. The supply curve of labour shows the relationship between the real wage and households' supply of labour and this is a direct relationship: the higher the real wage, the greater the supply of labour.

Now consider Fig. 1, where the upper graph shows the aggregate labour market in equilibrium at a real wage of $0W_1$ and a level of employment equal to $0L_1$. The lower graph shows the total output that is produced when different quantities of labour are employed (it illustrates, in fact, the short-run production function). With $0L_1$ units of labour employed, output in the economy will be $0Q_1$. The classical economists called the equilibrium level of employment the 'full employment' level. According to them, any unemployment which existed at the wage rate $0W_1$ must be due to frictions or restrictive practices in the economy or must be voluntary.

Suppose, then, that the wage rate is flexible and that the economy is sufficiently competitive to ensure that labour market equilibrium is achieved. Can we be certain that aggregate demand will be sufficient to take up the $0Q_1$ units of output produced? The classical economists answered yes – whatever the full employment level of output, the income created in producing it will necessarily lead to spending which will be just sufficient to purchase the

Fig. 1. The labour market and short-run production function.

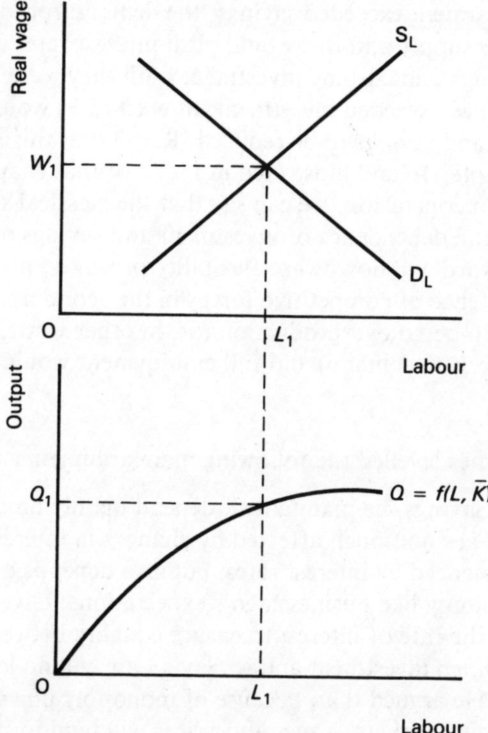

goods produced. In other words, *the supply of goods and services creates its own demand* and there can be no overproduction. This became known as *Say's Law*, named after the French economist Jean Baptiste Say (1767–1832).

To illustrate Say's Law, consider Fig. 2 which shows a simplified version of the circular flow of income diagram. It is simplified mainly by the omission of government and foreign trade activities. Households receive income equal to the value of goods and services produced; part of this income they spend and part they save. Consumption demand, then, falls short of the total value of production by the amount of savings. This shortfall is made up by investment demand and so long as investment and savings are equal, aggregate demand (which in this simple model is consumption plus investment) will necessarily equal the total value of production. The classical economists argued that, given a flexible rate of interest and a competitive market for loanable funds, savings and investment would always be made equal by changes in interest rates. For example, if

Fig. 2. A simplified flow diagram of an economy.

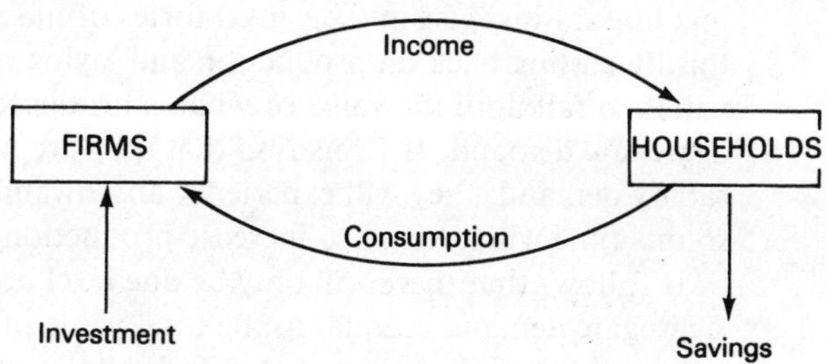

investment exceeded savings, the demand for loanable funds would exceed their supply and this would push interest rates upwards, bringing forth more savings and curbing investment until they were equal again. Similarly, if savings exceeded investment, interest rates would fall, causing investment to rise and savings to be reduced. Recall that this mechanism was discussed in Chapter 16 and illustrated in Fig. 4 of that chapter.

In conclusion, we can say that the classical system depends crucially upon: (a) the dependence of investment and savings on the rate of interest; (b) the upward and downward flexibility of wages, prices and interest rates; (c) the existence of competitive forces in the economy. Given these conditions, there could be no overproduction (or, in other words, no general deficiency of aggregate demand) and full employment would be assured.

Keynes' attack on the classical theory

Keynes levelled the following main arguments against the classical theory.

(a) Savings, he maintained, depend mainly on the level of national income and are not much affected by changes in interest rates. Investment may be influenced by interest rates, but also depends on more volatile factors in the economy like businessmen's expectations. Given this, it is no longer possible for the rate of interest to ensure equality between *planned* savings and *planned* investment and so Say's Law will no longer hold.
(b) He argued that, because of monopoly power in both the goods and labour markets, wages and prices will tend to be inflexible, at least in the short-run and particularly in the downward direction. This means that in a situation where savings exceed investment, so that aggregate demand is less than the total value of production, firms will reduce output and lay off workers. It is in this way that demand-deficient unemployment is created.
(c) He argued that even if wages and prices were flexible, aggregate demand would not necessarily be sufficient to ensure full employment. This has been the subject of much debate and controversy, however, and we consider it in Chapter 23.

The Keynesian theory of employment

The main result of the Keynesian theory is that the level of real national income and therefore employment is determined largely by the level of aggregate demand. This is, of course, very different from the classical model where 'supply created its own demand': in the Keynesian model, it is demand which determines how much is supplied. The argument is that if firms find that they are producing more than is being demanded, they will observe an involuntary increase in their inventories of unsold goods and so will rectify this by cutting back on production and laying off workers. National income will then fall until the value of what is produced is equal to the value of aggregate demand. If firms find that they are not producing enough to satisfy demand, they will experience an unwanted fall in their inventories and so this time will attempt to increase production and hire more workers.

It follows that there will only be one level of national income at which aggregate demand is equal to the total value of production. This is called the *equilibrium level of income*. An important point to remember is that in the

Keynesian model, the equilibrium level of income is not necessarily the same as the full employment level of income. This is the reason Keynes called his theory a *general* theory – he regarded the classical theory as no more than the 'special case' where the equilibrium and full employment levels of income coincided.

Determination of the equilibrium level of income

In order to set out the Keynesian theory more formally, we must first make a number of assumptions. The following assumptions are intended to conform with the Keynesian view of the economy and to simplify the analysis in such a way that enables us to make useful predictions. Notice in particular that we set out the Keynesian theory more generally than we did the classical theory where we assumed no government and no foreign trade. The reason is that we want to deal with the Keynesian model in greater detail and derive policy implications from it.

Assumption 1: *Wages and prices are fixed.* The model is a short-run model and this assumption means that, in the short-run, producers will respond to changes in demand by changing the quantity they produce rather than price. This implies that the economy is at less than full employment.

Assumption 2: *We ignore the money market.* For now, we concentrate on the real sector of the economy (that is, the markets for goods and services and for labour). We consider the impact of money and the rate of interest in Chapters 21–23.

Assumption 3: *Consumption (C) and savings (S) are both directly related to income (Y).* For simplicity, we assume that both relationships are linear and so can be drawn as straight lines as in Fig. 3. The consumption line C represents the relationship between the consumption of home-produced goods and income. Notice that the slope of the consumption line measures the increase in consumption brought about by a one pound increase in income – this is called the *marginal propensity to consume* (mpc). Similarly, the slope of the savings line measures the increase in savings brought about by a one pound increase in income – this is called the *marginal propensity to save* (mps).

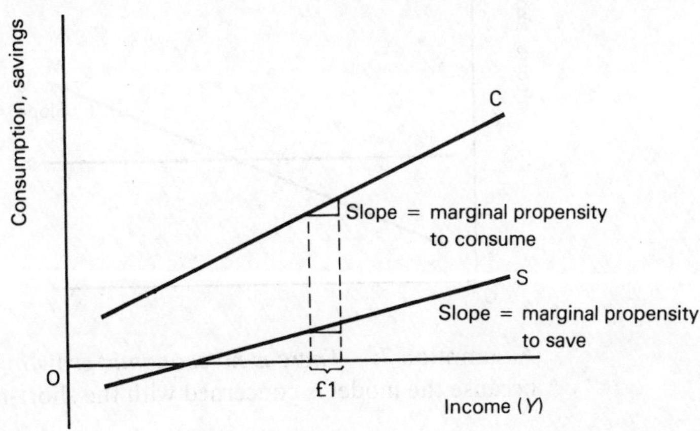

Fig. 3. Consumption and savings.

Assumption 4: *Investment (I) and government spending (G) are autonomous.* This means that they are both independent of income changes. Government spending is determined by government policy and investment depends to some extent on the rate of interest (which for now does not appear in the model) and businessmen's expectations. Plotted against income on a graph, therefore, they would simply be represented by horizontal straight lines, as shown in Fig. 4.

Fig. 4. Autonomous government spending and investment.

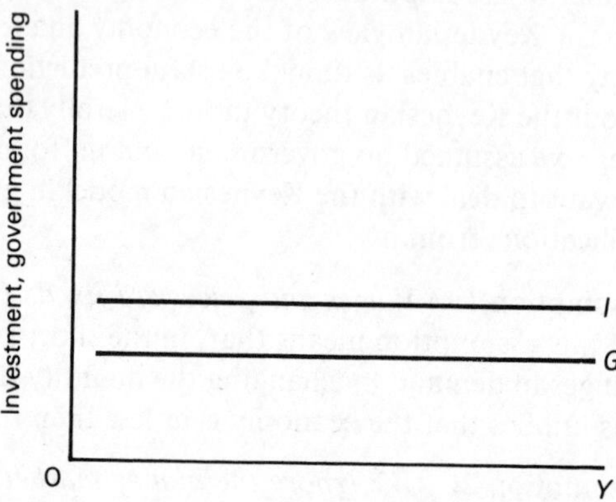

Assumption 5: *Taxation (T) is in the form of lump-sum taxes only.* This is a purely simplifying assumption: it enables us to see the role played by taxes in the model, but at the same time the analysis is kept simple.

Assumption 6: *Exports (X) are autonomous, but imports (M) depend directly on income.* Exports depend on such factors as incomes in other countries and the rate of exchange (which for now we assume fixed). The demand for imports, though, will be directly and, for simplicity, linearly related to income. These relationships are shown in Fig. 5. Notice that the slope of the import line is called the *marginal propensity to import* (mpm), this is the fraction of extra income spent on imports.

Fig. 5. Imports and exports.

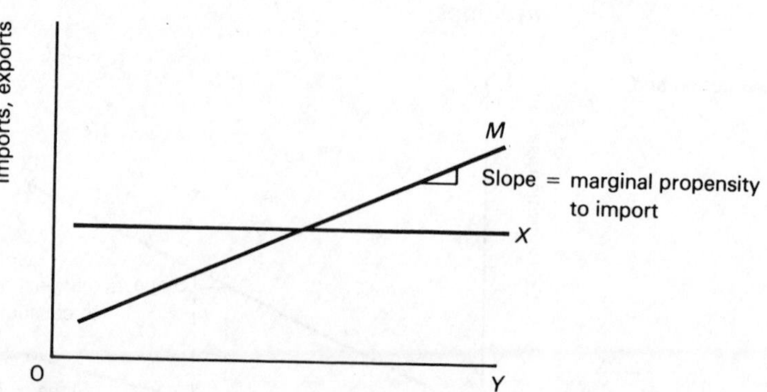

Assumption 7: *There is no economic growth.* This assumption is reasonable because the model is concerned with the short-run only. We extend the model

into the long-run and take account of economic growth in Chapter 25 where we deal with the Harrod-Domar growth model.

For equilibrium, we require that the aggregate demand for the economy's goods and services should be just equal to the total value of goods and services produced. As we saw in Chapter 17, aggregate demand consists of the consumption of home-produced goods, investment, government spending and exports (that is, $AD = C + I + G + X$). The total value of goods and services produced is measured by the national income (Y). The income received is either spent on home-produced goods, or withdrawn in the form of savings, taxes and spending on imports (that is, $Y = C + S + T + M$). So, as a condition for equilibrium, we can write:

$$AD = Y$$

$$C + I + G + X = C + S + T + M$$

$$\underline{I + G + X = S + T + M}$$

Investment, government spending and exports are sometimes called *injections* (J) into the flow of income, while savings, taxes and imports are sometimes called *withdrawals* (W) from that flow. Thus, the condition for equilibrium could be written more simply as:

$$\underline{J = W}$$

We have assumed that all the injections (I, G and X) are autonomous. This means that total injections will also be autonomous so that when plotted against income on a graph, we have a horizontal straight line. Of the withdrawals, we have assumed that savings and imports are both directly related to income but that taxes are lump-sum taxes. This means that total withdrawals will be directly related to income and when plotted against income on a graph will be an upward sloping line with a slope equal to the sum of the marginal propensity to save and the marginal propensity to import.

To illustrate these results, consider a simple numerical example. Table 1 gives hypothetical figures for consumption, savings, taxes, imports, investment, government spending and exports at different levels of national income for a simple economy. All the relationships conform to the

Table 1. Hypothetical statistics for a simple economy.

		Withdrawals			Injections					
Y	C	S	T	M	I	G	X	Total injections	Total withdrawals	Aggregate demand
10	7	0	2	1	8	4	3	15	3	22
20	13	2	2	3	8	4	3	15	7	28
30	19	4	2	5	8	4	3	15	11	34
40	25	6	2	7	8	4	3	15	15	40
50	31	8	2	9	8	4	3	15	19	46
60	37	10	2	11	8	4	3	15	23	52

assumptions we have already made. Note that the marginal propensity to consume is 0.6 (because for every £10 million rise in income, consumption rises by £6 million); the marginal propensity to save is 0.2 and the marginal propensity to import is also 0.2. The total injections, total withdrawals and aggregate demand lines for this economy are drawn together with a 45° line in Fig. 6. The 45° line joins together all those points which are equidistant from the two axes. The graph shows that there are two ways of identifying the equilibrium level of income: (a) *where aggregate demand is equal to national income* (that is, where the *AD* line cuts the 45° line); (b) *where total injections equal total withdrawals.* The equilibrium level of income (Y_e) in the example, then, is £40 million. At this level of national income, and only at this level, aggregate demand in the economy is just equal to the total value of goods and services produced. This can also be seen from Table 1: when *Y* equals £40 million, *J* and *W* are equal at £15 million, and *AD* equals *Y*.

This equilibrium can also be described as a *stable* one because at any other income level, economic forces will be generated to push the economy back towards the equilibrium position. For example, suppose that the prevailing level of income were £50 million: as can be seen from Table 1, this would mean that £50 million worth of goods and services were being produced when aggregate demand was only £46 million. Firms would find their inventories involuntarily building up and so would cut back production thereby reducing national income. Similarly, if income were £30 million, aggregate demand would be £34 million and so would exceed the total value of production, inventories would be run down causing firms to attempt to step up production and so increase national income. Note that the ability of firms to

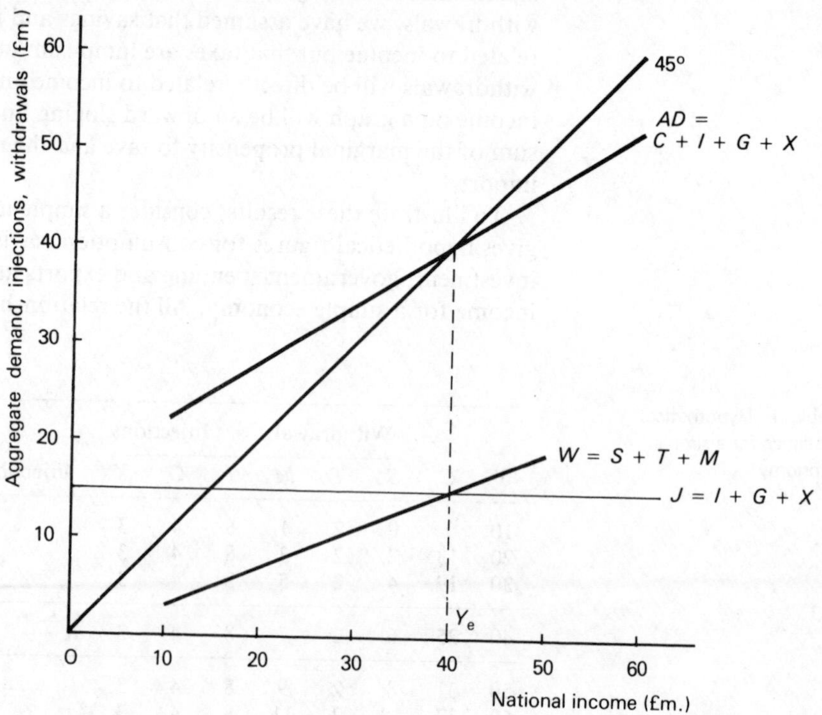

Fig. 6. Determination of the equilibrium level of income.

expand output in this situation depends upon the existence of unemployed resources in the economy.

The multiplier

We have already indicated that investment depends to some extent on the rate of interest and businessmen's expectations, government spending depends on government policy and exports depend largely on incomes overseas. If any of these should change, there will be an effect on the equilibrium level of income. Similarly, a change in taxation and autonomous changes in consumption, savings and imports will also affect national income.

Consider first the effects of an increase in one of the injections. Suppose that firms increase their investment spending on new machinery by £2 million (that is, from £8 m. to £10 m. in our numerical example). The immediate effect of this increased spending will be to raise national income by the full £2 million because the spending of one group in the economy is necessarily the income of some other group. Increased spending on machinery represents higher incomes for those involved in manufacturing the machines. The process does not end here, however, because the increase in income will bring forth additional consumption spending in the next period. In fact, since we have a marginal propensity to consume of 0.6, consumption will rise by £1.2 million when income rises by £2 million. This rise in consumption will create a further increase in income in the next period of £1.2 million over and above the initial increase and this in turn will bring forth more consumption spending. This process will continue with both consumption and income rising, but with the actual increases becoming smaller and smaller over time until eventually they become insignificant. The first few stages of this process are summarised in Table 2, where the subscripts refer to time periods.

Table 2. The first few stages of the multiplier process.

Initial increase in I, ΔI	$=$ £2 m.	Increase in Y in period 1, ΔY_1	$=$ £2 m.
ΔC_1	$=$ £1.2 m.	ΔY_2	$=$ £1.2 m.
ΔC_2	$=$ £0.72 m.	ΔY_3	$=$ £0.72 m.
ΔC_3	$=$ £432,000	ΔY_4	$=$ £432,000
ΔC_4	$=$ £259,000	ΔY_5	$=$ £259,000
⋮		⋮	

The total increase in national income ($\Delta Y = \Delta Y_1 + \Delta Y_2 + \Delta Y_3 + \ldots.$) will clearly be much bigger than the initial increase in investment spending. To see how much bigger, consider Fig. 7 which shows the movement from the original equilibrium position ($Y_e =$ £40 million) to the new one after the entire process has worked itself out. We can work out the total increase in income by recalling that the slope of the withdrawals line is equal to the sum of the marginal propensities to save and import (given that, in this model, the marginal propensity to tax is zero). As can be seen from Fig. 7, this slope can also be written as $\Delta I / \Delta Y$. It follows that if $\Delta I / \Delta Y =$ mps + mpm, then, by a simple rearrangement, we can write:

Fig. 7. The multiplier effect.

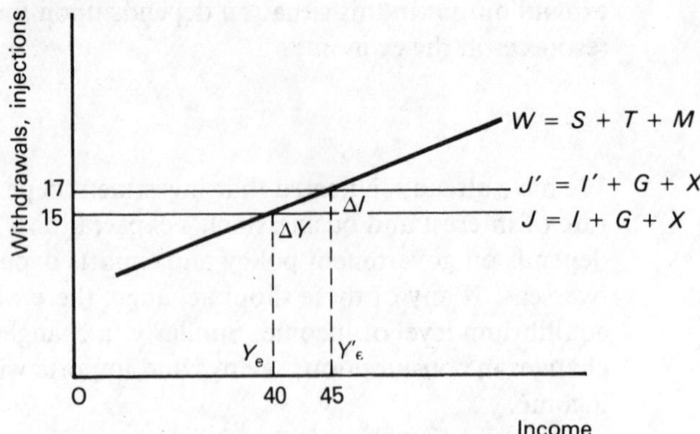

$$\Delta Y = \frac{\Delta I}{\text{mps} + \text{mpm}}$$

Substituting the figures from our example, we have:

$$\Delta Y = \frac{£2\text{ m}}{0.2 + 0.2} = £5\text{ million}$$

In other words, national income rises by £5 million following an increase in investment of only £2 million. This is called the *multiplier effect*, and the multiplier itself is the amount that the change in spending has to be multiplied by to obtain the change in income. That is,

$$\text{Multiplier} = \frac{1}{\text{mps} + \text{mpm}}$$

and this is equal to $2\frac{1}{2}$ in our example.

An important point to remember is that the size of the multiplier depends on the marginal propensities to save and import. The bigger these withdrawals from increases in income, the smaller will be the multiplier. To take an extreme example, if all the additional income received were withdrawn from the circular flow of income, the multiplier would be equal to 1 and the final rise in income would be just equal to the initial rise in spending and no more.

Now note the following important points about the multiplier.

(a) It comes into operation for any *autonomous* change in spending. So autonomous changes in investment, government spending, exports and consumption will all have the same multiplier effect on an economy's national income.

(b) The multiplier, 1 / (mps + mpm), is derived on the assumption that taxes are lump-sum only. If we had an income tax in the model so that some part of any extra income received was taken in taxes by the government, total withdrawals would rise and the multiplier would be smaller. This multiplier is derived algebraically in Appendix I.

(c) The multiplier, 1 / (mps + mpm), ignores foreign repercussions which could be significant for a country with a large foreign trade sector. Consider the effects of an increase in investment in the United Kingdom. As national income rises, some of it is spent on imports and this is equivalent to a rise in other countries' exports. So incomes in other countries rise (also by a multiplier effect) and some of this rise may in turn be spent on United Kingdom exports. As United Kingdom exports increase, there will be a multiplier effect on national income which we have not so far taken into account.

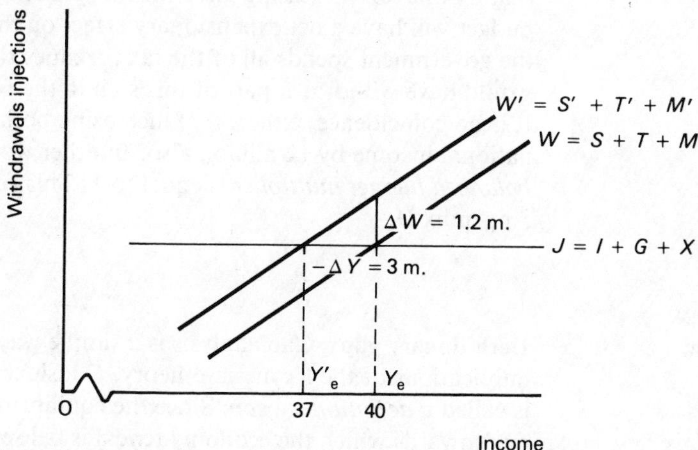

Fig. 8. The multiplier effect of a tax change.

Finally, we must consider the effect on national income of a change in the lump-sum tax (T) on the assumption that consumption, savings and imports depend on disposable income (Y_d) rather than national income (Y): recall that $Y_d \equiv Y - T$. Suppose that the lump-sum tax is raised by £2 million (from £2 m. to £4 m.). What will happen to the withdrawals line? The rise in taxes will reduce disposable income by £2 million so that savings will fall at every level of national income by £ (mps × ΔY_d) or 0.2 × £2 m. = £0.4 million. Similarly, imports will fall at every level of national income by £ (mpm × ΔY_d) which is also equal to £0.4 million. The withdrawals line, then, which is an aggregation of the savings, taxation and import lines, will be pushed upwards by £2 million because of the tax rise and downwards by £0.8 million because of the fall in savings and imports. Overall, it shifts upwards by only £1.2 million, as shown in Fig. 8. Given that $\Delta T = \Delta Y_d$, we can write the change in total withdrawals (ΔW) more generally as:

$$\begin{aligned} \Delta W &= \Delta T - (\text{mps} + \text{mpm})\,\Delta T \\ &= [1 - (\text{mps} + \text{mpm})]\,\Delta T \\ &= \text{mpc}\,\Delta T \end{aligned}$$

Notice from the graph that the slope of the withdrawals line is equal to $\Delta W / -\Delta Y$ = mps + mpm. Rearranging this expression, we have:

$$\Delta Y = \frac{-\Delta W}{\text{mps} + \text{mpm}} = \frac{-1.2}{0.2 + 0.2} = -\text{ £3 million}$$

So raising the lump-sum tax by £2 million will reduce national income by £3 million to £37 million. The general formula for the effect of a change in a lump-sum tax on national income is:

$$Y = \frac{-\text{mpc}\ \Delta T}{\text{mps} + \text{mpm}}$$

Notice that an increase in government spending of £2 million would increase national income by £5 million (via the ordinary multiplier), whereas an increase in lump-sum taxation of £2 million (to finance the government spending, say) would reduce national income by only £3 million. This means that a policy of increasing government spending but maintaining a balanced budget will have a net expansionary effect on the economy. This is because the government spends all of the tax revenues raised, whereas households would have withdrawn part of this sum in the form of savings and imports. It is no coincidence, either, that increasing both G and T by £2 million raises national income by £2 million also. In other words, in this model, the *balanced budget multiplier* is equal to 1. This result is derived algebraically in Appendix II.

Gap analysis

Deflationary gap Gap analysis is a simple way of describing the main policy implications of the Keynesian theory. Consider Fig. 9 which illustrates what is called a *deflationary gap*. Since the equilibrium level of income (Y_e) (the one towards which the economy tends) is below the full employment level of income (Y_f), the economy will be suffering from demand-deficient unemployment. The deflationary gap is the amount by which aggregate demand must be increased to push the equilibrium level of income, via the multiplier, to the full employment level. How can this increase in aggregate demand be achieved? The government has a number of possible policy instruments which it can use for this purpose. Consider the following:

Fig. 9. A deflationary gap.

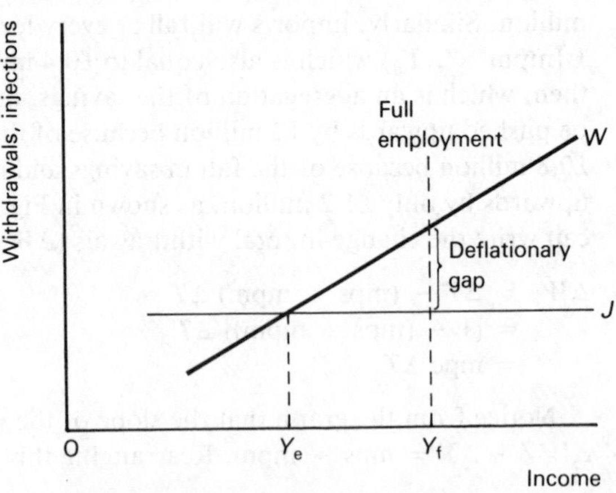

(a) *Increase government spending.* This will raise aggregate demand directly and, by increasing total injections, will have a multiplier effect on income. To achieve full employment in Fig. 9, it is necessary to shift the injections line upwards by the full amount of deflationary gap. If taxes are raised to finance the spending, the policy will still be expansionary and so reduce unemployment so long as the taxes raised do not exceed the increase in government spending by a certain amount.

(b) *Reduce taxes.* This will increase disposable income so that consumption spending will rise at every level of national income. Once again, the multiplier will come into operation and the equilibrium level of income and employment will rise. To achieve full employment in Fig. 9, the withdrawals line must be shifted downwards by the full amount of the deflationary gap. Note that, if the government's budget is balanced to start with, cutting taxes while leaving government spending unchanged means running a budget deficit.

It should be noted that changing the level of government spending and/or taxation is known as *fiscal policy*. In practice, governments can also use monetary policy and exchange rate policy to influence the level of aggregate demand. Monetary policy is considered in Chapters 21–23 and exchange rate policy in Chapter 28.

The major policy implication of the Keynesian theory, then, is that aggregate demand must be increased in order to combat demand-deficient unemployment.

Inflationary gap Now relax the assumption that wages and prices are fixed, and consider Fig. 10 which illustrates an *inflationary gap*. This time the equilibrium level of income is above the full employment level and so cannot actually be attained. The economy will be at the full employment level of output, but excess demand (equal to the inflationary gap) will still exist so that the general price level will be forced upwards. Appropriate fiscal policies to combat this *demand-pull* inflation would be a cut in government spending, or an increase in taxation. The objective this time is to shift down the injections line or to shift up the withdrawals line by the full amount of the inflationary gap.

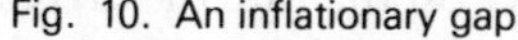
Fig. 10. An inflationary gap.

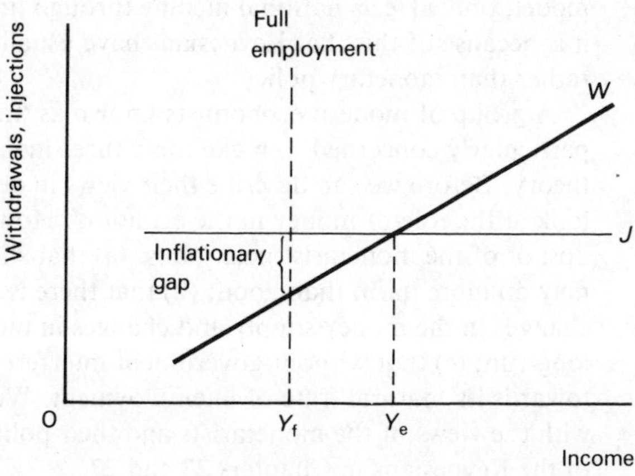

Limitations of the Keynesian theory

After the Second World War, Keynesian demand-management policies were used by the governments of most western countries in the attempt to keep unemployment levels down. Generally, these policies were successful in preventing heavy unemployment like that experienced in the 1930s, but unfortunately they tended to give rise to the phenomenon known as 'stop-go'. That is, in periods of high unemployment, the government would expand aggregate demand: this would reduce the unemployment but at the same time tend to create inflationary pressure so that eventually the government would have to reduce aggregate demand again. Thus, all 'go' periods tended to be followed by 'stop' periods and it became difficult to achieve long-term economic growth. Possibly the main problem is that the Keynesian model is only short-term and in the short-run, it is not always easy to predict the effects of policy changes, and the management of the economy, therefore, may become very erratic.

A second limitation of the Keynesian model as we have outlined it in this chapter is that it fails to take adequately into account the problem of inflation. Indeed, the basic model assumes that wages and prices are fixed and the only time we allowed them to rise was after the attainment of full employment. Experience in the 1970s in particular, though, has shown us that high rates of inflation can co-exist with high rates of unemployment and no explanation of this is provided by the Keynesian theory. Furthermore, the coincidence of inflation and unemployment makes the Keynesian policy recommendations very questionable. For example, if the economy is in the deflationary gap situation illustrated in Fig. 9, but is also suffering from a 15 per cent rate of inflation, an increase in government spending or a cut in taxation designed to combat the unemployment is likely to worsen the rate of inflation. We consider the post-Keynesian and other modern theories of inflation in Chapter 27.

A further criticism which has been levelled at the Keynesian model is that it tends to understate the influence of money on the real variables in the economy. Indeed, the model outlined in this chapter has taken no explicit account of the monetary sector and as such is sometimes called the 'simple' Keynesian model. We discuss the role of money in the Keynesian model in Chapter 23 where we see that a change in the money supply, according to this model, only affects national income through its effect on the rate of interest; it is because of this that Keynesians have usually put more faith in fiscal rather than monetary policy.

A group of modern economists known as 'monetarists' have been particularly concerned to make these three main criticisms of the Keynesian theory. Before we can describe their views in detail, we need to take a closer look at the role of money in the economy. However, we shall see that the upshot of the monetarist position is: (a) that short-term demand management may do more harm than good; (b) that there is a close relationship between changes in the money supply and changes in money national income in the long-run; (c) that without government interference the economy will tend towards its 'natural' rate of unemployment. We are particularly concerned with the views of the monetarists and their policy prescriptions vis-à-vis those of the Keynesians in Chapters 23 and 27.

Conclusion

This chapter has considered some of the major advances in macroeconomic thought in the twentieth century. The ascendency of Keynesian economics, which was reflected in policy making in the 1950s and 1960s, has become increasingly challenged in recent years. The growing disenchantment with Keynesian demand-management among policy-makers was due to its failure to overcome the coexistence of high rates of inflation and high unemployment.

Nevertheless, the way in which modern economists view macroeconomic problems owes much to the Keynesian framework. We turn now to an analysis of the main determinants of consumption and investment, two of the main components of aggregate demand.

Further reading

Brooman, F.S., *Macroeconomics*, Allen and Unwin, London, 1977 (Ch. 6, 8, 9 and Appendix).
Black, J., *The Economics of Modern Britain*, Martin Robertson, Oxford, 1979 (Ch. 4, 6 and 11).
Dornbusch, R. and **Fischer, S.**, *Macroeconomics*, McGraw Hill, New York, 1978 (Ch. 3).
Ackley, G., *Macroeconomics: Theory and Policy*, Collier Macmillan, London, 1978 (Ch. 4–8).

Exercises

1. Review your understanding of the following terms:

Say's Law	injections
loanable funds	withdrawals
equilibrium level of income	lump-sum tax
consumption	proportional income tax
savings	multiplier
investment	foreign repercussions
marginal propensity to consume	balanced budget multiplier
marginal propensity to save	inflationary gap
marginal propensity to import	deflationary gap

2. Consider a closed economy in which investment (I) and government spending (G) are assumed to be autonomous and taxes (T) are all lump-sum. Consumption (C) and savings (S) are both directly and linearly related to disposable income (Y_d). You are given the following information:

$$C = 22 + 0.6Y_d$$
$$I = 10$$
$$G = 20$$
$$T = 20$$

(a) Write down the equations relating consumption and savings to *national* income and plot these relationships on a graph.
(b) On the same graph, plot the $S + T$ and $I + G$ lines and identify the equilibrium level of income.

(c) Calculate the *net* effect on national income of an increase in G of 12 and a simultaneous increase in T of 20. Briefly explain the result.

3. Outline Keynes' criticisms of the classical theory of full employment.

4. Explain why a £10 million increase in government expenditure financed by a £10 million increase in taxation has a net expansionary effect on the economy.

5. Explain why the Keynesian model has come under increasing attack in recent years.

6. Discuss the effect on the equilibrium level of income and the level of total savings of an autonomous increase in the community's desire to save.

Appendix I Algebraic derivation of the multiplier in a model with an income tax

In equilibrium, $Y = C + I + G + X - M$ [1]
Consumption function, $C = a + b(Y - T)$ [2]
Autonomous investment, $I = \bar{I}$ [3]
Government spending, $G = \bar{G}$ [4]
Income tax, $T = tY$ [5]
Autonomous exports, $X = \bar{X}$ [6]
Import function, $M = d + m(Y - T)$ [7]

where a and d are constants, b is the marginal propensity to consume, m is the marginal propensity to import and t is a proportional tax rate. Substituting [2]–[7] into [1], we have,

$$Y = a + b(Y - tY) + \bar{I} + \bar{G} + \bar{X} - d - m(Y - tY)$$

$$= a + bY - btY + \bar{I} + \bar{G} + \bar{X} - d - mY + mtY$$

$$Y - bY + btY + mY - mtY = a + \bar{I} + \bar{G} + \bar{X} - d$$

$$Y(1 - b + bt + m - mt) = a + \bar{I} + \bar{G} + \bar{X} - d$$

$$Y = \frac{a + \bar{I} + \bar{G} + \bar{X} - d}{1 - b + bt + m - mt}$$

The effect of a change in investment is:

$$\Delta Y = \frac{\Delta I}{1 - b(1 - t) + m(1 - t)}$$

Thus, the injections multiplier in this model is $\dfrac{1}{1 - b(1 - t) + m(1 - t)}$.

Appendix II The 'balanced budget' multiplier

The increase in the equilibrium level of national income following an increase in government spending (in a closed economy with lump-sum taxes only) is:

$$\Delta Y_1 = \frac{\Delta G}{1 - b}$$

where b is the marginal propensity to consume.
The fall in the equilibrium level of income following an increase in lump-sum taxation is:

$$\Delta Y_2 = \frac{-b\Delta T}{1-b}$$

If the tax and government spending changes occur simultaneously, the combined effect on income is:

$$\Delta Y = \frac{\Delta G}{1-b} - \frac{b\Delta T}{1-b}$$

But if the budget is kept balanced, so that $\Delta G = \Delta T$, we can write,

$$\Delta Y = \frac{\Delta G}{1-b} - \frac{b\Delta G}{1-b}$$

$$= \left(\frac{1-b}{1-b}\right)\Delta G$$

$$= \Delta G$$

The balanced budget multiplier, therefore, is equal to 1.

20 Consumption and investment

Introduction

Consumption and investment are two extremely important aggregates in the economy. It should be clear from the last chapter that they both play a role in determining the equilibrium level of income and employment and that a change in any one of them will cause the level of national income to change via the multiplier effect. It follows, therefore, that if we are interested in deriving policies designed to secure full employment, we should first analyse the determinants of these variables. That is the purpose of this chapter.

First, we reconsider the definitions of consumption, savings and investment and discuss the distinction between consumption and investment. Secondly, we examine the Keynesian theory of consumption and savings: that is, the view that consumption and savings are both directly related to current disposable income. Thirdly, we make use of indifference curve analysis to examine the microeconomic foundations of aggregate consumption and we outline the 'permanent income' and 'relative income' hypotheses. Finally, we turn our attention to the determination of investment and outline the views that investment depends on: (a) the rate of interest; and (b) changes in national income (that is, the so-called 'accelerator' theory).

Definitions

Recall the definitions of consumption, savings and investment given in Chapter 19. Consumption is seen as households' spending on goods and services which yield utility in the current period, while savings are defined as that part of disposable income which is not spent. In a closed economy, it follows that by definition,

$$Y_d \equiv C + S$$

Investment, though, is seen as an activity of firms. It is firms' spending on goods which are not for current consumption but which yield a flow of consumer goods and services in the future.

These definitions enable us to say quite categorically that a household's expenditure on food is consumption – the food will be eaten within a short period of time and that will be an end of the matter. Similarly, we can say that the purchase of a new machine by a firm is investment – the machine itself will not yield utility to anyone in the current period but will produce (or help to produce) consumer goods probably for a long time into the future.

The distinction between consumption and investment is not so clear-cut, however, when we consider household expenditure on consumer durables, like cars and washing machines. These are goods which last for a long time and which yield the household utility-creating services both in the current period and in future periods. In a sense, then, the purchase of consumer durables is both consumption *and* a form of investment. Furthermore, it is sometimes useful to distinguish between consumption spending (meaning the actual amount spent on new consumer goods in the current period) and total consumption (meaning the 'using up' of consumer goods – both those purchased in the current period and those purchased in past periods but which are still providing services to the household).

To keep our analysis fairly simple in this chapter, we adhere to the definitions given above and ignore the complications created by durable consumer goods. For more advanced study, it is important for the reader at least to be aware of these complications.

Consumption and savings

It can be seen from Table 1 in Chapter 17 that consumption spending accounted for about two-thirds of total expenditure in the United Kingdom in 1978 and consequently is a very important component of aggregate demand. Small percentage changes in consumption can have a considerable effect on the equilibrium level of national income and therefore on employment. It is of some importance, therefore, to know what factors determine consumption so that appropriate policies to combat unemployment can be devised.

The 'absolute income' hypothesis

The Keynesian model we constructed in the last chapter was based on the assumption that both consumption and savings were directly and linearly related to current disposable income. This is sometimes called the 'absolute income' hypothesis to distinguish it from other more recent hypotheses of consumption: in particular, the 'relative' and 'permanent' income hypotheses.

The consumption and savings functions of the 'absolute income' hypothesis can be illustrated either numerically, graphically or algebraically. To show this, consider Table 1 which sets out a simple numerical example in which there is a direct linear relationship between disposable income and consumption, and between disposable income and savings. These linear relationships are plotted in Fig. 1 where both the consumption and savings relationships are seen to be straight lines. Notice that the slope of the consumption line is 0.8: this represents the fraction of additional disposable income which will be consumed and, as we saw in the last chapter, is called

Table 1. Income, consumption and savings for a hypothetical economy.

Disposable income (£m.)	Consumption (£m.)	Savings (£m.)
250	210	40
200	170	30
150	130	20
100	90	10
50	50	0
0	10	– 10

the *marginal propensity to consume* (mpc). Similarly, the slope of the savings line (= 0.2) represents the fraction of additional disposable income that will be saved and is called the *marginal propensity to save* (mps). Since the consumption and savings lines are straight lines and so have constant slopes, the mpc and mps are also constant in this example.

The *average propensity to consume* (apc) is equal to total consumption divided by total disposable income (C / Y_d) and this varies as disposable income varies. At point A on the graph, for example, the apc = 50/50 = 1; but at point B, the apc = 90/100 = 0.9. The apc is in fact equal to the slope of the ray from the origin to the appropriate point on the consumption line, so that at point A, the apc is equal to the slope of OA (= 1) and at point B, the apc is equal to the slope of OB (= 0.9). Exactly the same applies to the *average propensity to save* which is equal to total savings divided by total disposable income (S / Y_d).

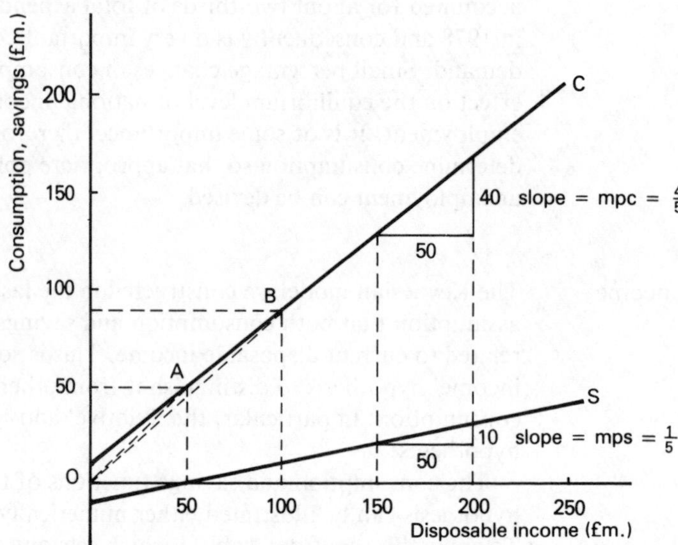

Fig. 1. The consumption and savings lines.

Algebraically, the relationships can be expressed in general form as follows:

$$C = a + bY_d$$

$$S \equiv Y_d - C$$

$$= Y_d - a - bY_d$$

$$S = -a + (1 - b)\,Y_d$$

It should be clear from Fig. 1 that the constant a is the intercept term for the consumption line (that is, the point where the consumption line cuts the vertical axis) and is equal to 10 in the example. Also, the coefficient b is the slope of the consumption line and so is equal to the mpc (0.8). Thus, the equation of the consumption line is:

$$C = 10 + 0.8\,Y_d$$

And the equation of the savings line is:

$S = -10 + 0.2\,Y_d$

Notice that it must always be true that $\underline{\text{mpc} + \text{mps} = 1.}$

The following points represent the major characteristics of the 'absolute income' hypothesis.

(a) Consumption and savings are stable functions of current disposable income. The relationships are direct ones.
(b) In our example, the relationships are linear. It is also possible in the 'absolute income' hypothesis, though, for the consumption and savings lines to be curved in such a way that the mpc falls as income rises and the mps rises as income rises. This is illustrated in Fig. 2.

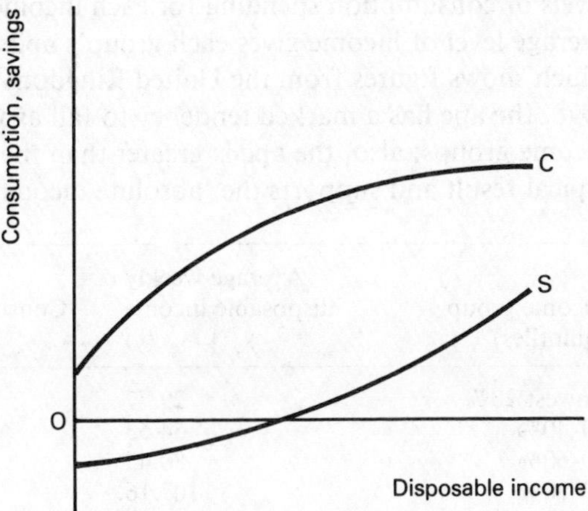

Fig. 2. Non-linear consumption and savings lines.

(c) The mpc lies between 0 and 1 ($0 < \text{mpc} < 1$). This means that for every additional pound of income received, consumption rises by some fraction of a pound. Of course, it is not impossible for the mpc to be greater than 1 or even less than 0, but such values are unlikely.
(d) *The apc falls as income rises and is greater than the mpc.* The hypothesis has this characteristic because the consumption line cuts the vertical axis at some positive point (that is to say, consumption spending actually exceeds income at very low levels of income). This is illustrated in Fig. 3 where the

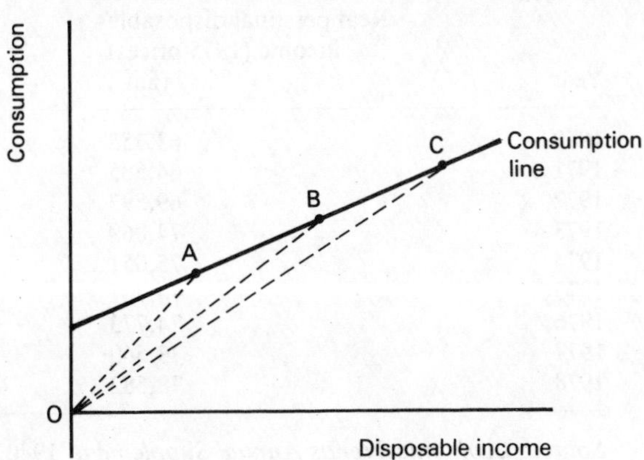

Fig. 3. Comparison of the apc with the mpc.

slopes of the dashed lines OA, OB and OC represent the apc's at points A, B and C respectively and the slope of the consumption line itself represents the mpc. Clearly, the apc's are all greater than the mpc and are diminishing as income rises. This characteristic is an important one because it is empirically testable. We turn now to a consideration of the different types of data that can be collected on the income-consumption relationship.

Different types of data Statistics on the relationship between income and consumption can be collected by means of three main types of empirical study.

(a) *Cross-section budget study.* This involves taking a sample of households and classifying them according to their income groups. Dividing the average levels of consumption spending for each income group by the corresponding average level of income gives each group's apc. As can be seen from Table 2, which shows figures from the United Kingdom Family Expenditure Survey of 1978, the apc has a marked tendency to fall as we move from lower to higher income groups; also, the apc is greater than the mpc in every case. This is a typical result and supports the 'absolute income' hypothesis.

Table 2. Cross-section budget study for the United Kingdom.

Income group (quintiles)	Average weekly disposable income (£)	Consumption (£)	apc	mpc
Lowest 20%	29.77	31.71	1.07	
20–40%	54.53	56.82	1.04	1.01
40–60%	80.45	77.56	0.96	0.80
60–80%	107.16	95.38	0.89	0.67
Highest 20%	165.01	139.81	0.85	0.77

Source: Department of Employment, *Family Expenditure Survey, 1978,* Tables 7 and 40.

(b) *Short-run time-series study.* This involves collecting annual data of real disposable income and consumption for the economy as a whole. Dividing consumption by disposable income for each year gives the apc and this is done for United Kingdom data (1970–78) in Table 3. This time, the results

Table 3. Short-run time-series study for the United Kingdom, 1970-78

Year	Real personal disposable income (1975 prices) (£m.)	Real consumption (1975 prices) (£m.)	apc
1970	63,352	57,676	0.91
1971	64,585	59,557	0.92
1972	69,597	62,999	0.91
1973	74,069	65,911	0.89
1974	75,051	64,418	0.86
1975	74,707	63,704	0.85
1976	74,773	63,852	0.85
1977	73,560	63,313	0.86
1978	78,682	66,728	0.85

Source: Economic Trends Annual Supplement, 1980, Table 18.

Table 4. National income and the average propensity to consume in the United States, 1869 – 1928.

Years	National income ($b.)	Average propensity to consume
1869–78	9.3	0.86
1874–83	13.6	0.86
1879–88	17.9	0.85
1884–93	21.0	0.84
1889–98	24.2	0.84
1894–1903	29.8	0.85
1899–1908	37.3	0.86
1904–13	45.0	0.87
1909–18	50.6	0.87
1914–23	57.3	0.89
1919–28	69.0	0.89

Source: Simon Kuznets, *National Income: A Summary of Findings,* NBER, Princeton University Press, 1946.

are not quite so clear-cut, but there is at least a tendency for the apc to fall as income rises and to rise as income falls. These figures, therefore, also tend to support the 'absolute income' hypothesis.

(c) *Long-run time-series study.* In this type of study, trend values of consumption and income are collected over a long period of time so that most cyclical fluctuations are smoothed out. The most famous studies of this kind were carried out by Simon Kuznets in the 1940s for the United States (1869–1938). The results of his study tended not to support the 'absolute income' hypothesis as outlined above. Instead, they exhibited an apc which was remarkably constant and had no tendency to fall as income rose or rise as income fell. His results are shown in Table 4. According to these results, the long-run consumption function is proportional, as illustrated in Fig. 4.

Fig. 4. A proportional long-run consumption line.

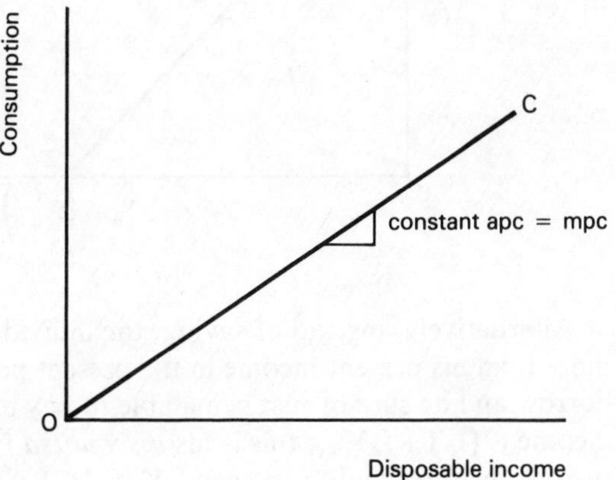

The 'absolute income' hypothesis appears to explain the cross-section and short-run time-series data well, but fails to explain the long-run time-series data. One objective of the more recent theories has been to try and reconcile this apparent conflict in the different sets of statistical results.

The influence of wealth on consumption To consider the influence of wealth on aggregate consumption, we should first examine the *microeconomic* analysis of an individual consumer choosing between present and future consumption. (This is, therefore, a good time to review your understanding of budget lines and indifference curves from Chapter 4.)

To simplify, we restrict the analysis to two time periods only: the present period, t, and the future period, $t + 1$. Suppose that we denote the individual's present income by Y_t and his expected future income by Y_{t+1}.

Now consider Fig. 5 where the individual's present consumption is measured along the horizontal axis and his future consumption along the vertical axis. Point A represents the combination of present income (Y_t) and expected future income (Y_{t+1}.) This is clearly one consumption possibility for the consumer – he can consume all of his present income in the present period and all of his future income in the future period. Point A must, therefore, be on the individual's budget line (or, as it may be called in this case, his consumption possibilities line). Other consumption possibilities exist as well and these are determined by the consumer's ability to lend and borrow. Suppose that the rate of interest for lending and borrowing is the same and equal to i. At one extreme, the consumer could spend nothing in the present period and save all of his present income so that in the future period he can spend as much as $Y_{t+1} + (1 + i)Y_t$; that is, his future income plus his saved present income plus interest. This is point R in Fig. 5 and represents another point on the budget line.

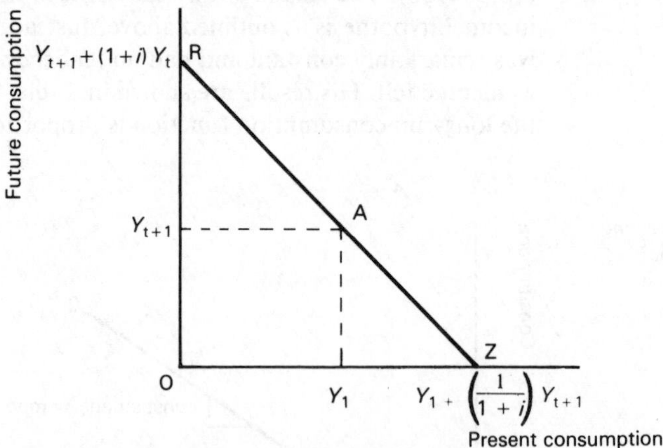

Fig. 5. The choice between present and future consumption.

Alternatively, instead of saving, the individual could borrow and so spend more than his present income in the present period. The most he could borrow and be sure of just being able to pay back the debt out of his future income is $(1/1 + i)Y_{t+1}$; this is his *discounted* future income. In the present period, then, he could just spend $Y_t + (1/1 + i)Y_{t+1}$, and this is shown as point Z on the graph. The line RAZ is the individual's budget line – it shows all the combinations of present and future consumption that the individual can just attain, given his present and future incomes and the rate of interest. Since *wealth* is the source of the individual's present and future incomes, we can say that the position of the individual's budget line is determined by his wealth and its slope is determined by the rate of interest.

Which point on the budget line will the consumer choose? This depends on his time preference for present and future consumption which, to some extent, depends on how patient or impatient he is. His preferences can be illustrated by means of a set of indifference curves which are likely to have the same shape as those depicted in Chapter 4 for the case of an individual choosing between two goods. The rational consumer will choose point W on the budget line which places him on the highest attainable indifference curve, I_1, in Fig. 6.

Fig. 6. The consumer 'equilibrium' position.

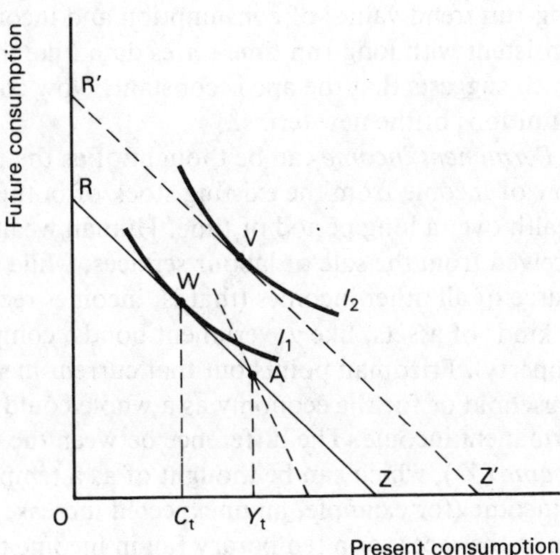

At point W, the individual is consuming OC_t and saving C_tY_t in the present period. This consumption and saving will change in the following circumstances.

(a) If there is a change in the individual's wealth which affects his present and/or future income. Such a change would cause the budget line to shift but remain parallel to the original one, as shown by line R′Z′ in Fig. 6, for an increase in wealth. The new utility maximising point is V where the increase in wealth has caused present consumption to rise.
(b) If there is a change in the rate of interest which will influence the lending and borrowing possibilities. In this case the budget line would pivot around point A, becoming steeper for an increase in the rate of interest, as shown in Fig. 6.

According to this microeconomic analysis of an individual consumer's behaviour, then, present consumption depends on wealth (which is the source of both present and future incomes) and the rate of interest. This result, however, is not reflected in the 'absolute income' hypothesis where consumption depends on present income alone.

To summarise, the 'absolute income' hypothesis may be criticised on two major grounds: (a) for not providing an adequate explanation of the different sets of income-consumption data; (b) for not taking into account the influence of wealth and the rate of interest on consumption, and so for not being consistent with the microeconomic analysis of consumer behaviour. Perhaps the most famous of the theories which attempt to overcome both of these criticisms is Milton Friedman's 'permanent income' hypothesis.

'Permanent income' hypothesis

The basic proposition of Friedman's 'permanent income' hypothesis is that *permanent consumption* (C_p) is proportional to *permanent income* (Y_p): that is, $C_p = kY_p$, where k is constant and equal to the average and marginal propensities to consume. Permanent consumption and permanent income are long-run trend values of consumption and income, so the hypothesis is consistent with long-run time-series data (like that collected by Kuznets) which suggests that the apc is constant. Now consider the following definitions of the new terms.

Permanent income can be thought of as the present value of the expected flow of income from the existing stock of both 'human' and 'non-human' wealth over a long period of time. Human wealth is the source of income received from the sale of labour services, while non-human wealth is the source of all other incomes (that is, incomes received from the ownership of all kinds of assets, like government bonds, company stocks and shares, and property). Friedman points out that current measured income (Y) for a household or for the economy as a whole could be greater or less than permanent income. The difference between the two, he calls *transitory income* (Y_T), which can be thought of as a temporary, unexpected rise or fall in income (for example, an unexpected increase in income resulting from a win at the races, or a temporary fall in income resulting from a short period of unemployment). Consequently, we can write:

$$Y = Y_p + Y_T$$

An important assumption of the hypothesis is that Y_T is *not* correlated with Y_p. In other words, a high permanent income is not necessarily associated with a high transitory income and a low permanent income is not necessarily associated with a low transitory income. This means that if we were to take a sufficiently large and completely random sample of households from all income groups, we would expect to find that the negative and positive transitory incomes would just cancel each other out so that the aggregate or *average* transitory income level ($\bar{Y}_T$) would be equal to zero. In this case, of course, the average permanent income would be just equal to the average measured income (that is, $\bar{Y}_p = \bar{Y}$). On the other hand, if we were to take our sample from those families with above-average *measured* incomes, we would expect to find that many of them had only temporarily high incomes so that average transitory income would be positive and $\bar{Y}_p < \bar{Y}$. Similarly, for a sample of families with below-average measured incomes, we should expect to find that $\bar{Y}_T < 0$ and $\bar{Y}_p > \bar{Y}$.

Much the same results apply to the economy as a whole. In a normal year (that is, not a boom year or a slump year), we should expect aggregate transitory income to be zero, so that aggregate measured and permanent incomes would be equal. In a boom year, though, when many people would be experiencing unexpectedly high incomes, aggregate measured income should exceed aggregate permanent income. Exactly the opposite would apply in a slump year. All these results are important because, as we see later, they help to explain the cross-section and short-run time-series data.

Permanent consumption can be thought of as the normal or planned level of spending out of permanent income and can differ from measured consumption (C) by any unplanned, temporary increases or decreases in consumer spending, called *transitory consumption* (C_T). We can write:

$$C = C_p + C_T$$

Friedman makes two important assumptions about transitory consumption. First, he assumes that it is not correlated with permanent consumption. Secondly, and more questionably, he argues that transitory consumption is not correlated with transitory income – in other words, temporary increases in income do not cause temporary increases in consumption. These assumptions make transitory consumption completely random, so that for any sufficiently large sample from any measured income group or in any year, we can expect the average and aggregate levels of transitory consumption to be zero. This means that average and aggregate levels of measured consumption must equal permanent consumption. Since we are concerned with average or aggregate data in macroeconomics, we need no longer make any distinction between measured consumption and permanent consumption. This means that we can write the basic consumption function in the 'permanent income' hypothesis as:

$$C = kY_p$$

This is illustrated in Fig. 7.

Friedman, then, has succeeded in introducing wealth into the consumption function, as the source of permanent income upon which consumption depends. The next question to be considered is how he explains the cross-section and short-run time-series data which yield an apc which falls as measured income rises.

Consider first a cross-section budget study in which a sample of families is classified according to their incomes. Recall that in a group of families with above-average measured incomes, $\bar{Y} > \bar{Y}_p$ – this means that the measured

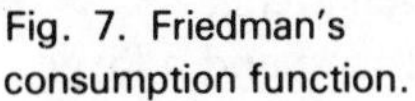
Fig. 7. Friedman's consumption function.

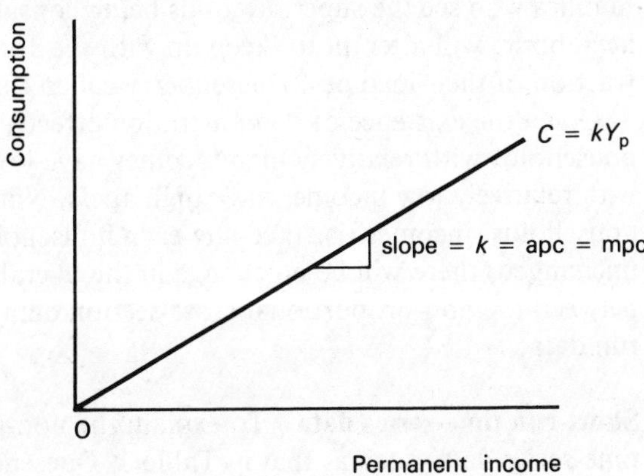

apc ($= \bar{C}/\bar{Y}$) will necessarily be less than the long-run apc ($= \bar{C}/\bar{Y}_p$). Now compare this with a sample of families with below-average measured incomes for which $\bar{Y} < \bar{Y}_p$ – in this case, $\bar{C}/\bar{Y}$ will be greater than the long-run $\bar{C}/\bar{Y}_p$. Since the long-run apc is the same for both samples, we would predict that the measured apc of the families with above-average measured incomes would be less than the measured apc of the families with below-average measured incomes. As we have seen, this result is supported by cross-section budget studies.

Next, consider the short-run time-series studies. Recall that in a boom year, aggregate measured income exceeds aggregate permanent income so that the measured apc is less than the long-run apc, while in a slump year (where $Y < Y_p$) the measured apc is greater than the long-run apc. So again we would predict that the measured apc would be higher in a slump year than in a boom year. This is the result supported by short-run time-series data.

In conclusion, we can say that the 'permanent income' hypothesis takes a long-term, wide measure of income as the main determinant of consumption. It proposes that the basic long-run relationship is proportional, yet predicts a non-proportional relationship in the short-run and for cross-section data.

'Relative income' hypothesis

The 'relative income' hypothesis was proposed by the American economist J.S. Duesenberry in 1949 and this theory can also be used to explain the apparent conflict in income-consumption data. Like Friedman, Duesenberry believed that the basic consumption function was long-run and proportional, as illustrated in Fig. 7. How, then, does the theory explain the non-proportionality of cross-section and short-run time-series data? Consider each one in turn.

Cross-section data To explain the observed non-proportionality of cross-section data, such as that in Table 2, Duesenberry argues that a household's consumption spending depends not only on its own income, but also on the incomes earned by neighbouring households. In other words, it is the household's *relative* income that determines its consumption spending. It follows that a household will spend more on consumption if it lives in a neighbourhood in which its income is relatively low than if it lives in a neighbourhood in which its income is relatively high. This is because poorer families who see the superior goods being consumed by their richer neighbours will attempt to 'keep up with the Joneses' and so spend a large fraction of their incomes. Duesenberry called this the 'demonstration effect'.

Given the existence of demonstration effects, it is not surprising that households with relatively high incomes have lower apc's and households with relatively low incomes have high apc's. Notice, though, that when all households' incomes rise (keeping each households *relative* position unchanged) there will be no change in the overall apc. So there is no conflict between the non-proportional cross-section data and the proportional long-run data.

Short-run time-series data To explain the non-proportionality of annual time-series data, such as that in Table 3, Duesenberry suggests that aggregate consumption depends not just on current income, but also on the ***highest level of income previously attained.*** To illustrate this, consider Fig. 8. As national income rises, consumption rises along the long-run consumption line LC. Suppose that national income reaches OY_0 and then begins to fall. Duesenberry argues that consumers (who have become accustomed to the income level of OY_0 and the standard of living that goes with it) will increase their apc in an attempt to maintain their level of consumption and will move down the consumption line SC_0. If national income rises again, consumers will move back along SC_0 until OY_0 is reached.

Fig. 8. The ratchet effect.

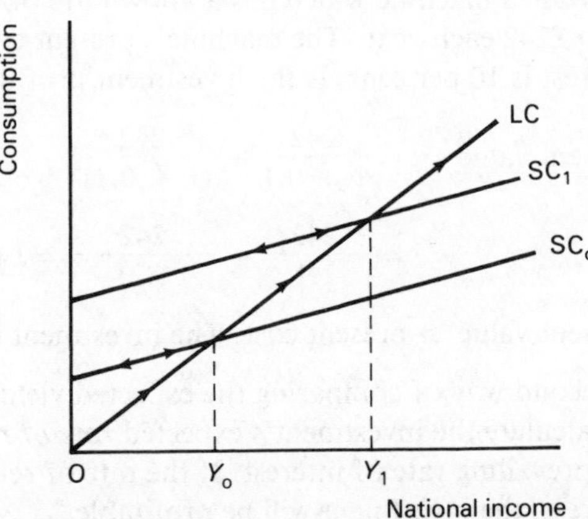

Now suppose that income reaches OY_1 and then again begins to fall. Consumers again will try to maintain their accustomed standard of living by reducing their spending along the consumption line SC_1. Duesenberry called this the *ratchet effect*. It explains the observed rises in the apc when income falls over the period of a trade cycle.

Investment

Total investment, which includes spending on all types of capital goods by firms, accounts for about a fifth of total expenditure in the United Kingdom. This is a relatively small proportion, but investment fluctuates more than any other component of national income and these fluctuations generate changes in income through the multiplier. Investment is sometimes thought of as the most dynamic element in the economy – it probably accounts for much of the cyclical instability in the economy and is an important determinant of economic growth.

Investment and the rate of interest

'Classical' economists viewed the rate of interest as the main determinant of investment. To summarise this approach, consider first the microeconomic analysis of a single profit-maximising firm deciding whether or not to undertake an investment (for example, to buy a new machine). When a firm buys a new machine, it presumably expects the *yield* of the investment to exceed its *cost*. Calculating the expected yield from a new machine, however, is not easy because yields are spread over a number of years in the future. Recall from Chapter 12 that an allowance has to be made for the fact that a given sum of money to be received in the future is worth less than the same sum received now.

One way of comparing the expected yield of an investment to its cost is to calculate the *present value* of the investment and to compare that with the *present cost*. If present value > present cost, the investment can be regarded as profitable; otherwise, it is unprofitable.

Example I:
Suppose a machine which has a known life of only two years is expected to yield £242 each year. The machine's present cost is £400 and the rate of interest is 10 per cent. Is the investment profitable?

$$\text{Present value} = \frac{242}{1 + 0.1} + \frac{242}{(1 + 0.1)^2}$$

$$= \frac{242}{1.1} + \frac{242}{1.21} = \underline{£420}$$

Present value > present cost. The investment is profitable.

A second way of comparing the expected yield of an investment to its cost is to calculate the investment's expected *rate of return* and to compare this with the prevailing rate of interest. If the rate of return exceeds the rate of interest, the investment will be profitable.

Example II:
Suppose a machine has a known life of only one year and is expected to yield £450 at the end of that year. The machine's present cost is £400 and the rate of interest is 10 per cent. Is the investment profitable?
We have to find the rate of return, r, which raises £400 to £450 in one year:

$$400\,(1 + r) = 450$$

$$r = \frac{450 - 400}{400}$$

$$r = 0.125 \text{ or } 12\tfrac{1}{2} \text{ per cent}$$

Rate of return > rate of interest. The investment is profitable.

It follows from the above examples that profit-maximising firms, operating under conditions of certainty, will invest in projects where the rate of return on the investment exceeds the market rate of interest. (The rate of return on an additional investment is sometimes called the marginal efficiency of investment or MEI.) A fall in the market rate of interest should make profitable some investments in the economy which were previously unprofitable, so that aggregate investment should increase. Similarly, a rise in the market rate of interest should make unprofitable some investments which were previously profitable, so that aggregate investment should fall. In other words, our microeconomic analysis of a single profit-maximising firm leads us to the conclusion that *aggregate investment is inversely related to the rate of interest*. This is illustrated in Fig. 9, where the curve II can be referred

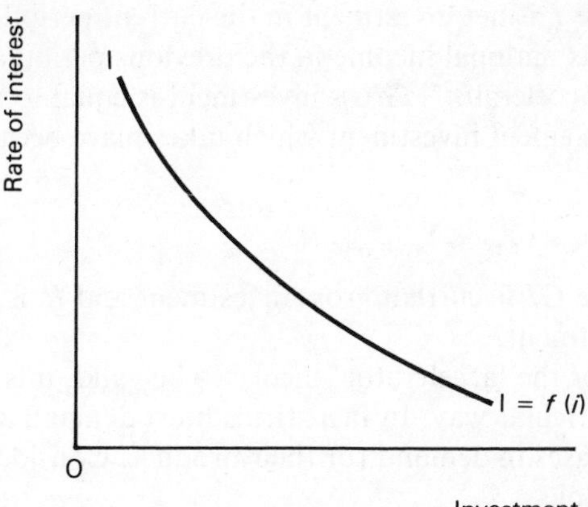

Fig. 9. The aggregate investment curve.

to as the demand for investment curve or the MEI curve.

Empirical evidence on aggregate investment tends to confirm that it is indeed *inversely* related to the rate of interest, but most evidence suggests that the relationship is a fairly weak one – for example, M. Evans estimated (for United States data) that a 25 per cent fall in interest rates would cause net investment to rise by 5–10 per cent over a two-year period after a one-year lag. Also, the results of many surveys in both the United States and the United Kingdom suggest that only a few firms explicitly take the rate of interest into account in deciding whether or not to carry out an investment project. There are two main reasons why investment tends to be fairly interest-inelastic.

(a) Investment is probably strongly influenced by businessmen's *expectations* of future economic activity. If businessmen are very pessimistic about the future, it is unlikely that even very low interest rates would induce them to increase their rate of investment. Similarly, if they are generally very optimistic about the future, high interest rates will not discourage them from investing.
(b) Yields on investment projects are notoriously difficult to estimate since they depend on the future demand for the firm's products. It could be that a firm may only be able to say with any certainty that it expects the rate of return on an investment project to be within a particular range, say 10 to 15 per cent. A small rise in interest rates would be unlikely to dissuade the firm from investing in this case. This would be particularly true if the investment were part of a long-term plan of expansion for the firm.

Now consider a second approach to the theory of investment – the view that it depends on changes in national income.

The accelerator theory

According to the 'accelerator' theory, the level of current net investment depends on past income changes. In its simplest form, this can be written as follows:

$$I_t = v\,(Y_t - Y_{t-1})$$

where I_t is net investment in the current period, Y_t is current national income, Y_{t-1} is national income in the previous period and v is a constant known as the 'accelerator'. Gross investment is equal to net investment plus any replacement investment which takes place because of depreciation. So we can write:

$$GI_t = v\,(Y_t - Y_{t-1}) + R_t$$

where GI_t is current gross investment and R_t is current replacement investment.

For the 'accelerator' theory to be valid, it is necessary that firms behave in a particular way. In fact, firms must demand additional capital to meet any increases in demand for their product. Consider the following simplified example.

Consider a single firm which initially has a stock of ten machines each of which is capable of producing 100 units of output per year. To keep the example simple, assume that there is no depreciation so that we do not need to worry about replacement investment. Suppose that to start with the total demand for the firm's product is 1,000 units. This is shown for year 1 in Table 5: notice that the *desired* capital stock to meet this demand is ten machines and since the firm already has ten machines, no net investment is necessary. So long as demand stays at 1,000 units, no net investment will take place. But now suppose that in year 2, demand increases to 2,000 units – the desired capital stock will rise to twenty machines and to achieve this, net investment of ten machines is necessary. In year 3, demand has risen to 3,000 units so that the desired capital stock goes up to thirty machines – since the firm already has twenty, another ten must be purchased. Notice here that although demand has risen from year 2 to year 3, net investment has remained the same. In year 4, demand continues to increase, but this time by only 500 units to 3,500 units: the desired capital stock goes up to thirty-five and so net investment of only five machines is necessary. Since demand has risen by a smaller amount than previously, investment has actually fallen. In year 5, demand levels off at 3,500 units – the firm, though, already has the thirty-five machines necessary to meet this demand and so no new investment is necessary.

Table 5. An example of the accelerator principle.

Year	Demand (*D*)	Desired capital stock	Net investment (no. of machines)
1	1,000	10	0
2	2,000	20	10
3	3,000	30	10
4	3,500	35	5
5	3,500	35	0

The example highlights the following important points about the 'accelerator' theory.

(a) To maintain net investment at a constant positive level, demand for the firm's product must be rising at a steady rate.

(b) For net investment to increase, demand must be increasing at an increasing rate.
(c) If demand should level off and remain constant, net investment will fall to zero.

Notice that the relationship expressed in Table 5 can be written algebraically as follows:

$$NI = 1/100\,(D_t - D_{t-1})$$

where NI is the firm's net investment measured in numbers of machines, D_t is the current demand for the firm's product and D_{t-1} is last year's demand for the firm's product. If all firms behave in a similar way to this, then we can say that *aggregate* investment in the economy will depend on changes in aggregate demand – both of these have to be measured in value terms and since the value of aggregate demand in equilibrium is the same as national income, we have:

$$I_t = v\,(Y_t - Y_{t-1})$$

which is the expression we started with.

Two main criticisms can be made of the accelerator theory as we have outlined it.

(a) It assumes that firms faced with increased demand for their products will immediately attempt to increase their capital stocks. This implies that there is no excess capacity (that is to say, all existing machines must be fully employed and there must be no possibility of overtime or shift working). This is extremely unrealistic – it is more likely that firms will be able to meet some of the increased demand by working existing machines harder and using whatever excess capacity does exist.
(b) It fails to take into account businessmen's expectations. If businessmen regard the increase in demand as temporary, they may not respond to it at all: this will be the case if they are generally pessimistic about the future level of economic activity. If, on the other hand, businessmen are generally optimistic and see the increase in demand as a signal for further increases, they may actually buy more machines than predicted by the accelerator theory.

Overall view of investment

In conclusion, we can combine our two approaches to investment theory and say that the level of net investment in an economy will depend on three major factors: the rate of interest (i), past national income changes and the state of businessmen's expectations (B). Using functional notation, we can write:

$$I_t = f\,(i,\ Y_t - Y_{t-1},\ B)$$

However, since it takes time for firms to adjust their capital stocks in response to changes in demand (remember that capital is a variable factor of production only in the long-run), it may be more realistic to introduce a lag into the accelerator part of the function and write:

$$I_t = f\,(i,\ Y_{t-1} - Y_{t-2},\ B)$$

Only empirical testing can determine which of the three independent variables is the most important.

Conclusion

Consumption and investment are two major components of aggregate demand. In this chapter, we have outlined the main theories which seek to explain the aggregate levels of consumption and investment. The chapter showed that these theories are based on microeconomic foundations.

An important point to note is that the existing theories are sometimes in conflict and the empirical tests have so far proved inconclusive.

Further reading

Levacic, R., *Macroeconomics*, Macmillan, London, 1976 (Ch. 3 and 4).
Glahe, F., *Macroeconomics: Theory and Policy*, Harcourt-Brace Jovanovich, New York, 1977 (Ch. 5 and 6).
Johnson, M.B., *Household Behaviour: Consumption, Income and Wealth*, Penguin, Harmondsworth, 1971.
Black, J., *The Economics of Modern Britain*, Martin Robertson, Oxford, 1979 (Ch. 5 and 7).

Exercises

1. Review your understanding of the following terms:

absolute income	permanent income
marginal propensity to consume	transitory income
average propensity to consume	permanent consumption
marginal propensity to save	transitory consumption
average propensity to save	relative income
cross-section data	present value
time-series data	marginal efficiency of investment
discounted future income	accelerator
time preference	replacement investment

2. Consider Table 6 which shows the results of a cross-section budget study.

Table 6. Cross-section budget study for the United Kingdom, 1971.

Income group (£ per week)	Average income (£ per week)	Consumption (£ per week)
Under 10	7.89	9.73
10–19.99	14.97	16.46
20–29.99	25.01	23.96
30–39.99	34.97	29.82
40–49.99	44.97	35.90
50–59.99	54.69	42.12
60–79.99	68.14	48.31
80 and over	112.26	70.92

Source: Department of Employment, *Family Expenditure Survey, 1971.*

Calculate the average and marginal propensities to consume for each income group and comment on the significance of your results for the theories of consumption outlined in this chapter.

3. Consider the view that the link between aggregate consumption and current measured income is a tenuous one.

4. In the permanent income hypothesis, Friedman makes a series of assumptions regarding the statistical relationships that exist between permanent and transitory consumption, permanent and transitory income and transitory income and consumption. Explain these assumptions and discuss their importance to the theory.

5. Consider a firm which initially has a stock of 100 machines, each of which can produce 50 units of output per time period. Assume that the 100 machines have been acquired at the rate of ten per time period for the last ten periods, so that from now on depreciation is equal to ten machines per time period. Table 7 shows the demand for the firm's product in time periods 0 to 5.

Table 7. The demand for the firm's product over time.

Time period	Demand
0	5,000
1	6,000
2	10,000
3	12,000
4	12,000
5	10,000

(a) Calculate the firm's gross investment in time periods 0 to 5.
(b) Write down the equations of the relationship between gross investment and changes in demand.
(c) Comment on the applicability of this model to the real world.

6. Discuss the influence of changes in interest rates on aggregate investment in the United Kingdom.

21 Money – I

Introduction

The objectives of this and the following two chapters are, first, to explain the meaning of money in a modern economy; secondly, to show how the supply of money might be influenced by government policy and other factors; and finally, to discuss the role of money in an economy. As we shall see, this is an area which has been central to the most fundamental controversies in macroeconomics. It is in the field of monetary theory and policy that many of the differences between Keynesians and monetarists are debated.

In this chapter, we are concerned primarily with the problems of defining and measuring a country's stock of money and with describing the methods employed in the United Kingdom to influence the money supply. To enable the reader to gain a good understanding of these methods of implementing monetary policy, we also outline the main functions of the more important financial institutions in the United Kingdom.

The nature of money

Money can be defined as any asset that is generally acceptable in transactions and in the settlement of debts. The key word is 'generally' and its interpretation does leave some room for discussion as to exactly which assets should be included as money. In a modern economy, banknotes and coins clearly form part of the money supply as they are generally acceptable in the settlement of all transactions. In addition, many transactions can be settled by the use of cheques drawn on bank deposits. Note that cheques are drawn on bank deposits in *current* accounts (sometimes called sight or demand deposits). Current account deposits, therefore, also form part of the money supply. It must be pointed out, furthermore, that people can readily transfer funds from deposit accounts (sometimes called time deposits) into current accounts or cash. Consequently, it can be argued that deposit accounts with banks or other financial institutions should also be included as part of the stock of money.

For official purposes in the United Kingdom, the Bank of England uses three alternative definitions of money:

(a) M_1 (the narrow definition) includes notes and coins in circulation with the public plus sight deposits (or current accounts) in sterling held by the private sector only.
(b) Sterling M_3 includes notes and coins in circulation with the public plus all current and deposit accounts in sterling held by United Kingdom residents in both the public and private sectors.
(c) M_3 (the wide definition) includes sterling M_3 plus all deposits held by United Kingdom residents denominated in foreign currencies.

In all three definitions, deposits are confined to those with institutions in the United Kingdom banking sector: this comprises British and overseas banks operating in the United Kingdom and the discount houses.

In December 1979, M_1 was £28.3 billion, sterling M_3 was £55.8 billion and M_3 was £61.1 billion. Because of the widespread use of cheques, bank deposits are the most important components of the money supply. In December 1979, while currency in circulation totalled £9.7 billion, private sector sterling sight deposits totalled £18.6 billion and private sector sterling time deposits totalled £25.9 billion.

Functions of money

The use of money in a complex economy, such as the United Kingdom, fulfils four main functions.

Medium of exchange Obviously, the use of money greatly eases the carrying out of everyday transactions. Without money, we would have to resort to barter: that is, the exchange of goods for goods. Barter is clearly inefficient and troublesome as it requires a 'double coincidence of wants'. Someone who wishes to obtain some food in return for some clothes, not only has to find someone who has some food, but who is also seeking some clothes. This might involve a prolonged search and thus discourage the specialisation that is so important in increasing output: in a barter economy, an individual would try to be as self-sufficient as possible because of the problems of trading. In a money economy, these problems are considerably reduced: clothes, for example, are exchanged for money which can then be used to purchase food. The food seller is willing to accept money in the knowledge that he in turn can use it in his purchases. Thus, with money there is no need for a double coincidence of wants.

Store of value Money enables an individual to delay a potential purchase to the most convenient time by providing him with a way in which to store his purchasing power. Clearly, if there is inflation, the efficiency of money as a store of value is reduced.

Unit of account The use of money with its units of measurement (pounds and pence in the United Kingdom) enables the prices of all goods to be quoted in these units. This facilitates the quick comparison of the respective values of different goods. In addition, money is the unit used in the financial accounts of all businesses and, for example, in expressing the values of a country's national income and balance of payments.

Standard of deferred payment Many transactions are conducted on the basis of credit. Thus, payment for work carried out now might be made several months later and it is convenient for the debt to be expressed and for the payment to be made in money terms rather than in terms of some commodity. For example, a sub-contractor on a building site may agree to do some work for the developer in return for a certain sum of money to be paid when the work is finished. Both parties to the agreement know how much money will change hands at the agreed date in the future. Once again, if there is inflation, money performs less efficiently as a standard of deferred payment. Some contracts, however, have cost-escalation clauses allowing the passing on of any increased costs.

The development of money

In the course of history, many different commodities have been used as money - for example shells, animals and metals. Over a period of time, the use of precious metals, such as silver and gold, became increasingly important. In the seventeenth century, goldsmiths acted as depositaries for the gold of the rich. The goldsmiths issued receipts for the gold deposited with them. When individuals wanted to settle debts, they came to realise that rather than withdrawing their gold, they could endorse the receipts instructing the goldsmith to transfer the deposits to the named creditor. In the course of time, the goldsmiths began to issue receipts for gold *payable to the bearer* rather than to any named person. As a consequence, the goldsmiths' receipts began to circulate as generally acceptable means of payment.

The goldsmiths noticed that a large proportion of the gold was not withdrawn from the vaults and as a result they seized the opportunity of making profits by granting loans through the issue of 'receipts' in excess of actual gold deposits. This was the origin of paper currency (or banknotes) as used in modern societies today. Note that by issuing 'receipts' in excess of gold holdings, the goldsmiths were acting as bankers and so laid the foundations of the modern 'fractional reserve' banking system. The goldsmiths learnt from experience what proportion of gold reserves they had to keep in order to meet day-to-day demands for gold withdrawals. Several goldsmiths developed into fully-fledged banks and issued banknotes. In the nineteenth century, however, the Bank of England, as the central bank, was granted a monopoly of banknote-issue. In modern times, commercial banks are still able to create money, but only in the form of bank deposits. This process of credit creation by banks is discussed below.

The central bank

In most countries, the central bank is at the apex of the financial system. It is responsible for ensuring the smooth working of the banking sector and other financial institutions. The primary aim of the central bank is to work closely with the government and so to operate in the public interest. The Federal Reserve System of the United States, the Bundesbank of West Germany and the Reserve Bank of India are all examples of central banks.

The Bank of England is the central bank of the United Kingdom monetary system. It was nationalised in 1946, and has the power to direct the actions of other banks. The Bank itself is subject to the direction of the Treasury. As far as is known the Bank of England has not issued any direction to any bank: it relies on 'moral suasion' and the co-operation of the banks.

Functions of the Bank of England

The Bank of England has several functions. Consider the following.

Responsibility for the implementation of monetary policy Monetary policy refers to control of the money supply by influencing the availability and cost of credit. The role of the Bank of England is to ensure that the supply of money is consistent with the attainment of the government's policy objectives. The government may, for example, specify a target rate of growth for the money supply and it will then be the Bank of England's responsibility to achieve that target.

The government's bank The Bank of England is responsible for looking after the government's finances. For example, it receives payments of taxes due to the government and pays out interest to the holders of the National Debt.

The bankers' bank The Bank holds accounts for other banks which use this facility to effect inter-bank settlements. Bankers' deposits at the Bank of England are regarded as being as good as cash by the banks because they can be turned into cash without delay.

Management of the foreign exchange reserves The Bank is responsible for the custody and use of the United Kingdom's foreign exchange reserves. These reserves, which are held in the Exchange Equalisation Fund, may be used to intervene in the foreign exchange market to influence the exchange rate between sterling and other currencies. Until the abolition of exchange controls in 1979, the Bank of England was also responsible for the enforcement of the exchange control regulations.

Management of the monetary system The Bank has among its responsibilities the management of the monetary system and the duty to ensure that sound banking principles are observed. It has a watching brief to keep its eye on the activities of banks and other financial institutions which are required to submit monthly returns to the Bank. The Bank also offers advice on monetary matters to the government.

Management and administration of the National Debt The Bank is responsible for issuing new government debt and arranging for its redemption. It aims to maintain an orderly market and the public's confidence in government debt.

The Bank of England's balance sheet

The weekly return in Table 1 illustrates the Bank's assets and liabilities: the division between the Issue Department and Banking Department is largely for historic reasons and has no real economic significance.

The Issue Department is responsible for the note issue. When notes are issued, the Issue Department receives interest-bearing government securities in return. The Issue Department frequently engages in open-market operations as part of the Bank's debt management. In order to avoid large cash payments to the public on a particular date, the Bank purchases government securities before they mature.

If an issue of a government security is under-subscribed the Issue

Table 1. Bank of England's balance sheet, 12 December 1979.

Liabilities	£ million	Assets	£ million
Issue Department			
Notes in circulation	10,089	Government securities	8,635
Notes in Banking Dept.	11	Other securities	1,465
	10,100		10,100
Banking Department			
Capital	15	Government securities	1462
Public deposits	20	Advances and other accounts	161
Special deposits	806	Premises and other securities	365
Bankers' deposits	462	Notes and coin	12
Reserves and other accounts	697		
	2,000		2,000

Source: Financial Statistics, Jan. 1980.

Department will purchase the remainder, which it will gradually sell to the public.

Turning to the Banking Department, *public deposits* refer to the government's account. The balance is kept to a minimum, and any temporary surplus is used to reduce government borrowing.

Special deposits are deposits of banks from time to time required by the Bank of England to be lodged in addition to normal reserve requirements. As we shall see, the Bank uses them to help control the level of bank lending.

Bankers' deposits are the deposits of the commercial banks, to which reference has already been made. *Other accounts* include the few private accounts the Bank still maintains for historical reasons, the accounts of overseas central banks and the accounts of its own staff.

The discount houses

The discount houses are unique to the British monetary system. In a sense, they are intermediaries between the Bank of England and the commercial banks. The discount houses attempt to make profits by creating a market in short-term financial instruments. They borrow short-term funds and use these funds to purchase higher yielding assets, such as Treasury Bills and commercial bills.

Definition: ***A Treasury Bill is an instrument of short-term borrowing by the Government, normally having a life of ninety-one days. Treasury Bills enable the Government to cover the difference between its revenues and expenditures on a week-to-week basis.***

Definition: ***A trade bill is an instrument of short-term borrowing by industrial and commercial companies.***

The discount houses borrow funds from commercial banks, accepting houses, overseas and other banks and from industrial and commercial companies. The banks are willing to lend funds to the discount houses at call, overnight, or at short notice because the banks earn some interest on these funds, while at the same time retaining a pool of liquidity. The discount houses have an arrangement with the Bank of England whereby they agree to tender for the whole of the weekly Treasury Bill issue. The price at which they bid for these bills determines the Treasury Bill rate. The higher the bid-price the lower is the rate of interest earned by holding them. For example, if the bid-price were £95 for a Bill with a face value of £100, the Government would be paying a 3-monthly interest rate of about 5 per cent; if the bid-price rose to £98, the 3-monthly interest rate would fall to about 2 per cent. Note that purchasing an asset for less than its face value is known as 'discounting'.

In return for guaranteeing the sale of the whole Treasury Bill issue, the discount houses have the privilege of borrowing from the Bank of England as 'lender of last resort'. If the commercial banks are short of cash they will recall some of their money at call or short notice from the discount houses. As these funds are tied up in Treasury Bills and other assets, the houses must turn to the lender of last resort – the Bank of England. The Bank will either rediscount (that is, buy) some of the bills or make loans against the security of such bills. The Bank will only deal in 'first class bills' – either Treasury Bills or commercial bills which bear at least two signatures of persons of an acceptable credit standing.

The Bank of England reserves the right to decide on what terms it will lend to the discount houses. The rate at which it will lend is called the *minimum lending rate*. This rate is fixed by the authorities with the approval of the Chancellor of the Exchequer. It is usually slightly higher than the market rate on Treasury Bills, however, and this means that when the discount houses borrow from the Bank they will be making losses on the loans they are repaying to the commercial banks. Thus, the discount houses will want to repay the loans from the Bank quickly and so will reduce the price at which they bid for the next issue of Treasury Bills, thus increasing the Treasury Bill rate. Because of the importance of the Treasury Bill rate for the money market, other interest rates will be forced up in sympathy. As funds are attracted into the Treasury Bill market from other parts of the money market, the reduced supply of loanable funds in these other markets will tend to push up other interest rates. This is one way, then, in which the Bank of England can influence interest rates. In fact, Treasury Bills now account for a relatively small proportion of the assets held by the discount market. As

Table 2. Distribution of discount houses' assets.

	£million	%
Treasury Bills	709	(14.4)
Other bills	2,638	(53.6)
Government stocks	764	(15.5)
Local authority stocks	373	(7.6)
Funds lent	280	(5.7)
Other investments	24	(0.5)
Other currencies	131	(2.7)
Total	4,919	

Source: Financial Statistics, Jan. 1980.

Table 2 shows, in December 1979, Treasury Bills accounted for less than 15 per cent of the discount market's total assets, although the actual proportion does vary from time to time.

Commercial banks

Commercial banks are deposit-taking institutions. They make profits by lending at a higher rate of interest than the rate they pay on deposits. Indeed, banks usually pay no interest on current account deposits. The banks operate the system of payment by cheques and offer a wide range of financial services to their customers.

Competition and credit control

Under the Competition and Credit Control System introduced by the Bank of England in September 1971, all banks are required to maintain a minimum ratio of 'reserve assets' to 'eligible liabilities' of $12\frac{1}{2}$ per cent. This is designed to ensure that the banks can meet the day-to-day demands of customers and also facilitates the Bank of England's control of the money supply.

'Eligible liabilities' consist mainly of sterling deposit liabilities (excluding deposits having an original maturity of more than two years) plus any sterling resources obtained by switching foreign currencies into sterling.

'Reserve assets' comprise:

(a) balances with the Bank of England (other than Special Deposits);
(b)Treasury Bills;
(c) money at call with the London money market;
(d) British government stocks with one year or less to final maturity;
(e) local authority bills eligible for rediscount at the Bank of England;
(f) commercial bills eligible for rediscount at the Bank of England (up to a maximum of 2 per cent of eligible liabilities).

The clearing banks have agreed to maintain as part of their minimum reserve assets ratio the equivalent of $1\frac{1}{2}$ per cent of their eligible liabilities in

Table 3. London clearing banks' assets, 12 December 1979.

		£ million
Notes and coin		937
Balances with Bank of England	Reserve assets	437
Money at call	Reserve assets	1,828
Treasury Bills	Reserve assets	474
Other bills	Reserve assets	674
British government stocks 0 to 1 year	Reserve assets	306
Special and supplementary deposit		393
Market loans		7,871
Other bills		72
Advances		23,758
Investments		2,742
Other currency assets		8,375
Miscellaneous		6,770
	Total	54,637

Source: Financial Statistics, Jan. 1980.

balances at the Bank of England. The London clearing banks' assets are illustrated in Table 3.

Fractional reserve banking

In managing their portfolios, the commercial banks have two aims that may conflict: first, they wish to maintain an adequate stock of liquid assets in case their reserve assets ratio comes under pressure; secondly, they wish to earn a high rate of return on their assets in order to maximise their profits. But the highest yielding assets tend to be illiquid – for example, a large proportion of advances to customers, though, profitable, are illiquid; similarly, equities are illiquid in that any attempt to sell a large amount of stock would depress stock prices and cause capital losses.

As mentioned above, under the Competition and Credit Control System, all banks are required to maintain a minimum ratio of reserve assets to eligible liabilities of $12\frac{1}{2}$ per cent. This means that for every £12.50 of reserve assets held by the banks, they can expand deposits up to a theoretical maximum of £100. This process is sometimes referred to as the multiple creation of bank deposits, or more simply as credit creation.

Credit creation To illustrate the *principle* of credit creation, consider a hypothetical example of a closed economy with a *single monopoly bank* which observes a minimum *cash ratio* rather than a reserve assets ratio. Suppose, in fact, that the bank wishes to maintain 10 per cent of its total deposits in cash in order to be able to meet the day-to-day demands of its customers. Table 4 shows the bank's initial position; it has total deposits amounting to £10,000 and is just maintaining its 10 per cent cash ratio by holding in its tills £1,000 in cash.

Table 4. The bank's initial balance sheet.

Liabilities		Assets	
Deposits	10,000	Cash	1,000
		Loans and investments	9,000
	10,000		10,000

Suppose now that a customer deposits an extra £2,000 in cash. The bank's new balance sheet is shown in Table 5. Notice that the ratio of cash to deposits is no longer 10 per cent, but is now as high as 25 per cent. Given that the bank's *desired* cash ratio is 10 per cent and that the bank wishes to maximise its profits, it will increase its total deposits to £30,000 so as to

Table 5. The bank's balance sheet after new cash deposit of £2,000.

Liabilities		Assets	
Deposits	12,000	Cash	3,000
		Loans and investments	9,000
	12,000		12,000

restore the desired ratio. The bank does this by granting new loans amounting to £18,000.

The final position is shown in Table 6. The cash deposit of £2,000 has led to an increase in loans and investments of £18,000, so that total deposits have risen by £20,000 – that is, by ten times the amount of the cash deposit. Thus, in this example, the *credit multiplier* (the figure any increase in cash deposits has to be multiplied by to obtain the increase in total deposits) is ten. This means that every £1 held by the bank in cash is capable of supporting total deposits of £10.

Table 6. The bank's final balance sheet.

Liabilities		Assets	
Deposits	30,000	Cash	3,000
		Loan and investments	27,000
	30,000		30,000

If, however, the bank's desired cash ratio rose to $12\frac{1}{2}$ per cent, cash holdings of £3,000 would only support total deposits of £24,000 (because £3,000 is $12\frac{1}{2}$ per cent of £24,000). Note that the credit multiplier in this case is only eight. It follows that there is an inverse relationship between the cash ratio and the credit multiplier and, therefore, the volume of bank credit.

Although this important principle of credit creation has been illustrated above for a single bank system, the same principle will operate in an economy with many banks provided that there is an efficient *clearing system*. When a bank creates a loan in a multi-bank system, the customers may write cheques in favour of customers of other banks and at the end of the day, all the banks have claims against each other. Most of these claims will be offset by counter-claims, so that only the net indebtedness has to be settled by using the banks' balances at the central bank.

Credit creation in the United Kingdom Although since 1971 the United Kingdom banking system has been required to observe, not a cash ratio, but the $12\frac{1}{2}$ per cent reserve assets ratio, the underlying principle of credit creation remains unchanged. Thus, if the banks' reserve assets are increased by £1 million, the maximum possible increase in the level of bank deposits is £8 million.

In practice, the credit multiplier is not as large as eight because of *leakages*. As stated above, if an individual bank creates loans, some of the new deposits will end up in different banks. If any individual bank expands lending faster than the other banks in the system, it will experience a drain of its reserve assets. This reduces the bank's capacity to create credit. Other leakages include: (a) the holding of *excess reserves* by banks – that is holding more than the minimum reserve requirement; (b) an increase in the public's desired cash holdings; and (c) a net outflow of currency overseas as a result of a balance of payments deficit.

Control of the money supply

There are several ways in which the Bank of England can seek to control the supply of money and to influence credit conditions.

Open-market operations This refers to sales and purchases of government securities on the open market by the Bank of England. If the Bank wishes to reduce the money supply it will sell securities through its broker on the open market. The buyers will pay for these securities with cheques drawn on their accounts with the commercial banks. The Bank of England which now holds these cheques will thus debit the accounts of the commercial banks with itself. This fall in bankers' deposits represents a fall in the commercial banks' reserve assets. If they were previously operating at the minimum $12\frac{1}{2}$ per cent ratio, the banks will now have to reduce their deposit liabilities, say, by calling in advances to their customers, by selling assets or by refusing to grant new advances. If the banks were previously operating with a reserve asset ratio above $12\frac{1}{2}$ per cent, however, the potential that exists for them to expand their deposits is reduced. Note that in this case if the Bank of England uses open-market operations to reduce the money supply, the official intention may be frustrated as long as the banks' reserve assets ratio remains above $12\frac{1}{2}$ per cent. Conversely, if the Bank of England wishes to expand the money supply, it will instruct its broker to buy securities on the open market and will pay for them with cheques drawn on itself. The sellers of the securities will deposit these cheques with the commercial banks, which will present them for payment to the Bank. The Bank will credit the commercial banks' accounts and this represents an increase in their reserve assets. The commercial banks will now be in a position to undertake a multiple expansion of bank deposits.

Interest rate policy Changes in the Bank of England's minimum lending rate are often linked with the use of open-market operations. Consider the case where the Bank of England sells securities in an attempt to reduce the money supply. The sale of securities depresses their price and so raises interest rates. As explained above, the commercial banks' reserve assets are reduced so that they may recall their loans from the discount houses. The discount houses may be forced to borrow from the Bank of England as lender of last resort. In order to influence the upward movement of interest rates generally, the Bank of England may announce an increase in the minimum lending rate. Alternatively, minimum lending rate may be raised initially, thus tending to force up other interest rates. This may be done in order to facilitate the sale of the government securities on the open market.

Special deposits The Bank of England has the power to require banks to lodge 'special deposits' with it. Calls for special deposits are normally expressed as a uniform percentage of each bank's total eligible liabilities. Special deposits do not count as a reserve asset, and normally earn interest at a rate equivalent to the Treasury Bill rate. As special deposits are compulsory, by using them the Bank can be sure of reducing the banks' liquid assets, and they are equivalent to an open-market sale, in that they reduce the banks' ability to increase credit (and hence the money supply).

Supplementary special deposits This scheme was first introduced in 1973 and is sometimes known as the 'corset' scheme because of the limit placed on the amount of bank deposits that the banks can create without having to place supplementary special deposits at the Bank of England. For example, in measures announced in November 1979 the banks' interest-bearing eligible liabilities (averaged over a 3 month period) were permitted to grow 1 per cent per month until June 1980. Faster growth would incur the requirement to lodge deposits at the Bank of England on a sliding scale, designed to make it unprofitable for the banks to expand their deposits too fast. For an excess rate of growth of 3 per cent or less, the banks would have to lodge supplementary deposits equal to 5 per cent of the excess; in respect of an excess of over 3 per cent but not more than 5 per cent, the rate was 25 per cent; thereafter, the rate was 50 per cent. Supplementary special deposits lodged at the Bank of England are not interest-bearing.

Ceilings The Bank of England can lay down quantitative limits on the growth of bank deposits. While ceilings have been used in the past (for example, in the late 1960s), since the introduction of the Competition and Credit Control System in 1971, their use has been discouraged. The banks argued that the overdraft system meant that it was impossible to control bank lending as precisely as quantitative limits would imply. Quantitative limits were also thought to restrict competition as they hampered efficient banks who were in a position to create new deposits.

Funding Funding is the term applied when the Bank of England attempts to lengthen the maturity of outstanding government debt. If the Bank restricts its Treasury Bill issue and sells longer dated securities, this reduces the commercial banks' reserve assets, and thus restricts their capability of expanding bank deposits.

Requests From time to time, the Bank of England requests banks to channel their lending into or away from certain areas. For example, in April 1978, the Bank of England asked banks to provide finance 'for both working capital and fixed investment by manufacturing industry and for the expansion of exports and the saving of imports'. To achieve these goals, banks were asked to restrain other lending, in particular 'to persons and property companies and for purely financial transactions'.

Changing the reserve asset ratio Of course, it is possible for the Bank of England to control the money supply by changing the minimum reserve assets ratio. As shown above, an increase in the reserve assets ratio reduces the credit multiplier. In practice, this action is not likely to be taken very often because it may have undesirable disruptive effects on the financial system.

Other sources of changes in the money supply

In addition to the methods of control used by the central bank, there are a number of other sources of changes in the money supply. Consider the following.

Government expenditure financed by borrowing from the central bank When the Bank of England issues new currency it obtains interest-earning government securities in return. The issue of currency may be regarded as helping the government to finance its expenditure. This method of government borrowing is sometimes described as 'turning the printing press'. In practice, the issue of new currency in the United Kingdom is geared towards meeting the expenditure requirements of consumers. Thus, there are seasonal variations in the issue of banknotes: in the holiday season and before Christmas, for example, the issue of banknotes is increased to meet the extra demand.

Government borrowing from the banking system If the public sector is running a deficit, the other sectors of the economy may deposit part of their consequent financial surplus with the banking system. These deposits form part of the money supply. The government might then borrow these funds from the banking system. This may lead to a further expansion of the money supply, as part of the public sector borrowing will be in the form of Treasury Bills, which count as reserve assets for the banks. Given the demand for borrowing by customers and assuming no offsetting action by the central bank, this increase in reserve assets may lead to an increase in the money supply.

A change in the public's desired cash holdings If the public decides to hold more cash and smaller bank deposits, the banks will need to replenish the cash in their tills by drawing on their balances at the Bank of England. As reserve assets fall, the banks may be forced to reduce further the level of bank deposits. This mechanism would work in reverse if the public decided to hold less cash and bigger bank deposits.

A change in the banks' demand for excess reserves Most mechanical models of the determination of the money supply assume that the banks will adhere to a constant ratio of reserves to deposits. More precisely, it is assumed that the banks will adhere to the minimum legal ratio, on the assumption that the banks will wish to expand bank deposits to the maximum. In practice, however, the banks may decide, or be forced, to hold reserves in excess of the legal requirement. This might happen, for example, if there were not enough potential borrowers of a satisfactory credit standing. This means that the Bank of England cannot be sure of success if it uses open-market operations to expand the money supply. The banks may simply allow their reserve assets ratio to rise.

Balance of payments disequilibrium A balance of payments *deficit* involves a net outflow of currency. In effect, the Bank of England has to finance the deficit by providing foreign currencies in exchange for domestic currency. Unless offset by an expansionary open-market operation, this will result in a contraction of the money supply. Conversely, a balance of payments *surplus* involves a net inflow of currency, and unless offset by a contractionary open-market operation, this will result in an expansion of the money supply.

Money and banking in less developed countries

The role of money

The stock of money has a relatively narrow base in less developed countries (LDCs) as it consists mainly of banknotes and coins in circulation. In these countries, habits of payment by cheque are still in their infancy so that bank deposits constitute a relatively small proportion of the total money supply. As a consequence, the volume of bank deposits has a minor influence on the general price level and total expenditure. The scope of monetary policy measures (such as discount rates, open-market operations and changes in reserve requirements) in regulating total expenditure is therefore limited.

Given the paucity of aggregate savings and the narrow base for taxation, most governments in LDCs resort to budgetary deficits, financed through the printing of money, as a means of speeding up the process of economic development. The resulting increase in the money supply can lead to a faster rate of inflation and a deterioration in the balance of payments. This is because domestic inflationary pressures generally lead to the diversion of foreign currency meant to be spent on imported plant and equipment to the importation of foodstuffs and other consumer goods.

There is, however, a counter-argument that the printing of money within 'safe' limits may not be inflationary. This is because in a growing economy, business units multiply and existing businesses expand, leading to an increased demand for cash holdings for reasons of safety and liquidity. In addition, part of the increased money supply may be hoarded as the non-monetised sector (in some cases as large as 20 to 30 per cent of the economy) is brought within the monetary sector of the LDCs economy. The non-monetised sector is characterised by barter and is known to have high hoarding propensities with respect to both commodities and precious metals.

The role of banking

In several Asian and African countries, central banks have been set up by statute and are based on the model of the Bank of England. Like the Bank of England, these central banks maintain two separate departments for the transaction of business: the banking department concerned purely with banking business; and the issue department concerned with the issue of notes.

In a number of LDCs commercial banks have also followed the English orthodoxy of branch banking. The operations of commercial banks in LDCs, however, are concentrated in major cities and towns. Additionally, loans and advances are concentrated on major industrial borrowers. The banks generally maintain large excess reserves with consequent loss of potential profits. The demand for personal loans and agricultural credit remains largely unsatisfied. Thus, small traders, indigenous producers and small farmers have to depend upon friends, relatives, landlords and money-lenders for loans. It is well-known that money-lenders typically charge exorbitant interest rates which are insensitive to interest rates in the organised money markets.

As indicated above, banks and financial institutions in most LDCs have not reached the same stage of development as those in the industrially advanced countries. Therefore, central banks in most LDCs have a statutory responsibility to promote the growth of financial institutions so that the latter can mobilise and channel the community's savings into planned investment. A notable feature of this policy has been the rapid increase in the number of industrial and agricultural banks and finance corporations during the past two decades. Some central banks also give positive encouragement to the growth of co-operative banks and credit societies and thus promote 'thrift' and 'self-help' at local and regional levels in the LDCs.

Conclusion

This chapter has considered the important topic of money: we examined the definition of money, its functions and traced its evolution from the days of the goldsmiths. Next the main activities of the central bank and the commercial banks were described, highlighting their roles in influencing the money supply. In order to appreciate fully the implications of changes in the money supply on other variables in the economy, we must first consider the factors influencing the demand for money. This is our objective in the next chapter.

Further reading

Crockett, A., *Money: Theory, Policy and Institutions*, Nelson, Sunbury-on-Thames, 1979.

Carter, H. and **Partington, I.,** *Applied Economics in Banking and Finance*, Oxford University Press, Oxford, 1979 (Ch. 5, 6 and 7).

Prest, A.R. and **Coppock, D.J.** (eds), *The UK Economy: A Manual of Applied Economics*, Weidenfeld and Nicolson, London, 1978 (Ch. 2).

Exercises

1. Review your understanding of the following terms:

supply of money	discount houses
medium of exchange	Treasury Bills
store of value	open-market operations
unit of account	special deposits
standard of deferred payment	reserve assets
central bank	excess reserves

2. A monopoly bank has the following balance sheet. It is required to maintain a ratio of cash to total deposits of 10 per cent.

Liabilities		Assets	
Deposits	2,000	Cash	500
		Bills	500
		Advances	1,000
	2,000		2,000

(a) Illustrate the bank's profit-maximising balance sheet on the assumption that it grants new advances.

(b) Suppose the bank has the original balance sheet and that the minimum cash ratio is increased to $12\frac{1}{2}$ per cent. Illustrate the bank's new profit-maximising balance sheet on the assumption that it wishes to maintain a 50 per cent liquidity ratio – that is, the ratio of cash and bills to total deposits.

3. Discuss the main disadvantages of an economy in which incomes are paid in kind and transactions are carried out by barter.

4. 'Money can only be defined in terms of its functions.' Discuss.

5. Consider the view that no banking and financial system can operate effectively without a central bank.

6. Describe the methods available to the Bank of England to control the supply of money in the United Kingdom. What are the limitations on these methods of controlling the money supply?

22 Money – II

Introduction

In this chapter, we examine the factors which influence the demand for money and the important question of how the economy reacts to changes in the supply of money. Economists are interested in the economy's reactions to such changes because society's ability to purchase goods and services may be affected. Additionally, changes in the money supply not only affect individual holders of money, but may also lead to inflation and so inject a degree of instability into the economy.

Discussion of the effects of changes in the stock of money goes back hundreds of years. In 1750, David Hume (in his essay, 'Of Money') gave an early account of the relationship between a country's stock of money and level of prices. This relationship is generally described as the 'quantity theory of money'. In 1911, an influential exposition of the theory was presented by the American economist, Irving Fisher. In more recent times, there has been a long running debate between monetarists and Keynesians as to the precise influence of money on individuals, businesses and the economy as a whole.

This chapter starts with a discussion of the quantity theory of money, setting out first the Fisher version and secondly, the Cambridge cash-balance version. The Keynesian theory of money is then considered and the liquidity-preference theory of the determination of the rate of interest is explained. Finally, we consider the 'modern quantity theory' which is the basis of the views put forward by monetarists.

The quantity theory of money

Fisher's version

Irving Fisher's version of the quantity theory can be explained in terms of the following 'equation of exchange':

$$MV \equiv PT$$

where M is the nominal stock of money in circulation and V is the transactions velocity of circulation of money (that is, the average number of times the given quantity of money changes hands in transactions); P is the average price of all transactions and T is the number of transactions that take place during the time period. Both MV and PT measure the total value of transactions during the time period and so must be identical. Thus, the 'equation' is really an *identity* which must always be true: it tells us only that the total amount of money handed over in transactions is equal to the value of what is sold. As an example, suppose that during a given time period, the number of transactions (T) is 1,000 and that the average price of these transactions (P) is £5, then it follows that the value of what is sold (PT) is £5,000. If the money stock (M) is only £500, then the average number of times each pound changes hands, the velocity of circulation (V), must be 10. As an identity, the quantity theory is no more than a way of calculating the velocity of circulation.

The identity, however, is converted into a *theory* of the determination of the price level by assuming: (a) that the money supply is determined by the monetary authorities; (b) that the number of transactions is fixed in the short-run because of the classical presumption that the economy operates automatically at full employment; and (c) that the velocity of circulation is also fixed in the short-run because it depends largely on institutional factors (such as whether workers are paid weekly or monthly) which themselves tend to remain constant for long periods of time.

With T and V constant, the identity can be re-written as follows:

$$M\bar{V} \equiv P\bar{T}$$

It now follows that changes in M, initiated by the monetary authorities, will cause proportionate changes in P. Notice that the direction of causation runs *from* changes in the stock of money *to* changes in the general price level.

Definition: ***The quantity theory of money states that the average price of transactions in an economy is proportional to the nominal quantity of money in circulation.***

According to the quantity theory, money is held only for the purpose of making payments for current transactions. Thus, the demand for money is called a *transactions demand*. When the money supply is increased, people find themselves holding more than they need for current transactions and so attempt to spend the excess. It is this extra spending which, given full employment and consequent constant *number* of transactions, pushes up the price level. As prices rise, the value of transactions rises and so the demand for money rises. This mechanism ceases when the demand for money and supply of money are equal again.

Cambridge version

A version of the quantity theory which concentrates on the factors that determine the demand for money was developed by economists at the University of Cambridge. These economists argued that an individual's demand for cash balances (or nominal money) is proportional to the individual's money income. If this were true of all individuals, then the aggregate demand for money (M_D) could be written as proportional to money national income (Y):

$$M_D = kY$$

where k is a constant. Notice that Y in this version represents the money value of spending on all final goods and services produced during the time period. This is much narrower than Fisher's notion of the value of all transactions (PT) which included spending on intermediate goods and financial assets, as well as final goods and services.

Since Y is money national income, it can be divided into its price and quantity components, so that

$$M_D = kPQ$$

where P is the general price level and Q is real income (or output). Notice that k is the reciprocal of the *income* velocity of circulation of money (which can be defined as the average number of times the money supply changes hands in financing the national income). This demand for money arises to enable the community to fulfill its planned expenditures during the intervening periods between receipts of wages, salaries or other forms of income.

If we continue to assume that the money supply (M) is under the control of the monetary authorities, we can write that in equilibrium,

$$M = M_D$$

Substituting from above, we have,

$$M = kPQ$$

With k constant, and Q fixed because the economy is assumed to remain at full employment, an increase in M will create an excess supply of money. This leads people to increase their spending directly on goods and services so that the general price level is pulled upwards. As this happens, the demand for money increases and eventually becomes equal to the money supply again.

Thus, both the Fisher and Cambridge versions of the quantity theory come to the same important conclusion: *that an increase in the money supply leads directly to an increase in spending and, with full employment, the general price level is proportional to the quantity of money in circulation.*

Keynesian theory of money

Keynes divided the demand for money into three types: (a) the transactions demand, which is the demand by firms and households for holdings of money to finance day-to-day transactions; (b) precautionary demand, which arises out of uncertainty and the desire not to be caught short of ready cash; and (c) the speculative demand, which is the demand for money as a financial asset and therefore part of a wealth portfolio. In (a) and (b), money is clearly held mainly for its role as a medium of exchange. In (c), it is held mainly for its role as a store of wealth.

What factors influence these three demands for money? Consider them in turn.

Transactions demand

The transactions demand for money arises because individuals receive their incomes weekly or monthly and yet have to pay for many of the goods and services they buy on a day-to-day basis. The amount of money held by an individual to finance these transactions, therefore, is likely to depend on the size of the individual's money income and on institutional arrangements, such as how often the individual is paid and how often he pays his bills and engages in monetary transactions. If we assume that these institutional arrangements remain unchanged, then money income is the main determinant. For the economy as a whole, we can expect the total demand for money for transactions purposes to depend directly on *money national income.* Using functional notation, we can write,

$$L_t = f(Y)$$

where L_t is the transactions demand for money.

Note that for a given level of income, the transactions demand for money would rise if more households were paid fortnightly or monthly rather than weekly. This is because such households would find themselves holding more money on average to finance the same total value of transactions. This is illustrated in Fig. 1 where a household, which at first is paid an income of £100 *per week*, is assumed to spend all of its income in a steady stream until, at the end of each week, it has nothing left until it receives its next £100. The household's average holding of money (that is, its transactions demand for money) is £50. If the household should now be paid £200 fortnightly, it can be seen that its average money holding increases to £100. So the household's demand for money has risen even though its income has remained unchanged.

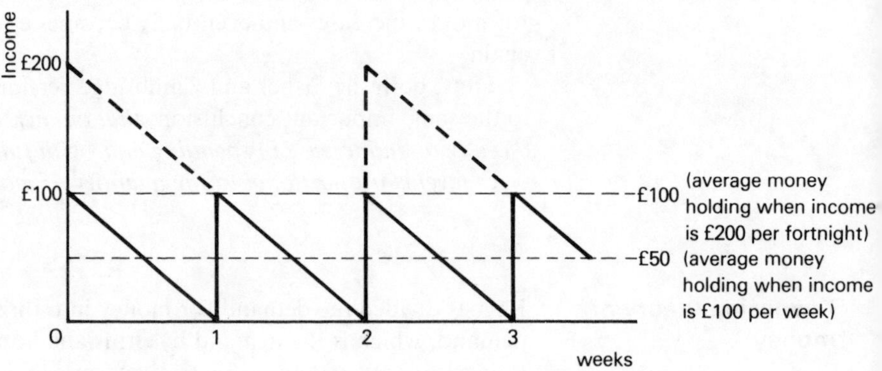

Fig. 1. The transactions demand for money.

In what follows, we ignore the possibility of such institutional changes and assume that the transactions demand for money depends only on money national income.

Precautionary demand

This demand for money arises out of consumers' desires to provide for unexpected, and therefore unplanned, expenditures. For example, a salesman on a business trip may carry some extra cash with him, not for expected transactions, but to guard against any unforeseen contingencies, such as his car breaking down, or the possibility of his coming across a cash bargain.

This demand for money is also likely to depend on national income: the higher the total value of transactions, the more money will be needed to guard against unexpected transactions. It can be argued that rates of interest may also influence the precautionary demand. The rate of interest is the opportunity cost of holding money: thus, if interest rates rise, consumers and firms may be tempted to reduce their precautionary holdings and hold interest-bearing assets instead.

For simplicity, however, it is convenient to assume that the precautionary demand does not respond to changes in interest rates (that is, it is completely interest-inelastic). This enables us to combine it with the transactions demand and to suppose that the total transactions and precautionary demand for money is a function of money national income. Indeed, in what follows, wherever we refer to the transactions demand, L_t, it should be understood that this includes the precautionary demand.

Speculative demand

It was in his analysis of the speculative demand for money that Keynes differed fundamentally from his predecessors. Before examining the nature of this demand for money, however, we first have to understand the relationship between the price of a bond and the rate of interest. Recall that a bond is an asset that earns a fixed sum of money for its owner each year. In a perfect capital market, the price of a perpetual bond (that is, one which is never redeemed) which earns £5 per annum for its owner will be £100 when the rate of interest is 5 per cent – this is because £100 invested in any other income-earning asset would earn a return of £5. If the market rate of interest now rises to 10 per cent, the price of the bond will fall to £50, because £50 invested in any income-earning asset will now yield £5. Similarly, if the rate of interest should fall to 2 per cent, the price of the bond would rise to £250. There is, then, an *inverse relationship* between the price of a bond and the rate of interest. It follows that an increase in the rate of interest, which reduces the saleable value of a bond, means a potential capital loss for an investor who purchased the bond at a higher price. Similarly, a fall in the rate of interest means a potential capital gain for investors.

Keynes argued that individuals would have some expectation or conception of the 'normal' rate of interest, although each individual's conception of what was normal might differ. If the prevailing rate of interest were greater than an individual's conception of the normal rate, that individual would expect the rate of interest to fall in the near future. It follows that the higher the prevailing rate of interest, the more people will anticipate that the next change will be downwards. Since a fall in the rate of interest implies capital gains for bond-holders, the theory predicts that an abnormally high interest rate will lead to a large demand for bonds and, consequently, a small demand for speculative money balances.

The analysis applies in reverse if the actual rate of interest is thought to be abnormally low. In this case, individuals will expect the rate to rise in the near future and so will expect potential capital losses for bond-holders. In this situation, bonds will appear less attractive and potential buyers will postpone intended purchases and bond-holders themselves will attempt to sell bonds before the fall in bond prices. Thus, if the prevailing interest rate is low, the theory predicts a low demand for bonds and, consequently, a high demand for speculative money balances.

In this way, Keynes derived an *inverse* relationship between the rate of interest and the speculative demand for money, as illustrated in Fig. 2. Notice that as the rate of interest falls from Oi_1 to Oi_2, the speculative demand for money increases from OL_s^1 to OL_s^2. But at the low interest rate, Oi_3, bonds become so unattractive (because their prices are high and expected to fall) that the speculative demand for money becomes perfectly elastic.

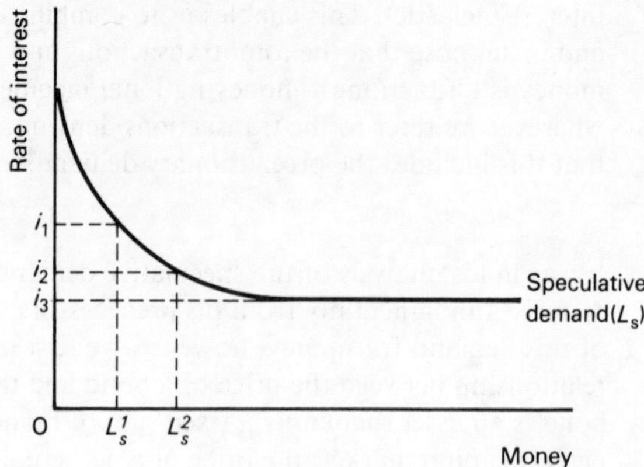

Fig. 2. The speculative demand for money.

Total demand for money

The total demand for money (or total liquidity preference) is found by adding together the transactions, precautionary and speculative demands. Figure 3 shows the total demand for money plotted against the rate of interest: L_s represents the speculative demand and L_t represents the transactions and precautionary demands for a given level of income. The horizontal summation of L_s and L_t yields the total demand for money curve, L. Note that a rise in income, which would cause L_t to increase, would shift the total demand for money curve to the right. Similarly, a fall in income would shift it to the left.

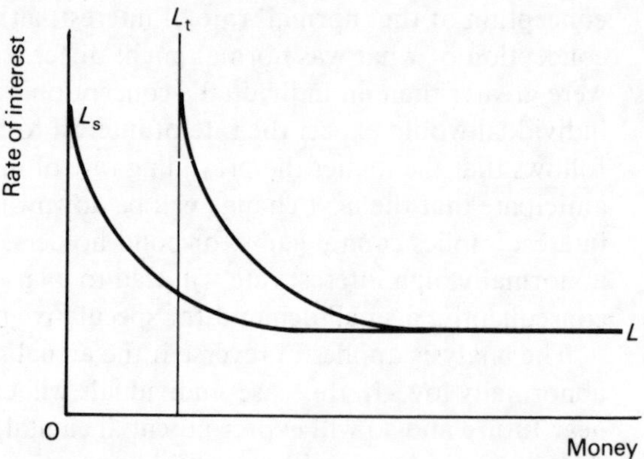

Fig. 3. The total demand for money.

Effects of a change in the money supply

In Fig. 4, L represents the total demand for money and M_s^1 the initial supply of money. Given competitive forces in the money market, the interaction of this demand and supply will determine the market rate of interest at its equilibrium level Oi_1. This is the Keynesian *liquidity-preference theory* of interest. Should the prevailing interest rate be greater than Oi_1, there would be an excess supply of money (or excess demand for bonds) which would push up the price of bonds and push down interest rates, back towards the equilibrium. Similarly, at interest rates below Oi_1, the excess demand for money exerts upward pressure on interest rates. The equilibrium at Oi_1 can, therefore, be described as a stable one.

Fig. 4. Effect of a change in the money supply on the rate of interest.

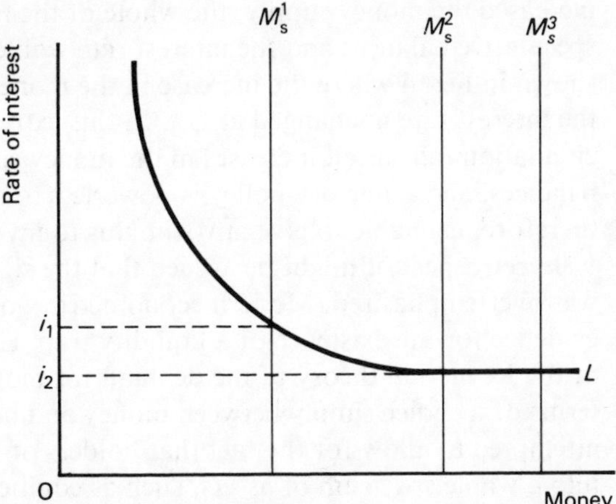

Now suppose that the money supply is increased to M_s^2. This creates an excess supply of money at the interest rate Oi_1. According to the Keynesian theory, firms and households will attempt to run down the excess money balances they are being forced to hold by buying bonds. But, in the aggregate, they are unable to increase their holdings of bonds and they only succeed in driving up the price of bonds. As we have seen, an increase in the price of bonds implies a fall in the rate of interest. As the rate of interest falls, so the speculative demand for money increases. Eventually, the rate of interest will reach Oi_2 at which point firms and households are induced to hold the increased money supply in speculative balances.

Note that the major effect of the change in the money supply is on the rate of interest. National income and employment will only be affected if the fall in the rate of interest causes a rise in investment and, possibly, consumption. In the Keynesian model, consumption and investment only respond weakly to changes in the rate of interest – that is to say, they are interest-inelastic. This implies that monetary policy is not very powerful as a means of influencing output and employment.

The analysis applies in reverse for a fall in the money supply. This time, firms and households find that their actual money balances are below their desired money balances. They attempt to build them up by selling bonds. In the aggregate, however, the community cannot reduce its bond holdings and the attempt to do so only drives down bond prices and, therefore, leads to an increase in interest rates. As the interest rate rises, the speculative demand for money falls and money market equilibrium is eventually restored.

The liquidity trap The horizontal part of the total demand for money curve shown in Fig. 4 is sometimes referred to as the liquidity trap, a theoretical possibility pointed out by Keynes in the *General Theory*. The liquidity trap occurs where the demand for money becomes perfectly interest-elastic at some very low interest rate. The argument is that at abnormally low interest rates (at or below Oi_2 in Fig. 4) virtually everyone would expect the interest rate to rise towards its normal level in the near future. In this situation, then, virtually everyone would be expecting a fall in the price of bonds and, therefore, capital losses for bond-holders. Thus, if the monetary authorities increased the money supply, the whole of the increase would be added to speculative balances and the interest rate would remain unchanged. This is shown in Fig. 4 where the increase in the money supply from M_s^2 to M_s^3 leaves the interest rate unchanged at Oi_2. In this extreme case, the velocity of circulation falls as all increases in the money supply are added to 'idle' balances, and monetary policy is powerless to drive down interest rates and, therefore, is unable to give any stimulus to investment or consumption.

In retrospect, it might be argued that the significance of the liquidity trap was over-emphasised. Modern econometric work has found no conclusive evidence for the existence of a liquidity trap. However, the major weakness of the Keynesian theory of the demand for money is that it is couched in terms of a choice simply between money and bonds. More recent work has attempted to allow for the fact that holders of money balances may switch into a whole spectrum of assets, such as equities, trade bills and certificates of deposit.

The modern quantity theory

Milton Friedman restated the quantity theory of money in 1956 as a theory of the demand for money, and this 'modern quantity theory' has become the basis of views put forward by monetarists. In this theory, money is seen as just one of a number of ways in which wealth can be held, along with all kinds of financial assets, consumer durables, property and 'human wealth'. A wealth portfolio, together with the rates of return on each asset, is illustrated in Table 1 where the assets are listed in decreasing order of liquidity. Recall from Chapter 20 that human wealth consists of all those

Table 1. The assets in a wealth portfolio and their rates of return.

Assets	Rate of return variables
Money	Price level (inverse relationship)
Bonds	The rate of interest on bonds (direct relationship) The expected rate of change of the rate of interest on bonds (inverse relationship)
Equities	The rate of interest on equities (direct relationship) The expected rate of change of the rate of interest on equities (inverse relationship) The rate of price inflation (direct relationship)
Goods	The rate of price inflation (direct relationship)
Human capital	---

physical and mental attributes possessed by individuals which enables them to earn income from selling their labour services.

Since money is seen as just one of the ways in which wealth can be held, Friedman sees the real demand for money (M_D / P) as depending on total wealth (W), the expected rates of return on the various forms of wealth (r), the ratio of human wealth to non-human wealth (w) and society's tastes and preferences (T). Using functional notation, we can write:

$$\frac{M_D}{P} = f(W, r, w, T)$$

Consider each of the independent variables in turn.

Total wealth The demand for money will be directly related to total wealth (which is the sum of human and non-human wealth) so long as money is regarded as a 'normal good' by wealth holders. Thus, as total wealth increases, the desire to hold money (one of the components of total wealth) will also increase.

Expected rates of return on wealth Since the rates of return on bonds and equities represent the opportunity cost of holding money, we can expect an inverse relationship between these expected rates of return and the demand for money. Notice that, in addition to the various market rates of interest, the expected rate of inflation should also be taken into account here. The higher is the rate of inflation, the greater is the negative return from holding money and the more attractive are the alternative interest-bearing assets. Thus, there is also an inverse relationship between the rate of inflation and the real demand for money.

The ratio of human wealth to non-human wealth Friedman includes this variable because human wealth is so illiquid. It cannot be sold (in the absence of slavery) and individuals have only a limited ability to transfer non-human wealth into human wealth (though an individual can, of course, invest in himself through education or by undertaking training courses). The higher the *w* ratio, the greater will be the demand for money in order to compensate for the limited marketability of human wealth.

Tastes and preferences Friedman argues that the demand for money also depends on a number of factors which are likely to influence wealth holders' tastes and preferences for money.

The main problem with this demand for money function is that of finding a method of measuring total wealth. Friedman suggested that *permanent income* (Y_p) may provide an acceptable proxy variable. Recall from Chapter 20 that this is a long-run measure of income which can be thought of as the present value of the expected flow of income from the stock of human and non-human wealth over a long period of time. It can be estimated as an average of past, present and expected future incomes. Incorporating this into the function, and assuming that *w* and *T* are constant in the short-run, we can write:

$$\frac{M_D}{P} = f(Y_p, r)$$

This formulation is not dissimilar in appearance from the Keynesian liquidity-preference function, $L = f(Y, i)$. There are, however, two crucial differences. First, the Keynesian function includes *current* national income, whereas Friedman is using permanent income as a proxy for total wealth.

Secondly, in the Keynesian function (where money is a close substitute for bonds), the demand for money is interest-elastic because if the rate of interest earned from holding bonds changes, wealth holders are assumed to react only by changing their money holdings; but in Friedman's function (where money is a substitute for *all* other assets, both financial and real), the demand for money is believed to exhibit low interest-elasticity.

Effects of a change in the money supply

Now suppose that the central bank increases the money supply – for example, by purchasing government securities on the open market. Assuming that the money market is in equilibrium initially, the policy will raise the supply of money above the demand for money, and wealth holders will find themselves holding more money than they desire in their portfolios. They will attempt to adjust their portfolios by spending their excess money balances on a wide range of assets, financial and real.

This brings us to the key difference between the Keynesian and monetarist models. In the Keynesian model, wealth holders attempt to spend their excess money balances on bonds, thereby forcing down interest rates. In the monetarist case, wealth holders attempt to spend their excess money balances on all types of assets, including physical goods. Thus, there is an effect on interest rates downwards (as in the Keynesian model), *but also a direct effect upwards on the output or prices of goods and services*. This is illustrated in Fig. 5 where the increase in the money supply is shown by the shift from M_s^1 to M_s^2. If the demand for money curve remained unchanged, the interest rate would fall to Oi_2. The increased demand for goods and services, however, leads to an increase in the output or prices of these goods and services, so that the nominal demand for money increases at every interest rate. The demand for money curve shifts from M_D to M_D^1 and the interest rate Oi_3 and a higher level of money national income result.

Notice that in Fig. 5, the demand for money curves are drawn fairly steeply. This reflects the monetarist view that the demand for money is interest-inelastic. A summary of the main tenets of monetarism and the monetarist policy recommendations are summarised at the end of the next chapter.

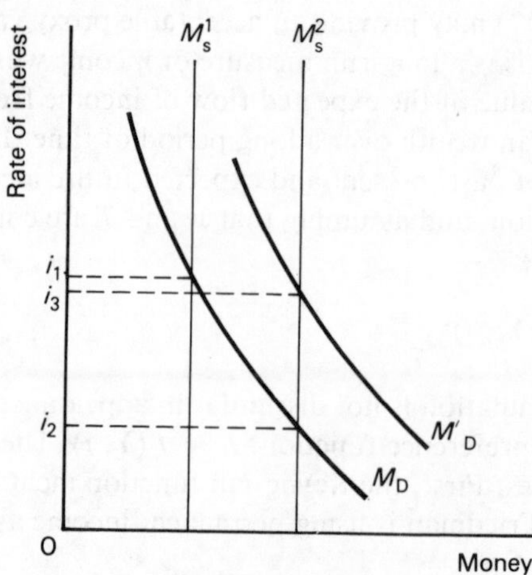

Fig. 5. Effect of an increase in the money supply.

Conclusion

In this chapter, we have considered the main determinants of the demand for money in terms of, first, the classical quantity theory of money; secondly, the Keynesian liquidity-preference theory; and finally, Friedman's modern quantity theory. In all three approaches, we have examined the effects on money national income of changes in the money supply.

This discussion is continued in the next chapter where, after deriving the IS–LM model and considering the contribution of Keynes to economic theory and policy, we turn our attention once more to the monetarist challenge to Keynesian economics.

Further reading

Crockett, A., *Money: Theory, Policy and Institutions*, Nelson, Sunbury-on-Thames, 1979 (Ch. 3 and 4).
Gowland, D.H. (ed.), *Modern Economic Analysis*, Butterworths, London, 1979 (Ch. 5).
Westaway, A.J. and **Weyman-Jones, T.G.,** *Macroeconomics: Theory, Evidence and Policy*, Longman, London, 1977 (Ch. 9 and 10).

Exercises

1. Review your understanding of the following terms:

Fisher's 'equation of exchange'	speculative demand for money
transactions velocity of circulation	liquidity-preference
income velocity of circulation	liquidity trap
Cambridge cash-balance approach	interest-elasticity of demand for money
transactions demand for money	modern quantity theory
precautionary demand for money	

2. A worker's average earnings are £100 per week, all of which he spends at an even rate throughout each period. What are his average money holdings if he is paid: (a) weekly; (b) monthly? Suppose his income increases by 25 per cent. How are the answers to (a) and (b) affected?

3. Consider the following information about a hypothetical economy:
Stock of money = £50 million
Each pound changes hands on average 3 times per year.
The number of transactions is 30 million per year.

(a) Find the average price level.
(b) Suppose the stock of money increases to £60 million, but that the velocity of circulation and number of transactions remain constant. What is the new average price level?
(c) Now suppose the velocity of circulation rises to 5 and the number of transactions increases to 40 million. What is the new average price level?
(d) Suggest possible reasons for the increase in the velocity of circulation.

4. Assuming an initial equilibrium in the money market, describe the effects of an increase in the money supply: (a) in the context of a Keynesian model; (b) in the context of the 'modern quantity theory'.

5. Explain why there is an inverse relationship between the speculative demand for money and the rate of interest in the Keynesian liquidity-preference theory. Under what circumstances might the demand for money be perfectly interest-elastic?

6. Discuss the qualitative effect on the demand for money of the following changes:

(a) an increase in the use of credit cards;
(b) an increase in the rate of return from holding bonds;
(c) a fall in the general price level;
(d) a decrease in the proportion of human wealth to non-human wealth.

23 Money and national income

Introduction

In Chapters 19–22, we examined the *real* and *monetary* sectors of the economy separately. Our objective in the first part of this chapter is to combine these pieces of analysis under Keynesian assumptions and so derive a more general model (developed originally by J.R. Hicks in 1937) in which the equilibrium level of income and the equilibrium rate of interest are determined simultaneously. This model is expressed graphically using IS and LM curves, so part of our task is to derive and explain these curves.

In the second part of the chapter, we discuss the value of Keynes' contribution to economic theory and policy. This involves outlining the neo-classical attack on Keynesian economics and the so-called 'reinterpretation' of Keynes as a disequilibrium economist by writers such as R.W. Clower and A. Leijonhufvud. Here, a distinction is made between *Keynesian economics* and the *economics of Keynes*. The final part of the chapter is concerned with setting out in some detail the monetarist challenge to Keynesian economics and with comparing Keynesian and monetarist policy recommendations.

A synthesis of the real and monetary sectors

The IS curve

In Chapter 19, we showed that the equilibrium level of income is determined at the point where total withdrawals from the flow of income ($S + T + M$) are just equal to total injections into that flow ($I + G + X$). Suppose now that we introduce the rate of interest into the analysis and thus provide a link between the real and monetary sectors of the economy. The variable most likely to be influenced by changes in interest rates is investment. Assume that a rise in interest rates causes a fall in investment and *vice versa*. With a given level of government spending and exports, it follows that total injections will also be inversely related to the rate of interest.

Definition: ***The IS curve joins together all those combinations of the rate of interest and the level of income at which the real sector of the economy is in equilibrium – that is, at which total injections equal total withdrawals.***

An IS curve is derived in Fig. 1 which shows four interconnected graphs for a hypothetical economy. Graph (a) shows the inverse relationship between total injections (J) and the rate of interest (i). Graph (b) represents the equilibrium condition that total injections should equal total withdrawals (W). Since J is measured along the horizontal axis and W along the vertical axis, the only points on the graph at which $J = W$ must lie along the 45° line from the origin (assuming, of course, that both axes are in the same scale). Graph (c) illustrates the direct relationship between total withdrawals and national income (Y).

Fig. 1. Derivation of the IS curve.

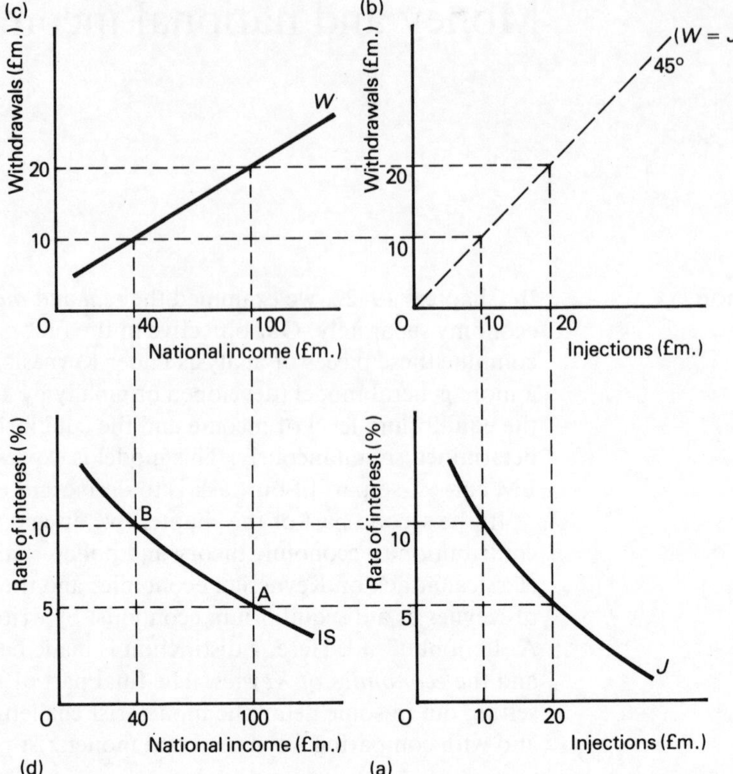

Notice from graph (a) that at an interest rate of 5 per cent, total injections amount to £20 million. Graph (b) tells us that, for equilibrium, total withdrawals must also be equal to £20 million. It is clear from graph (c), however, that there is only one level of national income at which W = £20 million. This is an income level of £100 million. It follows that an interest rate of 5 per cent and an income level of £100 million is one combination of interest and income at which the real sector is in equilibrium. This combination must be one point on the IS curve and is plotted as point A in graph (d).

Now consider an interest rate of 10 per cent. At this higher interest rate, total injections amount to only £10 million. This means that, for equilibrium, total withdrawals must also be £10 million and therefore that income must be £40 million. This gives us a second combination of interest and income (10% and £40 m.) which must also be on the IS curve. It is plotted as point B in graph (d).

Choosing other interest rates and finding the level of income required for equilibrium in each case will yield a series of combinations, all of which will lie along the downward-sloping IS curve shown in graph (d). It should be clear that for total injections and total withdrawals to remain equal requires that a rising interest rate be accompanied by a falling level of income, and *vice versa*.

The reader should be able to confirm that if investment were completely interest-inelastic so that the injections line in graph (a) were vertical, the IS curve would also be vertical. Given a stable withdrawals line, the steepness of the IS curve depends on the interest-elasticity of investment.

The LM curve

Now consider the monetary sector of the economy. We saw in the previous chapter that equilibrium is achieved in the money market when the total demand for money (which depends on the interest rate and the level of income) is equal to the money supply (which is assumed to be autonomous).

Definition: ***The LM curve joins together all those combinations of the rate of interest and the level of income at which the monetary sector of the economy is in equilibrium – that is, at which the demand for money equals the supply of money.***

An LM curve is derived in Fig. 2 using the same procedure as above. Graph (a) shows the Keynesian speculative demand for money (L_s) on the assumption that it is inversely related to the rate of interest between the interest rates Oi_0 and Oi_1: above Oi_1, the speculative demand is assumed to be

Fig. 2. Derivation of the LM curve.

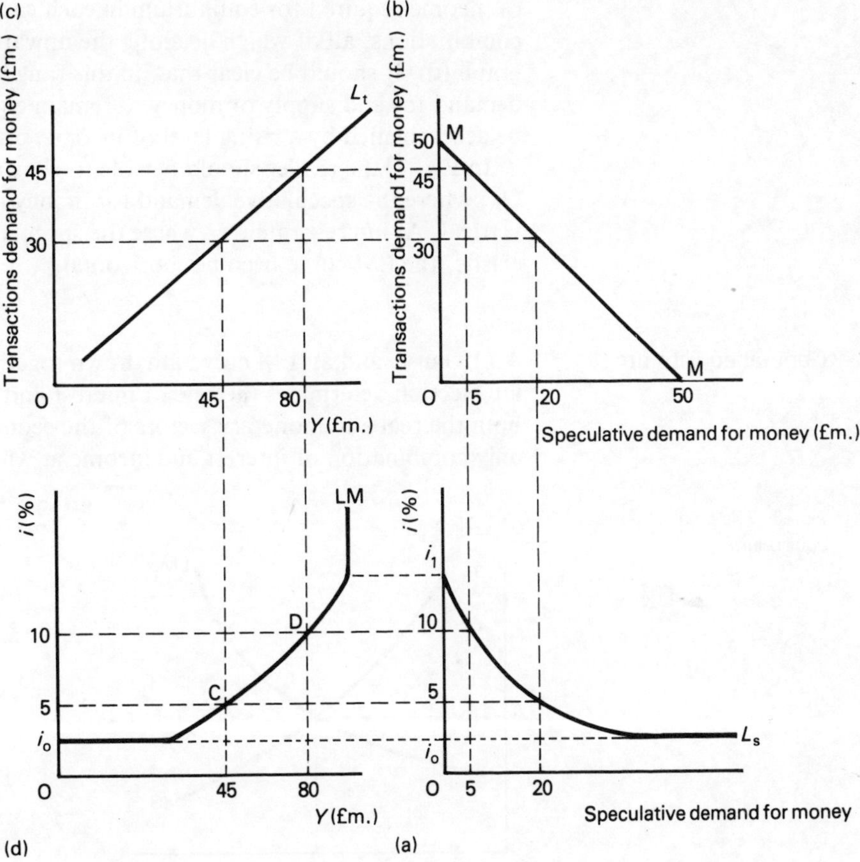

zero and below Oi_0, it is assumed to be perfectly elastic. Graph (b) represents the equilibrium condition that the sum of the speculative and transactions demands for money should equal the given money supply. The line MM shows how a money supply of £50 million can be divided between transactions and speculative holdings. Graph (c) shows the direct relationship between the transactions demand for money (L_t) and national income.

Notice from graph (a) that at an interest rate of 5 per cent, the speculative demand for money is £20 million. Inspection of graph (b) shows that with a given money supply of £50 million, equilibrium is achieved when the transactions demand is equal to £30 million. From graph (c), however, we see that the transactions demand will only be equal to £30 million when national income is £45 million. This gives us one combination which must be on the LM curve: it is plotted as point C in graph (d).

Now consider the higher interest rate of 10 per cent. The speculative demand for money is very low at this interest rate and equal to only £5 million. For equilibrium, transactions demand must be equal to £45 million and, from graph (c), we see that income has to be £80 million. The combination of a 10 per cent rate of interest with an £80 million level of income represents a second point on the LM curve, plotted as point D in graph (d).

Choosing other interest rates (between Oi_0 and Oi_1) and finding the level of income required for equilibrium in each case will yield a series of combinations, all of which lie along the upward-sloping LM curve shown in graph (d). It should be clear that, in this range of interest rates, for the demand for and supply of money to remain equal, a rising interest rate must be accompanied by a rising level of income, and *vice versa*.

In Fig. 2, the reader should be able to confirm that for interest rates above Oi_1, where the speculative demand for money is zero, the LM curve becomes vertical. At interest rate Oi_0, where the speculative demand is perfectly elastic, the LM curve becomes horizontal.

General equilibrium

An IS curve and an LM curve are drawn together in Fig. 3. The point of intersection determines the rate of interest and the level of income at which both the real and monetary sectors of the economy are in equilibrium. The only combination of interest and income at which both markets are in

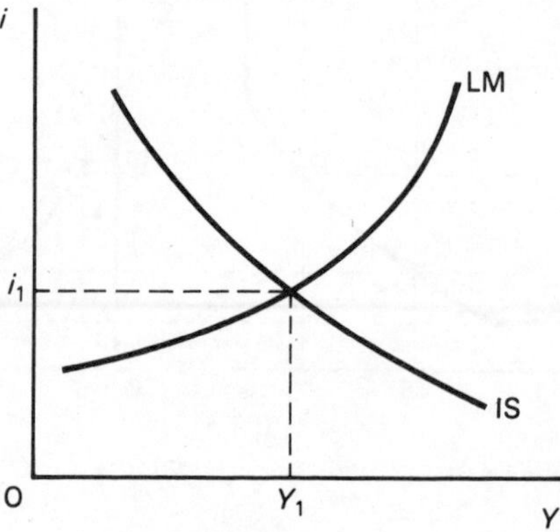

Fig. 3. The point of general equilibrium.

equilibrium is interest rate Oi_1 and income level OY_1. This is called the point of general equilibrium.

Stability of the general equilibrium Recall from Chapter 6 that an equilibrium is said to be a stable one when economic forces tend to push the market towards it. Figure 4 illustrates that the general equilibrium we have just derived is indeed a stable one. To show this, consider all the points to the left of the IS curve, like point A: at this point, with the given interest rate Oi_1, the level of income is too low for equilibrium to be achieved in the real sector. This means that injections exceed withdrawals and the total value of output is less than the economy's aggregate demand. In this situation, firms find their inventories being run down involuntarily and so act to increase output. This is the economic force which pushes up national income. For all points to the left of the IS curve, then, there is pressure on income to rise. Similarly, for all points to the right of the IS curve, there is pressure on income to fall.

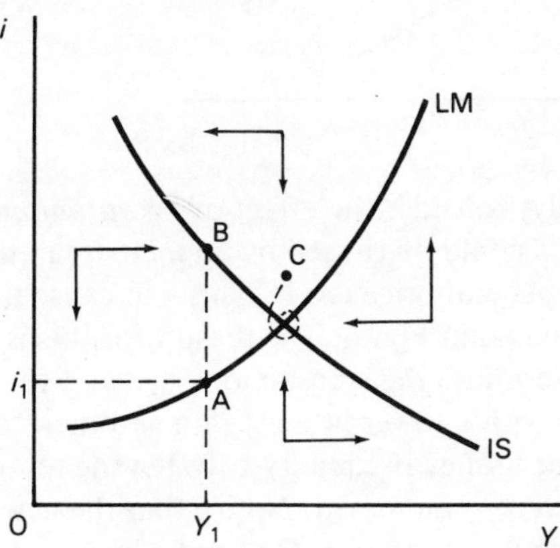

Fig. 4. The stability of the general equilibrium.

Now consider points above the LM curve, like point B: at this point, with the given level of income OY_1, the interest rate is too high for equilibrium to be achieved in the monetary sector. This means that the supply of money exceeds the demand for money and so downward pressure is exerted on the rate of interest. This is true for all points above the LM curve and it similarly follows that upward pressure will be exerted on interest rates at all points below the LM curve.

The directions of the pressures being exerted on incomes and interest rates in the four quadrants of the graph are indicated by the arrows in Fig. 4. It follows that at any disequilibrium point, such as point C, economic forces will be pushing the market towards the general equilibrium position. The actual path to equilibrium may be a spiral (as illustrated) rather than a direct route, but eventually, given sufficient time with other variables remaining unchanged, the equilibrium should be reached.

Shifting the IS and LM curves

Having demonstrated the stability of the IS–LM equilibrium, we can now consider what changes in the economy will cause the IS and LM curves to shift. Consider first the effects of an *autonomous increase in investment spending.* For equilibrium to be maintained, a higher level of withdrawals and therefore national income is required at every interest rate; this means that the IS curve shifts to the right, as shown in Fig. 5. This causes the equilibrium level of income to rise from OY_1 to OY_2 and the equilibrium rate of interest to rise from Oi_1 to Oi_2. Note that the reason for the rise in the equilibrium rate of interest is that the higher income level will have brought forth an increased transactions demand for money.

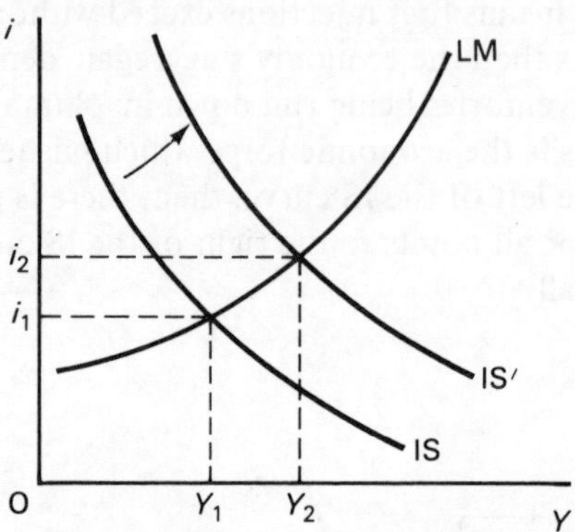

Fig. 5. A shift in the IS curve.

Secondly, consider the effect of an *autonomous increase in the real money supply* (this could be caused by an increase in the nominal money stock or a fall in the general price level). This will cause the LM curve to shift to the right, as shown in Fig. 6. The reason for this is that every income level (which determines the transactions demand for money) must now be associated with a lower interest rate and therefore a higher speculative demand for money if equality between the total demand for and supply of money is to be maintained. Notice that the new equilibrium is characterised by a lower rate of interest, Oi_2, and a higher level of income, OY_2. In this case, the increased money supply has reduced the interest rate which, in turn, has caused a rise in investment spending; it is this rise in investment which causes the increase in the level of income.

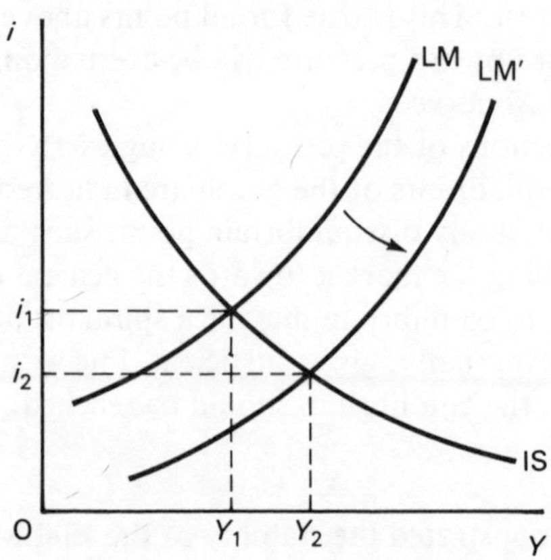

Fig. 6. A shift in the LM curve.

Table 1. Summary of the causes and direction of shifts in the IS and LM curves.

Increase in investment	IS shifts right
Decrease in investment	IS shifts left
Increase in consumption	IS shifts right
Increase in savings	IS shifts left
Increase in government expenditure	IS shifts right
Increase in taxation	IS shifts left
Increase in money supply	LM shifts right
Decrease in money supply	LM shifts left
Increase in price level	LM shifts left
Fall in price level	LM shifts right
Increase in the demand for money	LM shifts left
Decrease in the demand for money	LM shifts right

Table 1 summarises the changes in the economy which cause either the IS curve or the LM curve to shift. All the changes are autonomous in the sense that they are not themselves caused by changes in income or interest rates. The reader should be able to confirm the direction of the shifts either graphically or by reasoned argument.

Uses and limitations of the IS – LM model

It must be emphasised that the IS–LM model is a theoretical construction based on many assumptions. Since the assumptions we have made are the same as those in the simple Keynesian model and the Keynesian theory of money, the IS–LM model derived above is sometimes called the *general Keynesian model.* It can, however, be modified to take account of different assumptions and this means that it is a useful framework for illustrating the differences between the various schools of thought. For example, one major application of the IS–LM model is in comparing the effectiveness of fiscal and monetary policies in the Keynesian and neo-classical theories. This application is considered in Chapter 26.

It is important at this stage to point out two serious limitations of the IS–LM model and these should be borne in mind in all its applications.

(a) It is a comparative static equilibrium model and so ignores the time-lags which are so important in examining the effects of economic policy changes.
(b) The model does not enable us to examine the effects of changes in aggregate demand on *both* output and prices. On the one hand, the Keynesian version of the model assumes a *constant price level* and so cannot analyse the problem of inflation. On the other hand, in the neo-classical version of the model, which applies when full employment is reached, the price level is determined by the nominal money supply and output is assumed to be determined exogenously.

Keynes' contribution to economics

In the last few chapters, we have referred to Keynes and Keynesian economics on many occasions. Clearly, the publication of the *General Theory* in 1936 had an enormous impact on both economic theory and policy-making. In the field of macroeconomic policy-making, Keynes' contribution has undoubtedly been influential. The adoption in the 1950s and

1960s by western economies of demand-management policies to combat unemployment in the main kept unemployment rates down and we saw no return to the extremely high unemployment rates of the 1930s.

It is in the field of economic theory that Keynes' contribution has been questioned by neo-classical economists. Basically, the debate has been centred on the question of whether or not a competitive market economy with flexible wages and prices would automatically tend towards a full employment equilibrium position. The neo-classical economists argued that it would do so and, therefore, that all Keynes had done in effect was to add a single assumption to the neo-classical system: the assumption that wages and prices were inflexible downwards because of the existence of trade unions and other restrictive practices (which, of course, was well-known anyway). Keynesians, on the other hand, attempted to show that a competitive economy, even with completely flexible wages and prices, would not be likely to achieve full employment automatically. Consider how this debate progressed.

The neo-classical view The neo-classical view was that a perfectly competitive economy would always tend towards its full employment equilibrium position. This is illustrated in the three-graph diagram in Fig. 7. The upper graph shows the economy's initial general equilibrium position in the real and monetary sectors. The lower left-hand graph is the short-run aggregate production function and the lower right-hand graph illustrates the economy's labour market. Notice that for convenience the real wage is

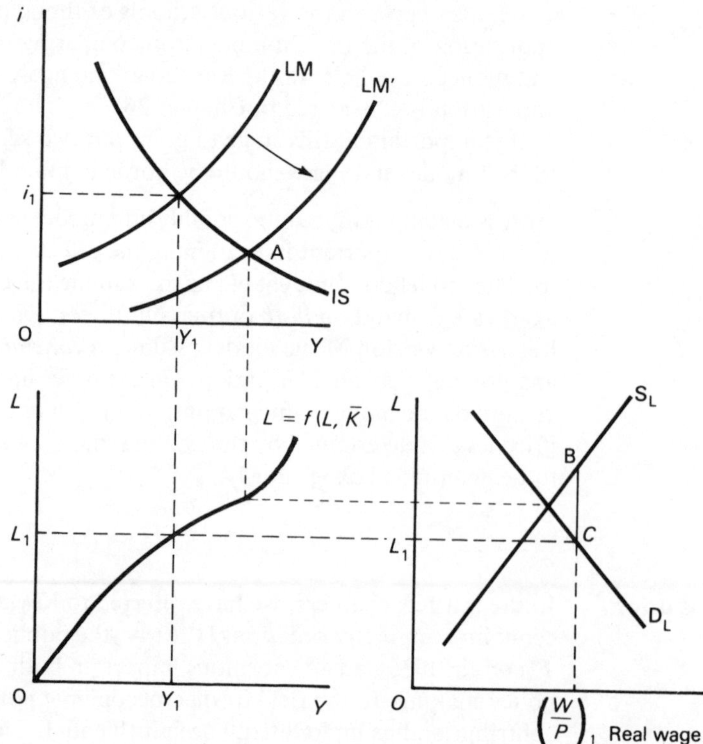

Fig. 7. The neo-classical attainment of full employment.

measured along the horizontal axis and the quantity of labour is measured along the vertical axis. As drawn, equilibrium in the real and monetary sectors exists at an output level of OY_1 which is produced using a quantity of labour OL_1. Unfortunately, this is not the full employment quantity of labour: there is an excess supply of labour (or unemployment) equal to BC. According to the neo-classical economists, this unemployment cannot persist. Assuming that wages and prices are flexible upwards and downwards, the excess supply of labour will cause money wages to fall. As the real wage falls, employment and output rise, but this spoils the equilibrium in the real and monetary sectors of the economy. In fact, there will be an excess supply of goods and services on the market which will exert downward pressure on prices. The result, then, is a general deflation of both wages and prices which leaves real wages unchanged but which causes the *real* money supply to increase, so shifting the LM curve to the right to LM′. This deflation, according to the neo-classical economists, will continue until the new equilibrium in the real and monetary sectors is just consistent with equilibrium in the labour market – that is, at point A in Fig. 7. Only when this point is reached will the unemployment in the economy have been eradicated.

The Keynesian view Keynesians were sceptical of the above mechanism, even assuming flexible wages and prices. In particular, they pointed to two barriers which might exist to prevent the full employment equilibrium from being reached: *lack of investment* and the *liquidity trap*.

The possible lack of investment is illustrated in Fig. 8 where the IS curve is very steep and cuts the horizontal axis at a point below the full employment level of income Y_f. Recall that the IS curve will be steep when investment is very interest-inelastic. In this case, as shown in the diagram, it is impossible for a full employment equilibrium to be reached by means of a shifting LM curve alone.

Fig. 8. Lack of investment.

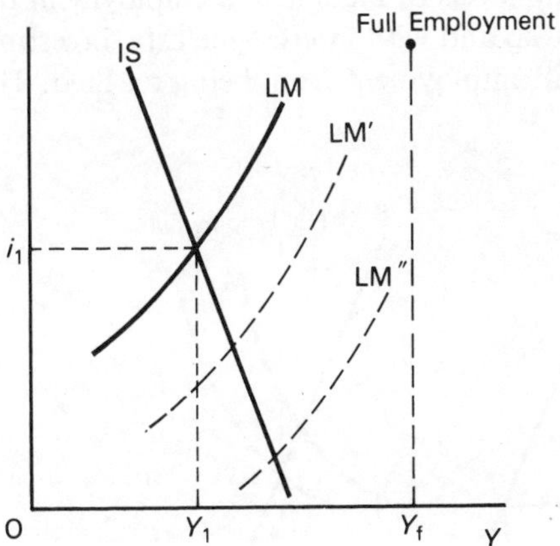

The liquidity trap was explained in Chapter 22. Recall that it exists where the interest rate is so low that the demand for money becomes perfectly interest-elastic. When the demand for money is perfectly interest-elastic, the LM curve is horizontal, as illustrated in Fig. 9. In this case, the equilibrium

Fig. 9. Liquidity trap.

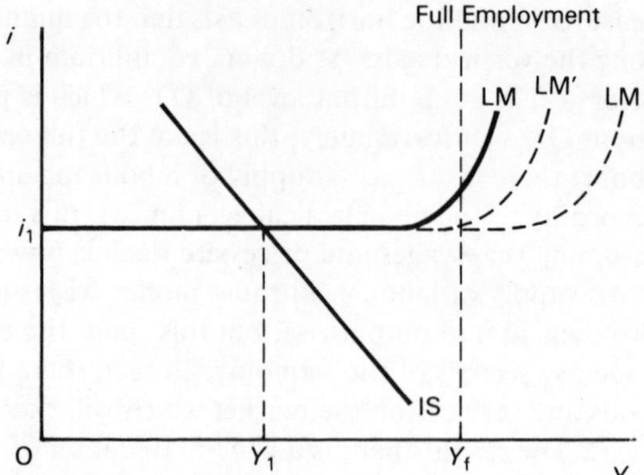

level of income is unaffected by the increase in the real value of the money supply. The LM curve shifts to the right, as shown, but the intersection of the horizontal part of the LM curve with the IS curve is unchanged. What is happening here is simply that the additional real money supply is being held in speculative or 'idle' balances.

The real balance effect The neo-classical economists, largely through the work of Pigou, produced a counter-argument to the above Keynesian cases in the shape of the real balance effect. According to this, with a constant nominal money supply, a general deflation of wages and prices will tend to increase the *real* value of people's holdings of money above their desired levels. Consequently, people will reduce their savings and increase their consumption in an attempt to reduce their 'real balances'. In the above cases, where full employment is not reached, as wages and prices fall and the LM curve shifts to the right, the IS curve will also shift to the right as consumption increases. With both curves now shifting to the right, the equilibrium levels of income and employment must increase (even in the liquidity trap and with interest-inelastic investment) and there is now nothing to stop full employment from being reached. This is illustrated in Fig. 10.

Fig. 10. The real balance effect.

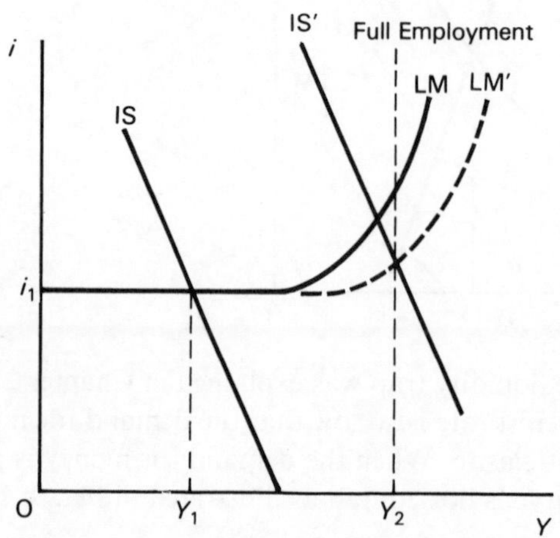

Theoretically, then, the neo-classical economists appear to have the stronger case. Only when it came to policy-making did the Keynesians have the upper hand, given the recognised inflexibility of wages and prices downwards. We turn now to a brief examination of a more recent attempt to give Keynes' economics some greater theoretical respectability.

The reinterpretation of Keynes

The economists Clower and Leijonhufvud have argued that a distinction needs to be drawn between Keynesian economics and the economics of Keynes. Keynesian economics, they say, is the comparative static equilibrium approach to macroeconomics which has developed from other people's interpretations of the *General Theory.* The true economics of Keynes, they argue, is a dynamic analysis of the macroeconomy in disequilibrium and as such represents a major contribution to economic theory as well as to economic policy-making. In other words, Clower and Leijonhufvud reinterpret Keynes as a *disequilibrium theorist*.

This reinterpretation sets Keynes' economics apart from the traditional equilibrium analysis of neo-classical theory which depended on some kind of 'tâtonnement' process (as described in Chapter 6) to ensure that all transactions took place in equilibrium. Given a 'tâtonnement' process or at least a perfectly operating price mechanism which disseminated the information necessary to co-ordinate the plans of households and firms, the neo-classical comparative approach would be justified.

Now consider Fig. 11 which illustrates a full employment equilibrium

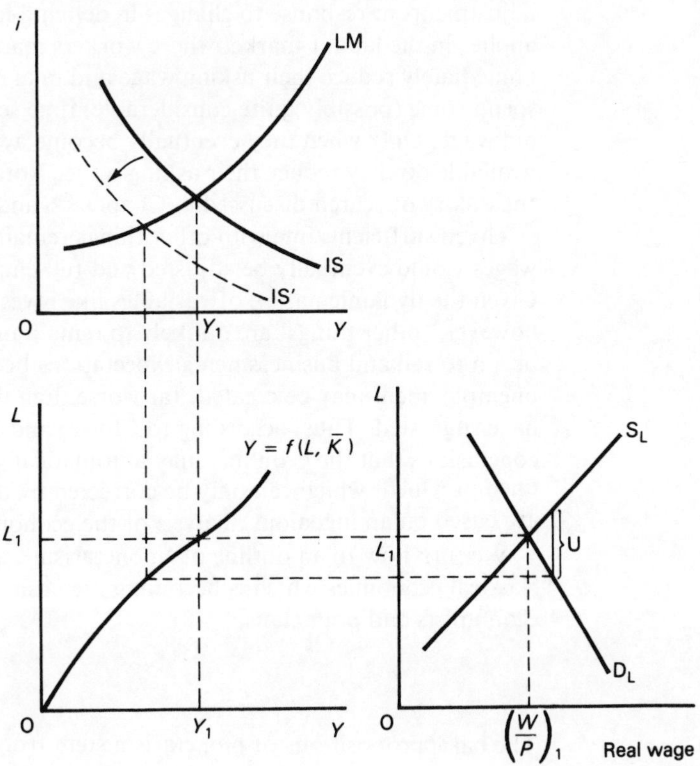

Fig. 11. Keynes as a disequilibrium theorist.

position. Suppose that some disturbance occurs - say, a fall in investment demand. The IS curve will shift to the left (from IS to IS′) creating an excess supply of goods and services and an excess supply of labour. In the neo-classical system, this excess supply would cause a lower wage and price level to be established and this deflation in turn would shift the IS curve back to the right (because of the real balance effect) and the LM curve to the right (as the real money supply rises) until the full employment were restored. With the help of the auctioneer and the 'tâtonnement' process, this new equilibrium position would be established instantaneously. The neo-classical analysis can be justified only if the new equilibrium positions are reached quickly.

Suppose now, though, that there is no auctioneer. Transactors will have to search for the new equilibrium values themselves. If they had perfect information, the new equilibrium values would be established immediately; unfortunately, information is far from perfect - there is ignorance and uncertainty instead. Searching for the new equilibrium values is time-consuming and in the meantime 'false trading' will take place at 'false prices'.

Firms which have experienced a fall in sales will have no idea whether the reduced demand for their product is temporary or permanent; they will be reluctant to cut their prices until they know that it is permanent. Whilst they are searching for the relevant information, their inventories of unsold goods will start to build up. This is involuntary and undesirable and many firms will react to it by reducing output and laying off workers. This is the essence of Keynes' analysis: that output or quantity adjustments come *before* price adjustments in response to changes in demand in the economy. The same applies in the labour market where workers made unemployed do not immediately reduce their asking wage and take up a new job - instead, they spend some (possibly quite considerable) time searching for a new job at the old wage. Only when they eventually become aware that no such jobs are available do they reduce their asking wage. Note that this analysis draws on the theory of search discussed in Chapters 6 and 15.

Given sufficient time with other things remaining unchanged, prices and wages would eventually be adjusted and full employment may be restored. Given the dynamic nature of variables like investment in the economy, however, 'other things' are unlikely to remain unchanged. Once income has begun to fall and businessmen's expectations become pessimistic, persistent unemployment may be created, far worse than the initial disturbance might have suggested. Thus, according to Clower and Leijonhufvud, Keynes' conclusions that the economy may automatically move to a position of high unemployment which can only be corrected by demand-management policies are based on an ingenious analysis of the economy in its disequilibrium state.

We turn now to an outline of 'monetarism', a modern version of neo-classical economics which is becoming increasingly popular among both economists and politicians.

Monetarism

The basic propositions of monetarism stem from the revival of the quantity theory of money, in particular by Milton Friedman, as described in Chapter 22. The contributions of monetarists to the analysis of inflation and unemployment are discussed in Chapter 27. Our intention in this section is simply to set out the main ideas of monetarism and to compare briefly monetarist policy recommendations with those of Keynesián economists.

Probably the most important assertion of monetarists is that the velocity of circulation of money, although not constant, is predictable, independent of the money supply and stably related to a limited number of variables. This assertion leads directly to the proposition that money national income and the nominal money supply must be directly correlated with each other. To show this, consider the following version of the quantity theory:

$$MV = PY$$

where M is the nominal money supply, V is the *income* velocity of circulation and PY is the money value of national income. Given V, all changes in M must be associated with changes in PY in the same direction. Friedman has written that 'there is a consistent though not precise relation between the rate of growth of the quantity of money and the rate of growth of nominal income'.

In 1963, Friedman and Anna Schwartz carried out extensive empirical tests of this correlation in their book *A Monetary History of the United States, 1867–1960*. The results they obtained suggested a close relationship between changes in the United States' money supply and changes in money national income over a long period of time. Correlation, of course, does not necessarily mean causation. Friedman and Schwartz, however, claimed that it was changes in the nominal money supply which *caused* changes in money national income (recall the mechanism described in Chapter 22) and, once again, they appealed to empirical evidence to support their view. For example, they looked in detail at each major recession and argued from their observations that the money supply declined for reasons other than the recession itself and that the fall in money national income generally followed the fall in the money supply. Critics of monetarism, however, remain unconvinced. Lord Kaldor, for example, has argued that the money supply is passively adjusted to the level required to accommodate the current level of economic activity.

A second assertion of monetarists is that in the absence of government intervention in the economy, there will be an automatic tendency towards the 'natural rate of unemployment' – that is, 'the level of unemployment which has the property that it is consistent with equilibrium in the structure of real wage rates'. Consequently, they argue, the effects of changes in the money supply will be largely on the general price level (P) rather than on real output (Y). They also believe that this will be a *lagged* response, with prices following an expansion of the money supply with a time-lag of up to two years. So, the short-term effect may be on output as firms strive to meet the increased demand, but the eventual effect will be almost entirely on prices. (Notice the similarity between this analysis and the reinterpretation of Keynes outlined in the previous section.)

Finally, monetarists assert that the economy (again in the absence of government intervention) will not be subject to any inherent instability.

Indeed, they believe that instability in the past has been caused, rather than smoothed out, by governments' futile attempts at demand-management policies.

Policy recommendations Unlike Keynesians, monetarists are almost entirely against the use of short-term demand-management policy. Instead, they recommend a steady, annual expansion of the money supply at a constant rate, determined by the predictable steady growth in the velocity of circulation and the predicted growth in the country's potential output. No attempt should be made to use monetary policy to offset any disturbances which may occur from time to time. Any such attempts would most likely fail and possibly make matters worse because of the difficulties of predicting short-run changes and because of the variability of the time-lags with which changes in the money supply affect nominal national income.

Similarly, fiscal policy, according to monetarists, has no role to play in demand-management. Since the economy will tend automatically to its 'natural rate of unemployment', any increase in government spending will increase the demand for money and so *crowd out* private spending through rising interest rates. This is the case illustrated in Chapter 26, in Fig. 3, where the LM curve is vertical. If the expansionary fiscal policy is accompanied by an increase in the money supply to counter the crowding out effect, the result will be nothing more than a higher rate of inflation.

Generally, then, we can conclude that the monetarists' major policy recommendation is: maintain a steady constant growth in the money supply, otherwise leave things well alone.

Conclusion

This chapter has drawn together the real and monetary sectors of the economy and shown how a general equilibrium may be determined. The IS–LM model is a method of illustrating the general Keynesian model and provides a useful means of analysing the effects of various policy changes.

We have seen that Keynes' contribution to economics has been challenged by neo-classical economists and reinterpreted by Clower and Leijonhufvud in terms of disequilibrium theory. The most serious challenge to Keynesian macroeconomic policies, however, has come from Friedman and the monetarists.

Further reading

Dernburg, T.F. and **McDougall, D.M.**, *Macroeconomics*, McGraw-Hill Kogakusha, International Student Edition, Tokyo, 1976 (Ch. 8).

Leijonhufvud, A., *On Keynesian Economics and the Economics of Keynes*, Oxford University Press, Oxford, 1968.

Barro, R.J. and **Grossman, H.I.**, *Money, Employment and Inflation*, Cambridge University Press, Cambridge, 1976.

Morgan, B., *Monetarists and Keynesians – their Contribution to Monetary Theory*, Macmillan, London, 1978.

Friedman, M. and **Schwartz, A.**, *A Monetary History of the United States, 1867–1960*, Princeton University Press, Princeton, 1963.

Exercises

1. Review your understanding of the following terms:

real sector
monetary sector
IS curve
LM curve
general equilibrium
real money supply
nominal money supply
wage and price flexibility
real balance effect
Keynesian economics
economics of Keynes
tâtonnement
disequilibrium analysis
price adjustment
quantity adjustment
monetarism
income velocity of circulation
crowding out

2. Consider a simple closed economy with no government. The following equations represent the investment and savings functions respectively:

$I = 20 - 2i$
$S = 0.5Y$

where i is the rate of interest and Y is the level of national income. Find the equation of the IS curve and plot it on a graph. If the equation of the LM curve is $Y = 4 + 2i$,

(a) find the equilibrium level of national income and the equilibrium rate of interest;
(b) calculate the effect on the level of income and the rate of interest of an autonomous fall in investment of 10;
(c) explain why the fall in income is less than that predicted by the multiplier.

3. 'The IS–LM model is based on comparative static analysis and ignores the dynamic processes of a modern economy.' Discuss.

4. In the context of the IS–LM model, illustrate the effects on the equilibrium level of income and the rate of interest of a change in the real money supply.

5. Discuss the view that completely flexible wages and prices would ensure the automatic attainment of full employment in an economy.

6. What observations would be required to support the view that the true economics of Keynes is an analysis of the economy in disequilibrium?

The economics of cycles and growth

24 Cyclical fluctuations

Introduction

Cyclical fluctuations in the level of economic activity in an economy can be observed by examining *annual* changes in real national income (or real output) over a long period of years; these changes are inversely related to variations in the rate of unemployment. Figure 1 shows the fluctuations in the rate of unemployment in the United Kingdom from 1878 to 1980. Notice that the fluctuations up to 1920 were fairly regular with an average of about eight or nine years from peak to peak and trough to trough. After the Great Depression of the 1920s and 1930s, however, the fluctuations were much reduced, possibly a result of the adoption of Keynesian demand-management policies by successive governments in the 1950s and 1960s. None the less, even in this period, the economy has been subjected to fairly regular cycles of minor expansions and recessions. In the 1970s, the trade cycle was masked by world recession, due in part to the energy crisis, which resulted in an upward trend in the rate of unemployment.

Fig. 1. The rate of unemployment in the United Kingdom, 1878–1980.

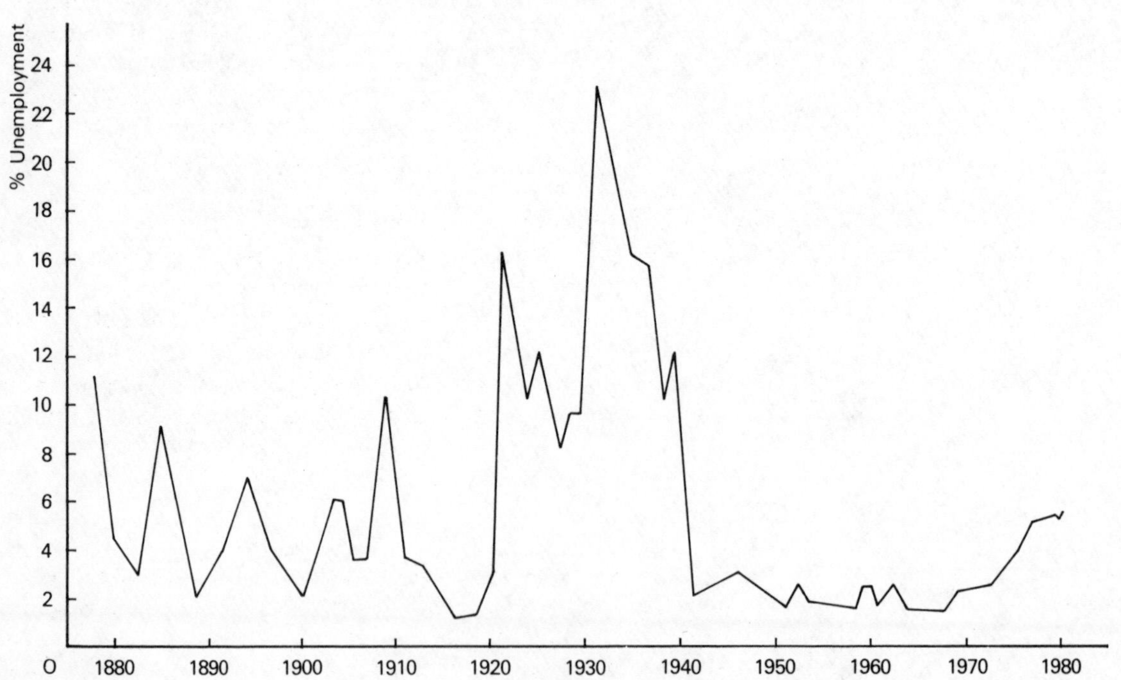

The phases of the trade cycle (sometimes called the business cycle) – slump, recovery, boom and deflation – are illustrated in Fig. 2. As pointed

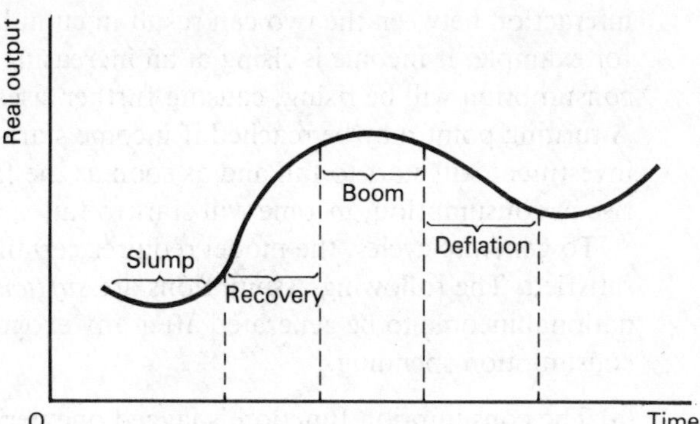

Fig. 2. The phases of a trade cycle.

out in Chapter 18, an economy in a *slump* or depression is generally characterised by high demand-deficient unemployment of both labour and capital. A low level of both consumption and investment demand leads firms to cut back on their production, lay off workers and leave capital equipment lying idle. Although money may be available for firms to borrow and interest rates may be low, investment will not be increased because of pessimistic expectations.

In the *recovery* phase, however, the level of aggregate demand is rising and consequently businessmen become more optimistic. Generally, this is a period of rising consumer demand, rising investment demand, expanding output levels and a falling rate of unemployment. Eventually, the economy reaches the peak of the cycle – the so-called *boom* period. This is a time of low unemployment, a high level of demand, firms working at full capacity earning high profits, an increasing rate of inflation and probably rising interest rates as investors compete with each other for limited loanable funds.

Finally, in the *deflation* phase, the demands of both firms and households start to fall, firms' profits dwindle and output and employment levels are reduced. Businessmen, once again, become pessimistic about the future level of demand for their product and so become extremely reluctant to invest in new capital, even for replacement purposes. Eventually, this contracting economy reaches the slump again and the whole process restarts.

The objective of this chapter is to consider the possible causes of this cyclical movement in economic activity. We concentrate on the famous multiplier-accelerator theory, so this is a good point at which to review your understanding of the multiplier process (Ch. 19) and the accelerator principle (Ch. 20).

Multiplier-accelerator interaction

Why do economies experience cyclical fluctuations? An interesting theory of the trade cycle was propounded by Paul Samuelson in 1939 and is based on interaction between the multiplier process and the accelerator principle. This simple model concentrates on the real sector of the economy and so excludes monetary variables. Recall that, according to the 'accelerator', investment depends on *changes* in income, and that according to the multiplier, changes in investment cause changes in income. Thus, it is not surprising that interaction between the two can result in cumulative movements in income – for example, if income is rising at an increasing rate, both investment and consumption will be rising, causing further rises in income in the next period. A turning point may be reached if income starts to rise at a decreasing rate; investment will start to fall and as soon as the fall in investment exceeds the rise in consumption, income will start to fall.

To generate cycles, the model requires certain important conditions to be satisfied. The following assumptions are *sufficient* for a cyclical movement in national income to be generated after any exogenous change in investment or consumption spending.

(a) The consumption function is lagged one period so that consumption in the current period depends on national income in the previous period. That is,

$$C_t = cY_{t-1}$$

where c is both the average and marginal propensity to consume.
(b) The accelerator is such that induced investment depends on the difference between national income in the last period and national income in the period before that. Thus, we can write:

$$I_t = I_o + v\,(Y_{t-1} - Y_{t-2})$$

where I_o is exogenous investment and v is the accelerator.
(c) The values of c and v must both lie below the curve shown in Fig. 3. For

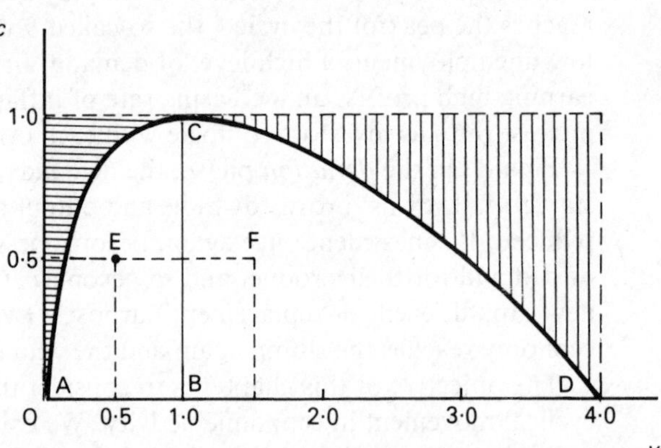

Fig. 3. Different values of c and v to generate cycles.

example, if the values of c and v lie in the area ABC (say, c = 0.5 and v = 0.5 as at point E) then any exogenous change in consumption or investment will generate a *damped* cycle like that illustrated in Fig. 4; it is said to be damped because the fluctuations in real output become smaller and smaller over time. But if the values of c and v lie in the area BCD (for example, c = 0.5 and v = 1.5 as at point F) then any exogenous change in spending will generate an *explosive* cycle like that in Fig. 5; in this case, the oscillations get larger and larger over time.

If the values of c and v should lie above the curve in Fig. 3, no cycles will be generated at all. If they lie in the area shaded horizontally, the new equilibrium Y_e is approached gradually, as shown in Fig. 6. If they lie in the area shaded vertically, national income will rise or fall explosively and

Fig. 4. A damped cycle.

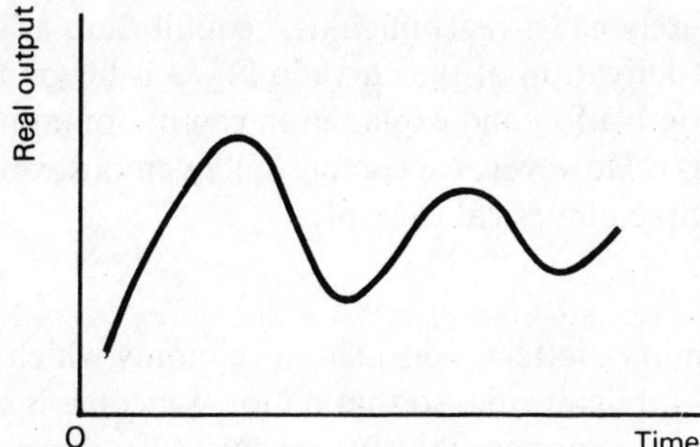

Fig. 5. An explosive cycle.

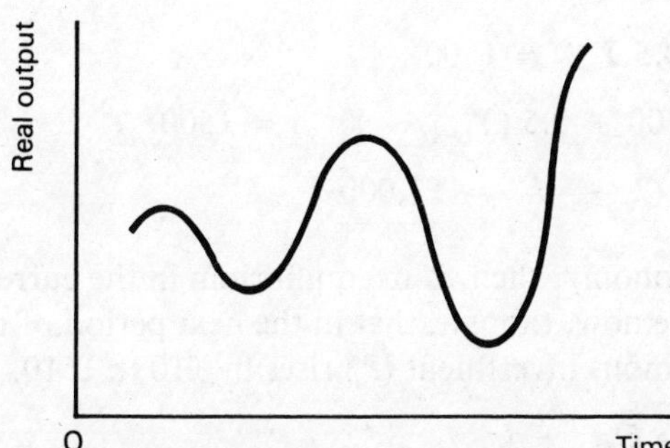

Fig. 6. No cycle, but damped.

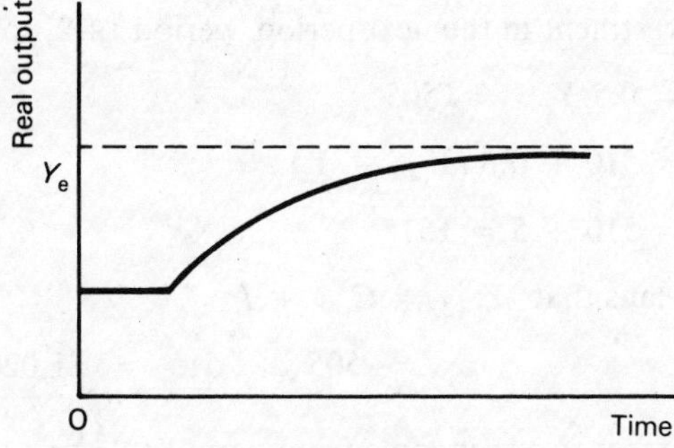

Fig. 7. No cycle, but explosive.

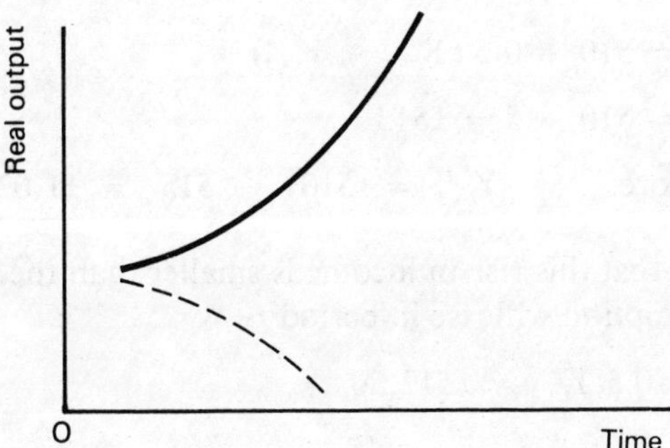

indefinitely never reaching a new equilibrium as shown in Fig. 7.

The derivation of the curve in Fig. 3 is beyond the scope of this textbook. A full derivation and explanation can be found in Chiang (see Further Reading). However, we can partially demonstrate its validity by means of two simple numerical examples.

Example I: a damped cycle

To simplify matters, consider an economy which has no government activity and no foreign trade, so that national income is equal to consumption plus investment. Suppose that for the last several periods of time, real national income has been constant at £1,000. Let $c = 0.5$, $v = 0.5$ (as at point E in Fig. 3) and suppose that initially autonomous investment (I_o) is equal to £500. We have,

$$C_t = 0.5\,Y_{t-1} = £500$$

$$I_t = 500 + 0.5\,(Y_{t-1} - Y_{t-2}) = £500$$

$$Y_t = C_t + I_t = \underline{£1{,}000}$$

This economy, then, is in equilibrium in the current period (called period t). Suppose now, though, that in the next period of time, period $t+1$, autonomous investment (I_o) rises by £10 to £510. Now we have,

$$Y_{t+1} = C_{t+1} + I_{t+1}$$

$$= 500 + 510 = \underline{£1{,}010}$$

This rise in income from period t to period $t+1$ will cause both consumption and investment in the next period, period $t+2$, to rise:

$$C_{t+2} = 0.5\,Y_{t+1} = £505$$

$$I_{t+2} = 510 + 0.5\,(Y_{t+1} - Y_t)$$

$$= 510 + 5 = £515$$

This means that $Y_{t+2} = C_{t+2} + I_{t+2}$

$$= 505 + 515 = \underline{£1{,}020}$$

This further rise in income from period $t+1$ to $t+2$ will cause consumption and investment in period $t+3$ to rise yet again:

$$C_{t+3} = 0.5\,Y_{t+2} = £510$$

$$I_{t+3} = 510 + 0.5\,(Y_{t+2} - Y_{t+1})$$

$$= 510 + 5 = £515$$

Therefore, $Y_{t+3} = 510 + 515 = \underline{£1{,}025}$

Notice that this rise in income is smaller than the previous rises. Consumption will rise in period $t+4$:

$$C_{t+4} = 0.5\,Y_{t+3} = £512.50$$

But investment will start to fall because, according to the accelerator, the *level* of investment depends on the *change* in income (which has now begun to decrease):

$$I_{t+4} = 510 + 0.5\,(Y_{t+3} - Y_{t+2})$$
$$= 510 + 2.5 = £512.50$$

Therefore, $Y_{t+4} = 512.5 + 512.5 = \underline{£1,025}$

So, after rising from periods t to $t+3$, income has now stayed the same from period $t+3$ to $t+4$. Consumption in period $t+5$ will therefore be unchanged:

$$C_{t+5} = 0.5\,Y_{t+4} = £512.50$$

But investment will fall again:

$$I_{t+5} = 510 + 0.5\,(Y_{t+4} - Y_{t+3})$$
$$= £510$$

Since investment falls and consumption stays the same, income in period $t+5$ will be lower than in period $t+4$:

$$Y_{t+5} = 512.5 + 510 = \underline{£1,022.50}$$

So far in the analysis, the single increase in autonomous investment of £10 has caused income to rise from £1,000 to £1,025 in the first four time periods and then to start to fall in the fifth. Taking the time-path to period $t+12$, we obtain a clearly *damped*, cyclical variation in real national income. This is summarised in Table 1 and graphed in Fig. 8.

Table 1. Cyclical variations in consumption, investment and national income following an increase in autonomous investment – damped case.

Time period	Consumption $C_t = 0.5Y_{t-1}$	Investment $I_t = I_0 + 0.5\,(Y_{t-1} - Y_{t-2})$	National income $Y_t = C_t + I_t$
t	500	500	1,000
$t+1$	500	510	1,010
$t+2$	505	515	1,020
$t+3$	510	515	1,025
$t+4$	512.5	512.5	1,025
$t+5$	512.5	510	1,022.5
$t+6$	511.25	508.75	1,020
$t+7$	510	508.75	1,018.75
$t+8$	509.375	509.375	1,018.75
$t+9$	509.375	510	1,019.375
$t+10$	509.6875	510.3125	1,020
$t+11$	510	510.3125	1,020.3125
$t+12$	510.15625	510.15625	1,020.3125
.	.	.	.
.	.	.	.

Notice that eventually the cycle will converge on the new equilibrium level of income of £1,020 (that is, an increase of £20 since the multiplier is 2 in this example). Only when income settles at £1,020 can we say that the full multiplier effect has taken place. However, no new equilibrium position is

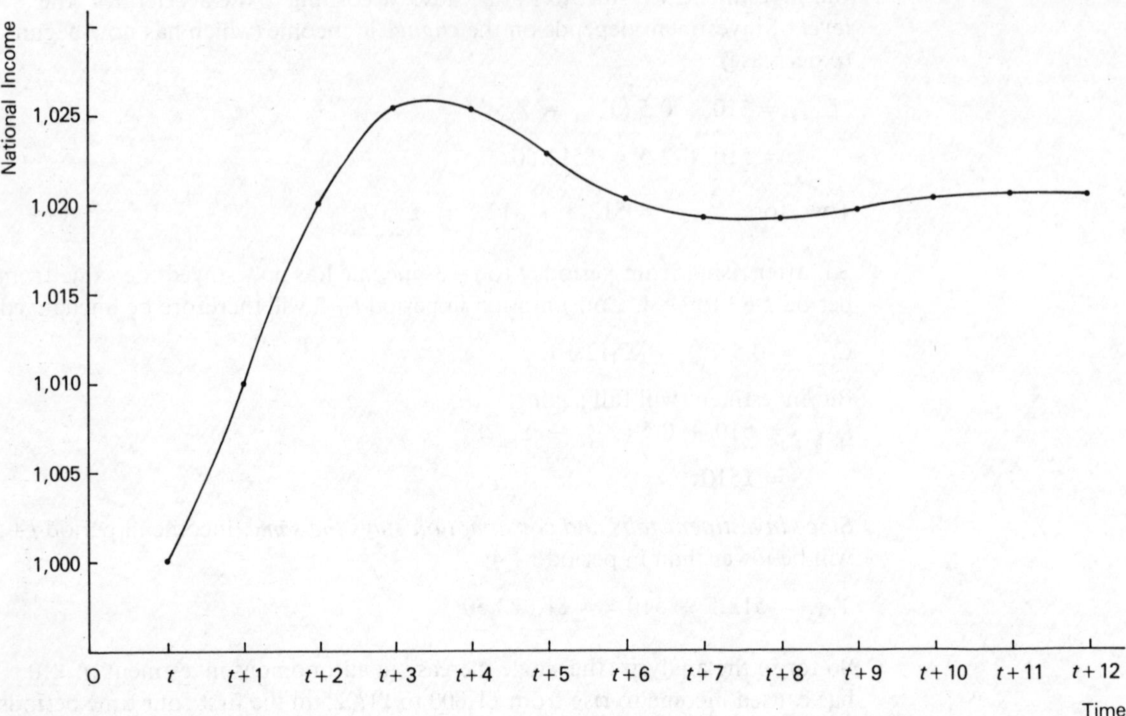

Fig. 8. Damped cyclical variation in national income.

reached in the case of an explosive cycle, as is shown in the next example.

Example II: an explosive cycle

In the same closed economy with no government, suppose now that $c = 0.5$ and $v = 1.5$ (as at point F in Fig. 3). Assume as before that national income has been constant for several time periods at £1,000, and that autonomous investment is initially equal to £500. This means that the economy is in equilibrium in period t. Now suppose, as before, that autonomous investment rises to £510 in period $t+1$. This rise in spending will raise national income to £1,010 in period $t+1$ and this will cause both consumption and investment to increase in the next period, period $t+2$:

$$C_{t+2} = 0.5\,Y_{t+1} = £505$$

$$I_{t+2} = 510 + 1.5\,(Y_{t+1} - Y_t)$$

$$= 510 + 15 = £525$$

This means that, $Y_{t+2} = 505 + 525 = £1{,}030$

Notice that both investment and national income have already risen above the levels reached in the previous example. The time-path to period $t+18$ is summarised in Table 2 and graphed in Fig. 9. An *explosive* cyclical variation in national income results. Although the arithmetic becomes quite laborious, it is a worthwhile exercise for the reader to work through the table carefully and confirm the results. Some further exercises, which include non-cyclical time-paths, are set at the end of the chapter.

Table 2. Cyclical variations in consumption, investment and national income following an increase in autonomous investment – explosive case.

Time period	Consumption $C_t = 0.5Y_{t-1}$	Investment $I_t = I_o + 1.5$ $(Y_{t-1} - Y_{t-2})$	National income $Y_t = C_t + I_t$
t	500	500	1,000
$t + 1$	500	510	1,010
$t + 2$	505	525	1,030
$t + 3$	515	540	1,055
$t + 4$	527.5	547.5	1,075
$t + 5$	537.5	540	1,077.5
$t + 6$	538.75	513.75	1,052.5
$t + 7$	526.75	472.5	999.25
$t + 8$	499.63	430.12	929.75
$t + 9$	464.88	405.75	870.63
$t + 10$	435.31	421.31	856.62
$t + 11$	428.31	489	917.31
$t + 12$	458.66	601.03	1,059.69
$t + 13$	529.84	652.38	1,182.22
$t + 14$	591.11	693.8	1,284.91
$t + 15$	642.45	664.03	1,306.48
$t + 16$	653.24	542.37	1,195.61
$t + 17$	597.80	343.69	941.49
$t + 18$	470.75	255.9	726.65
.	.	.	.
.	.	.	.

Fig. 9. Explosive cyclical variation in national income.

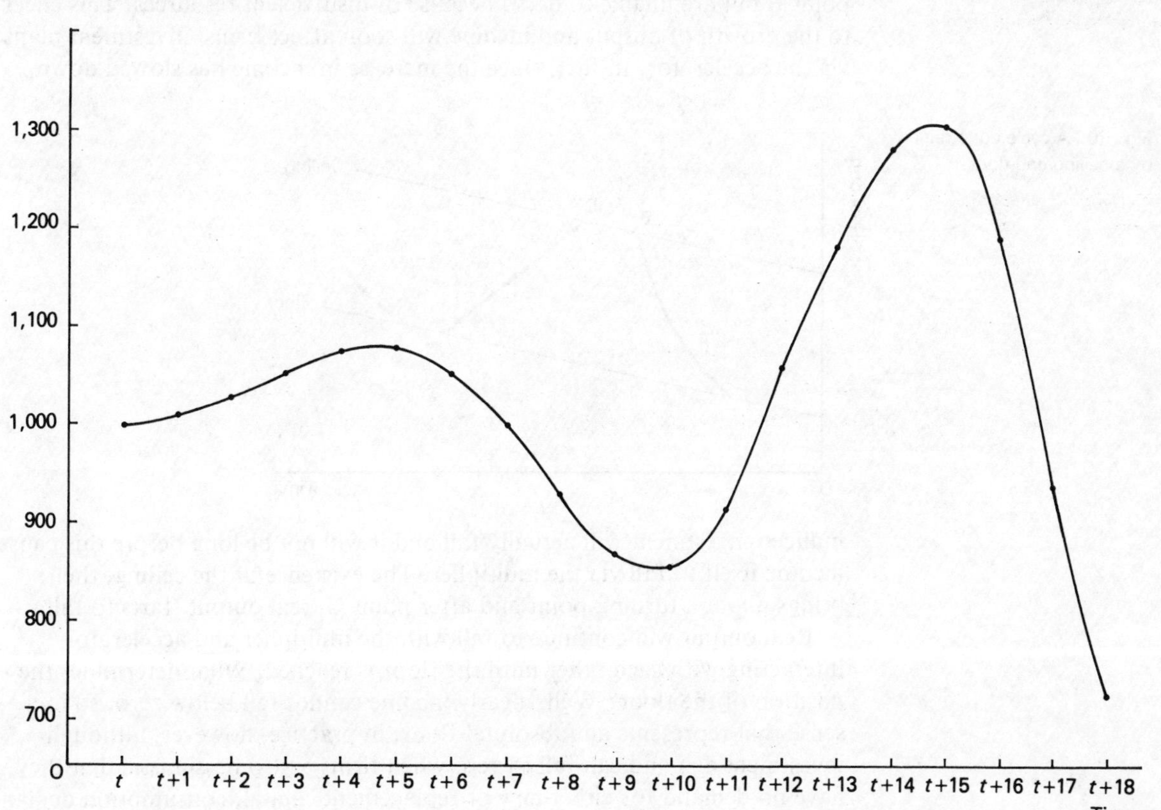

Ceilings and floors

We have seen that the multiplier-accelerator model outlined above is capable under certain circumstances of generating cycles automatically following any change in autonomous spending. Depending on the values assigned to c and v, the cycle may be damped or explosive. A re-examination of Table 1 shows that cycles in practice display no obvious tendency either to diminish or increase in amplitude over time - indeed, particularly in the nineteenth century, the amplitude of the cycles was remarkably constant. A possible explanation for this is that the cycle is inherently explosive, as in our Example II, but is constrained within a band determined by an upper limit above which real output cannot rise, called a *ceiling,* and a lower limit below which real output will not fall, called a *floor*. The cycle thus generated will tend to have a constant amplitude determined by the distance between the ceiling and floor. Such a cyclical movement in real output is illustrated in Fig. 10.

To explain how such a cyclical movement will develop, start at point A on the graph in Fig. 10. This is in the recovery phase: consequently demand is increasing, output is expanding and unemployment is falling. In terms of the multiplier-accelerator interaction, rising investment is causing national income to rise via the multiplier effect and the rising level of national income induces more investment to occur, after a lag, via the accelerator. Soon, though, full employment will be reached (point B on the graph); this determines the so-called ceiling because now real output can only rise as new net investment comes into operation. Firms may want to produce more at point B but are unable to do so because of insufficient resources. This check to the growth of output and income will soon affect firms' investment plans via the accelerator. In fact, since the increase in income has slowed down,

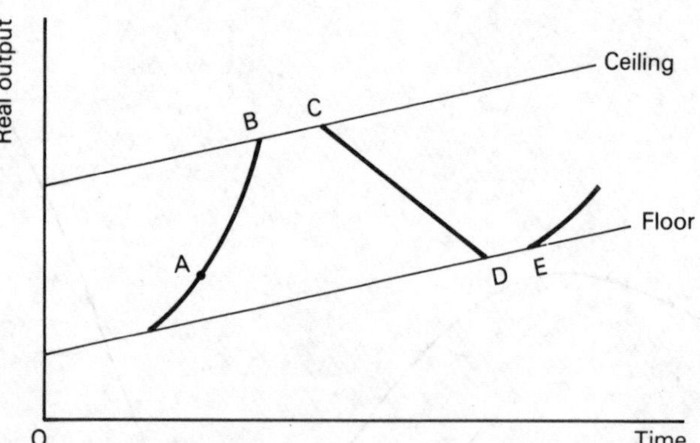

Fig. 10. A cycle constrained by a ceiling and floor.

induced investment will actually fall and it will not be long before this causes income itself to fall via the multiplier. The existence of the ceiling, then, brings about a turning-point and after point C, real output starts to fall.

Real output will continue to fall with the multiplier and accelerator interacting with each other until the floor is reached. What determines the position of the floor? Well, clearly income cannot fall below zero, so in a sense that represents an 'absolute' floor; in practice, however, although investment demand can fall to zero when firms are so pessimistic that they have no demand for either new or replacement capital, consumption demand must always be positive, if only to sustain life. This consumption spending must represent the floor below which the level of income cannot realistically be expected to fall. Furthermore. it is likely that some investment will be occurring somewhere in the economy so that aggregate investment is never likely actually to disappear completely. Once point D has been reached, output will have stopped falling and eventually, as existing machines wear out or become obsolete, some replacement investment will become unavoidable. This will set the multiplier-accelerator interaction into operation again.

The existence of the floor, then, brings about yet another turning-point so that after point E on the graph, real output is rising. This brings us back to the recovery phase and the whole process starts over again. Notice that each successive peak and trough is likely to be above all preceding ones because of underlying growth in the economy's productive capacity.

Random disturbances

The existence of ceilings and floors can help to explain the regularity of cycles when *c* and *v* are such that, without these constraints, cycles would be explosive. But suppose that *c* and *v* took on values consistent with damped cycles, how then could we explain the observed regularity of cyclical fluctuations? (In fact, this is an important question because empirical studies suggest that both *c* and *v* are less than 1, so damped rather than explosive cycles are likely.)

One possible answer has been suggested by the economist R. Frisch. He argues that, even though fluctuations around a country's equilibrium growth path are likely to be damped, random disturbances will be continually occurring to stop the equilibrium path from being achieved and to maintain the cyclical variations in a fairly regular pattern. No sooner has one cycle started to diminish in amplitude than another disturbance to the economy occurs, starting off a new cycle. The types of disturbances which could do this are *sudden changes in investment*, *balance of payments crises*, *changes in the money supply*, *rapid inflation and the policies designed to curb it*, *population movements*, *industrial disputes*, or even *wars*.

Of course, it is possible for more than one disturbance to occur at the same time so that the cyclical variations generated, although inherently damped, may be quite large. This means that the 'ceiling' and 'floor' analysis may become relevant here as well as in the explosive cycles case. Consider the hypothetical random disturbances shown in Fig. 11 which give rise to fairly realistic variations in real output.

In this kind of model, real output is volatile, occasionally reaching the ceiling or floor, with each successive random disturbance pushing real income upwards or downwards and with the underlying stabilising influences of the multiplier and accelerator.

Monetary influences

One of the random disturbances mentioned in the previous section was a change in the money supply. Consider now to what extent changes in a

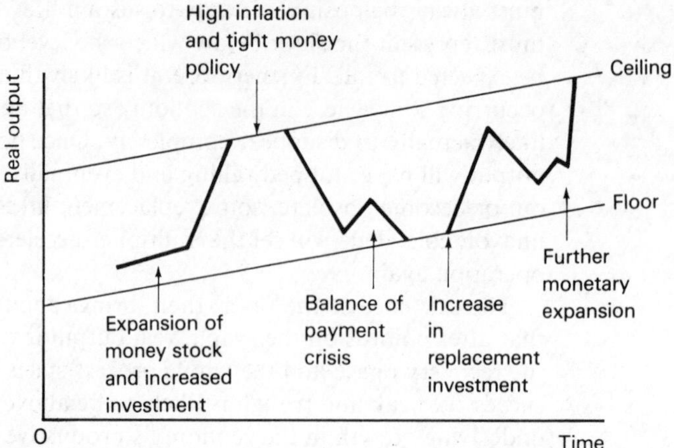

Fig. 11. A cycle caused by random disturbances.

country's monetary variables may be responsible for cyclical variations in real output.

Recall from Chapter 23 that the monetarists put a great deal of faith in the observed correlation between changes in the money supply and changes in national income. In particular, the study by Friedman and Schwartz emphasises the observation that all major recessions have been preceded by a fall in the money supply and all major inflations by an increase in the money supply. By attempting to show that the monetary changes were not associated with the changes in national income, they concluded that it must be the change in the money supply that causes the change in national income.

Non-monetarists also recognise the role that monetary changes may have on real output, though of course they do not assign them such a major role as the monetarists. For example, they recognise that in the recovery phase of the cycle, the demand for money will be increasing to finance the greater volume of transactions. If the money supply is not expanded sufficiently to meet this demand, interest rates will rise, this in turn will discourage some investment and so contribute to the slowing down in the growth of output and eventually lead to the upper turning-point. Similarly, in the deflation phase, the demand for money will be falling. If the money supply is not also falling at the same rate, interest rates will fall and so encourage new investment. This will contribute to the lower turning-point. However, notice that the effectiveness of this mechanism clearly depends on the interest-elasticity of investment which, as pointed out in Chapter 20, is likely to be very low in the boom and slump periods of a trade cycle.

Conclusion

There are many possible causes of trade cycles and we have only had time to consider some of the major ones in this chapter. In more advanced economics, it is possible to deal with more complex versions of the multiplier-accelerator model which require knowledge of difference and differential equations. Other theories concentrate on technological changes or on firms' investment in inventories to explain the cycles. There was even a theory that trade cycles were associated with sun-spot cycles, but this is not held in much regard these days.

Further reading

Westaway, A.J. and **Weyman-Jones, T.G.**, *Macroeconomics: Theory, Evidence and Policy*, Longman, London, 1977 (Ch. 15).
Matthews, R.C.O., *The Trade Cycle*, Oxford University Press, Oxford, 1959.
Mueller, M.G. ed., *Readings in Macroeconomics*, Holt, Rinehart and Winston, New York, 1966 (Ch. 18).
Chiang, A.C., *Fundamental Methods of Mathematical Economics*, McGraw-Hill, New York, 1974 (Ch. 17).

Exercises

1. Review your understanding of the following terms:

trade cycle	damped cycle
slump	explosive cycle
recovery	ceiling
boom	floor
recession	turning-point
deflation	random disturbance

2. Using the multiplier-accelerator model developed in this chapter, trace out the time-path for national income over 10 years when
(a) $c = 0.8$ and $v = 0.1$;
(b) $c = 0.5$ and $v = 4$.
Comment on your results.

3. Obtain data on gross domestic fixed capital formation, real national income and the number of unfilled job vacancies for the United Kingdom in the 1970s. Plot the data on a graph and comment on any cyclical variations.

4. Discuss the extent to which the cyclical fluctuations observed in question (3) may be a result of: (a) monetary variables; (b) random disturbances.

5. 'An essential characteristic of cyclical behaviour is not only that expansion and contraction follow each other, but that each phase of the cycle contains within it the seeds to generate the succeeding phase' (R. Levacic, *Macroeconomics*). How can this aspect of the trade cycle be explained?

25 Economic growth and development

Introduction

In Chapter 18, economic growth was defined as an increase in a country's productive capacity, identifiable by a sustained rise in real national income over a period of years. A country's annual rate of economic growth, then, can best be measured by taking the average percentage increase in national income over a long period of time, say five or ten years. The figure obtained will be an estimate of the average annual rate of growth in the country's productive capacity, assuming that the rate of unemployment is roughly the same at the beginning and end of the period. In Chapter 18, we also described the major advantages of economic growth (that it may increase living standards, reduce poverty and allow for a redistribution of income) and some of its major disadvantages (that it may harm some individuals or group, it has an opportunity cost, it may not be possible for much longer and it may cause negative externalities).

Economic growth and economic *development* are obviously closely related; for the purposes of this chapter, however, we draw an important distinction between them. A country is enjoying economic development when it is experiencing economic growth, as defined above, and at the same time is undergoing major structural changes in its economy, like a shift from agriculture to manufacturing. With this distinction in mind, we deal with economic growth in the context of an industrialised economy, such as the United Kingdom or the United States, and economic development in the context of a less developed country, such as India or Nigeria. In general, less developed countries can be identified by their relative poverty. They do have other characteristics which distinguish them from the 'developed' countries, but low national income per head is their major distinguishing feature.

In the first section of this chapter, we examine the main determinants of economic growth and their policy implications. In the second section, we consider some of the main problems of less developed countries and the possible ways of alleviating them.

Main determinants of economic growth

There are three main determinants of a country's rate of economic growth which we consider: the growth of its labour force; the growth of its capital stock; technical progress.

Growth of the labour force

A growing labour supply may enable a community to produce bigger combinations of goods and services and so bring about an outward shift in its production possibility frontier. This, in turn, can lead to an increase in output per head and hence a potential improvement in social welfare. The growth of the labour force itself will depend on the following main factors: (a) the 'natural' increase in the population; (b) international migration; (c) the participation rate. Consider these in turn.

(a) *The natural increase in population* is determined by the excess of the birth rate over the death rate. If a country's population is below its 'optimum' size (see below), then a natural increase in population will eventually lead to a rise in output of goods and services *per head*. The population growth rate, though, is influenced by complex social factors such as customs, attitudes and beliefs about marriages and family size. Death rates and birth rates are also influenced by such factors as the availability of medical facilities, old peoples' homes and ante-natal care, including help and advice on contraception.

In general, a fast growing population means that younger people form an increasing proportion of the labour force. A younger work-force may be presumed to be more energetic and diligent with a potential for greater geographical and occupational mobility than an older work-force. A slow-growing population, on the other hand, tends to lead to a rising proportion of older people in the economically active sector and a rising dependency ratio of the old and retired to the total population.

Finally, note that since population growth causes an increase in the number of consumers as well as an expansion of the labour force, the rate of economic growth caused by population growth must exceed the rate of population growth if output *per head* (and therefore potential social welfare) is to increase. If we denote the rate of economic growth by g and natural population growth by n, then, other things being equal, for an increase in potential social welfare, we require that $g > n$.

(b) *International migration* is the flow of people between countries and is largely determined by the degree of international labour mobility. Net immigration will tend to add to a country's labour force while net emigration will tend to reduce it. Such labour mobility, though, is influenced by differences in languages, customs and traditions between countries, job opportunities and promotion prospects, and perhaps more important, laws governing immigration.

(c) *The participation rate* is the proportion of the economically active population to the total population. A rise in this rate would amount to an increase in the size of the labour force. The participation rate is determined by the extent to which the different age groups and the sexes in the population are able by law, customs, tradition and trade union regulations and attitudes to participate in labour market activity. For instance, the equal pay legislation in the United Kingdom should tend to raise the participation rate of the female labour force (see Ch. 15). On the other hand, raising the school-leaving age and lowering the retirement age have the effect of reducing the participation rate.

Growth of the capital stock

An expansion of a country's capital stock through net investment, just like an expansion of its labour force, increases the country's stock of productive resources and so represents another possible source of economic growth. We have noted before that investment (which enables more consumer goods to be produced in the future) requires refraining from some current consumption so that resources can be channelled into the production of the various forms of capital. In other words, savings are required in order that investment can take place.

In our analysis of the simple Keynesian model in Chapter 19, we highlighted *one* role of investment in the economy: that it is a component of aggregate demand. Since that model is short-term only, we were able to ignore the fact that when net investment takes place, an addition to the country's stock of capital occurs (recall that by net investment we mean that over and above the investment required to replace worn out or obsolete equipment). In a long-term model, though, we must take into account the two roles of investment: that it is *a component of aggregate demand* and that it is *an addition to the stock of productive resources.* This is the objective of the Harrod-Domar model of economic growth – one of the simplest growth theories which extends the simple short-run Keynesian model into the long-run.

The Harrod-Domar growth model This model is named after its originators, the English economist, Sir Roy Harrod and the American, E. Domar. Since it is a simple model, we must start by setting out its major assumptions.

(a) We assume that the economy is closed and that there is no government economic activity. This means that there are no imports, exports, government expenditures or taxes in the model and the condition for equilibrium is that planned investment should equal planned savings.
(b) There are only two factors of production, labour (L) and capital (K), and in our simple version of the model, there is no technical progress.
(c) Labour is homogeneous, measured in its own units and grows at the constant natural rate of growth, n.
(d) There are constant returns to scale. This means that if both labour and capital are increased by a given proportion, output will also increase by that proportion.

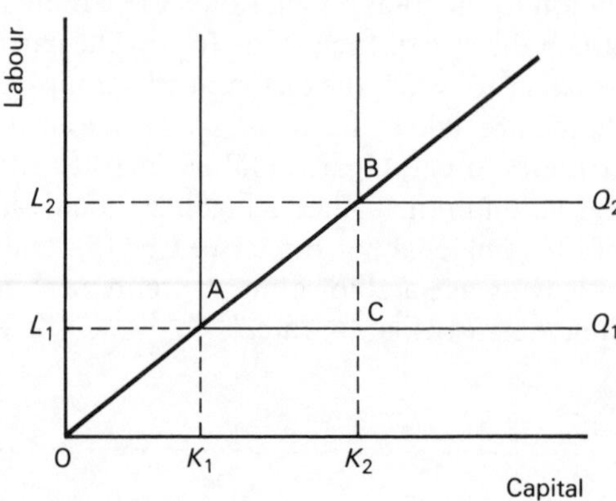

Fig. 1. Isoquant map illustrating a fixed proportions production function.

(e) Savings (S) are a fixed proportion of income (Y). That is, $S = sY$ where s is both the average and marginal propensity to save. Investment (I) is autonomous and there is no depreciation.

(f) The potential level of national income (Y_p) is proportional to the quantity of capital and to the quantity of labour. Thus, we can write $K = vY_p$ and $L = uY_p$, where v is a constant capital-output ratio and u is a constant labour-output ratio. This type of production function is called a *fixed proportions production function.* The isoquants illustrating such a function are L-shaped as shown in Fig. 1. Both labour and capital have to be employed in fixed combinations: in the graph, increasing labour and capital from OL_1 and OK_1 to OL_2 and OK_2 increases output from Q_1 to Q_2 (that is, from point A to B). Increasing only one of the factors, though, say capital from OK_1 to OK_2, keeping labour unchanged, leaves output unchanged at Q_1 (that is, from point A to C).

Now consider Fig. 2, starting at the equilibrium point A. The initial level of investment is I_1 which equals savings at the income level OY_1. Over time, however, the investment adds to the capital stock and so increases the economy's level of potential output, say to OY_2. The following analysis shows what the increase in potential output (ΔY_p) will be:

$K = vY_p$ (from assumption (f))

Therefore, $\Delta K = v\Delta Y_p$

But $\Delta K = I_1$, so we have,

$$\Delta Y_p = \frac{I_1}{v} \qquad [1]$$

The new level of income, OY_2, will only be an equilibrium level of income if aggregate demand increases. Assuming that the consumption and savings functions are stable, this increase in demand must come from an increase in investment. In fact, investment must rise to I_2 as shown in Fig. 2. Now I_2 intersects the savings line at point B where OY_2 is the equilibrium level of income.

As soon as the new capital from this extra investment comes into operation, potential output will rise yet again, say to OY_3. For this to be an

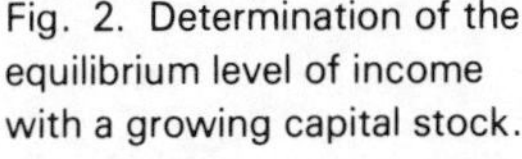

Fig. 2. Determination of the equilibrium level of income with a growing capital stock.

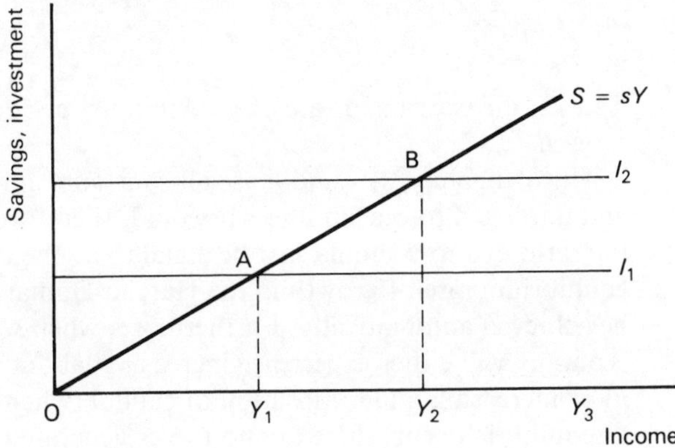

equilibrium, investment must rise again – and so on as the growth process takes place.

Harrod named that rate of growth of output which maintains equilibrium and keeps the capital stock fully employed, the *warranted rate of growth* (g_w). This rate can be derived as follows.

$$\Delta Y = \frac{I}{v} \quad \text{(from [1] above)}$$

In equilibrium, we have $I = S = sY$

By substitution, $\Delta Y = \frac{sY}{v}$

Rearranging, $\frac{\Delta Y}{Y} = \frac{s}{v} = g_w$

The expression $\Delta Y / Y$ represents the rate of growth of output required to keep the economy in equilibrium and at its potential output level. It is, therefore, Harrod's warranted rate of growth. As an example, suppose that the capital-output ratio, v, were equal to 4 and that the savings proportion, s, were equal to 0.2. The warranted rate of growth would be:

$$g_w = \frac{0.2}{4} = 5 \text{ per cent.}$$

This means that 5 per cent growth per time period would be necessary in this economy to keep the potential and equilibrium output levels equal. Notice that the warranted rate of growth can be increased by policies designed to increase the propensity to save or to reduce the capital-output ratio by increasing the productivity of capital.

Of course, given the fixed proportions production function in this model, output can only grow at the warranted rate, s/v, if sufficient labour is made available. The labour force, however, is assumed to be growing at the constant rate n: if this exceeds s/v, the warranted rate can be achieved but will lead to an increasing rate of labour unemployment; if n is less than s/v, the actual rate of growth will fall short of the warranted rate and unemployed capital will be created. Thus, for an equilibrium growth path which maintains full employment of both labour and capital, the following condition must be satisfied:

$$\frac{s}{v} = n$$

That is, the warranted rate of growth must be equal to the natural rate of growth.

Unfortunately, s, v and n are all constants in the Harrod-Domar model and unrelated to one another. It would, therefore, be a complete 'fluke' if the ratio of s to v should just be equal to n. We can conclude that the equilibrium rate of growth in the Harrod-Domar model is highly unlikely to be achieved automatically. Furthermore, when s/v is not equal to n, the economy will either experience increasing labour unemployment (when $s/v < n$) or increasing underutilisation of capital (when $s/v > n$). When such disequilibria occur, there are no forces generated to restore the equilibrium growth path. In other words, the equilibrium in the Harrod-Domar model is an unstable, or 'knife-edge', equilibrium.

Main drawback of the Harrod-Domar model The model's major drawback is its dependence on an inflexible production function where no substitution whatever is possible between labour and capital. For example, with a fixed proportions production function (illustrated by the L-shaped isoquants in Fig. 1), it is not possible to expand output by increasing the supply of one factor of production only – if more machines are acquired but the labour force is unchanged, output cannot expand; similarly, output cannot be kept unchanged by cutting back on the labour force and increasing the capital stock.

It is clearly more realistic to assume that there is some (though not perfect) substitutability between labour and capital. If there is some factor substitution, the isoquant map will have the more familiar shape as shown in Fig. 3. It is now possible to increase output from Q_1 to Q_2 by increasing the capital stock from OK_1 to OK_2 keeping the labour force unchanged, or by increasing the labour force from OL_1 to OL_2, keeping the capital stock unchanged.

Fig. 3. Isoquant map illustrating a neo-classical production function.

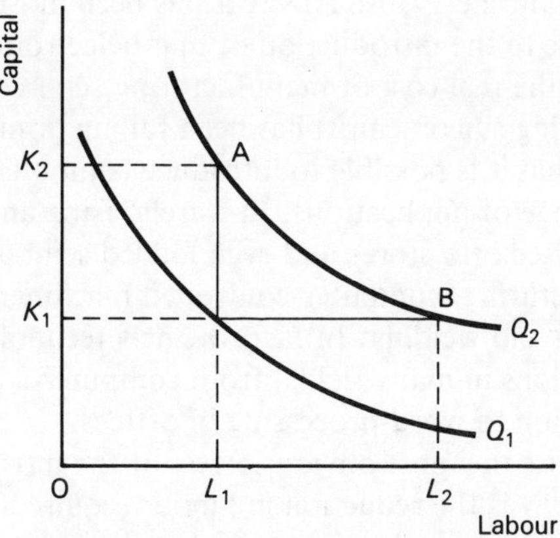

With a production function of this kind, the capital-output ratio (v) can vary: for example, v is higher at point A than at point B in Fig. 3. Suppose now that the warranted and natural rates of growth are not equal. As an example, let $s/v > n$; this means that the capital stock is growing faster than the labour force and also faster than output. Consequently, the capital-output ratio will rise and as it does so, s/v will fall. This tendency will continue until $s/v = n$ again.

This view, that any discrepancy between the warranted and natural rates of growth will be corrected by a change in v, is the basis of the so-called *neo-classical growth model*.

Technical progress

Technical progress which, as pointed out in Chapter 16, can either be neutral or non-neutral, is another possible source of economic growth. It can take the form of improved techniques of production, improved machinery, inventions or improvements in education; in other words, it is anything which improves the *quality* of the capital stock or labour force. The effect of technical progress is to raise the productivity of the stock of capital and labour. If it is neutral and so raises the productivity of capital and labour by the same proportion, then (given constant returns to scale) output will also rise by that proportion.

Note that the effect of technical progress on a country's equilibrium growth path depends on: (a) whether it raises in the same proportion the productivity of *all* capital and *all* labour, both old and new; (b) whether it raises the productivity of only new labour and capital, including those new machines which are created to replace those which have depreciated; (c) whether it affects only the productivity of capital (that is, capital-biased technical progress); (d) whether it affects only the productivity of labour (that is, labour-biased technical progress).

Technological unemployment A number of observers have expressed the view that rapid technological change in the two final decades of the twentieth century will lead to widespread technological unemployment. Some forecasts have suggested that total unemployment in the United Kingdom might rise to 5 million in the 1980s. This fear has been most frequently illustrated with reference to the introduction of microelectronic technology. As is well-known, the real cost of manufacturing semi-conductor integrated circuits (employing silicon chips) has been falling dramatically. This development means that it is possible to introduce computer-controlled equipment in a wide range of applications. In warehousing and distribution, products can be transported into stores and even loaded semi-automatically. In manufacturing, computer-controlled machinery can be used for paint-spraying and welding. In fact, the new technology has widespread applications in many fields, from computer-typesetting in newspaper production to word-processing in offices.

Because the most obvious effect of the introduction of microelectronic technology is the reduction in labour required to perform a given task, the fears of widespread technological unemployment have been expressed. A Department of Employment report argued, however, that the introduction of microelectronic technology would not in itself cause unemployment. Indeed, the report claimed that a bigger threat of unemployment would result from a failure by the United Kingdom to introduce the technology as this would make British industry uncompetitive in international markets.

To the extent that the introduction of new technology increases productivity and reduces costs, demand for products will increase and new jobs can be created. This has happened, for example, in the case of banking where, despite the introduction of computers, the level of employment has been maintained through diversification and the provision of extra services to customers. The introduction of new machinery also creates new jobs in their design and maintenance.

Growth policies We have seen that there are some disadvantages associated with a high rate of economic growth. Assuming, however, that a government's objective is to raise the growth rate, we can conclude that the appropriate policies must be those which influence the growth of the labour force, the growth of the capital stock and the quality of the country's labour and capital.

Fiscal and monetary policies could be used to try and shift resources from the production of consumer goods into the production of investment goods. As far as monetary policy is concerned, low interest rates and increased availability of credit may encourage firms to invest more and so increase the capital stock. Unfortunately, this policy tends not to reduce consumption spending – indeed, it is more likely to increase such spending and so possibly lead to the building up of inflationary pressures. We see later that a high rate of inflation can actually discourage investment.

Fiscal policy may have more chance of success. Assuming that the economy already has full employment and reasonably stable prices, the government may be able to keep aggregate demand unchanged by increasing taxes and directing the revenue raised into capital-creating expenditures. Such a policy should cut aggregate consumption (because disposable income is reduced) and increase aggregate investment and so lead to a higher rate of growth. Increased expenditures on retraining schemes, road-building, financial aid to firms setting up in depressed regions, education, health and research and development are the ones most likely to increase the economy's productive capacity. Unfortunately, policy conflicts still cannot be completely ruled out: raising taxes may lead to higher wage claims which, together with the increased government spending, may have a net inflationary effect on the economy.

In general, governments have given greater priority to the objectives of full employment and stable prices than the growth objective. Consequently, fiscal and monetary policies have been used mostly for the purposes of short-run demand-management and not for the longer-run objective of economic growth.

Indicative planning In planned economies (such as the Soviet Union), it is possible for the government to direct resources out of consumer goods industries and into capital goods industries as part of a long-term plan to achieve a higher rate of economic growth. In mixed economies (such as the United Kingdom), however, such direction of resources is not possible. One thing that governments in mixed economies can do is to *indicate* target levels of output for the various industrial sectors and for the economy as a whole. So in the United Kingdom, for example, the government could publish target growth rates for different industries and for national income over the next five years and set out a list of policies designed to assist the growth plan. If firms have confidence in the government's estimates, the figures should provide producers with information which would enable them to harmonise their production decisions more efficiently with those of related firms. Such planning is called 'indicative' planning and was practiced successfully in France after the Second World War. It was attempted in the 1960s in the United Kingdom with the setting up of the National Economic Development Council in 1962, the Department of Economic Affairs in 1964 and with the publishing of the National Plan in 1965. There was no coercion and no sanctions were imposed against firms which failed to achieve the stated targets; the aim was simply to indicate the growth path which the government regarded as desirable and thereby guide firms along it.

Indicative planning has both its proponents and opponents. On the one hand, proponents say that it creates growth by giving firms an expectation of increased future demand for their products and, perhaps more important, by helping to harmonise different firms' production decisions. On the other hand, opponents say that such planning represents nothing more than a waste of resources to produce inaccurate statistics. Confidence in the scheme will soon be lost, they say, when firms realise that the government's targets generally fail to be achieved.

Economic development

The problem of economic development

About one hundred less developed countries (LDCs) in Asia, Africa and Latin America are engaged in a struggle to escape from poverty. Within LDCs, there are often extreme inequalities of income and wealth with pockets of extreme poverty and high levels of unemployment. In the world as a whole, the LDCs have about 70 per cent of the total population but only 12 per cent of total income. The disparities of income between the poor and rich nations of the world are illustrated for selected countries in Table 1. Notice that per capita income in the United States is more than ninety times that in Bangladesh and more than fifty times that in India.

Table 1. Per capita incomes for selected countries in 1977.

Country	Per capita income ($)
Developed countries	
United States	8,520
United Kingdom	4,420
Less developed countries	
Venezuela	2,660
Iran	2,160
Brazil	1,360
Nigeria	420
Egypt	320
Indonesia	300
Tanzania	190
India	150
Bangladesh	90

Source: The World Bank, *World Development Report,* 1979.

In spite of some remarkable rates of growth in per capita incomes in the 1950s and 1960s, recent studies have shown that income inequalities have been widening in the LDCs. Perhaps more important, these countries' growth policies have failed to create employment opportunities to match the rates of growth in the labour force. For instance, in 1974, unemployment was estimated to be 28 per cent of the labour force in the Asian LDCs, 38 per cent in Africa and 25 per cent in Latin America. These, of course, are much higher than the rates of unemployment experienced by the developed countries.

Clearly, the problem of development is not merely that of increasing the national incomes of the LDCs. It is also the problem of finding ways to remove the related evils of poverty, inequality and unemployment. To devise appropriate policies, we must first examine the main causes of economic development.

Theories of economic development

The most frequently asked question in the study of development economics is: what initiates the process of economic development? Unfortunately, there is no single theory which fully explains the causes of development, nor can one draw general conclusions from the economic history of the rich industrial nations whose experiences have been unique. One lesson that can be learned from the industrialised countries is that growth and development are exceedingly complex processes – they combine changes in social and political institutions, the countries' sense of values and belief systems with changes in the methods of production and in the means of exploiting productive resources.

It is now being increasingly recognised that there are no 'laws' of economic development. No *single* theory can be used to explain the ways in which full employment might be achieved in LDCs which have diverse social, geographic and economic characteristics. The following summaries of development theories, therefore, should be treated with care. They merely highlight a few of the main factors which can contribute to industrialisation and economic development.

Classical theory of development This theory asserts that the major cause of economic development is the rate of investment which, in turn, depends on the share of profits in the national income. The higher the rate of profits, the faster will be the rate of investment and the rate of economic development.

Early classical writers, like Adam Smith, David Ricardo and J.S. Mill, made contributions to this theory. They maintained that the growth of capital would make more division of labour and specialisation possible and so lead to increased labour productivity and higher wages. As development proceeded, both profits and wages would be high. But high wages would encourage earlier marriages and a higher birth rate, leading to rapid population growth. In the course of time, as capital accumulated and population grew, with a fixed area of land, diminishing returns would set in, wages would gradually return to the subsistence level and profits would decline. Investment would then cease and the development process would come to an end. At this point, the economy was said to have reached a *stationary state*.

The fact that the economy reaches a stationary state in this theory is a direct result of the classical economists' belief in the law of diminishing returns and the Malthusian theory of population. They made little or no allowance for the effect of technological change on the process of development. The theory fails to provide any guidance to development planners as to the ways of generating increased employment opportunities and reducing poverty and inequality.

Marxian theory of development Karl Marx's theory strives to combine economics and sociology and views economic development as a continuous change in the social, cultural and political life of a society. Such a change is brought about by changes in the methods of production and in property rights by a class of people in society seeking economic power and prestige. According to this theory, the major factor in economic development is the rate of accumulation of 'labour surplus value' – that is, the rate of profit appropriated by capitalists from workers. Such surplus value arises in every society irrespective of its stage of development because labour, the sole producer of value, is capable of producing more than is necessary for payment of subsistence wages. Labour surplus value, then, is the difference between the value of what is produced and the amount paid in wages.

It follows that the nearer wages are to the subsistence level, the larger will be the surplus for investment. As we saw in Chapter 16, however, a fall in the rate of profit becomes inevitable when a capitalist society reaches an advanced stages of industrialisation. In an effort to arrest the decline in profits, capitalists resort to labour-saving technology and so add to the 'reserve army' of unemployed workers. This intensifies the struggle between capitalists and workers until capitalism is replaced by a new social order. Unlike the classical economists' belief in population growth as a limit to economic development, Marxist theory emphasises the organic composition of capital leading to the falling rate of profit.

Rostow's 'stage' theory of development This theory, developed by W.W. Rostow, asserts that the transition of an economy from being less developed to being developed is possible through a series of steps or stages. The most important of these is the so-called 'take-off' stage when resistence to change in traditional values and in the social, political and economic institutions of a less developed country is finally overcome and modern industries begin to expand.

The theory can be criticised for viewing development as simply a matter of higher savings and investment ratios. Many LDCs did, in fact, achieve remarkable growth rates (5 to 6 per cent) in the 1950s and 1960s, yet poverty, unemployment and income inequalities worsened.

Harrod-Domar growth theory This theory, as outlined earlier in this chapter, has a special analytical appeal to development planners. The planners have to make appropriate assumptions about capital-output and labour-output ratios, the sources of savings and the rate of population growth when formulating their development plans.

The modern view of economic development This new approach views economic development in terms of reducing poverty, income inequalities and high unemployment through a carefully selected strategy of development projects. The per capita income criterion of economic development is relegated to secondary place of importance.

In order that such strategies succeed in realising the goals of development, emphasis is placed on removing the structural rigidities in an LDC through such measures as land reforms, better farm practices and the improvement of access of farmers, craftsmen and traders to the marketing and credit facilities of the modern sector. In addition, a great deal of emphasis is placed on changes in attitudes and the belief systems of individuals and social groups so that these groups are able to evolve and enjoy their own sense of values, self-esteem and freedom from the degradation of poverty, unemployment and starvation.

The modern view of development perceives the problems of poverty and income inequality in an international setting – that is to say, between the rich and poor nations of the world. It focuses attention, therefore, on the need for reforming the United Nations' agencies, such as the World Bank, the International Development Association and other regional bodies such as the European Economic Community. The aim is the improve the access of the LDCs to the commodity and capital markets of the industrialised economies so as to effect a large-scale transfer of technology as well as real and financial resources from the rich to the poor nations of the world.

Population aspects of economic development

Students of economic development show considerable interest in the study of population. This is because a growing population, and hence a growing labour force, not only poses problems for full employment policies in the LDCs, it also has a direct effect on living standards and society's welfare. We have already noted that classical economists paid attention to the problem of population growth which they considered to be the major limitation on the process of development. T.R. Malthus, one of the famous classical economists, published his 'Essay on the Principles of Population' in 1798, a time when England's population was growing rapidly. The essay won immediate acclaim and became the major focus of controversy in the decades which followed.

Malthusian theory of population

Malthus's basic proposition was that there was a direct relationship between population growth and the supply of food. A given increase in food supplies and hence living standards would tend to cause an increase in the country's population. Malthus judged society's welfare by the strict criterion of the amount of food available to the people of the country.

Malthus employed the law of diminishing returns to support his view that food production grew *more slowly* than population. Indeed, he proposed that: (a) population tended to grow in a geometric progression, while (b) food production tended to increase in an arithmetic progression. These two propositions are illustrated in Table 2 for a hypothetical country with an initial population of 10 million in 1970. As can be seen from the Table, the population doubles itself every thirty years – that is, it increases in the

Table 2. Population growth and food supplies.

Year	Population (millions)	Food supply (millions of tonnes)	Food supply per head
1970	10	10	1.0
2000	20	20	1.0
2030	40	30	0.75
2060	80	40	0.5

geometric ratios 1, 2, 4, 8 etc. On the other hand, food supplies only grow in the arithmetic ratios 1, 2, 3, 4, etc. It follows that food supplies per head must fall as population increases. This imbalance between the growth of population and foodstuffs illustrates what might be called a 'population explosion'. Malthus painted a dark and depressing picture of future human societies.

The decline in food supplies per head could not continue indefinitely, however. Malthus argued that food shortages would eventually act as a check on population growth. In fact, he identified two types of checks: first, *positive* checks (like famine, disease, epidemics and wars) which increase death rates; and secondly, *preventive* checks (like late marriages, celibacy and voluntary restraint) which slow down birth rates. Being the son of a clergyman, Malthus was a strong advocate of preventive checks. He warned that if people failed to control the birth rate, Nature, which has a vengeance on mankind, would apply the more unpleasant positive checks to reduce population.

Can the Malthusian theory be applied to the LDCs? Because of rapid rises in their populations, countries like India, Bangladesh and Indonesia are heavily dependent on imports of food. Unfortunately, the greater the quantity of food imports, the smaller is the amount of foreign exchange available for importing machinery, equipment and technical know-how for economic development. In other words, the large food imports necessitated by the rapidly growing populations in the LDCs tend to slow down their rate of development.

As illustrated in Table 3, the LDCs as a group have recorded more than twice the rates of population growth of Europe and America. In contrast, the domestic production of foodstuffs in the LDCs has scarcely kept pace with population growth and, as a result, their dependence on imports from the developed countries has increased. Supporters of the Malthusian theory,

Table 3. Comparison of population growth rates.

Area	Average annual % increase in population, 1965–77
Europe	0.6
North America	1.0
Africa	2.7
Asia	2.2
Latin America	2.7

Source: United Nations Statistical Yearbook, 1978, Table 2.

therefore, have argued in favour of population controls. They point out that modern medical facilities have reduced death rates in the LDCs, but that it has not been possible to popularise modern techniques of birth control.

The following criticisms may be levelled against the Malthusian theory when applied to LDCs.

(a) It underestimates the impact on economic development in general and food production in particular of (i) technological advances, and (ii) international trade. These two factors enable a country to increase the production of food and other goods and so support a growing population and labour force. Historically, European countries experienced rapid population growth in their early stages of development, but they escaped the Malthusian catastrophe through increased food imports from the newer areas of North America, Australia and New Zealand.

(b) Malthus argued that population would not grow without growth in food supplies or a rise in living standards above the subsistence level. The populations of the LDCs, however, have grown without significant rises in food production or incomes per head.

The theory of optimum population

A country's 'optimum population' can be defined as that size of population at which, given the volume of all capital and land resources and the state of technology, income per head is maximised. This is illustrated in Fig. 4 which shows income per head for different population sizes. Income per head is maximised at population O*P* and this, therefore, is the optimum population. If the country has a population below O*P*, it can be described as *underpopulated:* this means that the country does not have sufficient labour resources to exploit all the other resources to the full and an increase in population will give rise to an increase in income per head. If the country has a population above O*P*, it can be described as *overpopulated:* in this case, the law of diminishing returns is operating and a decrease in population would increase income per head.

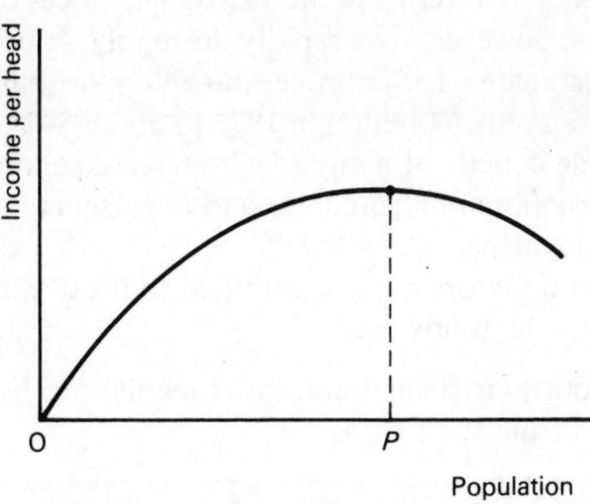

Fig. 4. The optimum population.

Note that for a developing country, the optimum size of population is not rigidly fixed, but will itself be increasing as economic development proceeds. As the state of technological knowledge improves and the volume of resources increases, so the optimum population shifts upwards.

One major difficulty that confronts the development planner is that of estimating the optimum population. Apart from the actual calculation problems, economic development involves continual changes in the data. This means that no sooner are the estimates calculated than they become out-of-date. Furthermore, the concept of the optimum population is based on a narrow economic viewpoint and fails to take into account social and political factors.

The roles of international trade and aid in the process of development

It has been argued that a major limitation on the speed of economic development is the volume of foreign exchange available to the LDCs. Foreign exchange is needed to fill several 'gaps' which characterise many LDCs; examples include the 'technological gap', the 'managerial and entrepreneurial gap' and the gap between domestic savings and the target level of investment. Foreign exchange is also needed to be channelled into those investment projects which benefit the poorer sections of the population and so reduce relative poverty. However, these needs have persistently exceeded the sources of foreign exchange earnings during the past two decades when effective international and regional action to augment the foreign exchange earnings of the LDCs has been lacking. Broadly, foreign exchange earnings arise from three sources: (a) export earnings from international trade; (b) foreign private investment; (c) development aid. Consider these in turn.

International trade

International trade is by far the largest earner of foreign exchange: it enables the LDCs to use their export receipts to pay for imports of food, capital goods and technical information. Most LDCs export primary commodities, raw materials and some finished manufactures. The export earnings of the very low income countries (with a GNP per capita below $300 in 1977) declined in real terms in the 1970s. The prices of many imports, including oil imports, however, rose rapidly during the same period. According to World Bank estimates, for example, the oil import bill of the developing countries rose from only $4 billion in 1972 to about $42 billion in 1980. Consequently, the trade deficits of many LDCs increased enormously with a mounting level of international indebtedness and a worsening of poverty and unemployment.

Several factors have contributed to the decline in export earnings. Consider the following.

(a) Quotas, tariffs and non-tariff regulations by the developed countries on imports from the LDCs.
(b) The development of substitutes by the rich countries for the exports of LDCs. One example is the increased use of synthetic rubber in place of natural rubber.
(c) Financial incentives, such as subsidies and tax rebates, to export industries in developed countries so that the exports of LDCs have been subject to

intense competition from the exports of developed countries in world markets.

(d) In some markets, the share of LDCs has fallen because of the low income elasticities of demand for primary products.

Many observers have urged that in order to augment the export earnings of LDCs, the rich nations of the 'North' must reduce the trade restrictions on imports from the poor countries of the 'South'. The Independent Commission on International Development Issues (or Brandt Commission) in a report called *North-South: A Programme for Survival,* published in 1980, placed a major emphasis on the need for expanding world trade between North and South as a means of overcoming the growing payments deficits of the LDCs and of averting the dangers of world-wide recession, poverty and starvation. The Commission took the view that increased North-South trade was also in the interests of the North and argued that economic growth in the South would provide new markets for exports from the North in the future. This partly explains the Commission's recommendations for a 'comprehensive trade institution combining the functions of UNCTAD and GATT'. Such an institution would be concerned with reducing trade barriers and implementing the rules of free trade.

Foreign private investment

Foreign private investment in LDCs is undertaken largely by multinational corporations mainly in extractive and manufacturing industries. In the 1960s and 1970s, it appears that investment by multinational corporations became less welcome to some countries. There has been some criticism, for example, that in many cases the net contribution to foreign exchange earnings and to the economic development of the host country has been relatively small. The capital inflows, including the transfer of technology, resulting from the activities of multinationals have often failed to create the anticipated employment opportunities for the local population. The machinery and equipment imported into the host country is typically capital-intensive, creating relatively few jobs. Secondly, repatriated profits and interest on loans impose strains on the host country's weak balance of payments position. Thirdly, host governments have been less able to influence the investment decisions of large multinationals with head offices in the developed countries. At the same time, some corporations, fearful of potential nationalisation and confiscation of their assets, have been reluctant to invest large sums of money in LDCs. Thus, the conflict of interests between the host countries and multinational companies has been a major element in the decline in the rate of growth of the inflows of foreign exchange into the LDCs from foreign private investment.

The Brandt Commission recommends the creation of a well-defined legal framework for reconciling the conflicting interests of host countries and multinational corporations. It calls for well-defined arrangements concerning transfer pricing, tax incentives and the avoidance of restrictive practices, for example. Given the right environment, the Commission sees an important role for multinational companies in bringing about a large-scale transfer of technology from North to South, as well as participating in a significant change in the pattern of world trade, mutually beneficial to North and South.

Development aid

Development aid comes directly from individual national governments of developed countries, largely in the form of concessionary loans and grants or technical assistance. Developed countries also provide aid indirectly through international agencies, such as the World Bank, the International Development Association and the Commonwealth Development Corporation. The emergence of surplus 'petro-funds' of the OPEC countries since 1974 opened up new sources of aid to the poorer countries of the Third World. Countries such as Saudi Arabia, Abu Dhabi and Kuwait consequently set up special development assistance funds to provide aid, especially to the poor Muslim countries. Because of the decline in real terms in foreign exchange earnings from international trade and foreign private investment, development aid is of critical importance to the economic development of the LDCs. Such assistance supplements meagre domestic savings and helps to relieve pressures on the balance of payments.

Major criticisms of aid, however, are that it is often 'tied' to the exports of donor countries and often results in a substantial debt repayment burden. Tied aid limits the freedom of the recipient countries to obtain capital goods and technical know-how at competitive prices in world markets. Official development assistance declined during the 1970s and averaged less than half the target. The World Bank set a target for developed countries to give an equivalent of 0.7 per cent of GNP in the form of aid. The Brandt Commission, conscious of the decline in development assistance, recommended that industrialised countries meet the 0.7 per cent of GNP target by 1985. The Commission also recommended that industrialised countries meet a target of 1 per cent of GNP by the end of the century. In the final analysis, though, the amount and nature of assistance will depend upon the willingness and determination of donor countries to reduce inequalities of income and wealth between the rich and poor nations of the world.

Conclusion

In this chapter, we have focused attention on one of the most important economic issues facing human societies. We first considered the main determinants of economic growth, outlined the simple Harrod-Domar growth model and briefly discussed policy measures designed to promote economic growth. We then defined the term underdevelopment, examined some of the major theories of development and the influence of population changes on economic development, and finally we turned our attention to the roles of international trade, foreign investment and aid in the process of development.

Further reading

Westaway, A.J. and **Weyman-Jones, T.G.,** *Macroeconomics: Theory, Evidence and Policy*, Longman, London, 1977 (Ch. 18).

Jones, H., *An Introduction to Modern Theories of Economic Growth*, Nelson, London, 1975.
Thirlwall, A.P., *Financing Economic Development*, Macmillan, London, 1976.
Todaro, M.P., *Economic Development in the Third World*, Longman, New York, 1977.
Report of the Independent Commission on International Development Issues, *North-South: A Programme for Survival*, Pan Books, London, 1980.

Exercises

1. Review your understanding of the following terms:

economic growth	less developed country
economic development	stationary state
natural rate of growth	labour surplus value
warranted rate of growth	subsistence wage
fixed proportions production function	positive checks to population growth
neo-classical production function	preventive checks to population growth
technical progress	optimum population
indicative planning	foreign aid

2. Consider Table 4 which shows comparative rates of growth for selected developed countries for the period 1970–77.

Table 4. Comparative growth rates of selected countries, 1970–77.

Country	Average annual growth of GDP, 1970–77
Japan	5.3
Australia	3.8
France	3.8
Belgium	3.7
Netherlands	3.1
Italy	2.9
United States	2.8
West Germany	2.4
United Kingdom	1.5

Source: The World Bank, *The World Development Report*, 1979.

Comment on the figures and account for the low relative rate of growth in the United Kingdom during this period.

3. Discuss the extent to which increased expenditure on education in the United Kingdom might contribute to a faster rate of economic growth.

4. Outline the arguments for and against the use of indicative planning in a mixed economy.

5. Describe the major economic problems facing a less developed country

of your choice. How might a study of the theories of development help the policy-makers to solve these problems?

6. Consider the view that foreign aid hinders rather than helps the economic development of a less developed country.

Macroeconomic policy issues

26 Macroeconomic policies

Introduction

In Chapter 18, we set out the five major macroeconomic policy objectives which most western governments strive to achieve: a high level of employment, stable prices, a high growth rate, external equilibrium and an equitable distribution of income and wealth. Having discussed the growth objective in Chapter 25, we turn in this final part of the book (Ch. 26–30) to a more detailed consideration of the problems of inflation and unemployment (Ch. 27), external balance (Ch. 28 and 29) and economic inequality (Ch. 30). In this introductory chapter, we start by discussing policy 'targets' and policy 'instruments' in general; then we outline the major policy instruments in turn – fiscal and monetary policies and their relative effectiveness; prices and income policy; and regional policy.

A most important point to make at this stage is that the policy recommendations made by economists are based on economic theories. This is why we have spent so much time setting out the current theories of employment, money and growth. Unfortunately, as we have seen, different schools of thought subscribe to different theories and this means that they also often disagree about which policies should be used. Probably the most marked disagreements exist between monetarists and Keynesians. In this and the remaining chapters, one of our aims is to give the reader a flavour of the important debate between these two groups.

Targets and instruments

The policy *targets* are the specific values which a government attaches to its various policy objectives. For example, if 'full' employment is thought to be attained when the rate of unemployment is 3 per cent, if prices are thought to be reasonably stable when the rate of inflation is 5 per cent per annum, and if the desired rate of economic growth is 4 per cent per annum, then 3 per cent unemployment, a 5 per cent rate of inflation and 4 per cent growth are all policy targets. Policy *instruments*, on the other hand, are those exogenous variables that can be influenced directly by the government (such as tax rates, government spending and the supply of reserve assets) and which are varied by the government in its attempt to achieve the policy targets.

The following is an important rule for economic policy-makers, demonstrated by Jan Tinbergen in 1952:

To have any hope of achieving all targets at the same time, there should be at least as many policy instruments as there are policy targets.

To illustrate this, consider a country with a high rate of unemployment and an overall deficit on its balance of payments (that is, the sum of the current and capital account balances is negative). Figure 1 shows how the combined policy instruments of fiscal policy *and* monetary policy can be used to achieve full employment and balance of payments equilibrium simultaneously on the assumption that the exchange rate is kept fixed. The use of only one of the policies, though, will (except by a remote chance) fail to achieve more than one of the targets.

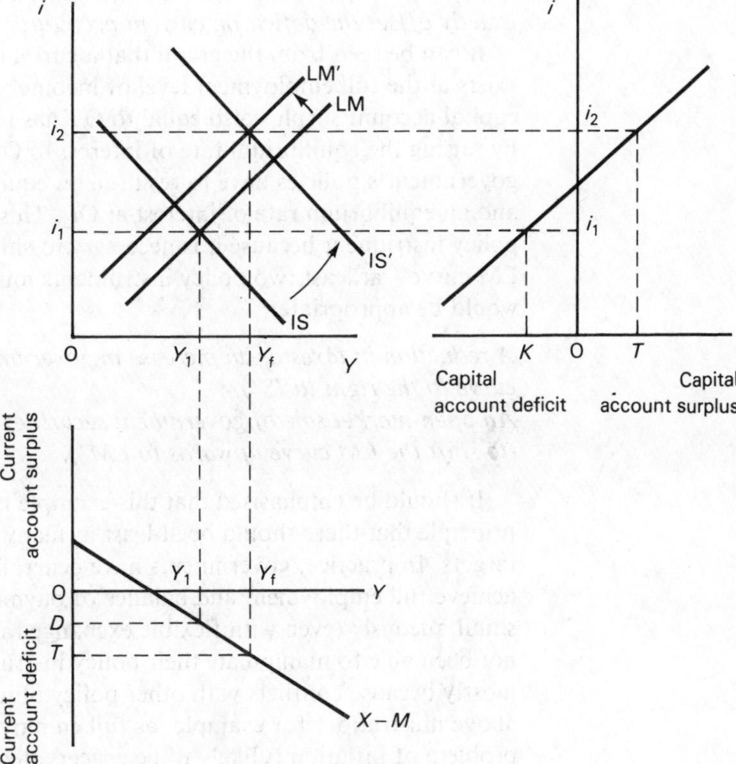

Fig. 1. The use of two instruments to achieve two targets.

The top left-hand graph in Fig. 1 shows the familiar IS–LM diagram. Initially, the equilibrium rate of interest is Oi_1 and the equilibrium level of income is OY_1 which is below the full employment level of income OY_f. The lower graph shows the relationship between the balance on current account (that is, total value of exports (X) *minus* total value of imports (M)) and national income. This relationship is based on two assumptions: first, that exports are determined exogenously and secondly, that imports are directly related to income. It follows that as income rises, imports will increase and the current account will move from a surplus into a deficit; conversely, as income falls, imports will fall and the current account will move back into surplus. Suppose that at the original equilibrium level of income, OY_1, there is a current account deficit equal to OD, as shown in the graph.

The upper right-hand graph shows the relationship between the balance on capital account and the rate of interest. A higher rate of interest (given interest rates in other countries) will attract capital inflows and lead to a surplus on capital account, while a lower rate of interest will encourage capital outflows and lead to a deficit. Suppose that at the original equilibrium interest rate, Oi_1, there is a capital account deficit equal to OK, as shown in the graph. This means that the *overall* balance of payments deficit at the initial equilibrium position is equal to OD + OK.

The government's two targets are: (a) *to raise the equilibrium level of income to the full employment level,* OY_f; and (b) *to achieve overall balance of payments equilibrium by creating a capital account surplus which will exactly offset the deficit on current account.*

It can be seen from the graph that a current account deficit equal to OT exists at the full employment level of income. To offset this, therefore, a capital account surplus also equal to OT has to be created; this can be done by raising the equilibrium rate of interest to Oi_2. In other words, the government's policies have to result in an equilibrium level of income at OY_f and an equilibrium rate of interest at Oi_2. This cannot be done with only one policy instrument because it is necessary to shift both the IS curve *and* the LM curve – at least two policy instruments must be used. The following would be appropriate:

A reduction in taxes or an increase in government spending (to shift the IS curve to the right to IS').
An open-market sale of government securities or a call for special deposits (to shift the LM curve upwards to LM').

It should be emphasised that this example is designed only to illustrate the principle that there should be at least as many policy instruments as there are targets. In practice, governments have generally found it impossible to achieve full employment and balance of payments equilibrium simultaneously (even with flexible exchange rates) partly because they have not been able to manipulate their policy instruments accurately enough, but mostly because conflicts with other policy objectives have arisen. In the above illustration, for example, as full employment is approached, the problem of inflation is likely to be exacerbated.

This brings us to a second important rule for policy-makers:

Since policy targets and instruments are not independent, it is essential to co-ordinate all the policy instruments in such a way that all targets are aimed at simultaneously.

This, of course, makes policy-making in practice a very complex affair indeed. Even in our simplified two-target, two-instrument example, it should be clear that the fiscal policy and the monetary policy both individually affect income and the rate of interest. That is to say, causality does not run from single instrument to single target; instead, each of the instruments influences *both* targets and this means that they have to be very carefully co-ordinated if the desired combination is to be achieved.

In the remainder of this chapter, we outline different policy instruments, starting with a comparison of fiscal and monetary policies.

Fiscal and monetary policies

Fiscal policy

Fiscal policy can be defined as the government's attempt to influence aggregate demand in the economy by regulating the amount of public expenditure and the rates of taxation. This policy is made more flexible by the fact that governments do not need to keep 'balanced budgets' – they can run a *budget surplus* by spending less than they raise in taxes or they can run a *budget deficit* by spending more than they raise in taxes. In this latter case, as we showed in Chapter 13, the excess spending can be financed either by borrowing or by 'printing money'.

In Chapter 19, we saw in the context of the simple Keynesian model how such policies could be used to affect the equilibrium level of income via the multiplier. An increase in government spending or a cut in taxes increased the equilibrium level of income, while a decrease in government spending or a rise in taxes reduced the equilibrium level of income. This can also be illustrated in the context of the IS–LM model. An expansionary fiscal policy (that is, an increase in government spending or a cut in taxes) will shift the IS curve to the *right*, while a contractionary fiscal policy will shift it to the *left*. This is illustrated in Fig. 2 where the IS and LM curves have their normal shapes and the original equilibrium is at OY_1 and Oi_1. As drawn, fiscal policy is seen to be reasonably effective – it causes a significant change in the equilibrium level of national income. Notice, however, that a change in government spending does not have a full multiplier effect on income. In this 'general equilibrium' model, a rise in government spending causes income to rise and this, in turn, causes the transactions demand for money to increase: with a constant money stock, less is now available for speculative purposes, so that interest rates are pushed upwards and this causes private investment to be cut back, so offsetting to some extent the effect of the increase in government spending on income. The new equilibrium position is at the higher income level OY_2 and at the higher interest rate Oi_2. Taking both the real and monetary sectors of the economy into account, fiscal policy is not necessarily so effective as it appeared in the simple Keynesian model.

Indeed, it is possible for fiscal policy to be *completely ineffective* so far as

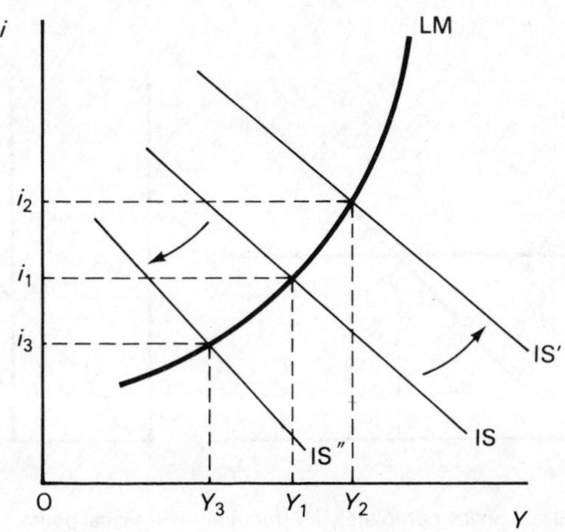

Fig. 2. Fiscal policy in the IS–LM model.

its influence over the equilibrium level of income is concerned. Recall from Chapter 23 that if the total demand for money were perfectly interest-inelastic, the LM curve would be vertical and there would only be one level of income consistent with equilibrium in the money market. In this case, as shown in Fig. 3 (a), the level of income remains unchanged whichever way the IS curve shifts. At the other extreme, fiscal policy will be very effective if the demand for money is perfectly interest-elastic. In the liquidity trap, where the LM curve is horizontal, interest rates are unaffected by fiscal policy, but income rises by the full multiplier effect. This is illustrated in Fig. 3 (b).

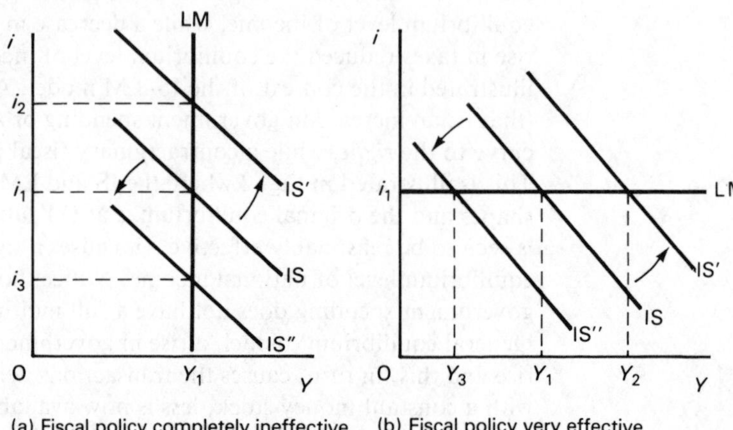

Fig. 3. The shape of the LM curve and the effectiveness of fiscal policy.

Result: Ceteris paribus, *the more interest-elastic is the demand for money, the more effective is fiscal policy.*

The effectiveness of fiscal policy, however, also depends on the steepness of the IS curve. The policy would be completely ineffective if the IS curve were horizontal, but would have its full effect if it were vertical. These cases are illustrated in Fig. 4 (a) and (b). The steepness of the IS curve depends

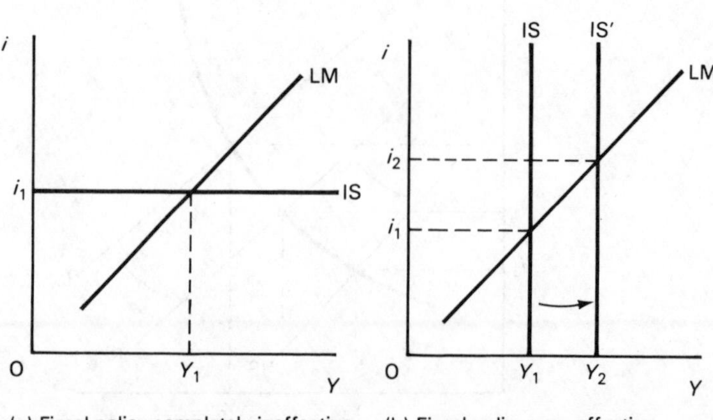

Fig. 4. The shape of the IS curve and the effectiveness of fiscal policy.

largely on the interest-elasticity of investment. Completely interest-elastic investment (highly unlikely) yields a horizontal IS curve, as shown in Fig. 4 (a); increased government expenditure leaves the IS curve unchanged so that the policy has no effect on income. Perfectly interest-inelastic investment would yield a vertical IS curve, as shown in Fig. 4 (b) and, in this case, an increase in government expenditure would have a full multiplier effect.

Result: Ceteris paribus, *the more interest-inelastic is investment, the more effective is fiscal policy.*

Monetary policy

Monetary policy can be defined as the government's attempt to influence aggregate demand in the economy by regulating the cost and availability of credit. We saw in Chapters 21 and 22 that in the United Kingdom, the government can influence both the cost and availability of credit by following measures designed to affect the country's supply of money - these include open market operations, special deposits and various forms of requests and direct controls over lending by banks and other financial institutions.

If we now analyse monetary policy in the context of the IS–LM model, this should enable us to compare its effectiveness with that of fiscal policy. Recall that an expansionary monetary policy will shift the LM curve to the right, while a contractionary monetary policy will shift it to the left. This is illustrated in Fig. 5 where the original equilibrium is at OY_1 and Oi_1. As was explained in Chapter 23, the increase in the money supply causes the interest rate to fall (assuming that the economy is not in the liquidity trap); this lower interest rate in turn gives rise to increased investment spending (assuming that investment is not completely interest-inelastic) and this increased spending raises national income. In Fig. 5, the new equilibrium position is at the higher level of income OY_2 and the lower interest rate Oi_2.

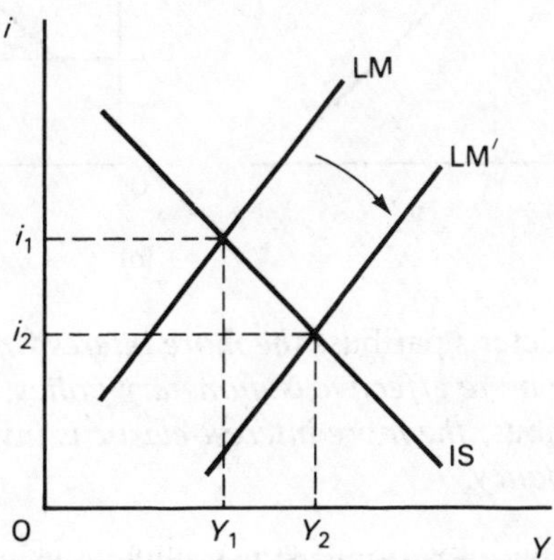

Fig. 5. Monetary policy in the IS–LM model.

As with fiscal policy, the effectiveness of monetary policy depends on the interest-elasticity of the demand for money and on the interest-elasticity of investment. The possible cases are illustrated in Fig. 6 (a), (b), (c) and (d). It can be seen that where the LM curve is vertical (perfectly interest-inelastic demand for money) and where the IS curve is horizontal (perfectly interest-elastic investment), monetary policy has its biggest effect on the equilibrium level of income and employment. These two cases are illustrated in Fig. 6 (a) and Fig. 6 (b) respectively. On the other hand, where the LM curve is horizontal (liquidity trap) and where the IS curve is vertical (completely interest-inelastic investment), monetary policy is completely ineffective. These two cases are illustrated in Fig. 6 (c) and Fig 6 (d) respectively.

Fig. 6. The effectiveness of monetary policy.

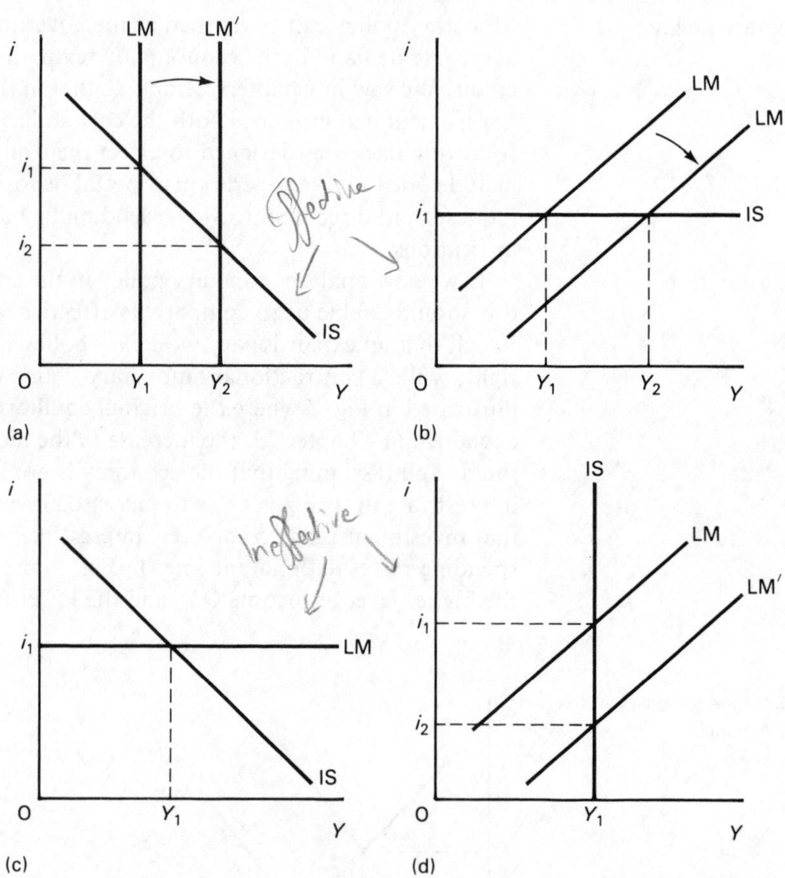

Results: Ceteris paribus, *the more interest-inelastic is the demand for money, the more effective is monetary policy.*
Ceteris paribus, *the more interest-elastic is investment, the more effective is monetary policy.*

Notice that these results concerning monetary policy are the opposite of the results concerning fiscal policy. We can conclude that fiscal policy is likely to be more effective than monetary policy, the more interest-elastic is the demand for money and the more interest-inelastic is investment.

Some empirical evidence

With reference to the different schools of thought, Keynesians generally believe the demand for money to be fairly elastic – after all, the liquidity trap is one (admittedly extreme) feature of the Keynesian model. Furthermore, they tend to cast doubt on the responsiveness of investment to interest rate changes. Consequently, they tend to regard fiscal policy as more effective than monetary policy. Monetarists, on the other hand, believe that the demand for money is fairly interest-inelastic and that changes in the money supply have a more *direct* effect on aggregate spending than is envisaged by Keynesians. This leads them to conclude that the money supply is a crucially important variable in the economy. Recall from chapter 23, however, that they do not support the use of monetary policy for short-term demand-management policies. This point is elaborated upon in the next chapter where we set out the monetarist theory of inflation.

The reader may reasonably think that since the effectiveness of the two policies depends on the interest-elasticity of the demand for money and the interest-elasticity of investment, the issue could easily be settled by considering the empirical evidence. Unfortunately, these elasticities are extremely difficult to measure accurately in practice. The evidence currently available suggests that the demand for money is fairly interest-inelastic (which supports the use of monetary policy). For example, the Bank of England used 1965–76 data for the United Kingdom to estimate the long-run interest-elasticity to be −0.3 (*Bank of England Quarterly Bulletin,* March, 1978). But evidence for the United Kingdom suggests that investment is also fairly interest-inelastic (which supports the use of fiscal policy). So even the available evidence leaves us in doubt as to which is the more effective policy.

Prices and incomes policy

A prices and incomes policy takes the form of exhortation or legislation in the attempt to reduce rates of price and wage inflation below what they would otherwise be. When a government requests (or exhorts) producers and trade unions to keep down the rate of increase of prices and wage rates, this can be described as a *voluntary* policy. When, on the other hand, a government introduces legislation that limits the rate of increase of prices and wage rates by law, this can be described as a *statutory* policy.

In practice, the distinction between a voluntary and statutory policy is not always clear-cut. With the so-called 'voluntary policy' that operated in the United Kingdom from August 1975 to July 1976 and limited wage rises to a maximum of £6 per week (with no increases for those earning more than £8,500 per annum), for example, the Labour government announced that any wage increase in excess of the guidelines would result in the whole increase being disregarded in any application to the Price Commission for an increase in prices. This was a powerful incentive for producers not to pay wage increases in excess of the guidelines.

In the United Kingdom, price increases were restricted by the operation of Price Codes from 1972 to 1979. The Price Codes defined the permitted price increases with references to increases in allowable costs and to profit margins. Critics of price controls argue that if profits are restricted, the level of investment will be reduced resulting in an adverse effect on the growth of output and the level of employment. The imposition of price controls is, in part, symbolic. If they were not introduced, the task of gaining acceptance for a policy of restraint of incomes would be made more difficult.

We now turn to the important topic of incomes policy and discuss the rationale for its introduction. We confine the discussion to controls on incomes from employment (as opposed to incomes from rent or shares). It is widely accepted that if a government introduces deflationary fiscal and monetary policies to combat inflation, this will result (at least in the short-run) in increased unemployment. An incomes policy can be seen as a way of attempting to reduce the rate of inflation without the undesirable side-effect of creating unemployment. In terms of the Phillips' curve (see Ch. 27), incomes policy is seen as a method of shifting the Phillips' curve nearer to the origin, thus easing the conflict between the objectives of full employment and stable prices. An incomes policy might be appropriate if the inflation results from cost-push factors, particularly from powerful trade unions exercising their monopoly power to force wage increases irrespective of the level of excess demand for or supply of labour.

If the inflation is due to generalised excess demand, however, an incomes policy is likely to result in disguised increases in earnings, as employers who wish to hire extra labour will attempt to find loop-holes or other ways round the policy. Even so, there is a logical argument for the introduction of an incomes policy in a situation of excess demand as a means of reducing inflationary expectations. As outlined below in more detail in Chapter 27, monetarists argue that inflation develops initially if the money supply is expanded faster than the economy's long-run growth of productive capacity. But once inflation is under way, it develops a momentum of its own because people expect further inflation and incorporate these expectations in their price fixing and wage demands. The duration and amount of unemployment above the 'natural' rate that is required to reduce the rate of inflation depends on the length of time that it takes for inflationary expectations to be reduced. Thus, if an incomes policy succeeds in reducing inflationary expectations, it will enable a government to reduce inflation with less unemployment than would otherwise be necessary.

There is, however, evidence from surveys that the imposition of an incomes policy does not in fact reduce inflationary expectations. This may be because the policy merely transfers money wage increases from the initial period of the policy to later years when the policy is beginning to crumble or when it is finally abandoned.

Problems of implementing incomes policies

Consider the following problems associated with the implementation of incomes policies.

(a) It is widely recognised that the operation of an incomes policy imposes costs on an economy. If, for example, a limitation on wage increases results in almost all workers receiving a similar wage rise, the allocation of labour through changes in relative wage rates is impeded. Companies that wish to expand may be penalised as they will find it more difficult to attract extra labour. An incentive will exist for such employers to evade the policy through relatively inefficient methods of remuneration (such as grants for children's education and cheap mortgage loans).

(b) If the government recommends a 'norm' or a target average pay rise for the whole work-force, trade union leaders and workers may regard the 'norm' as the minimum target that can be accepted. Thus, because of 'wage drift' (resulting from increased overtime, incremental payments and so on) average earning will increase by more than the 'norm'.

(c) A flat rate increase (such as the £6 per week maximum increase allowed in 1975–76) represents a bigger percentage increase for low-paid workers than for high-paid workers. This may result in the high-paid workers calling for further wage increases to restore their differentials.

(d) Workers in the public sector often claim that an incomes policy discriminates against them because the policy is typically pursued rigidly in the public sector. It is further claimed that in the private sector an incomes policy can often be avoided through the payment of fringe benefits or by other means.

(e) A government may be put in a dilemma as to whether it should introduce a voluntary or statutory policy. The problem with a voluntary policy is that powerful groups may break it, perhaps leading to a widespread sense of injustice and pressure from other groups to break through the policy. If the government introduces a statutory policy, the danger of confrontation exists. Indeed, in the United Kingdom, confrontation between the Conservative government, with Mr Heath as Prime Minister, and the miners led to the government calling an election in February 1974.

Are incomes policies effective?

There have been several periods in the United Kingdom when an incomes policy has been in operation. In the 1970s, for example, a form of incomes policy operated from 1972 to 1974 and from 1975 to 1979. The accumulated experience appears to indicate that the policy has the effect of reducing the rate of wage increase in its initial year or two of operation. After the policy has been in operation for a substantial period, unrest and pressure for greater flexibility develop. The United Kingdom policies have all been abandoned after a few years and typically been followed by a 'wages explosion'. Econometric evidence indicates that in the long-run incomes policies in the United Kingdom have had no significant influence on the increase in wage rates or the level of prices.

A study by Henry and Ormerod (in the *National Institute Economic Review* of August 1978) reported the results of an investigation into the effects of incomes policies on the rate of wage inflation in the United Kingdom. For the period under study (1961–75), the results indicated that, whilst some incomes policies appeared to reduce the rate of wage inflation during the operation of the policies, wage increases in the periods following the end of the policies were higher than they would otherwise have been. In other words, the incomes policies had no permanent effect on the rate of increase of wages.

Perhaps one problem with the use of incomes policies in the United Kingdom is that they have been introduced as a possible solution to a crisis when the balance of payments deteriorates or the rate of inflation accelerates. Some politicians have argued that in order to achieve long-term success in controlling inflation, a 'permanent' incomes policy is desirable and have remarked on the apparent success of such policies in countries such as Sweden and Austria.

Regional policy

Regional policy refers to those measures introduced by a government in order to discriminate in favour of less prosperous regions with a view to reducing certain economic disparities with the more prosperous regions. In the United Kingdom, several regions (for example, north-east England, Wales and Scotland) have higher unemployment rates, lower activity rates, lower incomes per capita and higher emigration rates than the average.

A regional policy can be justified on several grounds. It might aim to reduce the economic disparities between regions by increasing the level of economic activity in the relatively depressed regions. Apart from criteria of social justice, reducing the levels of unemployment in depressed areas will, *ceteris paribus*, increase the level of national income and the rate of economic growth.

Alternatively, a successful regional policy may enable the government to operate the economy at any given level of unemployment with a lower rate of inflation than would otherwise be possible. Consider an economy in which there exists initially widespread disparities in unemployment rates between regions. If the government attempts to achieve a high level of employment by introducing expansionary fiscal and monetary policies, full employment will be attained in the more prosperous regions while substantial unemployment still exists in the less prosperous regions. If the government persists in its attempts to reduce unemployment in the less prosperous regions, excess demand will develop in the more prosperous regions leading to inflation. If, however, a successful regional policy eliminates the disparities in regional unemployment rates, these excess demands are less likely to develop and the government will be able to achieve any given level of unemployment with a lower inflation rate than would otherwise be possible.

Finally, a regional policy might aim to prevent the decline of local communities in order to maintain a geographically balanced population and prevent possible underutilisation of social capital, such as schools and hospitals. Net outward migration tends to lead to congestion costs and severe pressure on social capital in the prosperous regions that gain population. This point has been made in relation to London and the south-east of England which have tended to gain population at the expense of other areas in the United Kingdom.

Policy instruments

In many cases, a regional problem exists because regions have adapted inadequately to changing economic conditions, such as the decline of old industries (like ship-building and coal-mining in the north-east of England and other regions in the United Kingdom). Typically, this results in an excess supply of labour in the problem region. Conceivably, a government might seek to promote a wages policy that led to a relative reduction in wage rates in this area in order to clear the regional labour market. In a country like the United Kingdom, however, there are severe limitations on this approach because of the prevalence of national wage agreements and trade union opposition. Thus, the government is left with two possible policy approaches: first, it can attempt to increase the demand for labour in the problem regions, perhaps by encouraging firms to move there or by increasing public expenditure in these regions; secondly, it could attempt to reduce the supply of labour by promoting labour mobility from these regions.

Policy measures in the United Kingdom In fact, the United Kingdom policy has been basically one of the former approach – that is, taking work to the workers. Large areas of the country are designated as 'assisted areas' which are eligible for assistance. Firms located in 'special development areas' are eligible for grants of 22 per cent on new plant and machinery and buildings; and firms in 'development areas' are eligible for grants of 15 per cent for the same purposes. The government builds advance factories in assisted areas which are then let at subsidised rents. There is, in addition, selective assistance available for individual firms or particular industries. These are *positive* inducements for firms to move to the assisted areas.

These is also a *negative* measure. Firms that wish to engage in significant expansion outside an assisted area have to obtain an Industrial Development Certificate from the government. If a certificate is refused, the government will hope that the project will take place in an assisted area. There is, however, the danger that the project will be abandoned with consequent adverse effects on employment.

In comparison, the help given by the United Kingdom government to promote labour mobility and migration away from the assisted areas has been of minor significance. This may be because of a feeling that migration from an already depressed region compounds its problems by further reducing demand and by draining the region of its young, well-qualified workers.

The United Kingdom regional policy has been criticised for having a capital bias in that subsidies are paid for the use of capital which, in many cases, substitutes for labour. This criticism has been strengthened since the Regional Employment Premium, introduced in 1967, was withdrawn in 1977. Critics have also claimed that frequent changes in government policy and in the type of aid available has led firms to play down the significance of regional aid when deciding on new investment projects.

The effectiveness of regional policy in the United Kingdom After more than fifty years of regional policy in the United Kingdom, significant disparities in economic indicators, such as unemployment rates, persist between regions. This does not necessarily imply that regional policy has been completely without success. As with assessing the effectiveness of any economic policy, there is the problem of estimating what would have happened in the absence of the policy. Defenders of regional policy might claim that the regional unemployment problem would have been more severe had the policy not been in operation.

A study conducted in 1972 by B. Moore and J. Rhodes of Cambridge

University used the industrial employment trends of the United Kingdom as a whole to predict what the industrial employment pattern might have been in the development areas had no discriminatory regional policy existed. Their study indicated that between 1963 and 1970, regional policy probably created or maintained 220,000 jobs, whereas somewhere between 750,000 and 1,000,000 jobs were needed to eliminate the regional unemployment problem at that time.

The Moore and Rhodes study is one of the most authoritative to appear, but one can safely predict that attempts to estimate the effectiveness of regional policy will continue to occupy the attention of economists. In the absence of complete information on its effectiveness, political pressures alone will be a powerful incentive for any government to continue with a regional policy in operation.

Conclusion

In the first part of this chapter, we stated two important rules to which policy-makers must adhere when using policy instruments to achieve policy targets. We then employed the versatile IS–LM model to compare the relative effectiveness of fiscal and monetary policies. Finally, we considered the main features, particularly in the context of the United Kingdom economy, of two additional macroeconomic policies – prices and incomes policy and regional policy.

Further reading

Black, J., *The Economics of Modern Britain: an Introduction to Macroeconomics*, Martin Robertson, Oxford, 1979 (Ch. 11, 17 and 21).

Westaway, A.J. and **Weyman-Jones, T.G.**, *Macroeconomics: Theory, Evidence and Policy*, Longman, London, 1977 (Ch. 17 and 19).

Prest, A.R. and **Coppock, D.J.** (eds), *The UK Economy: a Manual of Applied Economics*, Weidenfeld and Nicolson, London, 1978.

Peston, M.H., *Theory of Macroeconomic Policy*, Phillip Allan, Oxford, 1974.

Exercises

1. Review your understanding of the following terms:

policy targets	pay 'norm'
policy instruments	voluntary policy
fiscal policy	statutory policy
monetary policy	regional policy
prices policy	assisted area
incomes policy	industrial development certificate

2. Using the IS–LM model, illustrate an economy in the liquidity trap. Show graphically and explain carefully the effects of: (a) an increase in government spending; (b) an increase in the money supply.

3. Consider an economy with three policy targets: 3 per cent unemployment, 5 per cent rate of inflation and balance of payments equilibrium. Discuss what policy instruments are available to a government to achieve these targets.

4. Consider the view that since the economy is dynamic, the IS–LM model (a comparative static equilibrium model) cannot assist in the formulation of policies designed to achieve full employment equilibrium.

5. Discuss the costs and problems that result from the introduction of an incomes policy which specifies a maximum annual rise in wages for all workers.

6. Discuss the view that both regional policy and a prices policy create a misallocation of resources by impeding the operation of the price mechanism.

27 Inflation

Introduction

Inflation is a phenomenon which affects everybody in one way or another. It can be argued that mild inflation (say, no more than 5 per cent per annum) may have beneficial effects on an economy; for example, it may be consistent with a low level of unemployment and, if prices tend to be inflexible downwards, it may enable the price mechanism to work more effectively. However, inflation can have adverse effects on the economy, and it may give rise to the fear of a hyperinflation – a very rapidly accelerating inflation which usually leads to the breakdown of the country's monetary system. Germany experienced a hyperinflation in 1923 when the price level increased by more than ten billion fold in just over one year! The existing currency had to be withdrawn and replaced by a new one whose supply was subjected to greater control.

In Chapter 18, we defined inflation as *a persistent tendency for the general price level to rise* and we defined the 'rate of inflation' as *the percentage increase in the Retail Price Index over the period of one year.* Table 1 shows the United Kingdom Index of Retail Prices and the annual rates of inflation from 1964 to 1980. Notice that from 1964 to 1970, the rate of inflation did not exceed 6 per cent, but after 1970 it began to increase rapidly to levels never before experienced in the United Kingdom. Table 1 also provides

Table 1. Prices and unemployment statistics for the United Kingdom, 1964–79.

Year	Retail Price Index (1975 = 100)	Annual rate of inflation (%)	Rate of unemployment (excluding school-leavers)
1964	41.4	3.3	1.7
1965	43.2	4.8	1.4
1966	45.1	3.9	1.5
1967	46.2	2.5	2.3
1968	48.4	4.7	2.4
1969	51.0	5.4	2.4
1970	54.2	6.4	2.6
1971	59.3	9.4	3.4
1972	63.6	7.1	3.7
1973	69.4	9.2	2.6
1974	80.5	16.1	2.6
1975	100.0	24.2	3.9
1976	116.5	16.5	5.3
1977	135.0	15.8	5.7
1978	146.2	8.3	5.7
1979	165.8	13.4	5.4
1980	195.6	18.0	6.8

Source: Economic Trends, 1975–80.

statistics on another important variable to which we shall be constantly referring: the rate of unemployment.

In the remainder of this chapter, we first describe some of the main effects of inflation on both the economy as a whole and the groups and individuals within it. Secondly, we consider the conflicting explanations of inflation, including the demand-pull and cost-push theories, together with an examination of the view that there is a trade-off between inflation and unemployment (the Phillips' curve). Thirdly, we consider the current debate on the causes of inflation. Finally, we consider the pros and cons of alternative policy measures: for example, fiscal and monetary policies, prices and incomes policy, and indexation.

Effects of inflation

Inflation can either be *anticipated* or *unanticipated.* If it is fully anticipated, then all groups and individuals in the economy expect it and are able to gain full compensation for it. In this case, the inflation will have no appreciable effect on the distribution of income and wealth in the economy. Inflation, however, may be unanticipated for three possible reasons: (a) if there is a general failure on the part of the economy as a whole to predict the inflation correctly so that the actual rate of inflation exceeds the expected rate; (b) if certain groups or individuals in the economy fail to predict the inflation correctly so that they seek lower money wage increases than are actually necessary to maintain real wages; (c) if certain groups or individuals, even though they may correctly predict the inflation, are unable to gain full compensation for it (for example, if they have weak unions or if they earn contractually fixed incomes).

Where the inflation is unanticipated (either by the economy as a whole or by groups or individuals within it), there will be a *redistribution effect*: that is to say, some people will be made better off while others are made worse off. Whether the redistribution effect of inflation increases or decreases the economy's total welfare is an equity consideration and therefore a question of normative economics.

The following are some of the possible redistribution effects of unanticipated inflation.

From fixed-income earners and weakly-unionised workers to strongly-unionised workers Anyone earning a fixed income (for example, some rental income) or anyone relying on the return from fixed-interest investments will find the real value of his income being eroded by inflation. Furthermore, weakly-unionised workers who cannot gain full compensation for price rises will lose at the expense of strongly-unionised workers who can do so.

From lenders to borrowers Lenders will lose and borrowers will gain because when debts are repaid, their real value will be less than that prevailing when the loans were made. Even where interest is payable, borrowers will still gain if the nominal rate of interest is less than the rate of inflation – a situation where the *real* rate of interest is negative. For example, if the nominal rate of interest is 10 per cent per annum but the rate of inflation is unexpectedly high at 15 per cent, then the real rate of interest is approximately *minus* 5 per cent.

From taxpayers to the government As money incomes rise, earners with the same real income move into higher tax bands (unless these are adjusted) and so pay a bigger proportion of their income in tax. This is known as *fiscal drag*. This applies, of course, only to a country with a progressive income tax system. Since the government may redistribute the extra revenue back to consumers in some way, the final redistribution effect is uncertain.

From public sector employees to private sector employees If the government is trying to control inflation by means of a prices and incomes policy, it may set an example by resisting the wage claims of public employees. If private employers are more willing to concede wage increases, there will be a redistribution from public sector employees to private sector employees. This does depend, though, on the relative strengths of the public and private sector unions and on the ability of the private sector to provide wage increases.

From profit earners to wage earners If wage demands are met by squeezing profit margins, then the share of profits in the national income will fall and the share of wages will rise.

Some effects of inflation exist whether it is fully anticipated or not. These are the *administrative costs of adjustment* and the *international effects.* Both of these effects can reasonably be described as *costs* of inflation since they are both adverse effects as far as the country with the inflation is concerned. Remember that this cannot be said of the redistribution effects which may be costs or benefits depending on the form of social welfare function employed.

Administrative costs of adjustment arise because, with inflation, both households and firms incur costs of adjusting to the new sets of prices. Households have to intensify their search for the most favourably priced goods, while firms have to incur the costs of determining the new prices and disseminating the information (for example, new labelling, advertising, new price lists and so on). In addition, there are obvious costs to the economy when unions decide to take some form of industrial action in order to gain the wage increases which compensate their members for inflation. Strikes, go-slows and working-to-rule all have the effect of reducing the economy's total output.

The international effects of inflation depend on whether the country has a fixed or flexible exchange rate. With a fixed exchange rate, a country with a faster rate of inflation than its major trading partners is likely to develop a deficit on its balance of payments (because the domestic inflation makes its exports less competitive and its imports relatively more competitive). The deficit will tend to deplete the country's reserves; it may eventually require deflationary policies which will conflict with the domestic goal of full employment; and it may lead to speculative pressure against the country's currency on the foreign exchange market. With a flexible exchange rate, the country with the faster inflation is likely to experience a depreciating currency. Although many economists believe that the international costs of inflation are minimised by the adoption of flexible rates, there are two dangers which should not be overlooked.

(a) The currency depreciation itself may create some further inflationary pressure on the domestic economy. After all, the depreciation has the effect of increasing the price of the country's imports so that, unless there is a fall in some domestic goods' prices, the general price index will rise. This higher rate of inflation will, of course, put even greater downward pressure on the exchange rate, so that there is a danger that the situation will become unstable.
(b) Speculators, seeing the depreciation, may increase their sales of that currency in anticipation of further depreciation. This speculative activity is likely to cause the exchange rate to fall by more than would otherwise have been necessary.

These costs, together with the fear of the extremely destructive phenomenon of hyperinflation, have made the control of inflation one of the major policy objectives of governments. Before we can consider some of the possible means of reducing inflation, we must first examine the (sometimes conflicting) views about what causes it.

Demand-pull, cost-push and the Phillips' curve

During the 1950s and early 1960s, the two main conflicting theories of inflation were the demand-pull theory and the cost-push theory.

Demand-pull inflation exists when aggregate demand exceeds aggregate output at (or close to) full employment. Demand-pull theorists argue that it is excess demand which initiates inflationary pressure. The inflation may then give rise to wage claims which increase firms' costs, but the inflation is actually caused by excess demand. The excess demand itself can originate in either the real or monetary sectors of the economy – that is, it can be caused by autonomous increases in government spending, investment, consumption or exports in the real sector; or by an autonomous rise in the money supply or fall in the demand for money in the monetary sector. These possibilities are illustrated in the IS–LM graphs of Fig. 1 (a) and (b). A rise in the money supply or fall in the demand for money shifts the LM curve to the right to LM′, as shown in Fig. 1 (a). This raises the equilibrium level of income to OY_1 which is above the full employment level of income OY_f, and so opens up the inflationary gap indicated. Note that as prices rise, the real value of the money supply falls, so shifting the LM curve back to the left again. Similarly, an autonomous increase in real spending shifts the IS curve to the right to IS′, as shown in Fig. 1 (b), and this also opens up an inflationary gap.

It can be argued that the government is a likely source of demand-pull inflation: through policy measures, the government has some control over the money supply and can finance its own spending by raising taxes, borrowing or by printing money. Households and firms can only increase their spending by using their savings or by borrowing – they are not in the

Fig. 1. Inflationary gaps in the IS–LM model.

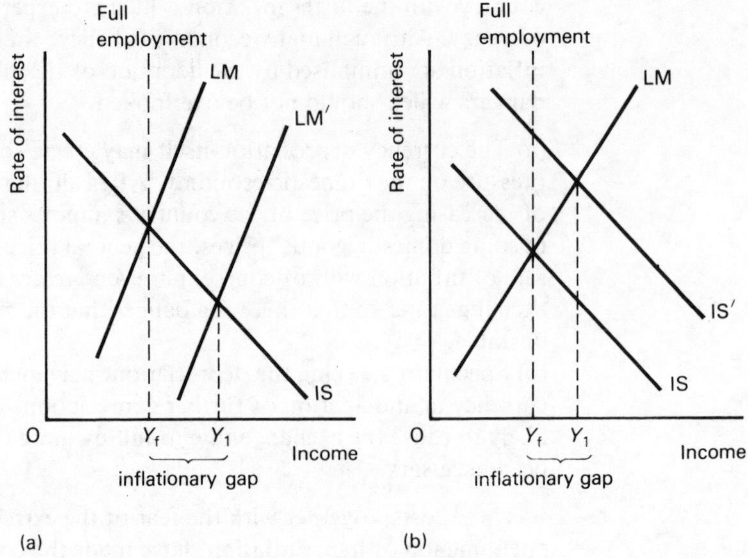

position of being able to raise taxes or print money for themselves.

Cost-push inflation exists when rising money wages or other production costs (for example, the costs of imported raw materials) are passed on to the consumer in the form of higher prices. As prices rise, so *real* wages fall and this gives rise to another round of wage claims so that an inflationary spiral develops. Most cost-push theories are based on the existence of imperfect competition in the labour market, particularly the existence of strong trade unions who make use of their monopoly power in the control of the supply of labour to push for wage increases in excess of those required to offset rising prices. Although cost-push inflation can exist when there is less than full employment, it is reasonable to suppose that wage claims are more likely to be successful when the economy is at (or close to) full employment because then employers will be competing with each other for the existing work-force.

Both the demand-pull and cost-push theories were consistent with the following result: *that the closer the economy is to full employment, the greater the inflationary pressure; the greater the rate of unemployment, the less the inflationary pressure.* Keynes argued that with unemployed resources, money wages would be more or less constant, but at low levels of unemployment, money wages would start to rise as bottlenecks occurred in the labour market. As full employment was reached, money wages would rise rapidly as employers competed vigorously with each other for the existing workers. All this suggests that there may be a trade-off (or inverse relationship) between the rate of unemployment (U) and the rate of money wage inflation ($\dot{W}$).

This relationship was analysed statistically by A.W. Phillips (in *Economica*, November, 1958). Using United Kingdom data, he examined annual figures for U and $\dot{W}$ first for the fifty-two year period 1861–1913, and then for the periods 1913–48 and 1948–57. Phillips' best-fitting curve through the scatter of observed combinations of U and $\dot{W}$ is reproduced in Fig. 2: this curve has become known as the *Phillips' curve*.

Fig. 2. The original Phillips' curve.

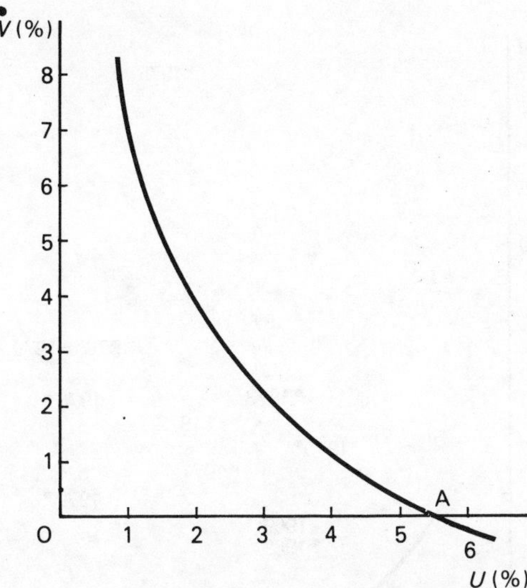

The Phillips' curve appears to have been a remarkably stable relationship for almost a hundred years and, indeed, the continued existence of such a stable relationship would have extremely important policy implications for a modern government. It would mean that the control of inflation and the maintenance of full employment were conflicting objectives, but (perhaps more important) that the attainable combinations were known. For example, from Fig. 2, it is clear that zero wage inflation could only be achieved at a cost of a 5.5 per cent rate of unemployment; similarly, a 1 per cent rate of unemployment could only be achieved at a cost of about 7.5 per cent rate of wage inflation. There is little doubt that this trade-off relationship between unemployment and inflation influenced policy-making in the United Kingdom during the 1960s.

One of the main critics of the original Phillips' curve was Friedman who argued that the vertical axis of the Phillips' curve graph should be labelled the rate of change of *real* (rather than money) wages. Theoretically, point A on the Phillips' curve in Fig. 2 is achieved when the total demand for labour is equal to the total supply of labour, so that the existing unemployment OA is 'natural'. At this point, Friedman argues, it is the real wage that will be in equilibrium and therefore constant, not the money wage. To see this, reconsider Fig. 1 in Chapter 19, where the real wage is measured on the vertical axis, rather than the money wage. When the real wage is constant, the money wage need not be constant: in fact, it can be rising at any rate so long as the price level is rising at the same rate.

Despite Friedman's theoretical assault, many economists throughout the 1960s continued to regard the Phillips' curve as a stable relation, useful for policy purposes. After 1966, however, some strange things began to happen as both high rates of inflation and high rates of unemployment were experienced at the same time. Figure 3 shows the original Phillips' curve together with points on the graph representing the combinations of *U* and $\dot{W}$ for the period 1964–80. The points after 1966 lie nowhere near the original Phillips' curve and it is safe to say that the empirical evidence shows the

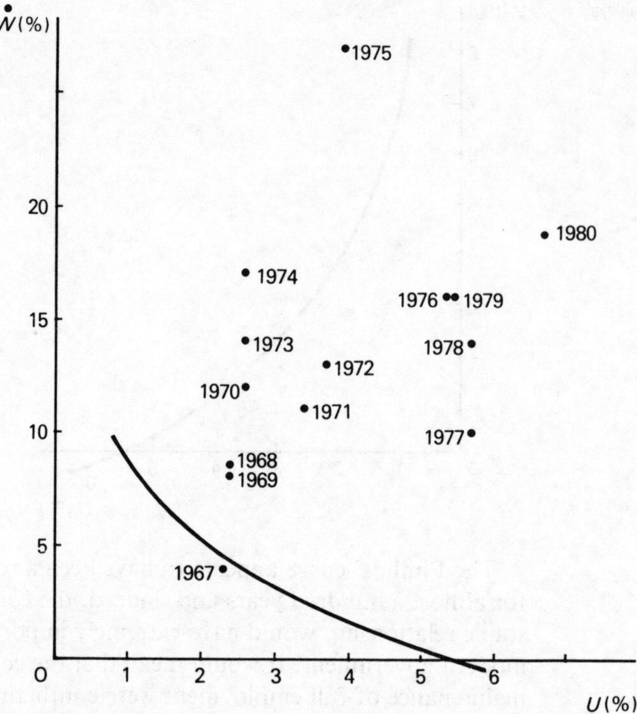

Fig. 3. The empirical breakdown of the Phillips' curve after 1966.

original Phillips' curve relationship to have broken down after 1966. Furthermore, the breakdown of this historical relationship between U and $\dot{W}$ was repeated in other industrial countries.

The main problem in the 1970s, then, was to modify the demand-pull and cost-push theories in an attempt to find an explanation for the co-existence of high rates of inflation with high rates of unemployment.

The modern debate

During the 1970s, two main contrasting views of the causes of inflation developed: the first is a modification of the demand-pull theory and the second is a modification of the cost-push theory. Consider each of them in turn.

The view that inflation is caused by excess demand and sustained by expectations

This view is held in an extreme form by monetarists who argue that sustained and severe inflation can be produced only by excessive increases in the money supply. Indeed, Friedman has said that 'inflation is always and everywhere a monetary phenomenon'. As discussed in Chapter 23, this view is backed up by an impressive amount of empirical evidence showing a correlation between increases in the money supply and consequent increases in the price level. Less extreme forms of the view that excess demand is the main cause of inflation tend to place more emphasis on fiscal, rather than monetary, factors as the source of the excess demand – that is, government overspending, however financed, is seen as the main cause of inflationary pressure.

How do these more recent views account for the apparent breakdown of the original Phillips' curve relationship after 1966? They do it by introducing expectations into the analysis, in the *expectations-augmented Phillips' curve*. This was originally developed separately by Friedman and E. Phelps and in what follows, we examine the proposal put forward by Friedman.

Friedman believes that an inverse relationship may exist between the rate of wage inflation and the rate of unemployment in the short-run, but that there is no such relationship in the long-run. Instead, the long-run Phillips' curve is vertical at the 'natural' rate of unemployment. (Recall that the 'natural' rate of unemployment is that rate established by market forces.) He claims that there must be a different short-run curve for every different expected rate of inflation: the higher the expected rate of inflation, the further up and to the right will be the relevant short-run Phillips' curve. This is illustrated in Fig. 4 where curve A is relevant when the expected rate of inflation ($\dot{P}_e$) is zero, and curve B is relevant when $\dot{\mathbf{P}}_e$ is 4 per cent.

Starting at point U_n on the graph, the natural rate of unemployment prevails and there is zero wage and price inflation. The expected rate of inflation is also zero so that expectations are being realised and there is no pressure being exerted to change either prices or the level of employment. Suppose now, though, that the government tries to reduce unemployment by following some expansionary policy (for example, by increasing government spending financed by printing money). As aggregate demand increases, firms will attempt to increase output, and to attract the required labour, money wages will rise, say by 4 per cent. Although this rise in money wages will soon be followed by a rise in prices, workers will at first interpret the rise in money wages as a 4 per cent rise in *real* wages – that is to say, in the short-run, the workers suffer from *money illusion*. The existing unemployed workers respond to this apparent increase in real wages by reducing their search periods (see Ch. 15) and total unemployment falls, say to U_1 in Fig. 4.

This, then, is the short-run trade-off: 4 per cent inflation is the price being paid for the reduction in unemployment. Friedman argues, however, that in the long-run, all money illusion will disappear as the workers come to realise that price inflation is depriving them of their increased real income. Search

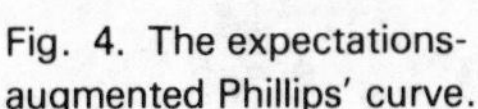
Fig. 4. The expectations-augmented Phillips' curve.

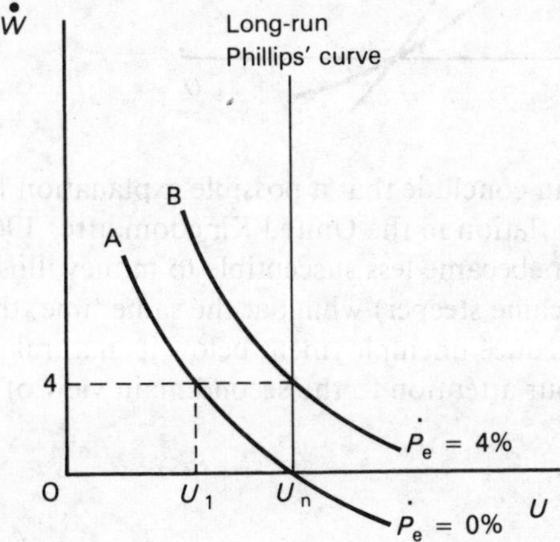

periods will be lengthened again and some workers will withdraw their labour. At the same time, employers who initially demanded more labour in response to the increased prices (which led them to believe that real wages were falling) eventually come to realise that real wages have not fallen at all and so revise their employment plans downwards. As some workers withdraw their labour and employers reduce their demand for labour, unemployment rises back to the natural rate. But now there is an actual and expected rate of inflation of 4 per cent. If the government should again attempt to reduce the rate of unemployment below U_n, the economy would this time move along the short-run Phillips' curve, B, which is relevant when the expected rate of inflation is 4 per cent.

It is the complete absence of money illusion in the long-run which ensures that any trade-off between unemployment and inflation can only be temporary so that the long-run Phillips' curve is vertical at the natural rate of unemployment. This means, of course, that any rate of inflation is possible at the natural rate of unemployment. The vertical Phillips' curve is of little use to policy-makers except as a warning that continued attempts to reduce unemployment below its natural rate can only lead to *accelerating* inflation.

Less extreme views of the expectations-augmented Phillips' curve allow for some long-run money illusion, and in this case, the long-run Phillips' curve does slope downwards from left to right, but is much steeper than the short-run curve. Since a trade-off does exist in this case, it becomes possible for a government to reduce the rate of unemployment so long as the economy is prepared to accept a high rate of inflation. This is illustrated in Fig. 5.

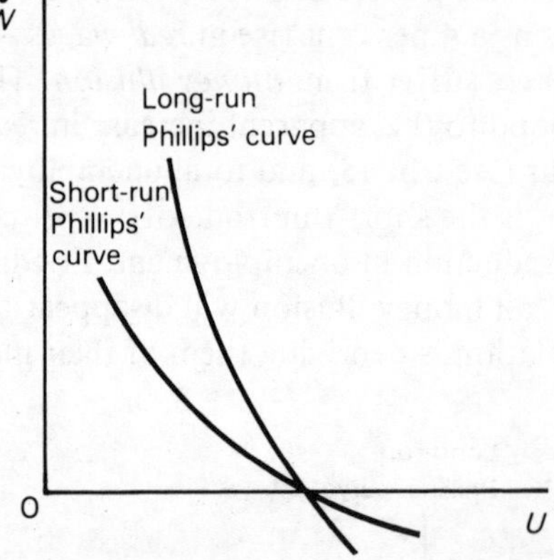

Fig. 5. A non-vertical long-run Phillips' curve.

We can conclude that a possible explanation for the rapid increase in the rate of inflation in the United Kingdom after 1966 is that workers and employers became less susceptible to money illusion (so that the Phillips' curve became steeper) while, at the same time, the government continued to try and reduce unemployment below its natural rate. It is time now, however, to turn our attention to the second main view of the cause of the recent inflation.

The view that inflation is caused by the activities of trade unions

There are a number of different versions of this view. One version is that trade unions put in for wage increases in an attempt to gain a bigger share of the national income for members, and that in doing so they take little or no account of the possible effects of their actions on the economy as a whole. In this approach, unions may be seen to be in conflict with capitalists as both groups strive to achieve bigger shares of the national income. Alternatively, each union may be seen as competing with other unions for bigger wage increases regardless of whether more inflation or more unemployment result. To explain the breakdown of the Phillips' curve in these terms requires that trade unions for some reason became more irresponsible during the 1960s.

Advocates of this view argue that the rate of wage inflation depends on the degree of *militancy* exerted by trade unions and a number of attempts have been made to test this hypothesis empirically. The main problem, of course, is that of measuring trade union militancy. In a study by A.G. Hines (in the *Review of Economic Studies,* October, 1964), militancy was proxied by 'the rate of change of the labour force unionised', the argument being that rapidly rising union membership would tend to make union leaders more militant, would strengthen the union's bargaining position and would generally raise the morale of the workers. Hines obtained good results for this hypothesis obtaining for the period 1949–61, a best-fitting line with the equation:

$$\dot{W} = 5.392 + 4.219\,\dot{T}$$

where $\dot{W}$ is the rate of change of money wages and $\dot{T}$ is the rate of change of the labour force unionised. The coefficient of determination (R^2) was 0.562. This was a significant relationship, but Hines' approach was later criticised by Purdy and Zis who carried out further tests and obtained far less favourable results. A second possibility is to use strike activity as a proxy for trade union militancy. In studies by Taylor and Godfrey, 'the number of stoppages at work due to industrial disputes' was used as a measure of strike activity, but as yet no conclusive results have been obtained.

A reconsideration of Fig. 9 in Chapter 15 might lead to the conclusion that if unions are successful in their wage claims, unemployment must rise as an excess supply of labour is created. It should be remembered in this discussion, however, that in the real world, collective bargaining typically takes place between imperfectly competitive firms and trade unions (both of which possess some monopoly power in their operations). As unions put in for wage claims, firms may be able to concede them in the knowledge that when they raise their prices to cover the extra costs, their rivals will follow suit so that a big loss of sales will not result. When this happens in the economy as a whole, all that is required to stop unemployment from increasing is an increase in the money supply so that the greater value of transactions can be financed. In this case, the unions' actions will create inflation rather than unemployment. Monetarists would say that it was the increase in the money supply which was inflationary, not the unions' actions. (Herein lies the monetarists' main objection to the whole idea of cost inflation: that it is impossible without accompanying increases in the money supply.)

Other cost factors

In addition to rising wage costs, a number of other cost increases may be sources of inflationary pressure. In the United Kingdom, it has been claimed that *rising import prices* have raised the cost of many fuels, raw materials and semi-finished products to industry and also led to wage claims because of the rising prices of imported food and consumer goods. Import prices may rise for two main reasons:

(a) *Rising world prices.* If world prices are rising, there is little a single country can do to isolate itself from inflationary pressure. In the 1970s, for example, the shortage and rapidly rising price of oil in the world exerted inflationary pressure on the United Kingdom and many other countries.

(b) *Currency depreciation.* A country with a flexible exchange rate and a persistent deficit on its balance of payments will tend to experience a depreciating currency. This will have the effect of raising the domestic price of all imported goods (thereby creating some cost-push inflationary pressure) and, at the same time, will increase the demand for exports and import-substitutes (which may create excess demand inflation if the country is at or close to full employment).

Multi-causal inflation

We have seen that there are a number of conflicting views about what causes inflation. Some blame excessive increases in the money supply; some blame excessive government spending or overspending by other groups in society; some place the blame squarely on the shoulders of the trade unions. It could be, of course, that there is some truth in all of these views – that is to say, inflationary pressure may stem from a number of causes all acting simultaneously. If this is so, then it is only by further analysis and empirical testing that the main cause will be determined.

With multi-causal inflation, no single policy measure will be sufficient to control it. For example, if the recent United Kingdom inflation has been caused by government overspending financed by excessive increases in the money supply, at a time when unions have been pushing for large wage increases, a single policy measure (such as a cut in the money supply, or a cut in government spending, or an incomes policy) is unlikely to be very successful. What is needed is some combination of policies.

We turn now to an examination of the various policy alternatives, including the suggestion that a policy of indexation might alleviate some of the adverse effects of inflation.

Alternative policy measures

Fiscal and monetary policies These have been much used in the attempt to control inflation. These policies affect the level of aggregate demand in the economy and so are often called *demand-management* policies. It follows that they are only likely to be effective against inflation caused by excess demand. A cut in government spending, an increase in taxation or some combination of the two (that is, deflationary fiscal policy) will directly reduce aggregate demand; a cut in the money supply or a reduction in its rate of growth (that is, deflationary monetary policy) should have the same effect. As we have seen, Keynesians place emphasis on fiscal policy as a means of controlling aggregate demand. Monetarists attach a greater degree of importance to the influence of the money supply. Nevertheless, most monetarists do not favour the use of monetary policy for short-term stabilisation purposes because of the uncertain length of the time-lags involved. They argue that variations in the money supply affect expenditure decisions after an uncertain lag, with a further lag before the price level is affected.

If Friedman is right and the long-run Phillips' curve is vertical, so that a high rate of inflation can exist at the natural rate of unemployment sustained by inflationary expectations, then the appropriate action to bring down the rate of inflation will be to keep a tight rein on the growth of the money supply. This will increase the rate of unemployment above its natural rate and reduce the *actual* rate of inflation below the *expected* rate. Expectations will then be revised downwards and eventually the natural rate of unemployment can be restored at a lower rate of inflation. As we explained in Chapter 23, the monetarists then favour a rule according to which the long-run growth of the money supply is kept at a constant annual rate, preferably announced in advance by the monetary authorities.

If, on the other hand, inflation is caused by the actions of trade unions, fiscal and monetary policies are both inappropriate. Deflationary policies will not necessarily reduce the militancy of unions and may create unacceptable unemployment.

Prices and incomes policy This is the main recommendation of those who support the view that inflation is caused by the unions. As we explained in Chapter 26, such a policy involves the direct intervention of the government in an attempt to moderate union demands for wage increases and to prevent unjustified price increases. This type of policy action can take a number of forms which can be summarised as follows.

(a) Government exhortation to firms to avoid unjustified price rises and to unions to avoid unjustified wage claims.
(b) The setting up of a prices and incomes board to examine proposed price increases and to contribute to collective bargaining between employers and unions.
(c) The bringing together of employers' and unions' organisations (the Confederation of British Industries and the Trades Union Congress in the United Kingdom) in an attempt to obtain some voluntary agreement from both parties to keep prices and incomes down; this may also involve the setting up of a 'norm' for wage and price increases.
(d) The imposition of legislation to regulate or even freeze wages and prices.

It should be pointed out that, even if inflation is caused by union militancy, a prices and incomes policy may still not work. Some groups inevitably find ways of evading it and some unions may become so frustrated with the policy that they take industrial action against it: this is particularly likely when wages are controlled more strictly than prices. If inflation is caused mainly by excess demand, prices and incomes policy is inappropriate

– during the course of the policy, the excess demand will build up so that when the policy is relaxed, prices and wages may increase faster than ever.

Indexation This policy, sometimes called index-linking, works by linking economic variables (such as wages, salaries and interest payments) to an index of price inflation, like the Retail Price Index in the United Kingdom. This means that if the price index rises by $5\frac{1}{2}$ per cent, then all wages, salaries and interest payments should rise automatically by $5\frac{1}{2}$ per cent. It is a method of removing the main redistributive effects of inflation so that a society can live with inflation in such a way that no individuals or groups suffer disproportionately.

There are, however, two main objections to indexation.

(a) It may itself be inflationary. Indexation cannot be a direct cause of inflation since it only comes into operation after prices have risen. But it could be an indirect cause: since unions no longer have to negotiate for money wage rises to compensate their members for price inflation, they are free to use their full bargaining strength to push for real wage increases. Thus, total wage increases may be greater than they would have been without indexation.

(b) Indexation does nothing to reduce the other costs of inflation. The administrative costs of adjustment and the international costs of inflation are not likely to be much affected by a policy of indexation.

In spite of these possible disadvantages, and given that inflation appears to be very much part of the way of life of many economies, any policy which makes it less uncomfortable to live with may have much to commend it.

Conclusion

This chapter has considered the problem of inflation – one of the burning issues of modern times. It examined the adverse effects that inflation can have on an economy and then analysed its principal causes. In this connection, we outlined the monetarist theory and the competing view that rising costs are the major source of inflationary pressure. We noted that the different theories of inflation lead to different policy prescriptions. Finally, we briefly considered the major alternative policy measures.

Further reading

Westaway, A.J. and **Weyman-Jones, T.G.,** *Macroeconomics: Theory, Evidence and Policy*, Longman, London, 1977 (Ch. 16).

Trevithick, J.A., *Inflation: A Guide to the Crisis in Economics*, Penguin, Harmondsworth, 1977.

Trevithick, J.A. and **Mulvey, C.,** *The Economics of Inflation*, Martin Robertson, London, 1975.

Exercises

1. Review your understanding of the following terms:

- price inflation
- wage inflation
- anticipated inflation
- unanticipated inflation
- demand-pull inflation
- cost-push inflation
- Phillips' curve
- trade-off
- expectations-augmented Phillips' curve
- natural rate of unemployment
- money illusion
- trade union militancy
- multi-causal inflation
- indexation

2. Examine the statistics shown in Table 1 of this chapter. Discuss the main causes of the rapid rise in the rate of inflation during the 1970s in the United Kingdom. Can you account for the simultaneous increase in the rate of unemployment?

3. Discuss the redistribution effects of the rapid rise in oil prices since 1973: (a) between countries; and (b) within a country.

4. 'Inflation is always and everywhere a monetary phenomenon.' (Milton Friedman). Discuss.

5. According to the monetarist theory, what will be the effect on the rate of inflation if the government attempts to reduce unemployment below its 'natural rate'?

6. Suggest ways in which trade union militancy may be measured in order to test the cost-push theory of inflation.

28 The balance of payments and exchange rates

Introduction

We saw in Chapter 7 that international trade based on differences in comparative costs can be beneficial to the countries that take part in it. Unfortunately, international trade also presents countries with a number of policy problems. In this chapter, we are concerned with those problems, like balance of payments disequilibria and unstable exchange rates, which are largely monetary in nature and arise because countries use different currencies.

In the first part of the chapter, we set out and explain the United Kingdom balance of payments accounts for 1977 and 1978 and discuss the implications of a deficit and a surplus. Secondly, we outline the main functions of the foreign exchange market and discuss the determination of the equilibrium rate of exchange. Thirdly, the effects of a change in the exchange rate on the balance of payments and on the level of income and employment are considered. Finally, the advantages and disadvantages of different exchange rate systems – the gold standard, a common currency area, a completely flexible exchange rate system, the IMF system and various forms of 'managed flexibility', including the European Monetary System – are set out.

As we indicated in Chapter 18, it is of crucial importance to recognise that international policy objectives cannot be considered in complete isolation from the internal objectives of full employment and stable prices. Indeed, policy conflicts can and often do arise and these should always be borne in mind when proposing policies designed to correct a payments deficit or to stabilise the international value of the pound.

The United Kingdom balance of payments

Consider Table 1 which shows the summary balance of payments accounts for the United Kingdom for 1977 and 1978. Recall that the accounts are designed to show all the economic transactions which take place between United Kingdom residents and the residents of all other countries during the relevant year. The accounts are divided into two main sections – the *current* account and the *capital* account, the latter including the autonomous 'investment and other capital flows' account and the accommodating 'official financing'.

The years 1977 and 1978 are interesting years to consider because the balance of payments in the United Kingdom changed considerably from one year to the next. In 1977, there was a small surplus on current account and a very large surplus on the investment account, yielding an overall surplus of £7,361 million. In 1978, although the current account was still in surplus, a substantial deficit had appeared on the investment account, adding up to an

Table 1. Summary figures for the United Kingdom balance of payments, 1977–78 (£m)

	1977	1978
Current account		
Visible trade: exports	+ 32,148	+ 35,432
imports	− 33,892	− 36,607
Visible balance	− 1,744	− 1,175
Invisible trade: exports	+ 16,413	+ 18,335
imports	− 14,376	− 16,128
Invisible balance	+ 2,037	+ 2,207
Current balance	+ 293	+ 1,032
Investment and other capital flows balance	+ 4,406	− 2,931
Balancing item	+ 2,662	+ 773
Balance for official financing	+ 7,361	− 1,126
Official financing		
Net transactions with overseas monetary authorities	+ 1,113	− 1,016
Foreign currency borrowing	+ 1,114	− 187
Official reserves (drawings on +, additions to −)	− 9,588	+ 2,329
Total official financing	− 7,361	+ 1,126

Source: United Kingdom Balance of Payments, 1978- and *1979*.

overall deficit of £1,126 million. Consequently, although £9,588 million were added to the reserves in 1977, £2,329 million were drawn from them in 1978. This highlights the importance of taking a *long-term* view of the balance of payments accounts – a deficit in one year will not necessarily have any serious consequences for a country as it may be offset by a surplus in the following year. Only if a country has a deficit which persists for several years can we say with certainty that it is suffering from balance of payments difficulties.

Similarly, caution should be exercised in interpreting figures relating to only parts of the accounts. For example, the *visible trade* balance was in deficit in 1977 but there was still an overall surplus. Even the current account balance only tells half the story and of course all of the entries in the current account and the investment and other capital flows account are subject to errors and omissions which can be quite substantial for any single year – notice that the 'balancing item' amounted to £2,662 million in 1977, more than nine times the size of the current account balance! *So far as the state of a country's international indebtedness is concerned, it is the overall balance of payments position, indicated by the amount of official financing required, over a period of years which should be consulted.*

Suppose now that a country does have a persistent deficit or surplus on its balance of payments. Such an imbalance will have two major implications:

(a) In the case of a deficit, the country will be losing its reserves of foreign currency and getting more and more into debt with overseas monetary authorities. Clearly, this cannot go on indefinitely as both reserves and sources of borrowing are limited. In the case of a surplus, the country will be accumulating reserves (though only at the expense of other deficit countries) and may be experiencing inflationary pressure as the net currency inflow boosts the domestic money supply.
(b) In the case of a deficit, there will be downward pressure exerted on the country's exchange rate; in the case of a surplus, upward pressure will be exerted. Whether or not the monetary authorities allow the exchange rate to change depends (as we see shortly) on the exchange rate system.

Now consider briefly what actions can be taken by a country with a persistent payments imbalance. There are three main possibilities.

It could adopt demand-management policies In the case of a deficit, a contractionary fiscal or monetary policy would be appropriate – it would reduce aggregate demand, including the demand for imports, and may at the same time reduce inflationary pressure and so make exports more competitive in world markets. It follows that an expansionary policy would be appropriate in the case of a surplus. Unfortunately, such policies may conflict with the domestic objectives of full employment, stable prices and economic growth. In particular, if a country has both a deficit and high unemployment, a demand-reducing policy designed to correct the balance of payments will tend to worsen the rate of unemployment.

It could impose import controls The advantages and disadvantages of import controls together with other trade restrictions are considered in Chapter 29.

It could allow the exchange rate to change Normally, a currency depreciation is appropriate to correct a deficit and an appreciation is appropriate to correct a surplus. However, before we can analyse this in any detail, we must first of all examine the foreign exchange market and the meaning and determination of the equilibrium rate of exchange.

The foreign exchange market and the rate of exchange

Since different countries use different currencies, there is an obvious need for the conversion of domestic currency into foreign currencies and *vice versa* so that international transactions can take place. The *foreign exchange market* permits the conversion of currencies in an efficient way and can be thought of as the market in which rates of exchange are determined.

Definition: ***A rate of exchange, as its name implies, is the rate at which one currency can be exchanged for another and can be regarded as the price of one currency in terms of another.***

We should at this point mention the distinction between the 'spot' rate of exchange and the 'forward' rate. The spot rate is the rate at which one currency can *currently* be exchanged for another, while the forward rate is an agreed rate at which one currency can be exchanged for another at some pre-arranged date in the future (usually 90 days). The existence of the 'forward' exchange market enables traders to *hedge* against the 'foreign exchange risk' and it gives rise to certain types of *speculative activity* and *interest arbitrage.* Consider briefly these three activities in turn.

Hedging An importer may incur a debt which has to be paid at some date in the future. The 'foreign exchange risk' is the risk that the exchange rate will change in the meantime involving the importer in a possible loss. The trader can hedge against this risk by buying 'forward' foreign exchange. This means that he enters into a contract with a bank to purchase an amount of foreign exchange at the appropriate future date at a rate of exchange agreed upon now (the 'forward' rate). Banks levy a small charge for this service.

Speculation Some speculators attempt to take advantage of the difference between the 'forward' rate for some given time period and the 'spot' rate which they expect to prevail at the end of that time period. As an example, consider an American speculator and suppose that the 90-day forward rate is £1 = $2 and that the speculator believes that the spot rate at the end of 90 days will be £1 = $2.20. He would take up a *long* position by buying, say, £1,000 forward-sterling for $2,000. In 90 days, he would receive his £1,000 and (provided the spot rate does rise to £1 = $2.20 as expected) he could sell it for $2,200, making a profit of $200.

Interest arbitrage The objective of interest arbitrage is to allocate funds between financial centres in response to interest rate differentials and so realise the highest possible rate of return. If, for example, 90-day interest rates are higher in New York than in London, it may be worthwhile for investors to transfer their short-term funds from London to New York. To do so, though, they will have to convert pounds into dollars at the spot rate and at the same time they can avoid the 'foreign exchange risk' by arranging to convert the proceeds of the arbitrage back into pounds at the forward rate. It follows that whether or not this transaction is worthwhile depends on the interest rate differential between the two financial centres and the difference between the 90-day forward rate and the spot rate.

Determination of the rate of exchange

Since we can regard the rate of exchange as the price of one currency in terms of another, its equilibrium level must be determined in a free market by the forces of demand and supply. The demand for and supply of a currency in international markets are in turn determined by the activities of traders, speculators and interest arbitrageurs. To simplify our analysis and yet to give some insight into the determination of rates of exchange, we make two important assumptions in this section.

(a) We consider trade between two countries only, say the United Kingdom and the United States. This means that there are only two currencies, pounds and dollars, and we define the rate of exchange as the price of a pound in terms of dollars.

(b) We ignore the activities of investors, speculators and arbitrageurs. This means that the demand for pounds depends only on the US demand for UK exports (because UK exporters require payment in pounds) and the supply of pounds depends only on the UK demand for imports from the United States (because pounds are supplied in exchange for dollars to pay for US goods and services).

Consider first the *demand for pounds.* This arises because US importers wish to buy UK exports. We should start, therefore, by examining the US demand for UK exports. This is illustrated in Fig. 1 where DD represents the US demand curve for UK exports. The price of UK exports is measured in pounds on the vertical axis and the quantity of UK exports is measured on the horizontal axis. Suppose that the initial position is at point A so that the total demand for pounds (equal to the total value of UK exports) is $p_o q_o$. Now suppose that the exchange rate depreciates, say from £1 = \$2 to £1 = \$1.50. This reduces the dollar price of UK exports and so makes them cheaper to US buyers. This should lead to an increase in US demand for UK goods at every pound price – in other words, the US demand curve will shift to the right, to D′D′ in Fig. 1. As can be seen from the graph, the sterling

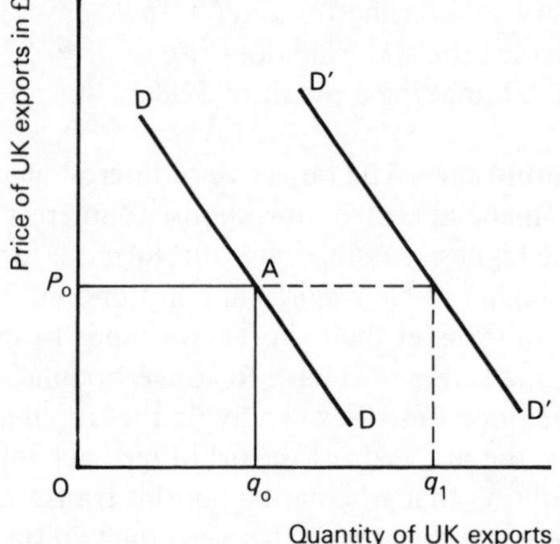

Fig. 1. The effect of a depreciation of the pound on the US demand for UK exports.

value of UK exports increases to $p_o q_1$. It follows that a fall in the exchange rate causes an increase in the demand for pounds; this means that the demand curve for pounds must be downward-sloping from left to right, as shown in Fig. 2.

Next, consider the *supply of pounds.* This arises because UK importers wish to buy US goods. In this case, then, we should examine the UK demand for imports which is shown in Fig. 3, where DD represents the UK demand curve for US goods. The initial position is at point B so that the total supply of pounds (equal to the total value of UK imports) is $P_o Q_o$. Now suppose, as before, that the exchange rate depreciates. This has the effect of raising the sterling price of US goods, making them more expensive to UK importers. The UK demand for imports will fall and this is shown as a movement along

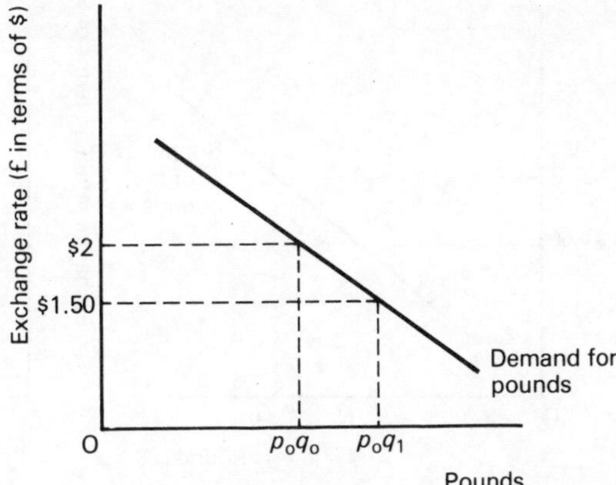

Fig. 2. The demand for pounds.

the demand curve in Fig. 3 from point B to point C. The new supply of pounds is P_1Q_1.

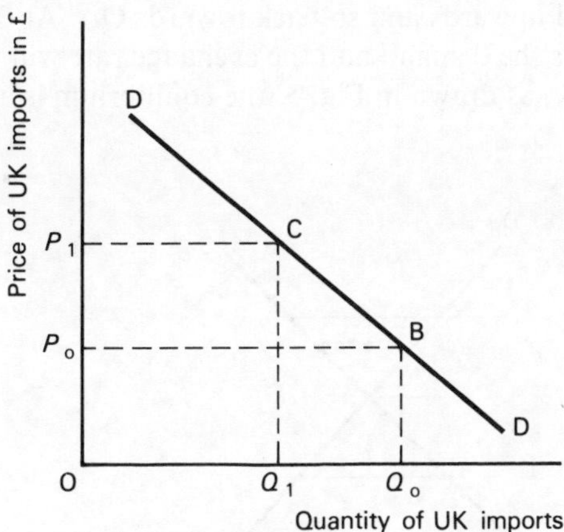

Fig. 3. The effect of a depreciation of the pound on the UK demand for imports.

We now have to determine whether the supply of pounds has increased or decreased following the depreciation - in other words, we have to determine which is bigger, P_1Q_1 or P_0Q_0. The answer depends on the *elasticity* of the UK demand for imports. If it is elastic, the quantity of imports will have fallen by a bigger proportion than their price will have risen, so the total value of imports and the total supply of pounds will have fallen. In this case, the supply curve of pounds will slope upwards from left to right as shown in Fig. 4 (a). If it is inelastic the quantity of imports will have fallen by a smaller proportion than their price will have risen, so that the total supply of pounds will have risen. In this case, the supply curve will be abnormal and slope downwards from left to right as shown in Fig. 4 (b). If the demand curve had unitary elasticity, the supply of pounds would remain unchanged and the supply curve of pounds would be vertical.

Stable and unstable equilibria The equilibrium rate of exchange is determined where the demand for pounds is equal to the supply of pounds.

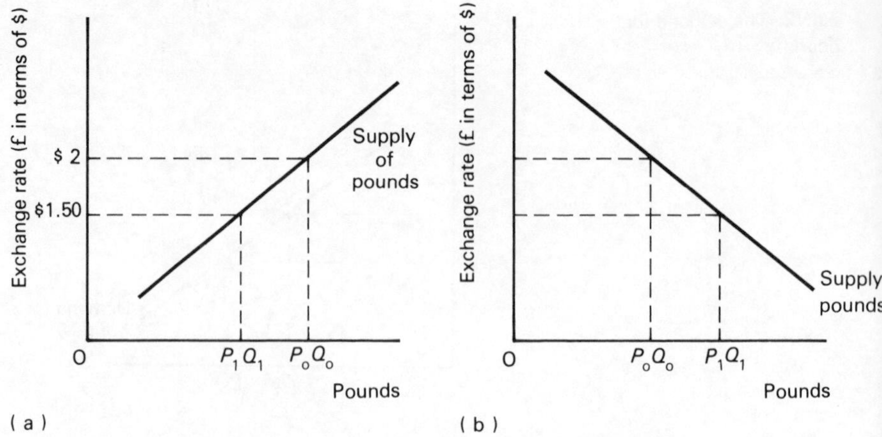

Fig. 4. The supply of pounds.

This is at Or_1 in Fig. 5. All other rates of exchange are disequilibrium rates. For example, at Or_2, the demand for pounds on the foreign exchange market exceeds the supply. Given free competitive forces, the exchange rate will be pushed upwards and so back towards Or_1. At Or_3, the supply of pounds exceeds the demand and the exchange rate will fall, back towards Or_1. Clearly, as drawn in Fig. 5, the equilibrium is a *stable* one.

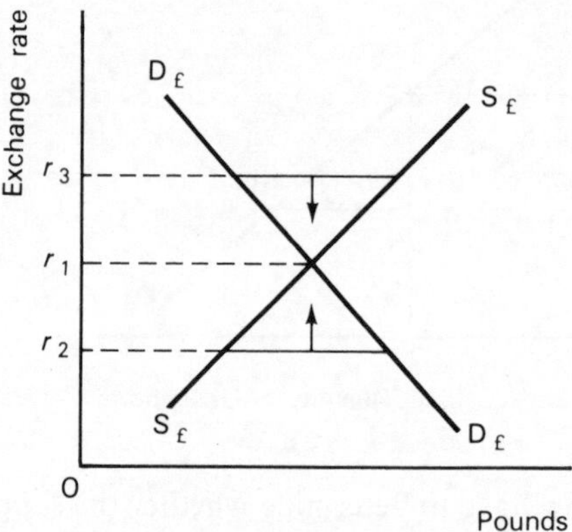

Fig. 5. A stable equilibrium in the foreign exchange market.

Now consider Fig. 6 where the supply curve of pounds slopes downwards from left to right and is less steep than the demand curve. The exchange rate, Or_4, is an equilibrium rate, but this time is *unstable.* At the disequilibrium rates, Or_5 and Or_6, competitive forces act to push the exchange rate further away from the equilibrium position.

As we shall see, the stability or instability of the equilibrium in the foreign exchange market has very important implications for exchange rate policy.

The effects of a change in the exchange rate

In this section, we examine the effects on the United Kingdom economy of a *fall* in the exchange rate – that is, a depreciation of the pound. As in the previous section, we keep the analysis fairly simple by considering two-country trade only, so we continue to refer to the United States as if it represented the 'rest of the world'.

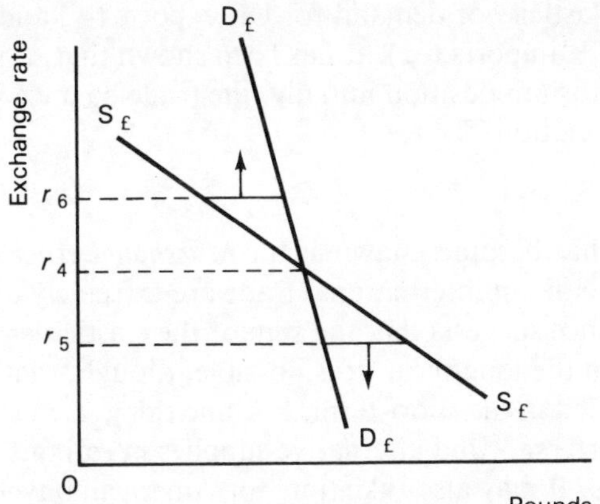

Fig. 6. An unstable equilibrium in the foreign exchange market.

A depreciation of the pound will immediately affect the relative prices of traded goods: the dollar price of UK exports will fall and the pound price of UK imports will rise. These price changes will in turn cause a rise in the demand for UK exports and a fall in the demand for UK imports – so long as these demand changes can be realised, they will affect the UK balance of payments. The price effects of the depreciation, however, do not tell the complete story because it is likely that UK national income will also be affected: changes in income will cause changes in the demand for imports and this will exert a further influence on the trade balance.

Consider first the *price effects* of the depreciation under the following two assumptions: (a) that supply elasticities are very large so that increases in demand can easily be met, and (b) that for now we ignore income changes. The UK trade balance (B) can be defined as:

$$B = \begin{matrix}\text{Total Value of}\\ \text{UK Exports}\end{matrix} - \begin{matrix}\text{Total Value of}\\ \text{UK Imports}\end{matrix}$$

An increase in B will represent a movement from a deficit towards a surplus and so can be regarded as an 'improvement'. We saw in the last section that the depreciation will, with almost complete certainty, *raise* the total value of UK exports – the pound prices of exports are not affected directly by the depreciation, but demand increases as dollar prices fall. *The greater the elasticity of demand for UK exports, the bigger will be the increase in the total value of exports following the depreciation.* Only if the demand for UK exports is perfectly inelastic will the total value remain unchanged.

The effect of the depreciation on the total value of UK imports is less certain because this time the pound price is raised directly by the depreciation and a significant decrease in demand is required for their total value to fall. We can summarise the result as follows, where e_m is the elasticity of demand for UK imports:

If $e_m < 1$, depreciation will raise the total value of imports.
If $e_m > 1$, depreciation will reduce the total value of imports.

Clearly, what happens to the UK trade balance depends crucially on both the elasticity of demand for UK exports (e_x) and on the elasticity of demand for UK imports (e_m). It has been shown that, assuming that we start from an equilibrium position initially, the trade balance will improve following a depreciation if:

$$e_x + e_m > 1$$

This has become known as the *Marshall-Lerner condition.* Although demand elasticities in international trade are extremely difficult to estimate, existing evidence suggests that the sum of the elasticities is considerably greater than one in the long-term. It is possible, though, that the condition may not be satisfied in the short-term. For one thing, it may take time for the country's importers to find alternative supplies in response to the increase in import prices. It may also take time for American buyers to increase their purchases of UK exports following the fall in prices. So a depreciation may at first cause the trade balance to deteriorate. Eventually, though, perhaps after a year, importers and exporters should respond to the changed prices and the trade balance should improve.

Absorption approach Now consider the *income effect* of the depreciation. This is important because an increase in the value of UK exports will induce, via the multiplier, an increase in national income which in turn will raise the demand for imports. This mechanism must be taken into account, therefore, in examining the effects of a depreciation. This analysis is sometimes called the *absorption* approach.

Consider this problem in the context of a simple Keynesian model. Ignoring government spending and taxation, and using the familiar *injections = withdrawals* condition for the equilibrium level of income, we can write:

In equilibrium, $J = W$

$$I + X = S + M$$

or $X - M = S - I$

In other words, the equilibrium level of income is achieved when the planned value of exports minus imports ($X - M$) is equal to the planned value of savings minus investment ($S - I$). The determination of this equilibrium is illustrated in Fig. 7, where savings and imports are, as usual, directly related

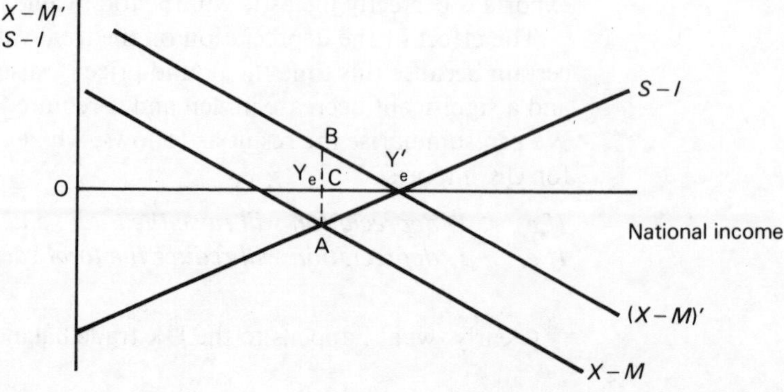

Fig. 7. Effects of a depreciation on the trade balance and the level of national income.

to income and investment and exports are autonomous of income. The ihitial position, then, is at OY_e and there is a small trade deficit equal to AC. Given that the Marshall-Lerner condition is satisfied and that there are some unemployed resources in the economy, a currency depreciation will have the effect of shifting the $X - M$ line upwards to the right to $(X - M)'$ raising the equilibrium level of income to OY_e', removing some of the unemployment and at the same time eliminating the deficit. This is one case where the two policy problems of unemployment and a trade deficit may be tackled by the one policy action of currency depreciation. Notice that the improvement in the trade deficit is less than that suggested by our analysis of the price effects alone: with the income change ignored, the trade balance improvement would be AB in Fig. 7, but with the increase in income taken into account, the improvement is only AC.

In fact, the rise in real income is of considerable importance. To show this, suppose that the economy is initially at full employment, as shown in Fig. 8 where the original equilibrium is at OY_f, the full employment level of income. A currency depreciation will now shift $X - M$ to $(X - M)'$ as before, but this time will open up an *inflationary gap* equal to BA. Since output cannot be expanded in the short-term, the increased demand for exports and import-substitutes creates excess demand inflation. This inflation of money prices and money incomes will make UK exports less competitive in world markets and at the same time imports will become relatively cheaper to domestic buyers. In short, the inflation offsets the effects of the depreciation and the $(X - M)'$ line moves back towards the original $X - M$ line. There has been much discussion in the literature about the possible ways in which this inflation might reduce domestic expenditure (sometimes called 'absorption') and thereby allow the trade balance to improve as resources are released from industries producing for the home market into industries producing for the export market. Of these, the income redistribution effect, the money illusion effect and the real balance effect have received most attention. Briefly consider them in turn.

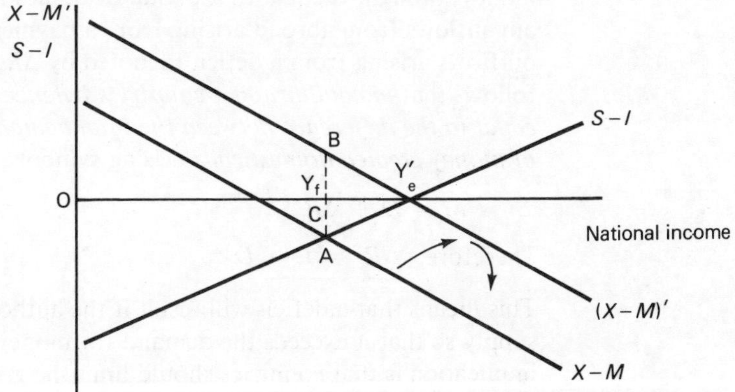

Fig. 8. Effects of a depreciation under conditions of full employment.

(a) *Redistribution effect.* In the short-term, a currency depreciation may increase profits (particularly in the export and import-substitute industries) at the expense of wages. If the marginal propensity to consume of profit earners is smaller than that of wage earners, then domestic expenditure will fall.

(b) *Money illusion effect.* The argument here is that higher prices will induce people to reduce their spending in spite of the fact that, on average, incomes have risen at the same rate as prices. For this to work, people have to have a price fixation in the sense that they observe prices rising, but fail to observe that their wages are rising at the same rate.

(c) *Real balance effect.* According to this effect, with a constant nominal money stock, people will see that rising prices are reducing the real value of their money balances: they will attempt to restore this real value by reducing their spending and increasing their savings.

If we can rely on one or more of the above effects to reduce absorption, then it is possible for a depreciation of the pound to improve the UK trade balance, even if there is full employment or near full employment initially. Too much reliance cannot be placed on these effects, however, and most governments have found it necessary to accompany a currency depreciation with *expenditure-reducing* fiscal and monetary policies. If, in addition, it is felt that rising import prices will exert some cost-push inflationary pressure on the economy, a government may find it necessary to impose some direct controls on domestic factor costs (for example, by means of an incomes policy) at the same time as the currency depreciates.

The monetarist approach

Monetarists argue that balance of payments problems are 'fundamentally monetary in nature' and they emphasise the role played by a country's money market in determining its balance of payments position. Their theory, which is more general than the absorption approach in the sense that it applies to the overall balance of payments rather than just to the trade balance, assumes that the total demand for money is a *stable* function of money national income and rates of interest.

As we know, equilibrium in the money market requires that the demand for money (L) should equal the supply of money (M). The total supply of money, though, is equal to the total of domestically created money (D) *plus* any inflows from abroad arising from a payments surplus, or *minus* any outflows arising from a deficit (denoted by ΔR, or net change in reserves). It follows that *in equilibrium a country's balance of payments position will be equal to the difference between the total demand for money and the quantity of money created domestically.* Using symbols, we can write, in equilibrium,

$$L = M = D + \Delta R$$

$$\text{Therefore,} \quad \underline{\Delta R = L - D}$$

This means that a deficit will result if the authorities expand the money supply so that it exceeds the demand for money. The obvious policy implication is that countries should limit the growth of their money supplies if they wish to maintain balance of payments equilibria.

The effects of a devaluation in this context would be to correct a deficit by creating a general inflation (with the country initially at the 'natural' rate of unemployment) which would reduce the *real* value of the money supply until the demand for and domestic supply of real money balances were equalised.

It is this mechanism of adjustment that leads most monetarists to support increased flexibility in exchange rates, as well as the fact that flexible rates tend to insulate countries from inflation in the rest of the world. It also follows from the above analysis that the concept of *domestic credit expansion* is the most relevant measure of changes in the money supply. Basically, domestic credit expansion can be defined as the actual change in the country's money supply plus any deficit or minus any surplus in the country's overall balance of payments. It thus yields a measure of the increase in the money supply that would have occurred in the absence of a payments imbalance.

Exchange rate systems

One of the most important international decisions that modern governments have to make is what kind of exchange rate system to adopt. In other words, they have to determine how their own currency should be related to other currencies in the world. If they choose to fix the value of their currency in terms of other currencies, how is this to be accomplished and what balance of payments adjustment mechanism will exist? If, instead, they choose to allow the value of their currency to fluctuate against other currencies, how much flexibility should be permitted and how can a reasonable degree of certainty and stability be safeguarded?

We attempt to answer these questions in this section by outlining some of the possible ways in which exchange rate systems can be arranged. Some of these have been tried and tested in the past, others are in current use, while others are still only proposals. We start by considering a completely fixed exchange rate system; secondly we look at the advantages and disadvantages of a completely flexible exchange rate system; thirdly, we examine the International Monetary Fund's adjustable-peg system which was set up at Bretton Woods in 1944 and existed until 1972; finally, we consider some of the proposed variations of 'managed flexibility'.

The efficiency of any exchange rate system can in part be judged by the extent to which it achieves three desirable characteristics.

(a) *Adjustment.* The system should enable countries to correct payments disequilibria without placing too much strain on their domestic economies.

(b) *Confidence.* The system should be such that traders have confidence that international payments can be made efficiently and safely without the danger of large losses.

(c) *Liquidity.* If the adopted system requires central banks to intervene in the foreign exchange market to stabilise exchange rates, there should be a sufficient quantity of reserve assets to enable this to be done efficiently.

These three characteristics should be borne in mind in considering the efficiency of different international monetary arrangements.

Completely fixed exchange rate system

The main characteristic of this system is that each country's currency is fixed in terms of all other currencies. One notable example of this was the *gold standard* system which was employed in one form or another until 1931 in the United Kingdom. A more extreme example of fixed exchange rates is the *common currency area*. Consider these two in turn.

Under the *gold standard*, the value of each currency is fixed in terms of gold and this necessarily means that the value of any particular currency must be fixed in terms of any other currency. For example, if £1 is worth so many grains of gold in the United Kingdom and the same quantity of gold is worth $2 in the United States, if follows that £1 must exchange for $2 – if not, any individual could buy £1 worth of gold in London, ship it to New York and sell it for $2. (Note that the exchange rate £1 = $2 is then called the 'mint parity'). In fact, the exchange rate can vary within a narrow band around the mint parity because of the transport and insurance costs involved in shipping gold from one country to another. The permitted variation is so small, however, that exchange rates can be regarded to all intents and purposes as fixed.

In its most extreme form, the system requires: (a) that gold be used as the only international means of payment; (b) that there be a rigid relationship between a country's gold reserves and its supply of money; (c) that there be flexible wages and prices and the operation of the 'quantity theory of money'. The *adjustment* of imbalances should then occur by means of David Hume's so-called 'price-specie-flow' mechanism:

Deficit countries lose gold; their money supplies fall; wages and prices fall making exports more competitive – the trade balance improves.
Surplus countries accumulate gold; their money supplies rise; wages and prices rise making their exports less competitive – the trade balance returns to equilibrium.

The main problem with this adjustment mechanism stems from its dependence on the flexibility of wages and prices and the quantity theory of money. It is more likely that the fall in the money supply experienced by deficit countries will create unemployment rather than falling prices.

Assuming that the exchange rate is kept permanently fixed under the gold standard, traders should have *confidence* in the system. They will know with certainty what exchange rates are now and what they will be in the future. A problem of *liquidity* could arise, however, because the world supplies of gold are finite and a point may be reached where it becomes impossible to increase supplies further: this could lead to problems if the total value of trade continued to rise. Finally, a major disadvantage of using gold so extensively is that it is so much more costly to produce than paper forms of currency – after all, gold has to be mined and manufactured into ingots before it is suitable for use as an international currency. On the other hand, some economists have seen a virtue in the limited supply of gold as a check to any temptation on governments to expand the money supply excessively.

Turning now to a *common currency area,* this is a very extreme form of fixed exchange rate system where different countries simply adopt identical currencies which, of course, can be exchanged for each other on a one-to-one basis. Such a system is highly unlikely ever to be established on a world-wide basis, but it is possible for a group of countries to use the same form of money whose supply would then have to be controlled by a centralised monetary authority. Indeed, it is proposed that the Common Market countries should eventually adopt a common currency and have both a centralised monetary and fiscal policy. Economically, the countries of such an area would become indistinguishable from regions within a country.

With reference to our three desirable characteristics, a common currency area would have no need for reserves to cover internal balance of payments deficits and traders would have no worries about possible exchange rate changes (at least, within the area), so that the criteria of *liquidity* and *confidence* should be satisfied. However, as in the case of the gold standard, the main problem arises in the *adjustment* mechanism. To show this, consider an imbalance which can arise between the regions of a single country. Suppose, for example, that there is a shift in demand from one region (say, region A) to the rest of the country – with wages and prices inflexible downwards, the result will be an increase in unemployment in region A. In a sense, we can say that region A is likely to develop a deficit with the rest of the country as it will probably find itself consuming more than its income. Such overspending will be financed, not by using reserves, but by borrowing from financial institutions and by receipts of government transfers in the form of unemployment benefits and social security payments. At the same time, of course, the amount of tax paid by the region will decrease.

The big problem with a common currency area is that adjustment to imbalances cannot take place through exchange rate changes (because exchange rates are permanently fixed) or through monetary changes (because a country's money supply cannot be separated from the area's money supply). In fact, if the price level is inflexible as well, then none of the traditional adjustment mechanisms exist. The only way in which adjustment can take place is through factor mobility – the unemployed resources must move into alternative activities either within the home country or in other countries of the area. With this in mind, an *optimum currency area* has been defined as an area of countries which can employ a common currency efficiently without serious regional problems arising. Such an area should have a reasonable degree of labour and capital mobility and integrated monetary and fiscal arrangements so that the adverse effects of any imbalance may be reduced by borrowing and transfer payments.

Completely flexible exchange rate system

In this system, exchange rates would not be stabilised by monetary authorities in any way, but would be allowed to fluctuate in response to market forces. This means that a United Kingdom deficit (which gives rise to an excess supply of pounds on the foreign exchange market) would put downward pressure on the exchange rate, and a surplus (which gives rise to excess demand) would put upward pressure on the exchange rate. As we have seen, these are *usually* the appropriate movements in the rate to correct the imbalances.

It has been claimed by some economists that this automatic adjustment mechanism is the great virtue of a flexible exchange rate system. Indeed, many proponents of flexible rates have claimed that governments could concentrate their policies on the domestic problems of inflation and unemployment, leaving automatic exchange rate changes to deal with any external imbalances. Another advantage claimed for flexible rates is that governments would no longer need to hold large quantities of international reserves – after all, if monetary authorities were not intervening in the foreign exchange market to stabilise rates, reserves would be unnecessary. According to these claims, it would seem that a completely flexible system should satisfy our criteria of *adjustment* and *liquidity*. Such a system, though, may also suffer from a number of disadvantages, some of which could make it unworkable. Consider the following.

The Marshall-Lerner condition may not be satisfied If the elasticities condition (that $e_x + e_m > 1$) were not satisfied, a flexible exchange rate system would run into difficulties. To show this, consider what would happen if a deficit developed. The excess supply of the country's currency would cause an automatic depreciation which would make the deficit bigger. Similarly, with a surplus, the excess demand for the currency would cause an appreciation which would lead to an even bigger surplus. We commented earlier that the elasticities are likely to be quite large in the long-term, but may be small in the short-term. If this is the case, a completely flexible exchange rate system may be subject to extreme fluctuations in the rates in the short-term. Such instability would cast doubts on the efficiency of the *adjustment* mechanism.

Uncertainty Since the adjustment mechanism depends on automatic exchange rate changes, it can be argued that importers and exporters may be discouraged from trading because of the 'exchange rate risk'. They can 'hedge' against this risk by operating on the 'forward' market, but this may involve them in costs which would not exist if rates were fixed. The uncertainty introduced by flexible rates may cause traders to lose some of their *confidence* in the system.

Destabilising speculation A further reason for doubt to be cast on the *adjustment* and *confidence* aspects of the system is the possibility of large fluctuations in the rates caused by the activities of speculators. There has been much debate in the literature about whether speculation has a stabilising influence or a destabilising influence on flexible exchange rates. Consider the following two cases, the first of which suggests that speculation is destabilising and the second of which suggests that it is stabilising.

(i) Suppose that when speculators see the pound depreciating, they expect it to continue depreciating. They will sell pounds and buy stronger currencies so as to make a capital gain later. This activity will tend to put even greater pressure on the pound to depreciate. Similarly, when they observe the pound appreciating, they will increase their purchases of pounds and so put even greater upward pressure on it. In this case, we should expect speculative activity to cause faster and bigger exchange rate changes than would have occurred without speculation. This is illustrated in Fig. 9 which shows the

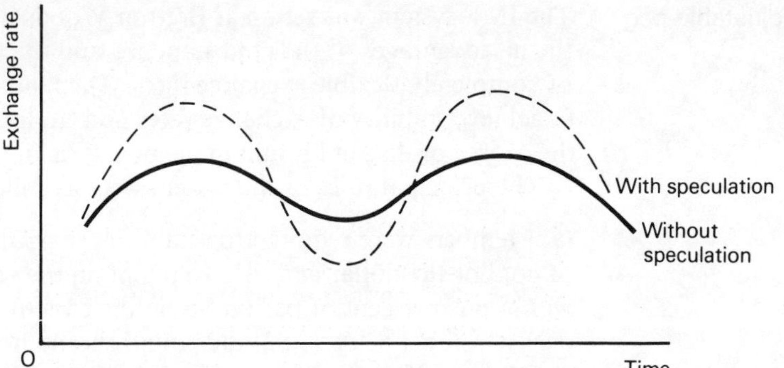

Fig. 9. Destabilising speculation.

hypothetical time-paths of the exchange rate with and without speculative activity.

(ii) It can be argued that in order to make profits speculators in general must buy a currency when its exchange rate is below its average level and sell when

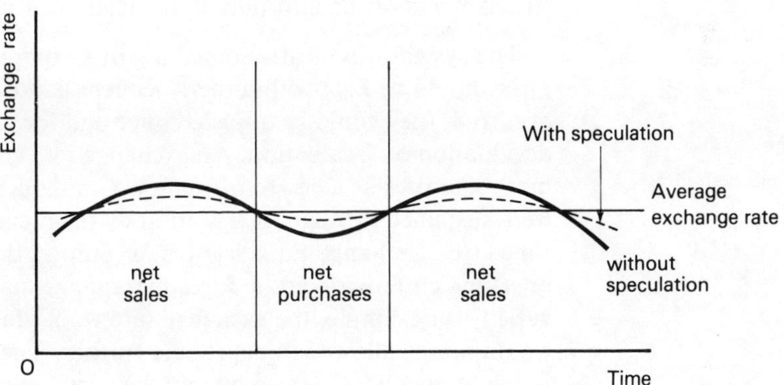

Fig. 10. Stabilising speculation.

its exchange rate is higher than its average level. Since purchases push the rate upwards and sales push it downwards, this activity should tend to stabilise the rate. Friedman has argued that since speculators tend to be well-informed and make profits, their activities must be stabilising. Stabilising speculative activity is illustrated in Fig. 10.

It may be inflationary for deficit countries A country with a persistent deficit will experience a depreciating currency. As we have seen, such a depreciation will raise the price of imports and, at the same time, increase the demand for the country's exports and import-substitutes. It may, therefore, exert both cost-push and demand-pull inflationary pressure on the domestic economy. Strong trade unions may, for example, resist any fall in real wages by pressing for compensating money wage increases. This may be particularly severe if the country is close to full employment.

The IMF adjustable-peg system

The IMF system was set up at Bretton Woods in 1944 in an attempt to avoid the disadvantages of the gold standard and the 'instability' and 'uncertainty' of completely flexible exchange rates. The main objectives of the system were to achieve stability of exchange rates and 'to lessen the duration and reduce the degree of disequilibrium in members' balances of payments'.

The principal rules of the system were as follows:

(a) Members were required to establish the parity of their currencies in terms of gold or the dollar and then to maintain the values of their currencies within one per cent of parity. So, in the case of the United Kingdom, if parity were set at £1 = $2, the pound should not be allowed to exceed $2.02 or fall below $1.98.
(b) No members were allowed to alter their parities without notifying the IMF, but the IMF could not object if the change was to be less than 10 per cent. If the proposed change was to be greater than 10 per cent, the Fund's permission was required – the member countries made their decision by means of a majority vote.
(c) Before changing the parity of its exchange rate (that is, devaluing or revaluing), a country should be faced with what the IMF called a 'fundamental disequilibrium' in its balance of payments.

The system was clearly something of a compromise. Normally, exchange rates should be kept within the 1 per cent band, but if a persistent imbalance occurred, they could be adjusted once and for all by means of a policy of devaluation or revaluation. An exchange rate change, however, was seen by most countries as a last resort policy. Consequently, short-term imbalances were sustained through intervention by the member countries' stabilisation funds (the Exchange Equalisation Account in the United Kingdom), buying or selling currencies on the foreign exchange market. In the case of a UK deficit, for example, the exchange rate would fall to its lower limit, but would not be allowed to depreciate further. The Exchange Equalisation Account would be used to buy up the excess supply of pounds. Similarly, in the case of a surplus, pounds would be supplied to the foreign exchange market to meet the excess demand which would otherwise push the rate above its upper limit.

If a deficit persisted, countries could not continue to sustain it indefinitely. Eventually, reserves would reach uncomfortably low levels and further loans from overseas would become difficult to negotiate. Countries would then typically follow domestic policies to try and correct the deficit. The appropriate policies would be deflationary fiscal and monetary policies designed to reduce the domestic rate of inflation and to cut the demand for imports. Only if these policies failed and the deficit still persisted, would a country consider a devaluation of its currency.

We can identify three main drawbacks to the IMF system.

(a) It was not easy for a government to decide *when* and *by how much* to devalue. Most countries tended to put off devaluation until the last minute by which time some international monetary crisis may have arisen. Consequently, when the devaluation came, it was often quite large and so

represented a severe shock to traders, particularly those in the devaluing country.
(b) Policy conflicts arose, particularly for deficit countries with high rates of unemployment. The deflationary policies required to correct the deficit tended to worsen the unemployment.
(c) Speculation may have been destabilising. Speculators, predicting a devaluation, could lose very little by selling the weak currency and purchasing stronger currencies, thereby adding even greater downward pressure on the weak currency. It can be argued that such activity may have brought about a devaluation which may otherwise have been unnecessary or may have brought about a bigger devaluation than was actually necessary to restore equilibrium.

It was partly for these reasons that the IMF system was abandoned in 1972 and more flexibility was introduced into the international monetary system.

Managed flexibility

By the term 'managed flexibility', we refer to an exchange rate system in which the rates are determined in the main by the conditions of demand and supply, but in which monetary authorities intervene at times to stabilise the rates or influence them in some way. Managed flexibility can take on a number of different forms. Consider the following.

Dirty floating With 'dirty floating', the fluctuations in a country's exchange rate are smoothed out whenever the country's monetary authority regards the upward or downward movements as becoming excessive. Thus, in the case of the United Kingdom, if the pound were depreciating rapidly, the authorities would sell part of the reserves of foreign currencies and buy pounds – this should help to reduce the rate of decline. Similarly, if the pound were thought to be appreciating too rapidly, the authorities would sell pounds on the foreign exchange market to smooth out the rise.

In 'dirty floating', the decision when to intervene and by how much is an arbitrary one. The main objective is to have reasonable stability in exchange rates and so maintain *confidence* in the system. Since the system does have some degree of flexibility, it is also hoped that the *adjustment* mechanism will work with reasonable efficiency, though it is possible that central bank intervention may lead exchange rates away from rather than towards their equilibrium values. Unlike countries with completely flexible rates, those whose monetary authorities intervene in the foreign exchange market will still have a need for international reserves – this means that 'dirty floating' will not necessarily overcome problems of *liquidity*.

Exchange rate bands This is a form of managed flexibility in which central bank intervention is determined more rigidly than in 'dirty floating'. In this system, a country will allow its exchange rate to fluctuate against some other currency (like the dollar) or against some 'average' of other currencies within a pre-arranged band. This would, therefore, be similar to the IMF system, but in most proposals the band is wider. One possibility would be for a country to allow its currency to fluctuate in value against some average

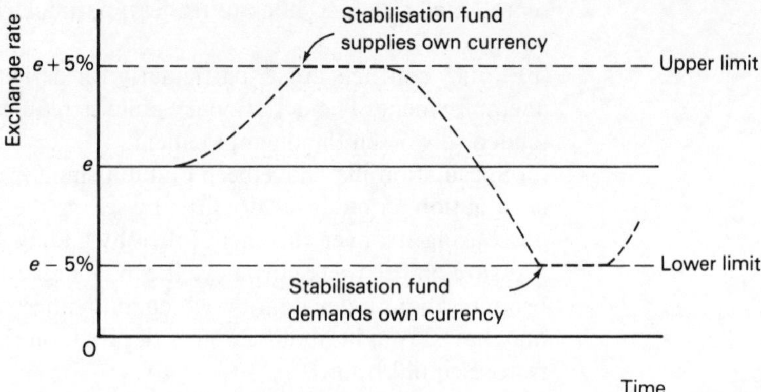

Fig. 11. A band proposal.

'basket' of other currencies by plus or minus 5 per cent around some initial central value. Such a system is illustrated in Fig. 11. The country's stabilisation fund would intervene only when the exchange rate reached the upper or lower limit of the band.

Band proposals, then, represent a compromise between fixed and flexible rates. One problem, though, is that once a currency reaches the upper or lower limit, the position is very similar to that of a disequilibrium in the IMF system and the same disadvantages apply.

Joint floating and the European Monetary System Another possibility is for a group of currencies to be pegged to each other in some way and then to float freely (or within a band) against outside currencies. Such a joint float was set up by a number of European countries in 1972 and became known as the 'snake'; the maximum allowed variation between any two of the participating currencies was $2\frac{1}{4}$ per cent. At first, the 'snake' was a joint float against the dollar, but this link with the dollar was broken in 1973.

In 1979, the 'snake' arrangement was replaced by the European Monetary System which can be described as follows. First, a new currency unit was established, called a European Currency Unit (or ECU) – this is a weighted average of the members' currencies identical in value to the existing European Unit of Account and initally equal to 67 pence. Secondly, each of the European currencies had to establish a 'central rate' against the ECU and a maximum fluctuation of up to plus or minus $2\frac{1}{4}$ per cent around this central rate is permitted and no currency can be more than $2\frac{1}{4}$ per cent apart from any other currency in the system. When any two currencies do move apart by more than the permitted margin, both countries' monetary authorities are required to intervene. It is, therefore, very similar to the 'snake' arrangement except that the 'snake' did not have the new currency unit. Note that the United Kingdom did not participate fully in the scheme from its inception largely because of fears that membership might prevent depreciation of an overvalued pound. It is eventually intended that a common currency area be set up in the European community and the new system should be seen as an important step towards that goal.

Conclusion

In this chapter, we have attempted to show what is meant by balance of payments 'problems' and how countries can tackle these problems, in particular by exchange rate policy. The types of policies used to maintain a balance of payments equilibrium depend crucially on the type of exchange rate system which prevails. We have seen that there are a wide variety of possible systems because there are so many possible compromises between completely fixed and completely flexible exchange rates. No country can insulate itself entirely from external forces, many of which stem from monetary factors. It is not surprising, therefore, that international monetary theory has developed into an extremely important branch of modern economics.

Further reading

Milner, C. and **Greenaway, D.,** *An Introduction to International Economics*, Longman, London, 1979 (Ch. 5–8).
Kindleberger, C.P. and **Lindert, P.H.,** *International Economics*, Irwin, Homewood, Illinois, 1978.
Prest, A.R. and **Coppock, D.J.,** *The UK Economy: A Manual of Applied Economics*, Weidenfeld and Nicolson, London, 1978 (Ch. 3).

Exercises

1. Review your understanding of the following terms:

foreign exchange market	absorption
'spot' rate of exchange	adjustment, confidence, liquidity
'forward' rate of exchange	gold standard
foreign exchange risk	common currency area
hedging	optimum currency area
interest arbitrage	flexible exchange rates
demand for pounds	destabilising speculation
supply of pounds	IMF adjustable-peg system
Marshall-Lerner condition	European monetary system

2. Consider the following data for the United Kingdom in 1979:

Sterling effective exchange rate (Dec. 1971 = 100): Jan. 1979 63.5
Dec. 1979 69.7

Rate of inflation during 1979: 17.2%
Current account deficit in 1979: £2,437 million
Balance for official financing in 1979: + £1,711 million
Account for the rise in sterling's effective exchange rate in 1979 when the United Kingdom had a rate of inflation appreciably higher than its major trading partners and a large current account deficit.

3. Outline the monetarist approach to the balance of payments. Critically evaluate this approach.

4. Discuss the view that currency depreciation may be inflationary and therefore ineffective as a means of correcting a balance of payments deficit.

5. What considerations are relevant in identifying the boundaries of an optimum currency area? Discuss the implications for the United Kingdom of an EEC decision to adopt a common currency.

6. Under a regime of flexible exchange rates, do speculators have a stabilising or destabilising effect?

7. What are the objectives of the IMF and how does it seek to achieve them?

29 Trade policy

Introduction

We have seen in Chapter 7 that free trade and consequent specialisation along the lines of comparative advantage potentially maximises world welfare in a world of perfectly mobile factors of production and of no externalities. Nevertheless, much attention has been devoted to the important question of whether protection can increase the welfare of a single country. By 'protection', we refer to barriers to free trade which tend to 'protect' the domestic industries against foreign competition.

Protection can take several forms. Much of the technical discussion has concerned the effects of an imposition of a *tariff* – that is, a tax on imported goods. A *quota* is the establishment by a government of a physical limit on the quantity of a good that can be imported over a given period; a quota may be expressed in physical, value or market share terms, but all imply that when a given quantity has already been imported, no more of that good will be allowed into the country. An *exchange control system* requires residents to obtain central bank permission to buy foreign currency for certain purposes, and perhaps multiple exchange rates with adverse exchange rates for luxury goods or unapproved uses.

Subsidies to domestic industries and *export subsidies* both have the effect of protecting domestic industries against foreign competition. An *import deposits scheme* requires importers to lodge some money with the central bank for a given time period. The effect is to increase the cost of importing and to tighten up on credit conditions. In recent years, new types of non-tariff barriers have been given increasing attention. Non-tariff barriers include *special regulations* that have to be met and the official form-filling necessary for goods to be imported into a particular country. Many regulations are imposed by governments on the grounds of consumer protection or public safety, but the effects may be to protect domestic production. There has been suspicion that some countries have imposed safety and other regulations as a means of discriminating against imports. In addition, a *public procurement policy* which requires some proportion of public expenditure to be spent domestically is a form of protection. Some countries, which officially adhere to free trade principles and are signatories of liberal international trade agreements, have become concerned at the levels of imports of particular products (for example, television and car imports into the United Kingdom from Japan) and have negotiated *voluntary agreements* with the overseas producers, which are designed to limit imports. We see from this brief discussion that protection can take many forms.

In the following discussion, we concentrate on the arguments for and against tariffs, but much of the discussion applies to the concept of protection as a whole. In the first part of this chapter, we start by considering the adverse effects of a tariff, including that of resource misallocation, at the microeconomic level. Later, we discuss the microeconomic arguments in favour of a tariff and consider the case for import controls at the macroeconomic level. In the second part of the chapter, we turn our attention to free trade areas and customs unions and discuss the European Economic Community.

Adverse effects of tariffs

Consider the imposition of a tariff on a particular good *X*. For simplicity, we assume that the world supply is infinitely elastic, that the good imposes no externalities, that the marginal utility of income is constant and that perfect competition prevails in both commodity and factor markets. In Fig. 1, S_w is the world supply curve of good *X* which is infinitely elastic at price Ow_1. D_dD_d and $S_d S_d$ are the domestic demand and supply curves respectively.

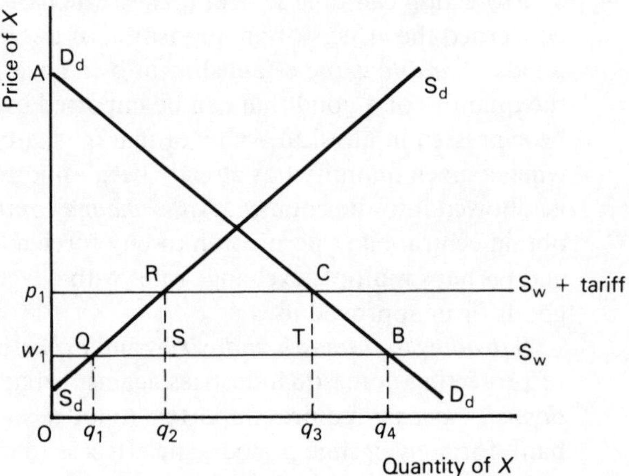

Fig. 1. The resource allocation effects of the imposition of a tariff.

Prior to the imposition of the tariff, consumers buy the quantity Oq_4, of which domestic producers supply quantity Oq_1. Thus, quantity q_1q_4 is imported initially. Now assume that a tariff equal to w_1p_1 is imposed on each unit of *X* imported, so that the effective world supply curve to this country shifts up to S_w + tariff. At the new domestic price Op_1, consumers buy a smaller quantity Oq_3, of which a larger quantity, Oq_2, is produced domestically. Imports fall to the quantity q_2q_3.

The imposition of the tariff imposes a cost on society in the form of *resource misallocation.* Consumer surplus, which was equal to the area ABw_1 prior to the imposition of the tariff, is reduced to the area ACp_1. Part of the reduction in consumer surplus accrues to producers as an increase in producers' surplus – that is, area w_1p_1RQ. Another part of the reduction in consumer surplus, rectangle RSTC, is collected by the government as tariff revenue. The resource misallocation costs of the tariff are represented by the areas of triangle QRS and triangle CTB. These areas are called *deadweight loss* of the tariff.

The *consumption loss* represented by triangle CTB arises because consumers are prevented by the tariff from buying X at the world price Ow_1. At the new price Op_1, consumers reduce the quantity bought by amount q_3q_4. Consumers value these units more highly than the world price, and thus the tariff imposes a loss on them. The *production loss* represented by triangle QRS arises because the quantity q_1q_2 is produced domestically after the imposition of the tariff. Under competitive conditions, the domestic supply curve S_dS_d represents the marginal cost of producing extra units. Thus, the total cost of producing quantity q_1q_2 domestically is represented by the area q_1QRq_2. Prior to the imposition of the tariff, the country imported this quantity at a cost represented by the area q_1QSq_2. Thus, triangle QRS represents the extra cost of domestic production.

Enforcement of the tariff will require resources to be diverted to this task, such as extra customs officials and civil servants. Thus, part of the tariff revenue accruing to government will probably be spent on enforcement. If so, this socially unproductive use of resources increases the deadweight loss of the tariff.

Another argument against a tariff kept in force over a long period is that it may enable inefficient firms to survive, which would otherwise have gone out of business. As a result, resources may be prevented from transferring to other industries in which the country has developed a comparative advantage. Similarly, a tariff may result in the creation of a domestic monopoly if foreign competitors are excluded, with the dangers that the monopoly may exploit the consumer and allow costs to rise unnecessarily.

Microeconomic arguments for protection

It appears that there are formidable microeconomic arguments against the imposition of a tariff, but now consider some microeconomic arguments in favour of a tariff.

The *strategic industry argument* is basically non-economic; it is that certain industries are of strategic importance in times of crises or armed conflict. Thus, a government might wish to expand the capacity of domestic production of a strategic industry through protection. It can be argued that industries such as agriculture, aerospace, armaments, ship-building and fuel industries are strategic. A decision to protect an industry on strategic grounds is clearly political. The economist can only point out that protection of an industry with a comparative disadvantage has an economic cost, and attempt to quantify that cost.

Another argument for the imposition of a tariff is the *terms of trade argument*. If, after the imposition of a tariff on a particular product, the tariff-imposing country imports less of the product, it may be able to force the suppliers to reduce their price as a result of excess supply. Clearly, this will only be effective if the importing country is a major buyer with some monopsonistic power. The United States, for example, has some degree of monopsonistic power with respect to some commodities. But a small country, like Belgium, could not realistically hope to improve its terms of trade for, say, wheat, as Belgium is a price-taker in the world wheat market. Even if a country which is an important buyer of a particular product succeeds initially in improving its terms of trade, other countries may retaliate by imposing tariffs on their imports. If this happens, with a consequent fall in the volume of trade, the welfare of all countries is likely to be reduced.

Perhaps the oldest and most widely accepted argument for protection is the *infant industry argument*. This argument is often applied to new industries in developing countries. When the industry is first established, the argument runs, it will be unable to compete effectively with the already well-established industries in other countries. The infant industry is likely to be producing on a small scale, and thus will not benefit from economies of scale. It is also likely to have a relatively inexperienced and less productive work-force. If, however, the industry is given some temporary protection, it will be able to develop a comparative advantage, and will ultimately be able to survive without protection. Thus, this argument incorporates a dynamic element, as the industry is held to develop a comparative advantage over time.

This argument appears valid and many economists have endorsed it, including Alexander Hamilton in 1791 and Friedrich List in 1841. But in recent times, some economists have put the infant industry argument under close scrutiny. If the infant industry will make temporary losses, but will ultimately be profitable, then surely entrepreneurs should be willing to withstand those initial losses in return for the prospect of future profits. If this does not in fact happen, it could be due to an imperfection or distortion in the capital market. In fact, many of the cases when protection has been called for an infant industry are examples of imperfections or distortions in the economy. Perhaps the capital market is inefficient in raising funds, or perhaps entrepreneurs are poorly informed about the future prospects of the industry. Alternatively, the development of the infant industry might result in external economies for other sectors of the economy. It might, for example, train a skilled work-force, some of whom will eventually transfer into other sectors of the economy. However, the entrepreneurs in the infant industry may not provide sufficient training from the viewpoint of society, as they recognise that some of the benefits will accrue to other industries.

Recent analysis has argued that if a distortion, imperfection or externality exists, then protection is an indirect and relatively inefficient method of dealing with the problem. Although protection can help the infant industry, it results in resource misallocation. The government should aim to remedy the imperfection, distortion or externality problem more directly. In the case of an imperfect capital market, for example, the government could provide loans, perhaps on preferential terms, to the entrepreneurs in the infant industry. If the entrepreneurs are poorly informed about the future prospects for the industry, the government can improve the flow of information through publications and counselling services.

Where entrepreneurs are not willing to provide the socially optimal amount of job-training, the government can give specific subsidies for training, or can set up government training centres. In the case where a government wishes to encourage production of a good domestically, because of external economies, national prestige or whatever, a production subsidy will be more efficient than protection of the industry. Such a subsidy stimulates production without introducing a distortion on the consumption side, as would a tariff.

Thus, when the infant industry argument is subjected to closer scrutiny the case for protection does not appear very strong. The argument is further weakened because of the danger that a protected infant industry may never grow up. It may never be able to discard its protection and compete effectively. A subsidy for training or to encourage domestic production is also more visible in the government's budget than a tariff, and is more likely to intensify public pressure for the industry to stand on its own feet. The United Kingdom government has allocated large sums of assistance to the microelectronic industry for the development and application of silicon chip technology. An argument for this support is that a successful microelectronic industry in the United Kingdom will generate many benefits, some of which will not be appropriated by the industry itself – for example, increased employment, a faster rate of economic growth and increased exports.

Another microeconomic argument for protection is as a counter-measure *against dumping*. Dumping occurs when a firm sells a product in an overseas market at a price below the price in the country of origin, after making appropriate allowances for differences in taxation, transport and insurance costs and tariffs. A firm acting as a discriminating monopolist, for example, may sell a product at a lower price in an overseas market. Recall from Chapter 10 that a discriminating monopolist can increase profits by selling a product at different prices in separate markets which have different demand elasticities.

Another motive for dumping is the intention by a firm to increase its market by driving its competitors out of business; this is sometimes known as 'predatory dumping'. The dumping firm may be able to sell temporarily at a loss-making low price in a particular market through cross-subsidisation from other markets. It is generally accepted that protection against predatory dumping is justifiable. In theory, persistent dumping benefits the consumer and no good case for protection against this form of dumping can be made. In practice, it is virtually impossible to distinguish the motives for dumping or to predict how long it will continue.

Dubious arguments

Some arguments advanced for protection do not stand up to careful inspection and have little validity. *Special interest groups,* such as producers and workers in a particular industry can, of course, benefit from protection of this industry. But the special interest groups will gain at the expense of consumers who are forced to pay higher prices and the community as a whole, as resources are diverted away from their areas of comparative advantage. It is common for producers and trade unions to call for protection against 'unfair competition' from lower paid foreign labour. If this argument were pursued to its logical implication, the United States and most of western Europe would refuse to trade with the United Kingdom, as wages in the United Kingdom are below those in these countries. As we have seen in Chapter 7, differences in comparative costs lie at the heart of the reasons for trade. If all countries had the same costs of production, there would be no gains from trade.

Pleas for protection often arise when an old established industry finds itself losing its comparative advantage and moving into a period of decline.

In these circumstances, the resources freed from the declining industry should move to new expanding industries. But often this transfer is slow and painful and structural unemployment results. Permanent protection would mean supporting an inefficient industry. One could, however, put forward a case for some *temporary* protection with a strict time limit and specific measures laid down to encourage adjustment. The appropriate policies for the government are to subsidise the retraining of the work-force and to encourage the development of new industries. It can be argued that the burden of adjustment should be borne by the whole community rather than only by those directly involved.

Macroeconomic arguments for protection

We now turn from the effects of protecting a single industry to a consideration of the wider macroeconomic arguments for protection. We consider the effects of widespread protection - if not on all imports, at least on a significant proportion of imports, such as manufactured goods. It will be convenient to consider the case for and against import controls as each point arises. There is a significant body of opinion in the United Kingdom, for example, that supports the view that a system of import controls would improve the economy's performance. Proponents of this view include the Cambridge Economic Policy Group (CEPG) and the Trades Union Congress.

The CEPG argue that in a situation of full employment the United Kingdom has a propensity towards a balance of payments deficit, which conventionally in the recent past has forced the government to impose deflationary policies. Even when deflation cured the balance of payments problems, it was at the expense of increased unemployment. The CEPG claim that the introduction of import controls would enable the growth in imports to be restricted to the level that can be financed from export earnings and full employment to be achieved through fiscal policy. Thus, the major advantages claimed are increased output and employment. In the longer run, the CEPG argue, the growth of effective demand will stimulate confidence in industry and investment, which will improve the United Kingdom's competitiveness and rate of economic growth.

The CEPG reject the use of devaluation to improve the United Kingdom's competitive position, arguing that devaluation would mean a worsening of the terms of trade and would require a cut in real wages. If workers tried to maintain the long-run growth trend of real wages, this might lead to a higher rate of inflation that would wipe out any competitive advantage gained through the devaluation.

The CEPG's views have been challenged on several grounds. In an era when there are already strong undercurrents of protectionist sentiments in various parts of the world, it is argued that by imposing import controls the United Kingdom might spark off a generalised trade war. Other countries might retaliate by imposing controls on their imports from the United Kingdom. Eventually, the whole liberalised trading structure of the western world might be undermined. If there were a large fall in world trade, the existing high living standards based on international specialisation would decline.

When the possibility of foreign retaliation is considered, it is not certain that the imposition of import controls by the United Kingdom will lead to a net improvement in the balance of payments and level of employment. There are several other factors that throw serious doubt on the ability of import controls to effect a lasting improvement in the balance of payments. Consider the following.

(a) When the United Kingdom imports less from other countries after the imposition of import controls, this will lead to a fall in the national incomes of these countries, *ceteris paribus.* As a result, their imports will fall which means that United Kingdom exports also decline.
(b) There is also the likelihood that some United Kingdom exports will be diverted to domestic consumption to make up for the fall in imports. Similarly, foreign goods now excluded from the United Kingdom market may be diverted to third country markets, where they may displace United Kingdom exports to some extent.
(c) If imports of particular finished goods are restricted, expenditure may increase on 'home-produced' goods that in fact contain a high proportion of imported materials. While imports of finished goods fall, imports of raw materials are likely to increase.
(d) Finally, if the import controls succeed in increasing the incomes of United Kingdom producers and their workers, part of the increased incomes will be spent on imports and on goods that would otherwise have been exported. Imports will increase and exports are likely to fall at every stage in the multiplier process, as the initial increase in incomes spreads through the economy.

Summary

We can note that both selective and generalised import controls have distinct disadvantages. Nevertheless, a case for protection of specific industries may be made (for example, a strategic industry or against dumping). It is by no means clear that generalised import controls will increase the level of employment or improve the balance of payments when the long-term implications are considered. Indeed, there is the risk that a trade war might result in lower living standards for countries such as the United Kingdom and it is no doubt largely due to this danger and to recognition of the benefits of trade that western governments have resisted some of the more extreme calls for the introduction of widespread protectionism.

With industries facing depressed markets, subsidies to protect industries have been introduced in many countries. Most countries in the European Economic Community (EEC) have, for example, given large subsidies to their steel industries. The EEC Commission introduced a cartel arrangement for the steel industry in the EEC which fixed minimum prices for steel. Under pressure from producers and trade unions, governments may be forced to introduce further protectionist measures.

We now turn to consider forms of economic integration and pay particular attention to the EEC.

Economic integration

There are varying degrees of economic integration among the groupings formed between countries with a view to encourage trade. In a *free trade area*, barriers to trade between the members are eliminated, but each member country maintains its own kind of restrictions and tariffs on trade with countries that are not members of the free trade area. With a *customs union*, tariff-free trade between member countries is created and, in addition, a common external tariff on imports from third countries is levied. In a *common market*, there is in addition to tariff-free trade and a common external tariff, free movement of labour and capital between member countries. The highest degree of integration is that of an *economic union* where the aim is to achieve a high degree of integration between the economic policies of the member countries.

The theory of customs unions

The traditional analysis of the formation of a customs union argued that the removal of tariffs was a move towards free trade and would, therefore, increase welfare. Jacob Viner showed that in fact the formation of a customs union might or might not increase welfare. Viner introduced the concepts of *trade creation* and *trade diversion*. Trade creation occurs when, after the formation of the union, production is shifted away from a higher-cost source towards a low-cost source within the union. Trade diversion occurs when production is shifted away from a low-cost source of production outside the union to a high-cost source of production within the union.

The effects of the formation of a customs union We can illustrate the concept of trade creation after the formation of a customs union with analysis that is the mirror-image of our analysis of the resource-misallocation effects of the imposition of a tariff.

Consider two countries A and B. Prior to the formation of the customs union, A imposes a tariff on the import of product *X*. In Fig. 2, D_dD_d and

Fig. 2. Trade creation after the formation of customs union.

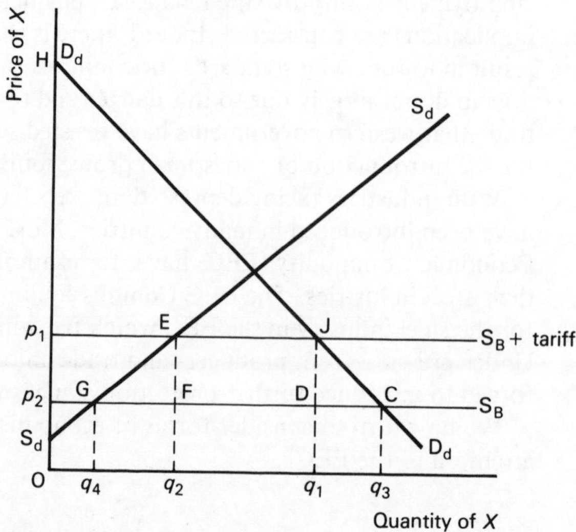

S_dS_d represent A's domestic demand and supply curves respectively. Note that for simplicity we assume that the supply of X from B is perfectly elastic. We assume that there is no other source of supply apart from B. Suppose that A is imposing a tariff of p_2p_1 on each unit of X imported so that the effective supply curve of X from B is S_B + tariff. Initially, A's consumers purchase Oq_1 of X, of which Oq_2 is provided by domestic suppliers and q_2q_1 is imported. Consumer surplus is represented by the area of triangle HJp_1.

When A forms a customs union with B, it removes tariffs on the import of X from B. Consumers in A can now purchase X from B at price Op_2. They purchase a total of Oq_3; domestic A production falls to Oq_4, and imports from B increase to $q_4 q_3$. This represents trade creation as production is shifted to lower cost supplies from B. Consumer surplus is now represented by the area of triangle HCp_2; thus, consumer surplus has increased by the area p_1 JCp_2 as a result of the formation of the customs union. But not all of the increase in consumer surplus represents an addition to welfare. Area p_1 EGp_2 is simply transferred from the producer surplus of domestic A suppliers of product X. The rectangle EJDF previously represented tariff revenue to the government. These areas then merely represent transfers to consumers from producers and the government respectively.

The net additions to welfare are represented by triangle JCD and triangle EFG. Triangle JCD represents a consumption gain since consumers in A are now able to purchase the extra quantity q_1q_3 at the lower price of Op_2. Triangle EFG represents a gain in production efficiency as the quantity q_4q_2 is imported at a lower cost than when produced domestically. In this example, *the formation of the customs union unambiguously increases A's welfare.* But now consider a case in which opposing effects on welfare occur.

In Fig. 3, D_dD_d and S_dS_d again represent country A's domestic demand and supply curves for product X. S_B is the perfectly elastic supply curve of country B and S_w is the perfectly elastic supply curve of the rest of the world. Prior to the formation of the customs union A is imposing a tariff of p_3p_1 on imports of good X. Consequently B's production is excluded from A's

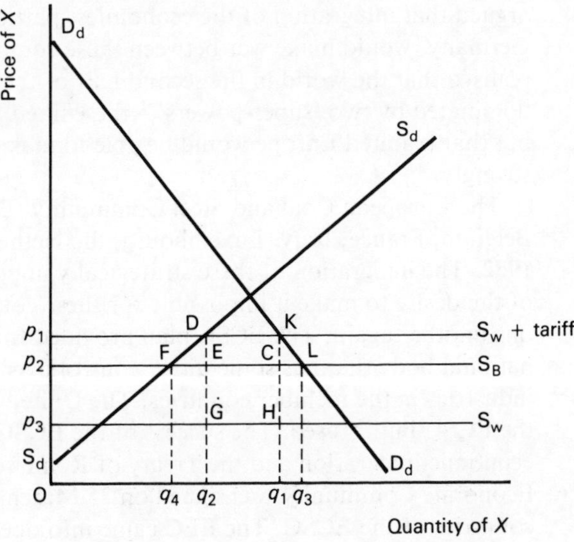

Fig. 3. Trade creation and trade diversion after the formation of a customs union.

market, and the effective supply curve from the rest of the world becomes S_w + tariff which is perfectly elastic at the price Op_1. Consumers in A buy quantity Oq_1 of which Oq_2 is produced domestically and q_2q_1 is imported.

Suppose now that A and B form a customs union so that imports from B now enter the A market without any tariff, while imports from the rest of the world still pay the original tariff of p_3p_1. Consequently, the imports from the rest of the world are displaced by imports from B. A's consumers now purchase a total quantity of Oq_3, of which q_4q_3 is imported from B. Domestic production in A falls to quantity Oq_4. As in previous analysis, there is an addition to welfare resulting from trade creation (triangle DEF) and increased consumption (triangle KLC). But there is also some trade diversion. Prior to the formation of the union, A imported quantity q_2q_1 and rectangle GDKH accrued to the government as tariff revenue. The resource cost of producing these imports was represented by the area q_2GHq_1. After the formation of the union, these imports are displaced by imports from B produced at the greater cost of q_2ECq_1 – that is the extra cost of producing this amount in B is represented by the area ECHG. Previously, this area was part of the tariff revenue accruing to government. After the formation of the union, it represents the resource misallocation cost of the trade diversion.

In this example, the formation of the customs union leads to trade creation which increases welfare (by triangles DEF and KLC), and to trade diversion which reduces welfare (by ECHG). The customs union only results in a net addition to welfare for A if the sum of the areas DEF and KLC is greater than the area ECHG. We have thus demonstrated that *if the formation of customs union results in trade diversion, it may or may not lead to an increase in welfare.*

The European Economic Community

The origins of the movement for a united western Europe go back to the tragedies of the two World Wars which brought so much devastation to Europe and the rest of the world. The 'founding fathers' of modern Europe argued that integration of the economies, particularly France and West Germany, would make war between these countries less likely. It was also realised that the world in the second half of the twentieth century would be dominated by two 'super-powers' – the United States and the Soviet Union, but that a united Europe would be able to make its voice heard more strongly.

The European Coal and Steel Community (ECSC) was formed by Belgium, France, Italy, Luxembourg, the Netherlands and West Germany in 1952. The integration of these strategically important industries was symbolic of the desire to make it impossible for these countries to go to war against one another again. The ECSC plan provided for a High Authority, a supranational body that has some direct control over the coal, iron and steel industries in the member countries. The United Kingdom was invited to join the ECSC but refused. The success of the ECSC led to pressure for more economic integration and the Treaty of Rome setting up the European Economic Community was signed on 25 March 1957 by the six member countries of the ECSC. The EEC came into operation on 1 January 1958.

The long-term aim of the EEC is to achieve an economic union – that is, to achieve a high degree of integration between the economic policies of the member countries and a measure of political unity.

The United Kingdom was involved in the early discussions on the proposal for some degree of integration, but it favoured the creation of a free trade area and withdrew from the discussions in November 1955. Various reasons have been suggested to explain the United Kingdom's reluctance to join the EEC as a founder member; in the mid-1950s the United Kingdom was still heavily involved in administering and developing the Empire into the Commonwealth; at that time its trade was weighted towards trade with the Commonwealth and colonies; the government also laid stress on its 'special relationship' with the United States. Thus, for these and other reasons, the United Kingdom did not join the EEC at its inception.

Perhaps partly because the United Kingdom government later realised that it had missed an opportunity by not joining the EEC, it initiated talks leading towards the formation of a free trade area in Europe. The Stockholm Convention which formed the European Free Trade Association (EFTA) was signed in 1960; its members were Austria, Denmark, Norway, Portugal, Sweden, Switzerland and the United Kingdom; Finland joined as an Associate Member in 1961. The EFTA agreement provided for free trade in industrial goods and, apart from a few exceptions, did not cover agricultural products.

The British government applied for membership of the EEC in 1961, and negotiations began. They were, however, broken off in January 1963 following a veto by the French President, General de Gaulle. The Labour government again applied for membership in May 1967, but once again General de Gaulle effectively vetoed the application and negotiations were not opened. Following M Pompidou's accession to the French Presidency, the original six members of the EEC indicated in 1969 that they were now favourably disposed to consider the application for United Kingdom membership. Negotiations were opened on 30 June 1970, following the general election in that month, which returned a Conservative government. The negotiations on the major questions concerning the United Kingdom's entry were completed by July 1971 and the terms of entry obtained were accepted in principle by the House of Commons on 28 October 1971. The Treaty of Accession of the United Kingdom (and Denmark, Eire and Norway) was signed in Brussels on 22 January 1972. The people of Norway subsequently voted against entry in a referendum, but the United Kingdom, Denmark and Eire acceded to the EEC on 1 January 1973.

When the Labour government returned to power in 1974, it made clear that it was not happy with the terms of entry obtained by the previous administration and would renegotiate the terms. After further discussions it obtained minor concessions on the maximum contribution to the budget and on the access of New Zealand butter and Commonwealth sugar to the EEC market. The government recommended the electorate to vote in favour of continued membership of the EEC in the Referendum held in July 1975. A two-thirds majority voted in favour of continued membership.

Benefits and costs of United Kingdom membership

When discussing the economic benefits and costs of EEC membership it must not be forgotten that major political advantages are claimed to result. Mention has already been made of the hope that integration would lessen the danger of war between European countries and that the United Kingdom would be able to make its voice heard more clearly as a member of an important economic bloc. In 1977 international trade involving EEC countries accounted for 34 per cent of world trade. Even prior to Britain's membership, its trade with the EEC was becoming increasingly important and was growing faster than its trade with the Commonwealth. The growing importance of trade with other EEC members in recent years is shown in Table 1.

Table 1. Area composition of UK visible trade, 1968 and 1978.

	Exports (%)		Imports (%)	
	1968	1978	1968	1978
EEC	26.7	38.6	27.6	43.5
Other Western Europe	15.0	12.8	14.0	13.9
North America	17.4	11.7	20.0	13.5
Other developed countries	12.5	6.5	10.7	7.0
Oil exporting countries	5.7	13.1	7.8	8.3
Rest of world	22.6	17.2	19.8	13.8

Source: Calculated by the authors from data in *United Kingdom Balance of Payments, 1979.*
Note: Some totals do not sum to 100 because of rounding.

Trade creation is a major potential advantage of joining a customs union. But empirical studies carried out prior to entry indicated that likely welfare gains to the United Kingdom from trade creation and losses from trade diversion were not likely to be large as a proportion of national income. The overall net welfare loss taking into account trade creation, trade diversion and the balance of payments effects of the common agricultural policy (CAP) was typically estimated at about 1 per cent of national income.

Prior to entry, British governments and economists placed greater emphasis on the *dynamic effects* of EEC membership; producers would have a 'home' market of 250 million people, which would enable many firms to benefit from greater economies of scale. The increased competition from EEC producers would, it was hoped, stimulate firms to greater efficiency and also lead them to invest more. With increased research and development expenditure, a higher rate of technological innovation was likely. It was argued that these dynamic effects would enable the economy to grow faster than it otherwise would. Because of the uncertainties regarding the outcome and future economic developments, no reliable estimates of the likely beneficial dynamic effects were possible.

Prior to entry, it was also recognised that there would be significant balance of payments costs for the United Kingdom. The budgetary agreements and the CAP which were formulated prior to British membership did not work to Britain's advantage. It was recognised that these two factors would have an adverse effect on the United Kingdom's balance of payments.

The EEC budget is financed by members handing over 90 per cent of the receipts from levies on agricultural imports and on customs duties, and by a contribution from the VAT receipts of each country. The maximum VAT contribution is equivalent to a 1 per cent rate of VAT. It is argued that this budgetary arrangement works against the United Kingdom because it imports a relatively high proportion of agricultural products, raw materials and other products from outside the EEC. But not only does the United Kingdom make a disproportionately high contribution to the EEC budget, it also receives relatively low payments. This is because the CAP accounts for about 70 per cent of expenditure from the EEC budget and Britain has a smaller proportion of its work-force in agriculture than any other EEC country.

By guaranteeing farmers artificially high prices for their output, the CAP has led to the appearance of various surpluses such as the 'butter mountain' and 'wine lake'. In 1977, for example, the purchase of surplus production by the intervention boards, the storing and disposal of surpluses cost the EEC taxpayers £1,850 million. The intervention boards were unable to sell the surpluses at low prices to consumers in the EEC because a major objective is to guarantee high prices to farmers. So, in many cases, the surpluses have been disposed of in ways that have resulted in anger from taxpayers. Well-known examples include the sale of butter to the Soviet Union on different occasions at prices below the production cost, and the subsidised use of skimmed milk as feed for dairy cattle. Recall from Chapter 6 that the operation of the CAP involves setting a price floor which might be higher than the equilibrium price.

The size of the United Kingdom's budgetary contribution remained a contentious issue in 1980. In 1980 the United Kingdom was the largest net contributor to the EEC budget, despite having only the seventh highest GNP per capita in the community. Table 2 shows estimates for net budget contributions in 1980 and relative GNP figures per capita for the member countries of the EEC.

Table 2. Net budget contributions and relative GNP figures per capita for EEC countries.

	Estimated net budget contribution 1980 (£m.)	GNP per head 1978 (Community average = 100)
United Kingdom	1,209	72.6
West Germany	699	136.7
France	13	116.1
Luxembourg	– 195	125.8
Denmark	– 247	143.7
Netherlands	– 281	123.1
Ireland	– 342	49.6
Belgium	– 367	128.9
Italy	– 489	60.2

Source: Economic Progress Report, February 1980.

Conclusion

Any attempt to assess whether membership of the EEC has benefited the United Kingdom cannot, of course, be solely concerned with economic issues; thus economics alone cannot answer the question. But neither can economics give a definitive answer to the question of whether EEC membership has on balance benefited the United Kingdom economy. There is no universally agreed social welfare function and, of course, one can only speculate on how the economy might have performed since 1973 if it had not joined the EEC. United Kingdom entry to the EEC coincided with the vast increase in oil prices in the mid 1970s and with the deepest worldwide recession since the 1930s. Some people have noted that the first few years after entry to the EEC coincided with high inflation rates, high rates of unemployment and slow economic growth. But it is almost redundant to point out that many other countries, not members of the EEC, suffered from similar problems. The extent to which EEC membership exacerbated these problems, if at all, can only give scope for speculation.

There is the view that in an increasingly hostile world economic climate, greater solidarity and mutual co-operation between the member countries of the EEC may enable these countries to avoid some of the more extreme dangers and economic problems confronting individual economies in the remaining part of the twentieth century.

Further reading

Lewis, D.E.S., *Britain and the European Economic Community*, Heinemann Educational Books, London, 1978.
Kindleberger, C.P. and **Lindert, P.H.**, *International Economics*, Irwin, Homewood, Illinois, 1978 (Ch. 6–9).
Milner, C. and **Greenaway, D.**, *An Introduction to International Economics*, Longman, London, 1979 (Ch. 2 and 3).

Exercises

1. Review your understanding of the following terms:

tariff	dumping
quota	free trade area
exchange control	customs union
export subsidy	common market
import deposits scheme	economic union
'deadweight' loss	trade creation
strategic industry	trade diversion
infant industry	EEC common agricultural policy

2. The following information shows the domestic demand and supply conditions for good X.

Price (£)	5	10	15	20	25	30
Domestic quantity demanded	100	90	80	70	60	50
Domestic quantity supplied	10	30	50	70	90	110

The world supply curve of good X is perfectly elastic at the price of £10 per unit.

(a) Using a graph, find the equilibrium total domestic consumption, domestic quantity supplied and the quantity imported.
(b) Now suppose a tariff of £5 per unit is imposed on the import of X. Calculate: (i) the reduction in total consumption; (ii) the fall in imports; (iii) the total tariff revenue and (iv) the deadweight loss of the tariff.

3. Consider the case for and against protection by tariffs and quotas of the United Kingdom microelectronics industry on infant industry grounds. Contrast this case with the arguments for and against financial support of the industry by the United Kingdom government.

4. Discuss the relative advantages and disadvantages of tariffs, quotas, voluntary agreements and an import deposits scheme as means of restricting imports.

5. Consider the extent to which the EEC common agricultural policy affects: (a) the welfare of different sections within a member country; and (b) the welfare of different member countries.

6. 'A customs union may or may not increase the welfare of the member countries.' Discuss this statement with reference to the theory of the second best.

30 Economic inequality

Introduction

This final chapter attempts to investigate the phenomenon of the inequality of incomes in human societies. The analysis of inequality is essentially the study of the distribution of personal incomes – that is, how the total income of a country is shared out among individuals and families. Inequality can be observed between different income groups, between different regions of the same country and, of course, between different countries – particularly, as we saw in Chapter 25, between the industrially advanced and the less developed countries of the world.

Economists are interested in both the pattern and trends of income distribution because these have a direct bearing on social welfare. As Chapter 8 showed, social welfare is a function of, amongst other things, the size of national income and the pattern of its distribution. This means that before any conclusions can be made about social welfare, both changes in the size of national income and changes in its distribution must be taken into account. This is equivalent to saying that both efficiency and equity criteria must be considered. As we emphasised in Chapter 8, the equity question as to what degree of inequality a society is prepared to tolerate is a value judgement and so part of normative economics.

In mixed economies, like the United Kingdom, the public sector plays a key role in implementing society's views about the desirable income distribution. We showed in Chapter 11 that one of the functions of the public sector is the redistribution of income and wealth through taxation and expenditure policies. Chapter 13 indicated some of the tax-expenditure legislative measures which have been directed towards the goal of reducing inequality. In this chapter, we reflect on the degree of success achieved by these redistribution policies in the United Kingdom. We consider the following aspects of inequality: the components of total personal income and the methods of measuring the distribution of income; the distribution of personal incomes before and after tax and the distribution of the income tax burden; the incidence of taxes and the benefits of social services; international comparisons of income distributions and inequality; and the major causes of inequality.

Components of total personal income

In any study of inequality, we need to know the composition of total personal income as this enables us to assess the pattern and trends in income distribution. As shown in Table 1, total personal income in the United Kingdom has three main components: earned income, investment income and transfer income.

Earned income is by far the largest of these components, making a contribution of almost 78 per cent to the total personal income of £125,143 million in 1977. This suggests that the distribution of earned income plays a key role in determining the shape of distribution over all income groups in the United Kingdom. However, although investment income only accounts for 9.8 per cent of the total, it is far more unequally distributed than other forms of income: in fact, in the United Kingdom, more than 60 per cent of all investment income accrues to the top 10 per cent of all tax-paying units.

Unfortunately, the statistical data available is not entirely reliable. The Royal Commission on the Distribution of Income and Wealth (upon which this chapter draws) obtained much of its information from the Survey of Personal Incomes and the Family Expenditure Surveys. These two sources of information have several deficiencies which we should mention.

Table 1. Major components of total personal income, 1977.

	£ million	% share
1. *Earned income*		
Income from employment	85,839	68.6
Income from self-employment	11,608	9.3
2. *Investment income*	12,324	9.8
(Imputed rent of owner occupiers, rent, interest, dividends *minus* mortgage and other interest paid)		
3. *Transfer income*	15,143	12.1
4. *Imputed charge for capital consumption of private non-profit-making bodies*	229	0.2
Total personal income	125,143	100.0

Source: Royal Commission Report No. 7, Tables 2.1 and 2.2.

The Survey of Personal Incomes is based on income tax returns and these suffer from the inherent difficulty of the under-reporting of incomes. Furthermore, the basic unit for the Survey is the tax unit – that is, a single person or a married couple who may or may not have children. From this data, there is no way of knowing the distribution of *individual* incomes. Allied to this is the problem of children leaving school and taking jobs half-way through the tax year and so becoming a tax unit, and single women getting married half-way through the tax year and ceasing to be tax units. Difficulties arise in these cases because if normal annual income is, say, £5,000, but work ceases after six months, the Survey statistics will record an actual income of £2,500 being earned for the whole year. Also, the Survey excludes low incomes which do not attract taxes and these, of course, are incomes which are of some importance in the study of inequality.

The Family Expenditure Surveys of the Central Statistical Office tend to suffer from the opposite difficulty – that is, the lower income groups are well represented, but the higher income groups are under-represented.

The concept of 'income before tax' which the Royal Commission uses is narrow in its scope and unrepresentative of incomes actually received by single persons or families in the United Kingdom. It applies the concept of 'taxable income', defined to include earned and unearned incomes only. It excludes unrealised capital gains, undistributed profits, imputed rents of owner-occupied dwellings, some gifts, non-taxable national insurance contributions and certain incomes in kind. In any study of income inequality, the question of what is and what is not income is of great importance. Only the adoption of a wide definition of income, including incomes from all conceivable sources, will yield an accurate representation of the distribution of income and hence inequality. A narrow definition will have the effect of distorting the picture of income inequality.

In what follows, it is very important to bear in mind the limitations of the data presented.

Pareto's Law

The Italian economist, Vilfredo Pareto, carried out a detailed study of the income tax data of several European countries, including Britain, towards the end of the nineteenth century. He discovered that there was some statistical regularity between a given income and the number of persons earning at least that income. This fixed relationship became known as Pareto's Law which stated that the number of income recipients earning at least a given level of income would tend to fall by a fixed percentage as that given level of income rose by a fixed percentage.

A most important implication of this law is that inequality is inescapable and so policy measures designed to reduce inequality are likely to be fruitless. It may, however, be argued that Pareto's Law is true only of high incomes and so does not throw much light on distribution between high and low income groups: the law is derived from income tax data, and as we know, income tax in the last century had a very narrow base, being levied mainly on property (or investment) incomes.

Pareto's work did, however, stimulate great interest in empirical research into personal income distribution in the years that followed. In the postwar years, F.W. Paish in 1957 and H.F. Lydall in 1959 studied the changes in the distribution of personal incomes in the United Kingdom. Using estimates from the National Income and Expenditure Blue Book, they compared personal incomes before and after tax between 1938 and 1955 (in the case of Paish) and between 1938 and 1957 (in the case of Lydall). Their conclusions were that there was a substantial reduction in inequality in the postwar years.

These conclusions, though, were criticised by R.M. Titmuss who stressed the inadequacies of the data. He pointed to the many rapid demographic and social changes following the Second World War which affected the pattern of distribution in the postwar years. These included changes in the age of marriage, changes in the proportion of the total married population and changes in the number of women going out to work – all of these would tend to affect the distribution of personal incomes regardless of the public sector's redistribution policies. R.J. Nicolson in 1967 suggested that the trend towards greater equality in the United Kingdom may have come to a halt after the 1950s because of the onset of rapid inflation and the attendant counter-inflation policies.

Methods of measuring the distribution of personal incomes

A common way of measuring income inequality is to arrange all individuals in descending (or ascending) order of personal income and then to divide the total population into distinct groups. For example, the population can be divided into successive fifths (called quintiles) or tenths (called deciles). From this arrangement, the proportion of total income received by each group can be determined. Table 2 illustrates this statistical method for incomes before tax in the United Kingdom in 1964 and 1976–77. The tax-paying units (or income recipients) are broken down into deciles in this example. The Table shows that the income share of the top 10 per cent of the population declined from 29.1 per cent in 1964 to 25.8 per cent in 1976–77, whereas there was an increase in the bottom 20 per cent's share from 5.2 per cent in 1964 to 6.3 per cent in 1976–77. This suggests that during the ten-year period there was a reduction in the inequality of personal incomes before tax in the United Kingdom. The ratio of the share of income received by the bottom 20 per cent of income recipients to the share received by the top 20 per cent provides a crude numerical measure of inequality: this ratio is shown in Table 2 for 1964 and 1976–77 and is seen to have increased during the ten years from 0.12 to 0.15. The larger this ratio is, the more equal is the distribution of income. A value equal to 1 would imply complete equality, but it must be remembered that the measure is based on extreme values only and ignores all those income recipients between the twentieth and eightieth percentiles.

Table 2. The distribution of personal incomes before tax, 1964 and 1976–77.

Income recipients (deciles) (%)	% share in 1964	% share in 1976–77
Top 10	29.1	25.8
11–20	15.5	16.1
21–30	12.6	13.3
31–40	10.9	11.1
41–50	9.2	9.2
51–60	7.4	7.5
61–70	5.8	6.0
71–80	4.3	4.7
81–90	} 5.2	3.8
91–100		2.5
No. of tax units (m.)	27.5	28.5
Measure of inequality (Ratio of bottom 20% to top 20%)	5.2/44.6 = 0.12	6.3/41.9 = 0.15

Source: Royal Commission Report No. 7, Table 2.11.

The statistical distribution of personal incomes, as shown in Table 2, tells us nothing about the locational and occupational sources of incomes. In other words, the incomes of doctors, solicitors, engineers, teachers and factory workers are all merged into relevant income brackets. In 1976–77, the lower limit of the income range for the top 10 per cent of income recipients was £5,686 per annum: a coal-miner working under hazardous and dirty conditions would be included in this range alongside executives, top civil servants and doctors. It is difficult to accept that the miner's welfare is the same as that of the others in the same income range.

Table 3 illustrates the effect of progressive income taxes on the distribution of income in the United Kingdom in the years 1964 and 1976–77. It can be seen from the Table that personal income tax is progressive in the sense that it has managed to reduce income inequality. This result is indicated by the changes in our crude 'measure' of inequality which in 1964 rose from 0.12 to 0.15 and in 1976–77 rose from 0.15 to 0.20. It should be emphasised, though, that taxation and public expenditure policies are capable of influencing the distribution of both gross and net incomes. For instance, personal income tax, including national insurance contributions, may influence gross earnings by affecting the willingness to work and the number of hours of work offered per week. Government benefits in cash and in kind may similarly affect gross earnings.

The Lorenz curve

Another way of illustrating inequality is to present the data of Tables 2 and 3 graphically. Such a graphical representation of the distribution of personal incomes is called a Lorenz curve, named after the American statistician, M.O. Lorenz. Figure 1 shows the Lorenz curves for the distributions of

Table 3. The distribution of personal incomes after tax, 1964 and 1976–77.

Income recipients (deciles) (%)	% share in 1964	% share in 1976–77
Top 10	25.9	22.4
11–20	16.1	15.9
21–30	12.9	13.4
31–40	11.1	11.3
41–50	8.8	9.4
51–60	8.0	7.9
61–70	5.6	6.8
71–80	5.1	5.2
81–90	} 6.5	4.6
91–100		3.1
No. of tax units (m.)	27.5	28.5
Measure of inequality (Ratio of bottom 20% to top 20%)	6.5/ 42 = 0.15	7.7/ 38.3 = 0.2

Source: Royal Commission Report No. 7, Table 2.3.

Table 4. The cumulative distributions of personal incomes.

Income recipients (%)	1964 (before tax)	1976–77 (before tax)	1976–77 (after tax)
Bottom 10	–	2.5	3.1
20	5.2	6.3	7.7
30	9.5	11.0	12.9
40	15.3	17.0	19.7
50	22.7	24.5	27.6
60	31.9	33.7	37.0
70	42.8	44.8	48.3
80	55.4	58.1	61.7
90	70.9	74.2	77.6
100	100.0	100.0	100.0

personal incomes in Tables 2 and 3. The curves are constructed in the following way:

(a) The percentage frequency distributions of Tables 2 and 3 are converted to *cumulative* percentage frequency distributions. As shown in Table 4, this is done by finding the percentage of income earned by the 'bottom 10 per cent', then the 'bottom 20 per cent', then the 'bottom 30 per cent' and so on – the final class interval is the 'bottom 100 per cent' which, of course, includes *all* income recipients who must therefore earn 100 per cent of total personal income.
(b) These figures are then plotted on a graph with 'percentage cumulative income' on the vertical axis and 'percentage of income recipients' on the horizontal axis. The resulting curve is called the Lorenz curve.

The 45° line, OB, drawn from the origin in Fig. 1 is called the *line of complete equality.* At every point on this line, the percentage of income received is exactly equal to the percentage of income recipients. Consider, for example, point E which is half-way along the length of OB. At this point, 50 per cent of total personal income is earned by 50 per cent of all income recipients. At point F, 75 per cent of income recipients receive 75 per cent of total income; at point G, 25 per cent earn 25 per cent of total income; and so on.

The curves a, b and c are the Lorenz curves for 1964 (before tax), 1976–77 (before tax) and 1976–77 (after tax) respectively. The further away a Lorenz curve is from the line of complete equality, the greater is the degree of inequality. Notice that the after-tax Lorenz curve, c, is the nearest one to OB, suggesting that the taxation policies of the United Kingdom do tend to reduce income inequality. Also, curve b is nearer to OB than curve a: this suggests that income inequality in the United Kingdom has declined in the twelve-year period up to 1976.

A commonly used measure of the overall degree of inequality in the distribution of income is found by calculating the ratio of the area between the Lorenz curve and the line of complete equality and the total area OBZ (in Fig. 1). This ratio is known as the 'Gini concentration ratio' or more simply, the 'Gini coefficient', named after the Italian statistician, C. Gini. It can be expressed as a percentage so that the closer the coefficient is to 100 per cent,

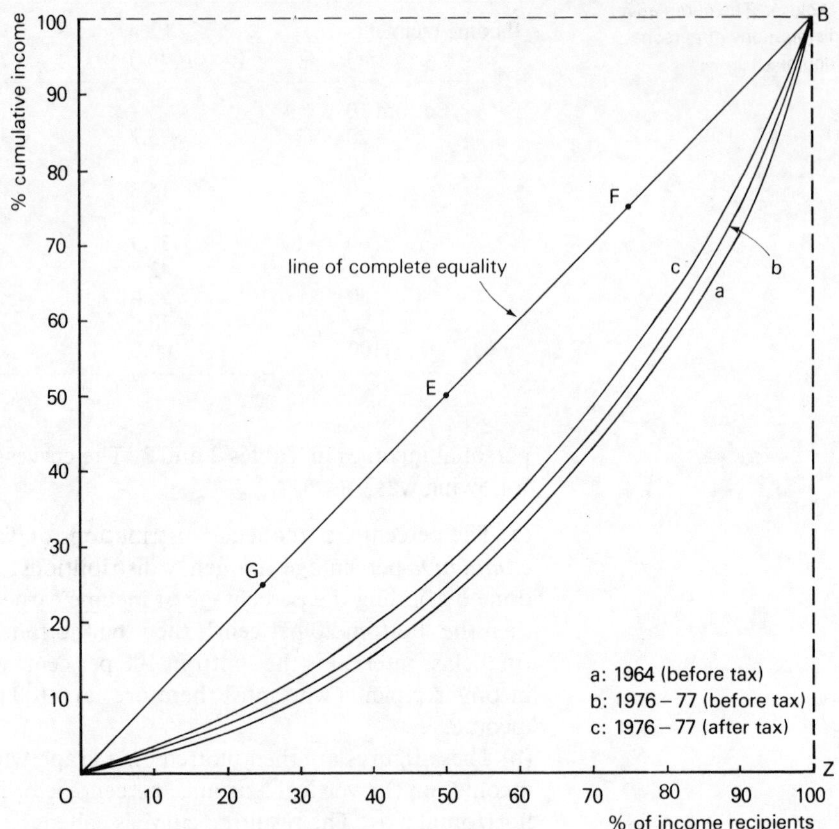

Fig. 1. Lorenz curves for the United Kingdom.

the greater is the degree of inequality; similarly, the closer it is to zero, the smaller is the degree of inequality. For the United Kingdom in 1976–77, the Gini coefficient for before-tax income was 36.5 per cent and for after-tax income 31.5 per cent.

It should be emphasised, however, that the Gini coefficient is not an ideal measure of income inequality. Figure 2 illustrates two Lorenz curves, A and B, which represent different distributions of personal income, but which have the same Gini coefficient. The problem with the Gini coefficient is that all the percentile information is collapsed into a single figure.

Distribution of the income tax burden

We showed in Chapter 13 that personal income tax, with its progressive rates, is not only important in terms of revenues, it is also a major instrument of redistribution policy in the United Kingdom. One would, therefore, expect a greater share of the burden of such a tax to be borne by higher income groups. Table 5 shows that the share of total tax paid by the top 10 per cent income group fell from 64.9 per cent in 1959 to 39.5 per cent in 1976–77. This means that for the remaining 90 per cent of the tax-paying population, the proportion of the tax burden borne rose from 35.1 per cent to 60.5 per cent. The middle income group (41–60 per cent) had its share almost doubled and the bottom 40 per cent had its share exactly doubled.

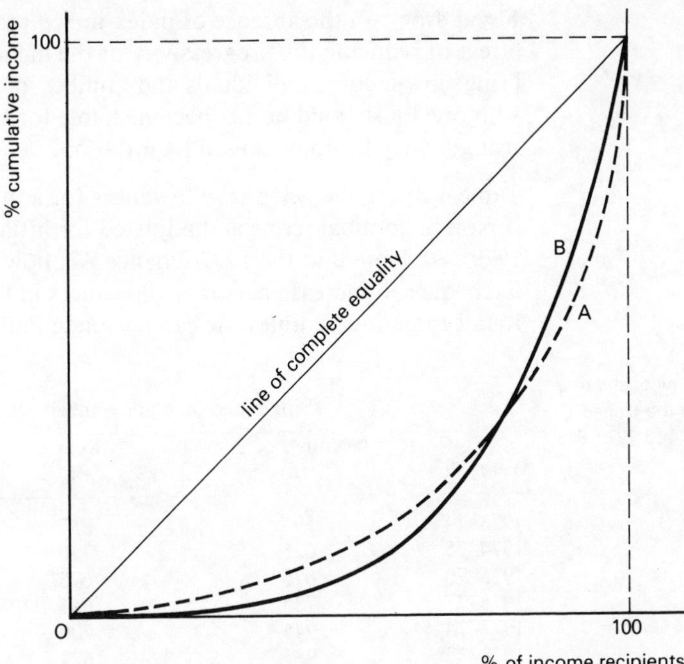

Fig. 2. Two intersecting Lorenz curves with identical Gini coefficients.

Note that average tax rates have risen markedly during the period 1959 to 1976–77, but the rates of increase have been spread unevenly over the different income groups in a way that has increased the tax burden on the lower income groups. It is possible to identify several reasons for this. Consider the following:

Table 5. The distribution of the income tax burden in the United Kingdom.

Income recipients (%)	Percentage share of tax paid 1959	1976–77
Top 10	64.9	39.5
11–20	11.6	17.3
21–40	13.1	23.8
41–60	7.8	14.0
61–80	2.6	4.8
81–100	-	0.6

Source: Royal Commission Report No. 5, Table 7 and *No. 7,* Table 2.6.

The system of reliefs and allowances The United Kingdom tax system is characterised by reliefs and allowances which tend to reduce its progressivity. Allowances include mortgage interest, certain other interest payments and the superannuation contributions of employees and the self-employed. By adding back these deductions to income and the imputed rent (net of mortgage interest payments) of owner-occupied houses, evidence shows that the income share of the top 10 per cent rises so that on equity grounds, they would be liable to bear a larger share of the tax burden.

Fiscal drag In the absence of index-linked income taxes, inflation has the effect of reducing the progressivity of the income tax system. Fiscal drag brings low-income individuals and families into the tax net. Thus, people who previously paid no tax become liable for tax simply because they have rising money incomes caused by inflation.

Table 6 shows the personal allowances for a married couple and a single person in nominal terms and adjusted for inflation from 1973/ 74 to 1979/ 80. Note that the 1977 Finance Act now requires the Chancellor of the Exchequer to increase personal allowances in line with the increase in the Retail Price Index, unless he can persuade Parliament to agree not to do so.

Table 6. The nominal and real tax allowances in the United Kingdom, 1973–74 to 1979–80.

	Single person's allowance		Married person's allowance	
Year	Nominal (£)	Real (£)	Nominal (£)	Real (£)
1973–74	595	857	775	1,117
1974–75	625	776	865	1,075
1975–76	675	675	955	955
1976–77	735	631	1,085	931
1977–78	945	700	1,445	1,070
1978–79	985	673	1,535	1,050
1979–80	1,165	703	1,815	1,095

Source: Financial statements and budget reports, 1973–74 to 1979–80.
Note: The *real* allowances are calculated in 1975 prices by the authors.

The incidence of taxes and social services benefits

The question of who pays taxes and who benefits from public expenditure is an exercise in the study of the redistribution policies of the public sector. In the United Kingdom, this study is undertaken by the Central Statistical Office which publishes its estimates from the Family Expenditure Survey (based on a sample of over 10,000 households) annually in *Economic Trends.*

We have shown in this chapter and in Chapter 13 that the public sector can attempt to reduce inequality: (a) through progressive taxes which directly reduce spending power; (b) through influencing the pattern of demand for finished goods by indirect taxes (like VAT and customs and excise duties); and (c) through influencing the allocation pattern of resources between private and public goods through its own expenditures.

In order to determine the standard of living of a person or family, the Central Statistical Office allocates taxes and benefits to the sampled households on highly simplified assumptions. It assumes, for example, that the incidence of direct taxes is borne by those on whom the taxes are levied and that the incidence of indirect taxes is borne by the consumers of the product. As regards the benefits allocated to households, the Central Statistical Office classifies these into: (a) direct cash benefits (for example, old age pensions, supplementary and other benefits); (b) direct benefits in kind (for example, National Health Service benefits, education and school meals); and (c) indirect benefits in kind (for example, housing and food subsidies). Non-allocable benefits, like defence, roads and museums, which form a significant part of total public expenditure are assumed to yield equal benefits to each individual in the community – a questionable assumption! Clearly, in any task of this nature, the inclusion or exclusion of particular taxes or benefits is likely to make a big difference to the estimates of the degree of inequality. The greatest problem arises with the benefits because, whereas all taxes are allocated to households, this is not the case with all benefits.

The overall conclusion of the Central Statistical Office's studies is that the four factors – direct and indirect taxes and benefits in cash and kind – make a major contribution towards reducing inequality.

International comparisons of income distribution

One way of judging the inequalities between societies is to compare the distributions of incomes of different countries. As we pointed out in Chapter 17, such inter-country comparisons are exceedingly difficult. Different countries collect data for different purposes; they tend to adopt different definitions of income and income units; and they employ different cost-of-living indices. Furthermore, exchange rates reflect only to a very limited extent the domestic purchasing power of different currencies and so are not necessarily the most appropriate way of converting from one currency to another. As might be expected, the difficulties of comparing income distributions are much more severe between the developed and less developed countries than between developed countries.

Table 7 illustrates the pattern of distribution of pre-tax total personal incomes for a selection of industrially advanced countries, subject to the limitations of the data mentioned above. We can see from Table 7 that the share of the bottom 20 per cent of income recipients in the United Kingdom (5.5 per cent) is the second highest after Australia (6.3 per cent). The lower degree of inequality in the United Kingdom and Australia is also reflected in the Gini coefficients – 34.8 per cent for the United Kingdom and 32.1 per cent for Australia – which are significantly lower than for France, Japan and the United States. As for other European countries, West Germany, the Netherlands and Norway have income distribution similar to France's, whereas Sweden has a more equitable distribution.

Table 7. The distributions of pre-tax personal incomes in selected countries.

Country and year	Top 20%	21–40%	41–60%	61–80%	81–100%	Gini coeff.
Australia (1966–67)	38.9	23.3	17.9	13.6	6.3	32.1
France (1970)	47.0	23.0	15.8	9.9	4.3	41.6
Japan (1971)	46.2	22.8	16.3	10.9	3.8	40.7
UK (1974)	40.1	24.4	18.1	11.9	5.5	34.8
USA (1974)	46.4	23.7	16.1	10.0	3.8	41.2

Source: Royal Commission Report No. 5, Table 62.

The centrally planned economies (such as the Soviet Union, Bulgaria and Poland) might be expected to have the lowest degree of income inequality. As we saw in Chapter 7, state ownership of resources other than labour means that the income from capital, land and property does not accrue to individuals and households. Inequality in these societies, then, is due mainly to variations in wage incomes between different sectors, skills and occupations.

Inequality is far more marked in the less developed countries. The average income share of the lowest 40 per cent of income earners in the less developed countries is typically about 12.5 per cent, and in some of the poorest countries, it is as low as 9 per cent. Table 8 shows the degree of inequality in a selection of less developed countries. It should be emphasised that a number of difficulties arise in studying the distribution of incomes in less developed countries. To start with, there is the difficulty of obtaining comprehensive data on family expenditures because households rarely keep records of their spending. Higher income groups often receive part of their incomes in kind and lower income groups (who comprise self-employed workers, tenants, farm workers and artisans) live mainly in rural areas and consume the bulk of their subsistence production themselves. This consumption of non-marketed goods by low income groups poses serious problems for statisticians seeking monetary valuations. The problem is accentuated by the fact that three-quarters of the population in less developed countries lives in rural areas where price levels differ widely for the same assortment of goods in urban areas. For instance, the costs of fuel, lighting and housing figure more prominently in urban living than in rural life. In the latter, the estimation of rent-free accommodation and virtually free fuel and lighting is an immensely difficult task. Rural communal life also provides for a collective funding of ceremonial functions of which there are plenty. This means that the conventional concepts of 'wage incomes' and 'capital incomes' are less relevant to the 'true' income distribution, though statisticians still attempt to apply such concepts.

Table 8. The distributions of income in selected less developed countries.

Country and year	Top 20%	40–60%	Poorest 40%
Argentina (1970)	47.4	36.1	16.5
Venezuela (1970)	65.0	27.1	7.9
Kenya (1969)	68.0	22.0	10.0
India (1964)	52.0	32.0	16.0
Malaysia (1970)	56.0	32.4	11.6
Peru (1971)	60.0	33.5	6.5
Taiwan (1964)	40.1	39.5	20.4

Source: H. Chenery *et al., Redistribution with Growth,* pp. 8–9

Causes of economic inequality

There are complex sociological, cultural, historical, political and religious factors which conspire to bring about economic inequality. A number of specific causes of inequality, however, can be identified. Consider the following:

Differences in wealth ownership Perhaps one major cause of inequality in the distribution of income is the unequal distribution of wealth. The holding of wealth represents not only direct command over goods and services (in that it can yield a cash income), it also confers status, security and potential spending power in the future. Life-time saving is one important source of wealth, but it may also be accumulated from gifts, inheritances, capital gains, and collections of rare stamps, coins and paintings. In developed societies, wealth may be held in the form of *physical assets,* like land, buildings and household goods, or *financial assets*, like cash, stocks and shares, building society accounts and life policies.

The actual measurement of the wealth held by individuals and families is by no means a simple task. This is because wealth holders in many countries are not obliged by law to keep records of their wealth, nor are they required to disclose the value of their wealth if they do not wish to do so. Another difficulty is that of putting monetary valuations on certain types of wealth, particularly those like pension rights, historic buildings and private estates, where there are no readily available markets for disposal. Problems of valuation contributed to the delay in the introduction of a wealth tax in the United Kingdom, proposed by the Labour government in 1974.

In most countries, then, only crude measures of personal wealth are available. In the United Kingdom, estimates are made by the Inland Revenue from estate duties – though there are some other independent estimates too. Table 9 illustrates the distribution of personal wealth derived from the Inland Revenue's estimates. It can be seen in 1975 there were about 21 million wealth holders in the United Kingdom (just over half the adult population) who owned about £190 billion of assets. Notice that the top 20 per cent of wealth holders owned over 63 per cent of total wealth, leaving only 37 per cent to be shared out amongst the bottom 80 per cent. Comparing these figures with those of Table 4, it is apparent that wealth is more unevenly distributed than personal income in the United Kingdom.

Table 9. The distribution of personal wealth in the United Kingdom, 1975.

Wealth owners (%)	% share of wealth	Absolute amount of wealth held (£b.)	Number of wealth holders
Top 5	35.0	66.6	1,051,000
Top 10	47.3	90.0	2,102,000
Top 20	63.3	120.5	4,204,000
Bottom 80	36.7	69.8	16,816,000

Source: Royal Commission Report No. 5, Tables 27 and 33.

Operation of factor markets Inequalities may result from the way in which factor markets operate. For instance, if the supply of a factor is scarce relative to its demand, it would command a high price and hence an economic rent. In markets where trade union monopolies and employers' monopsonies and oligopsonies prevail, the detailed rules of practice for labour and capital affect the shares of wages and profits in the national income. For instance, in labour markets, trade union rules may affect rates of pay, the standard working week, apprenticeship periods, redundancy and lay-off pay and the age of retirement. Studies indicate that workers in unionised sectors generally earn more for similar jobs than workers in non-unionised sectors. There may also be inequalities between the incomes of the economically active and inactive. The Royal Commission on the Distribution of Income and Wealth showed, however, that in the United Kingdom, the degree of inequality in the economically active population is less than in the inactive population (which includes the unemployed, the aged, the sick and disabled).

Differences in natural abilities, education, training and opportunities These differences all contribute to inequalities in earnings and wealth. In Chapter 15, we outlined in greater detail the reasons for wage differentials between different occupations and industries within the same country. Inequalities between countries may in addition be due to differences in factor endowments which, as we showed in Chapter 7, also affect the pattern of resource allocation.

Economic growth policies The postwar policies aiming for economic growth, both in the industrially advanced and the less developed countries, have lacked explicit redistribution objectives. Furthermore, it is possible that the growth of national income weights the income changes of individuals and families in proportion to their existing share of the national income. This would mean that economic growth would tend to benefit the higher-income groups more than the lower-income groups in absolute terms.

Conclusion

In the endeavour to increase social welfare, we have seen that decision-makers face policy choices. Perhaps the most fundamental and most difficult of these is the choice between efficiency and equity. In our imperfect world, policy-makers have to decide, for example, what loss of efficiency is acceptable in order to achieve a 'socially desirable' distribution of income and wealth. Such decisions can only be made using explicit value judgements, subject to the constraints of technology and the stock of renewable and non-renewable resources.

Further reading

Gowland, D.H. (ed.), *Modern Economic Analysis*, Butterworths, London, 1979 (Ch. 12).

Atkinson, A.B., *The Economics of Inequality*, Oxford University Press, Oxford, 1975.

Brown, C.V. and **Jackson, P.M.**, *Public Sector Economics*, Martin Robertson, Oxford, 1978 (Ch. 12–15, 20).

Chenery, H. *et al.*, *Redistribution with Growth*, Oxford University Press, Oxford, 1974.

Royal Commission on the Distribution of Income and Wealth, *Reports*.

Exercises

1. Review your understanding of the following terms:

personal income	Lorenz curve
earned income	Gini coefficient
investment income	line of complete equality
transfer income	fiscal drag
Pareto's Law	wealth

2. Consider the data on the distributions of wealth in France and West Germany shown in Table 10. Draw the Lorenz curves for the two countries and estimate the Gini coefficients. Comment on your results.

Table 10. The distributions of wealth in France and West Germany.

Top	5%	10%	20%	40%	60%	80%	100%
% share of wealth in France, 1975	36.2	51.7	71.0	91.8	98.3	99.6	100.0
% share of wealth in West Germany, 1973	18.7	45.3	57.4	73.4	84.5	92.9	100.0

Source: Royal Commission on the Distribution of Income and Wealth: Background Paper to *Report No. 7.*

3. Discuss the limitations of the official statistics on the distribution of personal incomes as a measure of economic inequality. Pay particular attention to the extent to which fringe benefits distort the pattern of inequality.

4. Account for the increasing income tax burden on the lower-income groups in the United Kingdom since 1959.

5. Explain why the distribution of income tends to be more unequal in less developed countries than in industrially advanced countries.

6. 'The British tax system fails to tackle adequately the problem of inequality in the distribution of personal wealth.' Discuss.

Index

KING ALFRED'S COLLEGE
LIBRARY